Larson's Book of World Religions and Alternative Spirituality

LARSON'S

BOOK OF

World Religions

~ AND ~

Alternative
Spirituality

BOB LARSON

Tyndale House Publishers, Inc.
WHEATON, ILLINOIS

Visit Tyndale's exciting Web site at www.tyndale.com

Larson's Book of World Religions and Alternative Spirituality

Copyright © 1982, 1989, 2004 by Bob Larson. All rights reserved.

Cover image of clouds © 2003 by William H. Edwards/Getty Images. All rights reserved.

Cover image of moon © Picturequest. All rights reserved.

Designed by Ron Kaufmann

Published in 1982 as *Larson's Book of Cults* by Tyndale House Publishers, Inc.

Published in 1989 as *Larson's New Book of Cults* by Tyndale House Publishers, Inc.

Unless otherwise indicated, Scripture quotations are taken from the *Holy Bible*, King James Version.

Scripture quotations marked NLT are taken from the *Holy Bible*, New Living Translation, copyright © 1996. Used by permission of Tyndale House Publishers, Inc., Wheaton, Illinois 60189. All rights reserved.

Scripture quotations marked TLB are taken from *The Living Bible*, copyright © 1971. Used by permission of Tyndale House Publishers, Inc., Wheaton, Illinois 60189. All rights reserved.

Library of Congress Cataloging-in-Publication Data

Larson, Bob, date.
   Larson's book of world religions and alternative spirituality / Bob Larson.
      p. cm.
Rev. ed. of: Larson's new book of cults. c1989.
Includes bibliographical references and index.
   ISBN 0-8423-6417-X
   1. Religions. 2. Spiritual life. I. Title: Book of world religions and alternative spirituality. II. Larson, Bob, date. New book of cults. III. Title.
BL80.3.L37 2004
200—dc22   2003022854

Printed in the United States of America

10   09   08   07   06   05   04
7   6   5   4   3   2   1

ACKNOWLEDGMENTS

To my wife and three precious daughters for allowing Dad
to fit this book into his already overworked schedule.
Thank you for your patience and understanding.
The spiritual fruit of this book will be your heritage.

CONTENTS

INTRODUCTION

I have been writing about cults and new religious movements for decades. The first *Larson's Book of Cults* was published in 1982. *Larson's New Book of Cults*, a revised and updated version, appeared in 1989. But almost before the ink was dry on the new edition, some of the information was already out of date, as groups changed their doctrines, their names, or their leaders. Also, over the past fifteen years, new groups with unique teachings have arrived on the scene and major transformations have occurred in contemporary spirituality that have affected what and how people believe.

The following trends are among the more significant developments of recent years:

- **The changing face of Western spirituality.**
  When I first started writing about non-Christian religions, they were a tiny minority in the United States. That is no longer the case. According to Harvard professor Diana Eck in *A New Religious America*, there are now six million Muslims in the United States—more than the number of Presbyterians, Episcopalians, or Jews. Los Angeles is now home to more varieties of Buddhist communities than any other city in the world.

- **The rise of the Internet.**
  In 1982, most people had never dreamed of today's nearly ubiquitous access to the Internet, but today it is one of the main ways in which religious groups communicate their ideas and recruit new followers.

- **Our shrinking world.**
  Improved travel links cities across the globe, and the Internet and other communication devices connect people instantaneously, even though they may be thousands of miles apart. These developments have enabled religious ideas and philosophies to spread more widely and more quickly throughout the world, creating a new global spiritual melting pot.

- **Changing attitudes.**
  As recently as a couple of decades ago, the cultural consensus that dominated Western religious thought was a worldview based on Judeo-Christian theology. Today, however, the majority of people are no longer committed to basic moral values such as those enshrined in biblical codes like the Ten Commandments.

Increasingly, sociologists talk about "spiritual seekers." These are people who are searching for God, but who tend to look anywhere but inside orthodox Christian churches. Over the last few decades of the twentieth century, there was a drastic increase in the variety of religious options available to these spiritual nomads.

The purpose of this book is to show how the world's religions and spiritual movements differ widely in their ideas and practices—differences that have eternal consequences. Each commentary is intended to be practical and is based on my personal encounters with spiritual movements in more than eighty countries.

HOW TO USE THIS BOOK

Part 1 of this book provides an overview of spiritual movements and a Christian perspective on world religions, alternative spirituality, and cults. We also establish guidelines for evaluating religious groups from a biblical perspective. In order to help you understand the growth of non-Christian groups, we examine the sociology and psychology of cults and discuss the appeal of non-Christian spirituality.

In part 2, the alphabetical entries of world religions and alternative spirituality summarize the key teachings and practices of various groups and philosophies. They also compare and contrast these ideas with the truths found in the Bible. In some cases, the differences are small, but in others they are significant. Readers need to be aware of these distinctions because many religious groups try to pretend that their views are compatible with Christian teaching even when they are unequivocally opposed to foundational Christian concepts. We have arranged the entries alphabetically for ease of use, and we've included an index in the back of the book that will allow you to search by the names of individuals and other keywords.

Some entries include information about other resources that will help you conduct further research, and some have "See also" references that will help you locate information on related groups and philosophies. We have documented our sources, whenever possible, and we have listed contact information for most groups. We don't necessarily recommend that you contact these groups, but we have provided the information for those who might want more information about a group's claims.

In the back of the book we have also included a recommended reading list that will help you understand world religions and alternative spirituality better. My prayer is that the material assembled here will help you find your way in today's increasingly confusing spiritual marketplace, and that you will be able to help others who may have lost their way.

Bob Larson
Denver, Colorado

PART 1

AN OVERVIEW OF WORLD RELIGIONS

~ AND ~

ALTERNATIVE SPIRITUALITY

1

FAITH MATTERS

Do you remember where you were during the final days of March 1997? That was when thirty-nine members of a group called Heaven's Gate dressed in identical black outfits, lay down on identical metal beds, and methodically killed themselves.

The members of Heaven's Gate had been told that death would be the portal taking them to another life in a galaxy far away (see the entry on Heaven's Gate for more information).

This whole idea sounds silly to reasonable people, but for the thirty-nine people who died because they believed this lie, the outcome was tragic.

Today many people believe that all religions teach the same thing, or that they are all equal, or that it doesn't really matter what someone believes. But the tragedy of Heaven's Gate reveals that it does matter. In some cases it's a matter of life and death. If you aren't convinced, check the entries on Jonestown, the Order of the Solar Temple, and some of the other deadly cults found in the pages that follow.

In most cases people don't die from believing a lie, but often their lives aren't all they could be. In the case of some controlling religious groups, people sacrifice their money, their relationships, and their free will for a self-proclaimed guru's promise of salvation.

TRUTH AND CONSEQUENCES

In recent years there has been a paradigm shift in the way people in the West think about religion. Concepts of truth are now considered less important than subjective experience. The late Joseph Campbell said as much in his book *The Masks of God:* "The swamis are coming from India, and they're taking away the flock. They're speaking of religion as dealing with the interior of life and not about dogmatic formulae and ritual requirements."

Today many people don't care whether a religion is based on solid truth like the historical resurrection of Jesus Christ from the dead. Instead, there is a voguish interest in experience and mysticism with little concern about truth or falsehood. If Marshall Applewhite, founder of Heaven's Gate, says that aliens in a spaceship are waiting to pick up the group's true disciples, some people respond by saying, "Well, that may be true for you."

Did Mormon founder Joseph Smith really discover golden plates buried in Palmyra, New York? Did Victor Wierwille (founder of The Way) actually hear the voice of God? Did Scientology's L. Ron Hubbard truly discover the essence of religion that has eluded saints and scholars for millennia? Millions of Americans have placed their faith in such questionable claims, regardless of whether or not they are true. In fact, it matters little to many mystics whether their system of worship is historically accurate. If we point out that Krishna's discourses with Arjuna in the Bhagavad Gita are mere legends, our assertion is dismissed with a shrug. Experience is what counts.

Consequently, the historical anchors of Christianity of a bloodstained cross and an empty tomb have little meaning to contemporary spiritual seekers. Whether Calvary and the Resurrection actually took place seems less important to them than what they see as the allegorical grandeur of the story.

But truth *does* matter! And when the myths of other world religions and New Age philosophies have been shattered, Bible-based Christians must be ready to offer disillusioned seekers an objectively valid response to the "whys" of life. We must be ready to present the claims of Jesus' divinity and his sufficiency as our Savior and Lord. "If anybody asks why you believe as you do, be ready to tell him, and do it in a gentle and respectful way" (1 Peter 3:15, TLB).

This book has been written to help provide those answers. The reader whose faith is experientially rooted in the living Word of God will find in these pages a concrete, intellectual rationale for pointing spiritual seekers to the historical Christ.

A SPIRITUAL BATTLEGROUND

Americans value independence, freedom of thought, and the entrepreneurial spirit. Therefore, it should come as no surprise that our nation has given birth to thousands of new religious groups. As a result, the United States has become one of the foremost battlegrounds in the struggle between Christianity and non-Christian faiths.

In a way, however, it's ironic this struggle has occurred here, because the deists and the devout Christians who settled this land were committed to a transcendent faith that recognized a God based on the Judeo-Christian model. However, a careful study of America's past reveals that the breeze of freedom that became the tumultuous gale of do-it-yourself spirituality in the late twentieth and early twenty-first centuries influenced even the early years of settling and exploration.

The promise of freedom of religious expression that originally lured people to this land also fostered utopian, communal, and apocalyptic dreams. American visionaries have always been enamored of idealistic, simplistic, and sacred explanations for life's purpose. This philosophy of manifest destiny has been most evident in times of cultural transition such as during the Armageddon-crazed days of the industrial revolution. Today's rapid growth in non-Christian religious and spiritual groups is the cultural by-product of this uniquely American attitude.

As an American, I support my country's commitment to freedom of religion. On the other hand, I believe that souls for whom Christ shed his blood deserve more spiritually fulfilling answers than those provided by modern myths.

As the reader, you have a right to know I am an evangelical Christian committed to a biblical theological perspective in this book. Does that mean I have slanted the information in an effort to recruit converts? No. But I have tried throughout to compare the teachings of various groups to the Christian faith taught in the Bible and proclaimed by the church for centuries.

However, I have not been commissioned by any church or denomination. Nor do I have a particular bias against any non-Christian spiritual group or leader. My analysis of each religion, spiritual movement, and philosophy in this book is based on orthodox Christian presuppositions alone.

Two basic theological principles have guided my study:

1. "In Christ the fullness of God lives in a human body, and you are complete through your union with Christ. He is the Lord over every ruler and authority in the universe." (Colossians 2:9-10, NLT)
2. "Don't just pretend that you love others. Really love them. Hate what is wrong. Stand on the side of the good." (Romans 12:9, NLT)

This book is not intended to be a sociological or theological treatise. Its purpose is to aid and inform the average person whose friends, neighbors, co-workers, or loved ones may be involved in a non-Christian religion or other spiritual movement. It is also intended to prepare readers to respond knowledgeably and in love the next time a canvassing missionary from a religious group rings the doorbell.

I bear a solemn obligation in writing this book. If Jehovah's Witnesses, for example, really do have inside information about the world's end, and if Scientology really can extinguish our hang-ups from past lives, then you, the reader, have a right to know. If Sun Myung Moon is the Messiah, or if Baha'u'llah was the Christ, then no personal prejudice on my part should stand in the way of proclaiming these facts.

But if these spiritual leaders and philosophers are in error, then every person whose life this book touches deserves to know the unvarnished truth.

SPEAKING THE TRUTH IN LOVE

Some people think it is wrong to criticize another person's religious beliefs. But is it better to smile and say nothing as people follow self-proclaimed messiahs to a false paradise or worse?

I believe it is my obligation as a Christian to talk to non-Christians about their faith, but in doing so I must follow the example of Jesus Christ, who attracted many people to his message through his grace, love, and compassion. Sound theology, doctrinal purity, and aggressive evangelistic techniques are not the whole answer. We are involved in a spiritual battle, but our weapons are not angry words or intimidating techniques. Rather, our mandate is to speak the truth in love.

John 13:34-35 reminds believers that love is the mark of discipleship. And love for our neighbors is the distinguishing characteristic of our love for God. Such is the message of the Good Samaritan parable recorded in Luke 10:30-35. A personal anecdote may emphasize this fact in a practical manner.

As I was writing the first edition of this book at the Colorado cabin where I did most of my writing, there came a knock at the door.

It was pouring rain outside, and when I opened the door, I saw two drenched Japanese-American girls standing on the doorstep. Once inside, they explained that the friends with whom they were traveling had slid off a muddy road and wrecked their car. They asked for a ride to a nearby lodge where they could call a tow truck.

No writer appreciates an interruption, but there was no choice but to render immediate assistance in their distress. The two girls, Harriet and Ellen, were soaking wet and covered with mud. Needless to say, my vehicle suffered the consequences! To make matters worse, on the way to the lodge, the heater fan conked out and the knob to the defroster fell off. One annoyance after another was heaped upon me to exacerbate the situation. After phoning for the wrecker, the girls asked me for another ride to the place where they had joined their friends and left their car—a half-hour's drive away.

There was no question that these young ladies needed my help. What concerned me was that their plight interfered with what I thought was a more important spiritual responsibility—writing this book.

On the way to retrieve their automobile, the conversation centered on the weather and how the accident occurred. Finally, Ellen asked what I did for a living. That led to a lengthy explanation regarding my personal faith in Christ, something neither girl seemed to understand.

"Where do you attend church?" I asked.

"We're Buddhists," they replied.

Suddenly I knew why God had allowed this interruption. What I had considered an annoying infringement on my time was God's way of reminding me that writing this book was not as important as showing God's love and helping someone in need.

The young ladies' devout Buddhist beliefs soon collided with my scriptural insistence that Christ is the only means of salvation. When we reached their car, Ellen's parting words climaxed the episode.

"Well, I guess we won't really know who's right until we're both dead," she concluded.

"But if Jesus is correct," I answered, "it will be a little too late for you to find out."

As I drove off, the Holy Spirit impressed upon me an important lesson: God loves mankind so much that he is willing to provide shelter and kindness even to those who reject his Son.

My knowledge of world religions, particularly Buddhism, would have enabled me to argue effectively on an intellectual level with Harriet and Ellen. But God was more concerned about my extending a Good Samaritan act of love than my winning a theological debate in defense of truth.

When I arrived back at the cabin, I was prepared to pursue this book with new resolve and enthusiasm. Most importantly, I felt the need to do more than simply issue a warning about the dangers of groups like the ones in this book. Dismantling the myth of false religious beliefs is not only the work of biblical apologetics; it is also a labor of love.

BALANCING LOVE AND TRUTH

I wrote this book out of genuine love and concern for people who follow other beliefs. As a Christian, I believe that God has revealed his will to humanity in many ways over the centuries. Most importantly, he revealed himself through Jesus, his only Son, who came to earth to redeem us. People are free to believe whatever they like, but I want them to be aware that there are consequences to their beliefs. Faith matters.

I also want to help people develop better critical thinking skills so that they won't be seduced when a charismatic leader declares that he alone has the key to understanding the secrets of the Bible.

God created all of us, and as it says in the Old Testament book of Genesis, we are created in God's image. This means we have a deep spiritual hunger. Over the years, people have developed thousands of different ways of filling that hunger. Can all these religions be true? Not when they teach different things.

It is only through studying what the various groups have to say and comparing that to the standard we find in the Bible that we can find our way through the confusing maze of today's religions, alternative spirituality, and cults.

It is my hope that this book will help you in your study.

2

A CHRISTIAN PERSPECTIVE ON WORLD RELIGIONS, ALTERNATIVE SPIRITUALITY, AND CULTS

It is important for Christians to evaluate other religious groups according to biblical criteria. Not every group will have obvious cultic characteristics, but what they teach—their principles and values—may be contrary to the truth of the Bible. As Dr. Walter Martin, one of the pioneers of cult research, has observed, "A person can be morally good, but if he sets his face against Jesus, his fruit is corrupt." Whether or not a particular religious group claims to be Christian is not our primary concern. Its members may quote the Bible and claim the endorsement of Christ for their efforts, but if their doctrine and practices are out of step with what the Bible teaches is true, then they are leading people astray. In determining whether a group is essentially non-Christian, we have based our analysis on two central factors:

1. They ignore or purposely omit central apostolic doctrines.
2. They hold to beliefs that are distinctly opposed to orthodox Christianity.

Deviation from either criterion rules out a group's inclusion in the Christian community. The ultimate gauge of truth and error is whether a belief system conforms to Scripture or the extent to which it departs from biblical precepts. Thus, any group that intentionally manipulates its language to mimic evangelical beliefs must have its semantic distortions exposed. Any group that places itself in opposition to historic Christianity should not be allowed to hide behind a cloak of religious goodwill or misleading terminology.

A CONFUSING LANDSCAPE

Christians are sometimes perplexed when others use spiritual-sounding phrases that appear to be in harmony with orthodox Christianity. Adherents to these groups may quote the Bible, profess devout reverence for Christ, and use familiar terminology. However, upon closer examination, it soon becomes apparent that they have redefined orthodox terminology to suit their own beliefs. In such cases, they should be compelled to assume an intellectually honest stance with regard to indispensable Bible doctrines. Only then will their treachery of language be exposed for what it is. Such individuals are "handling the word of God deceitfully" (2 Corinthians 4:2), an act that ensures their own destruction (2 Peter 3:16), and they should be warned.

Many spiritual leaders and their groups have made significant contributions to the social welfare of humanity. In some instances they are sincerely concerned about meeting the spiritual needs of seeking souls. Don't they deserve credit for their good works? Even though we recognize the positive elements of certain groups, it must not be forgotten that the Bible requires reproof and rebuke of any teaching that exalts itself against the necessity of salvation through Christ (2 Timothy 4:2-5).

According to scriptural criteria, false teachers are "enemies of the cross of Christ" (Philippians 3:18), "false apostles, deceitful workers, transforming themselves into the apostles of Christ. And no marvel; for Satan himself is transformed into an angel of light. Therefore it is no great thing if his ministers also be transformed as the ministers of righteousness; whose end shall be according to their works" (2 Corinthians 11:13-15). Gratuitous words in recognition of positive values should not be mistaken for an endorsement of what the Bible calls "doctrines of devils" (1 Timothy 4:1).

The good works and seemingly beneficial effects of a group's belief system are inconsequential considerations. Healing, for example, cannot validate the biblical credibility of a spiritual movement. The miracles of Pharaoh's magicians (as recorded in Exodus 7) illustrate that the supernatural is an arena where both godly and demonic powers operate. Only those with true scriptural discernment will be able to know whether good or evil is the source of any teaching. Jesus pointed out that apparent authority over evil spirits would not qualify one for entrance into heaven if the exorcist operated under a system of false doctrine (Matthew 7:21-23).

GUIDELINES FOR EVALUATING RELIGIOUS GROUPS

To evaluate a religious group according to biblical criteria, what areas of doctrine are vital for consideration? What are the scriptural parameters beyond which no religious group may lay claim to biblical orthodoxy? The basic fault of non-Christian spiritual movements is that they demote God, devalue Christ, deify humanity, deny sin, and denigrate Scripture. These groups may also be exclusive, elitist, organized under misplaced authority, and off track in their views of the end times, but these factors in and of themselves are not reliable measures for determining orthodoxy. We have identified five basic areas of doctrine that provide essential criteria for distinguishing truth from error, and we assert that correct theology regarding these doctrines is necessary in order for a group to be in accordance with historic Christianity:

1. The attributes of God
2. The person of Christ
3. The nature of humanity
4. The requirements of atonement
5. The source of revelation

On the basis of these historic Christian doctrines, we will lay a foundation on which we can evaluate individual groups. This is not intended to be an in-depth theological treatise; rather, our desire is to outline essential aspects of orthodox Christianity. This does not mean that the author and publisher consider theology to be unimportant. In fact, the lack of sound biblical theology in our culture has resulted in a post-Christian era that enhances the myth of the cults.

In the following discussion we will approach each doctrine in three ways:

1. A summary of basic biblical beliefs and the historic Christian position.
2. Five passages of Scripture that support the biblical doctrine. In most cases, dozens of biblical references could be cited as corroborating evidence, but for the sake of brevity, we'll limit ourselves to five. Please note that all Scripture quotations are from the King James Version because this version is the one most frequently quoted (and misquoted) by cultists.
3. An example of specific groups that promulgate an opposing, non-Christian viewpoint. The groups listed are representative examples only, not a complete catalog of all the groups that hold such views.

The Attributes of God

The Historic Christian Position

God is a personality who can speak and create and who possesses a mind and will (Genesis 1:1, 26; Jeremiah 29:11; Ezekiel 18:30). God's character is eternal (1 Timothy 1:17), omnipotent (Revelation 19:6), omnipresent (Psalm 139), omniscient (Romans 11:33), perfect (Deuteronomy 32:4), and holy (1 Peter 1:16). Both the Old and New Testaments proclaim the triune nature of God— Father, Son, and Holy Spirit. They are coequal, coexistent, and coeternal, three persons of the same substance (John 1:1-3; 14:26).

Supportive Scriptures
1. "There is but one God, the Father, of whom are all things." (1 Corinthians 8:6)
2. "Before me there was no God formed, neither shall there be after me." (Isaiah 43:10)
3. "And God said unto Moses, I AM THAT I AM." (Exodus 3:14)
4. "For there is one God." (1 Timothy 2:5)
5. "From everlasting to everlasting, thou art God." (Psalm 90:2)

Groups That Promulgate a Non-Christian Doctrine
1. Hinduism, Baha'i: God is an impersonal, unknowable essence.
2. Christian Science, Unity: God is a divine idea, principle, or example.
3. Jehovah's Witnesses, The Way: God is non-trinitarian.

The Person of Jesus Christ
The Historic Christian Position
The Apostles' Creed states that Jesus was "conceived by the Holy Ghost, born of the Virgin Mary, suffered under Pontius Pilate, was crucified, dead, and was buried. He descended into Hell; the third day he arose from the dead. He ascended into heaven and sitteth on the right hand of God the Father Almighty; from thence he shall come to judge the quick and the dead." Jesus Christ is the second person of the Trinity, the eternally begotten Son of God who became flesh and is now our "great high priest, that is passed into the heavens, . . . [who] was in all points tempted like as we are, yet without sin" (Hebrews 4:14-15).

Supportive Scriptures
1. "In the beginning was the Word, and the Word was with God, and the Word was God. . . . All things were made by him; and without him was not any thing made." (John 1:1, 3)
2. "And the Word was made flesh, and dwelt among us (and we beheld his glory, the glory as of the only begotten of the Father)." (John 1:14)
3. "Every spirit that confesseth not that Jesus Christ is come in the flesh is not of God; and this is that spirit of antichrist." (1 John 4:3)
4. "Far above all principality, and power, and might, and dominion, and every name that is named." (Ephesians 1:21)
5. "For in him dwelleth all the fullness of the Godhead bodily." (Colossians 2:9)

Groups That Promulgate a Non-Christian Doctrine
1. Church Universal and Triumphant, The International Community of Christ: Jesus is merely a human being without divinity who attained "Christ Consciousness."

2. Mormonism, Jehovah's Witnesses: Jesus is a created being.
3. Hinduism, Divine Light Mission: Jesus is one of many *avatars*, or revelations of God.

The Nature of Humanity

The Historic Christian Position

God created man in his own image (Genesis 1:26), perfect and without sin so that he could know and love God. Man is the highest distinction of God's creative genius, separate from him, made "a little lower than the angels" (Psalm 8:5), with dominion over all the earth (Genesis 1:28). In Eden, man fell by disobedience; henceforth all men are conceived in sin with a depraved nature destined for damnation unless they are spiritually reborn (John 3:3).

Supportive Scriptures

1. "By one man sin entered into the world, and death by sin; . . . all have sinned." (Romans 5:12)
2. "For as by one man's disobedience many were made sinners." (Romans 5:19)
3. "In sin did my mother conceive me." (Psalm 51:5)
4. "Their foolish heart was darkened." (Romans 1:21)
5. "The heart is deceitful above all things, and desperately wicked." (Jeremiah 17:9)

Groups That Promulgate a Non-Christian Doctrine

1. Theosophy and Rosicrucianism: Humanity is divine, an emanation of the infinite Impersonal.
2. Church Universal and Triumphant, Holy Order of MANS: Humanity is capable of attaining the same "Christ Consciousness" that Jesus did.
3. Mormonism: Humans are destined to be gods.

The Requirements of Atonement

The Historic Christian Position

The Old Testament sacrifices foreshadowed the atoning death of Jesus Christ, the Lamb of God "slain from the foundation of the world" (Revelation 13:8), whose shed blood would be the final sacrifice and cleansing for sin (1 John 1:7). Humanity, whose sinful rebellion has separated them from God, can now have "peace through the blood of his cross" (Colossians 1:20) and be reconciled to God (2 Corinthians 5:18-19) because of his vicarious, substitutionary death.

Supportive Scriptures

1. "Who his own self bare our sins in his own body on the tree." (1 Peter 2:24)
2. "While we were yet sinners, Christ died for us." (Romans 5:8)

3. "Neither is there salvation in any other: for there is none other name under heaven given among men, whereby we must be saved." (Acts 4:12)
4. "Without shedding of blood is no remission." (Hebrews 9:22)
5. "If we confess our sins, he is faithful and just to forgive us our sins, and to cleanse us from all unrighteousness." (1 John 1:9)

Groups That Promulgate a Non-Christian Doctrine
1. Baha'i, Unity: Good works and beneficent deeds will cause one to achieve "at-one-ment" with God.
2. Scientology, Krishna Consciousness: Reincarnation will fulfill the law of karma.
3. Christian Science, Mormonism: Universalism—the belief that all will eventually be saved.

The Source of Revelation
The Historic Christian Position
The Word of God in scriptural canon is inspired (God-breathed), inerrant, complete (Revelation 22:18-19), and the only infallible rule of faith. It reveals the origin and destiny of all things; it records God's dealing with mankind in the past, present, and future, and focuses on the person and work of Jesus Christ. The Bible inspires faith (Romans 10:17) and will make people "wise unto salvation" (2 Timothy 3:15).

Supportive Scriptures
1. "All scripture is given by inspiration of God, and is profitable for doctrine, for reproof, for correction, for instruction in righteousness." (2 Timothy 3:16)
2. "Holy men of God spake as they were moved by the Holy Ghost." (2 Peter 1:21)
3. "Thy word is a lamp unto my feet, and a light unto my path." (Psalm 119:105)
4. "The word of our God shall stand for ever." (Isaiah 40:8)
5. "For the word of God is quick, and powerful, and sharper than any twoedged sword . . . and is a discerner of the thoughts and intents of the heart." (Hebrews 4:12)

Groups That Promulgate a Non-Christian Doctrine
1. Mormonism, The Walk: The Bible needs additional subjective or written revelation for our age.
2. Jehovah's Witnesses, The Way: The Word of God needs to be properly translated with accompanying explanations.
3. Baha'i, Unity: The Bible is one of many equally divine, sacred books.

3

UNDERSTANDING THE GROWTH OF NON-CHRISTIAN GROUPS

In the 1960s and 1970s, people who researched the cornucopia of new religious movements sweeping across America referred to them all as "cults." Today there are many people who still refer to all non-Christian religions as cults. But is *cult* the best term to apply to world religions like Islam and Buddhism? Or international groups like Mormonism? Or movements like the New Age eclecticism, which is too broad and fluid to be considered a monolithic cult?

Merriam-Webster's Collegiate Dictionary, Tenth Edition, defines a cult as "a religion regarded as unorthodox or spurious." It also cites a wider parameter of "great devotion to a person, idea, object, movement, or work," a frame of reference to which this book in part ascribes. Ronald Enroth points out that the origin of the word *cult* can be traced to the Latin *cultus*, which "connotes all that is involved in worship—ritual, emotion, liturgy, and attitude." In this sense, academic researchers often speak of Christianity as a cult.

In Dr. Walter Martin's book *The Kingdom of the Cults*, Dr. Charles Braden is quoted as saying, "A cult . . . is any religious group which differs significantly in some one or more respects as to belief or practice from those religious groups which are regarded as the normative expression of religion in our total culture."

Thus, to designate any group as a cult requires an obviously subjective value judgment. Many respectable groups that are admired by society (such as the Mormons and Baha'is) were considered repugnant and were persecuted during their formative years. Who is to say which of today's nontraditional eccentrics will be considered socially acceptable in years to come?

THE SOCIOLOGY AND PSYCHOLOGY OF CULTS

The definition of a cult goes beyond theology to include sociological concepts concerning cultural definitions of normalcy and deviancy. Many of the groups that sociologists have identified as cults share the following common characteristics:

1. A centralized authority that tightly structures both philosophy and lifestyle
2. An "us versus them" complex, pitting the supposedly superior insights of the group against a hostile outside culture
3. A commitment for each member to proselytize intensively the unconverted
4. An entrenched isolationism that divorces the devotee from the realities of the world at large

The theology of cultic groups is diverse, ranging from the rigidly ascetic to the sexually permissive. And each group's character may change over time. At the outset, many groups display sincere expressions of a humble desire to improve society and follow God's will. At some point, the founder's teachings are codified into an organized system of revealed authority. Allegiance to the founder's ideals becomes an absolute requirement. What may have been one man's honest opinion is then presented as having the weight of divine endorsement.

If such a transformation takes place while the leader is still alive, he usually claims supernatural certifications for his beliefs. What then develops is a "type of institutional dogmatism and a pronounced intolerance for any position but their own," according to Dr. Walter Martin.

It is also helpful to look at the characteristics of people who are attracted to cults. Conventional solutions and institutions may have struck them as being sterile or unfulfilling. They are looking for an affirming community with which they can identify. Such a group will be all the more appealing if it offers a single, idealistic principle around which one's entire life can revolve. In a society that is biblically illiterate, the deception of a cult is particularly enticing if it claims to have "restored" certain truths that have been lost or undiscovered.

Loneliness, indecision, despair, and disappointment are the emotional characteristics that proselytizers notice. They approach the unwary recruit with an excessively friendly invitation to a lecture, free meal, weekend workshop, or other activity offering instant solutions to overwhelming problems. Surprisingly, few recruits bother to inquire about who is extending the offer, what is behind it, and what functions will take place. Vague answers are seldom challenged, leaving the recruiter an unassailable opportunity to obscure his intentions.

Cults generally attract prospects with an outpouring of attention and affection, the so-called love-bombing technique. Feeling, not doctrine, is the lure. In fact, the belief structure is seldom mentioned in the beginning. Cult leaders know that once initiates have been reconditioned to accept the group's particular worldview, and as soon as they feel a sense of meaningful belonging, their minds will be ready to accept any teaching, including a belief that the leader represents God.

Approval, acceptance, belonging, authority—all those things that were missing in a person's life are supplied by the cult. Motivation is generated by rewards for excessive zeal. Critical thinking is discouraged and corporate identification with some larger-than-life mission (as conveyed by the leader) causes members to equate what is good for the cult as being good for them.

FROM INTEREST TO INDOCTRINATION

When a recruit's mind shifts into neutral, the period of intensive indoctrination begins. The effectiveness of this tactic is often enhanced by sensory deprivation, extreme amounts of physical activity coupled with fatigue, severance of all ties with family and friends, and the forsaking of all belongings and material possessions. In a short time, the initiate becomes emotionally and spiritually dependent on the cult for decisions, direction, and even the physical necessities of life. The outside world appears more and more threatening. Finally his mind "snaps," and a sudden, drastic alteration of personality in all its many forms takes place.

Young adult recruits are the least likely to consider thoughts of abandoning the group. Severing the cult-fostered dependency would mean having to cope with hardships and to fend for themselves in a hostile world. Any consideration of leaving immediately conjures guilt feelings of forsaking God's calling, falling into Satan's hands, or even worse, risking the wrath and judgment of God.

Before a person joins up with an authoritarian religious group, he or she should be aware of what could result: neurosis, psychosis, suicidal tendencies, guilt, identity confusion, paranoia, hallucinations, loss of free will, intellectual sterility, and diminished capacity of judgment.

It will be much easier to avoid such consequences by identifying and recognizing the following psychological forms of cultic coercion:

1. *Absolute loyalty.* Allegiance to the sect is demanded and enforced by actual or veiled threats to one's temporal life or eternal spiritual condition.
2. *Altered diet.* Depriving one of essential nutrients and enforcing a low-protein diet can lead to disorientation and emotional susceptibility.
3. *Chanting and meditation.* Objective intellectual input is avoided by countering anticult questions with repetitious songs and chants.
4. *Conformity.* Dress, language, names, and interests take on a sameness that erodes individuality.

5. *Doctrinal confusion.* Incomprehensible "truths" are more readily accepted when presented in a complex fashion that encourages rejection of logical thought.

6. *Exclusivity.* Those outside the cults are viewed as spiritually inferior, creating an exclusive and self-righteous "us versus them" attitude.

7. *Financial involvement.* All or part of one's personal assets may be donated to the cult, increasing a vested interest in sticking with it and lessening the chance of returning to a former vocation.

8. *Hypnotic states.* Inducing a highly susceptible state of mind may be accomplished by chanting, repetitive singing, or prolonged meditation.

9. *Isolation from outside.* Diminished perception of reality results when one is physically separated from friends, society, and the rational frame of reference in which one has previously functioned.

10. *Lack of privacy.* Reflective, critical thinking is impossible in a setting where cult members are seldom left unattended, and the ego's normal emotional defensive mechanisms can easily be stripped away by having the new member share personal secrets that can later be used for intimidation.

11. *Love-bombing.* Physical affection and constant contrived attention can give a false sense of camaraderie.

12. *Megacommunication.* Long, confusing lectures can be an effective tool if the inductee is bombarded with glib rhetoric and catch phrases.

13. *New relationships.* Marriage to another cult member and the destruction of past family relationships integrates one fully into the cult "family."

14. *Nonsensical activities.* Games and other activities with no apparent purpose leave one dependent upon a group or leader to give direction and order.

15. *Skinnerian control.* Behavior modification by alternating reward and punishment leads to confusion and dependency.

16. *Peer pressure.* By exploiting one's desire for acceptance, doubts about cult practices can be overcome by offering a sense of belonging to an affirming community.

17. *Sensory deprivation.* Fatigue coupled with prolonged activity can make one vulnerable to otherwise offensive beliefs and suggestions.

18. *Unquestioning submission.* Acceptance of cult practices is achieved by discouraging any questions or natural curiosity that may challenge what the leaders propagate.

19. *Value rejection.* As proselytes become more integrated into the cult, they are encouraged to denounce the values and beliefs of their former life.

Such characteristics will not always be apparent with all cultlike spiritual movements or all adherents. One group may practice economic exploitation, while another allows its members to maintain a lifestyle that is financially independent. Certain spiritual movements entice members who are curious about their secret doctrines, whereas others openly evangelize by public propagation of their beliefs (though few cults qualify for this category).

The nineteen types of coercion listed above should serve as warning flags. Anyone who has become involved in a group that practices some of these techniques should be cautious. And if raising questions about a group brings responses of anger or condemnation, that's even more reason to be wary.

THE APPEAL OF NON-CHRISTIAN SPIRITUALITY

Why are non-Christian groups so attractive to so many people today? Is the recent explosion of cult activity indicative of societal or spiritual factors? Has America's proclivity for "inventive" solutions caused her to turn from rationalism to mysticism? Is it the fault of science for heralding the advance of problem solving by microprocessors? Can our innate spiritual hunger be blamed for our pursuing escapist solutions to desperate dilemmas? Or has humanity entered an age in which conflicting supernatural forces tug at our allegiances in one final bid for control of civilization before its last gasp?

The secular behaviorist would probably choose one or more of the above explanations, whereas evangelical Christians would most likely check off all of them.

There are other reasons we might add to this list. In his book *Those Curious New Cults*, William Petersen includes:

1. Disillusionment with American political life
2. Dehumanization by science
3. The advent of the drug culture
4. Future fright (fear of nuclear or environmental cataclysms)
5. The breakdown of the family
6. Popular culture (music and literature)
7. Psychology and the occult (Jung to Joseph Rhine)
8. The decline of the church
9. The ecology crisis

Because of these and other reasons, an estimated 1,500 to 6,000 non-Christian religions, spiritual movements, and cultic groups flourish in North American society. They range in size from groups of thousands of adherents to small bands of disciples numbering a few hundred or less.

Membership is divided between established groups with reasonably respectable followings (such as Mormonism, Christian Science, Unity) and less institutional movements (New Age). But fundamentally, all non-Christian groups have one thing in common: They consider the claims of Christ to be optional, not essential to salvation.

Idealistic young people whose quest for spiritual identity supersedes their desire for materialistic comfort are ripe for exploitation by cultic myths. The promise of psychic enhancement and raised consciousness has a powerful sway over the naïve and unsuspecting. Adolescents who want to intellectually shortcut the agonizing process of maturation can easily be victimized by a myth that offers a seemingly painless way to learn life's lessons.

New Age groups are particularly adept at beckoning the lonely and confused to step over the threshold to an altered perception of reality. Merging one's ego into the common good of the movement's vision for the future dismisses all the answers to humankind's great questions. The myth they offer is no passing fad. Their vision of remaking the world will endure even after the most optimistic predictions of cult leaders have been proven false.

A PARENT'S CONCERN

For as long as I have been writing about contemporary spirituality, I have heard many parents say, "It can't happen to my kids." Many of these parents have had their illusions shattered.

Instead of reaching out to meet the needs of a searching generation, they have offered the solutions of governmental control or deprogramming. Interference by the state in matters of religious convictions is a specter that could haunt religious freedom for years to come. Legislation aimed at bizarre groups could one day be turned into edicts that would hinder legitimate alternative expressions of faith.

Those whose responsibility it would be to establish religious norms might well someday officially repudiate the Bible in favor of paganism. What then? Temporarily stemming the tide of cultic brainwashing probably appeals to evangelicals, especially those whose children have become cult converts. But undermining First Amendment rights to achieve momentary suppression of an undesirable belief system might eventually invite suppression of biblically orthodox groups.

The plight of parents whose offspring have been unfairly captivated by mind-bending cults is a genuine concern of everyone, especially jurists. There is no way to calculate the emotional grief of a mother and father who suddenly find a family member undergoing a complete personality transformation. What are parents to do when their own child sees them as instruments of Satan and refuses to answer calls or letters?

For some, deprogramming, forcible kidnapping, and "coercive dissuasion" seem to be their last hope. Ted Patrick, possibly the most famous deprogrammer, charged as much as $10,000 to retrieve a child ensnared in a cult. After a while, his work was halted by courts that decided his tactics violated First Amendment guarantees of freedom of religion.

Even if a morally and legally acceptable method to extract cult members is found, the fundamental issue of countering cult evangelism still needs to be addressed.

The appalling number of cult devotees who have left the ranks of evangelical Christian churches poses a crucial question. How well is the church training its members to understand the foundation of their beliefs? Countering the cult invasion requires that Christians be properly grounded in biblical apologetics. Believers may need to be reminded that they have a sacred responsibility to "contend for the faith which was once delivered unto the saints" (Jude 3).

The prolific growth of the cults is not likely to abate anytime soon. As Dr. Walter Martin points out, Christians cannot sit back passively and assume that teachers who are not of God will eventually fade away. Some who adopt this passive attitude cite Gamaliel's advice to the Jewish council (Acts 5:33-39) as their theological pretext. When Gamaliel advised his brethren not to oppose the apostles lest they also oppose God, his counsel was directed toward a consideration of anti-Christian persecution. Thus Gamaliel's proposition cannot be used to justify a failure to counter false doctrines. Adopting such an attitude would be to concede godly origin to the successes of major world religions that oppose Christian beliefs.

To "just preach the gospel" and leave the cults to "hang themselves when they get enough rope" would confine the Great Commission to non-cult evangelism.

CULTIC TENDENCIES WITHIN THE CHURCH?

If Christians are to challenge the cults confidently, they must be spiritually prepared. "Judgment must begin at the house of God" (1 Peter 4:17), and confronting the myth of the cults also means the church first has to purge its own ranks.

Doing so requires facing some serious, introspective questions. What about the excessive authority conceded to Christian leaders who command large followings? How much attention is being paid to encouraging strong family units where young people find secure parental relationships that are too strong for cult authoritarianism to crack? Do laymen need carefully to weigh in light of Scripture the pronouncements of their respected leaders? (Even the apostle Paul acknowledged the necessity of such checks and balances in Acts 17:11.) Should the church be reminded of the supernatural gifts and spiritual spontaneity that characterized its early growth and are now indicative of what sometimes attracts youth to cults?

To dismiss the success of aberrant groups with the excuse that Satan has blinded the eyes of the cultists could be a way of ignoring the fact that the true church is also at fault. The apostle Paul's love for the church caused him to do more than merely issue a warning about "grievous wolves." His command to defend diligently the cause of Christ went forth day and night "with tears" (Acts 20:28-31). Paul's impassioned appeal, coupled with Christ's advance notice ("Behold, I have told you before," Matthew 24:25), leaves some churches in the embarrassing position of having abdicated the throne of dominion over men's souls to the more energetic cult groups.

A COMMON CALLING

Not everyone who reads this book will immediately become a missionary to counter cults and non-Christian spiritual movements, but all Christians are called to be prepared for opportunities to share their faith with others. I hope the knowledge found in the following pages will result in more prepared vessels whom the Lord can use when an appropriate opportunity presents itself.

Some may choose to actively invade Satan's kingdom, being filled with the Spirit and determined to dismantle the myth that holds millions in spiritual servitude. Others will reach out with new love and empathy for those who sorrow because a family member has joined a cult. Still others may sense the need for rehabilitative follow-up programs that will minister to the emotional needs of those who have been ravaged by cult ideology.

Any of these fruits will make this book worth its investment of time and energy. May God show you, the reader, what part you should play in helping to destroy the myth of cults and the allure of alternative spirituality.

This book is primarily written for the layperson who wants to know where a certain belief system originated, how it developed historically, the nature of its main teachings, and its relationship to biblical truth. Though some religious movements exhibit an arrogant air of superiority, care has been taken not to counter this attitude with a spirit of antagonism.

The unlimited grace of God that the apostle John so eloquently described (1 John 2:2) is extended to all who have not experienced salvation by grace, including the cultist. Members of religious cults may wonder why evangelical Christians would dare to dispute their beliefs, which the cults presume to be the "restored" or "revealed" truths of God. But such a response must be met with love, because apart from God's gracious intervention, the reader might also be ensnared in the same spiritual bondage.

PART 2

AN ENCYCLOPEDIA OF WORLD RELIGIONS

༄ AND ༄

ALTERNATIVE SPIRITUALITY

THE AETHERIUS SOCIETY

One of the best-known UFO groups, the Aetherius Society encourages members to be willing channels of communication with extraterrestrial beings.

FOUNDER: Dr. George King

TEXTS: King's books, as well as the society's newsletter, *Cosmic Voice*

OVERVIEW: Human beings have long been fascinated by the possibility of alien life forms and flying saucers. For the Aetherius Society, such fascinations are fundamental aspects of their faith.

The group was founded in 1954 by Londoner Dr. George King. In 1955 an alien leader named Master Aetherius of Venus, representing the "cosmic brotherhood" of "space masters," selected King to be the "primary terrestrial channel" for the Interplanetary Parliament.

King's involvement in Spiritualism and various forms of occultism prepared him for leadership of this strange cult. According to a society document, King receives teachings from "Cosmic Masters from other Planets" as well as Master Jesus when he is in "positive Yogic Samadhic trance."

The society's goal is to enlist terrestrials on the side of the "space masters" in their war against certain "black magicians" living on earth.

Society teachings, which appear in King's books and the group's newsletter, *Cosmic Voice*, echo common occult tenets found in many earth-based faiths:

- Reincarnation: "People have lived thousands of lives as people before and they will live endless more 'lives.'"
- Humans are divine: "Man came forth from God and all things are a part of God."
- The Law of Karma: "Everything and everyone is subject to the great all-encompassing Law of God expounded by Jesus in these words: 'As you sow, so shall you reap.'"

The group has reaped few members, though. Its newsletter mailing list has fewer than one thousand names.

Society members are encouraged to maintain contact with orbiting spaceships and assist the occupants of these circling saucers, whose mission it is to direct their "energy" through the minds and bodies of King's followers. Members celebrate a number of holidays, including King's birthday and July 8, which is said to be the date that a gigantic space ship channeled cosmic energies to earth.

SOURCES: The Aetherius Society, "Some Basic Principles Included in Its Teaching"; Ronald Enroth, *The Lure of the Cults* (Chappaqua, N.Y.: Christian

Herald Books, 1979); J. Gordon Melton, *Encyclopedia of American Religions*, 6th ed. (Farmington Hills, Mich.: Gale Research, 1999).

ACCESS: 6202 Afton Place, Hollywood, CA 90028

See also UFOs.

TONY ALAMO

Music Square Church; Holy Alamo Christian Church, Consecrated

This man, once described as a cross between Jim Jones and Elvis Presley, believes he alone speaks for God and makes his followers respond accordingly.

FOUNDERS: Tony Alamo; Susan Alamo and Elizabeth Alamo

OVERVIEW: The year was 1970. I stood at the front door of a small frame house just off Sunset Strip in Hollywood. Outside, a sign read "Alamo Christian Foundation." Inside, a coed crowd mingled in a somewhat disorderly fashion.

When I inquired about the nature and purpose of their group, the "elder brother" in charge quickly informed me that I was sent from Satan and ordered me to leave. This small communal flophouse was the inauspicious beginning of an Alamo empire that would eventually stretch from a California ranch to a quiet town in Arkansas.

People in Hollywood like fashionable clothes, and for years, a complex figure named Tony Alamo supplied some of their needs. One of Alamo's for-profit companies specialized in rhinestone-studded jackets that earned him the nickname "Designer to the Stars."

When others weren't talking about him, Alamo had plenty to say about himself. He has proclaimed himself the instigator of the "Jesus Revolution" of the 1960s and 1970s. He also claims to have been a successful entrepreneur who "had the touch of Midas" in his business dealings.

Alamo even boasts that he was "exceedingly well-known in the music industry," and that he advised artists like Elvis, the Beatles, and the Rolling Stones. (Mysteriously, he is not mentioned in biographies of these or other artists.)

Most of the media attention Alamo has received has focused on his bizarre beliefs and the regimented, cultlike conditions in which his small band of followers live and work.

A 1983 *People* magazine article is typical of the coverage Alamo has received:

"In a darkened prayer room inside a sprawling mansion atop a remote, guarded ridge in rural Arkansas rests a coffin. Inside the coffin rests the embalmed body of Susan Alamo, patiently awaiting resurrection. The cult leader has been dead more than a year. Encouraged by Susan's husband, Tony, her followers kneel by the coffin in two-hour shifts, twenty-four hours a day, every day, to pray for Susan's return."

Pilgrimage to a Hollywood Commune

Tony Alamo was born Bernie Lazar Hoffman in 1934 in Missouri. He fancied himself a country gospel star and eventually changed his name to Tony Alamo. In California he met Susan, born Edith Opal Horn in Arkansas or Missouri in the 1920s, who was married to a small-time Los Angeles hood. She and Tony were married once in Tijuana and twice in Las Vegas, to be "triple sure."

This flamboyant couple with extravagant tastes fashioned an effective organization using Pentecostal-like theology and cultic control techniques. Neither was ordained as a minister. They simply walked up to hippies and drug addicts and asked, "Why are you destroying your mind, your soul, and your body?"

They found people who were ready to try religion. The ranks of recruits were made up of disillusioned street kids who found solace in the regimented lifestyle of the Alamo ranch complex. These converts seldom questioned their deplorable living conditions, though Tony and Susan lived in secluded splendor. Most foundation members seldom saw the Alamos except when their Cadillac Fleetwood zoomed by or when they were bused to Los Angeles to witness a taping of the Alamos' TV show.

On the Move

The Alamos shifted operations to Alma, Arkansas, in the mid-1970s amidst embarrassing press stories and investigations by various California agencies.

Susan's daughter left the group, charging that the couple was growing rich while taking advantage of their followers. In another ugly scene, a foundation member severely beat her own mother, aided by Susan's top lieutenant.

The foundation quickly settled into its new Arkansas home. The Alamos owned as many as twenty-nine businesses in the small town, and soon their businesses spread into several other states. Their business practices sparked new controversies.

Foundation members were expected to consider themselves "volunteers," running the businesses in return for meager living conditions. The U.S. Department of Labor became interested, and in a case taken all the way to the

U.S. Supreme Court, the Alamos were ordered to pay at least minimum wage to those followers who worked their businesses, from hog farms to hotels.

Even with minimum wage, foundation members experienced living conditions that were far from pleasant. In both California and Arkansas, recruits existed on a diet of harsh sermons and hard labor. Brainwashed into viewing noncult members—including families—as "agents of Satan," they shunned people from their former lives and unquestioningly worked long hours. They lived under a siege mentality, and the Alamos occasionally called "alerts," predicting imminent enemy attack.

If a member needed anything—from clothes to surgery—the Alamos required a written request called an "ask" memo. Members were only allowed to have books approved by the Alamos. They had no pets, no radios, no vacations, no movies, no newspapers. Single men and women in the foundation were not allowed to speak to each other. Even in marriage, privacy was hard to find. Susan decided who would have how many children.

One woman who left the cult stated that when she and her husband were finally allowed a house, it had no phone and they could not use the kitchen because all cult members were required to eat in the group cafeteria. They could turn on the heat for only ten minutes in the morning and ten minutes in the evening, even on the coldest days of winter.

Hellfire Humbug

Tony Alamo's theology mixes end-times paranoia with old-time, hellfire Pentecostalism, though some say their practice of speaking in tongues appeared to be a hypnotically induced utterance. The Alamos taught that all churches except their own were corrupt. In one of the organization's newsletters, a section called "Message from God" contains this bold proclamation from Tony:

"When God opened my heart, my mind, and my eyes to what He requires of men in order for them to be saved and ensure their eternal salvation, I was shocked to see that almost every pastor, preacher, and teacher was preaching and teaching the exact opposite of what the Bible teaches."

Members ate discarded foodstuffs and labored long hours in order to "crucify the flesh," and they zealously believed they were the vanguard of God's spiritual army. The press repeatedly raised charges of sensory deprivation, enslavement, and brainwashing. These allegations only served to reinforce the persecution paranoia that permeated the cult's thinking.

In the 1980s Tony Alamo spearheaded several campaigns, including a crusade condemning the Catholic church and calling for the impeachment of then president Ronald Reagan, "one of the pope's little helpers." He also launched a campaign to recruit unwed mothers to join or give their children to the foundation.

Members were instructed to pray diligently for the healing of Susan Alamo, who died of cancer in April 1982. Susan had been the "handmaiden of God"; she had been expected to miraculously cure herself and then with Tony lead a world crusade. Her death shook the faith of many followers, and Tony ordered members to pray unceasingly in shifts at her coffin.

Tony married his second wife, Elizabeth, in 1985. They guided the declining cult during the 1990s, a time of further trouble. In 1991 U.S. Marshals raided the group's 265-acre compound in order to force Alamo to comply with a $1.8 million child abuse court judgment.

A few years later Alamo was convicted of understating his income and failing to file tax returns from 1986 to 1988. These and other troubles led many fashionable Los Angeles stores to pull his line of clothing from their racks.

Once again Alamo claimed the agents of Satan were attacking God's anointed. "I'm fighting for the freedom of religion," he proclaimed. But few people listened and fewer still believed Alamo's heretical views or overinflated claims about his own importance.

SOURCES: Elizabeth Alamo, *It Was All a Lie!* testimony booklet; Tony Alamo, "Biting the Bullet" and "Message from God"; "Arkansas Sect Accuses Catholics of Variety of Ills," *Charisma*, August 1984, 98–100; Chet Flippo, "Siege of the Alamos," *People*, 13 June 1983, 29–33; G. W. Hunt, "Of Many Things," *America*, 25 May 1985, inside cover; Mary T. Schmich, "God and Glitz," *Chicago Tribune*, May 1991; "Wages and Religion," *Christian Century*, 8 May 1985, 464.

ACCESS: Music Square Church, P. O. Box 398, Alma, AR 72921; 501/782-7370; www.alamoministries.com

ALEPH

Aum Shinrikyo

The group behind a 1995 nerve gas attack in a Tokyo subway has changed its name and some of its tactics but not its extremist, apocalyptic teachings.

FOUNDER: Shoko Asahara

LEADER: Fumihiro Joyu

OVERVIEW: March 20, 1995, seemed like an ordinary day for the people of Tokyo. But before the morning was over, an extremist cult then known as Aum Shinrikyo had terrorized the city's residents and soared into the international spotlight.

Members of the cult filled plastic bags with the nerve gas sarin and placed the bags throughout the Tokyo subway system. When the bustling city's morning rush hour was in full swing, cult members used umbrellas to puncture the bags.

The subways quickly filled with the deadly gas. Twelve people died and 5,500 became ill. Thousands more were afflicted with a host of physical and psychological ailments.

Years later, news reporter Julie Chao summarized the event: "Long before anthrax entered America's daily vocabulary, a doomsday cult in Japan led by a half-blind guru was experimenting with the substance in a search for ways to kill as many people as possible. . . . The Aum Shinrikyo cult's forays into germ warfare and chemical weapons didn't start or end with anthrax. It also did research on the botulism microbe, poisonous gases, and at one point tried to obtain samples of the Ebola virus."

Why would the cult, which blends aspects of Buddhism and Hinduism and practices like yoga and meditation, want to cause widespread death and destruction? The answers can be found in the group's unusual history.

End-Times Enthusiast

A visually impaired man named Shoko Asahara founded Aum Shinrikyo (which means "Supreme Truth") in Japan in 1987. By the 1990s the group claimed it had fifty thousand members in Japan, Russia, and other countries, including a small contingent in the United States.

Asahara was fascinated with biblical prophecy and end-times scenarios, and he taught his followers to prepare for such eventualities. He studied the book of Revelation in the Bible and the writings of Nostradamus. He made predictions that World War III or Armageddon would happen in the late 1990s.

Critics said Asahara was an insecure, fearful, and demanding guru with a deep persecution complex who manipulated his followers more than he guided them, using drugs to keep them docile when necessary.

Asahara and other members of Aum Shinrikyo made an unsuccessful bid to run for office in national elections in Japan in 1990. Their political involvement raised public awareness regarding Asahara's prophecies. Many people believe the subway attack was his effort to kick-start his own end-times scenario.

Preparing for Survival

Asahara developed a training method that included teachings from tantric yoga, Buddhism, and Taoism and was intended to get students in touch with their true self. Believing that a worldwide apocalypse was coming, Asahara's teachings focused on making the preparations necessary to survive such a tragedy.

An article in USA Today said the group's training focused on surviving the predicted end of the world. Followers were told they could achieve salvation and become a Buddha in one lifetime by progressing through courses on spirituality that stressed the following elements:

- yoga and meditation
- psychic development
- isolation from mainstream society
- monastic lifestyles in group compounds
- three levels of initiation, including earthly, astral, and causal
- evangelistic efforts designed to recruit new members

USA Today also reported that the group operated a number of commercial facilities, including discount computer shops and a library.

Under the Spotlight

Of the many cults in the world, a fair number talk about the end of the world. Most people pay little attention to such groups, but the Tokyo subway attacks exposed Aum Shinrikyo to government investigations and unprecedented media scrutiny.

Investigators and reporters found much about the group that was troubling, and in a criminal trial Asahara and other members of the group were sentenced to prison.

One of those imprisoned was Fumihiro Joyu, who claimed that he had no advance knowledge about the subway attacks since he was in Russia at the time. Although Joyu was convicted of perjury, he was released from prison in 1999 and became the group's new leader.

As with many other cults whose teachings and practices get them into trouble, Joyu embarked on an aggressive public relations campaign. He changed the group's name to Aleph, which means "new beginning," and claimed it had rehabilitated itself.

Many aren't so sure. In an interview published in The New York Times, Joyu tried to distance Aleph from Aum Shinrikyo: "Japanese society has nothing to fear from us. I think that the most important factor in resolving this conflict is time. We need time to adapt ourselves to the real world, without losing our basic beliefs, and Japanese society needs time to get used to our different kind of philosophy and values."

But the group's leader simultaneously claimed the old and new groups were linked, telling the Times: "Just like you wouldn't stop your connection with physical fathers and mothers who commit a crime, we will not sever our connection with our spiritual father."

Some believe Joyu is sincere, but the Japanese government isn't taking his words at face value. Instead, it has placed the group under intense monitoring by the police and other agencies.

Perhaps that's not a bad idea for a group that in the past has been very serious about honoring Shiva, the Hindu god of destruction.

CHRISTIAN CRITIQUE: Although the group cites the Bible, it is very selective in the passages it cites, preferring the book of Revelation and other texts that are easily misinterpreted. In addition, the group blends together so many different teachings and techniques that in the end its doctrine resembles Asahara's paranoia more than it resembles any of the sources it cites.

The Bible clearly teaches that the end of the world will happen at a time and means dictated by God. No one should attempt to hasten this final apocalypse.

SOURCES: Julie Chao, "'95 Attack Sparked Fear but Few Changes in Japan," *Atlanta Journal-Constitution*, March 19, 2002, A6; Peter Hadfield, "Japanese cult in subway killing is back," *USA Today*, 21 April 1998; Calvin Sims, "Under Fire, Japan Sect Starts Over," *New York Times*, 28 February 2000, 7A. Other recommended resources include: Christopher C. Harmon, "Comparative Terrorism," *Books and Culture*, March/April 2002, 16; Haruki Murakami, trans. A. Birnbaum and P. Gabriel, *Underground: the Tokyo Gas Attack and the Japanese Psyche* (Vintage, 2001); Anthony Tu, *Chemical Terrorism: Horrors in Tokyo Subway and Matsumoto City*, 2002.

AMERICAN INDIAN SPIRITUALITY

See Native American Spirituality.

ANANDA MARGA YOGA SOCIETY

Yoga is supposed to promote inner peace, not outer chaos.
But this group's controversial tactics have caused problems in both
India and the United States.

FOUNDER: Shrii Shrii Anandamurti, also known as Prabhat Ranjan Sarkav

OVERVIEW: What Hindu-oriented group would dare consider its founder a *Maha-Guru (avatar*—incarnation of God) even after he had been sentenced to life in prison for murder?

The Ananda Marga Yoga Society claims that distinction. The group was founded in 1955 by Shrii Shrii Anandamurti, whose name means "one upon seeing him falls into bliss." His 1976 murder conviction was overturned in a later trial.

Still, the Ananda Marga Yoga Society remains a source of controversy in India. In 1982 more than a dozen members of the group were attacked and killed by a Calcutta mob that was incensed by reports the society was kidnapping and indoctrinating local children.

The Indian government frowns on the organization, insisting it is fascist and teaches ritual murder.

In the United States, the group has cultivated a more positive image and has attracted three to four thousand followers. The FBI has, however, investigated the group's alleged ties to international acts of terrorism.

Bliss or Blood?

Ananda Marga's leaders preach a message of joy and teach that the group offers followers a "path to bliss." This path of joy and bliss is laden with yogic principles and practices, including initiation by a guru and daily mantric meditation. Special emphasis is placed upon *Kiirtan* dancing, a swaying routine with raised arms. This motion is accompanied by a chant known as *Baba Nam Kevalam,* which means "the cosmic father is everywhere." These choreographed steps are designed to increase spiritual vibrations and help one realize that "all of creation is a manifestation of the Lord."

In addition to the *kundalini* yogic techniques, charitable service to society is encouraged as a way to "break down the ego-bound mind."

But the group is better known for recurring charges and accusations than it is for any good works. In Australia, where the group has a sizable following, three members were imprisoned for conspiring to murder one of the country's political figures.

At one time the group claimed to have five million members in one hundred countries, but few today accept such claims.

SOURCES: Karen Cooke, "Ananda Three Pardoned," *The Age (Melbourne, Australia)*, 16 May 1985; *Denver Post*, 15 August 1975, 4BB; "FBI Probes Yoga Group for Link to Terrorism," *Boston Globe* (United Press International), 28 August 1982; Pat Means, *The Mystical Maze* (San Bernardino, Calif.: Campus Crusade for Christ, 1976).

ACCESS: 97–38 42nd Ave., Corona, NY 11368. The group's publication, *Sadvipra*, is available by writing 854 Pearl St., Denver CO 80403.

ANGELS

"Fools rush in where angels fear to tread," wrote Alexander Pope two centuries ago. Today millions are rushing in where they believe angels are treading, but are these beings "angels" or deceptive devils?

The empire of angels is as vast as God's creation. If you believe the Bible, you will believe in their ministry. They crisscross the Old and New Testaments, being mentioned indirectly nearly 300 times.
BILLY GRAHAM, *ANGELS*

The angels are the dispensers and administrators of the divine beneficence toward us; they regard our safety, undertake our defense, direct our ways, and exercise a constant solicitude that no evil befall us.
JOHN CALVIN, *INSTITUTES OF THE CHRISTIAN RELIGION*

TEXT: Angels are mentioned hundreds of times in the Bible and are regular features in literature and myth. In the 1990s an avalanche of new books and magazine articles portrayed angels in new and unorthodox ways.

SYMBOL: Today angels are usually portrayed as beautiful creatures dressed in white and surrounded by gold.

OVERVIEW: Angels have been around longer then people have, but the 1990s was the decade that brought about a sudden burst in their popularity.

During that time these celestial messengers were the subject of cover stories in *Time, Newsweek, Ladies' Home Journal, Redbook,* and other major magazines. In 1993 five of the ten best-selling paperback books were about angels. In 1994 ABC aired a two-hour, prime-time special entitled "Angels, the Mysterious Messengers." That same year brought the premiere of a popular new TV drama series called *Touched by an Angel,* which won awards from many religious groups for its supposedly biblically based approach to life.

But not all the angels popular in the 1990s were so theologically correct. The year 1994 also saw the debut of a new magazine called *Angel Times.* Its premiere issue featured this impassioned statement from publisher Linda Vephula: "I believe it's time for a major spiritual paradigm shift. It's not about dogma, it's not about ceremony, it's not about chanting, it's not about preaching. The message is simple. It's love. Live love. Be love. We are all one."

Time magazine's cover story "Angels among Us" illustrated some of the problems involved in much of the angel euphoria. Writer Nancy Gibbs pointed out that Protestants and Catholics alike expressed concern about much of the current thinking about angels, saying it goes beyond orthodox theology and can turn Christian doctrine into a touchy-feely mysticism that ignores or distorts the truths of Scripture.

Accentuating the Positive, Ignoring the Negative

Like so many other popular contemporary religious and spiritual trends, the recent angel hysteria has focused only on the good: angels are seen almost solely as positive spiritual forces that help people in their daily lives. What's been lost is a more balanced biblical view that sees angels as more complex. The biblical perspective includes two important concepts that are ignored by many modern angelologists:

- Angels are created by God to do his will, not ours.
- Not all angels are good angels.

Like humans, angels were created with free will, which was abused by some of the earliest angels. Lucifer, one of the grandest and most important angels, decided to rebel against God. His rebellion and pride are powerfully described by the prophet Isaiah:

How art thou fallen from heaven, O Lucifer, son of the morning! how art thou cut down to the ground, which didst weaken the nations! For thou hast said in thine heart, I will ascend into heaven, I will exalt my throne above the stars of God: I will sit also upon the mount of the congregation, in the sides of the north: I will ascend above the heights of the clouds; I will be like the most High. Yet thou shalt be brought down to hell, to the sides of the pit. (14:12-15)

Divine Intermediaries

The Bible teaches that angels are superhuman beings who serve as intermediaries between the divine and human realm. Both Jewish and Christian traditions emphasize the important role angels have played through the ages. But when angels are removed from this biblical context, confusion creeps in.

As recently as two centuries ago angels were conjured by magicians, wizards, "wise women," and witches. In addition, angels were blamed for plagues, wars, and other tragic events. Much of this fascination with angels ended with the dawn of the Age of Enlightenment, which emphasized rationality and scientific experimentation over faith and myth.

Today that kind of intellectual thought is losing ground, and misconceptions about angels are growing like weeds. Other factors in the growing popularity of angelology include:

- increased interest in spirituality
- perceived endorsement by orthodox religions that teach about angelic beings
- a belief that angels are more accessible than other forms of spiritual aid and comfort
- the mistaken belief that all angels are always good and helpful

One cult researcher found that contemporary ideas about angels have little in common with the Bible: "These 'angels' foster a spirituality without sin, guilt, and God. They are contacted by various occultic means. They bring new revelations that contradict the Bible."

Only by turning to the authoritative words of the Bible will we be able to separate truth from falsehood concerning the nature and role of angels.

CHRISTIAN CRITIQUE: Historically, Christianity has taught that angels were created by God to do his will. However, the Bible gives an important additional perspective: some angels followed Lucifer in his rebellion against God and were banished from God's presence.

Today angels are almost universally seen as existing for the benefit of humanity, which ignores biblical teaching about fallen angels. It is also important to note that many non-Christian religious groups, such as Mormons and Jehovah's Witnesses, claim that their views were inspired by angels. While this may be true, the only angels who would depart from God's truth as revealed in the Bible are those who joined Lucifer in his rebellion against God.

While many people may find solace in supposed angelic comfort, it is important that their understanding of angels is based on God's truth rather than contemporary anecdotes, visionary experiences, or metaphysical speculation.

SOURCES: Nancy Gibbs, "Angels Among Us," *Time*, 27 December 1993, 56–65; Linda Vephula, "About Angel Times," *Angel Times*, undated 1994 collector's first edition (the magazine's Web site is said to be "under angelic construction").

ANTHROPOSOPHICAL SOCIETY

Rudolph Steiner; Waldorf Schools

Rudolph Steiner, who sought to combine religion and modern science, founded an international movement based in part on ancient occultic practices.

FOUNDER: Rudolph Steiner

TEXTS: A prolific writer who authored more than one hundred books, Steiner summarized some of the key aspects of his religious philosophy in these three volumes: *An Outline of Occult Science; Knowledge of the Higher Worlds and Its Attainment;* and *Theosophy: An Introduction to the Supersensible Knowledge of the World and the Destination of Man.*

OVERVIEW: Steiner was born in 1861 in an area of eastern Europe known for both its Lutheran heritage and devout Catholicism. Although raised in the Catholic church, Steiner soon looked outside of Christianity for new sources of spiritual revelation.

At age eight he experienced clairvoyance, and by the age of fifteen he had become associated with Felix Kotgutski, a teacher of occultism and herbalism. Both of these subjects would appear in his later work.

Steiner's esoteric dabbling became more focused when he was nineteen and began studying with a spiritual "master" who helped him define his mission in life: "to develop a knowledge that synthesized science and religion."

Many founders of new religious movements have had similar objectives, but Steiner knew more about science than most. An intellectual (his followers call him a genius) who was educated at some of Europe's finest schools, he studied mathematics and science at the Technische Hochschule in Vienna and received a doctorate at the University of Rostock in 1891.

An Insatiable Curiosity

But academic learning wasn't enough to satisfy Steiner, a man who felt compelled to experiment with numerous spiritual traditions. Following his formal studies, he published two books in 1894: *The Philosophy of Spiritual Activity* and *The Philosophy of Freedom.* He became a Theosophist and headed the German division of the Theosophical Society, which was chartered in 1902. But he split with Theosophy over its growing emphasis on Eastern religious philosophy.

Steiner went on to work on his own religious philosophy, which he called Anthroposophy (which means "the wisdom of man"; from *anthropos,* "man," plus *sophia,* "wisdom"). He called his new "spiritual science" a form of "true

Christianity." His complex blend of various sources has also been called "Christian Occultism."

Steiner founded the Anthroposophical Society in 1913. In 1923 Steiner reorganized the society as an international entity with headquarters in Dornach, Switzerland.

Borrowing from East and West

Steiner borrowed heavily from a variety of traditions, including the Christianity of his youth and the Eastern religious concepts he had criticized in Theosophy.

He was a prolific writer who authored more than one hundred books. In these volumes he imaginatively developed a complex history of mankind, including the mythology of Atlantis.

He theorized that humanity and earth have embarked on a progressive evolutionary journey overseen by certain beings of the "supersensible" spirit world. Reincarnation, *karma, chakras,* and meditation are all concepts of his system, which proposes that human perfection comes through a succession of embodiments.

Even the earth goes through evolutionary cycles, the current stage being its fourth reincarnation. Some of Steiner's views on the earth and agricultural methods have been of interest to members of the environmental movement. Decades before contemporary concerns over issues like pollution, he advocated something called "bio-dynamic farming," which emphasized chemical-free farming and gardening. He also developed guidelines for holistic medicine and pharmacology which are still popular in some circles today.

Corrupted Christianity

In 1919 the Roman Catholic Church declared Steiner a heretic. The church's reasons for doing so become clear when one understands how Steiner corrupted basic Christian teaching.

Instead of seeing Christ as the divine Son of God, Steiner saw Christ as the "one great arhat that transcends all others." He also taught that through certain techniques of meditation, all who follow Anthroposophy may also receive the Christ within them.

Steiner taught that Jesus was human until receiving the Christ-Essence at his Jordan River baptism. In addition, he contradicted the Bible by teaching the resurrection of Jesus was not a bodily resurrection. His spiritual, "phantom" (not bodily) resurrection was clairvoyantly perceived by the disciples.

Conflicts with the Bible don't worry Anthroposophists, who consider the Bible to be a valuable document of secret knowledge; they pay more attention to Steiner's works, which assume an authority above and beyond

Scripture. By meditating on Steiner's words, the acolyte becomes capable of mediumistically communicating with initiates and departed beings of the spirit world.

Other concepts of Anthroposophy include:

- *eurythmy*, a form of rhythmic movement;
- the founding of Waldorf schools, institutions dedicated to awakening spiritual consciousness in children;
- and the "fall" of humanity that reduced human beings to a baser consciousness, rendering them incapable of knowing their true origin and destiny.

A sacramental branch of the Anthroposophical Society offers a liturgical form of "Christianized" Anthroposophy called the Christian Community. With its priests and ministers looking after the flock, the Christian Community maintains a separate identity with no formal ties to Anthroposophy, though it also has no accommodation with orthodox Christianity.

Waldorf Schools

Steiner also turned his attention to the subject of education. The result was the first Waldorf School for Boys and Girls, which opened in 1919 in Stuttgart, Germany.

Today Waldorf schools make up an international school system that supporters claim has more than seven hundred schools in dozens of nations around the world. Many of these schools boast a low teacher-to-student ratio, a warm and accepting educational environment, and a curriculum that is more child-directed than program-directed.

The Waldorf schools don't publicize their links to Rudolph Steiner and his occultic philosophy. In fact, some of the schools even deny any such link exists. As a result, many parents who enroll their children in these schools are unaware of their true spiritual origins.

Harper's Encyclopedia of Mystical and Paranormal Experience says that "the Waldorf system is now the largest nonsectarian system of education in the world."

If true, this statement may indicate that the Waldorf Schools are a much more effective vehicle for promoting some of Steiner's views than the nearly three dozen Anthroposophical Society offices located around the world.

CHRISTIAN CRITIQUE: Steiner was an intelligent man who believed that religion and science could work together. He also anticipated some of the major intellectual movements that would develop after his death, such as the West's interest in ecology and the Muslim world's critique of Western consumerism. He has attracted the attention of many people who are interested in leading a more spiritual, simpler, and less commercial life.

Even though Steiner taught that a form of mystical Christianity replaced the outdated Eastern religions, his syncretistic result was an occult system more attuned to Spiritualism than the Good News. His faulty view of Jesus has more to do with Eastern religion than true Christianity.

Rudolph Steiner was unquestionably an articulate man, but his perception of Christ as the "Lord of Karma" was clouded by his own subjective interpretation of occult phenomena.

SOURCES: *Harper's Encyclopedia of Mystical and Paranormal Experience* (San Francisco: HarperSanFrancisco, 1991); J. Gordon Melton, *The Encyclopedia of American Religions*, vol. 2 (Wilmington, N.C.: McGrath, 1978); *Spiritual Counterfeits Project Newsletter*, vol. 3, no. 1, February 1977, 4–7.

ACCESS: 1923 Geddes Ave., Ann Arbor, MI 48104-1797

See also Theosophy.

ARICA INSTITUTE

Who wouldn't want "body vitality," "mental clarity" and a "perfect society"?
These things and more, like "a permanent higher level of awareness," are promised
by this organization that had its beginnings in Latin America in 1971.

FOUNDER: Oscar Ichazo

APPEAL: In its offer to restore the essence of man's perfection, Arica attracts many who are emotionally disturbed or disenchanted with other self-improvement therapies. Ironically, Oscar Ichazo blames the ills of humanity on society's failure to adopt his ideas wholeheartedly. Consequently, he now offers forty-day courses, instead of the original three-month training, for universities and retirement communities.

OVERVIEW: In the Quechua language of the Andes Indians *arica* means "open door." Arica is also the name of a Chilean town to which fifty-four Americans were lured in 1971. They were invited by a Bolivian philosophy teacher and mystic, Oscar Ichazo. Ichazo offered to take these seekers of truth beyond the inhibitions of their egos to "the Permanent 24," a secret name describing the mysterious state of "unity with emptiness."

That original small group has now grown to an estimated twenty-five thousand adherents (by Arica estimates) who have undergone Ichazo's training, plus some twenty-five hundred new candidates, who each year shell out $995 apiece for induction into Arica.

Arica instructors practice what they call "scientific mysticism," claiming it will uncover *toham kum rah*, "the mystical name of the radiant being," inside each person.

Although Arica literature proclaims it is "not a religion," the institute draws from the religious philosophies of Hinduism, Zen, and Tibetan Lamaism in order to develop psychocalisthenics, a series of twenty-three movement-breathing exercises designed to awaken vital energy.

One such exercise, the *Audicon Plantar*, teaches students to lie on the floor and absorb sound with their feet. In addition to breathing techniques, African dances, Egyptian gymnastics, Hindu mantras and incantations, the seekers engage in "mentations." This odd practice requires the student to concentrate on a separate section of his or her body for specified time periods: eight minutes, forty seconds for the colon and kidneys; ten minutes forty-five seconds for the liver, etc.

SOURCES: Arica promotional advertisement, copyrighted 1973; *East-West Journal*, June 1976; *Time*, 29 May 1972, 88; Ibid., 9 November 1981, 20.

ACCESS: 145 Palisades St., Dobbs Ferry, NY 10522

See also Esalen.

ASATRU FREE ASSEMBLY

See Odinism.

ASCENDED MASTERS
I AM Movements

Spiritually superior beings who supposedly lived in centuries past are now said to send their followers messages from the spirit world.

FOUNDER: G. W. Ballard

TEXTS: Selected portions of the Bible; various works of G. W. Ballard (pen name Godfre Ray King), including: *Unveiled Mysteries* and *The Magic Presence*; *The Ascended Master Discourses* by "Various Ascended Masters"; *The "I AM" Discourses* by "The Great Divine Director"; and *I AM* magazine, which the Ballards published in the late 1930s and early 1940s.

SYMBOLS: A winged flame, reading from left to right, *AIM*, with the *I* twice as high as its flanking letters; seven rays representing life, with rays of varying colors representing various aspects of the "I AM" belief.

APPEAL: The various self-proclaimed representatives of the Ascended Masters promise to give people control over their spiritual and physical being, leading to interplanetary alliances and peace. Followers are encouraged to trust these disembodied leaders, who are supposed "to give help from their octave of life."

Some leaders of the "I AM" movements claim that believers must join their groups immediately, for no other creed or system, no outer activity in the world today, can solve the world's problems or stop the destruction that human beings are releasing against each other.

OVERVIEW: In Yugoslavia schoolchildren see supernatural manifestations. Throughout the United States crosses of light are reportedly seen in the sky. At a remote faith-healing center in the slums of Nairobi, Kenya, Sister Mary Akatsa welcomes a guest speaker into her fold. His name, she claims, is Jesus Christ.

Across the nation and around the world, followers of so-called Ascended Masters are proclaiming that the appearances of superior spiritual beings portend the second coming of Jesus. Virtually anyone can claim to be speaking for the Ascended Masters, and not all who do so agree about what these disembodied leaders from a higher spiritual plane are saying.

Still, there are many people in the world who pay close attention when a teaching or prediction is ascribed to these spiritually superior beings.

Benjamin Crème is one of the most popular representatives of the Ascended Masters in recent history. Crème claims that a person known as Maitreya (or the metaphysical Lord of the Second Advent, also known as Jesus) arrived on earth on July 19, 1977. Alive and well in London's Pakistani community, Maitreya is apparently in no hurry to reveal his identity to the world. Crème says that when Maitreya is ready, he will announce his return by appearing on television.

A Bridge to the Beyond

Many religions venerate deceased spiritual leaders, and the New Testament talks about "the fellowship of the saints." But Ascended Masters encourages communication with these and other departed adepts.

The first person in modern times to talk about the Ascended Masters ideology was G. W. Ballard. He claimed that while he was at Mount Shasta, California, in 1930, he was visited by Saint Germain, a spiritual being who had attained "Christhood" during his time on earth.

Following this meeting Ballard used the pen name Godfre Ray King and published his first two books, Unveiled Mysteries and The Magic Presence, to promote his new teachings.

Ballard's Saint Germain series proclaimed to the world the "I AM," or the individualized God Presence within us. Today, many groups signify their links to Ballard's ideas by using the words "I AM" in their teaching and literature.

Ballard's books also declared the existence of a cosmic government, whose hierarchy consisted of former earthly residents. Believers in Ascended Masters claim that, as members of the earth's governing body, these discarnate entities provide necessary instruction on purifying, energizing, and harmonizing human thought. Through correct ideas, Ascended Masters' teachings profess that anyone can obtain perfection, stop all suffering, and become divine.

Twenty-six years after G. W. Ballard's introductory encounter with St. Germain, the Ascended Masters allegedly initiated contact with confirmed atheist Pauline Sharpe. Born of Jewish parents in Brooklyn, New York, in 1925, Sharpe was told to prepare for the second coming of Jesus, the Christ. Chronological excerpts of her channeled communication with the Ascended Masters from 1958 to 1970 are compiled in her 1974 book MAPP to Aquarius.

Claiming to have been anointed by her master teacher, Sananda/Jesus, Sharpe is known as Nada Yolanda to followers of the Ascended Masters. The name Nada, taken from her past incarnation as a high priestess of the Sun Temple, represents her "reborn" self-identity, while Yolanda is her soul aspect.

Together with Charles Boyd Gentzel, "reborn" as Mark Age, Yolanda developed the Mark-Age of Ascended Masters, a partnership that spanned twenty-one years. In death, the former Boyd Gentzel channels to Yolanda as El Morya, Chohan, or Director of the First Ray of Will and Power.

Another member of the loose-knit "I Am" fold is Lori Adaile Toye, whose channeled "I AM America" map predicts that major portions of the world will be covered by water within a few hundred years.

More recently, a group called the Trinity Foundation claimed that an

Ascended Master named Kuthumi had sent a transmission to Norma Milanovich, the group's executive director. The transmission urged Milanovich to enroll students in twelve fifty-dollar classes that "are designed to accelerate our spiritual evolution . . . to facilitate bringing peace on Earth in the millennium."

Mixing Movies, Mysticism, and Metaphysics

Some aspects of G. W. Ballard's version of the Ascended Masters sounded similar to plots of science fiction movies of the 1930s and 1940s. In later years the movement adapted other aspects of Eastern mysticism and metaphysics and techniques such as astral projection, trance channeling, and reincarnation.

Sananda, a member of the Council of Seven, or highest ruling body of the solar system, reportedly had previous earth incarnations, including Jesus of Nazareth, the biblical figures Melchizedek, Elijah, and Moses, as well as Gautama Buddha and Socrates.

In Ascended Masters' theology, God is defined as a "creative force that has a negative and positive polarity, as each atom in creation has its negative and positive poles." He is comprised of seven major groupings: will and power; intelligence and wisdom; personal love and feeling; crystallization; unity, integration, healing, and balance; transmutation, cleansing, and purification; and divine love, peace, and rest. The Son is the product of God's duality of Father-Mother.

Life is lived under the tutelage of guardian angels. Strife enters our lives via negative thoughts. Criticism, condemnation, and judgment cause all suffering, including disease. Death supposedly occurs when the body is not purified, and the guardian angel's life ray is withdrawn. Once dead, the spirit takes on new dimension and remains in this form until it receives additional cosmic instruction.

CHRISTIAN CRITIQUE: The beliefs of the Ascended Masters are sprinkled with heresies. The movement discounts the importance of Jesus Christ, placing him on the same level as other religious teachers. Even though many in the movement use Christian jargon, their metaphysical approach downplays Christianity and emphasizes Eastern influences, mysticism, Gnosticism, pantheism, Pelagianism, and syncretism. Followers of the Ascended Masters claim control over their spiritual and worldly destinies and assert that increased consciousness leads the way to a new interplanetary dimension. Their belief that man's fall from grace occurred following the Second Golden Age 2.5 million years ago contradicts Scripture.

SOURCES: Mrs. G. W. Ballard and Donald Ballard, *The Purpose of the Ascended Masters "I AM" Activity* (Santa Fe, N.M.: St. Germain Press, 1942).

ACCESS: Among the major groups: "I AM" Religious Activity, St. Germain Foundation/St. Germain Press, 1120 Stonehenge Dr., Schaumburg,

IL 60194; Ascended Masters Teaching Foundation, Box 466, Mount Shasta, CA 96067.

For decades, the group has not responded to inquiries from the media or religion researchers.

See also Benjamin Crème and Church Universal and Triumphant.

ASSEMBLIES OF YAHWEH

Sacred Name Movement

Descended from groups founded to honor the name and Old Testament holy days of God, the movement is now splintered and divided.

FOUNDERS: The Assemblies of Yahweh faith derived in the 1930s from the Sacred Name Movement among some Church of God (Seventh Day) ministers. Some of the individual Assemblies and their founders are: Institute of Divine Metaphysical Research—Dr. Henry Clifford Kinley, 1931; Assemblies of Yahweh, Holt, Michigan—C. O. Dodd, 1939; Scripture Research Association—A. B. Traina, 1940s; Assembly of Yahvah—L. D. Snow and E. B. Adam, 1949; Assemblies of Yahweh, Bethel, Pennsylvania—Jacob O. Meyer, from *The Sacred Name Broadcast*, 1966; Assembly of YHWHHOSHUA—Laycher Gonzales, 1970s.

TEXTS: Several Assemblies of Yahweh groups have issued their own translations of the Bible. Among these are *The Restoration of Original Sacred Name Bible*, Missionary Dispensary Bible Research; *The Sacred Name Bible*, translated by A. B. Traina; *The Sacred Scriptures*, Bethel edition, Assemblies of Yahweh, Bethel, Pennsylvania.

SYMBOLS: The Assemblies of Yahweh of Bethel, Pennsylvania, display Hebrew lettering on the cover of their Bible, *The Sacred Scriptures*. They also partake of unleavened bread and grape juice as symbols of the Savior's body and blood during their Passover observance.

APPEAL: Many are attracted by the strict morality of the Assemblies of Yahweh faith. Some join out of a sincere desire to change their lives and obey God's commandments.

OVERVIEW: In 1979 the U.S. Supreme Court declined to review a Colorado suit brought against the state's motor vehicle division by two members of the Assembly of YHWHHOSHUA.

David Johnson and Anthony Virgil had been denied driver's licenses for refusing on religious grounds to have their photographs taken. They claimed their faith forbade making graven images. The Colorado State Supreme Court ruled that compelling reasons exist for requiring photographs on driver's licenses and that "no alternative less restrictive of religious freedoms" is acceptable. Unimpressed, members of the sect centered near Pueblo, Colorado, promised to continue driving, with or without licenses.

An aversion to photography is only one trait of the fundamentalist Assembly of YHWHHOSHUA, whose members also oppose hospitals, doctors, medication, social security, banks, medicare, and unemployment insurance.

Honoring God's Name

The Assembly of YHWHHOSHUA was founded in the 1970s by Laycher Gonzales, who said he first learned of the name of God from a hitchhiking prospector named O. K. Skidmore.

Believing that the Hebrew words YHWH (Yahweh without the vowels) and Hoshua (Joshua) are the only true names for God and Jesus, they blot out of their books all other names for God.

The common names for the months and weekdays are not used, since they have pagan origins. Children are educated in church schools with Mennonite textbooks. Science is considered unnecessary and is ignored. A modest dress code requires wearing loose robes over street clothes at all times. Alcohol, tobacco, drugs, jewelry, dancing, dating, cologne, and haircuts are forbidden. Secular and religious artwork is considered blasphemous. Christmas and Easter are not observed as holidays.

As is the case with many separatist cults, perfectionism can lead to abuse. A year after the lawsuit over the driver's licenses, Gonzales was accused by a former member of using mind-control techniques on his followers.

A Complex Family Tree

Another offbeat organization with more mystical overtones was Dr. Henry Clifford Kinley's Institute of Divine Metaphysical Research, founded in 1931 after the doctor supposedly had a face-to-face conversation with God (who Kinley called Yahweh-Elohim). This divine revelation led to Kinley's lifelong preaching of the universal calamity that would mark the end of the modern age.

The Institute of Divine Metaphysical Research and the Assembly of YHWHHOSHUA are only two of many splinter groups derived from the 1930s Sacred Name Movement. Today the most common name for the faith is the Assemblies of Yahweh, though various spellings of the name are used.

Headquarters of the Assemblies of Yahweh, founded in 1939 by C. O. Dodd, are in Holt, Michigan. Originally known as the Assembly of Yhwh, it now uses the more easily pronounced spelling of God's name. The group publishes *The Faith* magazine and distributes literature through the Faith Bible and Tract Society. The loosely organized assembly has congregations around the country and proposes to restore the true names for God (Yahweh and Elohim) and Jesus (Yahshua).

The Pennsylvania-based Assemblies of Yahweh has its origins in *The Sacred Name Broadcast,* which Jacob O. Meyer began in 1966. The group publishes *The Sacred Name Broadcaster* magazine and offers free literature from its headquarters in Bethel, Pennsylvania.

Old Testament Law and New-Fangled Heresies

The Assemblies of Yahweh believes in keeping the Old Testament commandments first delivered to the Israelites. Members observe Saturday instead of Sunday as their day of devotion and celebrate Passover, Hanukkah, and other Jewish festivals. Because the Assemblies of Yahweh is based on the Old Testament faith, members closely follow the ancient Israelites' religious laws, which include observance of food restrictions and tithing.

Apostolic practices borrowed from the New Testament include baptism by immersion, anointing, and a belief in divine healing. Salvation comes through accepting the "revealed, personal Name of our Heavenly Father, YAHWEH, and the Name of His Son, our Savior, YAHSHUA the Messiah."

Both the Michigan and Pennsylvania assemblies reject the teaching about the Trinity. According to the Bethel group's statement of doctrine, such a belief has no basis in the Scriptures. The Holy Spirit is defined as "the mighty power from the Heavenly Father and the Messiah dwelling within us so that we may . . . bring our lives into a state of perfection." This power is imparted by Assemblies of Yahweh elders through the laying on of hands after baptisms. Members do not ingest addicting or illegal drugs, believing the Holy Spirit will abandon impure, unsanctified bodies.

The Bethel assembly's doctrine also rejects the traditional Christian concept of an eternal hell. They believe the wicked will be completely destroyed in a lake of fire known as Gehenna. They do recognize a personified devil and believe he will be destroyed at the end of the Millennium.

The Bethel assembly also stresses nonviolence. Members are advised to refrain from all military duty. The assembly recommends conscientious objection, with alternative service in other fields approved by the U.S. government.

The Bethel assembly patterns its church government after that of the early Christians. Individual assemblies are led by a pastor, who is assisted by a teaching elder and a deacon. Doctrinal matters are decided by bishops and ordained ministers, who preside over the appointed body of male elders. Appointments are lifelong, though faithless elders can be removed for transgressions. Women are forbidden to preach. Assemblies of Yahweh tithes feed into a general fund at Bethel, from which local assemblies take allowances.

Members do not take each other to court over legal matters. Family life is important, and divorce is discouraged. Parents teach their children religion, since the Assemblies of Yahweh believes there is no scriptural basis for Sunday schools. Women are required to cover their heads during services. Evangelism and conversion of others is the overall aim of the Assemblies of Yahweh, and each member is encouraged to witness to nonbelievers.

CHRISTIAN CRITIQUE: Assemblies of Yahweh members believe the commonly used names of God and Jesus are human inventions. Their purpose is to replace these words with the "true" and "divinely revealed" sacred names.

But for all their emphasis on such issues, these groups have succumbed to much more problematic heresies. They deny the Holy Trinity and the orthodox concept of hell as a place of eternal punishment, and they reject Christian holidays in favor of Jewish ones. They believe the only Christians who will be saved are those who use the sacred names and that obedience to the Old Testament religious laws can win spiritual salvation—a teaching directly at odds with the words of Jesus. In their words, "We affirm that it is necessary and most important to our salvation that we accept the revealed, personal Name of our Heavenly Father YAHWEH and the Name of His Son, our Savior YAHSHUA the MESSIAH. We affirm also that the most accurate transliteration of these Names from the Hebrew into the English is by the spellings employed."

Assemblies of Yahweh literature liberally cites chapter and verse of both the Old and New Testaments, drawing upon biblical support for all tenets and practices. In reality, they have made the Old Testament more important than the New. Assemblies of Yahweh proponents write lengthy articles about their faith, carefully deleting when possible the vowels from the words *God, Lord,* and *Christ.* This approach to theology places more emphasis on how to spell God's name than living faithfully by his Word.

Other major departures from orthodox Christianity include: the necessity of "backwards" baptism in the name of Yahshua for salvation; observing the Saturday Sabbath; determining months scripturally by moons; the strict keeping of Jewish feasts; adherence to the Levitical laws concerning unclean meats; payment of an obligatory tithe to the ministry headquarters; women covering their heads for worship and witnessing; avoidance of military service. Such doctrines clearly separate the Sacred Name Movement from mainstream Christianity, a schism which would be quickly repaired by the movement's careful reading of Paul's epistle to the Galatians.

SOURCES: *Denver Post,* 10 October 1979, 1–2; Henry Clifford Kinley, Infallible, Biblical and Scientific Proof of How, When, and for What Purpose the

Universe Was Created (Hollywood, Calif.: Institute of Divine Metaphysical
Research, 1969); J. Gordon Melton, *Encyclopedia of American Religions*, vol. 1
(Wilmington, N.C.: McGrath, 1978), 476–479; *Pueblo Chieftain and Star-Journal*, 13 December 1980, 1, 6A; *Rocky Mountain News*, 2 October 1979, 10, 42;
The Sacred Name Broadcaster, April 1983, 2–5; *The Sacred Scriptures* (Bethel,
Penn.: Assemblies of Yahweh, n.d.), 102; *Statement of Doctrine* (Bethel, Penn.:
Assemblies of Yahweh, 1981), 2–10.

ACCESS: The Assemblies of Yahweh, Bethel, PA 19507

ASSOCIATION FOR RESEARCH AND ENLIGHTENMENT

See Edgar Cayce.

ASTARA

This group claims to honor all religions but simultaneously says its own
syncretistic approach is better than all earlier traditions.

In all Astarians there's no dogmatic trace,
We see the light of God in every face;
In mosque, cathedral and in synagogue,
Wherever man may lift his cry to God.
"AN ASTARIAN" BY EARLYNE CHANEY

FOUNDERS: Robert and Earlyne Chaney

TEXT: Genesis 1:1-3 is paraphrased without any indication that the
Chaneys' version is extrabiblical: "And God said, 'Let there be Light in the
minds of men.' And God created channels through which the Light might
come. And one of them was Astara. And God looked upon Astara and He saw
that it was good."

SYMBOLS: Seven-pointed "Star of the West," merging inside the "Lotus of the East." Astara literature also incorporates the symbols of many other religions.

APPEAL: Astara appeals to people with an interest in occult and psychic phenomena and a need for a historical basis for discovering hidden truths. Its secret ceremonies and promises of miraculous healing are also an attraction. Another appealing aspect to many is the group's unique blend of Eastern religious philosophy and ancient mystery schools (especially Egyptian) with Christian concepts.

OVERVIEW: "It is possible that I may have erred in receiving them [messages from the teachers of the spirit world]. Therefore if errors are brought forth in the lessons, it is I who am to blame. I alone must be held fully responsible," says Astara founder Earlyne Chaney in *Astara's Book of Life*, "First Degree Lesson 1."

Mrs. Chaney's admission of fallibility is rare among spiritualists. But lest anyone should think she approaches the teachings of Astara with ambivalence, she confidently declares (in the same booklet from which the above quote was taken): "It [Astara] guides the disciple toward the inner mysteries of life, death, God, man—and the ultimate initiation: immortality."

Contradictory teachings are common for this group, which on the one hand says it respects and welcomes members of all faiths, but on the other claims that people never really excel spiritually until they leave other religions behind and join Astara on a "cosmic expedition" like no other: "In whatever placid and contained reservoir they have drifted heretofore, at Astara they find the shining high tide of understanding and personal spiritual fulfillment."

From Death to Light

Astara means "a place of light" and is taken from the name of the Greek goddess of divine justice, Astraea. The group's teachings form an eclectic cult that encompasses spiritualism, Theosophy, yoga, Christianity, mystery schools, Rosicrucianism, and various occult orders and disciplines. For those who ask, "Why then follow Astara?" Mrs. Chaney answers, "Astara has come forth as a Light Bearer in the latter part of this century."

When she was twenty-eight years old, Earlyne Chaney's world was shattered by the death of her fiancé. The event had been prophesied by a spirit being named Kut-Hu-Mi, with whom she had communicated clairvoyantly since she was a child. (Kut-Hu-Mi taught her to develop psychic powers, including a methodology called *The Great Work of the Pentralia*, which contains a secret yoga system called *Lhama Yoga*.)

Two years after this tragedy, she met and married Robert Chaney, a spiritualist who had his own spirit guide named Ram. Earlyne then left the acting profession, and in 1951 she and Robert moved to California where they formed the Astara Foundation.

In creating Astara's complicated theology, the Chaneys drew from Masonic, Rosicrucian, and Theosophical beliefs. But their central doctrines are said to be rooted in the teachings of Hermes Trismegistus, the ancient Egyptian magician who is believed to be the organizer of the original mystery school from which all others were derived.

Another Egyptian named Zoser is the Chaneys' current spiritual guide. His god name is Nekerkeht, which literally means "God in flesh," and Astarians are told to call on his name if in need of healing. Members have been known to see materializations of Zoser, whom it is said gives of his efforts exclusively to Astara.

Despite these pagan overtones, Astara still endeavors to hide itself behind a veneer of Christian beliefs. While accepting the tradition of avatars, including Buddha, Astarians insist that God was most completely revealed in Christ, whom the Chaneys profess to revere as "the Light of the World." This "cosmic Christ" is said to be "the Lord of our planet, begotten before the beginning of our time and age."

The Astarian denial of Christ as Creator God, eternal and the only begotten of the Father, is consistent with the minor role he actually plays in Astara. Issues of the *Voice of Astara*, the foundation's monthly publication, abound with messages from Kut-Hu-Mi, but few biblical references are cited. The lessons do quote certain scriptural passages, but only out of context to support occult principles.

A "Cosmic Bank Account"

Astara promises soul progress, the solving of life's enigmas, the developing of "inner faculties," the healing of illnesses, spiritual brotherhood, expansion of consciousness, self-unfoldment, and God-realization.

Membership in Astara is said to be like a "cosmic bank account" where you earn interest in peace of mind and enlightenment. Members are told that when death comes they will "fade from consciousness and go to the Valley of Rewards" where they will "find again all they have deposited in the Cosmic Bank."

Though regular services are held at the organization's headquarters in Upland, California, most of the teaching is carried on through correspondence courses. Astarians are led through four degrees containing at least twenty lessons each.

The first few instructions explore elementary occult mystical practices. As the studies progress, the initiate is gradually introduced to secret documents revealing the Astarian sign, word, and handgrip. At this point the techniques of Lhama Yoga are taught. Almost every kind of psychic phenomena is pursued, with the exception of Ouija boards and automatic writing. Chaney acknowledges the demonic nature of such practices by warning members against the "disastrous consequences of those who indulge in them."

Healing plays a central role in Astarian philosophy. The *Voice of Astara* is filled with testimonies from those who have experienced supposedly miraculous cures. Members are encouraged to send their healing petitions to the headquarters' shrine, where a group of four Astarians, known as the Circle of the Secret Seven, will intercede on their behalf. Neophite Astarians are told that these individuals are "dedicated ones who touch and influence the cosmic powers of etheric realms for cosmic assistance."

The whole system of Astara is highly complex and includes phenomena such as arcane biorhythms, *prana* breath techniques, ethereal bodies, astral projection, polarity, and laws of vibrations and correspondence. The sacred word, sign, and handgrip are apparently taught during trance states.

Members are told that the "Divine Hierarchy of Great Beings" who once brought wisdom and knowledge to man have come again from the "Universal Brotherhood" to reveal life's mysteries through Astara. Considering the possibility that these "Great Beings" may be evil spirits, there is little comfort in Earlyne Chaney's admonition that "the presence of Astarian Masters overshadows your life."

CHRISTIAN CRITIQUE: Much of Astarian teaching should be of concern to committed Christians. Astarians decree verbally, "I am perfect," denying man's sinful nature. Without historical evidence, Astara claims Christ traveled to Egypt, Tibet, and India and was initiated there at mystery schools. The Bible is said to have hidden truth that requires special interpretation to be "rightly understood." The founders of Christianity are said to have "brought forth the doctrine of the resurrection of the physical body at the Judgment Day. A blind, believing humanity accepted the doctrine, and some still do."

The exclusive nature of Christ's salvation is denied by Astara's teaching that many paths lead to the "Infinite Being." In fact, all religions are simultaneously honored and declared bankrupt by this syncretistic group that claims "Astara is a complement to any religion" but denies any religious claim of exclusivity.

Astara ignores the Bible's warning against consulting "familiar spirits," or spirits of the dead (Isaiah 8:19); spirit guides (demons) are revered and elevated above Christ. When the founders of Astara claim to be "light bearers," they are apparently unaware that this is also the meaning of *Lucifer*, the name of the devil.

SOURCES: Miscellaneous Astara literature, including: "If You Are a Seeker . . . ," "Astara's Book of Life," "You and Astara," *Voice of Astara* (various issues); Robert Chaney, pamphlet/flyer from Astara, 24 March 1987; J. Gordon Melton, *The Encyclopedia of American Religions* (Wilmington, N.C.: McGrath, 1978), 183–184.

ACCESS: 792 West Arrow Highway, P.O. Box 5003, Upland, CA 91785

See also Spiritualism.

ASTROLOGY

Want to make a decision, find love, or earn a fortune on Wall Street? Astrologers claim that all the answers you need are in the stars.

FOUNDERS: Chaldeans of the ancient Babylonian Empire

TEXTS: Various occult volumes and oral traditions, including some Bible passages that are taken out of context to condone astrology

SYMBOLS: The twelve zodiac signs

APPEAL: In an age of uncertainty, people look for something to bring structure to their lives. Political, economic, and social turmoil create fear and uncertainty, which some feel could be assuaged by knowing the future. Astrology becomes a faith system, with the horoscope as its liturgy. Many who have abandoned the church find solace in astrology's tenets.

Astrology postulates that human lives are influenced (and in some cases predetermined) by the fixed position of certain heavenly bodies at the moment of birth. Earthly events are also affected by the relative positions of the planets and stars. Important decisions and momentous occasions should be considered with respect to their relationship regarding the horoscope.

OVERVIEW: Fifty centuries ago the Chaldeans of the Babylonian Empire observed the influence of the sun upon the earth and the moon upon the seas. They concluded that the planets were gods, and therefore certain conjunctions of their movements would have an effect upon wars, governments, and the destinies of men. Other methods of fortune-telling, such as surveying the entrails of animals, often proved unpredictable. The positions of the stars were dependable.

Today the techniques originally developed by these ancient astrologers are still used by millions of people who read the horoscopes and astrology sections in their daily newspapers or see them in women's magazines like *Glamour*, *Vogue*, and *Cosmopolitan*. Times and communication technology have changed, but the basic concepts—and the basic problems—of astrology have remained amazingly constant.

Many people believe there is nothing wrong with reading their horoscopes. "I don't really believe in it," they say. "Maybe it's all a bunch of bunk, but it's good for a laugh. What harm is there in seeing what my horoscope says?"

As a result, astrology is probably one of the most popular occult arts the world has ever seen. Pollster George Gallup says that one in five adult

Americans believe in astrology and eight in ten can name the sign under which they were born. There are three times as many astrologers as there are clergymen in the Roman Catholic Church. Nearly two thousand newspapers carry a daily horoscope. Astrology shows run on cable TV stations, and horoscope Web sites keep thousands of people glued to their computer monitors.

Even Nancy Reagan, the wife of President Ronald Reagan, acknowledged consulting an astrologer and attempting to use the information she gained to influence her husband's political decisions. The American public reacted to this revelation with a collective yawn.

But indifference and even skepticism can turn into gullibility when the horoscope's predictions seem to come true or when it promises love, a raise or promotion, or some other wonderful event. Such warm feelings and rationalizations don't change the fact that astrology—along with palmistry, witchcraft, numerology, and other practices—is identified in the Bible as a forbidden occult practice.

Science or Bunk?

Part of astrology's appeal is that it appears to be based on the scientific laws of astronomy. But when 186 distinguished scientists issued a statement on astrology, they clearly pointed out it didn't work: "The time has come to challenge directly and forcefully the pretentious claims of astrological charlatans. It's simply a mistake to imagine that the forces exerted by stars and planets at the moment of birth can in any way shape our future."

In spite of such scathing condemnation, belief in the effect celestial bodies can exert over human affairs continues unabated. This has been helped, no doubt, by the fact that some renowned people—the late psychologist Carl Jung, for example—believed in astrology.

Still, much has changed since the ancient Chaldeans looked at the stars. In their day, the Chaldeans held a geocentric view of the universe. In other words, they thought the earth was the center of the cosmos. Copernicus and later astronomers revealed that the cosmos is much bigger than anyone had thought and that the sun was the center of our solar system, not the earth. But astrology continues to be based on the ancient, outmoded, geocentric view. The sun signs and the various predictions are based on this prescientific approach.

Astrology uses a model of the universe that is like a spoked wheel. According to the geocentric view, the center where the spokes meet indicates the location of the earth, and the outer rim signifies the path the sun takes through the heavens each day as it revolves about the earth. Astrologers say the area indicated by the outer rim is about sixteen degrees wide and represents the zones of the zodiac. What concerns zodiac consultants are certain star constellations that appear within the pathway of the sun as it travels through the heavens. This band is divided into twelve equal sections representing the twelve divisions, or "houses," of the astrological zodiac.

During the course of a year, the twelve constellations, or signs of the zodiac, move through each of the twelve houses. In addition, each of the nine planets as well as the moon and sun move through each house every twenty-four hours. Just why the ancients did not take into account the many other constellations besides these twelve is uncertain. It may be that they reasoned the sun's rays would have to shine through the constellations to affect the people on the earth below, keeping in mind that the earth is at the center of the model of the universe to which we're referring.

To determine one's horoscope, the exact geographical spot of birth is coordinated with the date and hour of delivery. The conjunction and relative positions of all heavenly bodies are considered by the angles they form with relationship to each other. From this information the horoscope is eventually computed.

Astrology's faulty geocentric approach isn't the only factual discrepancy astrology faces. The earth has an uneven wobble as it spins on its axis. As a result, the zodiac has shifted. Today the sun's rays actually enter each of the constellations about one month earlier than they did centuries ago, when the present astrological charts were finalized. This means that current horoscope readings are inaccurate by a factor of thirty days. Even if the predictions of astrology were true, the characteristics of each sign would not apply to the months they have been assigned.

One astrologer wrote a book entitled *Astrology Fourteen*, which asserts that there are actually fourteen constellations in the zodiac. If the predictions of astrology were to be scientifically correct, these two extra constellations would have to be included when casting a horoscope. And what about the billions of other celestial bodies outside our own galaxy? Why aren't their influences considered? This astrologer's answer is that the heavens were not fully explored when the practice of astrology was developed.

Some people are born without a horoscope. What about those who live north of the Arctic Circle? No planet assigned to the zodiac is visible there for several weeks out of the year. Does this mean that Eskimos and some Norwegians have no celestial influences upon their lives and no astral destinies to guide their behavior?

Differences of Opinion

Astrology is a universal practice in pagan religions, but no two religions agree on the same attributes for each sign. If you were to have your horoscope computed by a Hindu in India, it would read much differently from that of a Buddhist in Bangkok.

55

The arbitrary characteristics assigned to constellations seem inconsistent. One horoscope may say Aquarians are practical and patient, while another designates them as restless and skillful. The only constancy appears to be a suitable ambiguity designed to apply to almost any personality.

The predictions of horoscopes are not only capricious, but the prophecies are also prone to a high degree of error. If most astrologers had their forecasts periodically reviewed for accuracy, their reputations would fade quickly.

Syndicated columnist Carroll Righter once predicted that Spain's Francisco Franco would remain healthy (he died) and that J. Edgar Hoover would have an improved physical condition (he, too, expired less than five months later).

Jeanne Dixon, who credited her foreknowledge to the Almighty, once declared that Jackie Kennedy would not remarry. Apparently her zodiac charts never bothered to consult a Greek shipowner by the name of Aristotle Onassis.

Another sad example is found in the case of Linda Goodman, who was once one of America's most popular astrologers. After her daughter Sally committed suicide, Goodman refused to accept the truth. Instead, she relied on the stars to find her "lost" daughter. Goodman died in 1995, haunted by death and disappointed by the stars.

Those who say their astrological talent is a "gift from God" need to be reminded that the Lord's qualifications for a prophet leave no room for error (Deuteronomy 18:22).

Astrologers depend heavily upon the accuracy of determining the exact moment of birth in relationship to the position of heavenly bodies. But who determines when a child is born? Mother Nature? Often the doctor decides the hour of birth, for the convenience of his schedule or for the mother's welfare. Would it then be possible for a physician to thwart one's astrological destiny by using drugs to manipulate the moment when the baby emerges? And since life begins at conception, wouldn't that moment more accurately determine one's astrological sign?

Astronomers, those who engage in the true science of stargazing, completely reject astrology, relegating it to the ranks of superstition. Yet millions of people waste hours and dollars studying the signs of the zodiac. In the end, they usually learn nothing about themselves except what they read into their horoscope, which generally is of a complimentary nature.

The Bible and Astrology

Probably the first Bible reference to astrology is in Genesis 11, which describes the building of the tower of Babel. The Bible says the purpose of the tower of Babel was to "reach unto heaven" (v. 4). This biblical metaphor could more accurately be paraphrased, "a tower whose top may be used to reach out unto the heavens." Archaeologists now believe that this structure and similar towers were actually ziggurats, which the early Chaldeans erected to survey the heavens. Some ziggurats that have been discovered give evidence of zodiac signs actually inscribed on the circumference at the top.

The Chaldeans were not simple and ignorant but were a highly advanced civilization. They had sense enough to know it was not literally possible to build a tower that would extend that far into the atmosphere. There is little doubt its real purpose was to survey the stars for astrological purposes. Because these men sought to discover their destiny in the stars rather than communicate with God, judgment was brought upon them.

The Bible explicitly denounces astrology in many other passages. In Jeremiah 10:2 we read, "Learn not the way of the heathen, and be not dismayed at the signs of heaven; for the heathen are dismayed at them." The prophet goes on to equate astrology with idolatry and describes the vain way in which heathens seek to please and follow their astrological gods.

The clearest command against astrology is found in Deuteronomy 18, beginning with verse 9. As the children of Israel were about to enter the Promised Land, God issued severe warnings against the practices of the heathen in that territory. One such warning is against any Israelite becoming an "observer of times," which is an astrologer. This practice, God declares, is "an abomination unto the Lord." The penalty for its practice was death by stoning. Therefore, consulting one's horoscope, whether seriously or casually, is an act defying one of the most solemn warnings of Scripture.

The futility of trying to use astrology to interpret God's dealings with man is portrayed in Daniel 2:27-28 and 4:4-8. In both instances Nebuchadnezzar's dreams confounded the wisest of the court astrologers. Even though they were pagans, these seers were quick to recognize that true perception of the unknown is an attribute of "a God in heaven that revealeth secrets."

Many years later (Daniel 5), Belshazzar was reminded of the dilemma his father Nebuchadnezzar faced when he, too, was confronted by a mystery that his most trusted soothsayers could not unfold. Once again the Lord's servant, Daniel, was called upon because his wisdom excelled that of Satan's prognosticators.

Those who consult astrology are displaying an anxious and fretful attitude. Jesus said in Matthew 6:25 that we should "take no thought" for what might happen in the future. He declared that the necessities of life would be provided by our heavenly Father if we would seek him first. People do not need to know what lies ahead. The Christian may not know the future, but he does know the One who holds the future in his hands.

Psalm 19:1 says, "The heavens declare the glory of God; and the firmament showeth his handywork." The emphasis of astrology is upon nature rather than the God of nature. This psalm points out that the purpose of the heavens is to declare the glory of God, not the affairs of men.

CHRISTIAN CRITIQUE: The scientific discrepancies are well documented. Even more apparent are the numerous Scripture passages that denounce astrology for its erroneous prophecies and its false worship of the creation rather than the Creator.

The underlying philosophy of astrology declares that one's destiny can be found in the stars. In contrast, Christianity teaches that the events of life are determined by a combination of God's sovereign will and man's personal moral choices. Astrology, on the other hand, attempts to destroy man's accountability to God. Horoscope devotees may think they can fall back on blaming the stars for their actions. But the Bible teaches that someday all mankind will stand before God to be judged (Romans 14:12). Humans are responsible for their conduct, and the Lord will not take into consideration the excuse that certain stars and planets were in the wrong conjunction.

Christians are to trust the Holy Spirit to guide their lives, knowing that "the steps of a good man are ordered by the Lord" (Psalm 37:23). The guesswork predictions of astrology should hold no interest for believers who follow "a more sure word of prophecy" (2 Peter 1:19). God in his mercy has veiled the future from man's eyes (except for those events detailed in eschatological biblical references). If it were possible to know the events of tomorrow in detail, most people would not place their confidence in God's wisdom to look lovingly after our future. Satan, who according to Isaiah 14:14 wanted equality with the Lord, still desires to be man's substitute god. Astrology is a tool the devil uses to entice man to replace trust in God with dependence upon the whimsical uncertainties of the horoscope.

SOURCES: Bob Larson, *Hell on Earth* (Carol Stream, Ill.: Creation House, 1974); Cynthia Sanz, "Lost in the Stars: Linda Goodman Lived Guided by Astrology and Haunted by Death," *People*, Nov. 27, 1995, 139–141; Charles Strohmer, *What Your Horoscope Doesn't Tell You* (Wheaton, Ill.: Tyndale, 1988); *The Toronto Star*, 16 April 1977, A3.

AMERICAN ATHEISTS

Atheism; Madalyn Murray O'Hair

Once only a minority of people denied the existence of God.
Today atheism is a rapidly growing worldview.

In practice, atheism denotes a way of life conducted in disregard of any alleged superhuman reality. Existential atheism is a positive form of the teaching: it argues that if humans are to be authentically free in the universe, then it is necessary that God not exist since that would limit human liberty.
THE HARPER-COLLINS DICTIONARY OF RELIGION

FOUNDER: Madalyn Murray O'Hair

LEADER: Ellen Johnson

OVERVIEW: For decades, a feisty woman named Madalyn Murray O'Hair was the public face of atheism in America. O'Hair didn't think her son William should be forced to recite the Lord's Prayer or read from the Bible in his public school classroom. She took her case all the way to the U.S. Supreme Court and won a landmark decision in 1963 that helped change public education forever.

Emboldened by her victory, she founded a group called American Atheists, which fought other court battles, rallied like-minded supporters, and used media appearances to promote the atheist message throughout the country. But even before O'Hair was reported missing in 1996 and declared dead in 2001, atheism had outgrown her. In 1994 Christian thinker Ravi Zacharias declared that many people today—including some in our churches—are "functional atheists," even if they aren't card-carrying members of American Atheists or any other group: "We often think of atheism as a dogma, or as a position that has taken a definitive stance against the existence of God, and that, of course, is true academically. But there are many in this country who are *functional* atheists who may not openly disavow the existence of an infinite being but make their day-to-day decisions as if God did not exist or did not matter. In all of the vital institutions of the land, we're already atheistic—at least functionally."

A Pugnacious Pioneer

Even though the movement she supported eventually transcended her, there's little doubt that Madalyn Murray O'Hair played a crucial role in both popularizing atheism and changing U.S. public policy so that religion received fewer privileges than it had before the 1960s.

O'Hair was passionate about her cause and energetic in her organizing efforts. In addition to founding American Atheists, she founded the International Free Thought Association of America, Poor Richard's Universal Life Church, the Society of Separationists, and the Charles E. Stevens American Atheist Library and Archives.

AA was also active in a host of activities and programs, including the following:

- organizing atheist conventions and gatherings throughout the United States, including "atheist pride" marches in state capitals
- demonstrating and picketing throughout the country on behalf of atheist rights and church and state separation
- publishing over 120 books about atheism, criticism of religion, and church and state separation, including O'Hair's *Why I Am an Atheist*
- publishing newsletters, magazines, and member alerts and hawking bumper stickers, flyers, posters, and other products
- building a network of representatives throughout the nation who monitor important First Amendment issues
- providing speakers for colleges, universities, clubs, and news media

While American Atheists grew, O'Hair's personal life was often troubled. The woman who once called herself "the most hated woman in America" watched in horror as William, her son who had been at the center of the school prayer case, broke away from the family and its atheistic creed in 1977 to set out on a spiritual search that took him through Buddhism and Judaism to Christianity.

William Murray announced he had become a born-again Christian, wrote a book about his experiences called *My Life Without God*, and became a popular speaker, engaging in debates with atheists and preaching at churches throughout America.

In the 1990s AA's membership began to decline. In the late nineties the group reported 2,400 members in more than two dozen U.S. chapters. In 1995, O'Hair, her son Jon Murray, and her granddaughter disappeared. Their bodies were found in 2001, and an associate named David Waters was charged with their murders.

"It's a shame," said William Murray, when notified that his mother's remains had been found, "because with her intelligence—if she had applied herself in the mainstream and worked within a civil society toward some change for the good—there's no telling what she might have become."

By then, Ellen Johnson had taken over the leadership of AA. But as Johnson sought to improve the organization's fortunes, atheism had already outgrown this pioneering group.

A Long Tradition

Atheism is much older than O'Hair. In fact, religious traditions such as Buddhism, Hinduism, and Jainism include significant atheistic populations.

There have been atheists throughout Western history, but in most periods they have been a small and invisible minority. During periods of social and intellectual upheaval, such as the Renaissance and the Enlightenment, atheism grew in popularity.

In the twentieth century, a number of factors have led to the growth in atheism: the atrocities experienced during global conflicts like World War I, World War II, and the horrors of the Holocaust; various intellectual movements like scientific investigation into the fields of geology and human origins; and religious movements like the "death of God" theology. All have contributed to a growing groundswell of disbelief in God.

CHRISTIAN CRITIQUE: Belief in God is the basis of Christian faith, so atheism is a direct contradiction of this faith. Still, such disbelief is made possible by God's grace. He created human beings with free will, and he loves them enough to permit them to exercise that free will, even if it means they do not believe in him.

"It is not the *absence* of evidence that is our problem but it is basically the very *suppression* of it—the evidence in creation, the evidence of the moral law," Zacharias has observed. "Even Immanuel Kant, the famed watershed philosopher of the Enlightenment on whose door we often park modern-day skepticism, said: 'Two things I forever hold in awe—the starry hosts above and the moral law within.'"

SOURCES: Laurie Goodstein, "It's a Harsh Political Climate for Believer in Nonbelief," *New York Times,* 16 September 2000, 8; Bill Hewitt, "An Ungodly Ending," *People,* 12 February 2001, 101–102; "The Real Face of Atheism: An Interview with Ravi Zacharias," *Christian Research Newsletter,* March-May 1994; Ravi Zacharias, *The Real Face of Atheism* (Dallas: Word, 1994).

ACCESS: American Atheists, Inc., Box 2117, Austin, TX 78767; www.atheists.org

MEHER BABA
Sufism Reoriented

An Indian mystic who claimed he was God, Baba attracted
a small but devoted following.

FOUNDER: Meher Baba, born Merwan Sheriar Irani

TEXTS: Baba was the author of three books: *Discourses*, *God Speaks*, and *Listen, Humanity*. He also quoted the Hindu scriptures.

APPEAL: For certain people with an authority vacuum in their lives, Baba provided a father figure as well as a deified object to worship. Devotees thus immersed themselves in Baba, tossing reason aside and heeding his call, "Come unto me."

OVERVIEW: When Jesus died, his fame spread because of his resurrection. When Meher Baba "dropped his body" (Baba's term for death) on January 31, 1969, it remained in the grave.

Baba remains famous decades after his death, but not because of any miracles he performed. In fact, he was prone to catch colds. He rationalized the seeming contradiction of being God yet not being disease-resistant by saying, "The physical body of even a God-realized Perfect Master is subject to ordinary contagion."

Today Lovers of Baba (as they call themselves) range from sophisticated socialites to college students on the latest Eastern-consciousness trip.

One of Baba's most famous disciples was Pete Townshend, who fronted the British rock group The Who. Townshend, an unabashed Baba-lover since the sixties, declared: "Baba is Christ," adding that being a Christian is "just like being a Baba-lover." He dedicated a solo album to Baba; it featured songs extolling reincarnation and a tune adopted from Baba's Hindu prayer, "Parvardigar."

Townshend's devotion exemplifies the status of deity accorded Baba by his followers. "A mere twitch of his nose could split the planet," Townshend said, "and a twiddle of his finger could save your life. Luckily his infinite power is used with compassion." If he were God, then why was there not more evidence of his omnipotence? Townshend explained: "Baba rarely interferes. He said, 'Why alter events that occur in a system that is self-perpetrating, self-correcting, and self-destructive when it goes too far?'"

Becoming God

Have you ever been kissed on the forehead? Probably lots of times, especially as a child. Most likely you responded with affection or embarrassment.

Meher Baba was kissed on the forehead, and he became God—or at least he thought so.

Meher Baba was born in 1894 in Poona, India, near Bombay. His parents were Zoroastrians and named him Merwan Sheriar Irani. While attending college, he developed an affection for an old Muslim woman believed to be a Sufi saint, one of the five Perfect Masters of the age. One day she kissed him on the forehead, an event that Baba claimed triggered an instantaneous God-realization. From that moment on, Baba was never the same.

Baba proceeded to spend seven years studying with the Perfect Masters of his time. One of them, Upasni Maharaj, threw a stone at Baba, hitting him in the exact spot where the old woman had planted her kiss. Presto! The event triggered another instantaneous God-realization, and he became aware of his new destiny as a Perfect Master.

From then on he became known to his followers as Meher Baba (compassionate father), the *avatar* (incarnation of God) for this age, in the lineage of Zoroaster, Krishna, Rama, Buddha, Jesus, and Mohammed. More than that, he claimed to be the final incarnation of the godhead.

A Silent Sadhu

In 1921 Baba gathered a group of disciples and established a colony, including a hospital and school. The unique distinction that set him apart from other sadhus and holy men of the East was the self-imposed silence he declared on July 10, 1925.

"You have had enough of my words, now is the time to live by them," he declared. By "my words" he meant the precepts of all the religious leaders of his previous incarnations. As Jesus and the others, he had said enough. Now was the time for his followers to act.

His communications continued by means of an alphabet board and hand gestures. Baba promised this self-imposed silence would someday be broken before he dropped his body. He predicted the words he would speak would bring a surge of spirituality throughout humanity.

Needless to say, Baba-lovers waited breathlessly at every public appearance, thinking each occasion might be the time for Baba's anticipated utterance. The Compassionate Father had indicated over and over, "I love you more than you can ever love me or yourself." This intensity of devotion to his disciples made them eagerly await his final words as if they were tantamount to the second coming of Christ.

Baba wasn't speaking, but he was furiously writing about his belief system. He crystallized his teachings by issuing the five-volume *Discourses*. He also published a document entitled "Chartered Guidance from Meher Baba for the Reorientation of Sufism as the Highway to the Ultimate Universalized."

A Modern-Day Yogi

Baba's religious philosophy was rooted in the impersonal concepts of divinity explicit in Hinduism; his theology was rooted in the Hindu tradition of *Bhakti Yoga*, which teaches that the pathway to God is facilitated by devotion to an earthly Yogi— all the better if the Yogi claims to be the ultimate avatar. And Baba was not shy about demanding that followers totally yield to him. He pompously declared, "I am neither a mahatma, nor a saint, neither a sadhu or a Yogi. I am the Ancient One. The Highest of the High."

What truths then did this new "god" expound? Basically, Baba introduced Western minds to a warmed-over, syncretistic combination of Hinduism, Buddhism, Zoroastrianism, and Islam.

Souls come to earth, he taught, from two sister planets. These souls begin their evolutionary journey upward by incarnating first in stones, then metals, then onward through vegetables, insects, reptiles, spiders, fish, birds, kangaroos, monkeys, and humans. The human form may dwell on one of seven planes of existence, decided by man's degree of adherence to what Baba called the "seven realities." The final plane is nirvana, where one's consciousness merges with God. But Baba-lovers must be careful. One false step of failed devotion to Baba, and they're right back down to the lowly rocks to start all over again.

"All religions are basically dear to me," Baba taught. "It is not so much what you believe that counts, but what you are." In other words, happiness in this life and preferential reincarnations in the next life are not dependent upon doctrine, but rather on devotion to Baba.

Was Baba's silence ever broken? What were those divine words he promised would transform mankind? No one knows, and it seems that Baba died before being able to utter the truths for which his "lovers" had longed. But that hasn't dimmed the devotion his followers feel for this mysterious guru.

CHRISTIAN CRITIQUE: Baba's claim of divinity must be accepted or ignored. He either was the Christ, an incarnation of God, or a deluded sham. Unlike Christ, Baba was a created being who died a normal human death. Thus, his desire to be worshiped as God falls under the judgment of Romans 1.

Jesus warned of false Christs and declared, "Go ye not therefore after them" (Luke 21:8). Romans 12:1 implores men to present themselves as a "living sacrifice" to God, not to a mustachioed Indian guru whose most important prophecy (breaking silence) was unfulfilled.

SOURCES: Meher Baba, *God Speaks* and *Discourses*, vols. 1–5 (New York: Dodd, Mead, 1955); William J. Petersen, *Those Curious New Cults* (New Canaan, Conn.: Keats, 1975); *Rolling Stone*, 26 November 1970, 25–27.

ACCESS: Lovers of Meher Baba, Meher Spiritual Center, 10200 Highway 17 N, Myrtle Beach, SC 29572

BAHA'I FAITH

Out of the Middle East came this nineteenth century world religion that proclaims universal peace and says Christ has been succeeded by a new messenger of God.

Ye are the fruits of one tree and the leaves of one Branch.

The well-being of mankind, its peace and security, are unattainable unless and until its unity is firmly established.

The world beyond is as different from this world as this world is different from that of the child while still in the womb of its mother.

ALL FROM BAHA'U'LLAH

FOUNDER: Mirza Husayn Ali (1817–1892), known as Baha'u'llah. He proclaimed in 1863 that he was the manifestation of God for the current age.

TEXT: The more than two hundred books and tablets of Baha'u'llah, Abdu'l Baha, and Shoghi Effendi provide the authoritative texts of the Baha'i faith. They include the *Tablets*, *The Most Holy Book*, *The Book of Certitude*, *The Hidden Words* and *The Seven Valleys*.

SYMBOLS: The number nine, a sacred designation dictating the structure of their temples (nine sides) and the size of local organizations (a minimum of nine members). The number nine also represents the nine historic manifestations of God: Moses, Buddha, Zoraster, Confucius, Jesus Christ, Muhammad, Hare Krishna, Bab, and Baha'u'llah.

APPEAL: In a world racked by cultural, ethnic, and religious divisions, the Baha'i faith promises world peace and the elimination of religious divisions. Many people see it as a gracious creed with high ideals. Unfortunately, Baha'is in the Middle East have experienced persecution, not the universal peace they proclaim.

In the 1970s, Baha'i and many other non-Western faiths were popularized by devoted rock and pop musicians who wrote songs about their devotion. "We May Never Pass This Way Again," a 1973 hit by Jimmy Seals and Dash Crofts, didn't directly preach about the pop-folk duo's faith, but their record contract with Warner Brothers said they could talk to fans about Baha'i after their concerts. Another song, "Year of Sunday," was more explicit: "People, return to the tree of oneness."

OVERVIEW: Baha'i is a faith of many ironies. It claims to offer the means of uniting all believers in all religions, but these claims result in a new exclusivity that rules out other faiths. It claims to hold the key to world peace, yet its followers have been hounded, persecuted, and killed in Iran, its country of origin, and in other areas.

Still, followers of this peace-loving faith continue to pursue its goal of reconciling religious opposites. Its devoted idealism has attracted millions of followers in at least two hundred countries, including more than one hundred thousand people in America.

Troubled Beginnings

The Baha'i concept of religious unity, international government, and planetary interdependence began in Persia (present-day Iran) over a century ago.

A twenty-five-year-old businessman, known as Mirza Ali Muhammad (1819–1850), announced in 1844 that he was the *Bab* (gate), who was the forerunner of the "Promised One," who would be a manifestation of God. Christians can see that this scenario has some intriguing parallels with the beginnings of their own faith.

According to the group's official teachings, after hundreds of soldiers had failed to kill the Bab, he was finally executed by a government firing squad. One of his followers, a Persian nobleman named Mirza Husayn Ali, known today as *Baha'u'llah* (the glory of God), came to believe he was the promised one prophesied by Mirza Ali Muhammad.

Baha'u'llah spent most of his life in prison for plotting against Persia's shah. In 1863 in Baghdad, he declared that he was the promised *Madhi* (messiah), the latest messenger of God in a long line of prophets including Abraham, Moses, Krishna, Buddha, Zoroaster, Jesus, and Muhammad.

Baha'i's syncretistic blending of so many faith traditions explains why its followers were hounded in its native Persia, where Islam and Zoroastrianism have large and devoted followings.

Baha'u'llah's claims of divinity were cut short in 1892 when he died at the age of seventy-five. His son, Abdu'l-Baha, brought the message of the Baha'i faith to the United States in 1912, laying the cornerstone at the attractive Baha'i Temple in Wilmette, Illinois.

Upon Abdu'l-Baha's death, the mantle of Baha'i leadership was passed on to his grandson, Shoghi Effendi, who died in 1953. Since then, the rulership of Baha'ism has been in the hands of more than one hundred National Spiritual Assemblies in countries around the world.

Teaching and Action

Baha'i belief has been summed up in the dictum, "The earth is but one country and mankind its citizens." And many Baha'is work to put these lofty goals into action.

The faith's belief system is based on twelve fundamental principles: the independent search for truth, the oneness of the human race, the unity of all religions, the elimination of all prejudice, the harmony of science and religion, the equality of men and women, universal education, a universal language, abolition of extreme wealth and poverty, world court, work as worship, and justice with universal peace.

Baha'is hold weekly gatherings, an annual fast, and follow a special calendar with New Year's Day occurring on March 21. There is no professional clergy, and leaders are forbidden to reveal exact membership figures to the public.

In a manner similar to Muslims, Baha'is are expected to pray at certain times during the day. They are also encouraged to make at least one pilgrimage to their mecca—the temple in the city of Ak'ka (near Haifa, Israel) where Baha'u'llah died and where Mirza Ali Muhammad was buried (on nearby Mount Carmel).

As Baha'is see it, mankind is currently headed toward a socioeconomic cataclysm. Out of this tragedy a "golden age" will dawn, and Baha'is will be the only ones prepared to rule in this new world order. "War shall cease," said Baha'u'llah, "and all men shall live as brothers." Unlike more passive cults, Baha'is evangelize vigorously to help fulfill their founder's prophecy.

But Baha'is aren't waiting for the end of the world to put their beliefs into action. The international Baha'i community is supportive of the United Nations and works with the U.N. Economic and Social Council (ECOSOC) and the U.N. Children's Fund (UNICEF). Its members are proponents of racial harmony around the globe.

Conflict and Controversy

As with most religious systems that emphasize their inclusiveness, the inherent result of Baha'i teachings is a new form of exclusiveness.

Baha'ism claims to be the ultimate fulfillment of Judaism, Buddhism, Islam, Zoroastrianism, Hinduism, and Christianity. While proclaiming the merits of all world religions, Baha'ism also insists that these faiths must now concede to the supremacy of God's fulfilled revelation in Baha'u'llah. As you might expect, followers of these other faiths aren't willing to concede that Baha'i is a superior creed.

The religious practices of Baha'ism are similar to Islam, with a modified Western twist, though the two faiths are entirely separate religious systems that are often at odds with each other.

In fact, the Baha'i faith seriously offends orthodox Muslims by teaching that the line of God's prophets did not end with Muhammad but includes Baha'u'llah and prophets yet to come. In Iran members of the Baha'i faith are severely persecuted and often sentenced to death for heresy.

A mob destroyed the House of the Bab in Shiraz, the Baha'is' holiest shrine. One apparent goal of the late Ayatollah Khomeini was to eliminate Baha'ism in the land from which it originated. Tens of thousands of Baha'is fled Iran after the Islamic Revolution in 1979 until the Khomeini regime stopped issuing them exit visas.

Many of the those escaping Iran settled in America, which granted them refugee status as victims of religious persecution. About a thousand refugees a year escape over the Iranian border into Pakistan and from there settle into communities around the world.

But in the land of its birth and elsewhere, Baha'ism is still a long way from achieving the goal of world peace and cooperation the faith proclaims.

CHRISTIAN CRITIQUE: The Baha'i faith promotes noble and altruistic goals. Above all, it desires to unify mankind into one religious kingdom. This attempt to be a watershed for all faiths in the oneness of God is laudable but impossible to achieve. The doctrines taught by the religions of this proposed union are in many instances quite contradictory. Thus any effort to accomplish a global, religious synthesis is a futile task.

Baha'is also teach that man cannot know God directly, but only through his messengers. Baha'is rob Christ of his incarnate deity by placing him on the same level as other religious leaders. He is also accorded a position inferior to that granted Baha'u'llah. Baha'is do not believe in the bodily resurrection of Christ, the inerrancy of the Bible, eternal punishment, a literal hell, or the blood atonement of the Cross. In place of these doctrines is a syncretistic religious system with Baha'u'llah as the central figure and fountain of all truth. The paradox of differences in the nature of God as he is viewed by various world religions is ignored in favor of the oneness theme of Baha'ism.

It is impossible for biblical Christianity to unite with Baha'ism. Those who believe that "all the fulness of the Godhead bodily" dwells in Christ (Colossians 2:9) would be unwilling to demote their Savior, accepting him as only one of nine manifestations of God. Acceptance of Baha'ism means that one must deny the substitutionary atonement of Jesus Christ and ignore the distinctions of other world religions. Baha'is teach that all major religions hold to essentially the same truths. If this is the case, why are the tenets of Baha'ism and Christianity mutually exclusive? The conclusion of this question cannot be ignored no matter how loving, kind, and considerate the followers of Baha'u'llah may be.

SOURCES: Fergus M. Bordewich, "Iran, Holy Terror," *The Atlantic*, April 1987, 28,30; W. Kenneth Christian, *Basic Facts of the Baha'i Faith* (Wilmette, Ill.: Baha'i Publishing Trust); *Denver Post*, 18 October 1974, 7BB; Ibid., 20 June 1975, 2BB; *East/West Journal*, December 1977, 80–83; Ruhiyyih Jahanpour, "Refusal to Give Up Her Faith Led to Imprisonment, Torture and Exile for an Iranian Baha'i," *People*, 9 September 1985; Walter Martin, *The*

Kingdom of the Cults (Minneapolis: Bethany, 1965), 252–258; National Spiritual Assembly of the Baha'is of Canada, "Do You Know in What Day You Are Living?", pamphlet; National Spiritual Assembly of the Baha'is of the United States, "A New Way to Bring People Together: The Baha'i Faith", pamphlet; *Newsweek*, 24 March 1980, 61; Kenneth L. Woodward with Janet Huck, "Iran's Holy War on Baha'is," *Newsweek*, 25 January 1982, 73; "The World Center of the Baha'i Faith," informational brochure handed to visitors of the Shrine of the Bab in Haifa, Israel;.

ACCESS: Baha'i World Center and International House of Justice, Haifa, Israel, is the group's international headquarters. U.S. headquarters and the main U.S. temple is in Illinois: National Spiritual Assembly of the Baha'is of the United States, 536 Sheridan Rd., Wilmette, IL 60091. Web site: www.bahai.org.

BLACK MAGIC

This ancient occult practice, which seeks to harness evil and destructive forces, is making a modern comeback.

Black magic is the art of spiritual transformation by working with and learning from dark and death deities, demons, and entities.

The black arts are the opposite of 'white magic' in the fact that they openly embrace and use the negative—destructive forces and energies.

The demons and deities of darkness guard this hidden knowledge, and only those who have overcome their own fear and conditioning and have replaced it with respect and sincerity will gain the lost knowledge.
FROM BLACK MAGIC INTERNET SITES

FOUNDERS: West African slaves brought their system of religion and superstition to the New World. This system incorporated supernatural and magical beliefs and practices.

TEXT: There is a large body of orally transmitted traditions and esoteric ceremonies as well as a flood of new books on the subject.

SYMBOLS: Several, including a gate that represents Ogu, the god of fire; a primitive head of a three-horned beast, which represents Bossli, the god of the sea; a simple heart, which represents Erzulie, the god of love.

APPEAL: Black magic attracts those who lust for power and want to dabble in the unknown, especially those seeking fame and wealth without working for it. For some, black magic supplies simple, cosmic answers to frustrations in a world of terrorism, starvation, pollution, and political strife. It seems to satisfy the need for order and discipline in a world of chaos.

Through black magic rituals, people find order and comfort in universal truths. Also, people are greatly fascinated by secretive things, which contributes to the macabre appeal of black magic and other occult activities.

The occult leads people to believe that spirits can be contacted and used for one's own benefit. People use black magic to control the future and other people's lives. Magicians practice their trade to get revenge on enemies or to protect themselves from bad spells. Black magic rituals are also used to intimidate or harm coworkers so the black magician can be promoted or gain more authority over others.

OVERVIEW: Popular songs like Frank Sinatra's "That Old Black Magic" or Santana's "Black Magic Woman" may have led some people to believe these musicians were singing about something that was harmless or silly. But for those who are truly dedicated to using this occult art, black magic is deadly serious.

The world saw an example of this in 1990 when former Panamanian dictator Manuel Noriega turned himself over to U.S. drug agents to begin serving a sentence for drug trafficking. When U.S. agents took custody of Noriega, he was wearing red underwear, which he believed would ward off demons. And when officials searched Noriega's Fort Amador headquarters near Panama City, they found a treasure trove of black magic tools and totems. A photo of former U.S. president Ronald Reagan was covered in red wax, a practice designed to immobilize Noriega's former foe. Other totems were intended for using magical powers against President George Bush, statesman Henry Kissinger, and the judge who presided over Noriega's trial.

An army expert on cults said items like those found in Noriega's headquarters are used by many in the drug trade. "They use it in a malevolent manner to protect themselves not only from police but also from rival drug dealers," said the expert.

Magic in Black and White

Black magic was first introduced to the New World by slaves from West Africa. But it isn't called black magic because these people had black skin. Rather, sorcery is considered to be black magic when it is used for harmful or malevolent purposes. In contrast, magic used for beneficent ends is called white magic.

"Black magic is the practice of harnessing the destructive as well as the creative power in darkness," says Jyade Cythrawl, who runs a black magic Web site.

"We understand and utilize the process of destruction, chaos, death and creation. We are able to create a completeness within ourselves that most will never achieve. Black magic is the art of spiritual transformation by working with and learning from dark and death deities, demons, and entities. Black magic is considered diabolical because it follows the reverse order."

Practically speaking, every shade of gray magic exists between black and white magic. Most black magic advocates believe that through the use of charms, spells, and potions, spiritual powers can be manipulated for one's own advantage. Thus, people who selfishly practice all types of magic to achieve their own ends seldom distinguish between black and white versions.

Black magicians concentrate on violence and devastation and believe man's savage nature is a counterpart of the universe and its nature. They suggest that man's turbulence and triumphs parallel the universe on a smaller scale. Human emotions such as pity, lust, love, and hate exist on both the universal and the mortal levels. These dynamic universal energies are named after gods and planets. The lifeblood of the world is the sun, since its light and warmth are necessary for life on earth. Mars, the Roman war god, is the name bestowed upon the ferociously destructive force of the universe.

Black magicians inflict disease, physical danger, and unfortunate circumstances on victims. Many people are tempted to use black magic to get even with enemies or get ahead in life. Charms and spells can eliminate an enemy or protect against someone else's black magic. Fetishes supposedly make one person love another or cause that person to follow someone else's wishes. They can also be used to persuade someone toward benevolence or to change a bad fate to a good destiny.

Today black magic is practiced by people of all races and ages for numerous reasons, ranging from rivalry to revenge. Ancient theory holds that demons dwell within every person and can be malevolently manipulated through black magic. These spirits are reached through the use of necromancy, spells, tarot cards, Ouija boards, astrology, and witchcraft. Examples of malevolent black magic can be found in such cults as voodoo and Santeria.

Products and Practices

Books on black magic are available on many Internet sites. In addition, the various kinds of equipment used in these occult arts are available on-line or at numerous retail stores.

Black magic advocates are known to carry fetish bags containing potions and animal bones, as well as an occasional human finger. Some black magicians poke pins into voodoo dolls to inflict pain or misfortune upon those who have angered them. Still others cast black magic curses on career opponents to frighten or intimidate them into resigning their positions. With the help of hexes, black magicians hope to advance in a world of professional rivalry.

The African slaves who brought black magic to America had a strong religious system of magical and supernatural beliefs and practices. In Africa religion and magic were not separated as they were in Europe and America, and black magic religion was deeply entwined in every phase of life. These Africans believed the sun to be omnipotent, and they worshiped river and thunder spirits.

Among African slaves black magic worship was primarily an individual practice, informal and ritualistic. This custom began when slaves were forbidden to gather in groups. Often a slave would steal into the woods at night to hold his own religious service. As in West Africa, he would worship a multitude of spirits and gods, praising in particular gods associated with natural objects.

In addition to their polytheistic belief system, many West Africans worshiped their ancestors and believed a person's powers did not end with death. Dead people simply moved to another plane of existence from which they watched over their descendants. If something went wrong in their lives, these spirits could intervene and protect their families.

Getting a Bad Rap?

Some practitioners claim that black magic is unfairly attacked by people who don't understand it and that it can bring about good. But satanic black magicians like the late Anton LaVey believe the power of the devil could be summoned and used toward evil ends. Some satanists employ black magic to manipulate spirits and supernatural powers to frighten or hurt others.

Some would argue that black magic is not always evil, that black magic medicine men also practice "good" magic. Witch doctors do sometimes attempt to use their knowledge and powers for beneficial purposes. These magicians create healing potions from plants, herbs, and minerals and also extend advice to those who ask for it. Frequently they counsel followers on how to protect against evil forces, as well as how to prosper or gain good fortune.

West African black magic includes witches, ghosts, and vampires as part of the belief system, concepts that constitute the closest similarities between African and European magic. According to the lore of European black magic, a witch's greatest desire was to eat people by sucking their blood. Many of today's witches carry on the malevolent heritage of their ancestors and use their powers for evil purposes, though most would not resort to such bloody tactics.

Even white witches acknowledge the danger of dabbling in black magic. They guard against these evil spirits by drawing magic circles around themselves. When witches call up a spirit, they know the summoned entity is powerful and dangerous. Ancient witches frequently used such drugs as belladonna, aconite, and hemlock so their minds and personalities would not be vulnerable to evil spirits. Mediums and witches who consort with spirits tell tales of others in their craft who became insane or committed suicide under the influence of evil spirits.

CHRISTIAN CRITIQUE: The New Testament teaches that black magic (witchcraft) is a "[work] of the flesh" (Galatians 5:19-20) and argues that dabbling in black magic will lead to spiritual enslavement by demons (Luke 11:24-26).

The rationale black magicians offer for their actions sounds seductively similar to the words of the serpent in the garden when he enticed Eve to partake of the apple: "For God doth know that in the day ye eat thereof, then your eyes shall be opened, and ye shall be as gods, knowing good and evil" (Genesis 3:5).

Black magic dealings with occult powers conflict with the Christian ethic of turning the other cheek. Christians deem emotions such as pride, lust, and hate to be wicked and self-defeating and are commanded instead to concentrate on love, forgiveness, and unselfishness. Christians believe in the personal power of God and his Son, Jesus Christ. To worship nature or any other gods is considered blasphemous.

Christians also recognize the destructiveness of playing in the devil's territory. They should refuse to be lured into the fascination of witchcraft and black magic. Instead, they should fill themselves with God's Word and "put on the whole armour of God" (Ephesians 6:11). Brewing up an evil spell is dealing with the devil and can only lead to spiritual death.

Other activities also considered part of black magic are condemned in the Bible. Necromancers attempt to foresee the future by contacting spirits of the dead. Scripture teaches that the entities mediums consult are not really dead but are the same demons encountered in other methods of fortune-telling.

Black magicians believe they are in control, but they are actually slaves to the demons guiding their activities. Black magic tends toward evil and selfish indulgence without moral restraint. Deuteronomy 18 lists the occult practices of black magic that the Lord has forbidden; 2 Corinthians 6:14-15 warns against any collusion with such secret works of darkness.

SOURCES: *Dallas Morning News*, 13 April 1984, 22A; *Encyclopedia Britannica*, 1986, 88; *Faith*, November 1977, 5; *Faith for the Family*, November 1977, 3–5; *Miami Sun*, 7 May 1983; "Manuel's Black Magic," *People*, 22 January 1990; *Newsweek*, 24 February 1986, 64; *Rocky Mountain News*, 16 August 1988, 8; *Witchcraft, Mysticism, and Magic in the Black World*, 1974, 13, 16–19, 26.

ACCESS: Originally found in Africa, black magic is now prevalent in Central and South America and in urban centers in the United States. Practitioners are not affiliated with any one organization, but their books and materials can be found in stores and on the Internet.

See also Aleister Crowley; Macumba, Umbanda, and Condomble; Voodoo, Santeria, and Yoruba; Wicca and Witchcraft.

BLACK MUSLIMS

See Nation of Islam.

BOSTON CHURCH OF CHRIST

See International Churches of Christ.

BRANCH DAVIDIANS

A 1993 fire near Waco, Texas, killed leader David Koresh
and nearly eighty members of this group but not the cultic,
Adventist splinter movement that started it all.

Branch Davidians believe they are God's chosen people for the Last Days prior to the end of the world. Because of this they believe that God will always send a prophet to guide them. Branch Davidians have had five prophets: Ellen White, Victor Houteff, Ben Roden, Lois Roden and David Koresh.
BRANCH DAVIDIAN WEB SITE

FOUNDER: Victor T. Houteff

TEXT: Davidians cite the Bible, particularly the book of Revelation. Other key texts include Victor T. Houteff's *The Shepherd's Rod* and a more recent work, *Hidden Manna: Branch Davidian Revelations*.

OVERVIEW: One of the enduring images of the 1990s is the scene showing the Branch Davidians' central Texas compound going up in flames. The fire was the horrifying culmination of a fifty-one-day standoff between members of the group and law enforcement officials who believed the group was stockpiling weapons.

Throughout much of the standoff, law enforcement officials were in contact with David Koresh, who talked to them about "the seven seals." Originally, officials thought he was talking about aquatic mammals, but soon it became clear he was referring to mysterious teachings found in the New Testament book of Revelation.

In fact, novel interpretations of the prophecies found in this complex book were what inspired the founding of the Davidian movement six decades earlier.

An Adventist Offshoot

In 1930 a Seventh-day Adventist named Victor T. Houteff declared himself a prophet and said God had called him to gather together the 144,000 true believers described in Revelation 7:4. Five years later, he founded the Mount Carmel Center near Waco, Texas. After the Adventist denomination dismissed him, he established an independent church called the Davidian Seventh-day Adventist Association.

Houteff died in 1955, and leadership of the group was passed on to Benjamin Lloyd Roden, who claimed he was the fifth angel described in Revelation 9:1. Upon his death in 1978, leadership of the group was assumed by Roden's wife, Lois, and his son, George.

A decade later a man named Vernon Howell used intimidation, guns, and sexual liaisons with Lois Roden to assume leadership of the group. (In 1989 George Roden was committed to a mental hospital, and he died in 1998 in an attempt to escape from a mental facility in Big Spring, Texas). Howell changed his name to David Koresh and took firm control of the Davidians. He began formulating his teaching, which stressed that the group should live as a community and submit to his rules and regulations.

A Troubled Messiah

Koresh was a disturbed man who had been emotionally scarred during childhood. He claimed his stepfather had been abusive and that a male relative had sexually molested him as a child. Perhaps it's not surprising that Koresh acted out his sexual hang-ups with members of his cult. In addition to sexual liaisons with Lois Roden, who was three years his senior, Koresh also engaged in "marriages" with younger women in the community. At least four of Koresh's teenage "brides" perished in the Waco siege, and some wives were possibly younger. Before his death, Koresh had declared that any single woman in the group was his wife.

Koresh also abused the children in the community. He instituted the practice that babies over eight months old should be spanked when they cried. These punishments could last for thirty-five to forty minutes.

Debbie Bunds, an ex-Davidian who had been born into the group, told *Charisma* magazine, "There were no adults that we kids trusted. We were non-humans to them. They didn't look at us as human beings, as people with feelings, rights and minds. They just looked at us as lumps of clay to mold and to do with as they wished."

As with Ellen White, who founded the Adventist movement, and Victor Houteff, who launched the Davidian group in 1930, Koresh believed he also had received "New Light" from God to lead his flock. His teachings focused on the idea that, in the end times, revelation about the second coming of Christ would be "unlocked" by a God-appointed prophet. He proclaimed that he was that prophet and by interpreting the book of Revelation's "seven seals," he would give his followers a totally new way of understanding the Bible.

A Fatal Confrontation

In the five years that he led the Branch Davidians, Koresh hammered home his message in lengthy, all-night preaching sessions, some of which were punctuated by his loud electric guitar playing. When he wasn't preaching, he was ruling over his community with an iron hand.

Koresh's end times beliefs included the idea that guns and other weapons were an essential part of the group's ultimate destiny. It was those guns and weapons that led to the deadly standoff with federal law enforcement officials.

Nobody knows exactly what happened on April 19, 1993. Some accounts claim that the people inside the buildings were trapped by fires and falling debris set in motion by the FBI. Others claim that Koresh himself set the fires that killed nearly sixty adults and more than twenty children.

The event has been the subject of numerous government investigations and is the flash point for conspiracy theories held by a variety of antigovernment groups. The truth about what happened may never be known, but one thing is clear: David Koresh was a troubled man who abused power and seduced followers into a damaging lifestyle that ended in tragedy for many.

SOURCES: Richard Abanes, "Escape from Spiritual Deception," *Charisma,* August 1996; "In the Line of Duty: Ambush in Waco" (1993 NBC TV movie); Laurence McQuillan, "Ghosts of '93 Still Found at Waco," *USA Today,* 31 August 2001, 6A; Kenneth Samples, Erwin de Castro, Richard Abanes, Robert Lyle, *Prophets of the Apocalypse: David Koresh and Other American Messiahs* (Grand Rapids, Mich.: Baker, 1994).

ACCESS: Information about the Davidians and their key teachings can be found at the Web site www.fountain.btinternet.co.uk/koresh. The site of the 1993 standoff is now a memorial to the nearly eighty members who died there. A new chapel was completed in 2001 by remaining Branch Davidians.

WILLIAM BRANHAM

Branham Tabernacle

Many preachers, like Oral Roberts, were famous healing
evangelists of the 1950s. William Branham was, too, but he departed
from mainstream Christianity.

FOUNDER: Baptist minister and healing evangelist William M. Branham,
1909–1965

TEXT: Branham's books include *Footprints on the Sands of Time* and *Conduct,
Order, Doctrine of the Church*. His teachings can also be found in *The Voice of
Healing* and *The Witness* newsletters. The Voice of God Recordings, Inc., sells
many of Branham's teaching tapes, which are circulated and studied by members of Branham-affiliated groups around the world.

APPEAL: Branham's teaching, which is still available in tracts, books, and
tapes, appeals to those who feel the organized church world is apostate and in
need of fresh, divine revelation through a prophet from God.

OVERVIEW: When a drunk driver killed William Branham in 1965, most
people assumed that the fame of this itinerant "Jesus only" (nontrinitarian)
preacher would fade into obscurity. But Branham was not just another evangelist. He claimed to be *the* prophet for this dispensation (presumed to be the
Laodicean Age), the voice of Revelation's seventh messenger.

Today the William Branham Evangelistic Association claims to have
more than half a million members around the world—a grossly inflated figure.
Still, Branhamites can be found from the backwoods of Appalachia to the prairies of Saskatchewan. They gather in small groups to study the few books
Branham wrote and listen to scratchy recorded tapes of his sermons. To such
zealots, there is one born among men greater than John the Baptist, and that
man is William Branham.

Apparitions and Spiritualism

Branham was born in 1909 in the hills of Kentucky, the son of a bootlegger. At
seven years of age, he experienced the first of several visions that were destined
to guide his life. On May 7, 1946, he spent a night in a cave where an angel
supposedly appeared to him and explained his past and future. The angel also
revealed how God would enable him to heal people.

Many of his contemporaries were concerned about the spiritualistic overtones exhibited by Branham's gift of healing. The presence of a disease would set off vibrations, causing his hand to swell. Sometimes he would see a fiery ball dance about the room and then hover over those upon whom he would pronounce healing. (I was present during a 1965 Branham meeting when a ball of fire supposedly appeared. No visible phenomenon was evident to the audience, but many of those present accepted Branham's explanation without question.)

But despite persistent warnings from fellow ministers that his visions might be demonic, Branham was undeterred.

Off the Beaten Path

As historian David Edwin Harrell reports, the 1950s were a time when Pentecostal evangelists like Oral Roberts traveled throughout the country, preaching in tents and offering healing to the afflicted.

Branham was one of the decade's better-known itinerant evangelists, traveling widely overseas and achieving a wide measure of acceptance among some mainline Pentecostal groups. But during the 1960s Branham's views started to diverge from orthodox Christian teaching. His small congregation in his hometown of Jeffersonville, Indiana, provided the primary channel for his teachings.

Branham told his parishioners that God spoke to him out of a pillar of fire and revealed the mysteries of Revelation 5–8. This led him to predict future events, including Hitler's rise to power (correct), and the destruction of America by an explosion in 1977 (incorrect). In fact, the book that contains this later prophecy, *The Seven Church Ages*, also designated 1977 as the first year of the Millennium.

During the forties Branham held large healing campaigns during which thousands claimed to experience miraculous cures. Those who knew Branham intimately claimed he was a self-effacing, withdrawn man who, in spite of an unlearned background, had a remarkable sense of spiritual understanding.

Did this humble, God-fearing man later succumb to doctrinal error because he lacked adequate theological training? Were his visions and angelic visitations of godly origin, or was he cleverly deceived by Satan?

Though it is impossible to judge Branham's heart, it is possible to decipher his theology and weigh its inconsistencies against orthodox Christian doctrine. Even Branham's most devout followers would have to admit that his unscriptural views generate some measure of skepticism regarding his claim to be a prophet for the end times.

Branham was nontrinitarian, claiming that Jesus was created and not the eternal Son of God. He also believed that Cain and Abel were born from separate impregnations, the former by the serpent's seduction and the latter by Adam. Though he accepted the existence of a literal lake of fire, he contended that it would be destroyed eventually. Some of his prophetic statements were fulfilled, while others contain glaring errors.

Analyzing the credibility of living cult leaders is relatively easy. But those vanguards who have passed away can only be judged by the written documents they leave behind. Without question, Branham sincerely believed he was a servant of God, whose revelations were from the Lord.

Assessing a Legacy

To question Branham's theology is not to suggest his conversion was false or that all he did was in error. But even if God did confer spiritual gifts upon William Branham, his current followers seem to have forgotten Paul's warning of 1 Corinthians 3. Christians are not to adulate men, no matter how dynamic or charismatic they may be. God alone deserves total devotion.

Branham is included in this book not only as an odd historical footnote, but because his legacy continues today. His sons still oversee his ongoing ministry. Joseph oversees the publishing of his father's books and tapes, while Billy Paul heads up The William Branham Evangelistic Association.

In addition, *Christianity Today* wrote in 1991 about a group of Kansas City leaders known as the "Kansas City Prophets." These self-proclaimed "prophetically gifted ministers" included some who were once influenced by Branham.

One of these disciples, Paul Cain, has attempted to distance himself from Branham, claiming that friendship does not equal doctrinal agreement. However, it is possible to detect worrisome parallels between certain aspects of Cain's claims of revelation and Branham's "supernatural" insights.

CHRISTIAN CRITIQUE: Branham denied the Trinity and eternal punishment, gave inaccurate foretelling of future events, provided an erroneous interpretation of Eve's fall into sin, and was subject to possible Satanic deception by engaging in behavior that bordered on the mediumistic.

He also had an inflated view of his importance, leading many of his followers to believe that he was God's appointed Elijah, as prophesied in Malachi 4:5, for today's so-called Laodicean Age.

SOURCES: Cal Beisner, Christian Research Institute, Western Tract Mission, Saskatoon, Saskatchewan, Canada: "William Branham," pamphlet; William Branham, *An Exposition on the Seven Church Ages*; "God's Word Came to the Prophet William Marion Branham," Spoken Word Publications, tract; Davin Edwin Harrell, *All Things Are Possible* (University of Indiana Press, 1975); Gordon Lindsay, *William Branham, A Man Sent from God* (Jeffersonville, Ind.: William Branham, 1950); Michael G. Maudlin, "Seers in the Heartland," *Christianity Today*, 14 January 1991, 18–22.

ACCESS: The William Branham Evangelistic Association and Branham Tabernacle, Box 325, Jeffersonville, IN 47130

BUDDHISM

Theravada, Mahayana, Tibetan, and Zen Buddhism

Theologically, Eastern Buddhism is a many splintered thing, but its essence—
a meditative life—has struck pay dirt in the materialistic West.

FOUNDER: Siddhartha Gautama, later called Buddha; also known as Shakyamuni, referring to the Kingdom of Shakya in which he was born; sometimes called *Tathagata* (truth winner) or *Bhagara* (lord); born 563 B.C., Lumbini, Nepal; died 483 B.C., Kapilvastu, India

TEXT: The *Tripitaka* canon, divided into the *Abidharma Pitaka*, the *Vinaya Pitaka*, and the *Sutta Pitaka*

SYMBOLS: Figures of Buddha, either standing with one arm raised, seated in a lotus position, or reclining

APPEAL: Buddhism is attractive to many seekers who are disaffected with Western faiths or who find objective belief systems to be sterile and devoid of spontaneous reality. Concepts of moral accountability in an afterlife are replaced with a passive approach to traditional religious issues. Enlightenment promises a state of bliss beyond human comprehension. Truth is said to have a subjective quality that can only be experienced, not objectively communicated.

Buddhism's Eightfold Path promises to rid followers of mankind's four basic evils—sensuality, the desire to perpetuate one's own existence, wrong belief, and ignorance. Those who attain Buddhahood will entertain only pure thoughts and be indifferent to wealth, pain, and pleasure. In brief, the goal is maximum well-being with a minimum of active effort.

OVERVIEW: Books by the Dalai Lama are best-sellers, and his lectures are standing room only. Movies like *Seven Years in Tibet*, which featured romantic leading man Brad Pitt, brought spiritual seekers into theaters and generated a *Time* magazine cover story on "America's Fascination with Buddhism." Even rock bands sing about their love for Buddha, who was a spiritual seeker himself more than twenty-five hundred years ago. And in one Wisconsin community, police officers and other public service employees are offered meditation instructions by a Buddhist monk, in the name of handling job-related stress.

But if consumer laws concerning full disclosure were applied to religions, few people seeking lives of peace and simplicity would convert to Buddhism, which is perhaps the most complex and paradoxical of all Eastern religions.

Millions of Westerners who reject the complexities and chaos of modern life have been drawn to Buddhism and other ancient faiths of India and Asia the rest of Asia. Many wrongly assume that the mystical road laid out by Gautama Buddha is a simplified path to truth. In fact, Buddhism's Eightfold Path to nirvana is an intricate system of rules and regulations that can require a lifetime to master.

Because Buddhism is having such an impact on Western society and because it is so complex, a number of pages are devoted here to the faith's founder, its teachings, and some of its major branches.

In Search of Enlightenment

The accounts given of Buddha's life are filled with facts and fables that are impossible to verify historically. As a result, the following information obtained from Buddhist tradition is partly legendary.

Buddha was born in 563 B.C. in the small town of Lumbini, near Nepal's border with India. Maya, his mother, was the wife of a ruler from the Kshatriya caste. One night she dreamed that a white elephant had a sexual relationship with her. Shortly thereafter she found herself pregnant, and she bore a son whom she named Siddhartha. His family name was Gautama, and later he would become Gautama Buddha.

Siddhartha was born a prince, and during his formative years he knew only the confines of the palace and its pleasures. When he needed cheering, his father, Suddhodana, would summon forty thousand dancing girls. At the age of sixteen Buddha married the princess Yasodharma, who bore him a son named Rahula.

Everything in Siddhartha's aristocratic surroundings went smoothly until his early twenties. Though forbidden to roam the countryside, he left the palace grounds one day and was abruptly confronted with the realities of life. Siddhartha witnessed a scene that shattered the illusions of his princely perception: a gnarled and bent old man was soliciting alms. This was Siddhartha's first encounter with poverty and the frailty of human existence. On other journeys beyond the palace walls he was confronted with death and disease.

The encounter that had the greatest impact on him happened the day he met a shaven, ascetic monk. The religious devotion of this monk was a sharp contrast to the leisure and wealth Siddhartha had known. From that point onward, he found his life unfulfilling. Finally, on his twenty-ninth birthday, Siddhartha left his wife and child behind to seek peace and discover the cause of all suffering.

Buddha began his search by studying with two yoga masters. Unsatisfied with this approach, he turned to extreme asceticism. Sometimes he would stand without sitting for weeks. At times his diet consisted of a single grain of rice each day. In desperation he even tried eating his own excrement. One night, on his thirty-fifth birthday, as a full moon shone above, he sat down under a pipal tree in a forest near Bodh Gaya.

He declared, "Until I have attained understanding, I will not rise from here." That night he entered a trance state and, according to legend, remembered his previous incarnations. His "divine eye" was quickened, and he was able at last to extinguish all his ignorance and desires.

Birth of Buddha

When Siddhartha arose from the foot of the *bodhi* (wisdom) tree, he became *Buddha,* which means "enlightened one." Life's problems were no longer an enigma to him.

In a sermon at the nearby deer park he revealed his "truth" to five disciples. "Birth is sorrow, age is sorrow, and death is sorrow," he told them. Suffering, he explained, is the result of man's desire to seek pleasure in the existence of this life. Grief can only be excluded when a man ends all his cravings.

Buddha's discovery may be summarized in these three premises:

1. Existence is suffering;
2. Desire causes suffering;
3. Ridding all desire ends suffering.

These precepts led to a fourth conclusion: Desire can be eradicated by following what Buddha called the Eightfold Path. Buddha's spiritual insights became known as the Four Noble Truths, a so-called middle way between asceticism and hedonism.

During Buddha's lifetime northeast India was embroiled in religious and political ferment. The parochial philosophy of the Brahmanistic Hindu leaders had disenchanted the masses. In this spiritual vacuum religious sects and charismatic leaders abounded. But Buddha was different. He dared to question the authority of the *Vedic* scriptures and advocated abolishing both the caste system and the priesthood. He also wanted to do away with prayers and rituals. Buddha even suggested that the concept of God be abolished.

For the next forty-five years of his life, until he died of dysentery at the age of eighty, Buddha traveled, begging for food and setting up communities to further his teachings. With missionary zeal he commissioned his followers: "Go ye now out of compassion for the world and preach the doctrine which is glorious." Buddha's *dharma* ("way" or "doctrine" or, literally, "work"; *dhamma* in his own Pali language) was aimed at ending the cycle of suffering through successive transmigrations. (He borrowed Hinduism's concepts of *karma* and reincarnation.)

Escape from the sorrow of existence would be possible by reaching nirvana, a condition of infinite bliss likened to an extinguished flame. Nirvana, meaning "blow out," would be the result of reaching a state where all desires are eradicated. Though local deities could be petitioned for immediate benefits, no god could facilitate the search for nirvana's enlightenment.

Buddha's Teaching

Buddha taught that only his Eightfold Path would lead to the exalted spiritual realm of nirvana. The eight steps to salvation in Buddha's system are as follows:

1. Right Belief—correctly understanding the Four Noble Truths frees one from illusion and superstition
2. Right Resolve—maintaining pure motives
3. Right Speech—speaking truthfully
4. Right Conduct—living peacefully and honestly
5. Right Livelihood—choosing an occupation that harms no one
6. Right Effort—seeking knowledge with self-control
7. Right Thought—keeping an active, self-critical mind
8. Right Concentration—practicing meditation and Raja Yoga with earnest zeal

Such high ideals were intended to dissolve the illusion of self and free one from the revolving wheel of existence. Buddha taught that self-effort is the key to understanding the truth. According to a pamphlet published by the Buddhist Church of America, patience and perseverance matter more than "the blood of crucifixion, [God] sacrificing his own being" on the cross. God "is not a Creator . . . does not judge or punish . . . is not transcendent" and is not a deity of "fear and mercy."

Buddha was indifferent to the question of man's origin and refused to recognize any supernatural authority in the cosmos. Man is the center of the Buddhist universe, and only what he does matters. Heaven and hell are conditions of feeling and emotion, not locations. No eschatological scheme is speculated, and no reason is offered for the reality of death and sin. Self-control, not the remission of sin, is Buddhism's central doctrine. In Buddha's own words, "Seek in the impersonal for the eternal man, and having sought him out, look inward—thou art Buddha."

A Complex Creed

Buddhism appears to be a simple system of belief. In fact, it is one of the most complex of all Oriental faiths. In addition to the Four Noble Truths and the Eightfold Path, the following practices and doctrines are considered essential to attaining Buddhahood:

1. The state of *Arahatship* (being worthy) contains thirty-seven precepts to be followed by the devout Buddhist. Twenty-nine of these are in addition to the requirements of the Eightfold Path.
2. Five obstacles hinder one's approach to enlightenment—sloth, pride, malice, lust, and doubt.
3. Three refuges must be affirmed by all who belong to the *Sangha* (the brotherhood of monks): refuge in Buddha, the dharma, and the Sangha.

4. Followers also must adhere to 227 regulations that, among other things, forbid them to touch a woman (even their mother) or drink unstrained water (lest they kill any living thing).
5. Man has no soul but rather exists in five conditions: body, feeling, ideas, will, and pure consciousness.
6. Ten commandments are propagated, the last five of which apply only to the Sangha. These "shalt nots" include killing, stealing, adultery, lying, drinking intoxicating liquors, eating after midday, being present at any dramatic or musical performance, applying personal adornment or perfume, sleeping on a comfortable bed, and owning silver or gold.
7. Three principles guide the Buddhist in his search for nirvana. The first principle designates thirty-one planes of existence, from higher spiritual beings on down through humans and lower beings-in-torment (who endure an existence similar to purgatory). The second principle teaches that one's karma determines his spiritual plane, though progression and retrogression are constant throughout successive transmigrations. Finally, the third principle promises "complete awareness" by practicing contemplation. The one who achieves this state is supposed to become immune to all feeling and emotion, including hate and love.

Four progressive stages of awareness await the seeker: *Sotapatti Magga*, *Sakadagami Magga*, *Anagami Magga*, and *Arahatta Magga*. Some Buddhists believe that an individual who attains Sotapatti Magga can no longer "kill, seduce . . . utter falsehood, take drugs . . . make evil utterances or have bad thoughts."

Buddhism's Later Developments and Conflicting Schools

For generations after his death, Buddha's teachings were orally communicated. In 245 B.C., a council of monks was held to decree the sacred teachings in written form. They drew up a three-part document in the Pali language that became known as the *Tripitaka* ("three baskets of law"). Kasyapa, an original disciple of Buddha, was credited as the source of the *Abidharma Pitaka*, a basic interpretation of Buddha's message. The *Vinaya Pitaka*, containing rules for the monastic life and the ten commandments mentioned above was the work of another disciple named Upali. The third "basket," or *Sutta Pitaka*, expounds Buddha's sermons and parables.

THERAVADA AND MAHAYANA BUDDHISM

During the so-called "Indian Empire" of the ruler Asoka, Buddhism spread rapidly throughout India and the rest of Asia. After Asoka's death, Buddhism split into two main schools, one liberal and the other conservative.

The conservative school became known as *Theravada* ("the way of the elder"; sometimes called *Hinayana*, "the lesser vehicle"). It was based on the writings of an early disciple of Buddha named Sariputta, and it emphasized monastic life as the pathway to nirvana. Theravada Buddhism became entrenched in Burma, Sri Lanka, Cambodia, and Thailand. The canon of the *Tripitaka* became its main source of doctrine.

Hinduism, which had become an abstract faith for many Indians, experienced a revival during the first-century-A.D. Gupta dynasty. It was at this time that *Mahayana* (the greater vehicle) Buddhism emerged. Its more liberal school is prevalent in China, Korea, Japan, Tibet, Indonesia, Nepal, and Vietnam. Mahayana Buddhism is more of a cult religion utilizing incense, magic, and occult rituals. Buddha figures are objects of deified worship. Standing, Buddha symbolizes compassion. Sitting, he signifies serenity. The Mahayana Buddhist does not strive to become a saint (*arhat*). More than anything he desires to be a *bodhisattva*—one who attains the supreme perfection of Buddhahood but denies his entry into nirvana to return and help mortals on their spiritual pilgrimage in this life.

Theravada (the way of the few) and Mahayana (the way of the many) are so distinct in their beliefs and practices that they almost represent two entirely different religions.

The godless, virtually atheistic system of Theravada is worlds apart from the Mahayana school with its polytheistic legends of gods and goddesses. The essence of Mahayana is faith in the divinity of Buddha (and a line of *bodhisattva*). Theravada pursues the more theologically abstract goal of nirvana.

A minor variant, *Tantric* Buddhism, borrowed the Hindu belief in *Shakti* sexual power and developed a cult devoted to idols and magic. The union of the individual with the divine is accomplished by ritual sexual intercourse. This is said to combine the opposite forces of the universe (positive masculine and negative feminine), resulting in the cohabitant's ability to perform supernatural acts.

A Renewed Popularity

With more than 350 million adherents, Buddhism is the world's fourth largest religion (behind Christianity, Islam, and Hinduism). Its numbers in North America are estimated between 100,000 and 250,000 and are growing rapidly.

The image of saffron robes and begging bowls may be foreign to the Western mind, but the concept of joining a cosmic flow to abolish the ego goes down well in an age that has turned inward. Those who look to the East for spiritual answers may find Christianity's promise of heaven less attractive than Buddhism's mystical, impenetrable "truths." To many spiritual seekers, problem solving by constructive action appears less desirable than the subjective quest for nirvana.

TIBETAN BUDDHISM

Ironically, one of the most complex forms of Buddhism has become increasingly popular in the West, thanks largely to the influence of one man: the Dalai Lama. "After Pope John Paul II and Billy Graham he is probably the most recognized religious figure on our planet," said *Christianity Today* in 2001. "He has also become the defacto leader of millions of spiritual seekers in the West."

But the faith he represents is an ancient and esoteric brand of Buddhism.

Taking Buddhism to Tibet

Padina Sambhava, a famed pagan exorcist, introduced Buddhism to Tibet in A.D. 747. His reputation so impressed the king that the entire land soon was following his blend of Hindu and Buddhist beliefs mingled with spells and secretive *tantric* ceremonies. Devotees preceded acts of sexual union with the ritualistic consumption of wine, meat, fish, and parched grains. They instituted a priesthood of *lamas* (superior ones) and designed prayer wheels with inscribed litanies.

Mantras and *mandalas* (mystic diagrams) were also adopted. The former were believed to possess a sound able to induce transcendent experiences. Mandalas, circular cosmograms of the universe, were also used as an aid in worship. The center of the mandala was thought to be a focal point of the universe. Adherents of Tibetan Buddhism were taught that merely glimpsing a mandala could start them on the road to nirvana.

They also developed the legend of *Shambhala*, an imaginary kingdom of enlightened citizens. This central Asian civilization was said to be the spiritual inspiration of the entire world. Their "warriors" were people of compassion and awareness who still serve as models of Tibetan Buddhist aspirations.

Chinese Suppression

In 1951 Chinese Communist soldiers invaded the mountaintop kingdom of Tibet. At that time the Dalai Lama (whose Buddhist name is Tenzin Gyatso, meaning "radiant oceans of wisdom") was worshiped by his 6 million fellow Buddhist citizens as a god-king. Tibetans bowed before the sight of his portrait and prostrated themselves outside his thirteen-hundred-year-old Jokka Temple.

The Dalai Lama finally fled the Communists in 1959, taking 110,000 refugees with him. He settled in Dharamsala, India, vowing he'd return someday to his native land. Today the Dalai Lama heads a government in exile, visiting world capitals and disciples in preparation for his awaited return as the spiritual and political leader of Tibet.

The advent of Buddhism in Tibet was so successful that by the time of the Communist invasion, as many as ten thousand monks studied at one monastery. Neighboring kingdoms in Nepal, Sikkim, and Bhutan also felt the Buddhist influence.

Because of Tibet's isolation and inaccessibility, some Buddhist scholars believe it has preserved the purest form of Buddhism. Devout Tibetan Buddhists insist they are custodians of the correct traditions and esoteric teachings of the Indian saints and sages.

A major Tibetan Buddhist text, *The Tibetan Book of the Dead* (or *Bardo Thodal*) has had great influence among America's youth. The volume is an occult guide to aid one's traverse through the existence of *bardo*, the dreamlike realm between death and reincarnation. In the sixties, some who experimented with LSD reported hallucinogenic visions paralleling experiences in *The Book of the Dead*, stirring Western interest in this exotic faith. Tibetan Buddhists believe that the demons, spirits, and powers of witchcraft encountered in *The Book of the Dead* are real forces to be avoided and appeased.

The theory of reincarnated *lamas* (*bodhisattvas*) came to prominence in the fifteenth century. According to this doctrine, the soul of a dead lama passes to a newborn boy. The current Dalai Lama, the fourteenth incarnation in Tibetan Buddhism's line of spiritual succession, was chosen at age two after oracles were consulted. Marks found on his shoulders (said to be remnants of a deity's two extra arms) established the proof required to designate his office. The young lad also had to identify correctly the crown of his predecessor from among five examples.

The Dalai Lama has toured the West, has had glowing praise from the press, and gratuitous plaudits from ecumenical religious leaders. He disarms reporters by insisting, "I'm just a humble monk."

The essence of Tibetan Buddhist philosophy is expressed in the Dalai Lama's view of life: "If the situation can be fixed, there is nothing to worry about. If it can't be fixed, there is nothing to worry about. After all, things are due to past karma."

A Growing Concern

The Dalai Lama's beliefs are of crucial concern to American evangelicals who lament Buddhism's growing foothold in North America. The first Western Buddhist university was established in Boulder, Colorado. Started by Chogyam Trungpa Rinpoche, a forty-two-year-old Tibetan exile, the Naropa Institute has effectively introduced tantric teachings in the West. The institution boasts thousands of summer students and a distinguished faculty, including the late poet Allen Ginsberg and theologian Harvey Cox. Rinpoche, who was believed to be an incarnation of a revered monk, developed an enticing curriculum that includes an array of mystical and spiritualistic disciplines.

I had the opportunity to witness a Naropa-sponsored ceremony held on the University of Colorado campus. Fifteen hundred students, many of them pursuing graduate degrees, paid eight dollars each to witness the Tibetan Buddhist Vajra Crown Ceremony.

His Holiness Gyalwa Karmapa was introduced as an incarnation of a lineage of bodhisattvas. As one having attained Buddhahood, he claimed the ability to transmit spontaneous spiritual insight. He was ushered to a ten-foot-high throne that had been constructed for the occasion. The ritual he performed consisted of his holding a black hat over his head for two minutes and forty-eight seconds! Nearly everyone in the highly educated audience was overwhelmed at the sight of such a "holy" and "enlightened" man.

Former Christian missionaries to Tibet report that Tibetan Buddhism is the most openly occult of all non-Christian world religions. Even the monks themselves make no pretense about their consorting with demonic demigods. This acknowledgment emphasizes the irony that this sect of Buddhism should gain such a powerful influence in a Christianized land.

Devotees in the homeland of the Dalai Lama have kept his bedroom untouched since the day he fled, awaiting his return. Perhaps the demonic forces behind Tibetan Buddhism have deliberately prolonged his exile as a means of exporting this ancient, shamanistic faith.

ZEN BUDDHISM

As he paces the sidelines at NBA games, coach Phil Jackson appears both intense and calm. As he wrote in his 1996 book, *Sacred Hoops,* Jackson grew up in a Pentecostal Christian home. But when he failed to experience the spiritual electricity that was promised every Sunday, he grew disillusioned.

Today Jackson is a disciple of Zen, an increasingly popular faith for many spiritual seekers. He credits his Buddhist faith with keeping him serene, not only at courtside but also in life.

Paradoxes and Imponderables

"What is the sound of one hand clapping?" Most people would easily recognize this riddle without knowing either its purpose or source. This conundrum and seventeen hundred others like it are known as *koans,* paradoxical questions concerning imponderable thoughts.

The perplexity posed by the koan is designed to lead the mind toward intuitive truth. In the world of Zen, logic and reason are taboo. As one Zen practitioner put it, "Be nothing, think nothing." Zen may be defined as concentration with an empty mind.

The ancient sage Bodhidharma, who is generally credited as being the founder of Zen practices, studied Buddhism in India for over forty years. He returned to China and encouraged the ruling emperor Wu to adopt the technique he had developed known as "wall meditation."

To prove his diligence at Zen, Bodhidharma sat in a cave while staring at a wall for nine years. He eventually lost the use of his legs through atrophy and even had to cut off his eyelids so he could sustain open-eye meditation.

Nearly seven centuries later two Japanese Buddhists developed what became the two prominent schools of Zen: Eisai originated the *Rinzai* sect in 1191, and Dogen initiated the *Soto* sect in 1227. Both disciplines strove to achieve the same goal of enlightenment, though Soto claimed it must be gradually attained while Rinzai insisted it could come as a flash of insight.

The koan is but one of several terms distinctive to the nomenclature of Zen. *Bodhi, satori, mondo,* and *zazen* are other words describing Zen concepts. Bodhi refers to the "awakening" of introspective truth. Buddhism has traditionally held that bodhi could only be possible after many lives. Zen purports to offer bodhi here and now, perhaps today, or at least in several years.

A Subjective Experience

Experiencing the immediate perception of truth is known as *satori,* a condition in which the meditator realizes all reality as one. In such a state, there is no such thing as right or wrong, only subjective reality pervades the consciousness. Alan Watts, the late writer and mystic, described the state of satori this way: "At this moment [the universe] is so completely right as to need no explanation or justification beyond what it simply is."

Though Zen offers enlightenment more quickly than traditional Buddhism, achieving satori is no easy task. Zen is an arduous training of the mind with koans and *zazen* (seated meditation). The *roshi* (Zen master) invites the initiate to enter a *zendo* (meditation hall) where an altar and idol of Buddha are the focal points.

Practicing zazen in the proper manner may require at least two three-hour periods each day. Hallucinogenic visions and demonic apparitions are common occurrences to persistent Zen meditators. A thin pillow is the only comfort provided, and correct physical posture is crucial. The back must be kept perfectly erect to be certain the ears, shoulders, and navel are in proper alignment. The teeth are to be firmly closed, and the eyes have to be left open at all times. During zazen, the meditator is instructed to free his mind of all earthly attachments and think of "neither good, nor evil."

A pool, a rock, a flower—any object can be used to focus one's attention. The roshi may verbally assault the student with *mondos,* a series of rapid questions. Chief of these is the koan. Abstract paradoxes are presented to boggle the meditator's mind. Contradictory and confused statements are posed so that he delves more deeply inward to fathom truth. If he dozes, the master may subject him to shouts and painful blows from a *keisaku* (warning stick). Such rigorous self-discipline accompanied by unanswerable questions is intended to trigger a newly conditioned view of reality. Ironically, in the words of Dr. T. Susuki, a former Western Zen master, "Zen teaches nothing."

While the precepts of Zen may not be based on specific theological doctrines, the inherent Buddhist worldview that results from zazen causes the meditator to see himself as an integrated part of the whole.

Buddhism presupposes that only one essence exists and that we are all somehow part of this one essence (monism). This teaching is contrary to the Christian assertion that the God, the Eternal One, created the world and man out of nothing. Thus, no part of this material existence is part of God. There is an eternal distinction between the Creator and the created. The inherent contradictory nature of the anecdotal koan conditions the devotee to reject reason and logic and instead rely on mystical experience to test truth. Zen is ultimately an egocentric search for subjective authority while inherently denying any objective authority for morality.

Since Zen has no God, the priests have no role of intercession for sin. There is no speculation on the nature of creation or the future of an afterlife, since everything considered important is embodied in the experience of the moment.

Zen adherents consider their practices to be the quintessential essence of Buddhism, liberating the devotee from all life's miseries. Christians may see satori as a false perception of spiritual insight. But many young Americans who have experimented with its rigorous spiritual disciplines are obviously fascinated with the idea of Zen's narcissistic non-answers.

CHRISTIAN CRITIQUE: Archaeologists have recovered a huge sandstone casket in the ruins of an ancient city near Kapilvastu, India. The inscription on the coffin indicates that the contents are the mortal remains of Buddha. "Be a lamp unto yourself," the sage declared before his death. This instruction sharply contrasts with the biblical claim to such guidance (Psalm 119:105).

Buddha's wisdom, backed by the evidence of his own decayed body, seems far less credible than the Word of God, which bears the authority of Christ's empty tomb. Whether the Good News of Jesus will prevail over the introspective appeal of Buddha is a fundamental choice that may well determine the spiritual direction of Western culture.

The original ethical ideals of Buddha degenerated into a system of theological dogmas with Buddha as a god and nirvana as a postmortem heaven. Idolatrous sects that advocate demonic ceremonialism and the propitiation of spirits constitute a form of witchcraft that is scripturally forbidden (Deuteronomy 18).

The greatest commandment of Jesus to love one's neighbor unselfishly (Matthew 22:35-39) contrasts sharply with the introspective egocentricity of Buddhism that has produced social indifference in the lands it dominated. Scripture presents an orderly universe under the control of a sovereign God.

Buddhists see karmic chance as life's only guiding force and make no attempt to explain the nature and origin of sin.

SOURCES: "America's Fascination with Buddhism," *Time*, 13 October 1997; James A. Beverly, "Buddhism's Guru," *Christianity Today*, 11 June 2001; Kenneth Boa, *Cults, World Religions and You* (Wheaton, Ill.: Victor, 1980); *Denver Post*, 11 March 1972, 8; Ibid., 18 October 1974, 6BB; Ibid., 8 August 1975; Ibid., 11 June 1976; 7BB; Ibid., 16 July 1976, 7BB; Ibid., 20 August 1976, 5BB; Ibid., 3 September 1976, 2BB; Ibid., 14 August 1981, 26; John Garabedian and Orde Coombs, *Eastern Religions in the Electric Age* (New York: Tempo Books, 1969); "Hollywood: Can It Save Tibet," *Tricycle* Winter, 1997; "Is There a God?" Buddhist Church of America, pamphlet; Michael H. Kohn, trans., *The Shambhala Dictionary of Buddhism and Zen* (Boston: Shambhala, 1991); Walter Martin, *The Kingdom of the Cults* (Minneapolis: Bethany Fellowship, 1977); Pat Means, *The Mystical Maze* (San Bernardino, Calif.: Campus Crusade for Christ, 1976); J. Gordon Melton, *The Encyclopedia of American Religions* (Wilmington, N.C.: McGrath, 1978); Naropa Institute promotional literature; *Newsweek*, 18 August 1980, 59; *Religions of the World* (New York: Barnes and Noble, 1965); *Time*, 14 February 1977, 86; Ibid., 27 July 1981, 71; *To The Point International*, 1 November 1976, 46; Ibid., 7 March 1977, 10; John Weldon, *Occult Shock and Psychic Forces* (San Diego: Master Books, 1980).

ACCESS: There are Buddhist churches and/or meditation centers in many American cities. The American Buddhist Congress provides networking between many unrelated North American groups (4267 W. Third St., Los Angeles, CA 90020). Popular magazines like *Tricycle* and *Shambhala Sun* cover the contemporary Buddhist scene. North America's only Buddhist liberal arts college is the Naropa Institute, 111 Pearl St., Boulder, CO 80302.

See also Nichiren Shoshu and Transcendental Meditation.

BURNING MAN FESTIVAL

This annual event, which climaxes with the torching of a gigantic effigy, combines art, spirituality, sex, drugs, and "radical free expression."

FOUNDER: Larry Harvey of San Francisco held the first Burning Man celebration in 1986 with a friend. He has repeated the ritual every year since then, and now tens of thousands of people attend the annual Burning Man Festival in the Nevada desert.

OVERVIEW: In a desert valley untouched by modern civilization, an eclectic group including hedonists, aging hippies, druggies, and spiritual vagabonds begins to gather. Slowly the crowd grows until some thirty thousand people are present.

Conditions are horrible. Daytime high temperatures reach over one hundred degrees. Nighttime lows can dip below freezing. And the ever-present dust stings the eyes and fills the lungs. But such harsh conditions hardly slow members of the crowd who are busy creating artwork, meeting and perhaps having sex with other people from around the world, drinking alcohol or doing drugs, and bartering for the basic necessities of food and water.

At the end of the week the whole community gathers around a seventy-foot-tall wooden statue of a man. At the designated moment the statue is set ablaze. As it burns, the crowd erupts in a frenzy of dancing and screaming.

Following this ritual the partying goes on all night. But in the morning, the crowd starts to disperse. People head back to their homes and their jobs, inspired by the time they have spent at an annual event called the Burning Man Festival.

Up in Smoke

San Franciscan Larry Harvey was recovering from a failed relationship in 1986 when he and a friend went to a nearby beach, built a little wooden statue, and set it on fire. The following year Harvey repeated his gesture. Only this time a small group gathered to participate with him.

Year after year the crowd attending Harvey's simple ritual has grown. When the beach patrol told him to quit doing it in San Franciso, he moved the event to the Nevada desert in 1990. Ever since, the event has attracted growing crowds to a unique mixture of cultural activities *Time* magazine summarized as "art, raves, nudity and spirituality."

As for the burning statue that culminates the week-long event, Harvey says it doesn't really mean anything. "Something bigger than they are—that's all people need," he told *Time*. "It's at least enough to inspire a leap of faith."

Spirituality without God

A stranger visiting the festival for the first time is bombarded by thousands of oddly dressed (or undressed) people, unusual sculptures and paintings, booths where one can barter for food or suntan lotion, and conversations about everything from French philosophy to comic books.

According to an article in the *Denver Post*, the makeshift community offers the world's largest rock-scissors-paper tournament, a workshop on sadomasochism, all-night raves, and updates on daily activities provided by newspapers and nearly forty low-power radio stations.

When pressed to define the basis of it all, the phrase Harvey and others repeat is "radical self-expression." From around the country and around the globe, people come to the Burning Man Festival to escape their humdrum jobs and rekindle their creative spark.

This annual event has now inspired a series of smaller celebrations held around the world.

The Burning Man Festival is an indication of what ancient pagan rituals may have looked like, and it also may provide a clue about what kind of shape godless, loosely defined spiritual gatherings of the future might take.

CHRISTIAN CRITIQUE: From the dawn of time, people have expressed their God-given spiritual nature in a variety of forms. The Burning Man Festival is one of the newest ways people try to express this spirituality without any reference to God.

The festival is symptomatic of modern post-Christian religious expression that lacks historical foundation or any dogma that holds faith accountable to reason. Devoid of moral boundaries, the festival celebrates each person's spontaneous responses to whatever whimsy compels his or her hormones or emotions.

Unlike Christianity, which teaches definable doctrine and responsible behavior, the licentious and erratic conduct of festival attendees mirrors the rebellion of Luciferian indulgence. The Burning Man may be seen as a symbol of classical satanism, which advocates extolling carnal and base desires—the animalistic nature of man—as the pathway to "freedom."

SOURCES: Ron Franscell, "Truth Elusive, Illusive at Burning Man," *Denver Post*, 9 September 2001, 1A; Joel Stein, "The Man Behind Burning Man," *Time*, 18 September 2000, 76–7.

See also Paganism and Neo-Paganism.

CARLOS CASTANEDA

Whether he was a sorcerer or a con man, this best-selling author helped popularize a mixture of Native American spirituality and psychedelic drug use.

FOUNDER: Carlos Castaneda

TEXTS: Castaneda's 1968 book *The Teachings of Don Juan: A Yaqui Way of Knowledge*, as well as nine other popular books, spins tales about drugs and a Mexican sorcerer. No one has been able to independently verify anything said in these books.

OVERVIEW: The report from the mortuary said Carlos Castaneda died of liver cancer and his ashes were taken to Mexico, the land he supposedly loved.

But a spokesman from the literary agency that represented the phenomenally popular author disagreed, saying Castaneda had simply disappeared from the earth like a cloud of steam evaporating into the atmosphere. The death report was simply a legal matter designed to facilitate the execution of Castaneda's will.

Much could be written about Castaneda, a man some consider a godfather of the New Age movement; certainly much has been written. But Castaneda acknowledged lying to journalists and interviewers, which makes separating truth from falsehood in his story complex, if not impossible.

One thing is clear: Beginning in 1968 Castaneda published a series of best-selling books purporting to be firsthand accounts of the author's apprenticeship with an Indian holy man named Don Juan. Everything else is pure conjecture.

Truth or Hallucination?

Castaneda was supposedly born in Peru in 1925. He later moved to Los Angeles, where he enrolled at UCLA and studied ethnobotany, which explores the use of psychotropic plants used by indigenous sorcerers and shamans throughout the Americas.

With the help of peyote, psilocybin, and other mind-altering substances, Castaneda says he learned how to stop time. He said drugs were a doorway to more spiritual states of existence, and he criticized people like LSD guru Timothy Leary, claiming Leary thought drugs alone could transform people's lives. But even though Castaneda said more than drugs was necessary to reach a state of "non-ordinary reality," the sources he turned to for his spiritual powers were indigenous spiritual traditions that acknowledge their origins in demonic rituals.

Castaneda claimed that he met a shape-shifting sorcerer with demonic powers named Don Juan Matus. He developed an apprenticeship with Don Juan between 1961 and 1965. This provided the basis of Castaneda's master's thesis at UCLA and his first best-selling book, *The Teachings of Don Juan: A Yaqui Way of Knowledge*, which became a huge best-seller among the youth counterculture of the 1960s and 1970s and inspired nine popular sequels that covered similar ground. In time Castaneda claimed he was selected to be Don Juan's successor.

Castaneda was also schooled in Tensegrity (from *tension* and *integrity*), the ability for human beings to perceive energy directly as it flows in the universe. The sorcerer Don Juan further explained that once those shamans of ancient times had established the validity of perceiving energy directly, which they called *seeing*, they proceeded to refine it by applying it to themselves, meaning that they perceived one another, whenever they wanted it, as a conglomerate of energy fields. Human beings perceived in such a fashion appear to the seer as gigantic luminous spheres. The size of these luminous spheres is the breadth of the extended arms.

Even though Castaneda's books sold at a fantastic rate, many critics and academics questioned whether the books were fact or fiction. No one has ever been able to verify the existence of Don Juan, and many anthropologists question the complete absence of Yaqui terms or culture in the books.

For many of his readers, it didn't really matter whether or not the books were true. They were interesting, and that was enough. But for Christians concerned about separating truth from fantasy, there's plenty to worry about in Castaneda's body of work. Or as journalist Thomas Ropp put it, "It's doubtful there's ever been a cult personage shrouded in more mystery."

CHRISTIAN CRITIQUE: Castaneda, like Timothy Leary, was just one of many academic mavericks in the seventies who enticed a generation seduced by the drug culture to explore alternative forms of consciousness. This led to the first modern melding of spirituality and psychotropic experiences. The danger of such an approach to reality lies in the lack of substantive evidence for any of Castaneda's claims. From his birth to his death, facts are shrouded in the same mystery that accompanied his metaphysical insights. This subjective quest for "truth" stands in contrast to the historical basis of Christianity, which is rooted in actual events recorded by eyewitnesses. No one other than Castaneda met the purported Don Juan, no one chronicled what went on between the two, and there is no proof that the ethnobiologist had anything other than a series of bad hallucinogenic trips which fueled his own internal fantasies.

SOURCES: Rosemary Ellen Guiley, *Harper's Encyclopedia of Mystical and Paranormal Experience* (San Francisco: HarperSanFrancisco, 1991); Thomas Ropp, "Author, 'Sorcerer' Castaneda Vanishes in a Mist, Says Agent," *Arizona Republic*, June 1998.

ACCESS: www.castaneda.org

EDGAR CAYCE

Association for Research and Enlightenment (A.R.E.)

This so-called "sleeping prophet" was raised in the Bible belt, but he left biblical moorings behind to become one of the twentieth century's most celebrated psychics.

FOUNDER: Edgar Cayce, born March 18, 1877, on a farm near Hopkinsville, Kentucky; died January 3, 1945, in Virginia Beach, Virginia

TEXT: Numbers 12:6: "If there be a prophet among you, I the Lord will make myself known unto him in a vision, and will speak unto him in a dream."

SYMBOLS: Dove and cross or the letters *A.R.E.*

APPEAL: Those suffering painful and incurable illnesses may turn to Cayce's physical readings when medical science cannot help. If their suffering is alleviated, they consider his life readings a source of truth explaining the nature of their cure. In addition, many believe Cayce's success in diagnosing physical ailments means he is a reliable guide to religious and spiritual questions.

OVERVIEW: As with many other cult leaders, things began simply for Edgar Cayce, a Sunday school teacher who discovered that he had the ability to go into a trancelike state and diagnose people's illnesses. But in time his psychic "readings" began to explore more complex areas, like the history of the universe, the hidden background of lost civilizations like Atlantis, and new ideas about human nature and religion.

Today a Cayce Web site—sponsored by the Association for Research and Enlightenment (A.R.E.), the organization founded in 1932 to preserve, research, and promote Cayce's ideas—boldly proclaims that he was "the father of holistic medicine."

Such lofty claims would have surprised those who knew Cayce and perhaps even the man himself.

Strange and Unusual Occurrences

Cayce's childhood was replete with strange phenomena. One story claims that as a baby he cried for the entire first month of his life until an old black woman suggested pricking the nipples of his breast with a pin. When that was done, milk came out. From that point on, young Edgar rarely ever cried.

Later in life he recalled that during childhood he was constantly surrounded by what he called "play folk." They disappeared when others were around, although his mother saw them occasionally. As Edgar grew older and increased in size, these play folk also seemed to increase in stature. One day they simply failed to show up, and that was the end of their communication with Cayce.

A turning point in his life occurred at age thirteen. The presence of a woman appeared and offered to grant him any request. Edgar responded in an altruistic manner, saying that he wanted to help others when they were sick. No sooner had his petition been stated than the apparition vanished.

He was not the first in his family to exhibit psychic tendencies. His father had a strange power over snakes, and his grandfather had a widespread reputation as a water witcher. The elder Cayce could also make tables move and brooms dance.

But Edgar's supernatural powers were even more strange. For one thing, he discovered at an early age that he could sleep with a book under his pillow and awake the next morning with its entire contents indelibly fixed in his mind.

When evangelist Dwight L. Moody was passing through town, Edgar shared with him his story of visions and voices. Moody warned him that evil spirits could create such things. But Cayce's official biography provides another interpretation of this encounter. According to *There Is a River*, the evangelist allegedly left open the possibility that Edgar might be a prophet as described in Numbers 12:6.

Edgar Cayce's psychic meanderings came to a crossroads at the age of twenty-four when he lost his voice. Doctors failed to offer a cure, so hypnotists were consulted. After being subjected to a deep trance state, Cayce's voice returned, and his throat was instantly healed.

Healing Others

Shortly after this, Cayce's technique of hypnotic self-cure was expanded to diagnose the ills of others. A. C. Layne, the hypnotist who had facilitated Cayce's voice restoration, suggested that Edgar self-induce a sleep-trance condition and attempt to see what was wrong in another person's body.

Cayce did just that and described in detail Layne's physical condition. Physiological, biological, and pharmacological terms were uttered from Cayce's mouth, although he had only a grammar school education and no medical training. Even Cayce admitted the voice was not his own.

Layne enlisted Cayce as an assistant to his lucrative practice of suggestive therapeutics and osteopathy. Layne told Cayce he had a clairvoyant gift and called his diagnoses "readings." Cayce started out with altruistic motives and refused to accept any money for his cures.

As his fame spread, he became convinced that all this success was the fulfillment of the request granted him by the woman who had appeared to him many years before.

Leaving the Truth Behind

Cayce continued teaching Sunday school and rationalizing his psychic experimentation by claiming it was his God-given calling. He remained reasonably orthodox in his doctrines until 1923. That's when he met Arthur Lammers, a student of Theosophy and occultism.

Lammers encouraged Cayce to go beyond his physical readings of illnesses to cultivate the practice of "life readings." These revelations contained analyses of spiritual and philosophical matters. From then on, Cayce departed sharply from biblical truth.

During his lifetime Edgar Cayce gave in excess of sixteen thousand readings. Of that total, 14,246 were stenographically recorded and are indexed and filed in the locked, fireproof vaults of the headquarters building of A.R.E. in Virginia Beach, Virginia. Cayce had prophesied that it would be a safe haven from earthquakes, floods, and other future cataclysms he believed would befall America.

The physical readings of Cayce were the main source of his attraction. Over a period of forty-three years he gave 8,985 readings proposing cures for the body and mind. In his state of altered consciousness, he expounded on diet, eating habits, and diagnoses for patients who sometimes were miles away.

His homespun remedies often had remarkable curative effects; however, some of his prescriptive suggestions were a little far-fetched. He told cancer victims they need never worry as long as they ate three almonds a day. (A.R.E. literature points out that almonds contain laetrile, but it has now been discredited as a cancer cure.) Patients who smoked moderately (six to eight cigarettes a day) were informed that their habit was harmless, a position not supported by modern research.

Some of Cayce's physical readings were undoubtedly beneficial for their practical, medicinal effects. Natural remedies for natural maladies should not be seen as being indicative of miraculous cures. And the success of such therapy should not validate the source of its information.

A Monument to a Man

The Association for Research and Enlightenment, founded in 1932 and located in Virginia Beach, Virginia, exists to index and catalog Cayce's readings for those seeking help for physical maladies. Inquirers may be referred to one of hundreds of physicians who are A.R.E. members and utilize Cayce's approach to health. Publications and lectures disseminate further information regarding Cayce's life readings on religion. The headquarters building houses a large occult/metaphysical library for research.

For years the A.R.E. was under the leadership of Cayce's son, Hugh Lynn Cayce. Today the A.R.E. Web site promotes classes, conferences, and international travel packages. The site also encourages people to visit A.R.E.'s visitors center, which claims to attract "tens of thousands of individuals from around the world—vacationers, scholars, researchers, philosophers, health care professionals, and students of all kinds."

Visitors can also see the A.R.E. library, which houses the transcripts of the more than fourteen thousand Cayce readings and a vast metaphysical library that indicates how far Cayce's group has departed from Christian orthodoxy. A nearby bookstore also offers books (like *The Edgar Cayce Bible Companion*), health care products based on formulas given in the readings, and gifts.

When I toured the site myself, I heard a confusing mixture of Christian and metaphysical lingo.

"All healing comes from God," declared the prim, pleasant-looking lady lecturing to our group of curious visitors. The statement seemed curious. She had already pointed out that in Cayce's theology "sin" is separation from that which is correct, such as wrong diet or negative thoughts. For an example, she explained that Cayce once declared constipation to be a sin since it disrupted the body's normal functions.

With that in mind, I wasn't going to let her comment on healing go unchallenged.

"Who is God?" I asked, thinking this was a logical question to pose.

"God is whatever you perceive him to be," was the reply. "The One Source, the Creator, the First Cause, that from which all emanates."

Such ambiguity certainly contrasts with the personal deity revealed in the Holy Scriptures. Perhaps that should have come as no surprise.

Cayce, the "sleeping prophet" who as a child aspired to be a missionary and claimed to have read through the entire Bible each year of his life, eventually departed from orthodoxy. His theology mixed metaphysics with mysticism, flavored by strong doses of teachings on reincarnation.

Reincarnation was a key part of Cayce's belief system. He admitted that reincarnation is not taught in the Bible but blamed the omission on third-century translators, who he claimed deliberately excised it from the canon.

Reincarnation is even used to justify sexual perversion. In the official A.R.E. publication, *Many Mansions*, a homosexual's conduct is excused as resulting from a psychological imprint from a former incarnation.

According to Cayce, God created all souls in the beginning, and they enter the material, earthly plane by choice to work out their faults and thus achieve atonement with God. Jesus Christ of Nazareth was appearing in his thirtieth incarnation, having been on earth before as Adam, Enoch, and Melchizedek, among others.

In Cayce's view Christ has now worked out his karmic debt and become a Christ-soul. Cayce referred to Jesus as "Master," and "our Elder Brother." The latter term probably came from the influence of a Mormon lady who lived in the Cayce home during Edgar's childhood. She claimed to have been a wife of Brigham Young.

Although Cayce was a well-meaning man who apparently had some kind of unusual abilities, the authenticity of Cayce's readings rests on whether his comments on scriptural matters are biblically sound. It is faulty logic to suggest that religious pronouncements can be trusted because the voice uttering them is also correct when analyzing people's ills. Psychic success is not a sufficient gauge for spiritual validity.

To trust Edgar Cayce because he was a sincere, devout man who read the Bible and taught Sunday school is dangerous reasoning. His charitable platitudes can't be used to judge the veracity of his readings, even when some of them seem to square with the Bible. Ardent altruism is no substitute for total harmony with the revealed truth of Scripture. By this measure Cayce's lofty sentiments fall far short of biblical standards.

CHRISTIAN CRITIQUE: A.R.E. literature calls Cayce's readings the "most impressive record of psychic perceptions ever to emanate from a single individual."

That may be true, but even his proponents admit his prophecies have proved to be only 90 percent accurate. Critics place his rate of accuracy even lower. He failed by underestimating Hitler's inclination for evil and struck out again by declaring that New York would be dumped into the sea in the seventies. People are still looking for the elusive Atlantis he prophesied would arise in the twentieth century.

Cayce's undocumented revelations of historical events, erroneous prophecies of geologic alterations, and unsubstantiated tales of lost empires should cause serious students of history and the Bible to question his credibility. If Jesus was once incarnated as Adam, then he is not a sinless redeemer. Cayce's solution for sin is not forgiveness in this life, but the promise of many future lives to make ourselves acceptable to God.

Much of what Cayce taught is extrabiblical. When questioned as to why he placed so much emphasis on the Essenes (a monastic sect not mentioned in Scripture), he replied, "We have received it [this information] psychically." Psychic revelation was also the source of information for his contention that Jesus was initiated into secret societies in India and Egypt.

Cayce also rambled on about souls descending from apes, and he expounded theories concerning advanced civilizations in the lost lands of Atlantis and Lemuria. He encouraged nearly every form of occultism from astrology to auras, from astral projection to ancient Egyptian mysteries.

How much of Cayce's readings came from his subconscious mind, influenced by outside sources, cannot be determined. Those familiar with demonic phenomena find in Cayce's readings a curious consistency with the kind of utterances associated with spiritism. One thing is certain: Though the extrabiblical aspect of Cayce's interests cannot objectively be evaluated, his claim to be a prophet is clearly without a scriptural base. One hundred percent accuracy (Deuteronomy 18:20-22) is the requirement for those who speak on behalf of God, whether awake or asleep.

SOURCES: Various A.R.E. publications, including Jess Stearn's *Edgar Cayce: The Sleeping Prophet*; Thomas Sugrue's *There Is a River*; and books by Cayce, including *The Edgar Cayce Reader*.

ACCESS: Association for Research and Enlightenment, Inc., PO Box 656, Virginia Beach, VA 23451. A.R.E. Press: 1/888-ARE-0050. Web site: www.edgarcayce.org.

CHILDREN OF GOD

See The Family.

CHRISTIAN SCIENCE

Church of Christ, Scientist

Emerging out of the superstition and spiritual ferment of the nineteenth century, the movement founded by Mary Baker Eddy remains a significant— if struggling—world religion.

FOUNDER: Mary Baker Eddy; born in 1821 as Mary Ann Morse Baker; died in 1910

TEXT: Matthew 9:2, supposedly an affirmation of Mrs. Eddy's own healing, which led her to formulate Christian Science beliefs. Eddy wrote numerous books, including the church's scripture: *Science and Health with Key to the Scriptures.* Bliss Knapp's controversial book *The Destiny of the Mother Church* claims that Eddy is a second Christ—a claim never dismissed by Eddy herself.

SYMBOLS: The seal of a cross ringed by a crown

APPEAL: The healing and health promised by Christian Science meets man's emotional need to overcome fear of pain and suffering. Eddy's teachings appeal to those seeking a philosophical basis for ignoring man's unregenerate nature and necessity of repentance. The reality of evil can be excused as an apparition of the mind.

OVERVIEW: Doug and Rita Swan had watched their sixteen-month-old baby convulse and scream with pain for twelve days. When they finally took him to the hospital, it was too late. Little Matthew died six days later.

As devout Christian Scientists, Doug and Rita had tried to follow their faith. Their church "practitioner" had told them to pray, tell no one, and ignore Matthew's anguished condition.

Rita Swan, who went on to run an advocacy group called CHILD (Child Health Care Is a Legal Duty) says she was threatened by the practitioner when she began to doubt. After all, "Mother" Mary Baker Eddy had declared that sin, illness, and disease are all illusions of the mind to be corrected by right thinking.

The tragic story of Matthew Swan is only one of many endured by Christian Scientists, who have historically rejected chiropractic treatments, vitamins, nutrition, and drugs, as well as immunizations.

Parents like the Swans are safe from prosecution for negligence in most states of the United States—forty-six at the writing of this book. But such freedoms are hotly debated.

In 1997 the American Academy of Pediatrics issued a policy statement that said such laws should be repealed and that federal funds should not be used to pay for care in Christian Science "sanitoria."

"Children are not mere property of their parents," said an AAP spokesman. "Adults may be free to martyr themselves, but they are not free to martyr their children."

Courts are also raising serious questions about laws that protect people from those who shun medical assistance for family members. One Sarasota, Florida, court found parents guilty of murder in the negligent death of their seven-year-old child.

In the midst of such church-state conflicts, Christian Scientists remain dedicated to their belief that when pain or sickness strikes, they must deny "material sense testimony" from their five senses. Even a mother's protective instinct is derided as a "false, mortal belief."

Church members like former Cleveland Browns running back Tommy Vardell may have broken bones set, but they aren't permitted any medical diagnosis because Mrs. Eddy taught that consulting a physician breaks the first commandment.

How can such an unenlightened and potentially fatal belief hold authoritarian sway over people?

Christian Science has so insulated itself from interaction with other religious groups that members feel a sense of isolation. They are reluctant to talk with outsiders and are forbidden to read any critical literature.

They have reason to be impressed with their church. Mrs. Eddy had declared, "There is one way to heaven . . . divine science shows us this way. The second appearing of Jesus is unquestionably the spiritual advent of the advancing idea of God, as in Christian Science."

Adding to the group's allure is the fact that weekly worship is carried on in expensive, beautiful buildings (though today many of the buildings are nearly empty). Reading rooms are well appointed and cheerfully staffed at highly visible locations. The *Christian Science Monitor*, the group's daily newspaper with a circulation of over 100,000, is a highly respected journalistic organ with several Pulitzer prizes to its credit.

A Founder's Faith

Mary Baker Eddy was certainly not modest in her claims, and most church members admire her as an infallible mother. She proclaimed that her teachings were God's "final revelation." Mrs. Eddy asserted divine inspiration for her book *Science and Health with Key to the Scriptures*.

The very choice of the word *key* in its title was based on her belief that she was the woman of Revelation 12. Many of her early followers accorded her a status of equality with Christ, a belief she did nothing to dissuade. Unfortunately for Christian Scientists, the historical record of her life gives one a decidedly different impression.

Mary Ann Morse Baker was the daughter of New Hampshire Congregationalists. Her childhood was characterized by emotional disturbances and frequent illnesses. At the age of 22 she married George Glover, who died seven months later. Her second marriage to a dentist, Dr. Daniel Patterson, ended in divorce.

It was while she was married to Dr. Patterson that her life changed abruptly. Seeking relief from a spinal illness in 1862, she visited a spiritual healer by the name of Phineas Parkhurst Quimby. He practiced a form of mind-over-matter healing that he called Christian Science.

While the depth of Quimby's influence on her is questionable, he stimulated her development of the religious teachings she eventually called Christian Science. Research has shown that Mrs. Eddy plagiarized heavily from a dissertation written by Francis Lieber, a German-American philosopher.

In 1866 Mary Ann Patterson fell and injured herself. She later claimed that the fall left her with only three days to live (though her physician denied such a diagnosis). On the third day she reported that after reading Matthew 9:2 she experienced a miraculous cure. From then on, she felt her mission was to spread this "new" discovery of Christian Science.

In 1875 she published her new faith's foundational book, *Science and Health with Key to the Scriptures,* which offered healing to those afflicted with any number of maladies. In 1877 she married Asa Eddy, her first disciple and the first Christian Science practitioner. The Church of Christ, Scientist, was incorporated in 1879.

An Alluring Doctrine

Many people are favorably disposed toward Christian Science in spite of its bad publicity regarding cases when medical treatment was withheld.

In fact, the church's teaching has grown more popular in an age when millions of people are interested in alternative medicine. In 1994 the church even launched an unprecedented promotional campaign to renew its image and increase its sagging membership.

Some have heard glowing testimonials of healing from church members. Others note the conservative, well-educated, upper socioeconomic types who attend Christian Science meetings. They certainly seem well intentioned, and few would condemn their effective ministry to those plagued with emotional ills and psychosomatic afflictions.

But the evaluation of any belief system must be based on substance, not image. The source of its authority and power, as well as the biblical validity of its views, are essential criteria to judge its worth. Such a critical analysis leaves Christian Science lacking in many areas.

Attending a Christian Science service immediately impresses one with its departure from mainstream Christian practices. There is no clergy, only lay readers and designated full-time practitioners who administer the church's healing techniques. No ordinances are recognized, and the service is ended with a reading of the Lord's Prayer interspersed with Mrs. Eddy's interpretations. Membership is restricted to only those who sever relationships with any other church or religious organization. *Science and Health with Key to the Scriptures* is read alternately with Bible quotations, giving the distinct connotation that the Word of God is useless without Mary Baker Eddy's illumination.

The government of the church is outlined in the *Manual of the Mother Church,* published in 1895. Mrs. Eddy continually revised this manual, intending that it would remain the authority in her church after she was gone. She entrusted the execution of the provisions of the manual to a self-perpetuating, five-member board of directors, who oversees the basically democratic framework of the branch churches.

Teaching and Terminology

The doctrines of Christian Science are not overtly unorthodox to the casual observer. Much of Eddy's terminology sounds good until the surface is scratched to reveal her semantic frame of reference underneath.

Influenced by the New Thought fad of her day, she underpins all her doctrines with the Hindu concept of an evil, illusory, material world. In this system, that which is spirit is the only true reality. This notion flavors her concepts of God, sin, and salvation.

Here is a sampling of her teachings: man did not fall; death is an illusion; angels are God's thoughts; God is divine Mind; Genesis 2 is a lie; the Virgin Birth was a spiritual idea; the Trinity is pagan; evil and sin are imaginary; disease can be removed by right thinking; Jesus was not God; heaven is a state of mind; hell is nonexistent; prayer to forgive sin is pointless; Christ did not die; his resurrection was spiritual and not physical; and the shed blood of Christ is ineffectual for sin.

The core of Christian Science teaching is the doctrine of healing. Nothing else the church propagates draws more potential members. Mrs. Eddy was constantly challenged by the medical leaders of her day to produce evidence of one bona fide healing of a medically diagnosed case of organic disease. She did not and could not.

Near the end of her life, though, even Mrs. Eddy turned to physicians and was treated with the painkiller morphine. Still, Christian Science maintains her belief that Jesus revealed to people their illusion of illness and thus cured them. Christian Scientists propose to go and do likewise.

Undeniably, there are some cases of Christian Science healing that deserve acknowledgment. Those who believe they have been healed are quick to embrace the entire scope of church teachings.

What really happens in these cases? Since medical verification before or after the fact is not allowed, no one knows how many cures were induced by alleviating the psychosomatic root of the problem. Emotional illnesses may have been removed by the psychologically soothing effect of the practitioner's therapy.

Some ex-members argue that in Christian Science healing, the symptoms are ignored, a decision that may later result in suffering that could have been alleviated with proper medical treatment.

In addition, Moses' encounter with Pharaoh's magicians in Exodus 7 illustrates Satan's ability to precipitate apparent miracles. In fact, supernatural healing is a trademark of many demonic cults, including satanism and Spiritualism. When a healing occurs, it should not necessarily be construed as an indication of divine approval of what the healer believes.

A Troubled Time

Like many mainline Protestant denominations, Christian Science has wrestled with the implications of a membership that is aging and declining in numbers.

Conditions worsened in the early 1990s when the church embarked on ill-fated ventures into media properties like cable television and magazine publishing. Hoping to duplicate the success of its flagship *Christian Science Monitor,* the church instead lost nearly half a billion dollars and was forced to dip into restricted funds. Its plans for a media empire crumbled under a deficit of nearly $7 million per month.

The church has kept its membership figures secret for more than a century, but those familiar with the organization say there are probably less than half the nearly 300,000 estimated in 1936 by the U.S. Census Bureau. The number of practitioners listed in the *Christian Science Journal* has dropped from about 12,000 in the 1950s to about 3,000. Interestingly, membership has increased in some other countries.

Before her death Mrs. Eddy prophesied that "in fifty years or less, Christian Science will be the dominant religious belief of the world." That prediction seems as misguided as her contention that "man is incapable of sin, sickness, and death."

CHRISTIAN CRITIQUE: Eddy taught a complex conglomeration of beliefs: the "myths" of traditional Christian belief must be eradicated; man is perfect and should strive for the same Divine Mind that Jesus attained; sickness can be eradicated once a person sees that pure thoughts will dispel the illusion of disease. As the one true church, members are encouraged to affirm that God is good and therefore good is God. In such a system, evil cannot exist since matter (evil) does not exist.

Few orthodox Christian doctrines are left unassaulted in Christian Science, a unique faith that is neither biblically based nor scientific. Its theology is universalistic. Jesus was said to be hiding in the sepulcher—he didn't die, so his resurrection holds no hope for believers, contradicting Paul's exposition in 1 Corinthians 15.

SOURCES: Kenneth Boa, *Cults, World Religions and You* (Wheaton, Ill.: Victor, 1980); *Christianity Today,* 10 October 1975, 6–11; William Dunn, "Conviction for Beliefs Ominous," *USA Today,* 7 April 1989, 3A; Marilyn Elias, "Pediatricians condemn laws on faith healing," *USA Today,* 11 February 1997, 1D; *Encyclopedia Britannica,* 15th ed, s.v. "Christian Science"; John Larrabee, "States Take On Power of Prayer," *USA Today,* 2 May 1988, 2A; Walter Martin, *The Kingdom of the Cults* (Minneapolis: Bethany Fellowship, 1977); "A Mild Matron Goes Modern," *Time,* 26 September 1988; *Newsweek,* 21 June 1976, 87; Gustav Niebuhr, "Christian Science Opens a New Era of Discourse," *New York Times,* 1 October 1994, 30; Richard N. Ostling, "Tumult in the Reading Rooms," *Time,* 14 October 1991, 57; *People,* 31 March 1981, 30–32; M. Thomas Starkes, *Christian Scientists and the Baptist Witness* (Home Missions Board, S.C.); Kenneth Woodward, "The Graying of a Church," *Newsweek,* 3 August 1987, 60.

ACCESS: The Mother Church and related businesses are at One Norway Street, Boston, MA 02115. There are local churches and/or reading rooms in most U.S. cities of reasonable size. About a third of the church's nearly three thousand congregations are located in fifty-six countries outside the United States.

CHURCH OF ARMAGEDDON
Love Israel; Love Israel Family; Love Family

Combining unique interpretations of the book of Revelation and a fondness for mind-altering drugs, this sixties group was still turning on and tuning out in the nineties.

FOUNDER: Paul Erdmann; later called Love Israel

TEXT: Revelation 16:16: "And he gathered them together into a place called in the Hebrew tongue Armageddon."

OVERVIEW: Funnyman Steve Allen was one of the most famous men in the early years of television. But Allen and his wife weren't laughing in the 1970s when their twenty-four-year-old son, Brian, sent them a letter saying he had joined a countercultural group then known as the Church of Armageddon, or the Love Family.

A decade later Allen was more philosophical. "We consider ourselves very fortunate and blessed when we look around at other families," said Allen, who wrote a book called *Beloved Son* that described both his relationship with his son and the profusion of unusual cults. "There are 1,001 worse other fates. The important thing is that we have a marvelous relationship."

Other families weren't so lucky. When their loved ones joined the cult, their names were changed and most contact with the outside world was cut off.

In Love with Love
Meekness, patience, and courage sound like admirable biblical qualities. But in the Church of Armageddon (sometimes called the Love Family), these virtues represent the newly adopted names of cult members. Since the Love Family considers all Christians to be descendants of the Israelites, Israel is added as a surname.

Presiding over the clan is Love Israel, a former salesman named Paul Erdmann, who formed the cult in the San Francisco Bay area in the 1960s and later relocated the group to Seattle. Erdmann gathered a group of followers around him who listened in rapt attention as he expounded his visions and teachings.

Taking his cue from Revelation 16:16, in which Armageddon is mentioned, Erdmann teaches his disciples that they are the true family of God. New members turn over all of their possessions to the church, cut off all communication with the outside world (including their parents and relatives, unless such contacts result in donations of money and materials), and devote themselves to the goals and person of Love Israel.

The disciples are also taught to adhere to some strange and unusual beliefs. Eating is considered to be a sacrament; the consumption of marijuana, hashish, and mushrooms are also sacraments; children are severely disciplined; marriage is replaced by "bonding" under Love Israel's authority; yoga is practiced; outside medical assistance is forbidden; and toluene (a solvent) vapors are inhaled as a religious rite. (After two members died from this practice, it has apparently been discontinued.)

Though Love Israel undoubtedly "transformed" his followers from insecure outcasts to self-confident zealots, they paid a great price in sacrificing personal freedom.

A mass defection in the early 1980s nearly destroyed the cult; departing members charged Love Israel with conning them into accepting his total control over their lives and income, while he lived in luxury and they struggled with necessities.

In the mid 1980s, after a brief period in Los Angeles during which he reexperienced an awakening to the world's troubles, he returned to Washington State to regain control of the Love Family. The early nineties found him working to rebuild the commune and dealing with the Snohomish County council on a range of zoning issues.

Fortunately, the growth of the group has never surpassed a few hundred members, but that's small consolation to the Allens—whose son Brian is now named Logic Israel—or to anyone else who has lost a loved one to this idiosyncratic cult.

With the personality of founder Love Israel as the focus of attention, the Love Family seems to be more an extension of his own personal ego rather than a "fulfilled" New Testament organ of Christ's body.

SOURCES: Robert Benjamin, "Family Cultivates New Names," *Springfield (Ohio) News-Sun*, 27 May 1982, 12; Ronald Enroth, *Youth, Brainwashing and the Extremist Cults* (Grand Rapids, Mich.: Zondervan, 1977).

THE CHURCH OF BIBLE UNDERSTANDING

Forever Family

A regimented cult that once attracted thousands, this group
has since hit hard times.

FOUNDER: Stewart Traill

OVERVIEW: His usual appearance has been a shaggy beard, stringy hair circling a bald forehead, military fatigues, Converse all-star yellow sneakers, a chain of brown leather pouches, a dozen colored, felt-tip pens in his breast pocket, and a large round pin proclaiming, "Get Smart, Get Saved."

This is hardly the image one would envision for a revered spiritual leader who likens himself to Elijah and hints that he may know the exact hour of the Lord's return. But then Stewart Traill, ex-atheist and former secondhand vacuum cleaner salesman, is not a typical Messianic cult leader.

After an apparent religious conversion in Allentown, Pennsylvania, in the early seventies, Traill began teaching Bible studies and collecting a following. With his wife and new converts in tow, he formed the Forever Family in 1971. Concerned that the name lacked respectability, in 1976 it was changed to the Church of Bible Understanding (COBU).

Traill continued to prosper until his far-flung fellowship grew to be 10,000 strong and he amassed a fortune, including a two-million-dollar-a-year rug-cleaning business and four airplanes, one of them a $300,000 turboprop.

In the wake of the Jonestown debacle, Traill's prospects soured. Today the group is believed to have only a few hundred remaining members.

Ex-members complained of being encouraged to work for a pittance (all earnings are turned over to church leaders) and being housed in rat-infested lofts.

The IRS put the rug-cleaning operation out of business, and the truth of Traill's divorce and remarriage surfaced: Traill, forty-six, and his wife had exchanged accusations of adultery in a messy divorce proceeding, after which he married his COBU secretary—half his age—only six weeks later.

A Closely Guarded Flock

An exact picture of COBU doctrine is sketchy, since few definitive statements have been published. Its communal lifestyle is regimented into categories known as *guardians* (active members who are leaders), *sheep* (advanced believers), and *lambs* (new converts).

Those who have left the commune report having been intimidated by suggestions that "backsliders" may meet a tragic end. The remaining COBU members devoutly believe that they have (via Traill) the one true access to "Bible understanding." Traill contends that God deliberately secret-coded the Scriptures and that only his "figure system" and "color-coding" scheme hold the keys to the true interpretation of the Word of God.

Though the basic appeal of COBU is directed toward a "personal acceptance of Christ" with "old-time religion" terminology, Traill's denial of the Trinity and his unsubstantiated berating of detractors (CCs—short for "contentious Christians") hardly endears him to mainstream evangelicals.

In addition, Traill challenges his converts to break off all familial relationships on the premise that those over thirty (excepting Traill) are too spiritually hopeless. He keeps his flock in line with a mixture of constant emotional abuse mingled with fatherly praise and kindness.

In spite of his attempts to improve his own personal appearance as well as COBU's image, the prognosis for any substantial growth of the cult seems doubtful. The question of whether or not most COBU members are "genuinely saved" is open to speculation, but their coercive and rigidly methodical methods of "witnessing" are unlikely to garner many adherents.

SOURCES: *Alternatives* 4, no. 6 (April-May 1977); Joseph Duffy, *Contemporary Christianity* 6, no. 3 (March-April 1977); Eric Pement, "Shepherd without Compassion: Stewart Traill and the Church of Bible Understanding," *Cornerstone* 11, no. 60: 32–33; *Sunday Record*, 25 September 1977; *Today Magazine (Philadelphia Inquirer)*, 24 June 1979.

ACCESS: Box 841, Radio City Station, New York, NY 10019

THE CHURCH OF
THE LIVING WORD
The Walk

With its confusing manipulation of Christian terminology and its founder's impromptu prophecies, this group has substituted truth for error.

FOUNDER: John Robert Stevens; born August 7, 1919, Washington, Iowa; died of cancer June 4, 1983

TEXT: Stevens uses Acts 9:3-4 to legitimize his apostolic authority by equating his visionary experience with Paul's Damascus-road encounter; he interprets John 16:13 to assume that subjective revelation should supplant and augment objective biblical truths. Stevens wrote a number of books, and Living Word Publications also offers many of his sermon tapes.

APPEAL: Disaffected Christians from nominal church backgrounds may find in The Walk a more spontaneous encounter with spiritual reality. Those familiar with Eastern religions and occult phenomena will easily recognize the similarities between these practices and Stevens's teachings.

OVERVIEW: John Robert Stevens, the founder of the Church of the Living Word, commonly called The Walk, was a classic example of what happens when one is raised in a Christian environment and departs into error.

Stevens used evangelical terminology to justify his private revelations. Consequently, the truth of Scripture was altered enough to be detected but not sufficiently to be obvious. The Walk members use colloquial Christian catchphrases that they have redefined. For example, when Stevens said he was "speaking the Word of the Lord" he was actually referring to a mediumistic revelation of his Christ-attained perfection. Those not familiar with his cult would assume that he was merely talking about preaching. Such a twist in logic and language is consistent with his whole approach to scriptural truth.

An Embattled Prophet
Stevens was reared in a preacher's home, though he later departed from Foursquare and Assemblies of God groups after a dramatic vision in 1954. He claimed this experience was similar to Paul's encounter on the road to Damascus.

Stevens's father, W. J. "Dad" Stevens, founded a congregation called the Church of the Living Word in 1951, and by the mid-1970s, the movement claimed more than eighty churches in the United States and other countries, with headquarters in Iowa and California.

But the father and son fell into a bitter dispute that culminated in a lawsuit John brought against his father. The younger Stevens accused his father and his father's associates of mishandling large sums of church money, bilking worshipers, and abusing their leadership.

Dad Stevens countersued, charging the John Stevens organization with conspiring to "take over the church . . . real and personal property" belonging to the elder Stevens and his associates.

John Stevens died of cancer in 1983 amid the legal battle, at which time his church claimed holdings that included ownership of a 1,100-acre farm in Brazil, a 300-acre commune called Shiloh near Kalona, Iowa, and a 150-acre retreat near Fresno, California.

In the son's scheme of teachings, the Bible was considered outdated and thus needed to be supplemented (and eventually replaced) by impromptu, spoken prophecies.

During frequent, lengthy, emotion-charged services, members were encouraged to deny reason and yield to extemporaneous utterances that represented "the living word." The one who spoke was more than a mere channel of Christ but was said literally to become Christ, a self-deification doctrine that was central to the church's beliefs.

Such individualistic revelations were important but always subject to the ones expounded by Stevens, who claimed apostolic authority. Members were taught that Scripture would confuse them unless they followed Stevens's interpretations.

This authoritarian manner of control also extended to the personal affairs of members. Day-to-day decisions had to be subjected to church supervision, since The Walk is assumed to be the only true church capable of guiding one's life.

As the church evolved, occult and psychic phenomena became more evident. Since a central doctrine having to do with perfectionism states that Christians become a part of God in a manner bordering on deification, their divine natures become willing recipients of mystical experiences.

This merging of one's nature with God negates the sense of personal identity, further opening up one's spirit to experience transcendent levels of consciousness. At some church services, participants are encouraged to raise the level of their vibrations, a practice bordering on the spiritualistic manner of inducing altered states of mind.

Many Walk members (there are about five thousand worldwide) are born-again refugees from sterile churches. They have been attracted by a sense of belonging due to the group dynamics and claims of supernatural gifts of tongues, prophecy, and healing.

These well-meaning people might overlook the occult nature of references to auras and "transference" of spiritual power. But their sincerity is no excuse for claiming superiority over all other churches and denominations. Such an exclusive attitude is not in harmony with 1 Corinthians 12, which emphasizes the unity of Christ's body in spite of its diversity.

Since the death of the elder Stevens, Shiloh is no longer affiliated with the California or Brazil factions. The vast wealth of the church is a source of contention between divisions of The Walk, some siding with John Robert Stevens's second wife, others aligning with contingents of the California church.

CHRISTIAN CRITIQUE: Members of The Walk are taught that all other churches belong to a false Babylonian system and that the Church of the Living Word is restoring the active presence of God's truth by the use of supernatural gifts and revelation.

Stevens's teachings rob Christ of his personhood by claiming that he is now embodied in the church and that Christians can be a deified extension of Christ. "Be robed with deity itself—God's very nature being reproduced in you," Stevens implores.

A conclusion of this belief is that the Church of the Living Word essentially represents the second coming of Christ, replacing the literal return of the person of Christ in the clouds (Acts 1:11). Romans 3:22-24 admonishes that Christians can and do sin. They are to repent and ask forgiveness (1 John 1:8-9), not strive for a sanctified state of self-deification.

SOURCES: "John Robert Stevens and The Church of the Living Word," *Spiritual Counterfeits Project Newsletter* 2, no. 7 (September 1976); Walter Martin, *The New Cults* (Santa Ana, Calif.: Vision House, 1980), 269–296; miscellaneous writings by John Robert Stevens, including *To Every Man That Asketh*.

ACCESS: Box 858, North Hollywood, CA 91603

CHURCH OF CHRIST

See International Churches of Christ.

CHURCH UNIVERSAL AND TRIUMPHANT

Elizabeth Clare Prophet

This "church" isn't even remotely Christian or universal.
And in the wake of controversies and its leader's health problems,
it's anything but triumphant.

FOUNDER: Mark L. Prophet (1918–1973) was succeeded by his wife, Elizabeth Clare Prophet, who was diagnosed with Alzheimer's disease in 1999. She was succeeded by Gilbert Cleirbaut.

TEXT: "I am that I am" (Exodus 3:14). In Scripture this statement affirms the eternal, omnipotent, omniscient nature of God. I AM cults say this phrase can be spoken to testify of the God-presence in each person.

Elizabeth Clare Prophet has also written many works of her own, including *The Lost Years of Jesus,* in which she supposedly reveals Jesus' experiences in the Orient as a young student of Eastern philosophy before returning to Palestine to complete his mission on earth. She followed this book with *The Lost Teachings of Jesus.*

SYMBOLS: Cross with dove emerging from center of the quadrants; flame representing the sacred fire; chart of "divine self" illustrating man's transition from lower self; pictures of miscellaneous Ascended Masters

APPEAL: Those interested in spiritualism and Eastern religions find a Christian frame of reference for pursuing these beliefs in a syncretistic manner. Some are attracted by the awe of receiving directly from Prophet's lips supernatural messages of departed spiritual masters.

OVERVIEW: Official literature from the Church Universal and Triumphant claims that its "church teachings are rooted in the Judeo-Christian tradition."

But one has to do an awful lot of digging to find any hint of orthodox Christianity in the doctrines of this group, which blends concepts from Eastern and Western religious traditions, along with a unique mix of insight from the Ascended Masters and controversial revelations from former leader Elizabeth Clare Prophet about imminent nuclear holocaust.

In January 1999 Prophet, who was formerly a dedicated student of Christian Science, was diagnosed with Alzheimer's disease and resigned from leadership of the organization.

Gilbert Cleirbaut, Prophet's successor as president of the group, reported a 35 percent membership decline since 1994 in the wake of Prophet's failed predictions that Russia would attack the United States.

These erroneous prophecies had led the group to build bomb shelters for thousands of people on its 33,000-acre property near Livingston, Montana. Even the usually sympathetic *New Age Journal* questioned the group's direction in a 1991 article entitled, "Trouble in Paradise?": "What's a self-described 'peace-loving' church led by a 'new age' mystic doing in rural Montana with high-powered rifles, bomb shelters, and a seemingly obsessive preoccupation with surviving nuclear Armageddon? That's the question on the minds of many in scenic Paradise Valley, home to The Church Universal and Triumphant and its spiritual leader, author and astrologer Elizabeth Clare Prophet."

But discerning people were asking questions about this group long before these problems developed.

A Self-Proclaimed Prophet

"I am that I am," says Elizabeth Clare Prophet as she conveys her blessing on the audience who has just heard her discourse. Guru Ma, as she is known to her followers, has not only plagiarized God's reply to Moses (Exodus 3:14), but she also makes some other phenomenal claims.

She purports to be a reincarnation of the biblical Martha, stating that in a former life Jesus spoke directly to her one day while she was kneading bread with her sister, Mary. Christ commanded her to keep incarnating until God's Spirit would be poured out at the dawning of the Aquarian Age.

Elizabeth Clare Prophet believes that hour has come, and she is the only present-day medium of truth endorsed by the Ascended Masters (beings who have passed on to an elevated spiritual plane). Those who follow her teachings, as received from the Great White Brotherhood (a community of Ascended Masters said to be sages of hidden wisdom and knowledge), will have their souls purified by the Violet Consuming Flame so that they may achieve Christ-consciousness.

To the uninitiated, such ideas may seem a little confusing. But to indoctrinated followers of the Church Universal and Triumphant, it's all part of an effort to transcend the laws of karma and acknowledge one's inner divinity.

Some cult groups can be explained in fairly simple terms. But the Church Universal has concepts and nomenclature that need defining before any analysis of church belief is possible.

Blending Diverse Traditions

During the early twentieth century, occultists and Theosophists such as Guy and Edna Ballard developed a system of religious philosophy around the concept of Ascended Masters. The theory is similar to a Gnostic belief that God, who is impersonal and unknowable, must be approached by deified, human intermediaries. These Masters are the messengers whom God uses to reveal his truth. They have passed beyond the cycles of reincarnation to merge their consciousness with God. Now these "elder brothers and sisters who have gone before" divulge the hidden mysteries of truth by discourses transmitted through selected human messengers. Elizabeth Clare Prophet claims to be their sole channel of communication for this hour. Foremost among these Ascended Masters is Saint Germain, a French eighteenth-century occultist. His associates in the spirit realm include Jesus the Christ, Mary, his mother, Master Kuthumi, Master Godfre, and El Morya (the main source for Prophet's message). This fraternity is known as the Great White Brotherhood.

Building on the spiritualistic concepts of the Ballards and other Theosophists/occultists, Mark L. Prophet founded the Church Universal and Triumphant (known then as Summit Lighthouse) in 1958. Prophet told his followers he was the second coming of the legendary Sir Lancelot. He also said that while driving a railroad spike one day in Minnesota he'd had a vision of El Morya, an Ascended Master. While serving as a medium, Mark met Elizabeth Clare Wulf at a meeting in 1961. They left their spouses, and two years later they were married.

The union seemed logical, since Elizabeth claims her first encounter with spirits occurred at about four years of age when she was surrounded by "angelic hosts." While she attended college, voices directed her to books about Saint Germain.

Through the years a variety of spirit beings communicated with Elizabeth. But it was not until she met Mark that she felt her calling in life was fulfilled. Mark Prophet, twenty years her senior, died of a stroke in 1973. He is now deemed to be among the other Ascended Masters, communicating with the spirit name Lanello. The mantle of serving as a messenger for the Ascended Masters fell upon her, and until her resignation, thousands of followers around the world (the group does not release membership figures) believed she was the absolute authority on all spiritual matters.

The Gospel according to Prophet

The gospel preached by the Ascended Masters and dictated through the medium Elizabeth to her *chelas* (disciples), is a mixture of Christian terminology and Eastern/mystical concepts.

Each person is believed to be on a spiritual pilgrimage (through a myriad of reincarnations) from his lower self to his higher self. Prophet ignores the warning of 1 John 2:22 that the spirit of antichrist denies Jesus is the Christ. She contends that the historical Jesus was a mere human who became a Christ. Thus, he is not God who is "able also to save . . . to the uttermost" (Hebrews

7:25), but merely an example of how we too can ascend spiritually by acknowledging our inner Christ-presence.

Chelas are assisted in their pilgrimage by a variety of occult/mystical practices. Foremost among these is the use of *decrees*, the mantra-like chanting of incantations. A favorite is "I am that I am," an affirmation of self-deity that ensures ascension. Devotees also seek to cleanse their karma by being surrounded by the Violet Flame, a sacred fire said to be made available by the spiritual merit of Saint Germain.

As a substitute for the blood of Christ, it provides a source of salvation from any negative influences. In addition to the Violet Flame, Prophet taught her followers how to enlist the aid of the seven archangels of God in their personal lives.

The spiritual smorgasbord in Prophet's theology also includes chakra purification, reflexology, healing, fasting, diet, auras, and cosmic astrology.

The cult is currently headquartered at the Royal Teton Ranch in Montana, where conferences attract followers each year and students take courses at Summit University. At one point members of the group outnumbered the population of Gardiner, a nearby town. Gardiner has since grown, the group's membership has dwindled, but controversy hasn't died down.

A local newspaper once discovered and printed a "hit list" that included the names of almost two hundred people against which the cult members pray daily, calling for the will of God to cleanse all opposition.

Unlike other cults which seek to cut off all contact with the outside world, the Church Universal and Triumphant seeks to reach out to other religious leaders and even its critics.

I have received letters of support and appreciation from organization followers and officials. This correspondence has been in regard to my books about the occult. In fact, these books were promoted and sold at public appearances of Mrs. Prophet.

In light of the presumption that the Ascended Masters might well be masquerading evil spirits and that Prophet's messages from them are demonic utterances, how could these same powers then promote the cause of one who represents orthodox, historic Christian theology?

The answer may be that Prophet and her followers are sincere in their religious devotion. In spite of their violation of scriptural commands against attempted communication with the dead (called necromancy; see Deuteronomy 18:11), they genuinely believe they are defenders of moral purity and opponents of witchcraft.

Prophet and her followers should be approached with loving concern so they might discover a personal faith in Jesus the Christ, who is above all principalities and powers, including the Ascended Masters (Ephesians 1:20-22).

CHRISTIAN CRITIQUE: Although the organization says it exists "To publish the teachings of the Ascended Masters and to shed light on the lost and distorted teachings of Christ," spiritual seekers who join the group invariably become entwined in a mix of occult practices and psychic experiences that portend a grave risk of spiritual bondage.

The biblical injunction against necromancy and consultation with familiar spirits (like Ascended Masters) is ignored (Deuteronomy 18:9-14). In this context (Leviticus 19:31), Elizabeth Clare Prophet fulfills the Bible's description of a witchcraft medium.

In Church Universal theology, Christ is not God in flesh, worthy of worship (Philippians 2:9-10) but rather "the mediator between God and man, the Christ-self, or the Christ-consciousness." Man's need is not forgiveness by God's grace but rather a purging of karma to ascend spiritually in future reincarnations, or to join the other Ascended Masters directly.

SOURCES: Church Universal and Triumphant literature and miscellaneous mailings, including "Pearls of Wisdom," "The Teachings on the Path of Enlightenment," "Only Love," "Sing a New Song," "Climb the Highest Mountain," and "The Coming Revolution," winter 1981; John Dart, "Sect Leader Continues to Spread Word Despite Uproar over Forecasts," *Los Angeles Times,* 23 February 1991, F16–17; Timothy Egan, "Thousands Plan Life Below, after Doomsday," *New York Times,* 15 March 1990, A1, A15; Walter Martin, *The New Cults* (Santa Ana, Calif.: Vision House, 1980), 203–236; "Put to the Test: Church Members Make the Grade as a Denomination," *Royal Teton Ranch News,* February-March 1995; Jim Robbins, "Trouble in Paradise?" *New Age Journal* (March-April, 1991): 16, 18.

ACCESS: PO Box 5000, Gardiner, MT 59047-1390. Web site: www.suonline.org.

See also Ascended Masters.

TERRY COLE-WHITTAKER

This speaker and author combines pop psychology, prosperity theology,
and Mind Science concepts to create "New Christianity,"
which is actually recycled ancient heresies.

FOUNDER: Terry Cole-Whittaker, a divorcée whose great-grandmother,
the family matriarch, was married six times and was also an adherent of Religious Science. Cole-Whittaker was trained in the teachings of *A Course in Miracles* as well as the beliefs of Ernest Holmes, who founded the Institute of Religious Science in 1927.

TEXT: Cole-Whittaker's book *Prosperity, Your Divine Right*, a gospel of success combining motivational psychology and selfish affirmations such as "It is right for me to prosper," as well as other books by Cole-Whittaker.

SYMBOL: A stylized fountain representing the flow of prosperity from the source of God. The fountain has seven points representing the perfection and completeness of God.

APPEAL: Cole-Whittaker has attracted three basic classes of people:
1. Participants in various New Age and human-potential disciplines looking for the latest promises of wealth and divine blessings on their own narcissistic motivations
2. Marginally churched people who want an ecclesiastical atmosphere with congregational services but want to avoid any theological demands pertaining to guilt and sin
3. Insecure and introverted individuals for whom Cole-Whittaker proves an alter ego, exuding the self-confidence and charisma they feel incapable of attaining

OVERVIEW: "To turn your life around requires that you live a new life in Christ. He overcame the world . . . so can you, now."

"Salvation must be an act of saving yourself from something. If you need to be saved, you must be in danger. The truth is, no one is in danger. You have never broken the laws of God. You are pure and innocent."

To Christians, such comments seem clearly contradictory. But to followers of Cole-Whittaker, they are the accepted truths of something called the "New Christianity."

A Metaphysical Phoenix

Cole-Whittaker, a perky, smiling, Doris Day look-alike and onetime third runner-up in the Mrs. America contest, has had more ups and downs than the stock market. In the 1980s she hosted a weekly half-hour television program which beamed her New Age "name-it-and-claim-it" message to more than a million viewers in major markets.

In the spring of 1985 Cole-Whittaker bade her followers farewell and called it quits. Some said she was burned out. It was also rumored that mounting debts—estimated between four and seven hundred thousand dollars—had become unmanageable. "I no longer want to be a religious leader. I want to be myself."

Cole-Whittaker searched through various contemporary human potential cults until she rose again like a phoenix.

Her quest took her to Ernest Holmes's School of Ministry, a Religious Science sect. Cole-Whittaker's California-style enthusiasm for the good life caught on in the San Diego area at the La Jolla Church of Religious Science. Rapid growth led her to form her own group, the Science of Mind Church International.

With a combination of pop psychology, New Age concepts, and beliefs borrowed from est (see separate entry) and the occult, Cole-Whittaker declared, "God doesn't forgive; you've never been judged except by your own thoughts."

Among the hodgepodge of disciplines she recommended are the following: A Course in Miracles, the occult volume dictated by automatic writing; group rebirthing, a breathing technique based upon yogic principles; body massage; nutrition; and affirmations.

Affirmations include declarations like these: to "visit only beautiful places . . . to wear only those clothes which are appropriate to upward mobility . . . to associate with those who are prosperous and happy."

The followers of Cole-Whittaker did not visit refugee camps or establish shelters for street people. On the contrary, Cole-Whittaker considered poverty the result of irresponsibility.

In 1990 she told a Canadian journalist that people starving in third world countries might have been put in that state to learn something about themselves. "Poor is a state of mind," she said.

She exhorted those in her church to attend "dressing to win" seminars so they could shed the old image of failure for the new personae of "divine wealth."

Such endorsements of hedonism and materialism appeal to the wealthy Mercedes-Benz crowd she targets. "Our ministry isn't into sin, guilt, disease, pain, or hunger," Cole-Whittaker was fond of saying.

What about the appeal of Jesus to deny one's self and take up the cross (Luke 9:23)? Cole-Whittaker declared, "God denies nothing in the world for you."

Confusing Lingo

Cole-Whittaker mastered the lingo of evangelicalism, further confusing her disciples. She spoke of her "prayer ministry" and "love offerings," and she went so far as to say, "Through the Holy Spirit I was saved." Her ministry tabloid, deceptively entitled *The Good News*, borrowed the trappings of more conventional media ministries.

Cassettes and books expounded her doctrines, along with special videocassette training programs in "Mastery of Living" and "Mastery of Faith." Those who digested the material eventually learned what she called "the principles," an eclectic cafeteria of New Age doctrines teaching that the major religions of the world are "woven together with the thread of light linking the ONE-beyond ISM."

With her chauffeured Cadillac and $180,000-a-year salary, Cole-Whittaker plugged into the good life. Her young and well-to-do parishioners didn't seem to mind, convinced that she really loved them and that they were "walking on the earth as sons of God," exactly as she said.

Critics argued she told people what they wanted to hear about themselves. She readily admitted the accusation was true. "I tell people they're wonderful. It's true!" she affirmed.

"I'm an explorer. I'm a metaphysical, evangelical, Pentecostal space cadet," Cole-Whittaker proclaimed. Her audience responded with whoops and hollers, apparently never stopping to ask themselves how someone who failed four marriages could hope to understand transcendent life and guide them out of their own insecurities.

On the other hand, her ever-absent injunctions against any divine moral code allowed people to live as they wished, as long as they chose "to look and feel beautiful." Cole-Whittaker affirmed her followers' hunger for affluence, saying, "The more I prosper, the more others prosper."

Déjà Vu All Over Again

Cole-Whittaker's message is about success and prosperity, but her own career has been a roller coaster-like succession of dramatic failures and self-promotional comebacks.

After her empire crumbled in the early 1980s, she resigned from apparent exhaustion and fatigue. She resurfaced in 1986 as a revitalized New Age advocate with her book *The Inner Path from Where You Are to Where You Want to Be*.

In this book she declared, "God is That Which Includes All Beings. God is All of it and the Everything, and God cannot be apart from any of it any way."

She made another unsuccessful comeback attempt in 1990 with a new marketing scheme called the "Women Unlimited Network" and a new book called *Love and Power in a World Without Limits: A Woman's Guide to the Goddess Within*.

Her promotional literature of the period proclaimed the nineties would usher in "the Golden age of planetary peace," and offered new affirmational nostrums such as "I am enough and there is enough, always," and "I am one with infinite supply."

Sadly, the woman who frantically markets such sentiments to gullible fans apparently hasn't experienced them in her own life.

CHRISTIAN CRITIQUE: Twisting Christian language until it is virtually unrecognizable, Cole-Whittaker teaches that conventional religion has failed because of its emphasis on sacrifice and guilt.

However, absence of guilt leads directly to absence of morality or common sense. No one bears blame for personal misconduct. A mass murderer is even considered sinless because his victims "created" their own fate.

Perhaps that's part of what she meant when she declared her purpose was to "bring you into oneness with God where you can have the direct experience of being limitless."

Cole-Whittaker borrowed from Christian Science to suggest that everything negative is an illusion, and each human is a "thought in the mind of God."

Whereas Jesus told the rich young ruler to sell all that he had and give it to the poor (Matthew 19:21), Cole-Whittaker's best-selling book is entitled *How to Have More in a Have-Not World*.

Though she spoke of the Holy Spirit in a personal sense, a closer examination of her theology reveals the term was used more for rhetorical purposes rather than orthodox references to any specific divine personage.

Terry Cole-Whittaker's Jesus was a Gnostic whose references to heaven and hell were merely figurative. Though Titus 2:1 warns us to "speak . . . the things which become sound doctrine," Cole-Whittaker contradictorily declares that the traditional dogma should be avoided: "Resist the temptation to buy into those beliefs," she said. She also denied a personal devil by teaching "there is no opposite to God."

SOURCES: various Terry Cole-Whittaker Ministries publications and fund-raising letters, including *Prosperity: Your Divine Right*, 1984, book and cassette, and miscellaneous copies of *The Good News*, a tabloid; *People*, 26 November 1984, 99–106; "A Self-Styled Evangelist Stretches God's Truth," *Christianity Today*, 21 September 1984, 73–75; Douglas Todd, "Lecturer Psyching Up for Another Comeback," *Vancouver Sun*, 19 May 1990; Paul Zuromski, ed., *The New Age Catalogue: Access to Information and Sources* (New York: Doubleday, Island, 1988), 44.

See also A Course in Miracles and Mind Sciences.

CONSPIRACY THEORIES

From Communism to the Illuminati to Y2K, well-meaning Christians
have frequently fallen victim to the paranoid lure of alleged
secretive, evil plots.

OVERVIEW: When Mel Gibson and Julia Roberts starred together in a movie called *Conspiracy Theory*, moviegoers were treated to an intense and entertaining film that featured heart-pounding chase scenes, bloody shoot-outs, moments of romance, and bouts of paranoia.

But there's nothing entertaining about real-life conspiracy theories, which have ensnared many sincere people over the past century.

Reds under Our Beds

When the 1917 Bolshevik Revolution brought socialists to power in Russia, evangelists like Billy Sunday railed against Marxists. But anti-Communist hysteria wouldn't really reach a fever pitch until the Red Scare of the 1950s.

Some troubled souls believed that Communism's tentacles had wrapped themselves around nearly every beloved American institution. Their fear-based fantasies led to ceaseless searches for signs of Communist subversion, an approach essayist Richard Hofstadter called "the paranoid style in American politics."

Christian historian George Marsden described this phobia as follows: "All the nation's problems were reduced to communist infiltration of the nation's liberal ecclesiastical, political, and intellectual establishments."

As Peter Lewis wrote in his book *The Fifties:* "No anti-Communist action or pronouncement could possibly be ridiculous. Fear infected Americans with a mass hysteria which had not been seen since the Great Crash."

At the height of the anti-Communist hysteria, some conservatives identified America with everything good and godly, equated Communism with everything evil and demonic, and demonized an ever-growing roster of enemies that included Hollywood, labor organizers, the United Nations, the National Council of Churches, the World Council of Churches, peaceniks, public school teachers, promoters of sex education, and the Revised Standard Version of the Bible. One excited crusader even claimed, "The largest single group supporting the Communist apparatus in the United States today is composed of Protestant clergymen."

Much of the Red Scare hysteria ended with the humiliating failure of U.S. Senator Joseph McCarthy. But decades later, David Noebel, who assumed leadership of the Christian Anti-Communism Crusade in 1998, warned believers not to be lulled into a false sense of security: "Indeed, this so-called quiet time should be a time for further preparation for the next Marxist threat which is even now raising its ugly head and preparing itself for an assault upon the West."

Long after Communism had ceased to pose a viable threat, evangelicals continued to exhibit their weakness for far-fetched conspiracy theories.

A Recurring Problem

Take secular humanism, for example. In the 1960s and 1970s, many Christian leaders said this nontheistic movement was the cause of the nation's ills.

In the 1980s and 1990s others declared that the main cause of America's rising divorce rate was a group of antifamily gay activists.

Over the years, conspiracy theories have developed around the 1969 U.S. moon landing (some say it was faked), John Hinckley's attempted assassination of Ronald Reagan (some say Reagan was killed and replaced by a body double), and the investigation into the shooting of John Fitzgerald Kennedy (Oliver Stone's movie *JFK* dramatized many conspiracy theories).

The Disaster That Wasn't

In 1993 a technology expert named Peter de Jager predicted a looming computer crisis he called "Doomsday 2000." Few people paid him any attention.

But by 1999 millions of people were worried about something called the Y2K glitch, which—depending on who you talked to—would cause minor inconveniences or hasten the end of the world.

While America's government and businesses sought to battle the Y2K bug, in conservative evangelical circles, fears about Y2K were combined with centuries-old traditions of world weariness and biblical prophecies about end times and the return of Christ. This apocalyptic anxiety led to a publishing tsunami of books and manuals, some designed to educate people and some seemingly designed to exploit people's fears.

Both Hal Lindsey and Jack Van Impe, who have made surprisingly successful careers out of promoting a never-ending, ever-changing stream of eschatological predictions and end-times scenarios, created videos about the Y2K crisis. Lindsey's, called *Facing Millennial Midnight: The Y2K Crisis Confronting America and the World*, promised to provide details about the unfolding crisis.

Jerry Falwell's pitch was even more urgent. "Y2K may be God's instrument to shake this nation," he said in his twenty-eight-dollar video, *A Christian's Guide to the Millennium Bug*. "He may be preparing to confound our language, to jam our communications, scatter our efforts, and judge us for our sin and rebellion against his lordship," warned Falwell, who said his own preparations included stocking up on food, gasoline, and ammunition.

A column on the Christian Coalition's Web site discussed the possibility of widespread "looting, robbery, (and) gang warfare," suggested President Bill Clinton might use the crisis to become America's "first dictator," and urged everyone to gather food, water, and bullets.

Christian publishers churned out dozens of ominous-sounding titles, like Grant Jeffrey's *The Millennium Meltdown;* Steve Farrar's *Spiritual Survival During the Y2K Crisis;* and Donald McAlvany's *The Y2K Tidal Wave: Year 2000 Economic Survival.* Michael Hyatt wrote circles around the competition, authoring three separate books: the best-selling *The Millennium Bug: How to Survive the Coming Chaos; The Y2K Personal Survival Guide;* and the fictional *Y2K: The Day the World Shut Down,* which provided an imaginative description of how things would unwind. Meanwhile, Shaunti Feldhahn, founder of a group called the Joseph Project 2000, said believers were overreacting, and he wrote *Y2K The Millennium Bug: A Balanced Christian Approach.*

But Gary North, a reconstructionist theologian who had been predicting the imminent destruction of the world for decades, continued to sow hysteria. He described the impending cataclysm in a newsletter topped with the bold headline, "The Day the World Shuts Down": "In a nutshell, the Y2K problem is the trigger that is about to cause a massive, date-sensitive worldwide computer crash—a crash of such gargantuan proportions that it will literally bring down governments. It may even bring down ours."

Things were so bad, said North, that concerned Christians should flee their homes, rush to the nearest bank, withdraw $299, and send it off to North for his "full 6-part Y2K Preparation, Protection and Survival Kit."

A Topeka, Kansas, group called the Prophecy Club offered videos and dehydrated emergency food. In an ad published in *Charisma* magazine, the group offered the *Y2K Chaos* video (which "briefly explains the Y2K problem, and why it WON'T be corrected in time") and three different food packages. The top-of-the-line Plan A promised "Food for 4 people for 1 year" for $4,100. Other suppliers hawked everything from human waste disposal systems, tooth extraction videotapes, an amazingly overpriced gold coin (the $20 coin was offered for $599), and magazines. *American Survival Guide* boasted it had a circulation of 60,000, and *Preparedness Journal* even sponsored a series of Preparedness Expos.

Not everyone was willing to go that far, but a July 1999 Associated Press article reported that one-third of Americans told pollsters they were going to stock up on essentials like food and water, and one-quarter planned on taking extra money out of the bank. The news brought a response from Federal Reserve Chairman Alan Greenspan, who predicted that fear-induced stockpiling would hurt the American economy more than the Y2K glitch itself.

As it turned out, the Y2K crisis didn't happen as the doomsayers had predicted. But for committed conspiracy theorists, the facts aren't allowed to get in the way of a good scare.

SOURCES: Robert G. Clouse, Robert N. Hosack, and Richard V. Pierard, *The New Millennium Manual: A Once and Future Guide* (Grand Rapids, Mich.: Baker, 1999); Mark A. Kellner, "Y2K: A Secular Apocalypse?" *Christianity Today*, 11 January 11 1999; Steve Rabey and Monte Unger, *Milestones: 50 Events that Shaped American Evangelicals in the 20th Century* (Nashville: Broadman and Holman, 2002); John Yemma, "Conspiracy Theories Go Mainstream," *Denver Post*, 29 September 1996, 32A.

A COURSE IN MIRACLES

Channeled messages about forgiveness and the supernatural are the basis of a complex creed recently popularized by Marianne Williamson, a spiritual advisor to political leaders and Hollywood stars.

FOUNDER: Helen Schucman, a channel of "the voice"

TEXT: *A Course in Miracles*, as well as the *Workbook for Students* and *Manual for Teachers*

SYMBOL: Stylized star with beams between the points on a slotted background circle, with the word *forgiveness* curved over the top of the circle.

APPEAL: Those who wish to affirm a reverence for Jesus are led to believe Christ has actually spoken through the *Course*. Without abiding by any ecclesiastical structure, adherents can claim to be in direct contact with the truth of Jesus.

OVERVIEW: For seven years "the voice" spoke to Helen Schucman. Claiming to be Jesus, the voice began, "This is a course in miracles. It is a required course. Only the time you take it is voluntary."

When first confronted by the voice, Schucman, a psychologist at Columbia University, transcribed its messages by automatic writing. She said the process made her uncomfortable.

Dr. William Thetford, Schucman's close friend and professor of medical psychology at Columbia University's College of Physicians and Surgeons, typed the manuscript for a book called *A Course in Miracles* from Schucman's notes. The voice dictated that 622-page text first, then the 478-page *Workbook for Students*, and finally the 88-page *Manual for Teachers*.

Schucman, who was a religious skeptic, took notes almost daily from the voice. It claimed that guilt is resolved by forgiving others, not through seeking forgiveness from a personal God. The essence of the *Course* is epitomized in this summation: "Nothing real can be threatened, nothing unreal exists."

In 1976 the *Course* was published by Robert and Judy Skutch of the Foundation for Inner Peace, which also offers pamphlets, audio and video cassettes, and other books.

The 1,200 pages of the three-volume set of books used in *A Course in Miracles* denigrates most Christian orthodoxy. Nevertheless, more than a million sets have been sold without benefit of advertising, and nearly two thousand study groups in the United States and Europe regularly dissect and discuss its teachings.

Miraculous Reinvention

The *Manual for Teachers*, channeled through Schucman during five months in 1972, states, "Christ takes many forms with different names." But this isn't the only way the *Course* reinvents Christianity.

It also claims man needs no help to enter heaven, since he's already there. Stripping Jesus of his divinity exemplifies the *Course*'s unconventional philosophy. Conversely, one of its stated aims is to emphasize "the importance of Jesus as our gentle teacher."

A Course in Miracles claims forgiveness is a "happy fiction," that it's unnecessary to forgive anything God has created. While denigrating God's forgiveness and criticizing Christianity for overemphasis on suffering, sacrifice, and sacrament, the *Course* proposes that peace becomes attainable only when humans forgive each other. Such borderline blasphemy constitutes a theme throughout the many pages of *A Course in Miracles*.

A Recent Revival

North America is a religiously diverse region where many groups compete for people's attention. During much of the twentieth century, *A Course in Miracles* was one of the quieter groups. But in the 1990s a fiery, outspoken woman named Marianne Williamson arrived on the scene. She helped popularize *A Course in Miracles* for a new generation of seekers.

A profile in *New Age Journal* summarized her impact on the group's visibility: "One-time cabaret singer Marianne Williamson is fond of saying that she gave up that career because she excelled more at stage patter than singing. These days she puts her public speaking skills to use in packed lecture halls and churches, preaching love and forgiveness and inner peace."

Williamson appeared on the best-seller list in 1992 when her book *A*

Return to Love, which is based on the teachings of *A Course in Miracles,* propelled this former nightclub waitress into the national limelight. In her book Williamson redefines key theological concepts:

- "Christ refers to the common thread of divine love that is the core and essence of every human mind."
- "The love in one of us is the love in all of us."
- "We are all part of a vast sea of love, one indivisible divine mind."

Williamson has no formal theological training but since 1992 has become one of the world's best-known promoters of feel-good spirituality. She has written a number of subsequent books on the general theme of love, has appeared on national television, including *Oprah,* created a successful seminar series, and in the late 1990s became senior minister at the Church of Today in Warren, Michigan. (She stepped down in late 2002.) She has spearheaded a spiritual activism group under the name of Global Renaissance Alliance.

During a stop on her 1992 book tour, Williamson explained the growing popularity for her book and *A Course in Miracles.* "People coming from a traditional religious viewpoint are ready for more sophisticated metaphysics and a more evolved understanding," she said.

Meanwhile, Christians remain convinced that there's nothing particularly sophisticated about trashing Christianity, twisting its core teachings, and deceiving people who are sincerely looking for God.

CHRISTIAN CRITIQUE: *A Course in Miracles* seeks to create peace and harmony through self-forgiveness and to correct what the *Course* views as the errors of Christianity. Removal of all personal guilt is the ultimate aim achieved by the act of forgiving others.

The *Course* teaches that salvation is available through self-help methods taught in the *Course,* not by God's grace, as stated in Ephesians 1:7. Humanity is already in heaven and needs to exert no special effort to attain what it already has.

The *Course* claims Jesus spoke through a channeler (Schucman) to deliver the messages that contradict basic tenets of Christianity and necessitate the biblically forbidden practice of transpossession mediumship.

If the *Course* holds such promises of unparalleled spirituality, it is fair to ask why Ms. Williamson, who officiated at Elizabeth Taylor's sixth (failed) attempt at marriage and counseled the Clintons at Camp David, dropped her role as *Course* spokesperson and resigned her Michigan "pastorate" for an undisclosed career change. Said one of her Renaissance Unity Church parishioners, "She told us the church is not a democracy," and she had an "anti-male" attitude.

My personal encounter with Ms. Williamson verified these concerns. At a public meeting in which queries from the audience were invited, I confronted her with the question, "How can you claim to be a religious organization doing the work of God and deny two essential qualities of spiritual faith—guilt and forgiveness?" There was no answer, only an abrupt refusal to answer the question and an embarrassing public chastisement for my supposed insolence. When I pressed her to respond, she flew into a rage and publicly excoriated me. After all, when the so-called voice of Jesus has supposedly revealed the "truth," what need is there for rational answers to earnest questions?

SOURCES: *Christian Research Journal* 21, no. 2; Foundation for Inner Peace, *A Course in Miracles* (Farmingdale, N.Y.: Coleman Graphics, 1975); Dean Halverson, "A Matter of Course: Conversation with Kenneth Wapnick, *SCP Journal* 7, no. 1: 8–17; *New Realities*, July-August 1984; Eric Pement, "The Pop Hinduism of *A Course in Miracles*," *Cornerstone* 20 no. 97: 19; *SCP Journal* 7, no. 1; Peggy Taylor and Eden Stone, "Miracle Worker," *New Age Journal* (March-April 1992): 47.

ACCESS: Foundation for *A Course in Miracles*, 41397 Buecking Drive, Temecula, CA 92590; www.acim.org. An affiliated organization, The Foundation for Inner Peace, operates a teaching facility in Temecula. For the Church of Today, in Warren, Michigan, see www.churchoftoday.com.

BENJAMIN CRÈME

Maitreya; Share International

Christians look forward to the second appearance of Christ, but one media-friendly Scottish mystic says this event has already happened.

FOUNDER: Benjamin Crème, who claims he was visited by Maitreya, one of the Ascended Masters and the true Christ.

TEXTS: Crème is the author of many books, including *The Reappearance of the Christ* and the *Masters of Wisdom*. Share International also publishes a newsletter.

APPEAL: Crème's message that Christ has returned with new words of wisdom is appealing to many, as is Crème's claim that Christ cares more about relationships, world hunger, and other issues than he does about theology or morality.

OVERVIEW: Benjamin Crème was born in Glasgow, Scotland, in 1922. At the time, nobody paid much attention, but now Crème is seeking and getting attention around the world by claiming he is the mouthpiece for a newly incarnated Christ.

But as is often the case with non-Christian groups, the things their "Christs" say are at odds with what Jesus taught in the New Testament. Benjamin Crème's Christ is not the Christ of the Bible, and his teachings are significantly different from orthodox Christian teaching.

The Masters Speak

Crème says that in 1959 he was contacted by a spiritual entity named Maitreya, who was said to be one of the Ascended Masters. Maitreya told Crème that Christ would return to earth within the next two decades.

Other encounters followed. Here's how Crème described one of these events:

> Towards the end of 1972, when I was rather in the doldrums and least expecting it, that Wise, and Wily One, whom I have the privilege to call Master, pounced. He took me in hand, and subjected me to the most intensive period of de-glamorisation [sic], disillusioning, training and preparation. For months we worked together, twenty hours a day, deepening and strengthening the telepathic link until it was two-way with equal ease, requiring the minimum of his attention and energy. He forged in this period an instrument through whom he could work, and which would be responsive to his slightest impression (of course, with my complete cooperation and without the slightest infringement of my free-will). Everything I see and hear, he sees and hears. When he wishes, a look from me can be a look from him; my touch, his. So, with the minimum expenditure of energy he has a window on the world, an outpost of his consciousness; he can heal and teach.

A Messenger Speaks

Crème began to speak publicly about this message in 1975. In 1977 he received more messages from Maitreya and passed these along to the public, becoming a major spokesman for this Ascended Master who had chosen Crème as his earthly representative.

Crème came to the United States in 1980 and was warmly received. Followers in the United States established the Tara Center in California. The center, along with Share International, Crème's publishing enterprise, are the major means by which he spreads Maitreya's message. (Neither is a membership organization, so no figures are available.)

Crème predicted that Maitreya would make a physical appearance to the people of the world in 1982 and vigorously tried to line up media coverage of the event. When the appearance failed to materialize, Crème blamed representatives of the media for their lack of interest in the subject.

But elsewhere, Maitreya wasn't so shy, as one can see from the following account in a Crème newsletter:

In 1988, Maitreya appeared in Kenya and allowed himself to be photographed. That picture has subsequently been reproduced and widely circulated. Meanwhile, Maitreya has appeared to hundreds of fundamentalist religious groups worldwide, while simultaneously potentizing water sources near each location with healing properties. Many other signs of Maitreya's presence are being documented. . . . Such "signs" include visions of the Virgin Mary, angelic encounters, "crosses of light," crop circles, and the September 1995 worldwide Hindu "milk miracles."

A Theosophical Christ

Just as Crème sees Maitreya at work in encounters with the Virgin Mary, crop circles, and Hindu miracles, he also sees Christ as a universalistic religious figure. In this and other ways, Crème's teaching borrows heavily from his training in Theosophy and the occult rather than from the Bible.

In a question-and-answer session featured on his Web site, Crème explains his views on his new Christ's mission to the modern world:

Q. What is the essence of his teaching for the new age?
A. Emphasis on the oneness of humanity . . . the need for sharing and right relationships . . . the need for harmlessness in all relationships . . . He will set about the inauguration of the new world religion, bringing together the approaches to God of the East and the West. . . . He will teach the Mysteries of the Path of Initiation, the scientific path to God. . . . He will reveal a new aspect of God.

Crème also teaches that people should experience something he calls transmission meditation, which will help them receive their own messages from the Ascended Masters: "Transmission Meditation is safe, scientific, nondenominational, and extremely potent. It will not interfere with any other religious or spiritual practice. In fact it will enhance your personal meditation and any other service activities in which you may be engaged. Many people find they can experience and demonstrate love more easily. Others report that their mind is more stimulated and creative. Some people receive healing, spontaneously, during the transmissions."

Another Appearance

Recently Crème has again been predicting that his new Christ will make an earthly appearance. Perhaps this time, the media will cooperate and Christ will appear.

According to Crème: "The Day of Declaration will be the day when Maitreya will reveal himself and appear on all media outlets. He will speak to the people of the world, many healings will occur, and Maitreya will be seen as the true Christ."

But no matter what Crème says, Christians know that Maitreya is not the Jesus who is described in the Bible as God's Son. He can't be, because Crème says Maitreya is God. He also teaches that God is everything and everything is God.

In addition, Crème says Jesus is not as important as Christians claim he is. To Crème, Jesus is just another in the long line of messengers of God who have appeared throughout time. As one of his newsletters pointed out, Crème teaches that "Maitreya 'overshadows' Jesus and is the true Christ. Maitreya is the one who has been operating through a number of World Teachers through the ages. Jesus now sits at the feet of Maitreya."

Crème conveys a messianic message that alternately offers the hope of a world transformed by Maitreya's intervention and a warning that there will be no place in the new order for those who resist Maitreya's appeal. Such spiritual arrogance makes Crème's Master the sole pivotal point of history's final chapter. Channeled spiritual messages by other Masters are not considered equally valid by Crème, which is heresy for Spiritualists who pride themselves on being open minded. For the Christian, this makes it easier to evaluate and confront Crème's message.

CHRISTIAN CRITIQUE: The extent of Benjamin Crème's devotion to Lord Maitreya leaves no room for compromise. Most Ascended Master traditions have opted for following any number of spiritually advanced beings, depending on one's spiritual predilections. But to Crème, there is only one choice—the true Christ, Maitreya. There is no vague spiritual inclusiveness to counter. Putting aside all talk of religious harmony and shared resources, the essence of the conflict between Christ and Crème has clearly drawn some apologetic battle lines. In a way, Crème has made Christian counterarguments much easier to posit, since he has already delineated an uncompromising position to debate.

SOURCES: John Moore, "In Search of Maitreya: An Evening with Benjamin Crème," *SCP Newsletter,* winter 1995–1996, 1.

ACCESS: Tara Center, Box 6001, North Hollywood, CA 91603; www.shareintl.org

ALEISTER CROWLEY

This iconoclastic guide to the spiritual dark side has been dead for decades, but his cultural and spiritual influence continues today.

"Magick" is "the science and art of causing change in conformity with will."
ALEISTER CROWLEY

FOUNDER: Aleister Crowley (1875–1947), poet, novelist, and author of books on magic and esoteric occultism

TEXT: Books of Aleister Crowley, including *Confessions*, *Magick in Theory and Practice*, *White Stains*, and *Snow Drops from a Curate's Garden*

SYMBOL: ∴

APPEAL: Crowley's philosophy encourages uninhibited moral abandon without a God to judge one's actions. Students of the occult who seek an evil rationale for total lustful indulgence discover justification in Crowley's teachings that one can conjure evil entities, devoid of accountability to an avenging God.

OVERVIEW: According to Aleister Crowley's autobiography, which was just a part of his ongoing campaign of self-promotion, his mother proclaimed him the beast, 666, from the book of Revelation, chapter 13. As a child he gleefully identified with the wicked, horned creature rising from the depths of the sea, blaspheming God.

As an adult he became the most infamous black magician and satanist of all time. And though he's been dead for years, Aleister Crowley, whose motto was "Do what you will," still inspires followers with his philosophies on satanism.

In recent years CDs like *The Beast Speaks*, which features some of his lectures, have been hot sellers. And paperback versions of his *Confessions*, one of an estimated hundred-plus books by Crowley in print, have sold at a rapid pace.

Part of Crowley's allure and mystique comes from the celebrity endorsements he has received over the years from pop culture icons like Jimmy Page (former lead guitarist for rock group Led Zeppelin who reportedly revered Crowley and purchased his Scottish Boleskine House) and Ozzy Osbourne (who before he was a TV star was the leader of a band called Black Sabbath that recorded the song "Mr. Crowley"). When the Beatles were deciding which figures would appear on the cover of their *Sgt. Pepper* album, one of the most influential recordings in the history of rock, Crowley made the list.

A Consuming Passion

Aleister Crowley's life was consumed by the occult. Born in England in 1875, Crowley rebelled against his strict, fundamentalist Christian upbringing.

In the 1920s and 1930s Crowley accomplished with satanism in England what Anton LaVey did for devil worship in America in the 1960s. Crowley's reputation as a bisexual with voracious sexual proclivities earned him a sinister worldwide reputation as "the wickedest man in the world."

At twenty-eight Aleister Crowley visited Cairo, Egypt. There a spirit appeared to him. He referred to the spirit as Aiwass (also spelled Aiwaz), holy guardian angel. Aiwass hailed himself as a representative of the Great White Brotherhood, ascended spiritual entities who rule the earth. Aiwass informed Crowley that a new, two-thousand-year eon would center on occultism and this simple dictum: "Do what thou wilt shall be the whole of the law."

Crowley's philosophy was set forth in a volume called *The Book of the Law*. It taught that history could be divided into two eras: the eon of Isis, the matriarchal period in Egyptian mythology; and the eon of Osiris, the patriarchal period of Judaism, Buddhism, Islam, and Christianity. In 1904, however, humanity entered the eon of Horus, the Egyptian child-god. During this time, the true self of man would predominate. There would be no allegiance to external authorities, priests, or gods. Crowley built on this concept and issued a creed declaring, "Lust. Enjoy all the things of sense. Fear not that any god shall deny thee for this."

Aleister Crowley believed sex had magical properties and practiced homosexuality, bisexuality, and child molestation. Borrowing from the Hindu idea of tantric yoga, he taught that sexual union reached its highest reality when the mind, the breath, and even the semen were held still.

Occult Organizations

Aleister Crowley founded the Britain magical association known as ∴ — Arganteum Astrum, or the Silver Star. The organization constituted the Inner Order of the Great White Brotherhood. The Outer Order was the Golden Dawn.

For a time Crowley coexisted with converts at the Abbey of Thelema (meaning "will") in Italy. Satanism was practiced, and sacrifices were offered to the devil by the devotees of Thelema. When the Italian government discovered evidence of black rituals and suspected infant sacrifices taking place at the abbey, Crowley was expelled from Italy. During the outbreak of World War I, Crowley shifted his activities to America.

An intellectual exponent of satanism, Crowley wrote several books, including *Confessions*, as well as his major work on the occult, *Magick in Theory and Practice*. (Crowley insisted on this spelling for *magick* to distinguish it from superficial stage magic.)

His pornographic novel *White Stains* was published in 1898. An equally illicit book was Crowley's *Snow Drops from a Curate's Garden.* Crowley frequently propositioned prostitutes as partners to practice his black magic. Eventually he acquired the name Baphomet, a Luciferian designation.

The Order of Thelema was founded as a Crowleyism study group. It rejects attempts by various branches of the Ordo Templi Orientis (OTO), which claims direct lineage dating to Aleister Crowley, to establish their authority by reference to a line of succession from Crowley. The order believes Crowley can reach them by psychic means. Such groups are profoundly devil-inspired and without conscience. No true Christian would follow Aleister Crowley's philosophy that uninhibited lust and total licentiousness lead to spiritual truth.

A Failed Mission

Aleister Crowley believed his mission in life was to destroy Christianity and build the magical religion of Thelema in its place. He failed to achieve that goal. Crowley became a heroin addict, and his son mysteriously died during a private ritual that only the two attended. Afterward, Crowley became a babbling, incoherent idiot. A black mass was performed at his funeral.

Despite such an ignominious end, thousands in England and America still follow his teachings of ignoring the conscience and adhering to one's will.

CHRISTIAN CRITIQUE: First Timothy 4:1-2 in The Living Bible declares, "The Holy Spirit tells us clearly that in the last times some in the church will turn away from Christ and become eager followers of teachers with devil-inspired ideas. These teachers will tell lies with straight faces and do it so often that their consciences won't even bother them."

Crowley rejected his family's Plymouth Brethren Christian upbringing. Most of his followers preach that Christian doctrine infringes upon their moral license. Though most of them do not participate in torture, child molestation, or criminal acts, those who adopt Crowley's motto have an excuse for private deviancy and overt support of satanism.

SOURCES: *The Book of the Law* (Kings Beach, Calif.: Thelema Publications); Richard Cavendish, ed., *Man, Myth, and Magic: The Illustrated Encyclopedia of Mythology, Religion, and the Unknown* (Freeport, N.Y.: Marshall Cavendish, 1983); *Passport Magazine*, March 1998, 4.

ACCESS: Golden Dawn Occult Society, PO Box 250, Oxford, OX1 1AP; www.uk.net/ogdos.htm; Thelema Publications, P. O. Box 1393, Kings Beach, CA 95719; Ancient and Mystical Order of the Rosae Crucis, San Jose, CA 95191

See also Black Magic.

DA FREE JOHN

Da Love-Ananda; Franklin Jones

This American-born, self-appointed guru promises that his disciples will
experience joy and laughter, but alumni tell a different story.

*My work is a new, refreshed, and living communication of Truth, which
also recapitulates the entire religious, spiritual, philosophical, and wisdom
experience of mankind.*

DA FREE JOHN, THE LAUGHING MAN INSTITUTE BROCHURE

FOUNDER: Da Free John, formerly Bubba Free John, was born Franklin
Jones on November 3, 1939. He changed his name to Da Free John in 1979.

TEXT: Hindu scriptures; also Da Free John's *Enlightenment of the Whole Body*

APPEAL: Da's claim to be an *atman*, a self-realized soul and avatar, is
stamped "made in America." His pompous claims of enlightenment are rare for
a Westerner and thus intriguing to students of Eastern mysticism. Some followers are drawn by hearing stories about his disciples experiencing a spontaneous kind of hilarity in his presence. Others are attracted by tales of devotees
receiving powerful psychic experiences by the mere touch of his hand.

OVERVIEW: What kind of God would sit by the bedside of a sick person and
mockingly tease him about his illness? Or accept a $250,000 gift from a disciple
and then forbid him to live in the spiritual resort purchased with the money?

Hindus have a term to describe such contradictory conduct on behalf of a
god-man: *lilas*, the humorous, irrational disregard of convention.

The American man who foists such lilas on his followers was born as
Franklin Jones. This nonconventional and controversial self-appointed guru
answers to no authority outside himself. He has operated under a number of
Eastern-sounding names, including Bubba Free John (*Bubba* meaning
"brother"), Da Free John (*Da* meaning "giver"), Heart-Master Da Love-
Ananda, Avadhoota Da Love-Ananda Hridayam, and Avatar Adi Da Samraj.

He has also founded a number of organizations since 1970, including the
Dawn Horse Fellowship, the Free Primitive Church of Divine Communion,
the Free Daist Communion, and Adidam.

Through it all one thing has remained constant: Jones has exhibited little
modesty about his person and purpose. He claims to be nothing less than an incarnation of God, a guru to be worshipped: "Surrender to me all your seeking,
the very sense of your separate self, all thoughts, all desires, every circumstance,
even your body."

Freedom or Bondage?

Those who follow Jones are promised "freedom" and the joy of constant laughter. All this supposedly comes from being in the presence of one (Da) who is "perfect love," a siddha guru "descended directly from God."

At one point his followers recited "The Great Confession," which proclaimed: "Da is the living truth. Da is the way of salvation. . . . I surrender body and mind and all self-attention to Da, the living God."

Jones started out his adult life rather normally. He was a college student at Columbia and Stanford; he studied at a Lutheran seminary; he experimented with LSD. In the late sixties he made several pilgrimages to India, where the Hindu Swami Muktananda influenced him so strongly that he experienced visions of the teacher. He also saw apparitions of the Virgin Mary, whom he considered to be Mother Shakti, the Hindu goddess.

By 1970 he felt he had attained enlightenment, and he formed the Dawn Horse Fellowship, later called the Free Primitive Church of Divine Communion. Other organizational entities under his leadership include the Free Community Order and the Laughing Man Institute.

In 1983 Jones's group purchased Naitaumba, one of the Fiji Islands in the South Pacific. On this tiny, isolated island Da's devotees built a retreat center called the Hermitage, where the guru has surrounded himself with certain followers. Others, if they are considered worthy, can come for short-term meditation retreats. Former top-ranking members have alleged that many in the guru's inner circle have used tithes and donations from rich benefactors to live in sensual luxury on Naitaumba and at another center in Hawaii. But devoted followers vigorously defend their leader.

Da's claim of divinity isn't unique in today's marketplace of mystical gurus and cult leaders. But he is one of the few American-born products available. Thus, when he claims to fulfill the traditions of Moses, Krishna, Jesus, and Buddha, he does so as one who (according to him) only assumed the identity of Franklin Jones to provide a lesson for his disciples.

The late Zen authority and Eastern religious gadfly, author Alan Watts, studied Da on videotape. Watts wept and declared, "It looks like we have an avatar here. I've been waiting for one all my life."

Submitting to a Guru

The teachings of Da Free John are dispensed by videotape, film, cassettes, pamphlets, and his four published works: *The Knee of Listening, The Method of the Siddhas, Garbage and the Goddess,* and *No Remedy.*

His doctrine is simple: Objective truth and reality do not exist. Life is an unexplainable mystery. One's only choice is to be subjectively absorbed by the impersonal Divine. This is done by sacrificing ego and consciousness and abiding in the presence of a guru. All negative karma will thus be dissolved spontaneously.

LARSON'S BOOK OF WORLD RELIGIONS AND ALTERNATIVE SPIRITUALITY

To embark on such a journey and join one of Da's communities, the seeker has to hold down a steady job (and tithe 10 percent to Da's work), adapt to a lacto-vegetarian diet, confine sex to marriage, and contemplate Free John's teachings every day. These doctrines include the Seven Stages of Life, through which the guru attempts to describe man's current state and the potential toward which he is evolving.

Significantly, Da Free John has acknowledged that in addition to himself, several of his disciples have achieved the Seventh Stage. The sect sees this as an indication that all human beings, not just a few, can attain enlightenment.

Following Bubba is not just a matter of intellectual acknowledgment. His avataristic claims are substantiated by what seem to be amazing supernatural phenomena. Disciples are privileged to see him heal and perform miracles.

They credit him with causing violent thunderstorms and creating coronas around the sun. Some students claim to have experienced dynamic kundalini phenomena such as *kriyas* (automatic purifying movements), *mudras* (spontaneous yogic postures), visions, revelations, and states of indescribable bliss (*samadhi*).

The close comparison of such experiences with similar occurrences in demonism and classical spiritualism should not comfort followers of Da Free John.

At press time Jones's group was currently known as Adidam. But that, too, will likely change before long.

CHRISTIAN CRITIQUE: Jones demands that his followers abandon independent thought and moral judgment in order that they might be absorbed by his guru (Da) and thus merge their consciousnesses with God (since the guru is God). "You do not even know what a single thing is. Then rest—abide in that ignorance," Da teaches. Presuming to know and think and be is the cause of all unhappiness. Seeking for solutions to problems is pointless. All dilemmas can be solved by one's abiding in a relationship to a God-realized guru.

Put bluntly in his own words, "Avatar Adi Da Samraj is not merely a highly developed human being. He is able to speak the Truth for Real because He is Himself the Living Divine Truth, Appearing on earth in a human body. In other words, He is the Eternal Real God—not the "Creator-God" of traditional religion, but the Very Divine Heart of Reality Itself—Appearing bodily for a time in our midst. He is the One Whom beings have prayed to and hoped for throughout the ages—the Promised and long-Awaited God-Man to come."

Independent thought and moral judgment are two important tools God has given humans so they can avoid being ensnared by false teachers like Jones. Second Thessalonians 2 describes the nature of the Antichrist, which is to exalt himself above God to the point of actually claiming to be God. Da Free John certainly possesses the same motivating spirit of self-deification. He makes himself the supreme source of truth and spiritual knowledge and claims equality with Christ as an incarnation of God.

SOURCES: "Da Free John Charged with 'Sexual Servitude,'" *The Cult Observer*, June 1985, 1–10; "Da Free John Followed Muktananda, Scientology," *The Cult Observer*, June 1985, 10; *East West Journal* (May 1976): 60, 67; Ibid, July 1976, 20–25; Bubba Free John, *No Remedy* (Los Angeles: Dawn Horse, 1976); Franklin Jones, *The Knee of Listening* (Los Angeles: Dawn Horse, 1972); David C. Lane, "The Paradox of Da Free John," *Understanding Cults and Spiritual Movements* 1, no. 2: 50–55; Don Lattin, "Free John's Island Paradise: Devotees Build Tropical Home for Their Guru's 'Spiritual Work,'" *San Francisco Examiner*, 14 April 1985, A22–23.

ACCESS: Adidam, 12040 N. Seigler Spring Road, Middletown, CA 95461

DEEPAK CHOPRA

This Indian-born medical doctor's charisma, media appearances, professional credentials, and commercial success have transformed him into one of the premiere promoters of Eastern-style alternative healing.

I satisfy a spiritual yearning without making [people] think they have to worry about God and punishment. In essence, we are immortal.
DEEPAK CHOPRA

FOUNDER: Deepak Chopra, an Indian-born medical doctor who has risen to fame and celebrity in the United States.

TEXT: Chopra draws his ideas from Hindu texts and the work of Maharishi Mahesh Yogi, the founder of the Transcendental Meditation movement. Chopra is the author of more than two dozen popular books and many more tapes and other products.

APPEAL: Chopra promises his fans a measure of spiritual and emotional stability with minimal requirements for moral behavior or religious observance.

He says his techniques will help people experience everything from reduced stress to curing of diseases. One popular book even promises readers a fountain of youth. *Grow Younger, Live Longer: 10 Steps to Reverse Aging* appeals to aging baby boomers and guarantees eternal health and the ability to control one's physical body.

OVERVIEW: Deepak Chopra is not an ordained minister and represents no official church, religious organization, or creed. But in our celebrity-obsessed age, his nonstop media coverage and the endorsements he has received from media figures like Oprah Winfrey and numerous Hollywood celebrities have introduced his teachings to millions and made his name a household word.

In 1999 *Time* magazine devoted an issue to the twentieth century's "Top 100 Icons and Heroes." Chopra, whom the magazine called "the poet-prophet of alternative medicine," made the list. *Newsweek* magazine featured Chopra on its cover, with the title "Spirituality for Sale." The article chronicled Chopra's seven spiritual laws and declared him to be "handsome, charismatic, an erudite amalgam of hard science and celestial seasoning, drawn selectively from the Vedic texts of ancient India."

Chopra's best-selling books, video tapes, musical CDs, and health-related products enjoy huge sales, but this marketing success is just one indication of the influence and impact this man continues to have in the fields of traditional and alternative medicine. His Chopra Center for Well Being in ritzy La Jolla, California, is a haven for well-heeled people seeking emotional and spiritual stability.

A regular guest on national TV shows, Chopra talks in a rapid-fire manner about his beliefs and his many products. But he is far less forthcoming about his past associations with Transcendental Meditation (TM) founder Maharishi Mahesh Yogi, whose reputation has suffered in recent years.

An Unlikely Background

Chopra's father, who died in 2001, was an Indian cardiologist. Deepak grew up in a privileged family and followed his father into the medical profession, entering medical school at the age of seventeen and later serving as a village doctor in rural India.

After moving to the United States, Chopra rose rapidly in his profession, becoming chief of staff at the Boston Regional Medical Center. But Chopra soon realized that Western medicine lacked soul, and he increasingly returned to the Hindu concepts that were part of his upbringing.

Chopra soon affiliated himself with Maharishi Mahesh Yogi, the founder of the Transcendental Meditation (TM) movement and one of Eastern religion's better-known apostles to the Western world. Chopra became a devoted follower of the Maharishi and adopted his approach to Ayurvedic medicine.

Ayurvedic medicine is an ancient Hindu practice that Maharishi and other figures have popularized in the West. It is based on a concept many Westerners now embrace: that both the mind and body of a person must be involved in medical treatment. Chopra later assumed control of one of the Maharishi's Ayurvedic clinics and helped established the American Association of Ayurvedic Medicine.

Over the next few years, Chopra would downplay his involvement with Maharishi Mahesh Yogi to concentrate on his own meteoric career. In 1992 he was appointed to a National Institutes of Health panel on alternative medicine, and in 1995 he and Dr. David Simon founded the Chopra Center for Well Being in La Jolla, California.

Meanwhile, Chopra's growing book sales and media interviews made him increasingly popular with millions of Americans.

Life and Work

As Chopra's fame and reputation have grown, few people have dissected his underlying philosophy or explored how this philosophy works itself out in his daily life.

For example, Chopra's winsome media appearances mask the fact that he views human beings as little more than a conglomeration of subatomic particles that are virtually indistinguishable from rocks and dirt.

As he told journalist Richard Scheinin, "Usually, I look at a tree and I don't see it as my lungs. I look at the rivers, the waters, and I don't see them as my circulation. I look at the atmosphere, I don't see it as my breath. But in fact, it is."

Such beliefs are totally consistent with Chopra's Hindu-influenced spirituality, which teaches that mind, spirit, and body have an indistinguishable oneness: "We are local expressions of the infinite universe and not individual beings."

A visit to the Web site sponsored by the Chopra Center for Well Being downplays Hindu distinctives and focuses instead on bland generalities that are designed to appeal to the nonreligious masses and increase the center's profits. The following quotes are taken from the Mission Statement and the Organizational Purpose, found on the Web site:

- "The Chopra Center for Well Being boldly explores new frontiers in the expansion of human consciousness through programs, products, and services for the integration of mind, body, spirit and environment in health care, education, business and personal development."
- "We believe by honoring creative transformation above all else we will create abundance for ourselves and our environment."
- "We pursue strategic alliances to expand current markets and create new opportunities."

- "We believe there is meaning and purpose in life and all knowledge comes from within."
- "We also believe there is an intimate connection between mind, body and spirit as well as between the individual and the environment."
- "By understanding and using these connections each of us can bring greater health, happiness and well being into our lives."
- "We are committed to learning and sharing knowledge with people to help enhance their lives."
- "We demonstrate this commitment through our message, which is to heal, to love, to transform, and to serve."
- "To heal we show others how to open their awareness to the infinite possibilities for understanding and renewal."
- "To love we accept people as they are and provide them with inspiration and support as we share our knowledge and programs."
- "To transform we help others to experience the balance and integration of mind, body and spirit, and we provide support and guidance while they incorporate these principles into their daily lives."
- "We share a vision of higher states of consciousness and embrace the path of enlightenment."

In addition, Chopra has been involved in financial and sexual scandals not even equaled by disgraced televangelists. But he uses his charm to keep such failures from dimming his allure or crimping his income.

As he told a writer for *Esquire* magazine, "Please understand, under no circumstances should you emulate me or set me up on a pedestal. One of the biggest mistakes we can make is to mistake the message for the messenger. What I write about is what I need most to learn."

What Chopra learned is how to market his message. His Global Network for Spiritual Success claims thousands of members in fifty countries, and his lecture fee tops twenty-five thousand dollars. His followers are undoubtedly attracted to his message of relative ease: "They say you have to give up everything to be spiritual. . . . I satisfy a spiritual yearning without making people think they have to worry about God and punishment."

CHRISTIAN CRITIQUE: Chopra's success is a sad commentary on our culture's obsession with the presumed expertise of anyone who has high-profile television exposure. His celebrity status has allowed him to mix traditional medicine with Hindu occult speculation about the body and come off sounding authoritative. The ancient ayurvedic approach to health is a combination of folk remedies and idolatrous devotion, though Chopra has jettisoned the latter for American audiences. By refusing to disavow his association with Maharishi, Chopra risks suspicion that his cures are more metaphysical than physical. Those who attend his centers will fall under the spell of his finely tuned public relations image as well as the dark forces operating through his pagan belief system of well-being. The same sinister powers that have propelled Maharishi have also catapulted Chopra to stardom for the sole reason of enhancing a nonobjective view of medicine that makes patients more open to spiritualistic explanations and remedies. It may also put patients at physical risk if they avoid the intervention of medical science in favor of ayurvedic speculation. The more serious consequence is eternal, if one believes Chopra's message that, "Although each person seems separate and independent, all are connected to patterns of intelligence that govern the whole cosmos. Deep inside us is an innermost core of being. This is who we really are."

SOURCES: Chip Brown, "Deepak Chopra Has (Sniff!) a Cold," *Esquire*, October 1995, 124; "Chopra on Oprah," *Christian Research Report*, July-September 1998, 1, 7; John Leland and Carla Power, "Deepak's Instant Karma," *Newsweek*, 20 October 1997, 56; Richard Scheinin, "Chopra Explores Life's Impermanence after Father's Death," *Colorado Springs Gazette*, 3 March 2001, Life3.

ACCESS: www.chopra.com

See also Transcendental Meditation; Holism and Alternative Medicine.

DIVINATION DEVICES AND TAROT CARDS

Business is booming for divination decks, those collections
of cards and manuals which claim to give users supernatural
access to information.

OVERVIEW: Divination—the attempt to communicate with divine or supernatural forces and learn about the past, the present and the future—has been practiced by many people throughout much of human history. But in the 1990s divination products became a booming business for bookstores and publishers, which are capitalizing on people's hunger for the transcendent by offering an unprecedented variety of card decks and other divination systems.

"Once the sport of wizards and kings, tarot, runes, astrology and more are now mainstream," said *Publishers Weekly* in a May 2001 article. Or as *New Age*

Journal executive editor Jonathan Adolph put it in an article entitled "Everyday Magic," published in the popular magazine's March-April 1993 issue, "It's hard to recall a time in history when consulting so many of the world's sacred oracles has been a simple matter of cracking some plastic wrap."

Shelves in New Age bookstores are overflowing with dozens of recently published systems, such as *Medicine Cards*, a beautifully illustrated card deck and companion manual which has sold more than 350,000 copies since it was published in 1988 by Santa Fe–based Bear & Company Publishing.

The Native American–inspired deck sells for $29.95 and promises users "the discovery of power through the ways of animals." As a promotional piece for the deck puts it, "Forty-four power animals are used in a variety of spreads to guide the way to healing of the body, emotions, mind, and spirit. Blank shields allow users to choose their own totem animals. An unsurpassed spiritual tool."

"What really makes these cards work is the illustrations," said a company spokesman. "They are very colorful and very accessible."

Some New Age stores report that as much as ten percent of their business comes from cards and other forms of divination systems. Not surprisingly, such systems are popping up at mainstream stores, too.

From Tarot Cards to Divination Decks

Stamford, Connecticut–based U.S. Games Systems Inc., a company which was founded in 1968, now sells more than seven hundred different products, including everything from playing cards to tarot cards and, increasingly, divination decks. A company spokesman says the growing mainstream popularity of divination and Tarot products has been nothing short of astounding.

"Twenty-five years ago we were selling the decks to people in the occult and in underground types of stores," he said. "But today, they're at the front counter at the Waldenbooks and B. Dalton stores."

The growing popularity of divination systems has lured many large, mainstream publishing houses into the business. HarperSanFrancisco's *Sacred Path Cards*, a system similar to the *Medicine Cards*, has sold more than one hundred thousand copies. And other big-name publishers are producing dozens of new offerings based on a grab bag of mystical, mythical, and literary traditions, including Simon and Schuster with *The Druid Animal Oracle*, St. Martin's with *The Lovers' Tarot*, and HarperCollins's Aquarian imprint with *The Norse Tarot* and *The Shakespearean Tarot*.

"Decks, decks, decks," wrote Karen Crane in the March/April 1992 issue of *New Age Retailer*. "It seems like everyone is coming out with a new deck of cards, each for a new kind of growth experience, these days."

No one's sure where tarot cards came from, although there's plenty of speculation. Interest in the cards flourished during the nineteenth-century occult revival which swept France, England, and America. Some believers claim tarot-like decks were used by the ancient Egyptians and Hebrews. But historians trace their origins to fourteenth-century Europe.

The most popular tarot deck is the Rider-Waite deck, created by British occultist Arthur Edward Waite in 1910. Like standard playing cards, the Rider-Waite tarot and other tarot cards are based on a series of suits, with tarot cards' *minor arcana* of wands, swords, cups, and pentacles corresponding to the clubs, spades, hearts, and diamonds of playing cards.

Tarot decks also include a *major arcana* of the fool, the magician, the lovers, the hanged man, the devil, strength, justice, judgment, and death.

In a tarot reading the reader shuffles the cards and arranges them on a table. The reader then observes which cards appear, what their placement is in the arrangement, and draws conclusions about what their appearance and placement means.

"People feel that there's something in the pictures or the colors or the symbology that touches on something else," says a professional tarot reader. This "something else" is a "gateway into the greater mysteries of the universe. But also, a lot of it is just common sense, just like anything else."

In recent years there's been an explosion of decks, some of which are patterned after the major and minor arcana. But the vast majority of the new decks dispense with traditional tarot systems and instead use a dizzying variety of traditions, all with attractive illustrations designed to appeal to virtually any taste or interest.

This profusion of divination systems puzzles skeptics, one of whom said divination was "a poor man's way of going to a psychologist. It's something like reading Shakespeare, or going to a play. People are projecting all of the meaning onto it."

The Allure of Divination

One thing is clear: Growing numbers of people are buying into the promise that the answers to life's most troubling questions can be found in the cards.

Authors, publishers, and users of divination systems claim they help people divine—or access—hidden information, whether it be spiritual or psychological, through mystical means.

While some users say the cards help connect them to mystical, psychic, and other supernatural powers, others say the cards are simple tools for self-help and analysis.

"I think the cards act as a mirror," said one user. "They help me process information that I already have inside." Or as Rachel Pollack, creator of the *Shining Woman Tarot* system put it, "The point of divination is to understand more about ourselves. I feel Tarot's structure has centuries of ideas and teaching behind it, and the accumulated, developed wisdom of all the interpreters who have worked with it gives a greater advantage to that structure."

One scholar says a big part of divination's growing popularity is people's desire for some kind of personal, spiritual connection to the cosmos at a time when they are experiencing an estrangement from traditional religious belief systems.

"We have a whole generation that has grown up not trusting government, institutions and churches," says the scholar. "But you can't grow up without something to trust. So now these people are finding non-traditional institutions they can trust. They are looking into Eastern mysticism and Native Indian cultures, and finding solace in all kinds of things in the New Age movement."

A marketing director for a publisher of books and divination decks agrees, saying that cards meet the spiritual needs of people who don't need or want "a commitment to an institution or a particular religious doctrine."

Understanding Divination

Tarot cards, divination decks and rune stones are some of the tools people use to access the unknown, the hidden, or the yet to be.

Broadly speaking, divination encompasses a number of disparate practices, including astrology, numerology, palmistry, Ouija boards, the reading of everything from crystal balls to tea leaves, and the pronouncement of various omens and oracles.

In ancient societies divination was often performed to complement royal and holy functions. Rulers sought knowledge from the gods to aid them in maintaining power and winning wars, while priests sought privileged information on natural disasters and famines.

According to Harper's *Encyclopedia of Mystical and Paranormal Experience*, the Chaldeans and Babylonians created elaborate divinatory systems in which priests sought occult knowledge through messages they read from the natural world. Egyptian priests slept in temples in order to receive divine input in their dreams. And in Rome, a class of priests known as augurs sought out wisdom from God in natural phenomena such as the flight of birds, the patterns of clouds, and the markings on the livers of sacrificed animals.

The Greeks, who helped popularize divination among their masses through astrological horoscopes, consulted special oracles who delivered messages from the gods through trancelike states. The most popular of the many Greek oracles was based at Delphi, near the foot of Mount Parnassus.

As *New Age Journal's* Jonathan Adolph put it, "Through the ages, soothsayers, seers, and shamans seeking otherworldly guidance and direction have managed to read significance into everything from the behavior of animals (zoomancy), to random passages in books (bibliomancy), to the astrological positions of the planets and stars (ReaganNancy)."

One of the oldest systems is the I Ching (pronounced *ee jeng*), or "Book of Changes," a system of sixty-four hexagrams consisting of solid and broken lines that dates back thousands of years. Originally I Ching practitioners would throw down fifty yarrow sticks, later modified to tossing three coins three times. The arrangement of the sticks or coins would be interpreted by a "superior man" whose life was guided by a proper flow of the yin and yang energies. The entire I Ching system was based on a concept of a unified and cyclical universe and was part of a wide-ranging social and political behavioral code.

Centuries later psychiatrist Carl Jung would express his appreciation for the "meaningful coincidences" or synchronicities found in the I Ching system, which relied heavily on introspection and intuitive knowledge for a proper reading of the signs.

A Changing Spiritual Marketplace

In today's fluid metaphysical and spiritual marketplace, one can find a baffling variety of diviners and dabblers. Some practice systems like the I Ching or tarot card reading in, accordance with strict traditions handed down over centuries. But others practice more of a patchwork-quilt approach, borrowing from a variety of systems and mixing them in unique, nontraditional ways.

Today people mix and match ancient occult systems with newer divination devices, using whatever they find appealing or whatever seems to "work" best. But many do not realize that in doing so, they are opening themselves up to the influence of harmful spiritual forces that are most certainly deceptive.

CHRISTIAN CRITIQUE: The Bible doesn't specifically mention tarot cards or divination decks, but the Old and New Testaments are crystal clear in their condemnation of divination as a dangerous and deceptive spiritual practice.

The instructions for God's people as they entered the Promised Land were clear: "There shall not be found among you any one that maketh his son or his daughter to pass through the fire, or that useth divination, or an observer of times, or an enchanter, or a witch, or a charmer, or a consulter with familiar spirits, or a wizard, or a necromancer. For all that do these things are an abomination unto the Lord" (Deuteronomy 18:10-12).

The prophet Ezekiel condemned "vain vision [and] flattering divination" which were misleading the people of Israel (12:24). In the book of Revelation the final words in the New Testament proclaim blessings for those whose lives are pure and will be able to enter the heavenly city, and condemnation for all practitioners of spiritual rebellion: "For without are dogs, and sorcerers, and whoremongers, and murderers, and idolaters, and whosoever loveth and maketh a lie" (22:15).

Interestingly, the Bible doesn't say that those who practice divination are always wrong in their findings. In fact, Acts records an incident in Philippi where Paul and Silas were preaching. One day on their way to prayer, the two evangelists encountered a slave girl who told fortunes for pay and earned a healthy income for her owners (16:16-24).

The girl told the gospel truth about Paul and Silas: "These men are the servants of the most high God, which shew unto us the way of salvation" (v. 17). But after a few days of this, Paul became troubled and cast a spirit out of the girl, an action that angered her owner and caused the two evangelists to be dragged before the town magistrates, who ordered them to be stripped and flogged.

Then, as now, followers of Christ proclaim a radically different way of knowing God and learning spiritual truth. Even if other means sometimes provide accurate information, it is knowledge that's retrieved by dark means and more often than not provides deceptive answers. Today, Christians who oppose divination may not get flogged, but there are increasing signs that occultic ways of seeking the truth are challenging the Christian worldview in the marketplace of spirituality.

SOURCES: Jonathan Adolph, "Everyday Magic," *New Age Journal* (March-April 1993); Karen Crane, "Working with a Full Deck, *New Age Retailer*, March-April 1992; Jan Ferris Heenan, "Divination = Divine Sales," *Publishers Weekly*, 21 May 2001, 46–48; Steve Rabey, "It's in the Cards: Business Booming for Divination Decks," *Christian Research Journal* (spring 1997): 7, 47–48.

DIVINE LIGHT MISSION

Guru Maharaj Ji; Maharaji

This group's adolescent leader became an overnight celebrity in the 1970s but just as rapidly fell from public favor.

FOUNDER: Balyogeshwar Param Hans Satgurudev Shri Sant Ji Maharaj (Guru Maharaj Ji); born December 10, 1957, Hardwar, India

TEXT: Hindu scriptures; selected Bible passages

SYMBOL: Pictures of Maharaj Ji seated on a throne wearing the crown of Krishna

APPEAL: During the early seventies youth rebelled against established institutions, which made them more susceptible to a strong disciplinary structure. The age of Maharaj Ji was an ironic contrast that appealed to the youths' loss of adult authority. Today's disciples tend to be older and better educated, responding to the Divine Light Mission's current goals of peace through meditation and selfless service.

OVERVIEW: "God has retired and now resides in comfortable affluence amid the placid splendor of a Malibu, California, mansion." That might well be the epitaph on the tombstone of Divine Light Mission.

In the early seventies, Guru Maharaj Ji commanded one of the largest and fastest growing followings of all imported cult leaders.

At one time he confidently declared, "The key to the whole life, the key to the existence of this entire universe rests in the hands of Guru Maharaj Ji."

Then it all fell apart. Reorganizational efforts failed to salvage the momentum of the days when he was worshiped as one "greater than God, because he showed men to God." Still, a hard core of an estimated several hundred to several thousand disciples still believes he is *the* incarnation of God, the Perfect Master for our age.

A Child of Affluence

Guru Maharaj Ji owes the founding of Divine Light Mission (DLM) to his wealthy, revered father, Brahman Samaj Shri Hans Ji Maharaj, who headed the Prem Nagar Ashram. Shri Hans was considered to be a *satguru* (perfect master) by many of his countrymen.

When Maharaj Ji was born December 10, 1957, in Hardwar, India, no one paid much attention. The family already had three older sons, and one of them was presumed to be next in line as satguru. But Maharaj Ji was remarkably precocious. By age two he was meditating and giving *satsang* (holy discourses).

When Maharaj Ji was eight years old, his father died. The boy addressed the grieving devotees by declaring, "Why are you weeping? Haven't you learned the lesson that your master taught you? The Perfect Master never dies. Maharaj Ji is here amongst you now."

As his father's disciples bowed at Maharaj Ji's feet, his mother, Rajeshwari Devi (usually known as Mata Ji), confirmed the passing of the spiritual mantle to him. He was invested with the crown of Krishna, and thirteen days later, while praying to his father's cremated ashes, an inner voice spoke. The message was simple: Guru Maharaj Ji was destined to become the savior of humanity.

To Delhi and the West

On November 8, 1970, Maharaj Ji led an entourage of thousands of followers through the streets of Delhi. Arriving at the India Gate, he declared, "I will establish peace in this world."

Strange words indeed for a ninth-grade dropout from a Catholic mission school. But several million Indian disciples believed his claim.

Only a handful of *premies* (devotees—literally "lovers") greeted his arrival in the West as he touched down at Los Angeles International Airport in 1971. Yet there was something fascinating about this pudgy teenager whose tastes ran from Baskin-Robbins to horror movies.

The turning point came the following year in Montrose, Colorado. Two thousand converts were solicited from an audience of five thousand, and suddenly Maharaj Ji was on his way. By the time another year rolled around, there were four hundred eighty DLM centers and thirty-five thousand members in the United States.

The organization opened up a variety of businesses and communes along with a record company, a film production house, and a printing establishment. Then came "Millennium 1973," an extravaganza held in the Houston Astrodome.

I witnessed the events of that festival, which was supposed to draw a potential attendance of 144,000. Though only approximately 20,000 showed up, the worship accorded to Maharaj Ji testified to his uncanny power.

Dopers-turned-devotees, fornicators-turned-celibates, hippies, and straights all united in their shouting praise: "Bholie Shri Satguru Dev Maharaj Ki Jai," a Hindi "hip, hip, hooray" to the Lord of the Universe. To my amazement, the entire audience of thousands prostrated themselves before Maharaj Ji's throne, which was elevated nearly forty feet above the AstroTurf.

Controversy and Dissolution

Controversy soon followed glory. A reporter who threw a cream pie in Maharaj Ji's face was mercilessly beaten by the guru's disciples. Maharaj Ji was accused by Indian customs officials of trying to smuggle eighty thousand dollars worth of jewels into his native land. The Astrodome gathering rang up huge debts, and questions were raised about the guru's true age and materialistic preoccupations.

Still, dedicated followers declared they would die or kill for the corpulent kid whom Rennie Davis, the ex-leftist radical, called "the power of creation itself."

The biggest upheaval occurred in 1974 when he married a former United Airlines stewardess who was eight years his senior. He pronounced her the incarnation of the ten-armed, tiger-riding goddess, Durga. When the new bride refused her mother-in-law access to their Malibu estate, that was the last straw.

Mother Mata Ji denounced her son as a drinking, dancing, nightclub haunting meat eater. She changed the name of the U.S. organization to the Spiritual Life Society and installed Maharaj Ji's eldest brother, Shri Satyapal Ji (Bal Bhagwan Ji), as the new Perfect Master. Even the birth of two grandchildren (Premlata and Hans Pal Singh) didn't mollify her anger. However, Maharaj Ji was unperturbed, wondering aloud how anyone could claim to tell God he was no longer qualified to hold office.

For a while things picked up. Maharaj Ji's income averaged over four hundred thousand dollars a month, mostly due to a mandatory tithe. His passion for automobiles extended to Mercedes-Benz, Maserati, Lotus, and a mobile van.

The *Divine Times,* a slick, four-color publication, circulated in communities in sixty-six countries, reporting on the guru's activities. He continued holding large festivals and *lilas* (god-games where audiences of disciples were doused with water and red paint from huge, pressurized nozzles). But as Goomerajee (as he is affectionately known by close associates) grew more obese, his following conversely diminished.

Plans for his divine city were shelved. Almost one hundred DLM-owned vehicles were sold. All but one of thirty-four food cooperatives were shut down. The Denver international headquarters was all but abandoned. Maharaj Ji's scores of handpicked evangelists, called *mahatmas,* were reduced to twenty and renamed *initiators.* His income plunged to less than one hundred thousand dollars per month. Estimates of followers worldwide remained slightly above a million, but in the United States that total went from a heyday high of fifty thousand to about ten thousand. Some critics suggested the figure might be closer to three thousand. Worst of all, his former head, Bob Meshler, left the DLM amid a series of accusations.

Today Guru Maharaji (as it is now spelled) is officially retired, though he does regularly speak to gatherings of Elan Vital, a nonprofit organization consisting primarily of former Divine Light disciples.

Teachings of the Child Master

But before any final obituaries on Guru Maharaj Ji are pronounced, it would be wise to ponder the teachings and practices that precipitated his sudden rise to power. In the seeds of his fame may be the genesis of other cult leaders having an Eastern inclination. Understanding what the DLM taught and represented may give a clue forewarning society of other personality cult figures.

Followers of Maharaj Ji are encouraged to live by his five commandments:
1. Do not put off until tomorrow what you can do today.
2. Constantly meditate and remember the Holy Name.
3. Leave no room for doubt in your mind.
4. Never delay attending *satsang* (one of Maharaj Ji's discourses of rambling stories and illustrations).
5. Always have faith in God (which is translated as complete devotion to Maharaj Ji).

The theology of DLM may be summed up by understanding its view of God, guru, mind, and knowledge. God is a form of energy, a cosmic vibration. As such, "the Word" extends itself to everything, making even man's soul a part of God.

I once heard Guru Maharj Ji exclaim in a speech that he did not desire a relationship with God. To do so would imply that deity is separate from man, undercutting the doctrine of oneness that is central to Hinduism. Hence, DLM has as its ultimate goal the merging of man's soul with the Infinite Absolute— the soul's energy being reabsorbed into the universal energy of God.

Guru Maharaj Ji's variant of Hinduism emphasizes the *Siddha Yoga* school of thought. In this tradition, God-realization can only be accomplished with the aid of a guru who leads one forward on the path of enlightenment. All the better if this guru is a Perfect Master greater than God himself. The Perfect Master is sinless, since his subjective consciousness is the only standard by which he is judged (God is inside him).

No external principles of absolute values guide him because he responds spontaneously to his own divinity. This living Master deserves and has the right to demand total submission from his followers. In Maharaj Ji's case, such subservience is reinforced by his ubiquitous visage, adorning every trinket and magazine produced by DLM.

But there is an impediment to following the Perfect Master on the path toward knowledge of God—the mind. Guru Maharaj Ji insists that the rationalistic West has given too much prominence to reasoning faculties. The mind, in his estimation, is delusive, unreliable, and imperfect. It is the spirit that contains the capacity for love and peace.

Therefore the knowledge of God is unattainable by objective information. It can only be received by experience. Maharaj Ji describes the mind as a snake to be killed so the direct revelation of divine knowledge can be transmitted. "Give it [your mind] to me," he implores. "I am ready to receive it. Because your mind troubles you, give it to me."

The devotee who surrenders his mental capacities is ready to receive the guru's knowledge. It is this experience that transforms the lives of his disciples and makes them into robots to do his bidding.

When pressed to explain this phenomenon, premies give glowing testimonials of its benefits but never reveal its process. Only diligent research has uncovered the fourfold procedure that consists of a blinding light (seeing the so-called third eye), hearing celestial music (supposedly referred to in Revelation 22), tasting a sweet substance called nectar (which presumably has curative powers), and sensing a primordial vibration (representing the internalized Word of God).

A devotee is considered ready to receive knowledge once his unfettered submission to Maharaj Ji has been proven. This may be evidenced by signing away one's possessions to DLM or listening to extended hours of satsang. At the appointed time, the candidate enters a darkened room. He may sit there, draped in a sheet, for several hours. All the while, a mahatma lectures him on the importance of the knowledge he is about to receive.

Finally the initiator places his thumb and middle finger on the devotee's temples and presses inward with the index finger at a spot near the center of the forehead (claimed to be the location of the spiritual "third eye," the pineal gland). The optic nerve is pinched, and a neurological light results from the pressure upon the retina. Premies learn how to duplicate this experience at will by merely closing their eyelids and letting their eyeballs roll back in their sockets.

Divine music is heard with the "third ear." The mahatma places his fingers in the initiate's ears long enough for the recipient to be conscious of the sounds of his own internal organs and systems. One premie described the sound as "loud rock and roll," while another insisted she was hearing the same vibrations she experienced in her mother's womb.

Tasting divine nectar isn't easy. The substance is said to be a fluid flowing from the brain, the very elixir that sustained Christ forty days in the wilderness. With the devotee's mouth open, the mahatma places his fingers in the premie's throat and forces his tongue backward until it rests against the uvula. The resulting mucus of postnasal drip is interpreted as being "sweeter than honey."

Finally, John 1:14 is quoted to justify the theory that God's Word is in man's flesh. The candidate is told that a repetitive pattern of rhythmic breathing actually constitutes a mantra. In reality, this experience of "primordial vibration of the divine word" is a hyperventilative technique that leaves the premie in an altered state of consciousness much like a drug-induced high. This concluding experience conveys a sense of omnipotence producing a feeling of oneness with the universe. Followers of the guru refer to this ultimate high as being "blissed out."

The dynamics of the four states of Guru Maharaj Ji's knowledge can be explained on a naturalistic basis. After the mahatma has predefined each experience, the candidate can easily be manipulated by autosuggestive hypnosis. At each stage he is prone to interpret the phenomenon according to the expectations his spiritual leader has previously explained.

Undoubtedly the passively receptive state of the willing devotee also allows demonic forces to enhance the dimensions of each aspect of the guru's ritual of receiving knowledge.

Today devotees have ceased the Indian custom of *darshan*, literally kissing Maharaj Ji's feet, but they continue to walk in his footsteps. Now affectionately known as Prem Rawat, Maharaj Ji's work is carried on by Elan Vital, a charitable organization incorporated in 1971 that promotes his message. Visions International, a trade name of Elan Vital, Inc., provides support for the production of global materials. At present, these materials are enjoyed in over eighty countries, with written and oral translations in more than sixty languages.

CHRISTIAN CRITIQUE: The DLM taught that the only pathway to God is by submission to an *avatar*, a fully God-realized guru. Guru Maharaj Ji was said to be this Perfect Master who helps one to remove the resistance of the logical mind that is the only block between man and his divine inner soul. His knowledge is equated with the Holy Spirit, an experience that conveys a heightened sense of well-being and union with the infinite.

All the requirements of DLM are based on pleasing God by submission and service, a contradiction of Ephesians 2:8-9. Since the experience of knowledge communicates a euphoric feeling, it is wrongly assumed to substantiate the teachings of Maharaj Ji. Proverbs 1:7 states that true knowledge is "the fear of the Lord," not a hypnotic series of psycho-neurological manipulations.

Clearly, according to 1 John 2:18-23 and Matthew 24:23-24, Maharaj Ji fulfills the role of an antichrist.

SOURCES: *Who is Guru Maharaj Ji?* (New York: Bantam, 1978); various issues of the DLM publication *Divine Times;* miscellaneous DLM pamphlets and materials published for release to the press; Bob Larson, *The Guru* (Denver: Bob Larson Ministries, 1974); Kenneth Boa, *Cults, World Religions and You* (Wheaton, Ill.: Victor, 1980); *Empire Magazine,* 28 April 1974, 52–61; *The Denver Post,* 2 April 1976; Ibid., 13 August 1976; Ibid., 18 February 1977, 3BB; Ibid., 15 December 1978, 3BB; *Time,* 28 April 1975, 75; Ibid., 13 March 1978, 39, *People,* 15 March 1984, 170.

ACCESS: The DLM is now defunct, and its former Denver headquarters was long ago abandoned; Elan Vital, P.O. Box 6130, Malibu, CA 90264.

DRUGS

People have used mind-expanding substances for millennia, but do drugs really deliver "better living through chemistry"?

OVERVIEW: "Timothy Leary is dead," sang the Moody Blues in their 1968 psychedelic anthem, "Legend of a Mind."

That lyric was fulfilled in 1996 when Leary died following a bout with inoperable cancer. The self-confessed "high priest" of LSD who coined the sixties' mantra of "Tune in, turn on, and drop out" died as outrageously as he lived—posting updates on his death on his Web site.

But the mind-expanding revolution Leary pioneered and promoted shows no signs of dying. Quite the contrary. New generations of spiritually curious young people are putting their faith in the cosmic consciousness-inducing properties of psychedelic drugs. Popular author and lecturer Terrence McKenna and magazines like *Psychedelic Illuminations* document the continuing interest in drugs.

Reports have found that the 40 million members of Generation X are contributing to a steady increase in drug usage, consuming both traditional psychedelics as well as a whole new crop of all-natural compounds like herbal ecstacy—and because they are considered nutritional supplements instead of drugs, they are cheap, legal, and easy to find.

"Between one and two million people in America use psychedelic drugs beneficially," says the publisher of *Psychedelic Illuminations*, a magazine that proclaims the spiritual benefits of LSD, MDMA (also known as ecstasy) and other psychoactive substances. "These people have discovered the therapeutic and mind-expanding usages of psychedelic drugs, and they are struggling to attain a higher understanding of humanity's history in connection with these sacred elements."

Instant Karma

On August 9, 1960, a thirty-nine-year-old psychiatrist named Timothy Leary bit into a mushroom sacred to the Aztec Indians. For Leary, and for millions of mostly young Americans, life would never be the same again.

Leary, who accepted a teaching position at Harvard University's Center for Personality Development the following year, became a true believer in and energetic evangelist for the spiritual power of psychedelic drugs, which he saw as a digestible, direct line to God.

"Listen! Wake up!" wrote a euphoric Leary in his autobiographical book, *High Priest*. "You are God! You have the divine plan engraved in cellular script within you. Listen! Take this sacrament! You'll see! You'll get revelations! It will change your life! You will be reborn!"

During his years at Harvard, Leary functioned as both pied piper and drug dealer. He distributed psilocybin, the synthesized form of the drug he had taken via sacred mushrooms in Mexico, and LSD, which was discovered by Swiss chemist Albert Hoffman in 1943.

Before being dismissed from Harvard in 1963, being arrested for drug possession in 1965, and being called "the most dangerous man in America" by Richard Nixon, Leary performed dozens of drug experiments with Harvard psychology and divinity students, many of whom reported the drug helped them have powerful mystical experiences.

He founded an organization called the League for Spiritual Discovery (LSD) and spread his gospel by sharing drugs with poet Allen Ginsberg, painter Willem de Kooning, jazz trumpeters Dizzy Gillespie and Maynard Ferguson, novelist Jack Kerouac, and Harvard associate Richard Alpert. Alpert had powerful drug experiences and later traveled to India, returning as Baba Ram Dass, the name he used when he authored the popular seventies' spiritual guide *Be Here Now*. He remains a popular speaker on today's New Age circuit.

From Bad Trips to Newly Hip

After a lot of bad press about bad trips, frightening flashbacks, and potential permanent brain damage, psychedelic drug use tapered off. But it never stopped entirely.

"Marketed by word of mouth as a spiritual awakener, acid is again tempting bright young people who are trying to make sense of the world and who want a more intense experience than pot can provide," *Rolling Stone* magazine reported in a May 1994 special issue on "Drugs in America."

Today author, speaker and ethnobotanist Terrence McKenna—a swashbuckling adventurer/shaman who's a cross between Indiana Jones and the late Jerry "Captain Trips" Garcia—is picking up where Leary left off. In fact, the *New York Times* called McKenna "the most forceful advocate for psychedelics since Timothy Leary."

McKenna is a hip, witty, and popular lecturer who can draw audiences of up to three thousand people to his talks about something he calls "the ethnopharmacology of spiritual transformation."

An author of half a dozen books and the host of a popular audiotape series called "The Search for the Original Tree of Knowledge," McKenna is an intellectual iconoclast who peppers his work with complex scientific jargon and humorous anecdotes about his own numerous drug trips.

"Life lived in the absence of psychedelic experience . . . is life trivialized, life denied, life enslaved to the ego," he says in "Vision Plants," one of his taped lectures.

McKenna believes that psychedelic mushrooms—which he says are far superior to LSD—are the missing link in humanity's evolution from its single-celled ancestors and suggests they may have an extraterrestrial origin. He boldly proclaims that psychedelic experiences are a superior spiritual path to Christianity, which he dismisses as "priestcraft and propaganda" or "a con game spun out by eunuchs."

During his appearance at a recent New Age symposiuim, I confronted McKenna and talked to him extensively about his outrageous views. He was even more preposterous in person than in his public comments. He raged against what he called the "pharmacological genocide" practiced against primitive cultures by missionaries bent on eradicating their use of hallucinogenic practices.

As he vented his anger, his mind seemed to radically and unexpectedly shift states of consciousness, undoubtedly due to his frequent mind-bending trips. Any mention of Christ caused his anger to flare, and I suspected that my very presence was no small irritation to the demonic forces that had contributed to his spaced-out view of reality.

As a psychedelic evangelist McKenna was persuasive to his indulgent peers, but speaking one-on-one with an informed Christian critic, he was by turns sarcastic and evasive. His one-note litany about the benefits of drug-induced states of altered consciousness was more boring than seductive.

God in a Pill

Throughout the centuries, mind-altering drugs have been used by sorcerers, holy men, and shamans as part of religious rituals in Asia, the Middle East, and South America.

But through the work of McKenna and others, psychedelics are becoming an increasingly important part of the spiritual lives of contemporary American seekers, helping millions to open what novelist and LSD advocate Aldous Huxley called "the doors of perception."

An editor with *Gnosis*, a quarterly magazine on esoteric religious practices, grew up in a family where he absorbed diverse religious influences, including Eastern Orthodoxy, Christian Science, and Roman Catholicism. But he rejected all three faiths for drug-influenced mysticism following his first psychedelic experience at age eighteen.

"Organized religion never touched me in any way," he says. "But through psychedelics, I could see beyond the dogma of organized religion to the essential truths undergirding all religions."

The editor even suggests that drugs are a timesaving way of achieving spiritual experiences.

"It's very hard for many people these days who don't have the time to spend on meditation, or spiritual exercises or whatever it takes to achieve that alternate state," he says. "Through psychedelic experience you can see, feel and touch the Other."

Natural High

Possession of LSD became illegal in America in 1966, but decades later people in search of a quick, mystical high take substances with names like Cloud 9 and Ultimate Xphoria, all of which are cheap, legal, and readily available through health food stores and novelty shops.

These products, which are made from combinations of organic sub-stances such as ephedrine, pennyroyal, and comfrey, are promoted as deliver-ing good times as well as "cosmic consciousness" and "inner visions," all without the troublesome side effects or legal risks of more traditional psyche-delic drugs.

As one young user told *Newsweek* magazine in a cover story on "The Natu-ral Drug Culture," "It's herbal so it's OK."

These so-called herbal supplements are a big part of a largely unregulated $6 billion market for nutritional supplements, a market that is growing by 20 percent every year.

The growth of the market has been helped by the Dietary Supplement Health and Education Act, a bill passed by Congress in 1994, which classifies vitamins, minerals and herbs as food supplements rather than drugs, thus re-ducing the Food and Drug Administration's control over them. Some people in the natural foods business feel the new drugs are giving their business a bad name, and FDA commissioner David Kessler has called the products "street drugs masquerading as dietary supplements."

Though promoted as safe if taken according to directions, food supple-ments have been linked with such medical problems as liver damage, heart pal-pitations, seizures, strokes, heart attacks, and brain damage. They have also been linked to more than a dozen deaths, which is leading some to urge the FDA to take stronger action. Several individual and class action lawsuits re-sulting from deaths attributed to such substances have only slightly slowed their popularity.

One of the most popular and most controversial supplements is the uniquely spelled herbal ecstacy, a pill which sells for two to three dollars and which, with the help of heavy advertising in publications like *High Times*, has emerged as one of the most popular new drugs, selling an estimated 150 million pills in the past four years.

Like other natural drug compounds, herbal ecstacy relies on a unique mixture of substances which the company claims are "synergistically blended to insure visionary vibrations." But many of these compounds rely heavily on ephedrine, a substance that can cause liver failure and circulatory prob-lems.

What's worse is that many users ignore recommended dosage warnings or combine these already complex compounds with other drugs and alcohol, a risky play with a pharmacological roulette wheel.

The United States of Drugs

America is perhaps the most heavily drugged country in the world, a place where the motto "Better living through chemistry" is more than merely a phrase from a DuPont advertising campaign. It has become a kind of national mantra.

Dieters pop pills to counteract the natural effects of too much food and fat. Athletes down drugs to improve muscle tone and enhance their competitive edge. Truckers use uppers to stay awake on the road. And consumers spend billions annually on Viagra, Celebrex, Allegra, aspirin, ibuprofen, and other substances that promise to relieve painful or bothersome symptoms.

In the 1950s American drug makers began hawking new substances with effects that went beyond the body. Mood-altering drugs designed to decrease depression were an immediate hit with American housewives, paving the way for more contemporary mood-altering substances like Prozac.

Prozac was introduced in the early 1990s, and according to the book *Listening to Prozac,* the substance "enjoyed the fastest acceptance of any psychotherapeutic medicine ever," selling 650,000 prescriptions a month within two years of the drug's introduction.

It shouldn't be surprising that in a culture where drugs are promoted as an answer to so many human problems, millions of people advocate the use of drugs for spiritual enlightenment.

But Robert Ellwood, a professor in the school of religion at the University of Southern California and author of the book *The 60s Spiritual Awakening,* says that many young people who started their spiritual journeys with drugs wound up on more traditional religious paths.

"For some people the drug experience did have the effect of opening the door to a mystical experience and showing them that something was there beyond their humdrum lives," says Ellwood. "After starting there, many of them went on to non-drug ways of continuing their spiritual growth, such as the Jesus movement, which was to a large extent ex-druggies and ex-hippies, or into yoga and other kinds of things."

Still, some seekers never advance beyond drugs in their search for bliss. And others wind up with damaged bodies and minds that make their search more difficult than it would have been otherwise.

CHRISTIAN CRITIQUE: Christian philosopher Os Guinness has been writing about the physical and spiritual dangers of the over reliance on drugs since 1973, when InterVarsity Press published *The Dust of Death,* his groundbreaking look at the youth counterculture; the book was just as relevant in 1994 when Crossway Books re-released it with a new introduction.

"Drugs have attained an almost sacramental importance," wrote Guinness in a chapter entitled "The Counterfeit Infinity." Guinness said psychoactive substances played a powerful role in spiritual lives of the young, serving as "virtually the bread and wine of the new community."

Through his work with the late Francis Schaeffer at the L'Abri community in Switzerland, Guinness saw how drugs' promises of instant paradise turned into a demonic and destructive delusion for many people.

"These drugs pose so many dangers, and there are so many people I knew who totally blew their minds," he says.

Guinness says drugs tell users far more about their perceptions of reality than they do about reality itself, and challenges the widely accepted idea that drug-induced states and traditional mystical states are the same.

"It's like comparing a seasoned Alpine climber who scales the Matterhorn to someone who was lowered there by a helicopter. The view from the top might be much the same, but the routes to the top would be very different in terms of the discipline, skill and strength demanded."

After more than three decades on the front lines of spiritual warfare, I'm convinced that drugs (or *pharmakia*—the form of sorcery spoken about in Revelation 21:8) are an open door to the demonization of partakers. To alter the mind's perception of reality by deliberate, rebellious sorcery affords evil spirits the opportunity to attack the mind.

While many psychoactive inner journeys are chemically induced, others are a combination of physiology and demonology. This is one explanation for the many horrible accounts people give of seeing hellish landscapes and preternatural evil beings that continue to haunt drug devotees long after their trips are over.

The only sure way to avoid such satanic encounters is to eschew all recreational drugs and bring one's thoughts into Christ's captivity (2 Corinthians 10:5) by natural means.

SOURCES: Ty Burr, "Dying in Oblivion," *Entertainment Weekly*, 10 May 1996, 77–78; "Drugs in America," *Rolling Stone*, May 1994; Robert Ellwood, *The 60s Spiritual Awakening* (New Brunswick, N.J.: Rutgers University Press, 1994); "Psychedelics and the Path," *Gnosis*, winter 1993; Steve Rabey, "The Psychedelic 90s: A New Generation Turns On with Mind-Expanding Drugs," *Christian Research Journal* (fall 1996): 6–7, 44; Sarah Sullivan, "LSD and the Mystical Agenda," *Cornerstone* 17, no. 87.

See also Ram Dass.

EARTH CHANGES MOVEMENT

According to some New Age "prophets," cities throughout the world will be covered with water as part of a new emerging order.

OVERVIEW: People in New York, Los Angeles, and Miami better buy boats and secure lodging elsewhere, because the oceans are rising as part of a new world order that promises to bring massive destruction and usher in an age of celestial harmony.

Channeler Lori Adelle Toye says these U.S. cities and major world metropolises like Bangkok, Buenos Aires, Manila, and Mecca will be covered with water in a few hundred years.

My descendants will be safe in Denver, which promises to be a beachfront city with a new name—The Golden Port. Future Denverites will have a breathtaking view of the Bay of Harmony, a huge new body of water that will cover most of California, Utah, and Nevada, as well as parts of New Mexico.

Toye says her view of this grave new world results from predictions she has received from Jesus and three other Ascended Masters who revealed these plans in dreams she began receiving in 1983.

"The spiritual masters started coming forward and talking to me," says Toye, who has sold more than forty thousand copies of her "I Am America" map, which displays new features and boundaries. "I felt like a telephone."

Toye isn't the only modern-day channeler who has received visions of a drastically different new world. She and a handful of New Age authors are at the forefront of what is known as the Earth Changes Movement.

Movement leaders claim to receive supernatural revelations about the earth, which they consider to be a living entity that is growing increasingly weary of humanity's spiritual and environmental misdeeds. While their predictions may vary in their details, Earth Changes leaders agree on one thing: The earth is ready to rebel.

"Mother earth's alarm clock is getting ready to ring," says one Earth Changes devotee who buys books and attends seminars on the phenomenon. "This is frightfully exciting."

Centuries of Predictions

Predictions about dramatic earth changes have been an important part of religious teachings since at least the time of Noah. But since then, the predictions have been wrong more than they have been right.

Nostradamus, a sixteenth-century French physician and clairvoyant, included earth changes among his one thousand published prophecies.

Edgar Cayce, a twentieth-century American psychic known as "the sleeping prophet," predicted before his death in 1945 that the mythical island of Atlantis would rise again from the seas by 1969.

And Jeffrey Goodman's 1978 book, *We Are the Earthquake Generation*, predicted that the Pacific Ocean would reach as far as Kansas by the turn of the millennium.

Today, Toye and Gordon-Michael Scallion are the best-known prophets of Earth Changes.

Toye's channeled "I Am America" map, which sells for eighteen dollars, was published in 1989 by her Payson, Arizona, company, Seventh Ray Publishing. The map shows a radical realignment of the North and South Poles, a new location for the earth's equator, and a complete redrawing of the world's continents.

In a video explaining the map, Toye suggests that the destruction of Los Angeles, New York, and other major cities may represent a modern-day parallel to the biblical description of the destruction of Sodom and Gomorrah.

"These are places where people have doubted their divinity the most . . . where people have co-created against the divine nature," she says.

Scallion, an ex-Catholic who says he started receiving spiritual visions after he had a severe illness, is the founder of Matrix Institute, Inc., in Westmoreland, New Hampshire. The firm publishes a monthly newsletter, *The Earth Changes Report*, markets videos and tapes, and offers Scallion's "Future Map of the World."

Differing Predictions

Scallion's map of the United States bears some superficial resemblance to Toye's map, but many of his predictions differ from hers in significant ways.

Scallion predicted massive death and destruction as the earth "cracks like an egg shell." He said much of California would fall into the Pacific Ocean by 2001.

Toye's predicted earth changes will take much longer—possibly hundreds of years—and will affect much of the entire globe. But she was apparently wrong about all the things she said would happen by 2001, which included predictions that a huge meteor would strike the Southwest, leading to a cloud of atmospheric ash, global warming, the melting of the polar ice caps, and increasing geological disturbances.

Another important difference between Toye and Scallion is their prospects for change. Toye says the earth changes she predicts can be avoided if enough people become spiritually attuned. But Scallion says environmental degradation—particularly underground nuclear testing—means that humanity's grace period is over.

"At this point, consciousness, prayer and repentance won't do it," he says.

One Woman's Date with Cosmic Destiny

Toye was raised in the Lutheran Church—Missouri Synod, married her high school sweetheart, and set up house on an Idaho cattle ranch that had been in her family for generations. In her spare time she read books on metaphysics, particularly those dealing with the teachings of the Ascended Masters. In 1983 she began experiencing lucid dreams.

She kept her dreams to herself for years. After she began talking about them, she divorced her husband, who had been raised in the Mormon church. She also grew distant from her family.

"When I first came out with my map, my whole family thought I had really gone off the deep end. They got too caught up in the idea that God is in heaven and on a throne, that God is inactive and cannot act through people."

Scallion has also suffered derision since he released his first map in 1982. "I can still hear the laughter," he says.

Once Toye made a decision to share her visions, she began receiving more channeled communications. One time as she worked on her map, one of the Ascended Masters ran his fingers along the drawing, helping her get every detail correct.

Scientists Disagree

Many scientists believe that continued ecological degradation and global warming will cause problems in the future unless humanity learns to live lifestyles that are less destructive and wasteful. In addition, many scientists believe that global warming will lead to a melting of the polar ice caps and a gradual rising of worldwide ocean levels, which will lead to changes in the world's coastlines. But no scientists agree that global calamities of the kinds Toye and Scallion predict are even a remote possibility.

"I would trust the U.S. Geological Survey before I would trust someone channeling information from another dimension, whatever that means," said one skeptic.

Another skeptic says Earth Changes prophets predict so many events that they're bound to be accurate sooner or later.

"Some day, a big earthquake will hit somewhere out West. Then all the psychics will be crawling out of the woodwork."

But for the rest of us, it's probably more reliable to listen to what geophysicists and geologists say than to trust our lives and our futures to self-proclaimed prophets who are wrong about what they say 99 percent of the time.

CHRISTIAN CRITIQUE: Christians adhere to a stewardship ethic based on Genesis 1:26-28 ("Let them have dominion"), an edict which conveys responsibility as well as control. Unfortunately, evangelical believers were slow to respond to public environmental interests in the last decade and have found their concerns for God's creation overshadowed by eco-extremists who have sacralized the creation rather than the Creator (Romans 1:25). As a result, regard for humanity's treatment of earth, water, and air has been championed by earth goddess movements and wiccan pagans who appear in the press to be more sensitive about earth's resources. The new millennium provides an opportunity for believers to regain the environmental high ground by expressing a well-articulated biblical basis for caring about the inexorable extinction of valuable species and the despoiling of God's handiwork. Such scriptural regard for beast and field will help to counter the pantheistic viewpoint of neopagans, for whom saving whales and rain forests has become a religious quest. A proper biblical view of humanity and the world will confront the god of immanence, worshiped by some environmentalists, with the God of transcendence, who has spoken the world into existence and given us the duty of watching over it to maintain it's beauty and provisions for future generations.

SOURCES: Steve Rabey, "Grave New World," (*Colorado Springs) Gazette*, 16 July 1994, E1-3.

ACCESS: Toye's "I Am America" map is available from Seventh Ray Publishing, PO Box 2511, Payson, AZ 85547. Scallion's maps and products are available from Matrix Institute, Inc., PO Box 87, Westmoreland, NH 03467.

See also Ascended Masters.

ECKANKAR

Though heavily promoted ever since its debut in the 1960s, this complex
and confusing faith has failed to catch on with the masses.

*You are Soul, a conscious spiritual being, a creative, divine spark of a loving
God. Your purpose on this earth is to grow spiritually—to gain experience,
to find truth, and to learn to love. To put it another way, to find your way
home to God. True religion is a link between God and you. It provides you
with a guide to help make the journey as direct as possible. ECKANKAR has
an inner and outer living guide who journeyed to the heart of God and returned
to help us on our spiritual journey home. This guide is the Mahanta, the Living
ECK Master.*

HAROLD KLEMP, *HOW TO SURVIVE SPIRITUALLY IN OUR TIMES*

FOUNDER: John Paul Twitchell, born between 1908 and 1912 in Paducah,
Kentucky. Twitchell's biography claims a birthdate of 1922.

SYMBOLS: A funnel-shaped series of ascending ovals representing the
eleven astral planes or "God Worlds of ECK"; a series of five stick-shaped human figures ascending horizontally, with the fifth figure encircled, representing spiritual progress on the path of ECKANKAR

APPEAL: ECKANKAR offers dramatic, psychic, out-of-body experiences
and purports to give the student direct access to departed spiritual masters,
who appear as light-being entities. These astral projection abilities supposedly
offer the opportunity to predict one's future, acquire healing, and eventually
obtain omniscience. One practitioner claimed he would leave his body while
driving to work so he could check traffic flows and avoid any bottled-up inter-
sections that might be ahead.

OVERVIEW: Of all the new religions to enter the spiritual marketplace in
this century, few are more confusing than ECKANKAR (or ECK). Perhaps
that's why those who study new religious groups say the group's claims to having 3 million followers worldwide are inflated. (Scholars say the real number is
probably closer to fifty thousand members.)

Though relatively new, the group claims ancient roots. It was once billed
as the "ancient science of soul travel," but ECK is now promoted as the "Religion of the Light and Sound of God."

People who come across the group's promotional pamphlets in the local
grocery store may be intrigued by the group's claims. And followers of
ECKANKAR are often intelligent, well-meaning people. Still, ECK's confusing

mix of Eastern, Western and occultic practices has prevented it from achieving more widespread popularity.

"Soul travel is the means we use as the vehicle of return to our true home." The stated purpose in ECK literature is to preserve the individual through all eternity. Once the techniques of soul travel have been mastered, seekers can travel in different realms, eventually reaching a level of awareness that makes them "coworkers with God."

Unproved Claims

Paul Twitchell, a journalist and frequent dabbler in occult and mystical practices (including serving as a staff member in the Church of Scientology), formed the first public ECKANKAR group in 1965.

His theology, a restatement of Hindu precepts, teaches that ECKANKAR (coworker with God) came into being as a result of his contact with two ECK masters, Sudar Singh in India and Rebazar Tarzs in the Himalayas. But there's only one problem: No documented proof has been presented that Twitchell ever visited either place or that either man actually existed.

Similar questions surround nearly every claim the group makes. The terminology of ECKANKAR is said to come from the Amdo dialect of the Tibetan language. Twitchell offered no explanation for claiming such expansive knowledge regarding this tongue, which is unverified by linguists. (One cult expert claims that ECKANKAR is a semantic perversion of "Ek Onkar," the name of the supreme deity in *Shabda Yoga*.)

The group teaches that Sudar Singh and Rebazar Tarzs designated Paul Twitchell to be the 971st Living ECK Master, a *mahatma* (living manifestation of God). Twitchell said such a person is "above the laws of man . . . omnipotent and omniscient."

The ECK Master's purpose in life is to lead the souls of men to "that realm of spirit which is known as the Kingdom of Heaven where God (known as SUGMAD) dwells." Life flows from SUGMAD in the form of a cosmic sound and light current called *ECK*. (ECK is also often used as an abbreviation for ECKANKAR.)

Twitchell taught a variety of occult exercises by which the ECK student could tune into this ethereal sound of God. Foremost among these phenomena is an out-of-body experience Twitchell originally called "bilocation" and later changed to "soul travel," which he declared is "the secret path to God." (Occultists generally refer to this phenomenon as "astral projection.") Twitchell claimed that Jesus, Buddha, and Paul indulged in the practice of soul travel.

Understanding ECK requires familiarity with many unfamiliar and unusual terms.

The *Shariyat-Ki-Sugmad* are sacred ECKANKAR scriptures, which Twitchell declared to be located in a monastery in the Tibetan mountains.

Anami Lok is the name given to the true heaven where SUGMAD dwells. *Atma Sarup* is the soul body, which travels astrally from the *Nari Sarup*, the physical ("light") body.

Such language (along with hundreds of other ECKANKAR-invented words) would be of little interest to the average person were it not for Twitchell's contention that by soul travel one can achieve "omniscience . . . through the release of the soul from the bondage of flesh." In fact, ECKANKAR claims to provide a "key to heaven."

Even the inventions of Alexander Graham Bell and the Wright brothers are said to be the results of astral journeys they made to a great museum in the capital of the spirit world, *Sahasra-dal-Kanwal.*

An Impersonal Universe?

The outward image of ECKANKAR is friendly and tolerant, but its fundamental theology is cold and impersonal.

An advertisement circulated in major newspapers stated that ECKANKAR "does not condemn any person or teaching. If a person is involved in any world religion, he is encouraged to stay there." However, other statements found in ECKANKAR literature do not necessarily support this declaration. Also according to this literature, ECKANKAR is not a cult since it promotes individuality and does not sponsor communal living.

But in his book, *ECKANKAR: The Key to Secret Worlds,* Twitchell described God as being "unconcerned about any living thing in this universe. He is detached and unconcerned about man."

Christ taught that love is the greatest commandment, but Twitchell asserted that Rebazar Tarzs has instructed man to "love only those whom you must!"

The group's teachings also reflect an anti-Christian hostility.

Kal (an ECK word denoting the devil) is identified in Twitchell's theology as the father of the Christian faith, and Jesus is "a son of Kal, King of the lower worlds."

As we can see, the inclusive, conciliatory language used in ECKANKAR ads is contrasted by its criticism of other faiths and its published claims to be "the path of Total Awareness," "the everlasting gospel," the one true source of religions, and "the most ancient religious philosophy known to man."

In Twitchell's booklet, "ECK and Music," he stated, "The ECK, therefore, is the Way. . . . Without this heavenly music, or the WORD, no one can reach God again." Other religions may not be openly condemned, but the teachings of ECKANKAR certainly relegate them to an inferior position.

Hindu-Style Salvation

To replace the Christian doctrines of sin and redemption, Twitchell proposed a Hinduistic concept of karma and reincarnation. Those who wish to avoid the countless cycles of rebirth must learn to ascend through a series of eleven astral planes by OBEs (out-of-body experiences).

Success on this journey depends on the guidance of a Living ECK Master, who is assisted by other spirit guides. This master will facilitate astral travel by helping the student discard the karmic debt he has accumulated in past lives.

The ECK master is no mere guide. He is believed to be God in the flesh, an incarnation of SUGMAD. The master teaches the student that by sensory deprivation, altered states of consciousness, mantra-chanting, trancing, and contact with spirit guides, he can advance to higher planes of enlightenment.

Twitchell claimed to have witnessed frequent appearances of entities who asserted they were "translated" (ECKANKAR for *dead*) masters. Students are encouraged to think upon the current living Master until he, too, manifests himself to them as a glowing light-entity.

On September 17, 1971, in a hotel room in Cincinnati, Ohio, Paul Twitchell suddenly died of a heart attack. Living ECK Master number 972 was Sri (an honorific Hindi title) Darwin Gross. Gross claimed to be God's guru for our age, "the most splendid specimen of manhood, the noblest of the noble," "the most gifted spiritual leader alive today," and "a healer who has rescued many from physical ills and mental anguish."

As the Divine One, he received Twitchell's Rod of Power, an event said to have taken place in the spirit world since Twitchell died too suddenly for an orderly transfer of leadership. Gross continued "the longest unbroken line of spiritual teachers on this planet."

The teachings of ECKANKAR according to Gross continue Twitchell's tradition. Of love he says, "Many are teaching the masses to love everyone, to love their neighbors, and that's fine, if it's with a detached love. You have to be very careful who you give love to." Morality is described as "an individual thing established by your own inner authority." He supports abortion by declaring that the soul does not enter the body until "after the child has been brought into the outer world, and sometimes later than that." According to Gross, animals have a soul and their own heaven, Christianity adopted the idea of the Virgin Birth from Hinduism, and the current spiritual awakening is "due to ECK Masters."

New Leader, New Directions

The current Living ECK Master (allegedly the 973rd person to hold this title) is Harold Klemp.

Born in rural Wisconsin, he grew up on a small farm and attended a two-room country schoolhouse before going to high school at a religious boarding school in Milwaukee. During a stint in the air force, Klemp was assigned to duty in Japan, where he first encountered ECKANKAR. He says he later traveled in his "soul body" to the planet Venus to visit the Moksha Temple of Golden Wisdom.

Today his full title is Sri Harold Klemp, the Mahanta, the Living ECK Master. As the Living ECK Master, he is responsible for the continued evolution of the ECKANKAR teachings.

A tireless traveler and promoter, Klemp has changed the emphasis of the group's promotional material, which now promises devotees will experience spiritual growth, emotional healing, and a better life.

Klemp also presided over the building of the Temple of ECK in Chanhassen, Minnesota, which was completed in 1990 and serves as the group's symbolic hub. The temple also hosts many seminars on topics like "Become the Spiritual Adventurer," "A Year of Spiritual Healing," and "Creativity, Leadership and Spiritual Growth."

CHRISTIAN CRITIQUE: In ECK teaching, every cardinal Christian doctrine is denied, including original sin, intercessory prayer (called "an occult form of black magic"), the Virgin Birth, Christ as Creator and sole incarnation of the Father, and the absolute goodness of God. Rather, Satan, or Kal, is a partial manifestation of God's character.

In addition, participants in astral travel may make themselves vulnerable to demon possession.

Christians have reason to be troubled by the spiritistic overtones of ECKANKAR. Others are skeptical about its deified, authoritarian leadership. In "Eck and Music," Twitchell addressed such apprehensions by saying, "If the individual is under the Living ECK Master, then he has no worry, for the Master is taking care of him." ("I am with you always," Twitchell's Master Rebazar Tarzs once told him, an adaptation of Christ's promise in Matthew 28:20.)

If ECK advocates believe that Twitchell's Master appeared to him, the stage has been set for Master number 971 (Twitchell) to appear to his followers. A masquerading evil spirit could easily assume the role, or possess Twitchell, to guide students of ECK onward to SUGMAD.

SOURCES: "ECKANKAR: A Universal Path," brochure, February 1983; Carey Quan Gelernter, "Soul Travelers: Teachings 6 Million Years Old," *Seattle Times*, 27 January 1983, E2; Sri Darwin Gross, *Your Right to Know* (Menlo Park, Calif.: Illuminated Way, 1979); "Mutation in ECKANKAR," *Forward* (Christian Research Institute), 5, no. 1, 1982, 13; "Open Letter to All Christians," advertisement placed in various newspapers and paid for by ECKANKAR; *Spiritual Counterfeits Journal* 3, no. 1 (September 1979); Paul Twitchell, *ECKANKAR: The Key to Sacred Worlds* (New Hope, Minn.: Illuminated Way, 1969), 42; Ibid., *ECKANKAR: Ancient Science of Soul Travel*, pamphlet; Paul Twitchell, "ECK and Music," pamphlet, 1971.

ACCESS: ECKANKAR Spiritual Center, P. O. Box 27300, Minneapolis, MN 55427; www.eckankar.org

ENLIGHTENMENT

A key concept in Buddhism and other Eastern faiths,
enlightenment is gaining ground in the West.

OVERVIEW: No matter what name it goes by, the goal is the same. It may be called heightened awareness, *nirvana*, *satori*, transcendental bliss, god-realization, expanded consciousness, altered perception of reality, or cosmic consciousness.

The discipline may be yoga, Zen, asceticism, or meditation. And the religious frame of reference may be Buddhism, Unity, Hinduism, Theosophy, or Scientology.

When all of the semantic externals are stripped away, what remains is the often nebulous concept of *enlightenment*.

Buddha experienced enlightenment one day sitting under a tree, and today the concept is a key part of Buddhist teaching, which claims the experience can help people see the true nature and causes of life's sorrow. But the concept has become much more broadly defined and more popular in the spiritual marketplace of the West.

John White, a scholar and author who writes for numerous New Age publications, said this: "So widespread is the urge to know about enlightenment that, for the first time in history, people and organizations claiming to understand it have developed into a thriving field of commerce. Today enlightenment is for everyone."

Reality or Illusion?

How is it achieved, and what separates it from biblical Christianity?

The first step toward enlightenment, in the mystical sense of the word, is the negation of one's rational faculties. Human rationality is seen as an obstacle on the pathway to a higher consciousness.

Truth is not perceived to be an absolute of objective revelation. Its reality must be experienced pragmatically by psychic or suprarational input.

Logic plays no part in finally determining that enlightenment has been achieved. I have debated many cultists who affirm the authority of their messianic leader. When pressed to explain how they decided to follow a man as god, the answer is the same: "I just know."

The subjectivized experience offered by many cult captains, whether it be the "knowledge" of Guru Maharaj Ji or the *shakipat* of Muktananda Paramahansa, is said to be its own proof.

When no rational attempt is made to judge intuitional experiences by objective standards, the enlightened cult member fails to ask, "Is it right?" He only concludes, "It works, and that is enough."

Some mystics would even admit that their altered perception of reality might be fantasized or hallucinogenic. That probability doesn't matter to them.

It's frustrating for a Christian who believes in absolute truth to debate a devotee of cosmic consciousness and try to proceed to a logical conclusion, only to have him roll his eyes back in his head and "trance out"! When he returns from his momentary trip, he dons a sweet smile declaring, "Try it, you'll like it," dismissing any further intelligent conversation.

When thinking has been replaced by feeling, the sea of subjectivism swallows up any effort to distinguish between reality and illusion.

Eastern Enlightenment or Christian Conversion?

While Christians may share glowing testimonies of conversion experiences, Hebrews 11 clearly designates the believer's life as one of faith. This transforming confidence in God is based on the objective criteria of his promises as revealed in the written Word. Jesus Christ declared that the basis of eternal life is knowing God (John 17:3).

Christians have a personal, conscious relationship with their Lord, one that combines the emotional dynamics of the new birth with the intellectual capacity to understand God's character by his creation (Romans 1:18-20). Man's faith does not rely upon some empirical foundation of truth that is being psychically communicated. The "power of God," as revealed in the miracles of the historical Christ, offers far more hope than the mythology of the mystic (1 Corinthians 2:5).

After the rational mental processes have been negated, the mystic next pursues enlightenment by seeking to release his spirit from the limitations of the body. One intention of enlightenment is "to be at one with the universe."

However, the "subtle" or "material" body clouds spiritual perception by its attachment to the world of senses. The mystic may release his spirit by yoga exercises or by astral projection. Once the shell of flesh is left behind, time and space have no boundaries, giving spiritual entities (demons) the opportunity to guide the "true self" as it searches for the essence of life out of the body.

The enlightenment resulting from shedding the bondage of the physical body is generally a perception of self-deification. This exaltation of the ego leads many to conclude that they are indwelt with a "Christ-consciousness," or even that they are God. In the monist view, such a conclusion is perfectly logical because the creator and the created are all of the same essence.

When enlightenment has been experienced in this manner, God is reduced to an impersonal principle. Gone is any concept of judgment and moral accountability. One's own enlightened self becomes the arbiter of all actions and the gauge of all truth.

All procedures leading to enlightenment and all cultic systems achieving their own illumination must operate on these propositions:

1. The mind and the body inhibit the attainment of truth by their confining sensory capacity.
2. A universal unity of spirit pervades the universe, the essence of which includes the nature of God and the souls of men.
3. Time, space, and matter are all illusory, therefore ignorant of good, with sin being a figment of the mind and not a state of conduct.

Jesus was interrogated by the Jewish leaders of his day, who demanded to know the authority by which he healed and forgave sins (John 5). Christ did not lure them down the road of speculative spiritual introspection. Instead, he offered himself and his words as the basis for determining the validity of his actions.

Jesus did not dispel their skepticism by suggesting they sit by a riverbank and think deep thoughts about the cosmos. "He that heareth [exercises objective mental comprehension] my word [which contain guiding spiritual truth], and believeth [compelling the intellect by faith] on him that hath sent me, hath everlasting life," Jesus declared (John 5:24).

Instead of dispensing enlightenment, Jesus offers the light of his life. The apostle John declared that Jesus is "the true Light, which lighteth every man" (John 1:9).

Why then do some men prefer the glimmer of a self-described state of higher consciousness to the penetrating glare of moral purity offered by the Lord? John tells us "that light is come into the world, and men loved darkness rather than light, because their deeds were evil" (3:19)

At last, we see the real reason behind the mystic's search for spiritual illumination. It is not truly the radiance of God he seeks but shelter from the penetrating searchlight of God's Holy Spirit. And the enlightenment upon which he stumbles is the false glow of one whom the Bible depicts as a deceiving "angel of light"—the devil (2 Corinthians 11:14).

SOURCES: John Ankerberg and John Weldon, *Encyclopedia of New Age Beliefs* (Eugene, Oreg.: Harvest House, 1996); Jonathan Z. Smith, ed., *The HarperCollins Dictionary of Religion* (San Francisco: HarperSanFrancisco, 1995).

ESALEN INSTITUTE

This holistic retreat center on the California coast helped give birth to the "human potential movement."

OVERVIEW: Hot tubs overlooking the Pacific Ocean. Encounter groups that sometimes featured drugs and sex. Everything about the Esalen Institute shouted the hippie hedonism of California in the swinging 1960s, which is where and when this organization was founded.

But even though it is small, this center had a profound influence on the shape and direction of twentieth century spirituality in America and around the world. And it is still going strong, celebrating its fortieth anniversary in 2002.

As writer Bob Morris said after a 1994 visit to the center, "Esalen is the Taj Mahal of group therapy and the Emerald City of massage and bodywork. It was the first big launching pad of the great American movement inward that began in the sixties."

Blending Psychology and Spirituality

Every year thousands of people pass through the gates of Esalen Institute to attend its hundreds of seminar offerings, wander through its groves, and give vent to whatever suppressed feelings haunt their psyches.

Founded in 1962 by Michael Murphy and Richard Price, Esalen Institute is one of the granddaddies of the so-called human potential movement. At its isolated location on Big Sur coastal shores, some of the early experiments with encounter groups and sensitivity training first surfaced.

Though Esalen's goals purport to emphasize psychological self-help, religious overtones are apparent to students of mystical thought.

Murphy founded Esalen (its name comes from the local Indian tribe) after studying at an *ashram* in India. His stated goal was to evoke Eastern-style spirituality by allowing participants to vent their true emotions in "the here and now . . . not to adjust, but to transcend."

In the process those who attend Esalen sessions may find themselves seated, facing a naked stranger, and sensuously stroking his or her body. This practice, known as "bodywork," is designed to stimulate self-awareness in attendees, who are also encouraged to pretend they are animals in distress or to simulate the sounds of lovemaking.

Sometimes those who attend Esalen sessions are made to stare at white squares until they see visions. Guided imagery and visualization exercise, gestalt therapy, and sensory awakening are a few of the seminars offered. The hot baths, which initiated members may attend in the nude, were once considered a rite of passage into a new life. (The age of AIDS led many participants to emphasize safe bathing.)

A World Force?

How could a small and isolated retreat center become a force that one former president of the American Psychological Association once called "the most important educational institute in the world"?

In part, that's due to the center's commitment to understanding the work of the twentieth century's most innovative thinkers, including Aldous Huxley, Alan Watts, Arnold Toynbee, Fritz Perls, B. F. Skinner, and Episcopal bishop James Pike.

These intellectual luminaries didn't always see eye-to-eye, but according to an Esalen catalog, their "complementary perspectives . . . inform Esalen's thinking and purposes today . . . and push us toward further discoveries."

In 1983 the Esalen Institute sponsored a Soviet-American satellite linkup with cooperation from the Soviet government and Academy of Sciences. In an attempt to develop relationships that would survive stressful political times, like-minded people in both countries shared—and still do—their common interests in meeting human needs through the development of paranormal perception, stress management, and healing.

Today Esalen continues to offer cutting-edge seminars, like "Techno-Pagans at the End of History: Psychedelics, the Internet, Virtual Reality and You." But participants aren't able to log on at the center, which shuns electronics and TVs so participants can soak in the hot tubs, gaze at the ocean, and discover their inner selves. According to Esalen, three hundred thousand people have done so over forty years, to indulge in the "Olympics of the body, mind, and spirit, committing themselves not so much to 'stronger, faster, highter' as to deeper, richer, more enduring."

SOURCES: Laura Bly, "Muddied Not Bowed, Esalen Still a Free Spirit," *USA Today*, 29 May 1998, D2; *The Esalen Catalog—25th Anniversary: The Early Years* (Big Sur, Calif.: Esalen Institute, 1987); John Garabedian and Orde Coombs, *Eastern Religions in the Electric Age* (New York: Grosset and Dunlap, 1969); David Landau, "Citizen Diplomacy," *New Age Journal* (January 1984): 35–38; George Leonard, "First Visit to Esalen: February 1965," 6–9; Richard Leviton, "Job's Body," *East West Journal* (January 1988): 61; Bob Morris, "Mind Games," *Vogue*, February 1994, 136–140; Connie Zweig, "Esalen's Soviet-American Exchange Program," *New Realities*, 6.

ACCESS: www.esalen.org; (408) 667-3000

See also Human Potential Movement.

EST

Werner Erhard

A consciousness guru or a con man? People can't agree about Erhard and his controversial techniques.

You and I possess within ourselves, at every moment of our lives, under all circumstances, the power to transform the quality of our lives.
WERNER ERHARD, EST TRAINING BROCHURE

FOUNDER: Jack Rosenberg; born September 5, 1935, in Philadelphia; Renamed Werner Erhard. The group was officially launched in 1971. In 1985 Erhard announced the burial of est and the birth of The Forum.

TEXT: Werner Erhard's words, "What is, is."

APPEAL: Those with a poor self-image learn to assert themselves by ignoring reality. For some it is another "trip" to experience, along with involvement in other consciousness-raising groups. People whose lives seem meaningless or who have experienced rejection and depression may view est as a quick, cheap form of psychotherapy. The appeal of The Forum is to those who are—or would like to be—upwardly mobile. The Forum also appeals to those who seek a vague and undemanding spirituality that combines with their own materialistic interests, which is a common characteristic of many cults.

OVERVIEW: "Obviously, the truth is what's so. Not so obviously, it's also so what." If that sounds like a conundrum, don't be fooled by the apparently harmless confusion of the statement.

Behind these words of Werner Erhard lies a system of religious philosophy rooted in Mind Dynamics, yoga, Silva mind control, gestalt psychology, Dale Carnegie, Subud, and most importantly, Zen Buddhism and Scientology.

Those who participated in Erhard's est training during the 1970s and 1980s were told they were "perfect . . . gods who have created their own world." This teaching led Erhard to conclude, "How do I know I'm not the reincarnation of Jesus Christ?"

Erhard's training is no longer offered under the *est* label. But Erhard has demonstrated an unusual ability to spring back from repeated defeats, and his basic principles are still promoted in new disguises.

Getting It and Selling It

Born Jack Rosenberg in 1935, Erhard left a wife and four kids in his early twenties. While traveling on a plane, he met a woman named Ellen who would become his second wife. (Ellen filed for divorce in 1984, citing Erhard's persistent adultery as the grounds.)

He happened to be reading an article entitled "The Men Who Made the New Germany." His longtime enchantment with the German nihilistic philosopher Nietzshe (who believed in a super race, the foundation of Hitler's political approach) compelled Erhard to choose a new identity with a German name. *Werner* came from Werner Heisenberg (not Werner Von Braun, as est literature claims) and *Erhard* from Ludwig Erhard.

In the company of friend Bill Thaw, he explored his interest in a succession of Eastern religions and mind-science cults. Finally (according to Thaw), Erhard read a book entitled *est: The Steersman Handbook*. The author, L. Clark Stevens, used the abbreviation *est* to denote "electronic social transformation."

Erhard borrowed the term and redubbed it Erhard Seminars Training—est (always lowercase) for short. While driving his wife's Mustang one day, he experienced a Damascus-road-type enlightenment. Erhard says he "got it," and est became the vehicle for selling "it."

Overcoming Obstacles

In the Zen Buddhist tradition of subjective, relative, intuitive enlightenment, no one in est (including Erhard) really knows what "it" is. But the goal of getting "it" is to conclude that there is nothing to get. In est there is no objective reality, only experience. Being is said to be more important than doing.

Logical thinking is forbidden, and terminology is twisted. "Wrong is actually a version of right. If you're always wrong, you're right," est declares.

On the surface such concepts might not make much sense. But est grew in popularity regardless, thanks in part to the endorsement of celebrities like singer-composer John Denver, an est advocate who was one of the most popular musicians of the seventies.

Denver extolled Erhard's view of life in his song "Looking for Space." ("If there's an answer, it's just that it's just that way.") "Seek and you shall find," Jesus said. In contrast, Erhard declares, "What isn't, isn't. You can't put it together . . . what you have to do is experience it being together."

Such doublespeak and intellectual dishonesty has been more than a clever way to dispose of the definitions used in normal language. It has also been an elaborate fund-raising vehicle ($16 million per year) and a public extension of Erhard's ego-oriented goal to remake the world. It all began when interested parties plunked down $250 to join 249 other people for two weekends of group-therapy encounter sessions, totaling sixty hours.

Inductees were initially greeted with smiles and hugs. But all that changed quickly once the hotel room doors were closed to begin the first fifteen to eighteen-hour period. Pens, papers, watches, tape recorders, and cigarettes had to be left outside. Participants needed to ascertain that they had not eaten or drunk too much before entering, since they were only allowed one bathroom break from start till finish (unless they had a doctor's signed statement indicating physical necessity). Later, numerous trips to the restroom were permitted.

An est seminar was a calculated process of breaking down the inductee's personality and then rebuilding it by harassment and intimidation.

A trainer began immediately to abuse the audience verbally with repeated obscenities. All ego defenses were ridiculed by means of demeaning epithets hurled at anyone who resisted the tactics of the trainer.

Eyewitnesses reported that scores of people urinated, defecated, convulsed, sobbed, screamed, and vomited (in specially provided silver-colored est bags). The only relief came in the form of "meditation practices" (to acquire an altered state of consciousness) and exercises of lying on the floor to "find one's space." The latter practice had its relaxing effect quickly ended by the trainer, who proceeded to create feelings of fear and danger, causing some to respond hysterically.

After three days of such psycho-manipulative and hemorrhoid-causing activity, participants were expected to "get it" on the fourth day. What they got was not an improved self-image but a totally transformed perception of reality consistent with a Buddhist/occult view of the universe.

"You are part of every atom in the world, and every atom is part of you," estians were encouraged to affirm. This all-is-one, merging-of-consciousness doctrine of Eastern thought is what led most est graduates to reject all other belief systems. After all, to know est is to know *you* are God.

Stuck on the Self

The elementary student of psychology can easily recognize est's potential for creating psychosis. By the confrontational stripping away of coping mechanisms, some emotionally unstable individuals can be left in a dangerous, vulnerable condition.

Even more serious to consider is the possibility that evil powers may take advantage of such a psychologically defenseless state to precipitate a demonic invasion. At the very least, the destruction of one's concept of self-worth may result in the violent release of suppressed traumas. Without an understanding of God's love, healing, and forgiveness to fill this void, the est participant can only deal with such feeling by retreating from reality and adopting a mystical view of life as an illusion.

In est Christ's commands to "love your enemies" (Luke 6:27) are replaced with a self-centered approach to life. Since there is no God but one's own ego, moral conduct is judged according to self-serving satisfaction. Est doesn't tell what not to do. It is understood that those who experience their "space" are practicing perfection, no matter what their moral beliefs may be.

What an estian graduate decides is good for himself is good. With no gods to worship, some est graduates adulate Erhard to a point of near perfection. His word is *the* word. What they do with guilt is another matter. No reinterpretation of reality can completely assuage one's conscience. That takes much more than four days locked in a hotel room, for it requires the shed blood of Jesus Christ (Hebrews 9:22).

Est's moral relativism was also displayed in an effort called the Hunger Project, which was founded by Erhard in 1977.

"I take responsibility for ending starvation within twenty years," he said. But unlike traditional relief and development agencies that actually give people food and train them how to grow it, the Hunger Project tried to end hunger by imagining away.

"The Hunger Project is not about solutions," said Erhard. "It's not about fixing up the project. It's not about anybody's good idea. The Hunger Project is about creating a context—creating the end of hunger as an idea whose time has come."

This sounded good, but behind all the mumbo jumbo was an empty promise. With the help of John Denver and other celebrities, the effort raised nearly $40 million but did little of value in the real world of starving people.

Moving On

By 1985 Erhard had shelved est in favor of his new baby, The Forum, which attempted to market his ideas to lucrative business customers. According to *Newsweek*, "Est was about 'getting it together,' The Forum is about 'making it happen.' "

An outgrowth of some of Erhard's satellite TV broadcasts, The Forum foregoes the abusive language of the intense est sessions and emphasizes "dialogue" between leader and participants.

The Forum seminars, stretched over two weekends and one evening, involve dialogue on virtually any subject. While the appeal of Forum seminars is to upwardly mobile yuppies (or those who would like to be), the latent mysticism of est still permeates the seminars.

Forum spokesmen say that the key element in the seminars is "being," which, they claim, is critical to motivating oneself and one's employees. No one gives a clear definition of what "being" is, and one spokesman happily admits that it is unexplainable, even though "being" is the "magic" of Forum.

This combination of business drive with vague mysticism is not unusual in cults today. Neither is the insistence of Erhard—and dozens of other propagators of cults—that one's logical capacities must be laid aside.

By the early nineties Erhard's enterprises were poised for global growth, but then a series of new controversies arose. Three lawsuits were filed against Erhard for wrongful discharge, wrongful death, and fraud. In addition, his daughters charged Erhard with raping them—a charge that was broadcast on an edition of the CBS newsmagazine *60 Minutes.*

In an age when image triumphs over substance, no wonder cults that teach "trust your feelings, not your mind" are popular. We must remember that, though logic has limits, we are called as children of God to love God with our minds.

CHRISTIAN CRITIQUE: Est compels people to get "it," though no one, including Erhard, can define precisely what "it" is.

The est manual fails to clarify matters: "The purpose of est training is to transform your ability to experience living so that the situations you have been trying to change . . . just clear up in the process of life itself." Life is not to be understood (understanding is irrelevant) but rather experienced.

Love, concern, compassion, sorrow, and other Christian and human values are considered illusions in the world of est. The Hunger Project proposed eliminating world famine by 1997, but this laudable goal was not supported by feeding the hungry but by simply declaring that "the end of hunger is an idea whose time has come."

Man is his own god, the center of the universe. Sin does not exist, and all personal conduct is justified by one's own perfection. As in Zen, reality is a matter of perception, not objectivity.

SOURCES: *Circus,* February 1976, 45; *Eternity,* March 1986, 55; "The Fuhrer over est," *New Times,* 36–52; David Gelman et al., "The Sorrows of Werner," *Time,* 18 February 1991, 72; Carol Giambalvo and Robert Burrows, "The Hunger Project Inside Out," *SCP Journal* 8 no. 1, 35–45; Walter Martin, *The New Cults* (Santa Ana, Calif.: Vision House, 1980), 105–141; *Newsweek,* 9 May 1977, 95; Ibid., 28 August 1978, 50; Ibid., 15 June 1981, 18–21; Ibid., 1 April 1985, 15; *SCP Newsletter,* March 1976, 2, no. 3; *Time,* 7 June 1976, 53; "Werner Erhard Flees in the Wake of Tax Liens and Child Abuse Allegations," *Christian Research Journal* (summer 1991): 5.

ACCESS: With a shift of emphasis toward The Forum, est centers are no longer operational.

See also The Forum and Silva International.

FALUN GONG

Persecuted in their homeland, members of this Chinese meditation group
are spreading throughout the world.

FOUNDER: Li Hongzhi, a former grain clerk who studied Buddhism and
Taoism and left his native China in 1996.

TEXT: Li has written books about Falun Gong, but reading them isn't a prerequisite for practicing the exercises.

SYMBOL: Falun Gong uses a Buddhist symbol that is similar to the Nazi
swastika but predates Hitler's use of that symbol. The swastika is surrounded by
Tai Chi symbols that express Falun Gong's debts to that ancient Asian faith.

OVERVIEW: Supporters say Falun Gong has more than 100 million adherents worldwide, including 70 million in China. But the Chinese government
says the actual number is closer to a few million.

How could these estimates be so different? Because China has declared war
on Falun Gong's members, who mix aspects of two ancient Asian religions—
Buddhism and Taoism—to create a new and increasingly popular faith. Communist authorities express concern over its leader's belief in aliens that inhabit
the earth and over his ability to give followers a "celestial eye" with supernatural powers. Such teachings have so captivated the Chinese masses that at least
fourteen imprisoned devotees of Falun Gong committed suicide to protest government persecution of the movement.

Humble Beginnings

Li Hongzhi worked as a Chinese grain clerk. In his spare time he studied Buddhism and Taoism. Over the years he developed his own hybrid faith which he
called Falun Gong, which means "Law of the Wheel Breathing Exercise."

The group doesn't emphasize doctrine but promotes five exercises—three
of which involve bodily movement and two of which involve prolonged periods of silence and inaction.

A *Time* magazine writer described Falun Gong (which is also called Falun
Dafa) as "a cocktail of religious beliefs and physical exercises aimed at leading
its practitioners to enlightenment."

Li made his faith public in 1992, and it immediately struck a cord with the
Chinese people, hundreds of whom could be seen in parks and public squares
practicing the group's trademark exercise, which is called "Buddha Showing
the Thousand Hands." The exercise consists of slow, meditative movements using the hands and arms and is designed to stretch both the body and the mind.

Li claims his group has no political aspirations. But in 1999 more than ten thousand Falun Gong came together in an area outside a residential compound for Chinese officials. The group members were protesting a plan by the government to label them a cult.

The gathering backfired. When officials saw the huge numbers of people Falun Gong could gather, they reacted by banning the group and its "evil thinking." They clamped down on the group hard, destroying millions of copies of its books and materials and interrogating many thousands of its followers. Thousands were imprisoned in Chinese labor camps, where hundreds died in captivity.

Li, who left China in 1996 and now lives in New York, defends the movement he founded. "I am just teaching people how to practice cultivation."

But Sophie Xiao, a Chinese member of the group, believes she knows why officials are so worried. As she told *Time* magazine: "I smile all the time, have no trouble in my life anymore. It changes you. You let go of a lot of human desires and become very peaceful, and then you don't fear anything. That's probably what the Chinese government is afraid of."

In addition to labeling the group a dangerous "cult," the government has made these claims about the group: it brainwashes its members; it has turned Communist officials into cult members in order to learn state secrets; and some members refuse to take any medications, leading to cases of paranoia, hallucinations, and suicides.

Group followers deny all such charges, and the government crackdown has generated strong international criticism. In 2001 members attempted group suicides at China's Tiananmen Square—a tactic that the government noted in its campaign to harass and ridicule the group. And in 2002 Falun Gong members in the United States attempted to use U.S. courts to bring lawsuits against Chinese officials visiting the United States.

Quiet at Home, Growing Worldwide

In China the government crackdown has ended Falun Gong's large public demonstrations. In addition, persecution and harassment have made it difficult to tell how many faithful devotees remain. But elsewhere in the world, the group is growing rapidly. People seem to like the fact that it takes some of the best aspects of Buddhism and Taoism without requiring strict adherence to these faiths' rules and regulations.

According to spokesperson Caroline Lam of Sydney, Australia, whose comments appear on one of the many Web sites dedicated to the group, "Falun Dafa is not a cult and not a religion and not a sect. There is no leader, there is no form of worship or rituals. Falun Dafa is not involved with politics or against any government."

In addition, at a time when growing numbers of people around the world are aware of the need for greater physical health and the connections between physical and spiritual well-being, the Falun Gong exercises seem practical and helpful.

CHRISTIAN CRITIQUE: In the world of alternative spirituality it is rare to find a movement that stirs political passions the way Falun Gong does. Some Christians, seeking a foothold in China's culture and the favor of the Communist regime, have sided with the Peking government's virulent opposition to Falun Gong. But such religiopolitical alliances are dangerous to the integrity of Christianity. Any official condemnation of a particular belief that Christians find repugnant could become a two-edged sword that later swings in the direction of biblical beliefs. Christians are on more firm ground if they oppose Falun Gong on theological rather than social grounds. Its real danger is the spiritual seduction of thousands by teaching a variant of godless Buddhism that promises unattainable organic cures by physical posturing. Worse yet, Falun Gong has addressed the spiritual vacuum in China with an empty offer of enlightenment and diverted the attention of many who might have turned to the gospel of Jesus Christ as an answer.

The fanatical devotion of Falun's members illustrates how dangerous mind control groups are, and even non-Christians have reason to fear what unthinkable actions such adherents might take if pressured by their leaders. The requirements of extended "stillness" and silence turn devotees inward, not outward to meet the needs of their neighbors. Falun is one of the most narcissistic of all contemporary movements, and its ethic of withdrawal from remedial social action is in sharp contrast to Christianity's message of feeding the hungry and clothing the poor. The worst danger may lie in exercises which claim to "penetrate the two cosmic extremes" to meld the cosmos and the body, and "Strengthening Supernormal Powers," originally a secret exercise and now declassified, that evokes paranormal abilities.

SOURCES: Matthew Forney, "How China Beat Down Falun Gong," *Time*, 2 July 2001, 48; "Inside the Falun Gong," *Time*, 9 August 1999, 48; "Mao Versus the Mystic," *Newsweek*, 9 August 1999, 43; Terry McCarthy, "Inside the Falun Gong," *Time*, 9 August 1999, 48.

ACCESS: One of the many Web sites that follows the group is www.religioustolerance.org/falungong.htm.

THE FAMILY

Family of Love; The Children of God

This group, formed during the Jesus movement, has changed its name
and address but not its faulty theology.

FOUNDER: David Brandt Berg, born February 18, 1919. The Children of
God (COG) coalesced into a viable organization circa 1970.

TEXT: The Bible, but more prominently the periodic "MO letters," rambling
discourses by which Berg communicated with his followers. Most letters had
strong sexual overtones and artwork and had titles like "Sex Works!" and
"Come on, Ma! Burn Your Bra!" Other letters discussed matters of doctrine and
railed against the "Systemites"—anyone not in agreement with the COG ideals.

APPEAL: In the seventies, COG recruiters concentrated on lonely young
people who were disenchanted with the establishment's economic or religious
institutions. Bible verses were quoted out of context. The group promoted a
positive image of happiness and brotherhood to suggest the COG were truly
dedicated Christians. Recruits were bombarded with threats that if they ever
left the group, they would become part of a condemned satanic system and
would never again have a chance to faithfully serve God.

Today the group seeks to portray itself as a Christian missionary group that
is more dedicated to Christ than mainstream churches. But these claims are deceptive at best.

OVERVIEW: "They went out from us, but they were not of us." The Apostle
John's appraisal of first-century heretics (1 John 2:19) might well describe how
early Jesus movement pioneers felt about the Children of God, an eccentric
group that has since changed its name to Family of Love and later The Family in an
effort to avoid identification with the bad publicity attached to the COG image.

Founded by David "Moses" Berg in the heyday of the Jesus movement, the
controversial group claimed to have ten thousand members in seventy-two
countries in 1981.

Berg died in 1995, and today a much smaller group, headquartered in Washington, D.C., claims it has reformed its beliefs and practices. But far more must
be done before this group is granted the orthodox Christian label it so desperately desires.

Radical Origins

David Berg was the son of a devout Christian and Missionary Alliance couple.
His father, Hjalmer, pastored and taught at a Christian college. Virginia, his
mother, was a radio evangelist.

David married Jane Berg in 1944 and entered Christian service as an evangelist. He gradually soured on organized religion and began to associate with fringe religionist O. L. Jaguers and TV evangelist Fred Jordan.

During the earlier years of the West Coast Jesus revolution, Berg joined his mother in directing a "Teen Challenge" coffeehouse. It was there that his radicalized, antiestablishment gospel took root among religiously zealous hippies, resulting in a group originally called Teens for Christ.

In August 1968 Berg's public declaration, "The War on the System," was printed in the Huntington Beach newspaper. In it he declared his "war on the system—the educational system, the church system, the parental system."

In 1969 Berg left the coffeehouse and with about fifty followers headed on a trek to Arizona, which he later described as a time analogous to Israel's wanderings in the wilderness. The ragtag group took organized form with members assuming new biblical names. Twelve groups were formed, named, and patterned after Israel's twelve tribes.

Maria, a Tucson church secretary, joined the movement and later was elevated to the status of Berg's mistress. Jane was nicknamed "Mother Eve" and was allowed certain sleeping "rights" with David. (Eventually she left the cult.)

The group couldn't return to California because Berg had twice "prophesied" the exact date the entire wicked state would slide into the ocean. Their meandering ended when Fred Jordan invited them to settle on his Texas Soul Clinic Missionary Ranch.

Heresy and Controversy

When the first wave of controversy hit the COG with charges of kidnapping and brainwashing, Fred Jordan kicked them out. By this time the COG numbered at least two thousand.

A subsidiary called THANK COG (consisting of favorably disposed parents of COG members) was activated to counter the charges of FREE COG parents, who claimed their offspring were unfairly controlled by Berg.

Communal organizations were divided into colonies. To communicate with his increasingly fragmented followers, Berg hit upon the concept of circulating periodic newsletters that came to be called "MO letters," which he continued after he withdrew from the daily operation of the group in the early 1970s.

The rambling and grammatically shabby content of Berg's epistles evolved into what were considered divinely commissioned pronouncements. MO letters were said to be God's inspired word for today, far superior to what was written in the Bible thousands of years ago. Letters were categorized according to the ranks of insiders who had access to them.

Though no official systematic theology was promulgated, a philosophical and methodological structure did emerge. A pyramid system of leadership (with Berg at the apex) placed "babes" (new converts) at the bottom and ensured that Berg's "Royal Family" (members of his immediate family and a few select others) remained in total control.

As an autocratic messiah, Berg claimed to have direct communication with God—the Lord's "Moses" for today. His word was unquestioned, and even "murmuring" against his views was considered a mortal sin.

Commune members languished in unsanitary quarters, were sometimes refused medical treatment, and were kept on a subsistence diet of food "procured" from local supermarkets. The "Revolutionary Contract" they signed turned over all possessions to the COG, and most contacts with past friends and family were abruptly severed unless such individuals could be considered sources of revenue for the group.

No member was ever left alone. Parents were hated and despised along with the corrupt political system of the United States. (At one point Berg prophesied that the comet Kahoutek would collide with earth and destroy America.)

Daily hours not spent pouring over MO letters were dedicated to "litnessing"—evangelizing by literature distribution. Litnessing was also a primary source of cult income, with strict quotas set as a barometer of fervency for the cause. (The group's Web site now claims that the group has distributed more than 850 million pieces of literature, 1.4 million videos, and 8 million audiotapes.)

The other basic source of income came through a bizarre form of religious prostitution, called "FFing" ("flirty fishing") in COG parlance. Female members were encouraged to offer their bodies as an inducement for men to join the organization, though the "fish" were expected to pay for such favors.

Children conceived through FFing were called "Jesus babes." (Unwed mothers were euphemistically referred to as "widows.") Husbands were admonished to offer their wives as a symbol of their devotion to the cause. If venereal disease was contracted, it was seen as a sign of one's willingness to suffer for the cause of Christ. Berg admitted he himself was afflicted with it.

Berg even asserted that Jesus practiced sexual intercourse with Mary and Martha and deliberately contracted venereal disease to illustrate his identification with human infirmities.

A Sex-Obsessed Cult

Sex was a central theme of the salacious MO letters. Nothing was forbidden. Even homosexuality and sodomy, once considered taboo, were legitimized "within the limits of the love of God." Topless bathing was promoted, girls were admonished not to wear undergarments, and most went braless.

According to David Berg's daughter Deborah, who later left the group and wrote a book about its errors, the COG "perpetuates all forms of adultery, fornication, deception, sodomy, homosexuality and lesbianism, child sex, adult/child relations, and teaches as doctrine incest."

A marriage relationship (approved of first by colony leaders) consisted of simply going to live with the chosen partner—legal civil ceremonies were seen as part of "Babylon's" corrupt system. Lesbianism and incest were considered particularly desirable.

Berg's system of sexual philosophy also included the following: wife-swapping, justified by the "all things common" passage of Acts 2:44; punishing female members by requiring them to masturbate before male observers; fondling children and sleeping with them in the nude; and the belief that God had intercourse with Mary to procreate Jesus! "God is in the business of breaking up families . . . salvation sets us free from the curse of clothing and the shame of nakedness," Berg wrote.

"God is a pimp," he blasphemously declared. "Experience a spiritual orgasm by being filled with the Spirit." When questioned about his personal sexual excesses, Berg argued that he was God's King David and that, like his namesake, his own promiscuity had been condoned by the Almighty.

The most startling aspect of Berg's sexual obsession was his claim to indulge in succubus relationships—sexual intercourse with spirit beings whom he called "goddesses." In fact, Berg had a long history of flirtation with the occult. He said that "spiritual counselors" visited him regularly and even entered his body to speak through his mouth. One of them, Abrahim, was supposedly a gypsy king who had been dead for over a thousand years. Berg was also involved in palmistry, fortune-telling, and astrology. "Spiritualistic churches are not so bad after all," he concluded.

Prophecies and Profanities

In Berg's eyes the COG were the 144,000 of Revelation 7 and 14, the restored Israel. He prophesied that after the United States fell to Communism, the Antichrist would briefly reign until Satan took over. The majority of professing Christians would take the mark of the beast, but the COG would remain the Lord's faithful.

In spite of his unimpressive record of past prophecies (the comet Kahoutek failed to destroy America), the end, according to Berg, was supposed to come in 1993. Berg died in 1995, and America was still going strong.

Due to the group's unfavorable reputation in the United States, the COG moved its international headquarters to Zurich, Switzerland. Berg also applied for Israeli citizenship but eventually turned violently anti-Semitic. He even courted the favor of Libya's Muammar Qaddafi and said about Jews, "Devils incarnate . . . if I had a gun I'd shoot them myself!"

One bulletin published by a parents' organization reported that Berg, sheltered by Qaddafi, had organized an international call-girl ring. The bulletin also stated that many COG members lived as vagabonds in West Germany.

In Britain officials investigated the COG solicitations for money, finding leaflets that amounted to "instruction in prostitution" for COG girls "working in 'escort' agencies in London." Called Heaven's Magic in the Philippines, COG members are making their presence felt in that country.

Over the years Berg's coarse language (MO letters were spiced with four-letter expletives) and immoral philosophy finally took their toll. Defectors abound, including members of his immediate family and even Barbara Cane (Queen Rachel), who was Berg's heir apparent.

Defections and Dissolution

Berg's own wife and children left the cult. His son Paul leapt to his death in the Swiss Alps in 1973, no longer able to cope with the bizarre teachings and abusive authority of his father.

Berg's daughter Deborah Berg Davis eventually left with her husband, Bill. In 1972 her father gave her the title of Queen, but when she refused his sexual advances, she was denounced, and her sister, Faithy, succeeded her. Deborah left in 1978 after her husband was excommunicated. In 1984 Deborah, who now professes orthodox Christianity, published a book exposing the COG's secret cult practices. Her husband, Bill, stated that the COG "preached the gospel of rebellion. . . . We would teach them . . . how to tell your parents you hate them, how to rebel against the government, how to fight the 'System.'"

Throughout the nineties scandals continued to rock the group even as it sought to improve its public image by working with the news media. The group sang at a 1992 Christmas event at the White House and created a top-notch Web site that makes the group look clean-cut and normal.

In 1993 police in Argentina raided the group's offices there, where they took custody of three hundred minors, confiscated many pornographic videos, and charged adult members with sodomy, involuntary servitude, and kidnapping.

Throughout the nineties, articles in both Christian and secular publications routinely declared that despite the group's claims, it remained heretical and destructive. The Family's promotional materials and Web site give no hint of its unsavory past. Retooled as the Fellowship of Independent Missionary Communities, its emphasis is now on providing comfort to the needy through their twelve thousand full-time and associate adult volunteer members working out of more than fourteen hundred centers or communities situated in over one hundred countries. They still continue the practice of maintaining a cooperative lifestyle, sharing material possessions and resources.

CHRISTIAN CRITIQUE: Berg wanted to start a revolution that would "Pull down, destroy, and throw out the old order." He said mankind is in the last generation, and the United States is the "great prostitute that sits on many waters" and the "Babylon" of Revelation.

He claimed that only the COG would remain true to God, escaping the world's impending doom to eventually rule the earth as an elitist group through whom God's promises would be fulfilled.

Today we can see these claims as the fruit of a fanciful mind that twisted scripture and denied key Christian doctrines.

Berg denied the Trinity. But on other occasions he promoted a Father, Mother, and Son conglomerate. The Holy Spirit, "Holy Queen of Love," was portrayed as a half-naked woman. Christ was declared to be a created being, in a misinterpretation of Revelation 3:14.

Scriptural injunctions against consulting familiar spirits were ignored (Deuteronomy 18:9-14; Jeremiah 14:14) by communicating with what Berg calls "God's witches." He also denied God's promises of blessings to the Jews (Acts 2:18-26; Romans 9:4-5), and he even cursed them.

By encouraging fornication, polygamy, incest, and adultery, Berg stood in opposition to the biblical view of sex in marriage as expressed by Paul in Hebrews 13:4 and Ephesians 5. In the words of anticult researcher Jack Sparks, Berg "managed to transform a gigantic personal temper tantrum against authority into a worldwide movement."

Today doctrinal errors still abound, including the belief in communicating with the departed spirits of the dead and isolated communalism in the name of "forsaking of the vain pursuit of material wealth, as well as all other worldly and materialistic ambitions and endeavors."

SOURCES: "Children of Children of God," *Eternity*, July-August 1984, 24; "Children of God Revamp Image, Face Renewed Opposition," *Christian Research Journal* (fall 1993): 5–6; *Christianity Today*, 28 February 1977, 19–23; Ibid., 25 February 1980, 40–41; Deborah (Linda Berg) Davis, *The Children of God: The Inside Story* (Grand Rapids, Mich.: Zondervan, 1984); *Encyclopedia Britannica*, 15th ed, s.v. "Family of Love"; Ronald Enroth, *Youth Brainwashing and the Extremist Cults* (Grand Rapids, Mich.: Zondervan, 1977); Anthony Erickson, "Same Candy Bar, Different Wrapper: A 'New' COG Returns to the United States," *Cornerstone*, 23, no. 104, 33–36; "Ex-Children of God 'Queen' Tells Story," *Eternity*, January 1983, 10; *Fundamentalist Journal* (October 1985): 22; Bob Larson, *Strange Cults in America* (Wheaton, Ill.: Tyndale, 1986), 70–71; Water Martin, *The New Cults* (Santa Ana, Calif.: Vision House, 1980); Joe Maxwell, "Have Children of God Cleaned Up Their Act?" *Christianity Today*, 14 December 1992, 42–43; Eric Pement, "Children of God Still Active," *Cornerstone*, 30; Ibid., "Built on a Lie," *Cornerstone*, 4; Jack Sparks, *The Mindbenders* (Nashville: Thomas Nelson, 1977).

ACCESS: The Family, 2020 Pennsylvania Ave., Suite 102, Washington, DC 20006-1846; www.thefamily.org/family

THE FARM

Stephen Gaskin

Hippies from San Francisco drove to rural Tennessee to establish one of the twentieth century's most famous communes.

FOUNDER: Stephen Gaskin

OVERVIEW: When a convoy of hippies came to Tennessee, they stopped in a rural backwoods area better known for its historic ties to the Ku Klux Klan than any support for the hippies' utopian beliefs.

Still, this is where a group of psychedelic pilgrims founded The Farm, one of the best known and most enduring of the many communes that emerged from the lifestyle experimentation of the 1960s and 1970s.

Some folks in the surrounding area viewed this commune with alarm. Others begrudgingly bestowed kudos for its self-sufficiency and apparent industriousness. But few really understood the historical facts concerning The Farm or comprehended the teachings and practices of its founder and leader, Stephen Gaskin.

Once supporting up to fifteen hundred members, The Farm now has closer to three hundred. Its many programs include a school, health clinic, recording studio, and computerized typesetting facilities for a publishing company.

The Farm proudly promotes its Bronx, New York, voluntary ambulance crew (which was covered in *People* magazine and the *Wall Street Journal*) and its relief organization, PLENTY, which dispatches members to provide aid for Third World countries.

In 1992 Gaskin (who was then fifty-seven) and the group showed their age by starting a holistic retirement community called Rocinante, which is named after Don Quixote's horse.

But Gaskin and his followers are far from being the respectable, mainstream group their publicity materials suggest, even though their image makeover has resulted in them being granted tax-exempt monasterial status by the U.S. government.

From San Francisco to the South

In the psychedelic sixties Stephen Gaskin was an assistant to S. I. Hayakawa at San Francisco State College. He dropped out to drop acid and eventually became a local guru celebrity.

Gaskin held Monday night counterculture rap sessions, attended by as many as two thousand supporters. He expounded at length upon revelations from his drug experiences, which were enhanced through his studies in a variety of occult and Eastern practices.

In the fall of 1971 he headed a ragtag caravan of sixty school buses carrying his 250 flower children. After meandering across the United States, they settled fifteen hundred miles away on roughly seventeen hundred acres of farmland near Summertown, Tennessee, sixty-five miles south of Nashville.

The Farm was once recognized as one of the few American communes to have achieved long-term success. In the mid-1980s, however, The Farm was de-collectivized. Each member is now a self-supporting, dues-paying member, although they still help each other and contribute part of their earnings to the land payments.

In the early days commune members lived a carefree life in squalid conditions and frolicked in the effects of peyote, psilocybin, mushrooms, and marijuana (all of which Gaskin proclaimed to be sacraments).

The Farm was eventually raided by police, and in spite of legal appeals all the way to the Supreme Court, Gaskin and three fellow members each spent a year in prison.

Group marriages with full sexual privileges were tried (with Gaskin once again leading the way), but that experiment also proved somewhat unsuccessful. Now, nuclear families are the rule, and members are, as in the past, complete vegetarians who wear no leather (this would harm animals) and do not eat dairy products.

Visitors to The Farm—there are about ten thousand each year—must obey the no hunting, no smoking, and no drinking rules in this idyllic spot that is a veritable nature preserve.

A Stoned Spiritual Messenger?

Though monogamy reigns and marijuana is no longer a Farm crop (members freely admit many of them still toke up frequently), Gaskin has not abandoned his spiritual mission.

Ex-members accuse him of openly declaring to be a messenger from God. Mystical religious experiences are encouraged, along with a mixture of beliefs ranging from tantra (ritualistic sex), karma, and mantras, to *bodhisattvas* (incarnations of God in Buddhism), the latter fitting nicely into Gaskin's claims of spiritual leadership.

His writings declare that Jesus and Buddha were each incarnations of God for their age. For this modern era, another *avatar* is required. Sin is a concept that "is no longer necessary," and the crucifixion of Christ "wasn't exactly what he wanted to teach."

Gaskin is no Jim Jones, and the Farm is no Jonestown. Still, the community's blend of drug-enhanced mysticism, Zen, and agriculture haven't created the benign utopia some in Summertown, Tennessee, or elsewhere may believe it to be.

SOURCES: *East-West Journal* (May 1981): 11; Stephen Gaskin, *Hey Beatnik!* (Summertown, Tenn.: The Book Publishing Co., 1974); Ibid., *The Caravan* (New York: Random House, 1977); Marty Meitus, "After The Farm," *Rocky Mountain News*, 3 August 1984, 70; *Newsweek*, 10 August 1981, 14; *San Francisco Chronicle*, 21 September 1981; *SPC Journal*; Michael Waldholz, "In an Emergency, South Bronx Turns To Hippie Commune," *Wall Street Journal*, 15 April 1981, 1; Craig Wilson, "Still Havens for Security, Spirituality," *USA Today*, 15 October 1991, 1-2A, 6D.

FENG SHUI

Some American architects and interior designers are adopting the Asian belief
that the shape of a building and the placement of its furnishings have
a spiritual effect on the occupants.

FOUNDER: Feng shui arose in China more than twenty centuries ago. One of its best-known contemporary popularizers is Master Larry Sang, who founded the American Feng Shui Institute in Monterey Park, California, in 1991. Sang's work has been recognized by a number of Fortune 500 companies, and he regularly consults with major firms on industrial design projects.

TEXT: The "Bible" of the modern American feng shui craze is Sarah Rossbach's *Feng Shui: The Chinese Art of Placement*, which contains a distillation of the philosophy of Lin Yun, an American Tibetan Buddhist who works at a temple in Berkeley, California.

SYMBOL: Many feng shui products include the yin and yang symbols, which are said to represent the opposing forces of the universe.

APPEAL: Feng shui appeals to the desire of many to experience an inner peace in the midst of frantic lives. The practice promises blessed harmony and markets this promise through beautifully wrapped and promoted products.

OVERVIEW: There are two kinds of places people can look if they are trying to understand the concept of feng shui.

One place is in the pages of scholarly reference books like *The HarperCollins Dictionary of Religion*, which discusses the concept under its entry for geomancy, which is a millennia-old method of harmonizing human beings and their natural environment. Here's what the dictionary says: "Chinese geomancy (feng-shui, literally 'wind and water') is an ancient system of site analysis to determine its suitability for grave, home, or temple. Diviners often used a special compass that indicated the main cosmic factors impinging upon a site."

Another place is in the glossy pages of women's magazines and catalogs marketing home decoration and consumer products.

For example, Bath and Body Works published a sales piece geared to pre-teen and teenage girls. Among it's offerings was an invitation to visit the feng shui section of the company's Web site, where consumers could use feng shui to "snap out of a funk or rev up for a big day."

As *New York Times* writer Molly O'Neill wrote in her article, "Feng Shui or Feng Phooey?": "Newly minted feng shui consultants are springing up in the telephone book, society pages and *Architectural Digest* to help Americans balance the chi in their homes. Pronounced 'chee,' these invisible fields of electromagnetic energy are believed to determine vitality, fortune and love life."

Writer Lori Lines went even further in an article for the newsletter *Especially for Women:* "It's happened! Feng Shui has shed its snake-oil-and-incense image and is now sweeping the nation. Why is this?" Ms. Lines provides her reasons for the growth of all things feng shui: because it works.

But does it work? And even if it does, should people be experimenting with this ancient form of divination?

Feng Shui Then and Now

Historians tells us that the Chinese people have been practicing some form of feng shui since at least four centuries before Christ. Like many New Age crazes that swept America during the last three decades of the twentieth century, feng shui, which borrows ideas from Tibetan Buddhism and Chinese Taoism, mixes the mystical with the practical.

Its current popularity surge in the West is based on claims that it will help people reduce their stress and increase their productivity and even their income or profits.

As Emily Yoffe writes in a *Newsweek* article entitled, "Ancient Art, Modern Fad": "Its age-old principles fit in nicely with New Age tenets. And when you throw in multicultural awareness and hard times, it's no mystery why feng shui is increasingly popular here."

Like many trends feng shui had its "early adapters" who embraced its concepts and became word-of-mouth evangelists to others. Entertainment celebrities like Rob Lowe and tycoon Donald Trump are among those who have tried it and swear by its results. Hong Kong's Disney park is being designed in accordance with feng shui principles.

Newspaper and magazine articles about feng shui are full of enthusiastic testimonials from people who have tried it and reaped the supposed benefits. One woman installed a window on a waist-level wall near her family room so that her family's good luck would stop leaking out the back door. As a result, profits increased at her husband's company.

But others aren't so sure. Robert Todd Carroll is a contributor to the *Skeptic's Dictionary* Web site. Carroll says feng shui has now joined the growing ranks of moneymaking philosophies that offer no proven benefit but load up consumers with a wide array of overpriced products.

Today feng shui is used to promote lotions, wallpapers, architectural firms, and business consultants. But one thing often gets lost in the marketing—the concept's ancient occultic roots.

Buyer Beware

America's vibrant consumer culture has been able to transform all kinds of noncapitalistic concepts into profitable products. Remember the antimaterialism of the hippies of the 1960s and 1970s? Companies quickly figured out how to market bell-bottom pants and tie-dyed tops to these countercultural bohemians.

Today the same kind of thing is happening with a host of Eastern spiritual concepts like feng shui. In many cases the watered-down versions of these concepts promoted in catalogs and shops contain little that would negatively affect Christians who are committed to following God's will for their lives.

However, it never hurts to be aware of the spiritual foundation of popular concepts like feng shui and to guard against unconscious involvement with evil spirits.

In its oldest and purest forms, feng shui is a spiritual technique that seeks to use divination—a practice forbidden in the Bible—to orient human life around pagan spiritual forces.

Of course, not everyone involved in promoting and marketing feng shui products and services today is aware of this occultic background. And not all contemporary practitioners are devoted to spiritual practices of divination. But some are. The only way for you to know is to ask.

If you buy a small waterfall device for your office because you find its sounds relaxing, that doesn't mean you will immediately begin communing with demons. On the other hand, if you consciously delve more deeply into feng shui's underlying philosophy and mystical practices, you are playing with fire.

When dealing with any Eastern lifestyle import having metaphysical roots, the best advice is to be aware of what you're dealing with and to be careful.

CHRISTIAN CRITIQUE: Americans are becoming increasingly obsessed with their surroundings, resulting in a boom of cable TV decorator shows and the spectacular growth of the do-it-yourself remodeling industry, making corporate giants out of companies like Home Depot. Feng shui fits nicely into this contemporary landscape by suggesting that there is a spiritual component to the colors, shapes, sizes, and arrangements of one's environment. Like many occult ideas, especially Eastern mystical ideas, feng shui operates on a measure of truth (increased comfort by enhancing one's surroundings) and overlays it with superstition and spiritism.

Though Western advocates of feng shui may downplay the occult overtones of this ancient, animistic practice, the historical evidence illustrates as its foundation the belief in a spirit world that parallels the one we objectively observe. Peace and harmony with one's accoutrements can only be achieved if there is accommodation and appeasement of these spiritual forces. The placement of furniture and the positioning of decorations may be more or less pleasing depending on an individual's tastes, but it's a leap in logic to believe that having one's surroundings "feng shui-ed" will enhance spiritual well-being. Christians realize it is our relationship to God and our placement of His Word in our lives that should be our spiritual focus, not how or where we set tables, chairs, rocks, waterfalls, or flowers.

SOURCES: Lori Lines, "Feng Shui Is Gaining Momentum in U. S.," *Especially for Women*, January 2002, 8; Molly O'Neill, "Feng Shui or Feng Phooey?" *New York Times*, 9 November 1997, B1, B101; Jonathan Z. Smith, ed., *The HarperCollins Dictionary of Religion* (San Francisco: HarperSanFrancisco, 1995); Emily Yoffe, "Ancient Art, Modern Fad," *Newsweek*, 23 December 1991, 42.

FINDHORN FOUNDATION

Located near the lochs and moors of northernmost Scotland,
this remote group has influenced many around the world to attempt
communication between plants and humans.

You have within you all that you need, so you do not have to waste time searching for it without.
EILEEN CADDY, *THE SPIRIT OF FINDHORN*

FOUNDERS: Peter and Eileen Caddy; Dorothy MacLean

TEXT: *The Spirit of Findhorn* by Eileen Caddy

APPEAL: Those concerned about man's desensitized relationship to his natural environment are drawn toward Findhorn's ecological ethic, which promises interplanetary harmony, renewed humanity, and the creation of a new civilization.

OVERVIEW: They don't believe in those who replace pulled teeth with coins or who fly through the air like Tinker Bell, but members of the Findhorn Foundation have faith in fairies and elves, *devas* that inhabit flowers and plants. Findhorn's purpose is to achieve oneness with God in order to contribute to the emerging New Age, which will herald a culture of world peace and renewed humanity.

Founded near Findhorn, Scotland, in 1962, the foundation gained early notoriety with its successful production of oversized vegetables and the establishment of elaborate gardens near the Arctic Circle, a horticultural triumph. The organization's founders, Dorothy MacLean and Peter and Eileen Caddy, credit this success to their communication with plant spirits. Professing other metaphysical New Age practices, such as trance channeling and the changing of man's consciousness toward the evolution of a new interplanetary world, the foundation claims to provide its membership with an international spiritual community, where members strive to create a wholeness of all life.

Through communal living, members contend they are part of the "living laboratory" where sacred works and spiritual ideals are tested and reinforced daily. Findhorn work departments and classrooms are structured to provide the basis from which to create peaceful lives and harmonious relationships. Activities for the foundation's reported two hundred members are carried on at several locations in and around the Scottish town of Forres and the Findhorn Village. Programs such as "The Joy of Sacred Dance," "Psychic-Spiritual Healing," and "Meditation" are offered throughout the year in a variety of languages.

In the 1980s the Scottish-based community consisted of Cluny Hill College in Forres, Cullerne House Gardens, Newbold House, the Isle of Erraid, and Caravan Park, upon which a "planetary village" has been planned.

Since then, the Findhorn Foundation has expanded its offerings to include courses at Findhorn Foundation College, which exists "to promote excellence in holistic education; which we define as integrating and balancing development of mind, body, emotions, spirit and relationships." The foundation also sponsors weeklong retreats at Traigh Bhan, a retreat house on the Scottish island of Iona.

Although the Findhorn Foundation is a registered, tax-exempt, charitable trust, recommended contributions for the weekly programs are not cheap. Most cost more than one hundred British pounds.

Although the foundation claims no formal doctrine or creed, its basic tenets center around New Age concepts of acquiring expanded consciousness, communion with supernatural beings, and enforcing the belief that God is found in every living thing. Unlike Christianity, which focuses upon the redemptive blood of Christ, the foundation promotes salvation based upon awareness of the God within us and cooperation with cosmic powers toward the creation of a new, more harmonious world.

CHRISTIAN CRITIQUE: Findhorn teaches that mankind is involved in an evolutionary expansion of consciousness which will ultimately create changes in world societies and promote a planetary culture infused with spiritual values. The Findhorn community is supposed to serve as a model of that utopian goal.

Like most New Age cults, Findhorn adopts a pantheistic belief identifying deity with the elements of nature. Metaphysical concepts of man finding oneness with God through his own actions, and unique rhythms of life are also promoted.

By sacralizing the earth, Findhorn worships the creation rather than the Creator, the sin that is illuminated in Romans chapter one.

SOURCES: Eileen Caddy, *The Spirit of Findhorn* (Forres, Scotland: Findhorn Press, 1977); *Findhorn Foundation Guest Programmes*, autumn-winter 1984–85; *The Findhorn Garden* (New York: Harper and Row, 1975).

ACCESS: Findhorn, Movay IV36 OTZ, Scotland; www.findhorn.org

THE FORUM
Landmark Forum

Werner Erhard, the controversial founder of est, launched a lucrative corporate education program in the 1980s.

Your participation in The Forum takes you beyond a mere understanding of being, beyond even an occasional, unpredictable experience of being, and provides you with direct access to the domain of being itself.
THE FORUM BROCHURE

FOUNDER: Jack Rosenberg, later called Werner Erhard; former used car salesman; born in Philadelphia

TEXT: The Forum materials are basically reworked Zen Buddhist concepts.

APPEAL: The Forum promises corporate clientele it will galvanize employees to greater productivity and creativity. Forum attendees are taught that man is in control of his life and is at the center of his own universe. There are no rules and regulations, only "being." Such a narcissistic emphasis readily appeals to the financially successful and upwardly mobile.

OVERVIEW: Although he has convinced thousands of people that he can help them "get rid of old baggage," spiritual entrepreneur Werner Erhard has had problems escaping his own troubled past.

Hounded by scandal and controversy, Erhard did what many New Age millionaires have done when they found themselves in similar situations: he altered his tactics, changed his organization's name, and started over.

Best known for founding est (see separate entry), Erhard announced in 1984 that est training was being "retired." In its place was a new course produced by Werner Erhard and Associates. In 1985 that course was redesigned and retitled the Landmark Forum. And in 1987 his company was again reorganized and renamed the Landmark Education Corp.

Erhard left the United States in 1991 for parts unknown. Critics say he was evading lawsuits. Supporters believe he was escaping from threats on his life. But even though he is gone, his work continues, albeit with changed tactics. His ideas are now marketed to corporations and managers. However, his basic message remains the same.

A Teenage Transformation

At age eighteen, a man named Jack Rosenberg had an experience about which he says, "I lost the kind of consciousness that locates one in a place. I became the universe."

This theology would eventually become the basis for two successful motivational organizations after Philadelphia-born Rosenberg changed his name to Werner Erhard.

For several years Erhard sold used cars, correspondence courses, and encyclopedias. He also studied Zen Buddhism and hypnosis and took courses from Scientology and California's Esalen Institute.

The next product he marketed was est (Erhard Seminar Training), which was reformulated as The Forum, an offshoot of est designed to teach people effectiveness in their lives. A series of addresses he broadcast via private satellite to eager est audiences was the basis for The Forum.

The organization advocates philosophical phrases like, "The Forum is about living in the question . . . much more powerful than having an answer, which closes possibilities." That premise is no clearer than another Forum dictum that states, "In all performance, 'being' is that one essential ingredient . . . which gives one human being a decisive edge."

The impoverished and infirm need not apply since The Forum welcomes only "successful, healthy people" looking for a "decisive edge" in their "ability to achieve."

Unlike Erhard's famous sixty-hour est seminars, which involved verbal abuse, the more casual Forum encourages dialogue between leaders and audience. The training is aimed at healthy, happy people who are already effective in their lives. It also includes a division called Young People's Forum for children between six and twelve. Creation of The Forum conveniently coincided with a substantial decrease in est enrollments, a drop of ten thousand within a three-year period. Some observers say The Forum is merely a marketing maneuver, designed to revamp est training. Critics of est have brought their complaints to court. Nevertheless, Erhard claims to have woven his work into the fabric of American culture.

Contemporary businesses are abandoning stress management seminars and assertiveness training courses in favor of motivational emphases that will inspire employees toward greater productivity and commitment. Consequently, Erhard has targeted successful corporate clientele and other upwardly mobile individuals, charging hundreds of dollars for two weekends and one evening during which participants will achieve "a breakthrough to a new dimension of possibility." He claims participants will consider the cost "a joke" after completing the course.

A New Age "Name-It-and-Claim-It"

Forum philosophy teaches advocates that commitment is vital, regardless of what the commitment is. According to Forum training, "You simply need to know what you want. . . . Whatever you want is fine. . . . Make a goal. . . . It doesn't make any difference."

The organization makes no guarantee of success, claiming results of The Forum's specialized training are unpredictable and difficult to define.

The Forum promises clients will experience "being" while simultaneously admitting the concept defies precise definition. "Your participation in The Forum takes you beyond a mere understanding of 'being' . . . and provides you with direct access to the domain of 'being' itself." Forum advocates are advised to forsake logic and reason before tackling the magic business of "being."

Excellence, Erhard says, is a matter of being excellent. He also claims creativity stems from being creative. This simplistic methodology recruited almost 7,700 people eager to discover the enigmatic essence of their "being" within a few months of its inception.

The Forum philosophy links strongly with Eastern mysticism. Erhard once stated that everyone is "part of every atom in the world." Eastern mysticism is also evident in Erhard's idea that, while "being" alive, one disappears as an identity.

Erhard himself confessed that est contained strong Zen Buddhism and Scientology influences, and the redesigned Forum is clearly an est offspring. While claiming not to be a cult, religion, or philosophy, one Forum leader stated that the organization is similar to religion, thus creating further ambiguity.

Christians should be wary of self-motivation training like The Forum, a modern masquerade of Eastern thought. Its obscure terms and aims are designed to conceal a satanic hoax, perpetrated by a man whose own biographer calls him "a liar, an impostor, and a rogue."

Instead, consult the real expert about "being," Jesus Christ. He uses simple language, and his intent is clear: "You can enter God's Kingdom only through the narrow gate. The highway to hell is broad, and its gate is wide for the many who choose the easy way. But the gateway to life is small, and the road is narrow, and only a few ever find it" (Matthew 7:13-14, NLT).

CHRISTIAN CRITIQUE: Designed to increase people's awareness of their inner selves and personal omnipotence, The Forum encourages laying aside all conventional religions and social ideas about achieving success. Supposedly, once The Forum's state of "being" is acquired, all one wishes will somehow materialize.

But Scripture teaches that God, not man, is the center of the universe. Under the guise of self-motivation, The Forum is an apologetic for Eastern mysticism. God's moral laws must be obeyed to gain salvation, but The Forum claims there are no rules or regulations. Since The Forum terminology is semantically ill-defined, the outcome of the training is equally ambiguous.

Workers who discover that The Forum or other New Age seminars are being offered or required as a part of their employee training should seek an acceptable alternative program.

SOURCES: J. Yutaka Amano, "Bad for Business," *Eternity*, March 1986, 55; John Bode, "The Forum: Repackaged Est," *The Cult Observer*, April 1986, 3; "Erhard's Forum: EST Meets the 80s," *Newsweek*, 1 April 1985, 15; "Est Training Changed to 'The Forum,'" *The Cult Observer*, February-March 1985, 2; Charlotte Faltermayer, "The Best of Est?" *Time*, 16 March 1998, 52–53; David Gelman et al., "The Sorrows of Werner," *Time*, 18 February 1991, 72; Barbara Zigli, "As Est Training Bows Out, Its Leader Founds The Forum," *USA Today*, 12 December 1984, 5D.

ACCESS: Landmark Education Corp. has centers in a number of U.S. cities. Check local listings.

See also est.

FOUNDATION FAITH OF GOD
Foundation Faith of the Millennium

This exotic extract of 1960s street culture has modified its most outlandish beliefs, but some still remember with concern its heretical roots declaring the reconciliaton between God and Satan.

FOUNDER: Robert DeGrimston; original group began in 1963 in London, England

TEXT: "Love your enemies—including Satan."

SYMBOLS: Formerly, a cross with a snake entwined upon it; now, a Star of David with two opposing Fs, one inverted. The symbol of the Crusade of Innocence is a Star of David with a lamb in the center.

APPEAL: In the early days of the cult, initiates were intrigued by the exotic doctrines that combined elements of satanism and Christianity. Because of its shift toward more orthodox Christian beliefs, the foundation currently appeals more to the general public, especially to families of acutely ill children, through its offshoot, Crusade of Innocence.

OVERVIEW: This church is part of a group whose name is difficult to define and whose evolving doctrines are even harder to pin down. In the beginning (1963) it was known as the Process Church of the Final Judgment, or simply the Process. In 1974, as a result of a break with its founder, Robert DeGrimston, its name was changed to the Foundation Church of the Millennium, with the word *Church* changed to *Faith* in 1977. Its current name is the Foundation Faith of God.

DeGrimston's original group followed his psychic teachings with rapt enthusiasm. But his theology of dualism (supposing the universe is dominated by two opposing spiritual forces, neither being omnipotently supreme) eventually received bad press. Even non-Christians didn't like being stopped on street corners by robed zealots wearing silver crosses entwined with a red serpent.

What Processians taught was even more offensive. "Christ said, 'Love your enemies,'" they declared. "Christ's enemy was Satan. Through love, Christ and Satan have destroyed their enmity and come together for the end, Christ to judge, Satan to execute judgment."

Therefore, to worship Satan was to worship Christ, and to kill in Satan's name was to kill in Christ's name. Growing out of this doctrine was the belief that "process" by spiritual knowledge would allow members of the church to provide moral leadership in a new age led by a God-sent messiah. All this would take place after a Bible-like apocalyptic period, when Christ and Satan would finally be reconciled. The Processian philosophy of duality appealed to Charles Manson, whom the group influenced heavily. The prosecutor in Manson's trial did not quite call Manson a member of the Process Church, but he pointed out that Manson stopped mentioning the group after two church representatives visited him in jail.

A Rift Develops

Eventually the black garb, somber theology, and satanic and Nazi symbolism became too hard to accept, even for Processians. DeGrimston was ousted, though he continues to lead smaller groups of leftover members under the original name.

The foundation's clothing was changed to blue suits and white shirts, and lately even these have been abandoned. The serpent cross was replaced by the Star of David with two Fs, one inverted. Occult practices such as tarot cards, psychic healings, and astrology persist, but elements of Judaism, including Sabbath ceremonies, have been added to upgrade the cult's image. The past and its spooky overtones are de-emphasized, though the belief in a soon-to-appear savior still undergirds foundation philosophy.

Father Lucius (Christopher de Peyer) and Father Malachi (Peter McCormick), one-time leaders of the foundation, claimed an estimated 500,000 people were affiliated with their efforts, including 20,000 hard-core members. Such figures were undoubtedly highly inflated.

Foundation advocates certainly seem more palatable since they no longer publicly promote the Christ/Satan reconciliation theory. But they have not abandoned their basic belief in a coming messiah. Bible students are left to wonder whether such a person might well be the Antichrist, the representative of the once-revered serpent that Foundation Faith advocates now seldom discuss.

In 1980 the Foundation Faith of the Millennium, which remained one of the more successful offshoots of the original Process Church, again changed its name to the Foundation Faith of God. It has a devoted clergy committed to a vow of perpetual celibacy as a testimony to "the existence of the Kingdom."

This group claims it has twenty ordained ministers with a growing number of followers. One new development is the Crusade of Innocence, a ministry offering counsel to families of seriously ill children.

The clown ministry is a hallmark of this crusade, entertaining children in hospitals and private homes. The foundation has established missions throughout the United States and appears to be growing through outreach programs and prayer fellowships.

A Move toward Orthodoxy

The Foundation Faith appears to be moving toward more orthodox Christian beliefs, including belief in the Trinity, Jesus' deity, salvation from sin, the need to be born again, and the second coming of Christ. Christ has a prominent role in the foundation's teachings, with special emphasis on spiritual healing.

However, the foundation's most distinctive doctrine maintains that everyone has a personal guardian angel who can be invoked for guidance in daily living. The clergy will conduct "angel listenings" (for a suggested donation of ten dollars), claiming they can actually hear the angel's voice and write down his instruction. Most angelic messages are generalized and concern removal of barriers preventing one's spiritual growth, but additional questions may be asked of these angels for a tax-deductible fee of three dollars per inquiry.

Two other prominent tenets of the Foundation Faith include reincarnation and the importance of controlling one's own life by personal choices.

CHRISTIAN CRITIQUE: DeGrimston set out to explain how a good God had created the devil and evil. His explanation—that the devil is not truly evil, and therefore, he will eventually be a cohort of God—was sadly mistaken.

Today the group's emphasis is more on understanding the nature of the coming Apocalypse and the role foundation members will play in the social order that follows.

Initially the Process Church exalted Satan as Christ's ally. The church philosophy held that Christ and Satan destroyed their enmity to judge and execute punishment on man. Although dissatisfaction with the growing emphasis on Satan worship in the Process Church led to ousting DeGrimston and the formation of the Foundation Faith of the Millennium/God, the church is still far from orthodox. The Foundation Faith of God is still rooted in the evil of the Process Church.

SOURCES: *Denver Post*, 27 July 1973; Ibid., 31 May 1974, 5HH; The Foundation Faith of God, *Statement of Belief*, "God and the Sin of Man," "Jesus Christ," "Salvation for Man," "Baptism," "Duties of the Believer," and "Jesus Lives"; J. Gordon Melton, *The Encyclopedia of American Religions*, vol. 2 (Wilmington, N.C.: McGrath, 1978), 229; Ibid., "Foundation Faith of God," *The Encyclopedia of American Religions*, 2nd ed. (Detroit: Gale Research), 578; *The Processians*, March 1974; *Toronto Star*, 24 January 1981, H6.

ACCESS: Foundation Faith of God, Faith Center, 3055 S. Bronco, Las Vegas, NV 89102

See also Charles Manson Cult.

FOUNDATION OF HUMAN UNDERSTANDING

Roy Masters

We've all been hypnotized by society, claims this group, which says it possesses the only means to return us to sanity.

FOUNDER: Roy Masters, born Reuben Obermeister; talk show host and author of eleven books

TEXTS: *How Your Mind Can Keep You Well* and other audiotapes and books promoting self-sufficiency through hypnosis

APPEAL: Masters's meditation philosophy and lifestyle appeal to emotionally susceptible or victimized people who have lost control of their lives. Foundation of Human Understanding participants venerate Masters as a perfected person who can save them from social disintegration. Masters likens the controversy surrounding his teachings to the persecution suffered by Jesus Christ.

OVERVIEW: He reportedly once declared, "Every religion in America is a cult. Only the Foundation is the true church." He claims America is a hypocritical country and that "preachers use the Bible as a fixation point of hypnosis." He considers himself a Christian mystic who can lead each person to perfection.

Roy Masters established the Foundation of Human Understanding in 1961. Once based in Los Angeles, the group offered his self-help brand of religion to millions of people who listened to his national radio show, "How Your Mind Can Keep You Well," during its peak years of popularity in the 1960s and 1970s.

That was then. Now headquartered at a ranch in Oregon, the group reaches a much smaller audience with the same basic message.

"The Foundation is one of the few, if not the only, organization in the entire world that teaches people how to deal with stress properly," said Masters in a 1991 fundraising letter which argued that his group should be considered a church and should be supported accordingly. "The FHU takes the words of the Bible and makes them relevant to people's daily lives."

From L.A. to Oregon

Masters has optimistically proclaimed, "All of us have a natural inclination toward right action," yet Masters believes nuclear Armageddon will occur in the future.

He considers himself a survivalist and has been accused of owning a small cache of arms. In 1982 Masters established a 378-acre ranch retreat near Grants Pass, Oregon, and invited like-minded radio listeners to join him. More than two thousand disciples packed up their belongings and moved to be near Masters, his wife, and five children. Masters holds seminars and weekend retreats at his ranch and is in the process of establishing Evelyn Street School, a Foundation of Human Understanding institute for kindergarten through twelfth grade.

In 1989 I debated Masters on a program of my nationally syndicated broadcast *Talk-Back*, at which time he claimed to have 150,000 people on his mailing list. Today his list is much smaller.

Hypnotized by Meditation

The British son of a Jewish diamond cutter, Roy Masters was born Reuben Obermeister in London, England. Fascinated with hypnotism as an adolescent, Obermeister traveled at age eighteen to South Africa and apprenticed as a diamond cutter. In 1949 at age twenty-one he journeyed to America to lecture on diamonds. Obermeister legally changed his name to Roy Masters in 1954, but he never became an American citizen.

Propelled by the popularity of the Bridey Murphy hypnosis case (in which an American woman appeared to reveal, under hypnosis, details of a previous life), Masters became a professional hypnotist and founded the Institute for Hypnosis.

He claims he can save people by teaching them self-sufficiency meditation hypnosis. In the early 1960s the American Medical Association incriminated Masters for practicing medicine without a license.

Masters claims that over 100,000 people have participated in his Foundation of Human Understanding meditation classes. According to Masters, America's problems stem from the deceptive works of preachers, educators, psychologists, and sociologists. He encourages followers to empty their minds and allow their spirits to guide them to understanding.

Masters scorns most men as "wimps" and condemns liberalism and intellectuals. Masters also maintains that rock music is "written by Satan" and declares that education brainwashes youth. He formerly published *The Iconoclast* magazine in protest of mainstream society.

In Foundation of Human Understanding training, Masters employs meditation exercises based on yoga, hypnotism, and Eastern concepts to help devotees obtain inner direction.

A Mixed Message

Masters often combines Christian terminology with gnostic beliefs. He claims, "One of the biggest curses in Christendom is the false idea that Jesus is God."

Yet he quotes Scripture and claims he has been saved by the blood of Christ. He says the Bible was written "by men inspired by mystical experiences." He maintains the Bible is merely a collection of words on paper.

In his meditation exercise, taught on three cassettes and in a book for a total cost of twenty-five dollars, Masters melodically encourages subjects to obtain an altered state of consciousness so as to contact God without thinking. He hypnotically tells disciples to discover the good within in order to grow in the grace of God.

Masters tells participants, "Do not analyze my words. Listen, but do not think." According to Masters, all that's needed to commune with the inner state of intuitive innocence is to empty the mind.

In his audio recording *How Your Mind Can Keep You Well*, Masters urges subjects to accept the "guidance of an invisible Divine Will" and to "wait, empty, for a new direction." He sells tapes on subjects like "controlling negative emotions and healing through understanding one's relationship to stress."

Masters also conducts exorcism seminars, in which he tells participants in a mesmerizing voice that something inside of them is evil and hateful. Then he waves a wooden cross at them until they break down emotionally. In one exorcism, Masters told a possessed person, "All you have to do is be sorry and you'll be all right." Participants pay twelve hundred dollars for week-long seminars or fifty dollars for one-day seminars across the country.

Roy Masters believes he's a sinless, perfected being appointed to save America and the world. He explains, "An intuitive innate knowledge . . . gave me a clear vision to see the world for what it was and it protects me from being caught up in various temptations." He boasts, "I can solve the world's problems in a week if I could get on television."

Masters says he wants to be remembered in the same category as Moses, Jesus, the apostles, Buddha, Gandhi, Martin Luther King, and John F. Kennedy. He maintains, "I'm not after political power; I only want to save souls."

But it's doubtful he can achieve this desire with his flawed theology and methodology.

CHRISTIAN CRITIQUE: Masters's Foundation of Human Understanding seeks to relieve stress and help people attain a perfected state through self-hypnosis and a new sense of inner direction. But humans can never attain a state of perfected being. The human race fell from grace and people remain sinners, though they may be saved by God's grace.

Roy Masters preaches a doctrine of sinless perfection and maintains that knowledge is the enemy of spiritual understanding. Although he doesn't believe the Bible is the inerrant Word of God and denies the deity of Christ and the Trinity, he uses Christian terminology.

Masters contradicts himself when he claims Jesus is not God and then says he's been saved by the blood of Christ. And 1 John 4 clearly states that spiritual authority only comes from one whose doctrine declares Jesus is God in flesh.

All Foundation of Human Understanding teachings revolve around Masters's meditation methods, which encourage emptying the mind and exposing it to demonic invasion. The participant clears his mind through a conditioning process that seeks to improve the meditator but gives no consideration to redeeming grace.

This false meditation prevents true spiritual renewal through the power of Christ. Foundation of Human Understanding participants believe they have the capability to perfect themselves. Thus they ignore accountability to God for their sins and deny the salvation Jesus Christ gained for us on the cross.

SOURCES: Lauren Kessler, "Roy Masters: I Can Do No Wrong," *Northwest Magazine*, 4 September 1983, 5–10; Walter Martin, *The New Cults* (Santa Ana, Calif.: Vision House, 1980); Roy Masters, *How Your Mind Can Keep You Well* (Los Angeles, Calif.: Foundation Press, 1971); Paul Taublieb, "Masters' Touch," *US*, 23 April 1984, 36–41; *Talk-Back with Bob Larson*, 27 July 1989 and 1 August 1989, radio broadcasts.

ACCESS: Foundation of Human Understanding, Box 811, Grants Pass, OR 97526

FREEMASONRY

A secretive fraternal order that claims it dates from the time of Solomon, Masons appear to be genial and philanthropic. But their clandestine vows and oaths link them to ancient, evil rituals.

[The Mason] must declare his faith in a Supreme Being before he may be initiated. But note that he is not required to say, then or ever, what God. He may name him as he will, think of him as he pleases; make him impersonal law or personal anthropomorphic; Freemasonry cares not.

CARL H. CLAUDY, *INTRODUCTION TO FREEMASONRY*, VOL. 2

FOUNDER: According to Masons, their history can be traced to Old Testament stonemasons who built King Solomon's temple. Hiram Abiff, purported builder of Solomon's temple, remains a hero in the eye of Masons because of his refusal to reveal the secrets of his trade to intruders. After the 1717 British revival of Freemasonry, Albert Pike and Albert Mackey were instrumental in laying down the laws of Masonry. Albert Pike is considered by Masons to be a great Masonic scholar and historian.

TEXTS: Albert Pike's *Morals and Dogma*; Albert Mackey's *A Lexicon of Freemasonry, Manual of the Lodge, A Textbook of Masonic Jurisprudence,* and *The Masonic Ritualist*

SYMBOLS: The compass and square combined with the G (gnosis, God-Deity). Other symbols are the apron, which represents the innocence of a lamb; the beehive, which denotes the fertility of a queen bee; the five points of fellowship, which symbolize a third-degree Mason; the Eastern Star; and the all-seeing eye of Horus.

APPEAL: Many people seeking social status join Masonic organizations. The society extends help to charities, leading some to believe it is an altruistic organization. Its many levels of membership and elaborate regalia appeal to those who live otherwise austere lives.

OVERVIEW: Masonic lodges are a part of the landscape in many communities around the world. And Shriners and other Masons regularly participate in parades that march through the centers of many towns.

But behind this positive public persona, Freemasonry has a more complex and controversial history.

An assortment of Masonic groups have been described as the "biggest, richest, most secret and most powerful private force in the world."

Some Baptist leaders have referred to it as "an ungodly brotherhood of satanic darkness," and the Roman Catholic church condemns it as incompatible with Christian beliefs and practices. Freemasonry has been denounced over the ages by the Christian community, which maintains Masonic rituals and tenets conflict with Christian beliefs.

In 1993 the Southern Baptist Convention stirred controversy when it concluded that the denomination could not prohibit its members from being involved in Masonry, saying that this was a decision to be made by individual Christians. Many disagreed with this decision, including cults researcher John Weldon, who wrote a book about the issue called *Bowing at Strange Altars*.

Meanwhile, members defend Freemasonry, saying it is a religious organization seeking human betterment and service to God. Sorting out these conflicting notions requires a review of Masonic history and theology.

Masonic History and Mythology

Freemasonry is a clandestine fraternal order revived in Britain in 1717. Masons claim their organization's roots can be traced to Old Testament stonecutters who built King Solomon's temple. Hiram Abiff, an apocryphal figure believed by Masons to have built Solomon's temple, is a celebrated figure of Freemasonry because of his death-defying refusal to reveal trade secrets to intruders. Inspired by Abiff, Masons met in lodges and guilds until the Middle Ages, when the group disbanded, awaiting its renewal in the eighteenth century. With the decline of the Mason's critical role in building construction, "operative" Freemasonry evolved into an esoteric order of "speculative" Freemasonry.

Condemned for centuries by the Roman Catholic church and banned by Greek and Latin American governments, Masons have often been active in politics.

Some of the most prominent American Masons were George Washington, Benjamin Franklin, Theodore Roosevelt, Harry Truman, Gerald Ford, and Chief Supreme Court Justices William O. Douglas, Potter Stewart, Hugo Black, and Earl Warren.

Early nineteenth-century explorers Albert Pike and Albert Mackey wrote and interpreted Masonic literature and rituals. Pike was an admitted occult Luciferian, espousing his beliefs in such books as *Morals and Dogma*, a text of Freemasonry.

A Complex Tradition

Followers of Freemasonry frequently belong to churches and claim the society's traditions are strongly rooted in religious thought. Most lodges of the organization require only the acknowledgment of a supreme being and life after death.

Masons diligently deny that Freemasonry is a secret society but admit it has secrets "just like other organizations." The secrets are Masonic rituals, in which advocates orate lessons about the brotherhood of man and Masonic teachings of good and evil. Masons are also required to utter bloody oaths, which they argue are symbolic.

The Blue Lodge is the basic Masonic organization representing the first three Masonic degrees: entered apprentice, fellowcraft, and master mason. The symbol for the master mason degree denotes a compass, exemplifying male force, and a square, depicting female force. They are combined with the letter G, symbolizing geometry and the Masonic Grand Architect of the Universe (God).

Other Masonic symbols include the apron, which must be worn at all meetings and to one's burial, as well as the star and its five points of fellowship. Master masons may receive more degrees in either the York Rite or the Scottish Rite Masonry.

In addition to the Shriners and high-degree Masons, Freemasonry also includes the Order of the Eastern Star for women, the Order of DeMolay for teenage boys, and the Order of the Rainbow for teenage girls.

Masonic members recite oaths to tear open their left breast or have their bowels taken out and burned to ashes should they reveal Masonic secrets. Mason handbooks threaten members who disclose confidences with curses of throat slashing, tongue removal, and burial at the edge of a lake or pond. Third-degree Masons, called Shriners, utter oaths to be penalized for violating rules by having their eyeballs speared and their feet flayed.

Growth and Decline

It's difficult to come up with precise membership figures for the various Masonic groups. Some experts say the group has more than 4 million members, while a 1998 article in *Time* magazine said the figure was closer to 2 million.

One thing is clear: The group's membership is declining in an age when men are finding plenty of new ways to get together and share the kind of comradeship that was once found only in groups like the Masons.

Here's how *Time*'s David Van Biema described Masons' efforts to boost their sagging membership numbers: "Are you tempted by the camaraderie of Promise Keepers but put off by the catharsis? If one must dabble in male-only culture, why not try something with a pedigree and an established philanthropic track record?"

Van Biema also quotes a Mason named John Hilliard who echoed these sentiments: "This elusive male bonding that people try to recover sitting in sweat lodges and drumming, the Masons have had it for generations. They never lost it."

Evaluating the Good and the Bad

Masons profess to be philanthropic, contribute to various charities, and strive to extend charity to Masonic families. Widows of destitute members of Freemasonry are supported, and nursing homes are provided for some elderly.

Freemasonry sponsors twenty-two Shriner hospitals for crippled children, which include three nationally recognized burn units. Recent reports, however, reveal Shriners give their hospitals less than one-third of the millions they raise each year, spending the remainder on travel, food, and entertainment.

But aside from all the good works Masons do, one cannot escape the conclusion that Freemasonry and Christianity are incompatible.

The symbolic physical penalties advocated by the Freemasons are violent and murderous. No faithful Christian can keep Freemason oaths, which endorse the death penalty for oneself and require members to persecute traitors of the organization. Oaths also obligate lodge members to protect lodge criminals and keep their secrets.

Most Masons join Freemasonry to be part of what they view as a prestigious, socially influential organization. But their society is based on misrepresentations and false explanations. Masons refer to their thirty-third degree Masons as "Worshipful Master" and believe Jesus was only a man and teacher.

The Bible clearly states that salvation can be attained only through Jesus, God's beloved Son. The brotherhood that Masons advocate is false. The only brotherhood spoken of in the Bible is the one entered into by the blood of Jesus Christ (1 John 1:3).

CHRISTIAN CRITIQUE: Masons pledge to better themselves through fraternal association and serve their God and their community by organized philanthropic activities. But do they do so at the expense of doctrinal orthodoxy?

Masons believe Jesus was nothing more than a man and teacher and require allegiance only to a supreme being. Though lodges in the South tend to be more Christianized, as a matter of dogma the Bible is only one of many sacred books, and adherents of all faiths are allowed membership.

By placing death curses on themselves and others, Masons violate the laws of Christianity. The teachings of Christ in Matthew chapter 5 clearly forbid the uttering of presumptive oaths that one does not have the power to perform (verses 33-37).

SOURCES: *Beaumont Enterprise,* 31 August 1985, 10A; *Birmingham News,* 12 August 1984; *The Courier Mail Saturday Magazine,* 22 May 1982, 23; Ed Decker, *The Masonic Lodge: What You Need to Know* (Eugene, Oreg.: Harvest House Publishers, 1997); Warren Hoge, "Who? Me a Mason? Britain Sees Threat," *New York Times,* 29 March 1998, "Week in Review," p. 5; George A. Mather and Larry A. Nichols, *Masonic Lodge* (Grand Rapids, Mich.: Zondervan, 1995); *Rocky Mountain News,* 30 June 1986, 27; David Van Biema, "Endangered Conspirators," *Time,* 25 May 1998, 65; John Weldon, "The Masonic Lodge and the Christian Conscience," *Christian Research Journal* (winter 1994): 21–23, 36–39.

ACCESS: Masons have local organizations throughout the United States, Canada, and Western Europe.

See also Rosicrucianism.

FUNDAMENTALISM

Back-to-the-basics believers populate Christianity, Judaism, and Islam,
with reactionary and sometimes dangerous ideas.

OVERVIEW: Millions of copies of a series of twelve booklets entitled *The Fundamentals* were published between 1910 and 1915, and they remain in print today.

Featuring articles by Christian thinkers like B. B. Warfield and edited by Rueben A. Torrey, the booklets covered everything from biblical inerrancy to personal testimonials about the efficacy of prayer in ninety loosely organized articles.

In 1919 some six thousand conservative Christians gathered for the inaugural meeting of the World Christian Fundamentals Association, which was created to counter the more liberal Federal Council of Churches, founded in 1908. And in 1920 a group of Northern Baptists called the Fundamentalist Fellowship became the first to claim the name *fundamentalist* for themselves.

But today the term *fundamentalist* is applied to everyone from Zionist Jews who settle in Palestinian-controlled areas of Israel to Islamic terrorists who attack Western interests around the globe.

How did a narrowly defined Christian term evolve into a label for the worst kinds of religious extremism? The answer can be found in some of the most important and wrenching social transformations of the twentieth century.

Faith vs. the Future

Charles Darwin's *Origin of Species* was published in 1859 and claimed to present indisputable scientific evidence for evolution, but Darwin's influential book was merely one of many troubling challenges to orthodox Christian assumptions during the nineteenth century.

Higher criticism subjected scripture to scholarly investigation, leading many to question the reliability of the Bible and its God. Protestant liberalism gained a foothold in many denominations and seminaries. The science of geology wreaked havoc on long accepted notions about both human and cosmic origins. Psychology and sociology subjected human behavior to unprecedented scientific scrutiny. And new religious movements like Spiritualism, Transcendentalism, Unitarianism, Christian Science, and Mormonism introduced religious diversity on an unprecedented scale.

Meanwhile, immigration and industrialization unleashed drastic social changes. There was an influx of Catholic and Orthodox Christians, as well as

Asians and European Jews. Many of these newcomers flocked to America's growing urban centers, where they fueled the industrial revolution and created unique cultural enclaves. Urban despair and poverty helped inspire a mainline Protestant "social gospel" movement which often placed greater emphasis on meeting people's physical needs than on securing religious conversions, while fundamentalists responded by organizing evangelistic crusades, promoting temperance, and lobbying for the passage of Sunday "blue laws."

Increasingly, fundamentalists could agree with the words of the revival hymn: "This world is not my home." And the popular *Scofield Reference Bible* led many to believe that human history was in its final "dispensation" and the end of the world was near.

The publication of *The Fundamentals* was an effort to hold off the corrosive effects of the future by returning to the traditional bedrock of the Christian faith. But such efforts proved counterproductive, as Christian fundamentalists adapted a combative approach to those who disagreed with them, as well as an anti-intellectual approach that ignored important developments in science and culture.

Edward John Carnell was a Christian thinker who had been raised a fundamentalist before receiving degrees from Harvard University and Boston University. He called fundamentalism "orthodoxy gone cultic" and described the movement's creed as "Believe on the Lord Jesus Christ. Don't smoke, don't go to movies . . . and you will be saved."

There was much to be applauded in the early years of the Christian movement toward fundamentalism. Biblical essentials were emphasized, the importance of a personal relationship with Christ was encouraged, and social trends that weakened belief in a sovereign God were resisted.

Unfortunately, such fervor sometimes becomes a culturally prejudiced tool to enforce legalistic restrictions of conformity regarding behavior that certain groups consider "sinful." These edicts were, all too often, based on provincial attitudes of an isolationist mentality more than they were on scriptural convictions.

Fundamentalism in Other Faiths

Around the world, Jews, Muslims, and others who believe in God have been confronted by a strange new world that seems to have little in common with the faith of their fathers.

Millions have left the countryside to live in massive cities teeming with poverty and opportunities for sin. Traditional values have been replaced by materialism and competitiveness. Pop music and movies—much of it coming from the West—have bombarded these cultures-in-transition with unrestrained images of sex, violence, and language that many find offensive and sacrilegious.

Like American Christians in the early part of the twentieth century, many of these bedrock believers have followed a back-to-the-basics philosophy that reveres the past and studiously avoids the future.

In its most radical forms, religious fundamentalism can even contribute to an absolute belief that the world is going to hell and this inevitable slide must be stopped at any price. Certain troubled souls take this concern to the next illogical step—using weapons and violence to attack those who are seen as corrupting the faith.

Forgetting the Mind

In their efforts to return to a purer form of devotion, many fundamentalists forget an important thing: God is a reasonable God who has given us reason to understand and interpret our faith.

Anti-intellectualism is a common characteristic of fundamentalism in various faiths. A Christian example of this trend can be seen in the words of fundamentalist preacher Billy Sunday, who once boldly proclaimed: "I don't know any more about theology than a jack rabbit knows about Ping-Pong, but I'm on my way to glory." Such sentiments may convey heartfelt emotions, but this viewpoint tends to belittle scholarly attempts to understand God's ways and purposes.

Historian Mark Noll's acclaimed 1994 book *The Scandal of the Evangelical Mind* detailed the continuing consequences of "the intellectual disaster of fundamentalism." An article published in *The Atlantic Monthly* in 2000 also explored the continuing consequences of this disaster: "Of all America's religious traditions, evangelical Protestantism, at least in its twentieth-century conservative forms, ranks dead last in intellectual stature."

Kenneth Kantzer, a former editor of *Christianity Today*, discussed this problem in a 1996 interview for the magazine's fortieth anniversary edition. "Most fundamentalists believed that the life of the mind was important," he said, "but they didn't know what to do about it." Some present-day evangelicals understand precisely how they felt.

Not all writers are so quick to dismiss fundamentalism. In *The Smell of Sawdust,* historian Richard Mouw writes, "Anti-intellectualism is a genuine danger, but so is a highly intellectualized packaging of Christianity. Otherworldliness is a threat to the Christian community, but so is a thoroughgoing this-worldliness. Ecclesiastical separatism is to be avoided, but we must also be on our guard against a vague inclusivism in our understanding of Christian unity."

SOURCES: Joel Carpenter, *Revive Us Again: The Reawakening of American Fundamentalism* (New York: Oxford University Press, 1997); George M. Marsden, *Fundamentalism and American Culture: The Shaping of Twentieth Century*

Evangelicalism, 1870–1925 (New York: Oxford University Press, 1980); Ibid., *Reforming Fundamentalism: Fuller Seminary and the New Evangelicalism* (Grand Rapids, Mich.: Eerdmans, 1995); Martin Marty and Scott Appleby, *The Glory and the Power: The Fundamentalist Challenge to the Modern World* (Chicago: University of Chicago Press, 1992); Richard Mouw, *The Smell of Sawdust: What Evangelicals Can Learn from Their Fundamentalist Heritage* (Grand Rapids, Mich.: Zondervan, 2000); Mark Noll, *The Scandal of the Evangelical Mind* (Grand Rapids, Mich: Eerdmans, 1994); Steve Rabey and Monte Unger, "Fightin' Fundies," *Milestones: 50 Events of the 20th Century That Shaped Evangelicals in America* (Nashville: Broadman and Holman, 2002); Alan Wolfe, "The Opening of the Evangelical Mind," *The Atlantic Monthly*, October 2000.

GODDESS WORSHIP AND FEMINIST SPIRITUALITY

Just as feminism has changed politics and society, feminist spirituality
has had a powerful impact on ideas about the fatherhood
of God and the identity of deity.

When a symbol as pervasive as that of the father-god begins to die, a tremendous anxiety is generated. Other images arise to take its place almost immediately.

NAOMI R. GOLDENBERG, *CHANGING OF THE GODS*

FOUNDER: Feminist spirituality was practiced since before recorded history. The New Testament talks about the role of goddesses like Diana (Acts 19). In recent decades many feminist theologians have adapted these ancient, idolatrous ideas to resurrect demonic mysteries which lead to God's judgment on human sin.

OVERVIEW: Today's growth in feminine spirituality can be seen on bumper stickers that say, "In Goddess We Trust" or in TV movies like *The Mists of Avalon*, which one Christian writer called a "neopagan pity party": "This would-be epic, based on a novel by the late Marion Zimmer Bradley, tells the 'true' version of the King Arthur tales, in which most of the heroes are goddess-worshipping feminists. . . . *Mists* makes feverish assumptions about religious suppression by evil and powerful men. . . . The film shows most Christians as superstitious and foolish, crossing themselves to ward off witches and fairies."

Today's feminism often calls on the gods of ancient feminist spirituality, with some writers arguing that the oldest forms of deity in ancient cultures were feminine. Foremost among these writers is Merlin Stone, who believes that deep down, we all know God is a woman: "For people raised and programmed on the patriarchal religions of today, religions that affect us in even the most secular aspects of our society, perhaps there remains a lingering, almost innate memory of sacred shrines and temples tended by priestesses who served in the religion of the original supreme deity. In the beginning, people prayed to the Creatress of Life, the Mistress of Heaven. At the very dawn of religion, God was a woman. Do you remember?"

In addition, many people in the environmental movement subscribe to the "Gaia" theory which describes the earth as a feminine goddess.

Neopagan author Margot Adler's book *Drawing Down the Moon* includes this testimony of feminist conversion:

It was Christmas Eve and I was singing in the choir of a lovely church at the edge of a lake, and the church was filled with beautiful decorations. It was full moon, and the moon was shining right through the glass windows of the church. I looked out and felt something very special happening, but it didn't seem to be happening inside the church.

After the Midnight Mass was over and everyone adjourned to the parish house for coffee, I knew I needed to be alone for a minute, so I left my husband and climbed up the hill behind the church. I sat on this hill looking at the full moon, and I could hear the sound of coffee cups clinking and the murmur of conversation from the parish house.

I was looking down on all this, when suddenly I felt a "presence." It seemed very ancient and wise and definitely female. . . . This presence, this being was looking down on me, on this church and these people and saying, "The poor little ones! They mean so well and they understand so little."

I felt that whoever "she" was, she was incredibly old and patient. . . . After that, I knew I had to find out more about her.

Stories like these are common in books about feminist spirituality, a diverse and growing movement that includes goddess worshipers, devotees of nature mysticism, lesbian spirituality leaders, and even some Christian feminists.

Their views are incredibly varied, but one thing unites these many women: the belief that traditional, male-dominated religions have overemphasized patriarchal ideas in both theology and life.

For decades feminist religious thinkers have been leading an assault on old forms of belief. Some of these women are on a holy crusade to dismantle Christian faith and worship. Naomi R. Goldenberg explains her mission in her book, *Changing of the Gods:* "God is going to change. . . . We will change the world so much that He won't fit in anymore. I found this line of thought most satisfying. I had no great tie to God anyway. He never seemed to be relevant to me at all. . . . Yet there was a magnificence attached to the idea of watching Him go. . . . I returned to graduate school to study the end of God. . . . The feminist movement in Western culture is engaged in the slow execution of Christ and Yahweh."

Origins of a Movement

What is it that some women find so offensive in traditional views of God? Most of them are repulsed by what they see as masculine supremacy in the Jewish and Christian religion and Scriptures. They see a seamless tapestry of male domination: from the male nature of God himself to the maleness of Christ and his disciples and many of the church leaders; from the early church fathers to the pastors, teachers, and seminary professors of our own day.

Some women accept the idea that Jesus came to earth as a man and chose twelve male disciples. But they argue that there were many women involved in the early church, some of them holding positions of influence. For these women the problem isn't theology but issues of sexism in the church.

Sexism, they believe, leads men to subjugate women, downplaying their role in God's work and minimizing their God-given talents and spiritual gifts. As Mary Daly, one of the leading feminist theologians, says in her book *The Church and the Second Sex,* "A woman's asking for equality in the church would be comparable to a black person's demanding equality in the Ku Klux Klan."

Many women remain active in Christian churches even though they are troubled by the sexism they see around them. This is especially challenging for professional women who are empowered to exercise their gifts in the workplace but are restricted to second-class status at church.

However, other women believe that churches are so antifeminine that they must find other forms of spirituality. This attitude has led to the creation of a vast feminist spirituality movement that begins by rejecting Christian theology and then looks elsewhere for meaningful spirituality.

Goldenberg describes one woman who told her, "I need the Goddess to love and pray to. But I need a male god to scream at for making life so sad."

Although feminist spirituality is very contemporary, it is also very ancient. According to *Harper's Encyclopedia of Mystical and Paranormal Experience,* the quest for the goddess has a long history:

> The beginning of the end of the Golden Age of Goddess commenced circa 1800 B.C. to 1500 B.C., during the time of Abraham. . . . During the spread of Christianity, worship of Goddess, along with all pagan deities, was routed or suppressed, and the deities were demonized. But the need for veneration of a female figure persisted, and in Christianity that need was transferred to the much-disputed adoration of the Blessed Virgin Mary. At times the cult of Mary has approached that of Goddess worship, but any similarities drawn between Mary and Goddess are discouraged by the Catholic church.

Finding New Gods

Many feminists begin looking for a female form of spirituality after participating in consciousness-raising groups where one of the cardinal rules is that there are no rules. With an emphasis on experience, all experiences are deemed valid and are treated with respect and empathy. Subjectivity reigns supreme in these forms of feminist spirituality. As one woman told Adler: "I am aware that my reality and my conclusions are a result of my unique genetic structure, my life experience and my subjective feelings; and you are a different person, whose same experience of whatever may or may not be out there will be translated in your nervous system into something different. And I can learn from that."

Other women are looking for an objective basis for feminist spirituality. One of the most impressive contributions to the field has been the research of Merlin Stone, whose book *When God Was a Woman* explores ancient goddess worship, matrilineal, and matriarchal societies.

Stone finds a wealth of evidence that some early civilizations prized women's contributions or even had female leaders. However, feminist scholarship is not perfect. In fact, some of it has many logical gaps and holes—some of which aren't filled by the mere repetition of charges of male bias.

For example, Stone's attempt at documenting the glorious past of goddess worship is often marred by remarks like these: "I could not help thinking of the ancient writing and statuary that must have been intentionally destroyed." But it's hard to make a case for feminist history if that case depends on the absence of evidence.

Other writers, including feminist witch Z Budapest, advocate a return to the ancient sexual rituals of Aphrodite and Diana: "The matriarchal Aphrodite always stood proudly naked, gently pointing out Her genitals as the Source of Life. . . . All women served in the temples of the Goddess of Love . . . extending Her life-giving powers to impotent men."

One important aspect of goddess worship is revering the so-called female life force. Such a force is said to reaffirm the power of feelings and senses, elements which many feminists say have been overlooked or intentionally avoided by patriarchal religious systems.

Budapest represents a sizable portion of the feminist spirituality that endorses lesbianism as a logical way of honoring women and rejecting the power of men. In her book *The Holy Book of Women's Mysteries* she ends many of her modern Wiccan rituals with all participants sharing the "Five-Fold Kiss," which involves kissing, genital manipulation, and orgasm, all of it accompanied by "sacred chants."

There is also a sizable feminist spirituality movement within the larger environmental movement. According to Elinor W. Gadon, author of *The Once and Future Goddess:* "In the late twentieth century there is a growing awareness that we are doomed as a species and planet unless we have a radical change of consciousness. The reemergence of the Goddess is becoming the symbol and metaphor for this transformation . . .(and) has led to a new earth-based spirituality."

A Time for Reflection

According to the authors of *The Goddess Revival*, a Christian study of feminist spirituality, the following factors are "the links in the chain" that connect the various aspects of contemporary feminist spirituality:

- Creation-centeredness
- Pantheism, polytheism
- A belief in humankind as cocreators with god/dess
- A belief in personal god/dess as archetype
- A belief in humankind as being part of the oneness that is god/dess
- An overemphasis on immanence as against transcendence
- A belief in the power of ritual to end alienation with god/dess
- A belief that the recovery of our sense of divinity equals salvation

As a Christian man, I can understand why so many women are so disappointed with the way they have been treated during nearly two thousand years of Christian history. At the same time, I am saddened by the fact that so many women feel they must leave the church and Christian orthodoxy in their desperate effort to find a form of spirituality that is both meaningful and affirms their feminine nature.

CHRISTIAN CRITIQUE: In Los Angeles a judge ordered a self-styled high priestess of the Church of The Most High Goddess to jail for one year on charges of prostitution. It seems that Mary Ellen Tracy, known as Sabrina Asset to her followers, claimed she had sex with 2,700 men in a "sin-cleansing" ritual. Most advocates of goddess worship are less provocative in their veneration but hold beliefs in ancient female deities who were fertility symbols and inspirations for pagan temple prostitution in the name of adoring the female principle of creation.

Today's goddess advocates draw upon the legacy of Diana, Aphrodite, Artemis, and other feminine deities, as well as the women's liberation movement, to argue for overthrowing what they see as an oppressive patriarchal society founded on Christian male chauvinism. The movement is fueled by the idea that the Judeo-Christian tradition has devalued women and inadequately fed their spirits. They snatch up replicas of Ishtar, Lilith, and Isis, as well as Inamma, a Sumerian goddess, depicted with pendulant breasts, signifying the nourishment of nature which they believe perpetuates life in the Cosmos. But such reversion to the witchcraft of ancient civilizations which God condemned will only bring judgment on those who embrace it. True liberation comes in Christ, in whom there is "neither Jew nor Greek, there is neither bond nor free, there is neither male nor female: for ye are all one in Christ Jesus" (Galatians 3:28).

Real freedom doesn't come from invoking a matriarchal system to overthrow male dominance. The ancient sites of goddess worship made women into sexual chattel, used by men in a cruel and brutalizing sport of carnal satisfaction. What feminist truly wants to return to those days? If goddess advocates can see past their prejudices, they will readily observe that women in Christianity are accorded far more liberties and status than any other major religion, most of which demand female subservience to men. Whom the son sets free is free indeed (John 8:36), whether male or female.

SOURCES: Elinor W. Gadon, *The Once and Future Goddess* (San Francisco: Harper and Row, 1989); Douglas LeBlanc, "Neopagan Pity Party," *Christianity Today*, 9 July 2001, 55; Aida Besancon Spencer et al., *The Goddess Revival* (Grand Rapids, Mich.: Baker Books, 1995); Merlin Stone, *When God Was a Woman* (New York: Harcourt Brace Jovanovich, 1976).

GEORGE GURDJIEFF

Subud; Renaissance; Fellowship of Friends; The Work

Although he died in 1949, this mystic who, according to his disciples, came to America following the Russian Revolution still has many followers of his "esoteric Christianity."

I ask you to believe nothing that you cannot verify yourself.
GEORGE GURDJIEFF, *VIEWS FROM THE REAL WORLD*

FOUNDER: George Ivanovitch Gurdjieff; born 1872; died 1949; teachings established in Fontainebleau, France, 1922

TEXTS: Various books by Gurdjieff and P. D. Ouspensky

APPEAL: Gurdjieff's teachings represent a thinking man's cult. Philosophical speculation and the potential for self-discovery attract some. Others are intrigued by the clandestine nature of Gurdjieff groups, which give the illusion of being an elitist corps possessing superior knowledge about the mysteries of life.

OVERVIEW: George Ivanovitch Gurdjieff didn't have the kind of household name that ensures popularity as a cult leader, and his personality traits weren't any more endearing. Gurdjieff was a despot with a habit of unpredictability. He was often known to drive down the wrong side of the road at high speeds, accelerating until he ran out of gas.

Even his death in 1949 didn't bring an end to his uncanny influence over people's lives. Today thousands of disciples are said to follow his teachings. They are organized into secret societies located all across the United States, from California to Washington, D.C.

The life of Gurdjieff was an enigma, but his teachings endure as the number of his followers continues to grow.

Mysterious Beginnings

The birth and background of Gurdjieff are shrouded in the same mystery that characterized his entire life. It is likely that he was of American origin. His father first interested him in the occult, and this fascination with the supernatural continued throughout his life. *Meetings with Remarkable Men,* his most widely read book, was made into a motion picture. The volume recounts his travels throughout central Asia, from Tibet to Russia and on to France, where he settled in 1922. It was there that his investigations into secret Sufi brotherhoods and Asian mystery schools prompted him to form the Institute for the Development of Man.

The actual teachings of Gurdjieff, which came to be called "esoteric Christianity," are hard to decipher. G-O groups (G for Gurdjieff and O for Peter Demianovich Ouspensky, his foremost contemporary disciple) don't advertise their gatherings. Disciples meet for the purpose of discussing Gurdjieff's books and indulging in whirling dervish–type dances, known as "spiritual gymnastics." Their intent is to embark upon "the great adventure of the search for self."

Waking the "Sleepers"

According to George Baker and Walter Driscoll, authors of "Gurdjieff in America: An Overview," found on a Web site dedicated to Gurdjieff: "Gurdjieff seems to have foreseen much of the present state of confusion in religious inquiry in the West. His teaching invites the religious seeker to develop in himself a moral sensitivity that is nourished, not by techniques or metaphysical answers, but by an ineffable opening to himself and others."

Gurdjieff sought to open up man's consciousness to higher planes of awareness. He believed that most people are "asleep," but they can be "awakened" by having a greater sense of self-awareness. Then they will be able to see their various egos and proceed to seek out which part of them is the real "I."

This "Fourth Way," as it is called, is the path to self-transformation. Seekers are encouraged to begin each morning concentrating on putting their real "self" into each part of their bodies, beginning with the toes and so on. Eventually such "self-consciousness" enables one constantly to observe his body and become aware of unconscious mannerisms.

The purpose of such exercises is to shatter the illusion that reactions and intentions are a choice of free will. The next goal is attaining "objective consciousness," by which a person finally discovers his true self. Human effort thus enables one to "save" his own soul.

There is definite value in recognizing that man's heart and his spiritual aims are in a state of disequilibrium. But looking to human merit as a source of right thinking overlooks the fallen nature of man, which clouds any attempt to achieve a truly objective state of mind.

Gurdjieff's teachings are found in books such as *All Is Everything* (sometimes known as *Beelzebub's Tales to His Grandson*), *Meetings with Remarkable Men*, *The Fourth Way*, and *Life Is Only Real When I Am*. In the first of these he speaks of a future prophet of consciousness.

Many believe that Muhammed Subuh, a Javanese government official, fulfilled that role. In 1925 a ball of light descended on Subuh and overwhelmed him, an event he called a *latihan* (God's power purifying the soul). Subuh combined three Sanskrit words to come up with the name of his movement—Subud.

Followers and Flaws

Subuh went to England in 1956 and gained a following among former disciples of the late Gurdjieff. He developed a process for surrendering to God's power (latihan).

Prospective recipients enter a darkened room and await contact with someone who has already experienced latihan. When the power enters, participants exhibit body contortions and vocal utterances. Healing may occur (along with moans and screams) as the goal of an altered consciousness is achieved.

One of the most visible and controversial offshoots of Gurdjieff's philosophy is the Fellowship of Friends. This monastic, well-educated group (generally called "Renaissance") was initially led by a former grade school teacher named Robert Burton. Burton intimates he may be the embodiment of the second coming of Christ. He lives with hundreds of his followers in affluent splendor on a northern California ranch called Apollo, located in Yuba County, California. The group operates the Apollo Opera and the Renaissance Winery.

Gurdjieff's ideals of self-improvement receive a special application from Burton. He contends that the quality of life is enhanced by a worship of beauty and materialism. Higher consciousness is possible by filling one's environment with beauty and comfort.

As a result, his disciples provided Burton with a Mercedes Benz and a lavish mansion filled with priceless works of art. Followers attend his bidding and provide free labor for the ongoing construction of cult facilities.

Most of Burton's time is consumed in world travel, a task he undertakes to scout for new paintings and porcelains to be added to Renaissance's growing collection of artifacts. He explains to critics that it is his duty to elevate the culture and tastes of those who surround him.

Burton also prophesies a worldwide economic collapse and nuclear holocaust. His hideaway in the Sierra foothills will escape this disaster. The priceless art objects he has purchased will allow him and his group to be surviving apostles of an advanced culture and civilization.

Such refined ideals seem hollow when compared with Burton's moral flaws. When his mother was dying in the hospital, he was practicing a period of self-imposed silence. In spite of her suffering, he refused to speak, an act he sees as exemplifying virtuous self-denial.

CHRISTIAN CRITIQUE: Christians can agree with Gurdjieff when he says happiness consists of that which is beyond immediate conscious perception (he called it the "something else").

Gurdjieff followed in the tradition of the ancient admonition to "first know thyself." The Work, as his teachings are now called, state that humans can evolve to spiritual understanding once they become aware of their own imperfections.

But was he right in teaching that the highest goal is to have self-knowledge? Proverbs 1:7 states, "The fear of the Lord is the beginning of knowledge." The quest for higher consciousness always portends the danger of invasion by an alien spiritual intelligence. That "something else" Gurdjieff sought with his blend of gnostic and occult philosophy is found in Christ, who transforms and regenerates the "I" to be a recipient of abundant life.

SOURCES: *Denver Post*, 9 December 1977; William J. Petersen, *Those Curious New Cults* (New Canaan, Conn.: Keats, 1975); *San Francisco Chronicle*, 20 April 1981; *SCP Newsletter* 5, no. 4 (June, 1979); www.gurdjiefffoundation.org.

ACCESS: Gurdjieff Foundation, 85 St. Elmo Way, San Francisco, CA 94127; www.gurdjiefffoundation.org. The foundation has centers in New York, Los Angeles and other major cities.

HARE KRISHNA

See International Society of Krishna Consciousness.

HEAVEN'S GATE

The leader of this UFO cult promised followers they would ascend to the "Level Above Human," but a group suicide was their tragic end.

FOUNDER: Marshall Herff Applewhite, a confused man who believed he was in contact with UFOs

TEXTS: Applewhite's rambling sermons, many of which were captured on audio and videotape

OVERVIEW: The attractive, nine-thousand-square-foot mansion was located in the ritzy Rancho Santa Fe area north of San Diego. Outside, a manicured lawn and blooming flowers greeted visitors.

But inside a much more grisly scene was on display when San Diego sheriffs arrived. There, thirty-nine bodies in varying states of decomposition were laid out on simple bunk beds, in near identical form.

The victims included eighteen men and twenty-one women. Their ages varied from twenty-six to seventy-two. But there was no variation in the manner of their deaths.

Each victim wore black pants, black shirts, and new, black Nike gym shoes. Their faces and torsos were covered by purple cloths. And to make things easier for those who found them, each body had identification papers nearby.

Most had ingested a mix of pain killers and vodka to help them relax, then they were asphyxiated with a plastic bag wrapped around their heads.

The house's master bedroom held the decomposing corpse of the unusual group's mysterious leader, a man named Marshall Herff Applewhite, who went by the nicknames "Do" and "Bo" (as in Bo Peep from the children's nursery rhyme.)

But there was nothing childlike about the death of these thirty-nine loyal members of Heaven's Gate. Applewhite had promised them that they would reach a "Level Above Human" if only they would shed their "containers" (bodies) and rendezvous with a space ship said to be hiding behind the Hale-Bopp comet.

"Planet earth is about to be recycled," said Applewhite in a videotaped message delivered in his clipped, robotic-sounding voice. "Your only chance to survive—leave with us."

All the victims had left packed suitcases and farewell statements.

"I look very forward to this next major step of ours," said one, "shedding these creatures . . . moving on to the next evolutionary level."

Another's farewell was more somber: "I don't have any choice but to go for it, because I've been on this planet for 31 years, and there's nothing here for me."

A Mixed-Up Messiah

Applewhite was a preacher's son who tried to support his own family by working as a freelance musician. But by his late thirties he could no longer contain his homosexuality, which ruined his marriage and his professional career, which included work with churches.

An affair with a male student at Houston's University of St. Thomas led to his firing and his admission to a psychiatric hospital. His nurse, Bonnie Lu Nettles, later known as "Peep," would become his lifelong soul mate.

Spiritualists had told Nettles that a man would come into her life shortly before she met Applewhite. She supported Applewhite's idea that his body was being influenced by otherworldly beings from the "next" level.

By 1973 the two became convinced they were the Two Witnesses prophesied in the New Testament book of Revelation. They left Houston for Los Angeles, where they started recruiting disciples for their offbeat cult.

Mixing New Age, UFOs, and Death

When two dozen people from Oregon left their jobs, families, and homes to follow Applewhite, people started to take notice. Press coverage followed, with articles full of Applewhite's odd mix of beliefs.

Nettles died of cancer in 1985, and after that point Applewhite became even more paranoid in his views. Followers were rigorously trained in exercises designed to prepare them for the rigors of extraterrestrial life. Members began adopting androgynous costumes and unisex hairstyles. Applewhite and a few of his male disciples had themselves castrated.

In the 1990s the group ramped up its recruitment tactics, perhaps because Applewhite feared that he himself might be dying of cancer.

The group designed an elaborate Web site and placed an ad in the newspaper USA Today that warned followers they might "experience such side effects as loss of marriage, family, friends, career, respectability, and credibility."

Even more shocking, the ad warned: "Continued use could even result in the loss of your membership in the human kingdom."

Few people knew that this warning would become a reality in 1997, when Applewhite and thirty-eight devoted followers killed themselves.

CHRISTIAN CRITIQUE: The errors that led to such catastrophic consequences with the Heaven's Gate cult are similar to those held by other UFO-type cults. The four basic errors the groups share are: an overdose of apocalyptic fervor; an eclectic approach to truth that accepts many notions and criticizes none; a complete abandonment of biblical teaching; and a combination of scientific ignorance and intellectual illiteracy. In the case of Heaven's Gate, these errors were combined in a fatal way.

SOURCES: Elizabeth Glick, "The Marker We've Been . . . Waiting For," *Time*, 7 April 1997; Douglas Groothuis, "Making Sense of Heaven's Gate," *Cornerstone* 26, no. 112, 22; Douglas LeBlanc, "Seeking Eternal Life through Death," *Christian Research Journal* (November-December 1997): 6–7, 44; James S. Phelan, "Looking For: The Next World," *New York Times Magazine*, 29 February 1976, 12.

HIMALAYAN INTERNATIONAL INSTITUTE OF YOGA SCIENCE AND PHILOSOPHY

Swami Rama

Combining ancient techniques and modern psychology,
this group developed a small but devoted following.

FOUNDER: Swami Rama (1925–1996)

OVERVIEW: Biofeedback, the psychophysiological technique of mentally controlling body functions and responses, owes its development to the expertise of Swami Rama. Dr. Elmer Green, a psychologist with the prestigious Menninger Foundation based in Topeka, Kansas, developed the principles of biofeedback by observing Rama, who studied with Gandhi, in meditative trance states.

Rama not only exhibited the ability to stop his heartbeat for seventeen seconds, but by psychokinesis (the supposed ability to affect physical objects by using mental powers) he was able to move an aluminum knitting needle while seated five feet away from it.

During the 1970s and 1980s up to five thousand students a month flocked to his Himalayan International Institute of Yoga Science and Philosophy, then located in Glenview, Illinois. By 1997 the group claimed to have fifteen hundred members in the United States and twenty-two branch and affiliated centers in the United States and abroad.

Disciples are taught via Raja Yoga to "exhale all problems" and "inhale energy" in order to become "a wave of bliss in the ocean of the universe."

Rama, who claimed to meditate eight hours a day and sleep only three hours each night, felt his mission was to combine Indian religious therapeutic techniques.

As a monk of the Shankaracharya Order, he spent the early years of his life traveling from monasteries to caves throughout the Indian subcontinent and living with various sadhus. Rather than just popularize the traditions in which he was trained, he sought to establish a clear scientific basis for practicing yoga and meditation.

As an Oxford-educated and Americanized guru, his life was dedicated to "creating a bridge between East and West." In creating this bridge, Swami Rama learned that many spiritually hungry people enjoy the exotic combination of ancient tradition and contemporary science.

SOURCES: J. Gordon Melton, *The Encyclopedia of American Religions*, vol. 2 (Wilmington, N.C.: McGrath, 1978); *People*, 24 October 1977.

ACCESS: Himalayan International Institute of Yoga Science and Philosophy, RR 1, Box 400, Honesdale, PA 18431

HINDUISM

With nearly a billion adherents worldwide, this ancient Indian faith is the world's third largest religion after Christianity and Islam.

FOUNDER: No founder or exact date of origin is known. The precepts of Hinduism go back at least four thousand years and have evolved over the millennia without a codified form.

TEXT: The Hindu scriptures Vedas, Upanishads, and other Sruti (canonical revealed scriptures), plus the Smriti (traditional, semicanonical writings)

SYMBOL: What has become known in the twentieth century as the Nazi swastika. In the Sanskrit language it was known as *svastika*, meaning "conducive to well-being." Originally it denoted the duality of the universe and implied good luck. The feet of the Nazi swastika are turned at ninety degree angles from the legs, the opposite direction of the Hindu version.

APPEAL: At least initially, Hinduism seems to promote an inclusive viewpoint, but ultimately, like all religions, it requires adherence to specific beliefs that set it apart from other devotional structures. Hinduism is an ancient, all-encompassing faith that strives to adopt other doctrines into its own interpretation and frame of reference. In the words of Radha Krishna, "While fixed intellectual beliefs mark off one religion from another, Hinduism sets itself no such limits." Its doctrines of karma and reincarnation insure even the most evil men that there will be a second chance to progress upward spiritually.

OVERVIEW: "Truth is one. They call him by different names," proclaim the Vedas, the most sacred of all Hindu texts.

In a nutshell, this is the essence of Hinduism, a religion that has no prescribed ecclesiastical order or hierarchical governing body. Instead, Hinduism might be viewed as religious anarchy in action.

For example, some Hindus are polytheistic (believing that there are many gods). Others are pantheistic (everything that exists is a part of God). Others are monistic (believing that all matter shares one essence). And other Hindus say they are atheistic (believing that no God truly exists). As the revered sage Mahatma (Great Soul) Gandhi once wrote, "A man may not believe in God and still call himself a Hindu."

Christians should try to understand this ancient and durable faith, which is perhaps the most absorptive and assimilative religion on earth. It's not an easy faith to understand, but it helps if we understand India's culture and history.

Evolution of a World Faith

Since the Aryan Indo-European people stormed into the Indian subcontinent from the north in 1500 B.C., Hinduism has grown in zeal and numbers. Even though its rituals and beliefs have now spread throughout the world, they are inextricably interwoven with the Indian social fabric.

The term Hinduism is derived from the Sanskrit word *sindhu* or *indus* (ocean or river), a geographical instead of theological designation first used by Persian invaders. This origin underscores the importance of understanding Indian history, which is divided into four periods.

First Period

The earliest stage of Indian history is called pre-Vedic and dates back beyond three millennia. Known as Dravidians, the earliest settlers of the Indian Peninsula were animistic. Local deities were worshiped in a fashion resembling witchcraft.

Second Period

The Aryan conquerors brought their own gods, such as Soma, deity of the hallucinogenic soma plant. The Vedas ("wise sayings" or "knowledge") dominated the religious philosophy of this second period.

Originally these texts were orally preserved, but by 1000 B.C. they were collected into written form (such as the ten-volume set of 1,028 hymns and prayers known as the Rig Veda).

The extreme polytheistic nature of Hinduism developed during this time. Hinduism proverbially has millions of gods, although the number is a metaphorical allusion to the seemingly infinite array of deities and is not intended to be a definitive numerical designation.

It was also during this second historical period that the caste system began developing. Castes were originally an outgrowth of vocational classifications: Brahmins were priests and scholars; Kshatriyas the rulers and soldiers; Vaishyas the merchants and farmers; Sudras the peasants and servants.

In later centuries this class division was presumed to be a justification for the doctrines of karma and reincarnation. One's caste became fixed at birth and was so immutable that a Brahmin dying of thirst would not take water from a Sudra lest he be polluted.

Eventually, a social mosaic of three thousand subcastes developed with those known as Untouchables at the bottom of the list. Untouchables were seen as virtually inhuman and good only to clean dirt, excrement, and blood.

Though Gandhi and other reformers persuaded the Indian Parliament to outlaw Untouchability in its 1949 Constitution, it remains a hallowed tradition in the villages where most Indians live. There, endogamy, marriage only within one's caste, is a socially enforced practice.

While other castes may not share the degradation of the Untouchables, they're intimidated with the knowledge that they were created from the feet of Brahma while the Brahmins sprang from Brahma's face.

Third Period

Beginning around 600 B.C. the Upanishadic period dawned on India. The Upanishads transformed the dominant religious outlook from a positive view of fulfillment to an escapist outlook seeking release from life.

In the Rig Veda the old Vedic gods were merely finite superhumans who indulged in licentiousness and debauchery. The Artharvaveda emphasized themes of exorcism and spell-casting in its six thousand verses. In contrast, the 108 poems of the Upanishads (which means "sitting at the feet of" and conjures images of sages instructing disciples) synthesized what would become the basic doctrines of Hinduism.

Hinduism had always been a grassroots religion of the masses, but the Upanishads developed it into a monistic, philosophic faith. Life was seen as an endless cycle of the soul's transmigration (samsara). Escaping the retributive law of karma and achieving liberation (moksha/mukti) from the wheel of life would occur only when the individual soul (atman) would be identified with and absorbed by the Universal Soul (Brahman).

This establishment of a religious worldview known as Brahmanism was the beginning of modern Hinduism as it is known today. Its two basic theological premises are rooted in pantheism (the belief that God is at one with and pervasive in all created matter) and monism (the idea that "all is one," the universe exists as a unitary principle).

Fourth Period

The final stage of Hinduism's development occurred after the beginning of the Christian era when the Vedantic literature became the dominant scriptures. Under the leadership of the philosopher Shankara, who expounded the theory of maya (all matter and reality is illusory), Hinduism enjoyed a revival from the corrupt and sterile forms that had developed. Self-renunciation and moral duty (dharma) became a pathway to freedom from the self and inclusion in the impersonal One (nirvana, a heavenly state).

Faith Meets Practice

As the home of Hinduism, India has been based on its principles for millennia. The results are not always positive.

I have walked the streets of Indian cities where millions sleep on sidewalks and naked children bathe in the gutters. Words seem inadequate to describe the sight of lepers and the congenitally deformed banging on the taxi window to beg for buchshesh (handouts) and wretched waifs with crippled bodies rummaging through garbage for morsels of food.

When I wondered about what all this meant, I learned how Hinduism is applied to daily life. Maya (or illusion), in all its ramifications, is the explanation the Westerner is given when he sees the suffering and poverty of India.

The Hindu has inoculated himself against any empathy for his fellow man. All of the universe is *lila*, God's cosmic game. And pain and pleasure are not absolutes but an illusion. The suffering one sees is not real, it is maya and therefore unworthy of any efforts to alleviate.

Furthermore, to extend kindness to those who are less fortunate would be to disobey the law of karma. That poor creature is suffering because of his sins in a past life, and lending any assistance to his state would violate the sacred principle of divine vengeance.

Common Characteristics

It might appear that Hinduism is a religion too complex to explain in terms of basic presuppositions. As one writer stated, "It rejects nothing. It is all comprehensive, all tolerant, all compliant." Still, there are some common denominators in Hinduism's past and present.

All Hindus do share the same basic scriptural foundation. Granted, certain sects may emphasize one school of literature over another, but the Vedas and Upanishads remain supreme. Other revered scriptures include the Mahabharata, Sutras, Ramayana, Aranyakas, and the Braham-Sutra.

The most popular Hindu writing is the portion of the Indian epic the *Mahabharata,* known as the Bhagavad Gita, or "Song of the Lord." It might well be called the bible of India. (This volume is discussed in more detail in the analysis of Krishna Consciousness.)

The Gita's message centers on developing indifference to desire, pleasure, and pain. Its message of "salvation" is found in Krishna's words, "Whoever surrenders to me is not destroyed."

Hindus also share a similar view of humanity's relationship to the divine. Reality is believed to be of one essence, but Hinduism also insists that it has many forms or expressions.

The human soul (atman) is divine and yearns for union with Brahma. This Brahma-atman unity produces an illuminating, mystical experience. In this state the self, or ego, is dissolved, extinguished by the oneness of God. Since man is ultimately God, and sin is merely an illusion, moral guilt and final judgment for one's conduct are moot concepts.

Different Ways of Worshiping the Gods

The divisions of Hinduism are more devotional than theological. An individual's favorite deity tends to classify the school of thought and form of ritual to which he ascribes.

Brahma is the Creator (Brahma is the masculine form of Brahman, which is neuter), Vishnu is the Preserver, Shiva (sometimes spelled Siva) is the Destroyer. These three comprise the so-called Hindu trinity.

Though there are hundreds of deities with whom a Hindu is usually familiar, it is Vishnu and Shiva who elicit the most devotion. Followers of these gods are divided into Vaishnavites and Shaivites.

Vaishnavites generally concentrate their attention on one of Vishnu's ten incarnations (such as Rama, Krishna, Buddha, or Kalkin, who is yet to appear). As the Vedic sun god, Vishnu's popularity was based on his power to reincarnate.

Shiva, however, attracts the most attention and devotion. The multiplicity of characters he assumes in Indian folklore has enhanced his popularity. A study of his disguises and forms says much about the essence of Hinduism. Here are some examples: Bhaiarave, the patricidal god of terror who uses his father's skull for a bowl; Ardhanarisvara, an androgynous, hermaphroditic sexual image; and Nataraaja, lord of the dance, with four arms. Shiva wanders naked about the countryside on his white bull, Nandi, overindulging in drugs and encouraging starvation and self-mutilation. The innermost sanctuaries of Shiva temples always feature a *lingam*, the stylized, erect phallus that symbolizes his rampant sexuality.

On a moral scale his female consorts assume no better role. Shakti, for example, encourages orgies, temple prostitution, and annual sacrifices. She is also credited with originating *suttee*, the sacrifice of a widow throwing herself into the fire of her husband's funeral pyre. (This practice was opposed by the nineteenth-century reformer Rammohun Roy, but it continues today in remote areas.)

But it is Shakti's manifestation as Kali that presents her most sinister and bloodthirsty image. Idols of Kali show her standing on a beheaded body, wearing a necklace of human skulls. I have personally witnessed animal sacrifices at Kali temples. When priests were questioned as to the bloody overtones of a god trampling corpses, they replied that the image of Kali portrays a "dualistic perspective of illusion and reality." Philosophy aside, even today there are a reported one hundred human sacrifice murders every year in India, all in honor of Kali.

Key Concepts

To comprehend fully the philosophical structure of Hinduism, one must first understand the concepts of karma, reincarnation, and the doctrine of avatars.

Karma is "an inexorable law of retributive justice . . . an internal law of nature independent of . . . the gods." Unlike the sowing and reaping law of Galatians 6:7, karma has no final judgment. Its consequences are felt in this life, and the next, and so on. Every act in this life influences the fate of the immortal soul's next incarnation. The wealthy and healthy are viewed as having accumulated good karma in a previous life, while the less fortunate are seen as getting their just reward for past sins. In other words, sin and punishment are mathematically adjusted on a divine scale.

In the system of karma, there is no forgiving Savior to redeem the consequences of one's deeds. The action of karma keeps moving onward, adding good or evil to its credit in a merciless manner. "Though all Hindus seek *moksha*, liberation from the bondage of karma, most resign themselves to the fact that they may need to be reborn millions of times to accomplish the feat.

Many Christians may find karma a difficult belief to understand since they are accustomed to the idea that, although each man is accountable to God, he can also become a new, forgiven creation in this life (2 Corinthians 5:17). John 9:1-3 is the most direct biblical account refuting karma: Jesus pointed out that a certain man's blindness did not result from sins in a previous existence.

The doctrine of reincarnation (which is covered in its own entry in this book) influences many New Age cults and is an integral belief of Hinduism.

Whereas the Christian anticipates a resurrection of his body, the Hindu views his physical nature as the source of his soul's bondage. Even animals are subject to the cycles of rebirth known as *samasara*. The Bible teaches that each human maintains his or her own personal identity throughout all eternity. In Hinduism, the consciousness of each individual is irrelevant since he might come back after death as a monkey or goat or even a plant (in extreme Hinduistic views).

In spite of attempts to cite biblical pretexts supporting reincarnation (e.g., the Transfiguration in Matthew 17 and Jesus' statement in John 8:58 that "before Abraham was, I am"), Hebrews 9:27 explicitly states that all men die once. In contrast to reincarnation's uncertain game of chance with life, in John 5:28-29 Jesus indicated but two destinations for living souls: "the resurrection of life" and "the resurrection of damnation." The basis for the theory of reincarnation is that man can eventually work out his own salvation, contrary to the Christian doctrine of grace. In addition, it marks a fundamental difference in the view of creation.

Hinduism sees each soul as but a portion of the First Cause, with only legendary explanations as to how each being came into its original state of existence. This is a sharp contrast to the Genesis account of man's origin as occurring from a divine act of creation by a purposeful God possessing a moral will.

Since the doctrines of karma and reincarnation leave man in a somewhat hopeless state, victimized by the forces of cosmic chance, the Hindu philosophers needed to inject some ray of hope.

Incarnations of God

The impact of Christianity forced Hinduism to come up with some method of illustrating the personality of an impersonal God and thus show the way to avoid endless transmigrations. The theistic branch of Hinduism made the Unknowable God more approachable by suggesting that he would occasionally incarnate in some illusory form visible to man.

Such a god-man is called an avatar. Avatars do not appear with any regularity but only once for each age, when man is in desperate need of such assistance.

Krishnaites cite Krishna in the Bhagavad Gita as the best example of God incarnating in flesh, though twenty-one other examples are also mentioned in the epic. Unlike Christ, who came to earth to be an eternal Savior by dying once for the sins of men (Hebrews 10:10-12), the Hindu avatar must return again and again to show men the way to God.

The god Vishnu, whose job it is to sustain the universe, takes human birth in the form of Narayana, the seed of all avatars. Of this belief the *Srimad Bhagavata* (a subtext of the Bhagavad Gita) states, "As countless rivers are born from an ocean that never goes dry, so countless are the descendants of the lord."

Below the rank of major incarnations (Krishna, Rama, et al.) there are "minor rays from the supreme radiance," partial or lesser avatars. Swamis are learned, usually celibate monks who follow the ascetic road to God. Sadhus are the less educated "holy men" who seek spiritual merit by meandering restlessly (and often naked with cow dung in their hair) across India.

A step up the Hinduistic ladder is the guru, a religious teacher who has mastered the path of yoga. He may be a Perfect Master, a satguru capable of transmitting instantaneous enlightenment and thus leading disciples directly to God-realization.

The avatar, on the other hand, is a human object of veneration and worship. He is supposed to possess supernatural powers (*siddhis*) and is said to be totally merged with God. His incarnation is seen as an act of love since he is totally enlightened. Thus, he has no karmic unfinished business to settle on earth, which would require his return. An avatar may show human emotion, since he is in a body, but his spiritual perception is supposed to be beyond the maya of time and space.

Seeking Salvation

Hinduism has no single system of salvation. Instead, the philosophy of Yoga (union with God) offers four different pathways to God, depending on the disposition of the seeker.

Bhakti Yoga (the way of devotion) is the most popular God-road in India. Love toward God is expressed by devotion to a guru who is the embodiment of divine grace. This way may also involve the recitation of God-name mantras.

Karma Yoga (the way of service) generally appeals to more active individuals who are willing to perform ceremonies diligently, make pilgrimages, and carry out actions of good works.

Jnana Yoga (the way of knowledge) requires that one seek out sadhus and gurus and also explore the sacred Hindu scriptures. By knowledge the seeker comes to realize the divine nature of atman.

Raja Yoga (the way of contemplation) inculcates meditation techniques that are known as the "royal road." The devotee must learn to discipline his body and mind to achieve *samadhi,* union with the Absolute.

On a practical level of daily life, these disciplines involve an endless array of idolatrous ceremonies and rituals. Deities kept in the home must be "awakened," "fed," "washed," and "put to sleep" each night.

These acts of *puja* (worship) are followed with exacting detail. There are temples to visit, offerings to deposit (money, flowers, fruit), and pilgrimages to make. Every devout Hindu hopes at least once in his life to visit the holy city of Banaras or the sacred source of the Ganges at Gaumukh, high in the Himalayas. He may settle for some major festival like the famous Car Festival of Jugannath in Puri, where devotees suicidally throw themselves in front of a huge chariot bearing a deity's image.

Despite the lofty philosophical ideals of Hinduism, its effect can be seen in the more bizarre outgrowths inherent in this ancient faith.

In some villages temples care for and feed sacred rats at a cost of thousands of dollars a year. Such vermin dispose of 15 percent of India's grain. The cobra, which is also worshiped, kills twenty thousand Indians each year.

Females, whom Hindu legends relegate to a decidedly inferior state, are so despised that some Indian mothers deliberately strangle their girl babies.

Sadhus, in the name of religious devotion, have been known to sit on a bed of nails and not speak for years, grow their hair into seven-foot braids, stand on a leg like a stork for months, or hold an arm outstretched until it atrophies.

But sacred cows get the most publicity. Since the cow is believed to be the mother-goddess of life, its urine is drunk to purify the soul. They freely roam the streets of urban centers like Calcutta, depositing dung everywhere. Aged holy cows are even provided with rest homes called *gosadans.* I once observed two Indian women fighting over a pile of warm, fresh cow manure. A swami nearby explained their zeal by declaring, "Since the cow is a god, the cow is holy. Therefore, whatever comes out of the cow is also holy."

Reform and Renewal

These and other less desirable aspects of Hinduism have sparked reform movements which, though initially successful, eventually splintered off into new religious faiths. Each of these groups is covered in more detail in its own section of this book.

- The most successful was that of Buddha, who developed the Hindu ideal of *ahimsa* (nonviolence to all living things) into a social creed.
- The Jains, led by the sixth-century ascetic Mahavira, enforce the

command against killing to such an extent that present-day followers of this sect still avoid even swatting a fly.

Jains strain the water they drink, sweep the path in front of them lest they step on an ant, and sometimes go on death-defying fasts as the ultimate way to avoid destroying any life-form.

Mahavira, the spiritual father of Jainism, proclaimed that spiritual truth could be found in the "three jewels" of Right Faith, Right Knowledge, and Right Living. In pursuit of these goals, the most devoted Jain monks never bathe, brush their teeth, or sleep in a bed. With such a rigidly ascetic view of life, it is little wonder that Mahavira's disciples number little more than a million worldwide.

- Another major reform movement in Hinduism's history was the fifteenth-century upheaval of Sikhism brought about by the guru Nanak.

Disavowing castes and idolatry, he grafted Islamic ideals onto a Hindu system of salvation by works, to which he added the grace of God (whom he called Sat Num, "True Name"). The Granth, a collection of poems and prayers from the first four Sikh gurus, is Sikhism's bible and is literally worshiped as a symbolic guru. Sikhism eventually turned into a militant brotherhood marked by five Ks: *kes* (long hair), *kangha* (comb), *kacha* (short pants), *kara* (iron bracelet), and *kirpan* (sword). It is said that if a Sikh ever unleashes his sword, its blade must draw blood, even if it is his own. Sikhism remains a vital faith for millions of people in Asia and more than a quarter million Americans.

- The final reform movement that needs consideration is the Vedanta movement, organized in the 1800s by Swami Vivekananda. India's conquest by England created a Hindu renaissance in response to the incursion of an alien culture and religion.

Vivekananda, a disciple of Sri Ramakrishna, insisted that man's greatest good was to express his humanity. In 1893 he created a sensation by addressing the Parliament of Religions in Chicago. His emphasis was on the unity of all religions with special importance placed on promoting Vedantic Hinduism with missionary fervor.

East Meets West

With thousands of spiritually curious Americans flocking to India's shores each year, the growth and exportation of Hinduistic variants will likely continue.

India's government regards Hinduism as a virtual state religion, providing institutional support and thwarting Christian missionary efforts. As the West embarks upon a post-Christian pilgrimage, Hinduism may continue to look ever more attractive in spite of its inconsistencies and abject failures to alleviate human misery in its own motherland.

Certainly the popularity of such award-winning films as *Gandhi*, *A Passage to India*, and *The Legend of Bagger Vance* (based on a book written as an allegory of the Bhagavad Gita) show that the West is more and more favorably inclined to India and its spiritual essence.

Rudyard Kipling's dictum suggesting that the East and West were diametric opposites that would never meet may prove to be hollow prophecy that could not have predicted spiritually bankrupt Occidentals looking for hope in the ancient Indus valley.

CHRISTIAN CRITIQUE: In addition to comments made above, it is important to point out the following ways in which Hinduism differs from Christianity.

In Hinduism, each soul is an immortal part of the Universal Soul from which it came. Reemergence into the Impersonal Absolute is the goal of each living creature. One must therefore choose the system of God-realization that will most expediently avoid the cycles of rebirth (reincarnation) and permit him to achieve oneness with God.

However, the polytheistic and idolatrous practices of Hinduism are pagan forms of worship that constitute collusion with demonic forces. Karma's system of salvation by conduct is contrary to the biblical doctrine of salvation by the sole grace of God.

The Hindu cannot acknowledge his need of a Savior without repudiating his entire belief system. As Vivekananda said, "It is a sin to call a person a sinner."

The Hindu strives to attain purity by becoming a god, instead of having his sins washed away by the imputed righteousness of a transcendent, personal God. Christ cannot be accepted as an incarnation of Vishna or Krishna. In the Bhagavad Gita, chapter 10, Krishna declares, "I am the prince of demons."

Romans 1 denounces those who worship the creation rather than the Creator. In this respect, consider this quote from the Vedas: "Worship, O Cow, to thy tail-hair, and to thy hooves, and to thy form."

SOURCES: Kenneth Boa, *Cults, World Religions and You* (Wheaton, Ill.: Victor, 1980); *East West Journal* (February 1978); Ibid. (July 1978): 49; John Garabedian and Orde Coombs, *Eastern Religions in the Electric Age* (New York: Tempo Books, 1969); *Great Religions of the World* (Washington, D.C.: National Geographic Society, 1971), 34–76; *Hamilton Spectator*, 6 March 1980; Joel Mathai, "Deciphering Hinduism," *World Christian*, January 2001, 24–26; *Religions of the World* (New York: Barnes and Noble, 1965); J. Gordon Melton, *The Encyclopedia of American Religions* (Wilmington, N.C.: McGrath, 1978); *Newsweek*, 1 April 1979, 68; Ibid., 4 May 1981, 89; Ibid., 4 June 1979, 50;

Stephen J. Rosen, *Gita on the Green: The Mystical Tradition Behind Bagger Vance* (New York: Continuum, 2000); *Time*, 11 March 1974, 6; Ibid., 16 March 1981.

ACCESS: Numerous Hindu shrines and temples are located throughout India and Asia, with lesser numbers in many major Western cities.

HOLISM AND ALTERNATIVE MEDICINE

Ancient mystics believed in a mind-body-soul connection,
but today this belief is gaining acceptance in modern medical science.

The most distinguishing characteristic of Holistic Medicine is that it is based on the fundamental belief that unconditional love is life's most powerful healer.
ROBERT S. IVKER, PRESIDENT, AMERICAN HOLISTIC HEALTH ASSOCIATION

FOUNDER: Ancient folk medicine and superstition, modernized for a new age

TEXTS: Various New Age books on self-healing

SYMBOL: A circle representing the wholeness of man's consciousness and the link of his body to the cosmos

APPEAL: The failure of conventional allopathic therapy causes some to turn to holistic approaches. Many such therapies are nutritionally sound and are partially beneficial, which is interpreted as an endorsement for the philosophy behind the cure.

OVERVIEW: Self-proclaimed holy men and wizards have been promoting healing through complex rituals and odd concoctions for millennia. But in 1991 the U.S. Congress authorized the formation of the Office of Alternative Medicine (OAM) which is now housed inside the National Institutes of Health (NIH).

Two years later journalist Bill Moyers hosted a popular PBS series entitled *Healing and the Mind.*

These and other developments speeded up a process many have called the mainstreaming of the Holistic Health Movement. In recent years powerful voices in the government, the media, and the medical establishment have observed a surge of interest in alternative medicine.

What does this trend mean, and should Christians be concerned about it?

Varying Beliefs and Practices

Laurie Cabot, a professional witch, puts a crystal in her moisturizing cream to improve her skin. Pop singer Tina Turner cuddles a crystal to combat loneliness before entering hotel rooms. Actress Jill Ireland meditated with pieces of quartz after her mastectomy. "Crystals are an access tool to other planes of awareness," she said.

Increasing discontent with traditional American health care encourages patients to adopt holistic healing as an alternative to excessively expensive hospital and doctor fees. Researchers report changing a patient's physical and emotional condition can profoundly transform his self-image and worldview.

Consequently, some proponents of holism believe anxiety about chronic, catastrophic diseases can be alleviated by guided meditation. The ultimate intent is to unite body, mind, and spirit in an integrated approach to health.

Holism proponents use crystals to promote health and happiness. Others adopt the theories of the ancient Greek philosopher Pythagoras, who urged students to cleanse themselves of fear and danger by daily singing. Advocates claim the appropriate music can cure depression, diagnose mental illness, and reduce the effects of surgery. To substantiate their theory, holistic healing adherents refer to the biblical example where David cured King Saul's despondency by playing the harp.

Holism is based on the idea that consciousness can be altered through meditation, visualization, or occult practices. In addition to crystals and music therapy, methods include metaphysical massage, naturopathy, pyramidology, yoga, iridology, reflexology, meditation, trance channeling, biofeedback, acupuncture, and other exotic techniques.

Iridology claims that the entire body can be treated by observing sympathetic body loci in the eye's iris. Reflexology proposes that all the body's organs have corresponding points in the feet, which, when massaged, can relieve physical ailments. Laughter, courage, and tenacity are touted as prime ingredients to holistic healing, since such emotional factors supposedly control the body's ability to heal.

Inner Dimension mail-order catalog offers everything from "tuning forks" that "balance the right and left hemispheres of the brain," to "tranquility mouse pads."

Multifaceted Methods

Holism is multifaceted:

- Macrobiotics, an Oriental theory that divides all energy into opposites, promotes a whole-grain diet, augmented by exercise, meditation, and prayer.
- Rolfing, deep muscle maniplation, is designed to straighten the body and make it more supple.
- Chromotherapy is used to view otherwise invisible auras.
- Herbology proposes that its prescriptions are preferable to drugs for treating illness.
- Polarity therapy, "acupuncture without needles," claims to balance the body's inner energies through deep massage.

Dr. Whit Reaves, certified acupuncturist in west Los Angeles, ran tests on a group of sprinters and found that inserting acupuncture needles in specific body points enhanced athletic performance. Runners reported feeling more energized and efficient. The two-hundred-year-old practice of homeopathy is based on the idea that "like cures like": A substance in large doses that would produce symptoms in a healthy person will, in small amounts, affect a cure.

Of course, not all such therapies are without controversy. One of the most hotly debated approaches is "therapeutic touch," which is practiced by tens of thousands of nurses and other care givers in the United States.

The therapy involves a practitioner who moves his or her hands around the patient without ever touching. Supporters say it relaxes patients and can even relieve pain and produce chemical changes in the blood. But others aren't so sure. One critic called therapeutic touch "pseudo science" and "paranormal and religious activity masquerading as science."

Some of these criticisms could be leveled at other alternative approaches. Still, their many supporters swear they see positive results, and more Americans are trying holistic methods.

A 1993 article in *The New England Journal of Medicine* reported that interest in alternative medicine was booming. Citing a 1990 survey, the *Journal* said Americans paid over 400 million visits to alternative medicine practitioners, spending nearly $14 billion, only about $4 billion of which was covered by their medical insurance. In this decade, the amount spent on alternative care has increased dramatically.

All such holistic theories hinge upon the idea that man is capable of curing his own diseases. Puncturing the body with silver needles, attaching electrodes to muscles, redistributing energy by laying on of hands, and the myriad other holistic healing practices may avoid the primary issue of the sinful origin of many diseases. The focus on eliminating symptoms could dangerously conceal far more serious and life-threatening disorders.

CHRISTIAN CRITIQUE: While the Bible does not endorse any particular approach to medicine, traditional Western medical techniques are viewed as too expensive and intervention-oriented.

Holistic therapies purport to be cheaper and more effective because they are based on a preventive approach. The ultimate intent is to restore the body to harmony with universal cosmological laws of health and well-being.

Unfortunately, severely ill people may circumvent prescribed treatments that are critical to their recovery. Through psychosomatic effects, a sense of immediate relief may be experienced, but the real cause of internal organic dysfunction may go unnoticed.

Holism purports to treat soul and spirit, as well as the body, without defining those terms in a Christian context. Thus, those who seek such cures are usually introduced to various kinds of mystical concepts and literature. They often adopt a metaphysical world view consistent with Hinduism or Buddhism.

SOURCES: Sharon Begley with Debra Rosenberg, "Helping Docs Mind the Body," *Newsweek*, 8 March 1993, 61; Pamela Bloom, "Soul Music," *New Age Journal* (March-April 1987): 58; Leon Jaroff, "A No-Touch Therapy," *Time*, 21 November 1994, 88; Susan Reed, "Mind over Medicine: Bill Moyers Examines the Role of Emotions in Sickness and in Health," *People*, 15 March 1993, 64; Paul C. Reisser, M.D., "Alternative Medicine: The Mainstreaming of the Holistic Health Movement," *Christian Research Journal* (summer 1997): 31; Carolyn Reuben, "It's a Whole New Game with Acupuncture," *East West Journal* (July 1986): 51; Ibid., "Homeopathy for Relief," *East West Journal* (July 1986): 52; Stephen Sutphen, "Increasing Crystal Power," Masters of Life, January 1987, 14.

ACCESS: Dozens of organizations and advocacy groups promote holistic methods. One of the main groups is American Holistic Health Association, founded in 1989, P. O. Box 17400, Anaheim, CA, 92817-7400, phone 714-779-6152, www.mentalhealth.about.com.

See also New Age Movement.

HOLY ALAMO CHRISTIAN CHURCH, CONSECRATED

See Tony Alamo.

HOLY ORDER OF MANS

Originally teaching ancient mysteries and esoteric concepts in Christian lingo, many members of this small group converted to Orthodox Christianity.

FOUNDER: Earl Blighton, who died in 1974, was an ex-engineer who claimed that "divine revelation" prompted him to start the order.

TEXT: The Bible (usually the New Testament), with mystical emphasis on the Pauline epistles; seminars and correspondence study

SYMBOLS: Golden cross overlaid with a flaming sword. *MANS* is an acronym denoting *mysterion* (mystery), *agape* (divine love), *nous* (knowledge), and *sophia* (wisdom).

APPEAL: Moral asceticism and ethical honesty are strongly emphasized to attract those who have been victimized by society's moral vacuum. The image of the order is noncontroversial, and so little is known about it that prospective members have no presuppositions about its secret teachings.

OVERVIEW: Publicly distributed literature describes the Holy Order of MANS as a "discipleship movement," not a religion. "Seekers" who inquire are told that the order's purpose is to teach the Universal Law of Creation, revealed by ancient Christian mysteries.

A list of "Twelve Rules of Living" guide the search, including admonitions to tithe (five dollars per month for beginners) and render absolute obedience to the Class Master to whom the inquirer is assigned.

Entry into the order (which is coeducational) starts when the initiate fills out an application form. He must also pledge his willingness to receive the teachings of Master Jesus. This nominal reference to Christ is consistent with the order's position that Jesus was a great teacher, but only one of several great avatars.

The Holy Order of MANS purports to have a Christian belief system. There are frequent references encouraging the seeker to maintain "high Christian morals." However, the order's true mystical nature is revealed by its allusions to concepts such as "Self-Realization," the "Aquarian Age," the "Christ Light Within," the "Esoteric Council," and "Attainment of the Illumination."

The so-called Basic Course takes about two years to complete. Then the entrant (who is now a Lay Brother or Sister) may proceed on to the Advanced Course, or may even pursue the highest level of Discipleship Instructor. From that point onward, each member is expected to exhibit qualities of self-control, charity, and detachment from material and physical desires.

A Rigorous Lifestyle

Dark-colored clothing with a clerical collar is standard attire, a dress style designed to spiritually distinguish members from "the common folk." Such garb also emphasizes the Catholic-type overtones of the order.

In fact, the order has reinstituted many monastic practices of the pre-Vatican II Roman Catholic Church. The order's emphasis on sacraments also reflects a spiritual tie to Catholicism, though some conscientious Catholics would find many of the order's tactics highly questionable. It is interesting that, after the changes in Catholicism following the Vatican II council, many disgruntled Catholics sought a religion that had the sacramental emphasis of pre-Vatican II Catholicism.

Rigid moral codes are not assigned. Instead, the order seems to assume that a subjectively acquired Christ-consciousness will dictate positive conduct. Members are told that they do not need to forsake their existing church or religious faith affiliations because the precepts of the order are "not doctrines."

For those who make a total commitment to MANS teachings, there are cloister and monastic orders. But by denying that Christ is the only Savior/Creator and relegating him to an infusion of "radiant energy," the Holy Order of MANS places itself in opposition to orthodox biblical belief. The order also denies the biblical concept of hell, claiming that the only hell we know is of our own making.

More serious spiritual dangers may be encountered by meditation techniques designed to "reach the higher beings and your own inner being." Such a solicitation may result in spiritistic practices, though there is no reason to suggest that any active attempt at spiritualism or necromancy is intended. They do, however, promote involvement in tarot cards, astrology, psychic power, Kabbalah, and parapsychology.

On a more positive level, the order does operate Raphael House, a San

Francisco shelter for the homeless and abused. Raphael House's inmates can stay until they find work or go on public aid.

The main thrust of the order is an appeal to achieve a higher consciousness. This exalted state is to be achieved by attaining the same "Christ consciousness" as Jesus, who was merely a God-realized man. Members will then be prepared to enter the New Age of man's spiritual understanding.

Their slogan, "And by their work ye shall know them," is paraphrased from Matthew 7:20. The substitution of the word *work* for *fruits* may or may not have been deliberate, but it does reveal the essential difference between the order and biblical Christianity. The ethical aims of the order are commendable but ultimately unattainable. The true Christian is to be known by the Spirit's fruit (Galatians 5:22-23), which comes from the indwelling person (not consciousness) of Christ. While the Holy Order of MANS is quick to report its acceptance by some Christians, no sensitive Christian can accept the order's unorthodox theology and its mingling of Christianity with the occult.

Later Developments

Following the death of founder Earl Blighton, the Holy Order of MANS experienced a period of change. In the 1980s many remaining members of the group committed themselves to core Christian concepts and were accepted into the Greek Orthodox Missionary Archdiocese of Vasiloupolis.

It is encouraging to see that remnants of a group that twisted Christian teaching have now become a part of Christ's family.

CHRISTIAN CRITIQUE: The Holy Order of MANS promises to reveal hidden, ancient Christian mysteries. These "truths" will elevate one's spiritual consciousness and prepare him for the new age that will soon dawn upon humanity. Members are promised entry into the "Greater Brotherhood," a company of "Christed" individuals who will someday reign with the "Cosmic Christ."

However, according to the group's teaching, Christ is not eternal God but merely a great teacher. God the Father is "the highest initiate among the humanity of the Saturn Period," Jesus is "the highest initiate of the Sun Period," and the Holy Spirit is "the highest initiate of the Moon Period." Mystical wisdom is considered to be a valid source of truth and equal in authority to biblical revelation.

In the 1980s remaining group members adopted the Christian faith and became members of a Greek Orthodox community.

SOURCES: Holy Order of MANS solicitation correspondence; *SCP Newsletter* 2, no. 2 (February 1976); "Steps along the Way," brochure.

ACCESS: Greek Orthodox Missionary Archdiocese of Vasiloupolis, 44-02 48th Ave., Sunnyside/Woodside, NY 11377

HUMAN POTENTIAL MOVEMENT

Combining humanistic philosophy, psychology and New Age concepts,
this influential movement taught people to look within—not to God—for salvation.

FOUNDER: Founded partially upon tenets brought forth in the 1933 Humanist Manifesto and restated forty years later in Human Manifesto II; beginnings can be traced to sensitivity, leadership, and group training of the 1940s.

TEXTS: Writings of late psychologist Abraham Maslow and self-improvement teachers such as Napoleon Hill. The literature of est, The Forum, the Esalen Institute, and other Human Potential Movement centers is revered.

APPEAL: Individuals seeking warmth and security in a confusing world turn to motivational therapies to rise above the masses. Promises of control over one's life and destiny draw those who feel powerless in a bureaucratic society. The belief that man can have anything he desires appeals to self-indulgent materialists.

OVERVIEW: Its influence is everywhere—in publications, daily conversations, in business, and on radio and television. As the Human Potential Movement gains momentum, people across the nation are striving to "Master Their Possibilities" and "Be All That They Can Be."

The Human Potential Movement (HPM) claims to provide a quick fix for a society that idolizes human control, comprehension, and expediency. Grounded in humanistic philosophy and psychology, man, not God, occupies the center of the HPM universe.

The movement disregards man's sinful nature and considers the universe as self-existing rather than created. Man's emotions and feelings are exalted at the expense of intellect. Jesus, declare HPM humanists, was merely a mortal teacher, who like Buddha before him, raised his cosmic consciousness to its full potential and became one with the universe.

Salvation and divinity are achieved by raising personal consciousness. The most extreme HPM adherents, such as Werner Erhard, founder of est and The Forum, insist man can be his own god.

To attain godship and achieve full human potential, one must regain what has deteriorated through modern scientific thought, specifically body and soul. Full human potential can be attained only with an elevated consciousness of the God within you, a recognition that everything in nature is God and all that exists is one. Through individual conversion to HPM ideals, a new, more harmonious world will evolve.

To achieve this transformation, several means are used. Past life regression therapy frees one from prior traumas and helps attain reunion with the universe. Rebirthing, transpersonal psychotherapy, and a combination of Western self-improvement techniques and Eastern wisdom are also employed.

From Sensitivity to Self-Actualization

Conceived in the sensitivity training of the 1940s, HPM concepts of leadership training and group dynamics took on renewed popularity with the self-help movement of the 1960s. As the psychodramas of so-called self-actualization evolved, HPM sessions took on a more therapeutic air.

By the 1970s the Human Potential Movement was entrenched nationwide and increasingly emphasized spiritual and transpersonal experiences. Interest in Eastern religions flourished. Psychic phenomena, including the study of man's relationship to the cosmos, took on new meaning and importance.

Today the Human Potential Movement remains the base from which many New Age tenets have emerged. From its roots have sprung such well-known programs, disciplines, and groups as Life Training, est, psychosynthesis, the Esalen Institute, bioenergetics, encounter groups, Gestalt awareness, and Arica training. In all cases participants are encouraged to be less analytical and judgmental and to focus on the present.

HPM training programs can be brutal. Its practices of marathon sessions, strict discipline, use of buzzwords, verbal abuse, fear, and humiliation to breakdown an individual's personality have been compared to brainwashing.

Negative thinking and past transgressions allegedly cause suffering; therefore, no mention of past failures or sins is allowed. Feelings and emotions are the means by which truth is measured so that one's psychological state becomes an example of pure awareness once all inhibitions are removed.

The San Francisco Bay area has emerged as the movement's unofficial center. At least twenty-five HPM growth centers are located within the Golden Gate region. A dozen or more universities and colleges conduct related research, and scores of therapists, teachers, and clergy engage in its activities in and around San Francisco.

Wherever they are found, HPM promoters charge anything from a basic processing fee to hundreds of dollars per session. Large donations are actively sought.

One distressing aspect of the Human Potential Movement is its blatant anti-Christian bias. While claiming to be nonreligious, its syncretistic, gnostic, and pantheistic ideologies diametrically oppose Christian doctrine.

CHRISTIAN CRITIQUE: HPM seminars promise to help people attain wholeness without reference to God by eradicating the errors of one's past and creating a future of unlimited possibilities.

All restraints pertaining to one's religious or social position will be ignored in favor of unlocking boundless powers dormant in each individual.

The error of Eden was the serpent's lie that man's understanding would allow him to be a god. HPM courses resurrect this falsehood with supposedly pure motives of enhancing self-esteem and improving business environments.

In the process God's sovereign will is ignored, and Christ's call to self-denial refused. A theocentric worldview is exchanged for a man-centered approach to problem solving and personal advancement.

SOURCES: Francis Adeney, "The Flowering of the Human Potential Movement," *SCP Journal* (winter 1981–82): 7–18; William E. Biewett et al., "The Human Potential Movement, est and The Life Training: A Background Paper," 14 September 1984; Marcia Greene, "A Christian Consideration of Human Potential," *SCP Journal* (winter 1981–82): 32–38; Ted Peters, "Discerning the Spirits of the New Age," *The Christian Century*, 31 August–7 September 1988, 763; A. J. S. Rayl, "Magical Mystery Tour," *Harper's Bazaar*, April 1988, 158; Donald Stone, "The Human Potential Movement," *The New Religious Consciousness*, 1976, 93–115.

See also Arica, Esalen, New Age Movement.

I AM INSTITUTE OF APPLIED METAPHYSICS

This now-defunct group balanced esoteric principles and practical application.

FOUNDER: Winfred Grace Barton; 1963; Ottawa, Canada

SYMBOLS: A pair of wings with an encircled human figure, arms raised in the center, with the motto "I AM All in All."

APPEAL: New Age seekers of wisdom who have dabbled in metaphysics were attracted to Barton's intellectual approach to the paranormal and the academic presentation of the courses.

OVERVIEW: "Take your metaphysics seriously, but take yourselves lightly." So advised Winifred Grace Barton, who in 1963 founded the I AM Institute of Applied Metaphysics.

Her first book, *The Inner Power,* was published in that year. That was followed by ten additional books, including her masterwork, *I AM—The Book of Life*. From her basement classroom in Ottawa, Canada, this occult organization grew to include campuses, facilities, and representatives on five continents and in nearly a dozen nations.

Barton said her goal was to provide a methodology for "building heaven on earth for all mankind." Like most New Age metaphysical approaches, Barton believed that an unfolding consciousness was the pathway to spiritual health and personal fulfillment.

In that sense, Barton said I AM was a kind of "finishing school" to polish the jewel of life so it may reach ultimate perfection. Study courses carried the seeker of higher consciousness through a series of stages with metaphysical designations.

The first is the Realization. It requires twenty hours of study. Next comes the Fulfillment. Barton referred to this as "sabbatical"; it was a time when students spent a month on one of her campuses. The Fulfillment drew students deep into I AM teachings, which were designed to free the mind from inhibiting constraints.

Next is the Opportunity, the stage at which Barton believed students would become "full co-creative partners in planetary transformation." During the Opportunity, I AM students were asked to commit five months of their lives, one month on an I AM campus, and the next four at home, after which they became licensed affiliates and "profit-sharing participants in the establishment of the New Age."

Barton admonished students to read her books faithfully. Topics in her volumes include human auras, psychic phenomena, meditation, astral projection, and dream power. The cost for a single course? Around $250, including textbooks—expensive for some, but for others it was a small price to pay to acquire "the super magic vibrance that fills the air."

CHRISTIAN CRITIQUE: The I AM Institute sought to develop a methodology by which dedicated people could change the world by changing themselves. This transformation occurs by an altered perception of reality, consistent with metaphysical explanations of being.

The I AM motto, "I AM All in All," suggested in a humanistic way that humans are the center of the universe and self-sufficient. In contrast, Christianity teaches that our universe is sustained by God's power alone. Humans are incapable of overcoming moral insufficiencies because of original sin. Instead of being "all in all," humankind is under the curse of Eden's sin.

SOURCES: I AM Institute of Applied Metaphysics promotional material

ACCESS: Group is now defunct.

See also Human Potential Movement; New Age Movement.

I AM MOVEMENTS

See Ascended Masters.

REV. IKE
United Church and Science of Living Institute

This prosperity preacher twists the Word of God without apology,
declaring that the lack of money is the root of all evil.

FOUNDER: Rev. Frederick Eikerenkoetter; born 1935

TEXT: "The lack of money is the root of all evil," a misstatement of 1 Timothy 6:10. Rev. Ike also restates John 3:16 to read, "God so loved all of mankind that he gave every man Divine Sonship. And whoever believes in his Divine Sonship, whoever believes in his relationship to God, shall not perish but shall have everlasting life."

APPEAL: Ike's goal is self-improvement and financial advancement by visualizing oneself in a positive frame of mind. Since all reality is a mental state, those who may not have natural or educational abilities to improve their socioeconomic standing are told that by a developed pattern of giving to Rev. Ike, they release some inner potential for wealth.

OVERVIEW: "The lack of money is the root of all evil." So says controversial preacher Rev. Frederick Eikerenkoetter, better known as Rev. Ike.

This distortion of 1 Timothy 6:10 is representative of Ike's Science of Living philosophy, a mixture of black Pentecostalism and Christian Science, laced with evangelical terminology. "Forget about the pie in the sky," this monetary messiah proclaims, "Get yours here and now. You can't lose with the 'stuff' I use."

What is Ike's "stuff"? While some cult leaders obscure their true doctrines with a veneer of orthodox Christian theology, Ike's aberrant beliefs are openly expressed.

He sees the Bible as "a book of psychology rather than a book of theology." Satan is "the negative thoughts of lack and limitation," and deity is "the Presence of God in you." Ike says the purpose of his preaching is to "teach the individual to be master of his own affairs by manipulating his own self-image." Heaven is replaced by "the eternal now" since there are no literal, spiritual realities. Sounding like Mary Baker Eddy, Ike declares, "Everything is a condition of the mind."

A Materialistic Messiah

The cornerstone of Ike's appeal is rooted in an admittedly materialistic view of success and happiness. He makes no apologies for insisting that those who give generously to finance his own extravagant lifestyle will, in turn, receive similar benefits from the god who is in them.

Ike's audiences at his Joy of Living meetings empty their pocketbooks in the hope of getting rich quick. Certain people who live in poverty and see little chance of upward economic mobility are easy prey for Ike's promises. As a result, the biblical concept of receiving from God by giving to God is set aside in favor of unadulterated greed.

"The Bible says that Jesus rode on a borrowed ass," Ike explains. "But I would rather ride in a Rolls-Royce!"

Ike's blatant materialism is typified in a mid-1980s mailing, which included this request: "As a man of God I feel that I am to ask you to give God exactly $18.02"—a small amount, it seems, but apparently the accumulation of such amounts have helped fill Ike's coffers for many years.

Ike also made this statement regarding poverty: "If it's that difficult for a rich man to get into heaven, think how terrible it must be for a poor man to get in. He doesn't even have a bribe for the gatekeeper."

The fallacy of such unbiblical motives may be easily recognized by the evangelical Christian. But for those who are biblically illiterate, Ike has cleverly filled a vacuum that may have been unwittingly left by the church.

Some segments of Christianity have experienced a dearth of strong biblical preaching coupled with an emphasis on the so-called "prosperity gospel." Consequently, some nominal church members feel justified in seeking financial gain in the name of religion. Marginal Christians infected with this "disease" may be concerned very little that Ike's doctrines are nothing more than a rehashed Science of Mind approach. It might be argued that the appeal of the Rev. Eikerenkoetter would be greatly diminished if Christians sincerely reflected God's concern for the poor and lived like they truly believe that "a man's life consisteth not in the abundance of the things which he possesseth" (Luke 12:15).

Today's edition of Rev. Ike comes complete with a Web site, which has an introduction in his welcoming voice. It features the entire scope of his ministry, including his latest gimmick, "Thinkonomics," an updated version of his Science of Mind theology. ("God is not somebody else, somewhere else, sometime else; but God is the Presence of Infinite Good within you HERE and NOW. . . . and this Presence is within everyone—Including YOU!")

Ike's message still resonates with many on the fringe of Christian belief, even after evangelicalism has suffered through a series of financial scandals. His ostentatious Christ United Church covers a city block in Manhattan. At the top of the church is the Prayer Tower with a twenty-three-foot candle, which serves as a "beacon and a blessing." It's there that Ike's Prayer Circle meets in response to reports of miraculous healings from those who seek the Reverend's blessing. His message is alluring to those in financial straits. He claims to have the "gift of money" to "prophesy money into people's hands." Such scriptural perversion is understandable, since Ike admits to interpreting the Bible psychologically rather than theologically. Without apology for any unbiblical distortion, Ike asserts, "I teach the individual that they can BE what they want to be, DO what they want to do, and HAVE what they want to have." For that matter, so does Satan.

CHRISTIAN CRITIQUE: Ike proposes to abolish negative thoughts that induce poverty and replace them with positive mind power, which produces unearned wealth. In reality, it is Ike's financial status that is most directly enhanced, as evidenced by his unabashed and ostentatious display of diamonds and sixteen Rolls-Royces.

Orthodox Christian beliefs in self-sacrifice, denial, a personal devil, a transcendent God, the hereafter, and the importance of spiritual values over material concerns are all negated.

These doctrines are replaced by a mind-science approach that emphasizes immediate financial gain over future moral considerations. Ike says, "There is no God outside of you to do a d— thing for you. Your only savior is your own realization that you are the Christ, the Son of the Living God."

His entire system is in contrast to the command of Christ in Matthew 6:33: "Seek ye first the kingdom of God."

SOURCES: Miscellaneous issues of *Action* magazine, published by United Christian Evangelistic Association; *People*, 1 November 1976, 101–103; *US*, 21 October 1985, 60.

ACCESS: United Church and Science of Living Institute, 4140 Broadway, New York, New York 10033

INTERNATIONAL CHURCHES
OF CHRIST

Boston Movement; Boston Church of Christ

Though it proclaims many orthodox teachings, this group's attitude of exclusivity
and its control of its members has led some to label it cultic .

FOUNDER: Kip McKean, a former pastor in the Churches of Christ denomination who has now founded his own international organization.

TEXT: The Disciples Handbook and other resources

OVERVIEW: Introducing lukewarm Christians to a more passionate faith is a good thing. Teaching these Christians to disciple other believers is a good thing. And evangelizing the world is a good thing. But when activities like these are conducted by a new group that suggests all other churches are erroneous and rules its members' lives with an iron hand, this could be a bad thing.

International Churches of Christ (ICOC) is a movement that was founded in the early 1990s by Kip McKean, a charismatic and effective leader. The ICOC's roots are in McKean's former church, the Boston Church of Christ, home of the so-called Boston Movement.

But some of the roots of the ICOC movement can be found farther back in the heavy-handed "shepherding" movement introduced by the Crossroads Movement, which had its beginnings in a Gainesville, Florida, congregation.

Shepherds and Sheep

The "shepherding" or "discipleship" movement that started with Crossroads sounds like it could be a good thing, too. After all, doesn't Jesus call all who follow him to be his disciples?

Yes, but the legalistic methodology that Crossroads used gave older "shepherds" almost absolute control over the lives of their younger sheep. This kind of authoritarian micromanagement of all aspects of people's lives, including career and family, isn't taught in the Bible and is rife with potential drawbacks.

Kip McKean converted to Christianity at a Gainesville Crossroads group. After moving to the Boston area in 1979, McKean encountered some opposition when he tried to incorporate his shepherding techniques into the life of a traditional Church of Christ (Non-Instrumental). These differences led to McKean's parting from the Church of Christ denomination.

Undaunted, McKean led his own congregation, the Boston Church of Christ, on an aggressive church planting campaign that began in 1981. The next year churches were started in Chicago and London, and more churches were introduced in the succeeding years.

In 1994 McKean introduced an even more ambitious plan to evangelize the world by planting a church in every nation that has a city with a population of at least 100,000. The group reached that goal by 2000, though admittedly some of these church plants are very small.

Questionable Techniques

Much of the ICOC's growth has come through questionable recruitment tactics that are used on college campuses. Using a technique called "love bombing," ICOC recruiters seem to befriend young people who are seeking spiritual answers.

But friendship is only used as a tool to attract new members; it is not a real effort at personal relationship. Those who show greater promise of joining the group are treated with greater warmth.

A former ICOC recruiter named Scott Deal explained the process to the Canadian Broadcasting Company: "Once you get them into the activity, you find out who's a little bit interested. Then you start becoming their best friend. That was the whole idea. We teach people that you need to get in there and become that person's best friend. Liking them had nothing to do with it. And also, doing it carefully enough where they don't alarm their parents. And if we ever met parents, we try coming off as innocuous and as harmless and as typical as the church on the street."

Recruits are challenged to become more committed and "count the cost" to follow Christ, but often aren't told what their commitment entails. They are told that water baptism is a prerequisite to salvation. Even if they have previously been baptized in another church, incoming ICOC members are rebaptized the ICOC way.

Part of "counting the cost" means agreeing to abide by the dictates of elder brothers and church leaders. If leaders tell a member to pick up and move to a new town to start a new church, obedience is mandatory.

For those who disobey or show too strong a tendency to independent thinking, "love bombing" is quickly replaced by "breaking sessions" designed to squash all vestiges of rebellion. These sessions, which can last for hours and can contain verbal abuse by one's shepherds, often conclude with the former rebel writing a detailed confession of sins that can later be used to enforce obedience.

These tactics have led many cult-watching groups to criticize ICOC and have led some college campuses to ban it altogether.

A Mixed Blessing

The ICOC has introduced many people to Christ, and it has inspired many believers to be more committed and disciplined in their faith. Along the way, it has founded some of the fastest growing churches in the United States, according to Dr. John Vaughn's newsletter, *Church Growth Today*.

Still, the ICOC has caused irreparable harm to many people who believed that it was the one true church for our day and trusted their souls to its care. Many people have been so damaged by their experiences in the ICOC that they have vowed never to set foot in another church again.

Much of what the ICOC teaches is consistent with orthodox Christianity, but its abusive approach to discipleship and its insistence that baptism is a prerequisite for salvation should cause people to be cautious.

As *Time* magazine religion writer Richard Ostling said of the ICOC, "Many are crying 'cult,' although dropout Rick Bauer thinks 'authoritarian sect' is a better label."

CHRISTIAN CRITIQUE: Former church members charge that they were told to engage in a daily ritual of Bible reading, lest they lose their salvation. In some cases they were also required to relinquish contact with family members, based on a faulty interpretation of Matthew 15, demanding that adherents place God above their parents. Water baptism is seen as essential to salvation, a prerequisite for receiving God's full measure of grace. More seriously, they claim to be the only true church and that other churches are "going to hell." The aggressive appeal is disarming when confronted with an ICOC recruiter who convinces the neophyte that every Christian experience they've had is invalidated, their whole relationship with Christ is a lie, and they are going to hell unless they are baptized into the ICOC. The catch is that you can't be baptized until you are first discipled, a rigorous process that includes weekly tithing, a listing of all the sins you have committed, and confession of those sins to one or more ICOC members. Only then can you belong to the one true church for one city, the local ICOC congregation, a biblical distortion that interprets early church history as a normative practice for all ages and localities.

SOURCES: *The Disciples Handbook* (Los Angeles: Discipleship Publications International, 1977); Bill Kellogg, "Confronting the Church of Christ," *SCP Newsletter* 15, no. 2: 11–13; Richard Ostling, "Keepers of the Flock," *Time*, 18 May 1992, 62; *Thresholds Newsletter: A Publication for Ex-members of the Boston Church of Christ*.

ACCESS: www.icoc.org

INTERNATIONAL COMMUNITY OF CHRIST

The Jamilians

Claiming he is restoring the lost doctrines of the church,
Eugene Douglas Savoy has created a brand new Jesus.

FOUNDER: Eugene Douglas Savoy; born May 11, 1927, in Bellingham, Washington

TEXTS: *The Essaei Document, Decoded New Testament, Lost Gospel of Jesus, The Jamilians,* and *Jamil, the Child Christ*

SYMBOL: A four-pointed cross with radiants of equal length

APPEAL: Those with a nominal Christian background and metaphysical inclinations may be fascinated by the idea that Savoy has discovered the true, hidden teachings of Jesus.

OVERVIEW: Would you be willing to believe that Christ came again in the form of Eugene Douglas Savoy's child, Jamil Sean Savoy, who was born in the United States in 1949 and passed away in the Peruvian Andes in 1962?

And would you also be willing to accept the fact that the miracles of Christ were performed by solar energy? If not, then this "secret community" based on "the System" as revealed by Gene Savoy is not for you.

If these beliefs do seem plausible, you are welcome to enroll in Jamilian University to discover the esoteric, true teachings of Jesus as revealed in *The Decoded New Testament*. People wanting to enter the institution were once required to fill out the "Spiritual Awareness Aptitude Test" advertised in major occult journals.

From Baptist Teachings to Modern Mysticism

Gene Savoy, a writer and explorer of some renown, was the grandson of a Baptist minister. At the age of six he witnessed the first of several visions and had psychic experiences that led him into a study of world religions.

At age twenty-eight he came upon the teachings of the Essenes and other Middle-Eastern mystic orders. Savoy became convinced that Jesus was a mere "inspired man of God" whose most important teachings were not included in the New Testament. He concluded that Christ orally communicated a secret, closed system to his followers that is only cryptically revealed in the Gospels. He believed the time had come to restore to the church this message that has been lost for centuries.

As a result of explorations in the Peruvian mountains, Savoy became convinced that ancient sun worship was based on the premise that all humans are actually "light-beings." By a technique of gazing at the sun, initiates of the cult are taught to absorb solar energy so they can experience a "new birth" and increase their life span by "15 to 20 percent." By feeding upon the invisible light that is being shed through the sun, each person can become more aware of his "true nature" as a "light body."

Savoy contends that "the creative energy of the universe begins in the sun." His ultimate goal is "intercommunication with some greater intelligence via the sun."

The rationale for his "co-solary" teachings lies in the assertion that his only child, Jamil, was actually a divine being who came to earth as Christ. Taking his cue from Christ's references to receiving the kingdom of God as a child (Matthew 18:3) and Isaiah's prophecy that "a little child shall lead them" (Isaiah 11:6), Savoy claims Jamil was the fulfillment of these Scriptures.

Jamil's purpose was to amend Christianity through his prophecies and restore it to its original form. Though any adept student of occult and Eastern philosophy will find nothing new in Jamil's discourses, Savoy is convinced that the child's words were divinely inspired.

When Jamil died in 1962 ("returned to the World of Light" is Savoy's way of putting it), Savoy came back to the United States. In 1972 he established the Community near Reno, Nevada. The ministry went public in 1975. There are presently a few hundred members worldwide.

Universal Salvation

In Savoy's scheme of theology, "Christ is a universal force to be experienced [instead of worshiped as a deity]" and "man, too, is a son of God."

His writings denigrate the blood atonement and promise to "open the Book of Life." When Christ returns, he will not be a "man-savior . . . to redeem mankind, but a new spiritual Sun, unlike any sun that ever shone."

Among the practices used to develop Savoy's concept of solar energy are pyramidology, dream analysis, altered states of consciousness, vision analysis, biorhythms, auras, the study of light and color bodies, and other indulgences from the world of spiritualism. The promotion of occult phenomena, along with persistent references to "light-beings," are uncomfortable reminders of the Apostle Paul's warning of 2 Corinthians 11:14—"For Satan himself is transformed into an angel of light."

Though Savoy's religion is a false one, civic officials are not so sure it's a religion at all. In 1986 county officials revoked the tax-exempt status of the group's large land holdings outside Reno. The county apparently did not feel that the group's sun-gazing ritual or the thirty crosses scattered around the property qualified the group as a church.

CHRISTIAN CRITIQUE: The Community claims to reveal the secret teachings Christ orally communicated to his disciples, now interpreted through the writings of Savoy. These doctrines are substantiated by the "prophecies" of Savoy's child, Jamil.

Savoy refuses to accept the Bible as inerrant and assumes that the supernatural power of Jesus was from solar energy. He believes that Christ was a mere prophet of no greater significance than others and that Jesus was a messenger, not the Redeemer.

The Community freely admits that salvation is attainable only by "secret procedure of regeneration: an application of supernatural, cosmic forces liberating and empowering the human spirit." These spiritual insights aren't available by reading the Bible, but rather "the restored oral gospel is taught in our present age through a tutorial program administered by authorized ministers in the Church's University of the Ordained."

SOURCES: "Dawning of a New Creation," *East-West Journal*, December 1976, 19–21; *East-West Journal*, March 1980, 40–49; Ibid., April 1981, 7; Gene Savoy, *The Emerging New Christianity* (Reno, Nev.: International Community of Christ); Ibid., *A Confidential Prospectus* (Reno, Nev.: International Community of Christ, 1975); Ibid., *Jamil, the Child Christ* (Reno, Nev.: International Community of Christ, 1973); Ibid., *Project X: The Search for the Secrets of Immortality* (Reno, Nev.: International Community of Christ, 1977); Ibid., miscellaneous Community documents, advertisements, and published texts; Ibid., membership solicitation letter, 19 May 1976.

ACCESS: International Community of Christ, 775-786-7827, www.communityofchrist.org; Jamilian University, 643 Ralston, Reno NV 89503, 775-786-7432.

INTERNATIONAL SOCIETY OF KRISHNA CONSCIOUSNESS

Hare Krishna; Krishna Consciousness

One of the most visible Eastern sects in the 1970s, it became a troubled Asian
import in the 1990s, plagued with scandals and defections.

FOUNDER: His Divine Grace A. C. Bhaktivedanta Swami Prabhupada;
born in Calcutta, India, September 1, 1896, as Abhay Char De; died of heart
failure November 14, 1977

TEXT: The Hindu sacred texts, especially the Bhagavad Gita according to
Prabhupada's interpretation

SYMBOLS: Traditional Indian-style devotional paintings of gods and
demigods, especially depicting Lord Krishna as the Supreme Personality of the
Godhead driving the chariot of Arjuna

APPEAL: Youth in the sixties were ripe for exotic, simplistic answers to questions unfulfilled by technological advances. Even today, those frustrated by the
vanity of materialism may resort to a system that totally rejects all pleasure from
sensory gratification. The authoritarian structure of temple life may fill a need
for the disciplinary lifestyle being sought by some victims of this permissive age.

OVERVIEW: At one time Krishna Consciousness devotees dressed in colorful robes were a common site on street corners and in airports, where they
raised money for their international movement.

But during the last two decades of the twentieth century, the most visible
thing about this esoteric Hindu offshoot was a series of misfortunes, including
internal power struggles, the moral failure of key leaders, and lawsuits from children of disciples who claim they were abused at the group's boarding schools.

The group is now trying to pull itself back together, but it is doing so with
far smaller numbers and with far less public respect than it enjoyed during its
heyday in the sixties and seventies.

Reviewing the group's history requires a step back into a time when U.S.
newspapers regularly covered emerging new cults and their recruiting techniques.

Aggressive Tactics

"Get out of here! You're a demon—a fornicating meat-eater." That kind of rebuke would be harsh anywhere, let alone in a crowded airport concourse.

The epithet was directed toward me for butting in on what, to that point, had been a successful attempt to con an unsuspecting tourist out of his money. He was an Israeli citizen visiting America. If I hadn't stepped in, he might never have known he was the victim of what Hare Krishna devotees call "transcendental trickery." The victim had been told he was giving his one-hundred-dollar traveler's check "donation" in exchange for a book about the Jewish religion.

Of all the imported cults to land on American shores in the turbulent times of the sixties and seventies, none was more ubiquitous and scorned than the International Society of Krishna Consciousness (ISKCON). Members were seen as deceptive, pushy beggars who frequented public places to prey on the naïve.

But beneath the *dhotis* and *saris* they wear is more than a collection of societal dropouts with brainwashed minds. Thirty percent of the devotees have spent at least a year in college, and 70 percent formerly attended church with regularity.

What they find in Hare Krishna is not just an exotic system of authoritarian asceticism. The 50 percent who remain permanently with the cult claim a deeply personal relationship to their Lord similar to the devotion expressed by evangelical Christians to Christ.

ISKCON members are dedicated to a set of sacred scriptures and seek to surrender their lives to a supreme power. They acknowledge man's inherent desire to worship a deity beyond himself and have plunged into their belief system with total commitment.

This is not to suggest that Christianity and Krishna Consciousness are in any way compatible. Far from it. An exploration of the history and nature of ISKCON readily establishes the pagan and mythological roots of this fervent faith.

Emergence of a Hindu Sect

The worship of Lord Krishna began in the sixteenth century in Bengal, India. It was then and there that Caitanya Mahaprabhu, inspired by the Bhagavad Gita (one of Hinduism's sacred books), sought to revitalize a religion that had become heavy on philosophy and weak on participative devotion.

Hinduism had split into two schools: those who worshiped Shiva as the greatest of the godhead (Brahma, Vishnu, Shiva), and those who considered Vishnu to be supreme. Caitanya insisted that Vishnu was actually an incarnation of Krishna (chief character in the Gita) and that Lord Krishna was the ultimate god. Even more revolutionary was his idea that Krishna would intimately commune with his devotees on a personal level, a foreign concept to the traditional Hindu perception of god's impersonality. This communion could be possible by the practice of exuberant chanting and dancing, known as *sankirtana*.

This concept of worshiping Krishna was revived in the early 1900s by the Indian sages Bhaktivinode Thakur and Sri Srimad Bhaktisiddhanta Saroswati Gosvami Maharaj. One of the latter's disciples was a University of Calcutta philosophy and economics major named Abhay Charan De. In 1922 Gosvami initiated Charan De into the discipline of Bhakti Yoga and instructed him to take a message of Krishna Consciousness to the Western world.

Abhay Charan De became known as *Bhaktivedanta Prabhupada* (at whose feet the masters sit). At age fifty-eight he left his wife and five children and a prosperous pharmaceutical business to pursue the life of a swami.

In 1965 he boarded a steamer for the United States and on September 18 sailed past the Statue of Liberty with eight dollars in his pocket. At the time of his death, His Divine Grace A. C. Bhaktivedanta Swami Prabhupada was chauffeured in black limousines and claimed to his credit forty Krishna temples and an estimated five thousand to ten thousand followers in the United States alone.

At any other time, this seventy-year-old man sitting in a Greenwich Village park and chanting strange words would have been an oddity. But in the burgeoning counterculture milieu of the sixties, he was considered hip.

Beat poet Allen Ginsberg, along with an array of hippie types, gravitated to Prabhupada's message. The late ex-Beatle George Harrison wrote a song extolling Krishna's virtues ("My Sweet Lord") and dedicated an entire album (*Living in the Material World*) to ISKCON belief. With the proceeds from these and other activities, Harrison bankrolled Prabhupada's efforts to evangelize.

In those days Bhaktivedanta had confidently declared, "This is a prediction that in all the villages and towns of the entire word, the Krsna [his preferred spelling] Consciousness movement will be known." For a while it looked like he might be right.

A Mystical Message

What was the message he brought? Many people have heard of the repetitive Hare Krishna chant and have witnessed devotees ecstatically dancing on urban street corners. But few understand the aim of such activity, and even fewer have any knowledge about their object of devotion, Lord Krishna.

Dismissing ISKCON antics as weird and offensive is an understandable response of Westerners. What may not be apparent to the Western mind is the complicated system of religious philosophy behind the conduct of Krishna devotees.

The religious philosophy of ISKCON is found in the Bhagavad Gita, a long Hindu poem written (according to most credible scholars) sometime in the first century A.D. (not five thousand years ago as Krishna devotees claim).

The Gita is a virtual bible to devotees, so long as it is consulted in the form of Prabhupada's commentary, *Bhagavad-Gita As It Is*. The *Gita* is an allegorical story of a certain war. The dialogue between Krishna and the warrior Arjuna is purported to represent a conversation between deity and humanity. This exchange is said to embody the ultimate wisdom of the ages.

Arjuna bravely enters the battle until he learns that his relatives are among the opposing forces. He hesitates to fight and is understandably overwhelmed with concern for the coming death of his kinsmen. Krishna spurs him on, advising him to avoid feelings of attachment to his loved ones. This approach of detachment from earthly desires and emotions is central to Krishna's message and ISKCON's theology.

Gita As It Is contains a picture of devotees calmly walking past the poor and suffering. The caption explains such indifference by quoting Krishna's command, "Those who are wise lament neither for the living nor the dead." Prabhupada agreed. He wrote, "Philanthropists who build hospitals and churches are wasting their time."

Such a callous rationale is nothing compared with the twist in logic necessary to justify Krishna's character. Hindu legends portray ISKCON's deity as a blue-skinned (blue symbolizes deity in Hinduism), flute-playing prankster. He hides the clothes of girls bathing in a river and entices the wives of other men to frolic with him in the moonlight. They become so overwhelmed by his romancing that each feels as if she is the only one having intercourse with him. Though Krishna does have a favorite mistress named Radha, he also consorts with 16,108 *gopis* (women cowherds). Over a period of one hundred twenty-five years he fathers ten children with each of them.

A Legalistic Lifestyle

Such orgiastic abandon is a far cry from the behavior demanded of present-day Krishna devotees. Their lives are carefully regimented in a fashion that eradicates the need for personal choices or decisions.

Everyone rises at 3:00 A.M. for a cold shower before "awakening" the temple idols. These "deities" are then dressed and "fed." Devotees chant, count their japa beads, and head for the street to solicit funds and fill the surrounding landscape with Krishna's praises. Evenings are spent with more chanting and idol worship before an early retirement. Six hours of sleep on a hard floor is all that is between most Krishna disciples and another day.

Life is austere in many other ways. No alcohol, drugs, coffee, meat, fish, gambling, or conversation unrelated to Krishna devotion is allowed. Reading of magazines or newspapers is strongly discouraged. Contact with the outside world, including family and friends, is infrequent and sometimes nonexistent. Personal possessions are disposed of, leaving the devotee solely dependent on the temple for food and shelter. Children born of temple-sanctioned unions are taken from the parents to be placed in special ISKCON schools.

In fact, the marriage relationship is viewed as an inferior state for those unable to answer the higher calling to celibacy. Couples live in separate quarters, and sexual intercourse is allowable only by permission of the temple priest.

At the most, conjugal relationships are restricted to one visit per month at the wife's optimum time of fertility, preferably at the time of a full moon, and only then for the purposes of childbearing, not pleasure. In addition, consummation is possible only after each partner has completed chanting fifty rounds of the Krishna mantra, a feat requiring about five hours. Finally, avoiding hand-holding and kissing, the act is performed to the accompaniment of a cassette recording of Prabhupada's voice. It should come as no surprise that one former member claims 90 percent of ISKCON marriages fail.

Obviously, the mind and body of a Krishna devotee is not his own. To signify this fact, every day each member places thirteen clay markings (*tilaka*) on his body. The clay is flown in all the way from India, and these marks signify one's total servitude to Krishna. Those who stay in the cult more than six months are given a new Sanskrit name and a secret mantra. Men must shave their heads, leaving a handful of hair (a *sikha*) by which Krishna can pull them up to heaven if he so desires.

The shaved heads also remove what Prabhupada declared is the symbol of man's vanity. Bald pates are to be indicative of denying any means of sexual attraction.

Women, who are said to have inferior brains and to be worthy only of serving men, must adorn themselves in plain Indian *saris*. This long, loose-fitting garment is prescribed as a deterrent to arousing male passion. Such practices are central to the Krishna doctrine that all desire must be suppressed. The body is the enemy of the spirit, and only by denying it comfort and attention can one reach the high goal of intimacy with Krishna.

The Krishna Gospel of Prabhupada

Prabhupada expounded a strict, fundamentalist form of Hindu philosophy. In essence, his main goal was to help disciples liberate their pure souls from the spiritually inferior nature of their bodies. "I am not this body," devotees are fond of saying. What they mean is that all matter is *maya* (illusory and transient), and only the spirit is worthy of eternal attention.

Man's primary dilemma in life is his ignorance of the Krishna god-nature of his spirit. This unfortunate state has been caused by the bondage resulting from the spirit's encasement in flesh. The only merit of having a human body at all is the alternative of having been incarnated in a lower animal form. At least having a human body means one's previous incarnation must have exuded good karma.

How does one escape the confines of the sensory temptations of flesh and blood? ISKCON teaches that the way of salvation can be shown only by a guru whose spiritual succession is legitimate. Prabhupada lays claim to such a lineage, insisting he is the spiritual heir of Caitanya, who was Krishna's incarnation for this present age. (Some devotees believe that Prabhupada was himself an incarnation of Krishna and thus greater than Christ.)

Prabhupada taught that liberation of the soul in this age, called *kali-yuga* (the dark age), is possible only by *kirtana:* reciting the Hare Krishna chant. The devotee who does this is freed from *samsara* (endless cycles of reincarnation) and begins his pilgrimage "back to the Godhead."

One must admire the zealous success of Krishna devotees. Their relatively few numbers have managed to familiarize the public consciousness with their sixteen-word chant: "Hare Krishna, Hare Krishna / Krishna, Krishna, Hare, Hare / Hare Rama, Hare Rama / Rama, Rama, Hare, Hare." Even though it is brief, amazing powers are claimed for the mere utterances of this *maha* (great) mantra. Accompanied by the "transcendental sound vibrations" of drums and finger cymbals, these words are said to embody Krishna himself. (*Rama* is an alternative name for Krishna and *Hare* expresses his creative energy.)

Devotees often do the chant in correspondence with each of the 108 japa beads on the "rosary" kept in a bag hanging around their necks. They may repeat the entire cycle as many as sixteen times a day.

It is of no concern to the chanters that the curious observers who watch them during public displays may mock or listen with disinterest. Prabhupada told them that "there is no need to understand the language of the mantra." Anyone who hears it will be automatically affected by Krishna's name.

For a similar reason, ISKCON's own "spiritual sky" incense is often burned during chanting to provide an aroma in which Krishna may dwell. Devotees believe that those who smell it will literally inhale Krishna. And there's more to chanting than that silly, blissful smile on the face of devotees. They are promised by His Divine Grace that eventually they may experience hair standing up on their bodies, dislocation of the voice, crying in ecstasy, and going into trance states.

The result of this form of suggestive hypnotism is that the participant may enter a condition that would facilitate control by demonic possession. At the very least, such an enforced method of divorcing the mind from reality can turn devotees into robots who will act blindly in response to whatever they perceive to be Krishna's will. The potential misuse of such exaggerated devotion should cause alarm to those initiates who are just beginning the pathway of temple service.

The Hare Krishna chant is essentially an invocation to the pantheon of Hindu deities. Such paganism is also evident in a variety of temple duties and rites. Krishna is believed to be resident in the metal and wood idols maintained in ISKCON facilities.

These statues are offered food six times a day, which is later eaten by devotees (an act called *prasada*) as a way of actually ingesting Krishna. (This ritual is a kind of Hare Krishna Eucharist.) When water is used to bathe the deities, it is collected for the disciples to drink. A sample of the Indian *Tulasi Devi* plant is kept in each temple as an object of worship to eradicate sin and disease.

In spite of all this, Prabhupada declared his religious system is not idolatrous. To him idolatry was the "worship of a material *form* of God." He insisted that in Hare Krishna the devotee is not worshiping a *form* of God. "The form is God," Prabhupada declared. In Krishna's case, "There is no difference between the form of the Lord and the Lord himself." Whatever the excuse, such practices are inconsistent with Exodus 20:4-5.

Facing Tough Challenges

But accusations of idolatry are mild aberrations to defend compared with the kinds of charges leveled at ISKCON during the eighties and nineties.

Since the passing of Prabhupada in 1977, the organization has faced accusations of drug smuggling, firearms hoarding, suicides, murder, and outright thievery.

In 1983 a California jury leveled a $32 million judgment against the organization for kidnapping and brainwashing a fifteen-year-old girl and actions that led to the death by heart failure of her father. Though the judge reduced the actual payment to $9.7 million, it was at the time the largest award against a cult.

The solicitation methods the group has used have fostered court investigations of tactics including shortchanging donors, participating in false pretense, and even using experienced thieves to train devotees on how to lift wallets.

Critics suggest that such sources of income enabled the cult to erect its most elaborate temple at its center in the West Virginia hills. This center, called New Vrindaban, is the largest of about three hundred centers worldwide. Its major feature is a massive structure known as "Prabhupada's Palace of Gold." Once called "West Virginia's Taj Mahal" by *The New York Times*, the site rapidly became one of the state's major tourist attractions. But underneath all the gold and incense, trouble was brewing.

ISKCON's magazine *Back to the Godhead* used to publish ads like this one to beckon readers: "Meet a Bona Fide Spiritual Master." The ads featured a photo of Swami Bhaktipada, New Vrindaban's guru/leader. But in 1996 Bhaktipada revealed that he had feet of clay, pleading guilty to a racketeering charge and agreeing that he had hired hit men to kill a critic who opposed his fundraising schemes.

Even before this, Bhaktipada had engaged in ethical and sexual offenses that led to ISKCON banning him and New Vrindaban from its membership. Following Bhaktipada's imprisonment, the West Virginia community completed a process that led to its being readmitted to the ISKCON family.

Picking Up the Pieces

Prior to dying of heart failure in 1977, Prabhupada appointed eleven gurus to carry on his work. After a governing body was established to help ISKCON iron out some of its problems, he excommunicated six of the eleven gurus for reasons such as seduction, violent behavior, homosexuality, and drug abuse. Clearly, even some of Prabhupada's most devoted disciples found it impossible to live up to the legalistic moral code ISKCON promoted.

But it appears that those who have been hurt most by this group aren't its failed leaders or even those innocent victims whose money was used to fund ISKCON programs. Rather, a lawsuit filed by children of Krishna disciples charges that the group regularly abused its most innocent members.

ISKCON members who married and had children were urged to place their children in boarding schools so that family obligations wouldn't distract from their religious duties. These boarding schools were called *gurukulas*, and according to a lawsuit filed in 2002, Krishnaites running these schools routinely engaged in physical and sexual abuse of the children.

Ninety former Krishna children are seeking $400 million in damages from the group, which admits the schools were mismanaged and has closed them all down. Sadly, a group that promised people they could find spiritual purity often gave them something quite different.

Today Hare Krishna faces a more skeptical world where promises of ecstasy by chanting will no longer keep either the coffers or the membership rolls filled.

CHRISTIAN CRITIQUE: ISKCON offers a highly religious life with the dedication and fellowship of like-minded adherents.

All rituals and devotions are designed to free man from the ignorance of having forgotten his true personal relationship with Lord Krishna. This can be accomplished only be freeing the spiritual body from the physical body.

Chanting Hare Krishna mantras bypasses the intellect to cleanse the mind and heart of a false concept of concern for the material world.

The entire religious system of ISKCON is built upon mythological scriptures of legendary events and people (including Krishna). There is no sin to be saved from; there is only the illusion of evil to be eradicated.

Jesus warned in Matthew 6:7 that "vain repetition" was a fruitless form of prayer. According to 1 Corinthians 8:6, there is but one Lord—Christ, not Krishna. Jesus died of his own choice and rose from the dead. Krishna expired from an arrow in his foot and failed to conquer death.

SOURCES: Kenneth Boa, *Cults, World Religions and You* (Wheaton, Ill.: Victor, 1980); *Circus*, 28 February 1977, 48; *Denver Post*, 11 July 1975, 3BB; Ibid., 15 April 1977, 4BB; Ibid., 26b August 1977, 2BB; Ibid., 17 March 1978, 1BB; Ibid., 6b March 1981, 5BB; Ibid., 29b May 1981, 1BB; *Forward* 4, no. 1;

John Hubner and Lindsay Gruson, "Dial Om for Murder," *Rolling Stone*, 9 April 1987, 53; Ibid., *Monkey On a Stick: Murder, Madness, and the Hare Krishnas* (New York: Harcourt Brace Jovanovich, 1988); "On Chanting Hare Krishna," ISKCON pamphlet; ISKCON, various issues of the periodical *Back to the Godhead*, especially vol. 10, no. 7; "Krishna Children Sue over Abuse," *Colorado Springs Gazette (Newsday)*, 3 March 2002, A14; *Life*, April 1980, 44–51; Sue Lindsay, "Krishna Devotee Linked to Crimes," *Rocky Mountain News*, 5 February 1989, 8; Pat Means, *The Mystical Maze* (San Bernardino, Calif.: Campus Crusade for Christ, 1976); Nori J. Muster, *Betrayal of the Spirit: My Life Behind the Headlines of the Hare Krishna Movement* (Urbana, Ill.: University of Illinois, 2001); *Newsweek*, 27 December 1976, 26; Ibid., 30 January 1978, 57; Ibid., 29 September 1980, 83; "New Vrindavana Rejoins ISKCON," *Hare Krishna Report*, May-June–July-August 1998, 1; "One Generation of Hare Krishna," *SDP*, 22 March 1987, 10A; Bhaktivedanta Prabhupada, *Bhagavad Gita As It Is* (Los Angeles: Bhaktivedanta Book Trust, 1975); Ibid., *The Nectar of Devotion* (Los Angeles: Bhaktivedanta Book Trust, 1970); Ibid., *The King of Knowledge* (Los Angeles: Bhaktivedanta Book Trust, 1973); R. E. Schecter, "$32 Million Judgment against Krishna," *The Advisor*, August-September 1983; Jack Sparks, *The Mind Benders* (Nashville: Thomas Nelson, 1977); "Swami Sentenced after Admitting He Committed Fraud," *Colorado Springs Gazette Telegraph*, 29 August 1996, A13; *Time*, 15 September 1980, 71; J. Isamu Yamamoto, *Hare Krishna, Hare Krishna* (Downers Grove, Ill.: InterVarsity, 1978).

ACCESS: International Society for Krishna Consciousness, 3764 Watseka Avenue, Los Angeles, CA 90034

ISLAM

Westerners can no longer afford to remain ignorant about Islam, a rapidly growing and increasingly influential faith that is the world's second largest religion. In America, the Muslim population has increased 25 percent in less than a decade.

FOUNDER: Muhammad the Prophet; born Ubu'l-Kassim in Mecca, A.D. 570; died in Medina, A.D. 632, in the arms of his favorite wife, Aisha

TEXT: The Koran, containing prayers, rules of etiquette, and calls to wage "holy wars." It is supplemented by the traditions of the Hadith. In addition, Muslims also revere the Tauret (Pentateuch) of Moses, the Zahar (Psalms) of David, and the Injil (Evangel) of Jesus.

SYMBOLS: Crescent moon and star

APPEAL: The simplicity of Islam's message is its chief attraction: one God, a rigidly defined method of worship, and a clearly explained destination of man's soul. Its system of salvation by good deeds and ardent devotion offers solace for those who want to conform to an outward display of piety without having to experience a spiritual rebirth of their inner nature.

OVERVIEW: "There is no god but God, and Muhammad is the Messenger of God." Those thirteen words comprise the *Shahada* (confession of faith) for every true Muslim (which means "one who submits").

Five times a day the devout, from Arabic sheiks to Palestinian camel drivers to American Muslims, respond to the *muezzins* (callers to prayer) and bow toward Mecca. Some Muslims display a round spot on their foreheads, an indelible souvenir memorializing the thousands of times they have touched the ground in respect to the Prophet's command.

Like Christians, Muslims accept Abraham and Moses as prophets. But Christians are taught to thank God for his blessings and to petition him for divine favor. This is not the case with Muslims. Their passive fatalism will not permit them to seek spiritual merit or to desire material provisions.

Islam is an Arabic term that means "submission," and that definition is the sum of a Muslim's faith. *Inshallah*—"if God wills"—is the byword of Arabic conversation. In *umma* (the world community of Islam), faithful Muslims view every event, the fortuitous and accidental, as an expression of Allah's divine will.

The major faith in many parts of the East, Islam in its many forms is growing increasingly popular in the West as well.

This entry will examine mainstream Islam, but two of its most influential offshoots, the mystical Sufi movement and the "Black Muslim" movement, are covered further in separate entries.

An Arabic Faith

Separating Islam from its Arabic cultural heritage is impossible. More than a religion, it is an all-encompassing way of life with its own jurisprudence system and traditional honor code.

It is an intolerant faith that has impeded progress and repressed women. Perhaps this is because the Muslim tends to see the world in black and white. There are only two classes of people: *Dar ul-Islam*, those who have submitted, and *Dur ul-harb*, those who resist.

The latter are fair game for missionary efforts, financial pressure (e.g., the oil embargo), and the "sword of Allah" in *jihad* (holy war), or whatever measures are necessary to bring them under the authority of Islam. Jihad is a concept that has been getting a much closer inspection in the wake of the September 11, 2001, terrorist attacks on the United States instigated by nineteen fundamentalist Muslims from the Arab world.

Today the crescent and star of Islam fly on the flag over a number of major world nations. Adopting the evangelism techniques of Christianity, Muslims have broken out of their mud huts and desert terrain to confront the world with the message of Muhammad. Saudi Arabia has even financed a communications satellite to beam the Koran's precepts. Since October 1973 when Egyptian soldiers stormed the Suez and the oil embargo brought the West to its knees, the cry *"Allahu Akbar!"* (God is great) has been heard with new fervor.

Revelation in the Desert

Islam began with the mystic visions of a nondescript camel driver named Ubu'l-Kassim (who became known as Muhammad). For six months he had been in solitary meditation in a cave at the foot of Mount Hira near Mecca. Had he not married a widow named Khadijah, fifteen years his senior, he might have spent his life on caravan journeys. Khadijah's wealth gave Ubu'l-Kassim the time he needed for ascetic reflection.

Muhammad was born in A.D. 570 in Mecca. He was yet a baby when his father died, and his mother passed away when he was six. Abu-Talib, an uncle, raised the young lad and took him on lengthy trips to Egypt and throughout the Near East. During these travels Muhammad engaged in lively conversations with Jews and Christians. From these encounters he learned the theological concepts that were later to influence his teachings.

In Muhammad's time the Arabian peninsula was populated by wandering tribes that practiced various forms of polytheistic idolatry. The pantheon of deities they worshiped included angels, demons *(djinn)*, and a supreme god known as Allah.

269

Ubu'l-Kassim seemed an unlikely challenger to confront such a firmly entrenched animistic religious system. He was afflicted by a strange disorder that caused him to foam at the mouth and fall into unconscious trances. Christians might well wonder in retrospect whether such phenomena reflect the symptoms of demonic possession as represented in the Bible. Muhammad himself questioned whether the seizures were divine or devilish, but his wife encouraged him to ignore any such considerations.

According to Islamic tradition, at forty years of age he entered the Hira cave and was confronted by a being who identified himself as the angel Gabriel. "Proclaim!" Gabriel declared, choking Muhammad into submission. "Proclaim in the name of the Lord the Creator who created man from a clot of blood."

During periodic return visits to Hira, the frequency of revelations increased. What he saw and heard was summarized in what became Islam's sacred book, the Koran (or Qur'an, meaning "recitation"). Over a twenty-two-year period, Muhammad memorized all 78,000 words of the Koran's 114 chapters and transmitted its teachings orally (he was illiterate).

A Controversial Message

The Koran's message encountered stiff resistance from the pagan populace. Wealth and material gain were their "gods," and Muhammad (which means "the Praised One") insisted they share their wealth with the poor in exchange for the promise of a glorious afterlife.

The God he preached was a transcendent being who was both lawgiver and divine arbiter. Muhammad's theology proclaimed a Day of Judgment with severe punishment for the unbeliever. This harsh warning of accountability was contrasted with a sensual heaven where green meadows, rivers of wine, and beautiful virgins awaited the faithful.

Few converts accepted this message in the beginning because Muhammad's denunciation of idol worship threatened the livelihood of Meccan businessmen. Those who followed Muhammad were stoned and beaten. In A.D. 622 he received a vision warning of mortal danger. His escape toward the oasis of Yathrib, 250 miles away, became known as the *Hegira* ("migration" or "flight"). This event marks the beginning of the Moslem era. Later the name Yathrib was changed to Madinat al-Naabi (Medina), the "city of the Prophet," second only to Mecca as a Muslim spiritual center.

To raise funds for his spiritual quest, Muhammad sanctioned plundering expeditions that raided caravans. Even during his native land's traditional month of peace, his followers mercilessly attacked innocent citizens.

During this time when Muhammad ruled as a king and prophet, he forged the Islamic concept of the *jihad* (exertion), the "holy war" that advocates military ventures in God's name. Those who died in battle were promised immediate transition into paradise. In 618, Muhammad led a force of ten thousand men toward Mecca and in a bloodless coup gained control of the city. Within ten years of his Hegira, all Arabia was under his control.

In 632 not long after his triumphal entry into Mecca, Muhammad died. One of his early disciples, Abu Bakr, was chosen as a successor, establishing the system of religious leaders known as caliphs. Filled with religious zeal, Muslim armies spread the message of Islam to India, across North Africa, and into Spain.

Had it not been for the Battle of Tours in 732, all Europe might have succumbed to the message of the Koran. A capital was established in Baghdad, and the caliph who ruled from there was the most powerful man on earth and headed a regime spanning three continents.

The Islamic empire was to last for a thousand years. Arabs developed the concept of algebra, and their skills in architecture helped them devise the pointed arch that was to grace Europe's lofty cathedrals. Sugar, paper, apricots, and rice were introduced to the West. Constantinople became the headquarters of the Ottoman Empire in 1453, which endured until Arab power diminished in the twentieth century.

A Rapidly Growing Religion

What is the key to Islam's current and past successes? The simplicity and directness of the Koran has left no room for compromise. Its history, fables, regulations, and threatening description of hell compel believers into single-minded devotion. Jews are damned by Allah, and Christians are told that faith in Christ as God incarnate is "blasphemy . . . whoever joins other gods with God—God will forbid him the Garden, and the Fire will be his abode." (The doctrine of shirk forbids associating anyone or anything with God's divinity.)

Islam does accept the virgin birth of Christ and even the scriptural account of his miracles. However, the Muslim's interpretation of how these events occurred is not compatible with biblical theology. The Bible is seen as a corrupt rule of faith inferior to Muhammad's message.

Twenty-eight prophets are mentioned in the Koran, but none compare with the last and greatest of all—Muhammad. Though he took ten wives and encouraged military savagery, his tomb draws millions of disciples who pay their respect with solemn admiration. He improved the condition of slaves, and although his ruling that a man could have four wives seems inconsistent with spiritual ideals, it was an improvement over the conditions of his day because he insisted that each spouse had to be treated equally and kindly.

Pillars of the Faith

The surahs (chapters) of the Koran are augmented by the Hadith, which contains traditions recounting the deeds of Muhammad. As a supplement it serves a role similar to that of the Jewish Talmud.

But the Koran is considered to be more than just another Islamic holy book. Muslims believe that every word was literally dictated by God and that its substance is eternal and uncreated. As a result, the Islamic Five Pillars of Faith are binding rules of conduct. These pillars are:

1. Reciting the Shahada. Every day the Muslim must publicly affirm the monotheism of God and the prophetic status of Muhammad.

2. Daily prayer toward Mecca. Morning, noon, later afternoon, sunset and before bedtime, all Muslims must say their prayers while kneeling with their foreheads touching the ground. Most Muslims go through the procedure in a mechanical manner, but such constant repetition serves to reinforce the piety of their faith.

3. Almsgiving (zakat). Charity was originally a voluntary act to aid the poor and purify one's remaining material possessions. Today the principle of donating one-fortieth of one's income has become an institutionalized tax in most Muslim countries, averaging 2.5 percent annually.

4. Fasting during the month of Ramadan. Between sunrise and sunset, no eating or drinking is permitted. This occasion is determined by the lunar calendar and commemorates the month Gabriel supposedly delivered the Koran to Muhammad.

5. The Hajj (pilgrimage to Mecca). Every Muslim must attempt to make this journey once in a lifetime as a deed of merit facilitating his salvation. Once there, he walks seven times around the kaaba (a cubical building housing a black stone). The kaaba is said to have been originally built by Ishmael and Abraham on the spot where Adam uttered his first prayers to God. If the jostling crowd permits, he must also kiss the rock (probably a meteorite), which Muslims believe was carried to earth by Gabriel.

Other holy sites in the area are visited, and a ritual sacrifice of goats, sheep, or camels may be performed. Pilgrims may also throw stones at the sacred pillar to "stone Satan," reenacting the stones Ishmael supposedly heaved at the devil when the Evil One attempted to dissuade Abraham's son from submitting to his father's plans to offer him as a sacrifice. (The Koran says it was Ishmael, not Isaac, whom Abraham laid upon the altar of Mt. Moriah.)

Principles and Practices

Other beliefs and practices associated with Islam are: using a ninety-nine-bead rosary to recount the unmentionable names of Allah (the camel is the only creature said to know the one-hundredth name); holding mass services for the dead; forbidding statues and music in mosques; insisting on circumcision; veiling women's faces with the purdah and draping their bodies in the ankle-length chador; permitting polygamy; abstaining from drinking alcohol, eating pork, and gambling; meeting for congregational worship at noon on Fridays; building minarets (towers from which to broadcast the call to prayer); abolishing a priesthood and having the Imam serve as spokesman for the faith; believing that Christ did not die but was taken up to heaven; teaching that Jesus will return in the last days to convert the entire world to Islam; and enforcing the "law of apostasy," whereby converts to other faiths (especially Christianity) may be imprisoned or lose their jobs and possibly their lives.

It should be noted that Islam is a complex faith, spanning many cultures and countries; therefore, the list in this paragraph should not be considered as categorical. The beliefs and practices of various Muslim sects are as diverse as those found in Christian denominations.

The code of ethics known as the *Shari'a* (the path to follow) enforces the morals and doctrines of the Koran. In the face of what the Muslim perceives to be encroaching decadent Western values, the Shari'a's stern application of "an eye for an eye" system of penal justice seems a reasonable deterrent to crime and immorality. Today, from Bangladesh and Pakistan to Iran and Saudi Arabia, flogging and stoning is again meted out to thieves and adulterers. Beheadings and amputations may seem gruesomely harsh, but to the Muslim the Shari'a represents fourteen hundred years of cumulative ethical standards that impose discipline for turbulent times.

Fortunately, such brutal punishment is rare, since exacting standards of proof are required. (Even usury is forbidden by the Shari'a, forcing some Middle-Eastern banks to come up with novel schemes to charge interest under another name.)

Not all Muslims regard the Shari'a with equal esteem. Like all religious movements, Islam is a fragmented faith with numerous sects. The three most prevalent are listed below:

1. Wahhabi

This group tends to be the most strict and puritanical. Mohammad Ibn Abd al-Wahhab founded the sect in the eighteenth century by preaching strict adherence to the Koran. Saudi Arabia's moralistic, authoritarian rule is an example of Wahhabi devotion.

2. Shiites (from shi'ah, meaning "partisans")

They believe that only descendants of Muhammad's family are the rightful heirs to spiritual leadership. Since Muhammad bore no son who survived him, his cousin and son-in-law, Ali (who married his daughter Fatima), are considered to be in the line of the Prophet's succession. Found mainly in Iran, Yemen, Algeria, and Iraq, Shiites tend to revere the Shari'a (though not as fervently as the Wahhabi). About 10 percent of all Muslims belong to this branch of Islam. Their leaders, Imams, wield dogmatic spiritual authority, as in the case of the late Ayatollah Khomeini of Iran.

Some Shiites believe that a twelfth Imam who disappeared in 882 will re-turn someday as a messiah, the *Madhi* (guided one), to establish a kingdom on earth. In Kashmir once a year young Shiahs parade through the streets of Srinagar, scourging their bodies with knives and chains. This self-mutilation ritual laments the martyrdom of Hussain, Ali's son and the Prophet's grandson, who was massacred in an attempt to restore the seat of Islam to Medina. A powerful Islamic leader named Muawiya had refused to recognize the succes-sion of Ali, taking the title of caliph himself and moving the headquarters of Is-lam to Damascus. This event lead to perpetual enmity between the Shiites and the Sunnites (discussed below), who followed Muawiya. Subsects such as the Ismailis, known as the *hashshashini* (hashish eaters), killed Muslim leaders while in a crazed, drugged state. (From this we get the word *assassin*.) They are firmly entrenched today as a merchant class in India and East Africa. The Aga Khan is their Imam.

3. Sunnites (from sunnah, "the tradition of the Prophet")

Ninety percent of all Muslims consider themselves adherents of this orthodox sect. Since Muhammad left no clear instructions concerning his successor, Sunnites decided their Islamic leader should be nominated by representatives of the community. The ulama, Sunnite religious scholars, have less authority than the Imam and are considered to be teachers and wise sages. Sunnites ac-cept the line of succession as passing on through four caliphs: Abu Bakr, Omar, Othman, and Ali.

An Adaptable Faith

The diversity of Islam is one of its greatest assets. On the steppes of central Asia, devout Muslims fill mosques every Friday. Iran's Imams assumed dictato-rial control to oust the Shah from his Peacock Throne. Across the vast Sahara, black Africans gather beside oases to study the Koran, a book written by an Arab whose descendants loaded their ancestors on slave ships to the New World. And in faraway Indonesia (with the world's largest Muslim popula-tion), students memorize the Koran while their elders mix entrenched local deities with Islam's fervently monotheistic system.

America's Muslims (estimated at 5 to 6 million) maintain a much lower profile. Evangelicals tend to approach them warily, remembering the massa-cres of Christians (5 million in Turkish Armenia) and the persecution of mis-sionaries for which Muslims are infamously known.

Of all major religious bodies, the conversion rate of Muslims turning to Christianity is probably the lowest because Islam pervades all areas of a na-tive Muslim's life. For him to turn to Christ is almost the same as committing suicide.

Few Islamic countries enjoy freedom of religion, and even where such freedom is sanctioned by the state, it is rejected by the culture. When a Muslim decides to place his faith in Christ, for all practical purposes he loses his family, his culture, his history, his economic stability, and his social life. One who leaves Allah for Jesus Christ walks from the life of the Islamic community to the death of being a social outcast.

Perhaps evangelicals should not resent the seeming arrogance displayed by the present Arabic spiritual descendants of Muhammad. God did promise to make of Ishmael's offspring a great nation (Genesis 16:9-11; 17:20; 21:13, 18; 25:12-18). Their ascent to world influence might well be viewed as a fulfillment of biblical prophecy.

Islam after 9/11

After nineteen "Islamic terrorists" attacked the World Trade Center in New York and the Pentagon in Washington, D.C., on September 11, 2001, many Americans who had never thought much about the faith of Muhammad suddenly became very curious about this growing religion. Many wondered whether all Muslims hated Americans and whether they intended to put that belief into practice by participating in suicide bombings or other terrorist acts.

Many Muslim leaders from around the world condemned the terrorist acts, arguing that the perpetrators had twisted the concept of jihad to pursue political ends. But still, many of the estimated 6 million Muslim-Americans understand the anger of their devout brethren who live in countries where U.S. political, military, or economic might has changed traditional cultures.

Small numbers of misguided fundamentalists in all major faiths believe they are taking matters of divine justice into their own hands when they use violence and destruction in an effort to punish sinners. But Christians shouldn't let the hatred of a few stop them from showing the love of Jesus to Muslims in their midst.

CHRISTIAN CRITIQUE: Although Christianity shares some ideals with Islam, the two faiths differ on most major theological issues.

Muslims view all other religions as satanic expressions of polytheism. Allah alone is to be praised and worshiped. Muhammad originally prayed facing Jerusalem and gave the Jews an opportunity to submit to his spiritual authority. When they refused, he persecuted them severely.

Christians must also be opposed, violently if necessary. In the eyes of a Muslim, if Jesus were God, it would have been unjust for God to have punished his own nature. All Muslims have a sacred mission: to bring the entire world under Allah's dominion by force of persuasion.

Though Allah is believed to be omniscient, merciful, and compassionate, the Muslim holds him in such transcendent awe that he is virtually unapproachable. The message of John 3:16 that "God so loved the world" is an alien concept to Muslims. God is to be feared and strictly obeyed, but his attributes cannot be personally experienced in man's heart.

Allah demands a codified system of submission, but he offers no immediate forgiveness of sin in return. The certainty of salvation known by the Christian (John 3:36; 5:24) is but a vague hope to the Muslim who awaits the Day of Judgment when works, not grace, will determine his destination in the next life. Christians cannot accept the authority of the Koran because it seeks to supplant the Bible.

SOURCES: "America's Facing Toward Mecca," *Time*, 23 May 1988, 49; James A. Beverly, "Is Islam a Religion of Peace?" *Christianity Today*, 2 February 2002, 32–42; Kenneth Boa, *Cults, World Religions and You* (Wheaton, Ill.: Victor, 1980); *Christianity Today*, 21 March 1980, 24–27; *Christian Life*, September 1977, 22–67; Timothy George, "Is the God of Muhammad the Father of Jesus?" *Christianity Today*, 2 February 2002, 28–35; *Great Religions of the World* (Washington: National Geographic Society, 1971); Asma Gull Hasan, *American Muslims: The New Generation* (New York: Continuum, 2000); *Newsweek*, 26 February 1979, 38–41; *Religions of the World* (New York: Barnes and Noble, 1965); Gabriel Said Reynolds, "Muhammad through Christian Eyes," *Books and Culture*, January-February 2002, 6–8.

ACCESS: Islam's disciples are found everywhere, primarily in the Middle East, Indonesia, and North Africa, where more than 90 percent of the population is Muslim. But Islam is a growing presence in the West as well, with mosques located in many major cities. For information, visit these Web sites: Islamic Society of North America (www.isna.net) and National Muslim Student Association (www.msa-natl.org).

See also Nation of Islam (Black Muslims), Sufism

JAINISM

This Indian faith has some similarities to Hinduism, but the strict demands it places on believers keep its numbers small.

Jainism at a Glance

God: Jains do not believe in a supreme being.

Good Deeds: Jains value good deeds toward animals and even insects, as well as toward fellow humans.

Creation: There was no creator of the universe.

Humankind: The human soul, like the universe, has no beginning and no end. Humans can come to perfection, omniscience, and omnipotence; it is possible for every person to become a god.

Sin: Like Hinduism, Jainism teaches that good deeds create good karma or good results, and bad deeds create bad karma or bad results.

The devil: There is no superhuman evil force, but everyone is capable of doing evil.

Judgment: There is no divine being who passes judgment; one's fate is determined by the balance of good and bad acts.

Heaven: Jainism accepts the idea of seven levels of heaven, but these are temporary stations for the soul between lives. The ultimate goal of the soul is moksha, or liberation.

Hell: Jainism also recognizes seven levels of hell.

FROM GAYLE COLQUITT WHITE, *BELIEVERS AND BELIEFS*

FOUNDER: Lord Mahavir

OVERVIEW: Jainism is as ancient as Buddhism, and its founder, a holy man named Mahavir, lived at the same time as Buddha in the sixth century B.C. But while Buddhists comprise about 6 percent of the world's population, Jains are much fewer in number. They number 3 to 4 million, 99 percent of whom live in India. But as a writer for *The New York Times* put it, they "make up in peace living intensity what they lack in numbers."

Jainism is a religion with many rules and restrictions, including a rule that restricts travel over water. That helps explain why people living in North America are far less familiar with Jains than they are with followers of many other faiths born in India.

To see Jains in action, one must visit India, which is what the *Times* writer did for a report from Sravanabelgola, one of the faith's sacred cities and the home to elaborate sculptures and temples. The report provides a vivid picture of this demanding, ascetic faith:

> From time to time, devotees amble past: dressed entirely in white, the color of purity, they wear veils over mouth and nose to avoid acciden- tally killing insects by breathing them in, and they carry whisks to sweep them from their path. That is typical: Jainism is an austere creed in which the respect for life, in all its forms, is absolute. As a result, the Jain are vegetarians. . . .
>
> Across from a small plaza is a plain temple with no sculpture; around 10 each morning it fills with digambara worshipers, Jain men who believe that nakedness is an essential part of religion.

Ancient Origins

Lord Mahavir, who was born in India in 599 B.C., was the last of twenty-four master teachers. He became a monk around the age of thirty and developed teachings about meditation and other spiritual practices that eventually led the follower to "liberation of one's self."

At the end of his twelve-year spiritual pursuit he "realized perfect percep- tion, knowledge, power, and bliss." For the next thirty years he traveled around India, teaching and preaching. He died in 527 B.C.

According to *The HarperCollins Dictionary of Religion*, Mahavir's message was similar in some ways to the doctrines of Hinduism: "The individual's soul- substance (jiva) is mingled with karmic substance to produce a person. All ac- tions, good and evil, past and present, produce karmic particles that weigh one down and bind one to endless rebirth. Liberation (moksha) consists in freedom from rebirth by halting the influx of new karmic particles and by eliminating those acquired from the past through disciplines of knowledge and ascetic practices. The most famous teaching of Jainism, noninjury (ahimsa) to every living being, is based on the notion that all forms of life possess jiva."

Jains also dedicate themselves to following the Five Great Vows of their faith:

1. Nonviolence
2. Truthfulness
3. Non-stealing
4. Chastity
5. Non-possession/non-attachment

Over the centuries, Jain has subdivided into sects. By the first century A.D. there were two main groups: the Digambara group taught that non-attach- ment required nudity; the Shvetambara group believed that wearing only one article of clothing was detachment enough from the body and nudity was not required.

Gurudev Shree Chitrabhanu, a Jain monk who came to the United States in 1971, established an organization that is now called the Jain Meditation International Center in New York City. But due in part to the group's strict lifestyle, it has found few converts in the United States.

SOURCES: Olivier Bernier, "The Extravagant Art of a Rigorous Religion," *New York Times*, 21 January 1996, 12; Gayle Colquitt White, *Believers and Beliefs* (New York: Berkley Books, 1997); J. Gordon Melton, *The Encyclopedia of American Religions*, 6th ed. (Detroit: Gale Research, 1999); Jonathan Z. Smith, ed., *The HarperCollins Dictionary of Religion* (San Francisco: HarperSanFrancisco, 1995).

ACCESS: International Mahavir Jain Mission, 722 Tomkins Ave., Staten Island, NY 10305; www.angelfire.com/co/jainism/mahavir.html

JEHOVAH'S WITNESSES

Founded amidst a nineteenth-century millennial mania, this exclusivistic sect continues witnessing to its unusual beliefs that contradict medical science and affront universal social customs.

Jehovah's Witnesses believe the New World Translation (their version of the Bible) is the best translation available today. They also believe that because they are the only group that refers to God by His "true" name, Jehovah, they are the only true followers of God.

RON RHODES, *THE 10 MOST IMPORTANT THINGS YOU CAN SAY TO A JEHOVAH'S WITNESS*

FOUNDER: Charles Taze Russell; born in 1852 in Pittsburgh, Pennsylvania; died in 1916

TEXT: "Ye are my witnesses" (Isaiah 43:10); *The New World Translation*

SYMBOL: The ubiquitous castle-shaped watch tower that appears on almost all their literature.

APPEAL: Those with an apocalyptic mentality may be enticed by the zealous desire of Witnesses who want to evangelize all the world before the end. Some people not well versed in Scripture may be attracted by what seem to be logical and reasonable explanations for hard-to-explain doctrines, such as the Trinity and the eternal punishment of the wicked.

OVERVIEW: She died on her sixth birthday, but like many others, she could have lived.

A blood transfusion would have saved the life of Ricarda Bradford, who was critically injured in a car accident. But her father, a chiropractor and devout Jehovah's Witness, refused the life-giving procedure. He quoted Genesis 9:3-4 and Leviticus 17:10-15, explaining that Witnesses consider taking blood in the veins to be the same as eating it.

Refusing to accept blood transfusions is just one of several distinctive beliefs associated with Jehovah's Witnesses. They do not donate vital organs or receive transplants. Until 1952 they refused smallpox vaccinations. They also refuse to vote, salute the flag, sing "The Star Spangled Banner" (or any nationalistic anthem), and will not serve in the armed forces.

And in everything they believe, members are utterly convinced they are right and the rest of the world is wrong. As Ron Rhodes wrote in his book, *The 10 Most Important Things You Can Say to a Jehovah's Witness*: "Jehovah's Witnesses are extremely exclusivistic in viewing the Watchtower Society as the sole possessor and propagator of God's truth. Other Christian organizations are viewed as deceptive and rooted in the work of the devil."

Unorthodox Doctrines

In 1879 a Bible study leader named Charles Taze Russell was looking for a way to expound his somewhat peculiar teachings. He had departed from orthodoxy by denying the existence of hell, the Trinity, and the deity of Christ, and felt compelled to reach a larger audience. He copublished *The Herald of the Morning* magazine with its founder, N. H. Barbour, and it is here that we find the first records of Russell's movement.

By 1884 Russell controlled the publication, renamed it *The Watch Tower Announcing Jehovah's Kingdom*, and founded Zion's Watch Tower Tract Society (now known as the Watch Tower Bible and Tract Society). The first edition of *The Watch Tower* magazine circulated only 6,000 copies a month. Today the Witnesses' publishing complex in Brooklyn, New York, churns out 100,000 books and 800,000 copies of its two magazines—daily!

Russell's theology established the foundation for the Witnesses' militant opposition to all other church organizations. Until his death in 1916 aboard a train in Texas, Russell insisted that the Bible could be understood only according to his interpretation.

At the heart of his system was a prophetical chronology that predicted the Gentile era would end in 1914. (Russell had already concluded that Christ had returned in 1874, but as a "presence in the upper air," not a visible manifestation.)

The end of the sealing of the 144,000 saints who would be "kings and priests in heaven" was also designated to occur in 1914. Those saved after that would belong to a servant class, "the great company," who would rule on earth under the tutelage of the 144,000. In the early days, strict doctrinal discipline regrading issues such as blood transfusions and conscientious objections was not mandated.

After the death of Russell, a Missouri lawyer named Joseph Franklin Rutherford took over the presidency of the Watch Tower Society. At a Columbus, Ohio, convention in 1931, he cited Isaiah 43:10 as the pretext for changing the name of the organization to Jehovah's Witnesses.

Thus, the stigma of Russell's questionable scholarship (he had only a seventh-grade education) and morals was resolved. Rutherford assumed total charge of the organization, and from then on his prolific writings were the source of divine mandate. This consolidation of power enabled him to discard some of Russell's less desirable teachings about the gathering of the Jews and the great pyramid theory.

After Rutherford's death, Nathan Knorr took over. In the same way that Rutherford had sought to supplant Russell's influence, Knorr ignored the works of Rutherford. Knorr was succeeded by Frederick W. Franz, who died in 1992.

Franz's successor was Milton G. Henschel, who resigned in 2000 along with six church board members in the wake of lawsuits that were filed against the group alleging child abuse. All denied the suits were the cause of their departures, but according to *Christianity Today*, all had enforced a policy that "instructs members to keep suspicions of abuse within the church."

A Binding Tradition

Witnesses live in a strictly legislated religious culture. The pronouncements that issue forth from the Brooklyn headquarters (known to members as Bethel) are binding, and no deviation is tolerated.

Witnesses who depart from such injunctions are "disfellowshiped" (their term for excommunication). From then on, Kingdom Hall worshipers (even family members) consider them as dead and are forbidden to speak with them.

The excommunicated "apostate" is told he will not rise from the grave on Judgment Day. Many former Witnesses have revealed that in the early 1980s, grounds for this shunning increased to include reading books written by ex-members, eating with suspected dissenters, and even, for some women, wearing pantsuits.

Strict theological control insures a consistency of doctrine. Witnesses avoid contact with outsiders, and the rare chance to meet one usually occurs when they knock on the door.

Society statistics indicate that 740 house calls are required to recruit each of the nearly 200,000 new members who join every year. During the 1970s the society grew 45 percent worldwide; in 1984 alone members spent nearly 600 million hours in missionary outreach worldwide.

In 2001 the Watch Tower Web site (www.watchtower.org) claimed the group had almost one million members in the United States and over 6 million worldwide. The site also said members spent over one billion hours that year preaching and had baptized 263,000.

These friendly but persistent zealots deserve high marks for perseverance. Although Witnesses never identify themselves when evangelizing, the first thing to notice once they're inside the front door is that they do bring a Bible, *The New World Translation*—their specially prepared version. Its translators are anonymous, so neither credentials nor their manuscript sources can be checked. But astute students of the Word will readily notice that the society's theological stance is enhanced by significant changes from the Authorized Version.

Debating a Witness requires skill and a thorough knowledge of Bible doctrines. They have been taught that all other beliefs are satanic, and they have been programmed with stock answers for questions that are often raised. Even if they don't know an answer, they're confident that their leaders back at the Kingdom Hall will provide the correct response.

An Informed Response

Evangelical Christians need to be aware of Witness beliefs so that a clever choice of words doesn't disguise their extremely unorthodox doctrine. The following paragraphs point out some of their more controversial views.

To begin with, the Trinity is seen as a demonic doctrine. The Holy Spirit is robbed of his personality, and Jesus is stripped of his deity. Their *Translation* renders John 1:1 "the Word was a god," introducing the Witnesses' belief that Christ, the archangel Michael, was created by Jehovah.

The appearance of Jesus on earth was not an incarnation but an example of human perfection in response to Jehovah's moral law. Witnesses do not consider Christ to be Eternal God, the Creator of the universe and our Great High Priest as declared in Hebrews 4:15 and Colossians 2:9-10.

Each year around March, Jehovah's Witnesses hold a "Memorial" service, which all members and potential members are expected to attend. This occasion commemorates Jesus' sacrifice, which began the covenant between the 144,000 and Jehovah. While it is similar to the biblical ordinance of Communion, only a few Witnesses partake of the meal. The Memorial is considered merely symbolic. No spiritual significance is attached to the event. Even October 2, their estimated date of Christ's birth, is largely ignored. (The only birthday the Witnesses acknowledge is that of the Watchtower Bible and Tract Society, which celebrated its hundredth anniversary in 1984).

Other Jehovah's Witnesses doctrines that may be encountered are soul-sleep and the annihilation of the wicked (along with Satan and his demons). They deny the existence of a soul that can exist apart from the body. To Witnesses, the soul is just the animating force that gives life to a material body. When a human being dies, his soul ceases to exist, and his body ultimately deteriorates.

There is no hell since there is no conscious existence after death. Hell, for the Watchtower, is the grave. Faithful Witnesses hope one day to be recreated (resurrected) from Jehovah's memory. Those destined for resurrection will inhabit either paradise, earth (the large earthly class), or heaven (the elite spiritual class, the 144,000 of Revelation 7 and 14). The earthly class will live as they have here, with a body and a soul. The heavenly class will "give up" any right to a resurrected body and will live as spirits, as they believe Jesus did after his "re-creation" or spirit resurrection.

Witnesses make much of their devotion to Jehovah and eschew any reference to God by another name. Ironically, respected Greek and Hebrew scholars tell us that the word *Jehovah* is nonexistent in the original Scriptures, no matter how many times it appears in *The New World Translation*. (No one is exactly sure how the Hebrew consonants referring to God—YWHW—were pronounced. It was probably pronounced *Yahweh*. The word *Jehovah* did not appear until William Tyndale's English translation of the Bible in the 1500s.)

There is no sufficient proof that any designation other than Jehovah is a deliberate distortion of God's name. The greatest challenge to Watch Tower Society doctrine is the fact that the Bible presents Jesus as God incarnate, a fatal blow to their entire belief system.

Paradise Postponed

But one need not be a Hebrew scholar to be aware of the most glaring inconsistency in the teachings of Jehovah's Witnesses. A brief study of the society's history shows a confused view of the end times as indicated by their record of erroneous dates for Christ's return. The world's end has been prophesied to occur in 1914, 1918, 1920, 1925, 1941, and 1975.

Since Adam's creation was presumed to occur in 4026 B.C., Witnesses taught that six thousand years of human history would end in A.D. 1975. When the date passed, thousands of disillusioned members left the sect. But President Franz had an explanation ready. The six-thousand-year chronology was set forward to begin with Eve's creation, and how long that occurred after Adam's advent is an interval not yet revealed by Witness leaders.

The delays in the coming of the kingdom are the cause of mental illness among some members, according to Jerry Bergman, author of the article, "Paradise Postponed . . . and Postponed: Why JWs Have a High Mental Illness

Level": "Many plod along for years, hoping that Armageddon will soon come to rescue them from their plight. In the meantime, their depression and hopelessness colors everything they do, even though they ostensibly may appear to be 'happy serving Jehovah.'"

Still, members believe the end can't be far off, and in fact the society has produced new mathematical reasons to delay Armageddon only until the early 2000s. They have been told that the war of Armageddon will be waged and the Millennium must dawn before all of the 144,000 "anointed class" from 1914 have died.

In the meantime Witnesses must wait to usher in the Kingdom Age of the Millennium and join Jehovah's forces, who will triumph at Armageddon. Only faithful Witnesses will survive the battle. Since the 144,000 already sealed will remain in heaven with Christ, most current-day Witnesses look forward to living eternally on a perfected earth.

CHRISTIAN CRITIQUE: Faulty biblical scholarship and out-of-context interpretations allow Witnesses to discard most orthodox doctrines. The 144,000 cited in John's Revelation obviously refer to 12,000 Jews out of each tribe of Israel, not a sealed company of heavenly "spirit brothers," as Witnesses contend. The death of Christ is not seen as a ransom for sin but rather as the procurement of a second chance to be offered in the Millennium.

SOURCES: Jerry Bergman, "Paradise Postponed . . . and Postponed: Why JWs Have a High Mental Illness Level," *Christian Research Journal* (summer 1996): 36; Kenneth Boa, *Cults, World Religions and You* (Wheaton, Ill.: Victor, 1977); Robert M. Bowman Jr., *Jehovah's Witnesses* (Grand Rapids, Mich.: Zondervan, 1995); *Christianity Today*, 12 December 1980, 60–71; Corrie Cutrer, "Witnesses Accused of Failing to Report Abuse," *Christianity Today*, 3 December 2001, 23; *Denver Post*, 10 June 1977; Walter Martin, "Jehovah's Witnesses," *The Insider*, March 1986; Ibid., *The Kingdom of the Cults* (Minneapolis: Bethany, 1977); Richard N. Ostling, "Jehovah's Witnesses Deny Legal Worries," *Denver Post*, 11 October 2000, 5A; David A. Reed, "Whither the Watchtower?" *Christian Research Journal* (summer 1993): 27; Ron Rhodes, *The 10 Most Important Things You Can Say to a Jehovah's Witness* (Eugene, Oreg.: Harvest House, 2001); Ruth Tucker, "Nonorthodox Sects Report," *Christianity Today*, 13 June 1986, 48; Watch Tower Society, *The Truth That Leads to Eternal Life*; *Time*, 11 July 1977, 64–65; "Watch Tower World View," *Christianity Today*, 22 November 1985, 43; Kenneth Woodard, "Witnesses for the Millennium," *Newsweek*, 15 October 1984.

ACCESS: Jehovah's Witnesses, 25 Columbia Heights, Brooklyn, NY 11201; www.watchtower.org

JOHN-ROGER

Church of the Movement of Spiritual Inner Awareness (MSIA)

After recovering from a coma, this group's founder said his body
was now inhabited by Jesus' disciple John.

FOUNDER: Roger Delano Hinkins

OVERVIEW: Prior to the coma, Roger Delano Hinkins, who was born in
Rains, Utah, to Mormon parents, seemed like an ordinary guy. After the coma,
though, he began making an unusual claim: his body was now inhabited by two
people—himself and Jesus' disciple John the Beloved.

Hinkins did what anybody would have done next: he renamed himself
John-Roger and founded a new spiritual movement.

Today the MSIA has fewer than five thousand students who take its
courses and buy its materials. But in the 1990s, the group received some un-
wanted publicity that raised its profile.

When a conservative California Republican named Michael Huffington
used millions of his own dollars to campaign for the U.S. Senate seat held by
Democrat Dianne Feinstein, Huffington's opponents announced to the media
that his wife, Arianna Huffington, a nationally syndicated journalist much
loved by some evangelical Christians during her conservative days, was involved with the MSIA. When Huffington (minus her ex-husband Michael)
made a run for California governor in 2003, she was again dogged by claims
that John-Roger was "her closest advisor." Mr. Huffington goaded his ex-wife
by saying, "[John-Roger] has more influence on her than anyone else in the
world. His religion is a religion of opportunity."

Newspapers labeled the group a "dangerous cult," and the popular
"Doonesbury" comic strip spent an entire week making fun of Arianna and her
so-called guru. Arianna claimed that John-Roger was only a friend, but the
damage had already been done. Michael Huffington lost his election bid, and
some think John-Roger was one of the causes.

What's surprising, though, is how well John-Roger had been able to elude
the media spotlight for so many years.

A Guru Is Born

MSIA teaches that in December, 1963, John-Roger became "the physical anchor point of the Mystical Traveler Consciousness," a mysterious being who
supposedly visits the earth every twenty-five thousand years.

MSIA was incorporated as a church in 1971, but before long John-Roger was being charged with plagiarizing the works of ECKANKAR. He was never convicted on these charges.

During the 1980s John-Roger wrote a number of best-selling books with Peter McWilliams, who joined MSIA in 1977–78. Books like *Life 101* and *You Can't Afford the Luxury of a Negative Thought* put John-Roger's name on the national best-seller lists, but this relationship soured in the 1990s as the two men fought over book royalties. McWilliams left MSIA and published a bitter expose entitled: *Life 102: What to Do When Your Guru Sues You.* A copyright ruling forced him to withdraw the book from circulation, but he remains bitter, telling *People* magazine, "John-Roger is a master of manipulation."

The self-congratulatory claims of John-Roger would be embarrassing to anyone outside New Age spirituality. But those in the movement are regularly bombarded by claims of advanced spiritual awareness. Still, the promotional claims of this egotistical guru are hard to swallow for even jaded spiritual sojourners, who are called to heed his invitation: "All that you want to be you already are. All you have to do is move your awareness there and recognize the reality of your own soul."

This newly polished version of the old spiritualistic claim of inner divinity compels anyone who is interested to get involved in one his many entities: Movement of Spiritual Inner Awareness, Peace Theological Seminary and College of Philosophy, Institute for Individual and World Peace, Insight Seminars, Heartfelt Foundation, Mandeville Press, University of Santa Monica, EduCare Foundation, Esprit Travel, The New Day Herald, Scott J-R Productions, and Network of Wisdoms Productions. All of that is available to find the "spirit within" and live a "loving, peaceful, and rewarding life."

CHRISTIAN CRITIQUE: John-Roger's claims of spiritual "transcendence" by being aware of yourself as a "soul and as one with God" denies the reality of humanity's separation from God by sin, a subject John-Roger predictably avoids. Borrowing from Eastern thought, he offers a "detached, nonmaterial state that is the source of our true wealth and prosperity." (One must wonder how that teaching squares with Ms. Huffington's personal comforts, including a $7 million estate and millions more in wealth.)

In typical New Age, syncretistic style, John-Roger promises that studying his teachings will not conflict with your prior theological convictions but will only amplify whatever religion you have chosen through "eternal wisdom." This embrace of all spiritual principles as one road, albeit enhanced by John-Roger, has already been adopted by Hinduism for millennia and is as old as the serpent's lie in Eden.

More dangerously, John-Roger belittles a hurting world beset by poverty, disease, child abuse, drugs, and scores of other real maladies, by declaring to his well-heeled clients, "The soul does not suffer. . . it looks at every situation as an opportunity to get more experience." That message may play well in upscale Hollywood ballrooms, but it would be a challenge to take that message to Liberia or Bangladesh or an urban American ghetto and convince the malnourished and disenfranchised that their deprivation is an experience opportunity! His dictum, "If you feel responsible for what is happening in the world, you can let that go," contrasts sharply with the command of Christ to "give even a cup of cold water to a little child, you will surely be rewarded" (Matthew 10:42, TLB).

SOURCES: Peter Sheridan, "Arianna, the Cult and Her Messiah Who Aim for the White House," *International Express*, 12 November 1994, 29; *USA Today*, 5 October 1994, 1-2A.

ACCESS: Church of the Movement of Spiritual Inner Awareness (MSIA), 3500 W. Adams Blvd., Los Angeles, CA 90018; John-Roger, P.O. Box 513935, Los Angeles, CA 90051

JONESTOWN

People's Temple; Jim Jones

The suicide deaths of more than nine hundred members of this cult in the South American jungle exposed the dangers of blind belief.

FOUNDER: Jim Jones

OVERVIEW: The aerial photographs revealed the scene in all its horrible detail. The bodies of hundreds of people lay swelling in the tropical sun, surrounding the metal-roofed compound where Jim Jones had once preached to his followers at all hours of the night and day.

Close-up photos showed dead parents huddled together with the decomposing bodies of their children. In addition, one could see the large metal vats that still contained the remains of a grape-juice colored concoction that all the members of the People's Temple had drunk.

The liquid contained fatal amounts of cyanide, and as far as investigators could tell, most of the people had voluntarily drunk the potion, then laid down calmly to accept their fate.

Drinking grape juice was a drill that Jones had perfected during his American group's brief tenure in the jungle. But on November 18, 1978, the drill was for real. At Jones's command, his followers obeyed, preparing the way for the most gruesome act of its kind ever recorded.

The Makings of a Mass Killer

Jim Jones was born in Lynn, Indiana, in 1931. A neighbor who was a member of the Church of the Nazarene told him about Jesus. Before long, the charismatic kid was carrying around a big Bible, preaching hellfire and damnation to other neighborhood children, and even performing elaborate funerals for dead animals and pets.

He later founded a congregation called the Christian Assembly located in a poor, racially mixed neighborhood of Indianapolis where he gained members by distributing food and becoming active in community issues. The church was renamed the People's Temple, and Jones was appointed director of the Indianapolis Human Rights Commission.

In 1961 the People's Temple Full Gospel Church became part of the Disciples of Christ, and Jones was later ordained in that denomination.

In 1965 Jones moved his People's Temple to Uriah, California, located near San Francisco. He had become increasingly fearful that parts of America would be destroyed in a nuclear war, and he had read that the Bay Area would provide a safer environment for riding out the chaos and death.

For the next decade the church grew and Jones again became involved in community issues, being appointed to the San Francisco Housing Authority.

But outside the public spotlight, questions were being raised about Jones's authoritarian and abusive methods. Ex-members complained of beatings and sexual abuse, and local officials and the news media began to investigate the charges.

Deborah Layton, a Jonestown survivor who wrote a book about her experiences, once described the punishment Jones gave to the group's children: "They would be taken to the Jonestown well in the dark of night, hung upside down by a rope around their ankles, and dunked into the water again and again while someone hidden inside the well grabbed at them to scare them."

Afraid that his carefully crafted empire would crumble, Jones moved the whole congregation to Guyana, a country in South America. Once there, his strong-arm tactics became even more abusive. People were fed poorly and forced to work long hours in agricultural fields. Criticism was reported to Jones's spies. Once they told the "father," Jones would humiliate his critics before all the church's members.

Complaints about the group continued, and California Congressman Leo Ryan decided to investigate, even though Jones told him to stay away.

As Ryan and members of his party were preparing to leave Guyana for

America on November 18, 1978, members of Jones's group gunned them down, killing five, including Ryan, and injuring others. That night Jones's paranoia got the best of him again. Afraid that Guyanese officials would investigate him, he ordered his followers to drink the cyanide-laced juice.

Guyanese soldiers approached the compound the following evening, but they kept tripping over obstacles in their path. These obstacles turned out to be the bodies of Jones' followers, which were covering the ground in all directions.

Lessons Learned

Following the March 1997 suicides of thirty-nine members of the Heaven's Gate cult in San Diego, *Chicago Tribune* reporter Laurie Goering traveled to Guyana to see what she could find of Jonestown nearly twenty years after it had gone silent.

Some of the trees Jones's followers had planted were still growing in the dense jungle, but remains of tractors, buildings and electrical insulators were disappearing into the overgrowth.

A Guyanese soldier who used to give Jones plane rides doesn't want the facility to totally disappear. "We need to keep Jonestown alive as an example," said Gerald Gouveia.

He is right. The blind faith and trusting vulnerability that led more than nine hundred people to their death in Guyana is a reminder to us all that we should "test the spirits" before we place our trust and our lives in the care of a persuasive leader who demands unquestioning allegiance.

SOURCES: "Cult of Death," *Time*, 4 December 1978; Christine J. Gardner, "Remembering Jonestown," *Christianity Today*, 11 January 1999, 31; Laurie Goering, "Lessons Remain to Be Learned from Jonestown," *Denver Post*, 1 June 1997, 24A; Deborah Layton, *Seductive Poison: A Jonestown Survivor's Story of Life and Death in the People's Temple* (New York: Anchor, 1998); James Reston Jr., *Our Father Who Art in Hell: The Life and Death of Jim Jones* (New York: Times Books, 1981).

KABBALAH

Thanks to stars like Madonna and Roseanne, an old Jewish mystical practice is finding new fans.

Understanding this means not just "believing in" the Creator, but identifying with Him in a way that magnifies and humbles us at the same time. To assert that each of us can become God might seem the utmost vanity— but no twhen the very essence of becoming God is to receive with the intention to share.

MITCH SISSKIND, "MEET GOD," WWW.KABALLAH.COM

OVERVIEW: Students who want to understand ancient Jewish practices usually have to look in historic theology books to find what they're looking for. But in recent years, Kabbalah has been covered in glossy magazines that people can find at the nearest supermarket.

"Mad about Judaism" was the title of a 1997 article in the magazine *Entertainment Weekly*. The story said Kabbalah's popularity has been helped by the entertainment industry's fascination with this form of mystical Judaism. Among the celebrities cited in the article were Madonna, Roseanne, Barbara Streisand, and Elizabeth Taylor, all of whom have become devotees of Kabbalah.

It is now trendy and hip among female entertainers, but when it was first introduced seven centuries ago, Kabbalah was a specialized practice that was restricted to men who were devoted scholars of the Torah, or the Old Testament.

How did this ancient practice become so popular today?

Uncertain Beginnings

In the thirteenth century, a Jewish man named Moses De Leon introduced a book called the *Zohar* to the Jewish world, which was mainly centered in Europe. De Leon claimed that "the book contained the mystical writings of the second-century rabbi Simeon bar Yochi."

No one had ever heard of this rabbi before, but to many people, it looked like the *Zohar* was authentic. It was written in Aramaic and claimed to be a commentary on the Torah.

Others weren't so sure, though. Some scholars maintained that De Leon himself wrote the book and passed it off as the real thing. Debates about Simeon bar Yochi, the *Zohar*, and Kabbalah's origins continue today. But nobody is debating Kabbalah's growing popularity, regardless of its origin.

Twentieth-Century Growth

In 1922 the first Kabbalah Centre opened in Jerusalem. Dedicated to spreading the practice of Jewish mysticism throughout the world, the group now supports centers in fifty locations worldwide.

A man named Philip S. Berg was one of the deans at the Centre in Jerusalem. After Berg moved to the United States in 1981, the movement caught on here. Berg has since become a prolific author. His most famous book is entitled *Kabbalah for the Layman*. This book helped make Kabbalah understandable to non-Jewish laypeople and helped spread the practice's popularity.

Rabbi Joseph Telushkin is the author of *Jewish Literacy*, which is a guide to millennia of Jewish traditions and theology. In this book Telushkin writes that Kabbalah looks into the mystical side of Judaism. It delves deeper into the essence of God and is less concerned with the laws and the more pragmatic issues of Judaism.

Historically, Jewish rabbis prescribed caution when exploring the mystical side of the Jewish tradition. In the seventeenth century rabbis taught that only "married men over 40 who were also scholars of Torah and Talmud" could study Kabbalah.

Today such cautions have been thrown to the wind. People who know little about Judaism or the Torah have begun dabbling in Kabbalah. What they encounter is often a watered-down and modernized version of this ancient practice.

Novel Teachings

The Old Testament describes God as awesome and holy. Old Testament figures like Moses hid their eyes from God so they wouldn't be overwhelmed by his overwhelming power. But today some Kabbalah practitioners have transformed God into a chummy, inoffensive force who sounds more like a New Age guru than the God of all the cosmos.

One book described it this way: At the core of Jewish mysticism is the practice of esoteric disciplines that tap into secret wisdom that can involve "ascent to and unitive experiences with the divine realm."

The www.kabbalah.com Web site describes God as Creator, but at times the site's comments make God sound as impersonal as one of the many Hindu deities: "The Creator desires to share his positive energy with us and this comes to us through manifestations."

The site also talks about "The Light of the Creator": "This Light comes to us in many forms, such as marveling at the beauty of nature, seeing the innocence of children. Light is just a small glimpse at the Creator's essence, and union with that essence is what we are searching for."

This site and other contemporary teachers say the emphasis of Kabbalah should be on putting its principles into action rather than worrying about theology and the nature of God. And as is often the case with New Age religions, the emphasis is on what's in it for us. In the case of the Kabbalah, its promoters claim it will bring people peace, joy, and fulfillment without any worries about moral codes like the Ten Commandments.

Telushkin says the essence of Kabbalah can be stated as follows: "God reveals Himself to mankind through a series of ten emanations, *sefirot*, a configuration of forces that issue from the *En Sof.*" These ten emanations are:

1. Crown
2. Wisdom
3. Understanding
4. Mercy
5. Power
6. Beauty
7. Victory
8. Splendor
9. Foundation
10. Kingdom

Some ideas promoted by contemporary Kabbalah teachers, such as reincarnation, seem un-Jewish to devout Jews. But you don't have to be Jewish to be concerned about a technique that claims to offer people mystical insights without any strong connection to an established faith tradition.

For example, the Kabbalah Web site promises a no-strings-attached approach to mystical experience: "Intellectual understanding is not the ultimate goal. Thinking about the concepts—and especially putting them into action in the real world—are what counts. Kabbalah gives us the tools to stay connected to the Creator's Light, and we accomplish this by drawing out the Light that is already within us."

Such comments from Kabbalah promoters indicate that no matter how much they claim they are teaching Jewish traditions that have been around for centuries, many contemporary seekers are getting little more than New Age spirituality with a few touches of Jewish window dressing.

SOURCES: Kristen Baldwin and Jessica Shaw, "Mad about Judaism," *Entertainment Weekly*, 24 October 1997, 8–9; www.kabbalah.com; Rabbi Joseph Telushkin, *Jewish Literacy* (New York: William Morrow and Company, 1991).

ACCESS: The Kabbalah Learning Center in Los Angeles is one of the most famous centers, due largely to its work with many Hollywood celebrities. There are also centers in other major cities around the world.

KIRPAL LIGHT SATSANG

Jesus taught that there is only one way to God, and this group claims it is through their divinely-appointed avatar.

FOUNDER: Sant Thakar Singh, born in 1929 in India of a pious Sikh family and educated as an engineer. He was inspired by his guru, Sant Kirpal Singh (1894–1974).

TEXT: *Kirpal Light Satsang International Newsletter*

SYMBOLS: Lighthouse on Kirpal Light Satsang stationery; slogans: "The masters come to fulfill existing religions, not create new ones" and "All mankind is one."

APPEAL: Kirpal Light Satsang appeals to the altruistic and to parents who feel society destroys the values they try to instill in their children. The emphasis on service to others contrasts with the obvious self-centeredness of most Hindu cults.

OVERVIEW: This organization is noted for its belief that one spiritual master (*avatar*) exists in the world at all times and that, by following him, devotees can burn away past karma.

Its advocates are vegetarians who meditate three hours daily and regularly practice introspection. Kirpal Light Satsang members are forbidden to participate in political campaigns and must pledge total obedience to their master.

Literature of Kirpal Light Satsang describes its organization as primarily service-oriented. According to the organization's founder, Sant Thakar Singh, it services the self/soul as well as the body's vehicle. Singh stresses, "Any service to the body which is not accompanied by service to the soul is of no use."

Initiation into the group is free, and the organization professes to be funded by private donations from members only. Thakar Singh tells his followers they must not believe in him until they verify the truth of what he says.

He insists, "If you follow blindly, there is a 99 percent chance you may be led astray because you have only blind faith, which leads to blindness."

Are Singh's followers blind? Not according to him. He travels around the world claiming he has no followers, only cherished brothers and sisters. He says he serves people and lives with them in harmony and in faith to God.

To Thakar Singh, success is achieved through the amount of service and love he teaches his cult members to give to each other. He believes this is a basic necessity and the "greatest service we can do for humanity."

From India to New York

Kirpal Light Satsang was founded by Sant Thakar Singh in 1976. The organization sells itself as a spiritual and social group dedicated to helping others. The organization's headquarters is in Kinderhook, New York. There are forty-five satsangs, or spiritual centers, located throughout the country.

The group does not release membership figures, but its followers have never been numerous. In the 1980s there were an estimated two thousand active Kirpal Light Satsang members in the United States. The national organization is operated by a board of directors and chaired by the U.S. national representative. At that time the organization also claimed 130,000 members worldwide, with branches in sixteen countries.

Sant Thakar Singh was born in 1929, the only child of a devoutly religious Sikh family. His father, a rural blacksmith and carpenter, died when Thakar was eleven years old. Thakar worked to support his family and finish his education. He gained admittance to an engineering school and worked as an engineer with the Irrigation Department of the Punjabi government.

Thakar Singh searched for truth and the perfect religion throughout his youth. His life was changed by Sant Kirpal Singh, a reputed Indian guru, whom he met in 1965.

Born in India in 1894, Sant Kirpal Singh was considered a leading spiritual figure in India during his lifetime. He was an avid religious scholar and wrote numerous books on spirituality. Sant Kirpal's master, Baba Sawan Singh, died in 1948, at which point Sant Kirpal became successor to a long line of spiritual masters. Sant Thakar Singh eventually followed in his footsteps.

In the twenty-seven years that followed Baba Sawan Singh's death, Sant Kirpal Singh organized and presided over the World Fellowship of Religions and sponsored the first World Conference on the Unity of Man. Sant Kirpal has traveled to more than fifty countries, talked with Pope Paul VI, and met with royalty, diplomats, and high government officials.

After days of questioning Sant Kirpal Singh about truth and religion, Thakar was initiated into Surate Shabd Yoga (the meditation of the Inner Light and South Current, which the group considers the Word of the Bible).

Before he was initiated, Sant Thakar struggled spiritually because his Sikh religion taught that Guru Gobind Singh was the last master and there could be no other living masters on earth. But once he accepted Sant Kirpal Singh's beliefs, Sant Thakar quickly advanced as a student of Surat Shabd Yoga. He practiced spiritual meditation six hours daily.

In 1974 he retired from the government of India to devote himself to the task assigned by his master, Sant Kirpal Singh. Sant Thakar Singh explains, "I was given this Mission by him: to carry on and share this help with other needy souls. It is by his orders and by the Will of God I am going on. These are his powers working. I am only being used as an instrument."

Sant Thakar Singh believes he accepted the "mission" from Sant Kirpal Singh because he had yearned to find God in previous lives. By establishing an organization based on the teachings of Sant Kirpal Singh, Sant Thakar Singh feels he found God. He teaches from the Bible when he is in Western Countries. When in the East, he teaches from the Hindu scriptures, such as the Vedas and Adi Granth, the Mahabharata (which includes the well-known Bhagavad Gita), and the Ramayana.

Sant Thakar Singh acquired from Sant Kirpal Singh the concept of the Manav Kendra of Man-Center. For Kirpal Light Satsang members, Manav Kendra services humanity. These man-centers offer free food, retirement homes, and free spiritual schools for orphaned children or those with poor parents. Handicapped people are also helped, and medical assistance is available through the man-centers. They also serve as an altruistic trap for spiritually searching individuals.

Teaching and Practices

Kirpal Light Satsang claims to be a worldwide spiritual and social service organization expanding to Western countries. Members come from all walks of life but must possess idolatrous devotion to their master and tolerance for his frequent and harsh discipline. Advocates are not asked to abandon their religions but must practice daily the ideals expressed in the scriptures of all the world's religions. Meditation, vegetarianism, and introspection are basic tenets of the cult.

Spiritual risk permeates Kirpal Light Satsang practices. Initiation, or the reconnection of the soul to its God-Source, is taught through Surate Shabd Yoga (literally, "the practice of light and sound"), the meditation practice of the organization. Kirpal Light Satsang enthusiasts believe light and sound can be awakened within every human being through initiation.

Meditation is single-minded attention on that highest entity—God—which is to be seen, heard, and enjoyed. Meditators are supposed to feel the blissful and peaceful "inner music of God." Initiation usually takes about two hours at the aspirant's home or at the Satsang Center. During initiation, the master "burns away" the seeker's past karma, which has "accumulated for ages," so the soul can be like new. Through daily practice of introspection, the student can realize and see for himself that God resides in his own soul.

For some, Kirpal Light Satsang meditation is not peaceful. Six former female disciples of Thakar Singh have publicly accused the guru of physical and sexual abuse. One woman described a forty-five-minute session of beatings, including karate chops to her head, that the guru inflicted to free her of negative emotions. Other women have complained of sexual assaults committed under the semblance of meditation massages.

Initiates into Kirpal Light Satsang are staunchly disciplined. Members must become vegetarians since meat, fish, fowl, and eggs are considered bad for the body and the soul.

Kirpal Light Satsang seekers are also expected to be ethical and honest, with an unwavering devotion to their master. They must meditate at least three hours daily and abstain from intoxicating drugs. Receiving the holy initiation does not signify joining any group or membership.

The charter of Kirpal Light Satsang, Inc., also forbids its members to participate in or interfere with political campaigns or legislature. Members may not own any kind of business in the name of the organization, which stresses that it is not a political or money-making group. Its sole function is to encourage people to attain God-realization.

The organization has a publication called *Kirpal Light Satsang International Newsletter*, which can be obtained by writing to the national headquarters address below. Sant Thakar Singh calls Kirpal Light Satsang a universal religion of love and service and wants to build a school in Oregon to have his concept carried on by younger generations.

At one point, the group's plan to create the Lighthouse School, a one-million-dollar boarding school to be constructed near Umpqua, Oregon, was the cause of much controversy. The issues of fire danger, water quality, and traffic control were raised by critics. In addition, Oregon citizens had already had nasty encounters with a fraudulent Eastern spiritual leader named Guru Bhagwan Shree Rajneesh, who was convicted of attempted murder and wiretapping.

In the end, controversy generated too many negative feelings, and the group went back to the drawing board to create plans for a less ambitious center.

CHRISTIAN CRITIQUE: Kirpal Light Satsang says its goal is to help others and to attain God-realization within oneself. The organization teaches its followers not to surrender personal religions but to connect with all humanity through universal love and brotherhood.

However, Kirpal Light Satsang conflicts with Christianity and the Bible. Christians believe Jesus Christ was God's only begotten Son, that he was the world's only Savior.

In contrast, Sant Thakar Singh says, "I think the Christians have not read all the other Scriptures. They are not wrong in saying Christ was the only begotten Son of Lord God, but as he himself said, 'As long as I am in the world, I am the Light of the world.' He was the Light of Life as long as he was in the world."

Sant Thakar Singh claims that since Jesus is no longer in the world, someone else (himself) must be the new master and the present light. The group exalts itself and its leader, not Christ or God. Kirpal Light Satsang is a dangerous cult that misinterprets the Bible and throws in Eastern philosophies and beliefs. Sant Thakar Singh manipulates his disciples spiritually and stands accused of assaulting some of them physically and sexually.

SOURCES: Kirpal Light Satsang, Inc., and the Lighthouse School brochure, 1 March 1988; publicity cover letter by Michael Robinson, 1 March 1988; biographical history cover letter with material, 1 March 1988; excerpts from interviews with Sant Thakar Singh; cover letter with material, 1 March 1988; *The Register-Guard*, 31 July 1988; Ibid., 2 August 1988, 1B.

ACCESS: Kirpal Light Satsang, Inc. National Headquarters, Merwin Lake Road, Kinderhook, NY 12106, (518) 758-1906

KRISHNA CONSCIOUSNESS

See International Society for Krishna Consciousness.

KRISHNAMURTI FOUNDATION OF AMERICA

Although others claimed he was a modern Messiah, Jiddu Krishnamurti refused to be worshipped.

FOUNDER: Annie Besant

OVERVIEW: Annie Besant, a guiding force behind the Theosophical Society, believed him to be an incarnation of God, the divine spirit in human form. A periodical, *Herald of the Star*, was printed and an organization was formed—Order of the Star of the East—to announce his appearance to the world.

Unfortunately for Annie and more than 100,000 members of the order, Jiddu Krishnamurti wasn't interested in being worshiped. He repudiated the ideas of his followers and commenced to travel the world, proclaiming his philosophy that mankind's crises are psychological in nature.

Though he was born the son of a devout Brahman, Krishnamurti declared, "Discard all theologies and all beliefs." Krishnamurti believed that all problems could be solved when human beings achieved a "right relationship with each other."

The Krishnamurti Foundation was not started by Jiddu Krishnamurti himself. Annie Besant, then president of the Theosophical Society, spotted the young teenager playing on a beach in southern India. Attracted by his "aura," she adopted Jiddu and raised him in Europe, all the while grooming him for the role she had in mind.

Besant, with other Theosophists, believed in a high entity called Lord Maitreya. She believed Maitreya had come to earth as Buddha and as Christ and would now manifest in Krishnamurti. In 1911 she founded the Order of the Star, with Jiddu as World Teacher.

Others weren't so sure. In 1926 American humorist Will Rogers called him "the amateur messiah from India."

A 1992 biography by a former associate claimed that what appeared to be his mystical calm actually came from the sexual pleasures he enjoyed with another man's wife: "Krishna had experienced his first sexual relationship, and . . . the new and joyful exuberance that he often expressed in those years was naturally taken by his followers to reflect his transcendent spiritual condition."

Another early follower, Lady Emily Lutyens, called him a "congenital liar." Clearly, Krishnamurti's legacy is complex and contradictory.

No Messiah, No Single Path

At first Krishnamurti accepted his followers' adulation, but in 1929 he dissolved the order, declaring that he was not the Messiah, was not divine, was not even a spiritual leader. Eventually he reconciled with Besant and the Theosophical Society. He spent the rest of his life traveling between England, India, and California. California was the site of his meditation and retreat center in Ojai.

Krishnamurti's most consistent teaching was that there is no path to truth. Man cannot reach it through creeds, doctrines, organizations, or knowledge. He stated over and over again that he believed in nothing. He encouraged those who looked to him for spiritual wisdom to "look within for the incorruptibility of self."

Even as an aged "non-guru" who disdained devotees, he continued to draw large audiences in the 1970s, composed mostly of young people anxious to observe a mystic of "elevated consciousness." Until his death in 1986 at the age of ninety, he traveled less frequently than when he was younger but still conducted several world tours each year. His trips to the United States were often sponsored by New Age consciousness groups.

Theosophists have not rejected him entirely; they carry his writings in their bookstores. In *The New Religions*, Jacob Needleman observed: "Many people still think of him as the World Teacher, even when he tells them to their faces that there is no such thing as spiritual authority and that he is not anyone's teacher. American students, who do not know his background and reputation, often hear his talks mainly as a profound expression of their own disgust with society, its hypocrisy, its ideas of national honor, duty, race and class, its bourgeois ideals and morality."

Today many people aren't quite sure what to make of this once-famed holy man.

SOURCES: Radha Rajagopal Sloss Bloomsbury, *Lives in the Shadow with Krishnamurti* (Addison-Wesley, 1992); *Denver Post*, 23 July 1976, 1BB; Jim Dreaver, "Krishnamurti's Shadow," *Yoga Journal* (January-February 1992): 88–90; Catherine Ingram and Leonard Jacobs, "I Don't Believe in Anything," *East-West Journal*, July 1983, 34–40; Paul L. Montgomery, "Followers Flock to Hear Mystic's Gentle Words," *New York Times*, 28 March 1982, 42; Jacob Needleman, *The New Religions* (New York: Dutton, 1970), 154; Gretchen Passantino, ed., "Jiddu Krishnamurti Dies at 90," *CRI*, 1986; Harriet Shapiro, "Picks and Pans," *People*, December 1985; Karin Stephan, "The Man Who Would Not Play God—The Life of Jiddu Krishnamurti," *East-West Journal*, July 1983, 36–39; "Milestones," *Time*, 3 March 1986, 79; Ibid., 7 June 1971, 4.

ACCESS: Krishnamurti Foundation of America, Box 1560, Ojai, CA 93024-1560

See also Theosophy.

SWAMI KRIYANANDA

Ananda Church of Self-Realization

Founded by a Westerner, this Hindu-based spiritual community practices yoga to achieve joy and fulfillment.

FOUNDER: Donald Walters, later called Swami Kriyananda

OVERVIEW: A former disciple of Paramahansa Yogananda, Swami Kriyananda's mystical name was conferred upon him by his spiritual mentor. It literally means "to do" (*kriya*) the way of "bliss" (*ananda*), or "to pursue and act upon the joyful path of yoga."

Kriyananda was born in Romania of American parents and was named Donald Walters. As an eloquent spokesman for Eastern mysticism, he has been called "the most respected non-Indian yoga exponent in the world."

Kriyananda was a vice president of the Self-Realization Fellowship until 1968, when he left to form his own seven-hundred-acre ananda commune near Nevada City, California. Commune members meditate at least three times daily and refer to each other by newly designated Indian names. Related business ventures cover the community's expenses.

According to J. Gordon Melton, the community and its branches currently have six hundred members, while the community's church has two thousand members.

Many devotees have been attracted by Kriyananda's "Practice of Joy" seminars that emphasize the attainment of outward boundless energy and inward fulfillment. "Joy," declares Kriyananda, "is the central fact of your existence."

To develop the state of ananda, groups are coached in chanting, meditation, "energization exercises," secret sacred yoga techniques, and Kriyananda's "Songs of Divine Joy."

"Belief is no barrier," he emphasizes. "Anyone can benefit: Christian, Jew, Hindu, believer, and agnostic." A closer inspection of *The Path: Autobiography of a Western Yogi*, Kriyananda's definitive work, reveals that his entire system presupposes a Hinduistic interpretation of life. These pagan concepts are considered to be the "original, pure essence" of the "ancient teachings." *Raja Yoga* is emphasized as a "science" to uncover the "truth" that man is an integral part of a greater Reality: "this Reality is conscious . . . infinite."

Pursuing Kriyananda's path supposedly neutralizes bad *karma* and enables one to "tune in to higher knowledge and guidance."

SOURCES: Miscellaneous Ananda publications and promotional literature.

KU KLUX KLAN
White Supremacy

Blending racism and religion, this prejudiced group attracts a new following of angry, young white males who feel disenfranchised by civil rights advances.

What the Klan Believes

1. That the White Race is the irreplaceable hub of our nation, our faith and the high levels of western culture and technology.
2. America should always be first before any alien influence or interest.
3. That the Constitution, as originally written and intended, is the finest system of government ever conceived by man.
4. That every American has the right to practice their faith, including prayer in schools.
5. That the family is the strength of our nation.
6. That abortion should be outlawed, except in the very rare case in which the life of the mother is endangered.
7. That all immigration should cease until all Americans are gainfully employed. Troops should be positioned at all borders to stop the flow of illegal aliens.
8. That the death penalty should be given to all convicted drug dealers and smugglers.
9. That the laws of the land should always be upheld. Criminal acts of any kind will not be condoned or tolerated.

WWW.AMERICANKNIGHTS.COM

FOUNDERS: Small group of ex-Confederate soldiers in Tennessee after the Civil War

TEXT: Bible passages quoted out of context and misused to justify racial intolerance

SYMBOLS: White hoods and robes; burning crosses

APPEAL: The economically disadvantaged ·have historically been exploited by scapegoating explanations. In this instance, America's problems of unemployment, crime, and civil strife are blamed on racial minorities. Such simple answers are attractive to the uneducated, who may not comprehend the complex causes of social unrest.

OVERVIEW: It was no ordinary picnic. White-robed figures mingled in the Alabama countryside with mothers and children, teenagers, and college students. People clustered around a hot dog stand. A man in a booth sold bumper stickers, belts, wallets, knives—all marked KKK.

Later, hooded Ku Klux Klansmen solemnly lit torches. At their leader's command, the disguised men tossed their blazing torches at the foot of a large wooden cross. Flames shot upward and to each side of the cross. A man nearby exclaimed proudly to his small daughter, "That's white power!" An attending Klansman attested, "We don't burn crosses, we light them!"

The KKK insists that it is a Christian organization and that torching a cross is a "religious celebration and ceremony . . . [not] an act of desecration." The group even claims its cross-burning ritual is an act of godly devotion: "We also light the Cross, as a tribute to Jesus Christ in recognition of his sacrifice, and willingness to die for our sins."

Many members use the Klan as a church substitute, citing the fellowship and support as reasons for joining. Its elitist tenets demand that prospective members be white, non-Jewish American citizens who favor a white government and racial separation. The Klan also targets homosexuals for harassment and physical violence, but it has changed its attitude toward Catholics and now accepts them as members.

Hate-Filled Origins

The Ku Klux Klan (from the Greek *kuklos*, meaning "circle" or "wheel") grew out of the Civil War. Alarmed at the changing social scene in the South— blacks were no longer slaves and the unscrupulous Northerners known as carpetbaggers had moved into the South, taking advantage of the defeated Confederates—many ex-Confederate soldiers and sympathizers formed the KKK out of desperation.

It was natural that in the changed South, with former slaves and sneering Northerners wielding political and social muscle, white Southerners would react in some way. But the Klan didn't become a serious social force until the movie *Birth of a Nation* was released in 1915. The film so romanticized the KKK and encouraged racial prejudice that, by the 1920s, the Klan counted nearly 5 million members.

For the next half century the Klan enjoyed a heyday that included substantial political influence, listing several senators and governors among its members. Throughout much of this century the Klan was a respectable—albeit secret—fraternal organization in many areas, and hooded Klansmen often marched en masse in civic parades, reminding both white and nonwhite onlookers that white supremacy was still a cherished concept.

Defending Whites

The KKK states that its primary goal is to protect and preserve the white race and ensure voluntary separation of the races. Its violent history has included lynchings, murders, and bombings.

In the late 1970s, 125 Klansmen wielding ax handles and guns clashed with a hundred black protesters in Decatur, Alabama. After the brutal brawl ended, the state prosecuted only one participant on a felony conviction: a black man who shot a robed Ku Klux Klansman. During the sixties and seventies many Klansmen went underground or quit the KKK because of internal splits and rivalry.

One young minister who refused to allow Klan recruitment in his Cambridge, Massachusetts, church was warned that he had only two weeks to live and would be shot in the pulpit. A large butcher knife was plunged into the upholstered backrest of his desk chair with a note that read, "You will be dead."

Lydia Jackson, president of Harvard University's Black Students Association, was threatened by the KKK with rape if she didn't "stop creating trouble and making noise on campus."

According to *Klanwatch*, a publication that monitors KKK activities, combined national membership of twenty-five public Klan groups in 1984 numbered fewer than ten thousand. *Klanwatch* stated that virtually all the groups claim their "Christian calling" is to separate or eradicate all minority races. A former Grand Wizard of the White Knights of America Klan said that "minorities were placed here by Satan to overthrow."

KKK leaders arbitrarily interpret various biblical passages to support their prejudices and to Christianize their viewpoints. One prevalent view is that Eve had sexual intercourse with Satan and bore Cain, from whom the Jewish race descended.

The Klan teaches that the Jews then fled to the forest where they had sex with animals, thereby creating all other minority groups. Only the chosen people—the white race—descended from Adam. Klan doctrine evades the issue of Jesus being a Jew by claiming that he descended from Adam and is, therefore, part of the Aryan race.

Nazism Reborn?

The KKK embraces neo-Nazism while claiming its solutions are more moderate than its swastika-emblazoned brother groups. During the 1970s a Klan revival was fueled by economic troubles, social changes, and a white backlash.

But its agenda of hate and elitism met with unprecedented opposition. Many states enacted laws dealing with racial and religious terrorism, also cracking down on paramilitary camps, where the KKK, the neo-Nazi National Socialist Party of America, and the National States Rights Party practiced guerrilla warfare. One such camp in Alabama, named My Lai, trained thirty boys and girls with M-16 rifles in the summer of 1979.

In recent years the KKK and its numerous offshoot organizations have worked overtime to repair its negative image. *Time* magazine reported about Thomas Robb, who tried to remake the image of the KKK by calling himself a director instead of an Imperial Wizard, eliminating robes, and making statements like, "We don't hate blacks. We just love whites."

But such efforts have done little to hide the evil at the heart of this group and have only generated criticisms from die-hard Klan members, one of whom dismissed Robb as "a poor example of a Klansman. He comes off as a young Republican, not as a racist."

Regardless of how Klan members attempt to spin their public relations, no greater travesty exists than when men play God and decide who is worthy of human dignity. The Ku Klux Klan abuses Christian charity by claiming godly direction in its diabolical schemes to eradicate minority groups.

Terrorism and murder are examples of satanic activity, devoid of the tolerance and love Christians should extend to others, regardless of race, color, or creed. Carefully crafted rhetoric cannot alter the fact that a burning cross symbolizes hatred and profound prejudice against God's handiwork.

CHRISTIAN CRITIQUE: The KKK proposes total separation of the races and the eradication of minorities. Some favor a back-to-Africa solution, while other racial separatists advocate partitioning the United States into segregated sections.

KKK followers believe they are elevating white ethnic pride, but they are also ignoring and twisting key biblical teachings. The New Testament teaches that all born-again believers are one family in Christ. To the Apostle Paul, there was no Jew or Greek, male or female, but all disciples of Christ were of one body (Galatians 3:27-28). Ironically, the theory of Eve's sexual seduction by the serpent was borrowed from occult Jewish rabbis.

SOURCES: One of the best regularly updated sources on the KKK is *Klanwatch*, a program of the Southern Poverty Law Center (see www.splcenter.org). Wendy Cole, "Re-Enter the Dragon," *Time*, 3 October 1994, 51; *Christianity Today*, 20 April 1984; *Cornerstone*, 1981; *Denver Magazine*, 1978; Martha T. Moore and Laura Parker, "Observers See Big Threat in Small Klan Groups," *USA Today*, 26 June 1998, 2A.

ACCESS: Found in urban areas of the United States, mainly in the Midwest; see www.americanknights.com.

FREDERICK LENZ

Zen Master Rama

Long accused of fictionalizing his biography, this controversial guru wrote fiction in the nineties before drowning offshore of his Long Island estate in April 1998.

FOUNDER: Frederick Lenz

OVERVIEW: He said he was one of about a dozen enlightened beings currently inhabiting planet earth—but he wasn't at liberty to reveal the other eleven.

He once claimed that people who spent an hour with him achieved the equivalent of what it would take a century to do through traditional meditation.

Females who spent time with him often engaged in other activities. "He claimed that it was a really special honor to sleep with him," reported one offended woman.

And one year he spent half a million dollars advertising his seminars with full-page ads in *The New York Times* and *Vanity Fair*.

Born in San Diego, Lenz formerly studied with Sri Chinmoy. But in a turn of events that should have served as a warning to the world, the group tried to discipline him for his arrogance. Instead, he left the group claiming that he, and not Chinmoy, was the truly enlightened one.

Retreating to Los Angeles around 1980, he founded an organization called Lakshmi, named for a Hindu goddess of fortune. By 1985 the group allegedly had eight hundred students.

Ever since, Lenz has been attempting to make a fortune for himself, allegedly using spirituality and his own disciples in the process.

In the 1990s he was charging as much as six thousand dollars for computer correspondence courses operated by a Delaware company called Advanced Systems, Inc. Earning as much as $15 million a year, he owned a fleet of luxury cars and mansions in New York, California, and New Mexico.

In 1995 Lenz wrote a novel about Zen Buddhism called *Surfing the Himalayas*. His publisher asked basketball coach Phil Jackson to endorse it. Jackson did so but then recanted when he learned more about who Lenz was.

"The message is fine," Jackson told *Newsweek* magazine. "The messenger is a guy who's done some things I don't agree with."

For example, one female disciple said Lenz forced her at gun point to have sex with him.

Lenz admitted he was an unconventional guru. "I am an American," he said. "I like cars, I like gals, I like success."

No wonder one journal called Lenz a "cosmic con artist."

SOURCES: John Leland and T. Trent Gegax, "Instant Bad Karma," *Newsweek*, 22 January 1996, 63; Joe Szimhart, "Snowboarding to Nirvana," *SCP Newsletter* (summer 1997): 1–7; "Who Is This Rama?," *Newsweek*, 1 February 1988, 58; "Zen Master Rama: Cosmic Con Artist?," *Christian Research Journal* (spring 1993): 5–6.

ACCESS: There is no current address for Lenz's latest group, Disciples of Rama.

LIFE TRAINING
The Kairos Foundation

In popular weekend sessions, this group teaches that people can achieve freedom without a savior.

FOUNDERS: W. Roy Whitten, M.Div., and K. Bradford Brown, Ph.D.; founded in San Jose, California

TEXT: Nothing specific. The Bible is quoted to those who want to hear it. During the training, certain exercises or disciplines are handed out in printed form.

SYMBOL: A squiggly line that represents the ups and downs of life

APPEAL: Life Training offers empowerment to transform oneself and the world through a simple set of psychological techniques similar to the rational-emotive therapy of Albert Ellis. Founders claim that "telling yourself the truth" can cure pain and suffering. Troubled persons with low self-image and feelings of powerlessness and hopelessness see Life Training as a solution to their maladies.

OVERVIEW: Promotional material crows, "NOW you can live your life powerfully and meaningfully. THE LIFE TRAINING: An intensive educational experience." Brochures proclaim, "You can ease the effects of . . . disorders in your life and begin to live . . . the vision you have always had!" Advertisements promise, "You become free to contribute what you are to the benefit of all."

This and more can be yours if you raise your consciousness and awaken your self, your heart, and your soul through the miracle of Life Training.

California Dreaming

In the late 1970s two California est-trained Episcopalian priests, W. Roy Whitten and K. Bradford Brown, founded Life Training. Rooted in the New Age and Human Potential Movement, Life Training tells students they can be free from fears, decisions, judgments, expectations, and beliefs—if they learn to change their basic reactions to life's problems.

Since 1979 thousands of students have sought to discover the truths of Life Training through reawakening or conscious awareness. Life Training is offered at several sites throughout the United States and England.

At the heart of Life Training is the humanist philosophy of noted psychologist Albert Ellis. According to Ellis, all suffering is created by illogical thinking. By his definition, man, not God, is the center of the universe, and all religious thought is irrational.

In spite of Life Training's founders' claims that it is "proto-evangelism," there is more similarity to New Age programs such as est than to Christianity. Specific examples include the two-weekend format, group size, the use of neutral hotel facilities, creation of a controlled environment, intimidation, transformational New Age buzzwords, group manipulation, a mystical worldview, public exposure of painful past experiences, and catch phrases such as "Transformation begins with Life Training."

Founder Whitten admits he believes that a nonreligious approach reaches more people than a religious one. As a result, man's sinful nature and the fallen state of the world are ignored. Though not directly stated, using this technique eliminates the need for a Savior.

Selling Secular Salvation

A slick manipulator of crowds, Whitten uses physical touch, eye contact, humor, and affirming applause to disarm people. He quotes the Scriptures but carefully avoids revealing his opinion of who Jesus is. He categorizes as holy books the Hindu Upanishads and the Bhagavad Gita, the Muslim Koran, as well as the Bible. He states his training would benefit members of all religions.

Life Training brochures declare the group's diversity, claiming that "approximately one-third of the participants are involved in a church, synagogue, or temple, another third consider themselves 'spiritual' but unaffiliated with a religious group, and the other third are burned out on the subject of religion or simply not interested."

Typical sessions consist of two weekends, seventeen hours per day, which conflicts with traditional Sunday worship. Instruction is intensive, running from 9:00 A.M. to 2:00 A.M. An average of 150 to 200 students are accepted per training session.

Detailed directions offer suggestions on seating, when and how to talk, and what to do in case of drowsiness. Chewing gum, watches, and outside reading material are forbidden, as are the names of Jesus, God, Christ, and Buddha. Members of the audience are encouraged to share painful personal moments. For additional instructions, "mastery training" is available. Once certified by Brown or Whitten, graduates assist in staffing weekend seminars.

Special programs, such as Lifework, provide routine follow-up lectures, workshops, and seminars to prevent graduates from slipping back into old habits. Life Training supporters claim this reinforcement gives followers the means to attain a higher mastery of self and service. Upon achieving higher consciousness, graduates are encouraged to bring guests to Lifetalks and are used as ringers in the crowd to evangelize and evoke appropriate cues and responses.

Life Training is operated by the Kairos Foundation, a nonprofit educational organization created in 1983 by Whitten and Brown. Potential participants are told the programs are free, a gift paid for by contributions of satisfied customers.

Through endorsements from celebrities like tennis star Billie Jean King and gushing testimonials from other alumni, Life Training continues to recruit people seeking to better their lives.

Although suggested donations range between $435 and $1,000, Life Training says its $20 nonrefundable processing fee is the only levied charge. That may be a small monetary investment, but the spiritual cost may be one's soul.

CHRISTIAN CRITIQUE: Life Training literature states its purpose is "to awaken you with an experience of life, which will radically enhance your ability to handle everything else in life."

According to Life Training, life's pain and suffering is the result of "mindtalk," which is counterproductive and untrustworthy. A psychological technique called "process" supposedly will solve all problems. Self-awakening is said to be a God-realization experience. In keeping with the Human Potential mind-set, Life Training contends that man creates his own universe.

The Training reveals a strong obsession with self and falsely claims human experiences and emotions can measure truth. Sin is ignored, and salvation is offered without Jesus Christ.

SOURCES: William E. Biewett et al., "The Human Potential Movement, est, and The Life Training," 14 September 1984; www.lifetraining.org.

ACCESS: Training centers are located in Atlanta, Houston, and Knoxville. For information contact The Kairos Foundation Administrative Center, 1508 Coleman Road, Knoxville, TN 37909.

See also Human Potential Movement and New Age Movement.

LIFESPRING

We already have everything we need inside ourselves, claim the founders
of this egocentric enterprise.

FOUNDERS: John Hanley and Randy Revell

OVERVIEW: Watch out for any group that feels it must contain a self-defensive statement like this one on its Web site: "There is no evidence of psychiatric harm from Lifespring courses."

The need for the statement is evident when one begins researching this group, which offers courses on personal development but which, according to alumni, achieves its ends through psychological abuse.

A 1994 story in *Redbook* magazine entitled "I Lost My Husband to a Cult" told an all-too-familiar story: "We joined a 'personal growth' group to bring us closer. But what we learned would shatter our marriage forever."

As author Anne McAndrews explains, "My experience was with a cult that arms itself not with rifles but with psychological manipulation. A cult called Lifespring."

The Best of est?

Cult researchers familiar with est (discussed earlier in this book) are aware that some of its concepts are rooted in Mind Dynamics, a San Francisco organization that taught mind power techniques until its demise in 1975. Werner Erhard (founder of est and The Forum) was a Mind Dynamics employee, as were John Hanley and Randy Revell, originators of Lifespring.

Hanley, who looks like the quintessential California golden boy, states that his movement is influenced by such thinkers as Søren Kierkegaard, Martin Heidegger, and Abraham Maslow. Hanley has chosen to be deliberately anti-intellectual and nonlogical.

Approximately 200,000 people have been trained through a program that now costs at least $995 and freely admits its similarities to est. (One difference is that Lifespring concentrates more on personal relationships than est did.)

In the course, "lecturettes" suggest principles against which participants can test their beliefs and habits, though the "lecturettes" do not present a particular doctrine that should be believed. Lifespring concepts reflect a mystical perception of reality. Even though no specific theological precepts are promoted, trainees are encouraged to indulge in parapsychology, meditation, and "guided fantasies." Self-love is promoted as being "the greatest love" one can experience. In fact, Hanley states that the first goal in the course is to get people to realize "they're enough."

Such practices and teachings inherently condition the trainee to view life in a non-Christian mode. Exposés in the media and lawsuits by former participants have marred the image of Lifespring and raised serious questions about its techniques, even though its promotional literature boasts it can help people discover their "core . . . a perfect, loving, and caring being."

SOURCES: "Lifespring—New-Age Danger," *Forward* 4, no. 1; Anne McAndrews, "I Lost My Husband to a Cult," *Redbook*, May 1994, 60–72; Elliot Miller, *Lifespring* (San Juan Capistrano, Calif.: Christian Research Institute, 1979).

See also est, The Forum

MACUMBA, UMBANDA, AND CONDOMBLE

Combining superstition, black magic, and voodoo, these practices have moved from Africa to South America to the United States.

FOUNDERS: West African slaves transported to Brazil

TEXT: Oral traditions

SYMBOLS: Many, including drawings in dirt, charms, signs, primitive idols representing the gods, offerings of money, liquor, cigars, and flowers

APPEAL: The promises of wealth, health, and revenge appeal to an illiterate majority. More educated devotees are fascinated by Macumba's promise of instant gratification and its immediate response to petitions. The popularity of spiritistic cults in Brazil can be traced to a hunger for transcendence many churches fail to satisfy.

OVERVIEW: The article was published in *The Washington Post* in 2001, but the shocking mysteries it described could have been the subject of an episode of TV's *The X-Files* or a bloody science fiction movie.

In short, someone was killing the young boys of Maranhao, a state in northeastern Brazil. In a decade, twenty young boys had been murdered in gruesome ways. All twenty had been castrated. Many had their jugular veins cut so that their blood could be drained for ritual purposes. Some bodies were even found near crosses or religious circles. Others were left near offerings of chicken blood, feathers and candles.

The killings created fear in the community, but one father who had lost his son was not afraid to speak out.

"Most people are afraid to talk about this, but I will say it because they have already taken what is most precious to me and I have nothing left to lose," said the father. "It is they—the ones who practice Macumba. They are the ones doing all these killings."

From Africa to Brazil to America

Ostensibly, Brazil is the world's largest Roman Catholic country. But underneath the veneer of mainstream religion are many disciples of more widely practiced, unofficial religions called Macumba, Umbanda, and Condomble.

An Afro-Brazilian cult that blends spiritualism, Catholicism, and voodoo, Macumba was imported by sixteenth-century African slaves who worked on sugar plantations. While most of the nation's cults tend to be regional, Macumba and the related cults of Umbanda and Condomble have adherents in most parts of Brazil. An estimated 25 percent of Rio de Janeiro's 10 million-plus people believe in Iemanja, goddess of the sea, and about 40 million Brazilians combine Christian beliefs with spirit worship.

Macumba stores are found on street corners throughout Brazil's major cities. The faithful choose their gods from a pantheon of Christian/African deities and make offerings to win their favor.

Roosters and Rituals

Black roosters with their throats slit, lighted candles tied with brightly colored ribbons, and bottles of sugarcane whiskey placed at special crossroads in Brazil are commonplace signs of Macumba. In a nation where hunger is epidemic, no one touches offerings of cooked chickens left at such road junctions, for fear of angering the gods of Macumba.

On New Year's Eve, Rio de Janeiro's world-famous Copacabana beach glitters with lighted candles placed in holes scooped out of the sand in ritual homage to Iemanja. White-robed, cigar-smoking *macumbeiros* (priests of Macumba) hold court in front of flower-strewn altars made of sand.

At midnight thousands of devotees wade into the water, carrying fresh flowers and other ritual offerings, which are floated away on toy boats to the goddess. Once the sea claims its gifts, those placating the gods believe their wishes are granted for the year ahead. On a recent Macumba holiday, about 2 million people gathered on Brazil's Atlantic beaches to honor Iemanja. They offered money, jewels, and champagne by tossing them into the ocean.

During Macumba rituals, gods speak through mediums in trance to offer help and advice. The Mother of the Gods, the ceremonial leader, is forbidden to enter into trances and oversees the rituals while making her own special contact with Macumba deities.

Condomble, like Macumba, blends African spiritism and Portuguese Catholicism. On any Catholic saint's day, Condomble practitioners pray and sing to the *orixa*, an African deity affiliated with the saint. But Condomble, unlike most cults, is monotheistic in its claims that the supreme being, Olorun, Lord of the Sky, created heaven and earth.

Umbanda is the newest cult of the Afro-Brazilian religious group. Combining aspects of Christianity and spiritism, the cult's rituals are led by priests and priestesses who oversee mediums. These mediums claim to become possessed by disembodied spirits so they can help people progress in their spiritual development.

A Growing Movement in a Shrinking World

Macumba and the other Afro-Brazilian cults are largely practiced by illiterate, middle, and upper-class advocates. The cults are embraced throughout Brazil, and an estimated 62,500 Macumba temples exist in the state of Rio de Janeiro alone.

A Brazilian state assemblyman won an election by promising state support of Macumba, and popular athletes and singers openly profess their adherence to the cult. One upper-class Macumba practitioner said, "It's okay to come out of the closet now."

To demonstrate his faith in a dead Catholic priest, canonized after allegedly turning the host into blood, a young Brazilian walked on ground glass and hot coals, swallowed razors, nails, and screws, ate light bulbs, and jabbed nails through his cheeks. He emerged unscathed from the Macumban practices, claiming he could do such things without feeling pain because of his faith in the dead Catholic priest.

When Portugal ruled Brazil, the Roman Catholic Inquisition tried to destroy heretical cultists, and failed. In the late 1800s a troublesome mystic, Antonio Conselheiro, persuaded thousands of followers to ignore the Catholic church and to deny the authority of the state. It took four military campaigns to obliterate the sect's stronghold by killing the mystic. Subsequent Brazilian regimes decided it was simpler and more prudent to tolerate the Macumban cultists.

Today disciples of Macumba, Condomble, and Umbanda are spreading their beliefs throughout the Western world. As growing immigration and improved travel have caused our world to shrink, these faiths have penetrated the United States, where they have established a powerful presence.

Initially, these faiths were popular primarily in South American immigrant communities, but now they have overflowed those boundaries and are becoming "mainstream" for many Americans.

CHRISTIAN CRITIQUE: Macumba and the other Afro-Brazilian cults support a pagan polytheistic belief system that refutes the Christian concept of one God.

Pagan deities are identified with Christian saints, compounded by the weakness of the Roman Catholic church in permitting such syncretism. Evil spirits, fetishes, charms, symbols, and signs are tools of Satan, as are all manifestations of witchcraft and black magic. Macumba spiritually oppresses a people already steeped in superstition and illiteracy and distorts Christian missionary work in Brazil.

SOURCES: "Brazil, Paying Homage to Goddess of the Sea," *To the Point International*, 26 December 1977, 12; "Brazil's Bizarre Cults," *Newsweek*, 27 February 1978, 39; Anthony Faiola, "Witchcraft Murders Cast a Gruesome Spell," *Washington Post*, 28 November 2001; Richard N. Ostling, *Time*, 21 July 1980, 43; David R. Phillips, "Brazil: The Spiritual Climate," *Christianity Today*, 4 April 1980, 32.

See also Black Magic, Voodoo/Santeria

CHARLES MANSON CULT

This disturbed and deadly figure who epitomized the dark side of the 1960s still influences followers from behind prison bars.

FOUNDER: Charles Manson, inspired by the Process Church and its Christ/devil duality

TEXT: Robert DeGrimston's *As It Is*, as well as issues of *The Process*, a magazine published by the Process Church in the 1960s

SYMBOLS: The official Process symbol is a form of inverted swastika. The Mendez goat of Satan is also used.

APPEAL: Charles Manson appeals to the socially maladjusted because of his hatred of society and visions to make things better. His fame as the mastermind behind the Tate-LaBianca murders also makes him a god to some.

OVERVIEW: He envisioned a racial holocaust and an elite "family" emerging victorious. Charles Milton Manson masterminded a plan to launch a bloody war between whites and blacks and convinced his slavishly faithful disciples to do the dirty deeds.

On August 9 and 10, 1969, Manson mandated the murder of several prominent Caucasians, heinous crimes he hoped would be blamed on the black community and ignite a racial battle. In all, seven people were slain, including actress Sharon Tate, coffee heiress Abigail Folger, and wealthy supermarket president Leno LaBianca. The Tate-LaBianca murders exposed the Charles Manson cult.

The philosophy Manson preached is based in the Process Church, also known as the Foundation Faith of God. In late 1967 Robert DeGrimston published *As It Is*, which spelled out the Process philosophy that Christ and Satan destroyed their enmity and came together for the end.

Christ is considered the judge and Satan the executor of the judgments made by Jesus. Therefore, to love the devil and kill for him is a divine mission of love for Christ. This duality of Christ and Satan greatly appealed to Charles Manson, who became known as the Christ/devil to his advocates.

Charles Manson and the "brothers and sisters" of his familial cult were also heavily influenced by Adolf Hitler. Vincent Bugliosi, prosecutor in the Charles Manson murder trials and author of *Helter Skelter*, wrote, "Manson looked up to Hitler and spoke of him often. He told his followers that 'Hitler had the best answer to everything' and that he was 'a tuned-in guy who leveled the karma of the Jews.'" The swastika Manson carved on his forehead testifies to his admiration of Hitler. Manson, like Hitler, is viewed by his devotees as a leader who strove to save the Aryan race, his all-white family.

The Process philosophy gained further popularity with the publication of *The Process*, a magazine devoted to the cult. In one issue, a band of marching Nazis spewed from the mouth of a fiery pink skull, trampling people perishing in a fire. In the same issue, Hitler's face appeared in a fun-house mirror, and a human being was shown burning to death. Fear was portrayed as power.

Vincent Bugliosi picked up on Manson's use of fear. Bugliosi said, "Manson's attitude toward fear was so curious I felt it to be almost unique . . . until reading a special issue of *The Process* magazine devoted to fear." Bugliosi said Manson preached about fear as an energizer and weapon, enabling a person to reach new heights and leave bitter failures behind, just as the magazine sermonized. Manson still favors fear and has been cited for behavioral problems in prison.

Manson's War Continues

Incarcerated for masterminding the Tate-LaBianca murders, Manson continues warring with society. He has repeatedly been denied freedom. Albert Leddy, chairman of the State Board of Prison Terms, declares Manson is "definitely a danger."

But many of Manson's family members await his return. (One notable exception is Charles "Tex" Watson, who is also serving a life sentence. Watson converted to Christianity, became a minister in prison, was married and has fathered four children.)

Still revered as the Christ/devil by disciples, Charles Manson serves as an inspiration for those who bastardize the Bible and attempt to justify murder, butchery, and such crimes as child pornography and sadomasochism. Racial Armageddon remains a vision for cult members.

The cult of Charles Manson has persisted over the years. Glorified by heavy metal masters like Ozzy Osborne in such songs as "Bloodbath in Paradise," Manson continues to lure fascinated followers.

In 1995 Manson released a musical album called *Commemoration* to celebrate his sixtieth birthday. The album was secretly recorded between 1981 and 1985 during his stay at the California Medical Facility at Vacaville.

And in 1999, on the thirtieth anniversary of the murders, followers were still singing the madman's praises, according to the *Los Angeles Times*: "The Charles Manson cult that carried out the seven killings haunts the Internet, and a new generation is oddly fixated on a bloody rampage that remains the nation's most bizarre and notorious."

Coprosecutor Stephen Kay told the *Times*, "It's sad, but Manson has become somewhat of a folk hero to young people. He gets more fan letters a day, more mail than any prisoner in the United States."

Testifying at his murder trial, Manson taunted, "You say there are just a few? There are many, many more, coming in the same direction. They are running in the streets—and they are coming right at you!"

People are attracted to the Manson cult because of its twisted philosophies of Aryan superiority and the worship of the devil and Christ as one. The torch that Manson lit in 1969 continues to blaze and singe the lives of those who revere him as a visionary leader and sanctified savior.

CHRISTIAN CRITIQUE: Followers of Charles Manson wanted to become part of his family. By being on Manson's side, if indeed a racial Armageddon occurred, that person would be saved along with the rest of the elitist family.

But the idea that Christ and the devil are no longer enemies is erroneous (Revelation 20:2). Manson followers feel that by killing for Satan they're conducting a noble mission for Christ. But Satan (which means "adversary") is the enemy of God. The two will never be allies, as John's Revelation clearly in-structs us.

SOURCES: Vincent Bugliosi, *Helter Skelter* (New York: Bantam, 1975), 637–638; Linda Deutsch, "Web of Deceit: Manson Following Grows on 'Net," *Denver Post*, 9 August 1999, 2A; "Mass Killer Manson Releases Album to Mark 60th Birthday," *Rocky Mountain News*, 1 August 1995; *Rocky Mountain News*, 9 February 1989, 33; Maury Terry, *The Ultimate Evil* (New York: Doubleday, 1987), 175, 177, 511–512.

ACCESS: Some cult members reside in California, while others are part of Manson's virtual community through a Web site maintained by former Man-son associate Sandra Good.

See also the Foundation Faith of God.

MARTIAL ARTS

Popularized through movies and exercise classes, this Eastern tradition has strong roots in the occult, despite its apparently benign adaptability to Western culture.

FOUNDER: Most historians credit the Buddhist monk Bodhidharma, in the sixth century A.D.

TEXT: Zen Buddhist doctrines; *Tao Te Ching*

SYMBOLS: So-called "spiral configuration" from the *I-Ching* representing the belief in reincarnation and cyclical evolution; double fish shown as a curved line in the shape of an S bisecting a circle. One side of the S is dark and the other is light. This represents the harmonizing opposites of yin and yang.

APPEAL: Self-defense as a crime deterrent; physical conditioning; sport; fascination with martial arts movies and TV idols; desire to achieve physical and spiritual composure; a way of life to arrive at immortality

OVERVIEW: One can hardly pass a video store today without seeing dozens of martial arts movies featuring characters who punch and kick their way across the screen.

Martial arts classes are taught in gyms, parks and church recreation rooms throughout the country. Even conservative radio star Dr. Laura Schlessinger has endorsed some forms of the martial arts, although she is Jewish and does not subscribe to Eastern religious ideas.

But few people understand the spiritual roots of this popular trend.

Exercise and Enlightenment

He stands motionless, draped in his flowing white uniform called a *chi*. Silence fills the room. With eyes closed in mute contemplation, one thought possesses his mind. Finally, he is ready.

Bowing slightly to his *sensei* (honorable teacher), he steps near the object of his concentration. In the center of the main room of the *dojo* (training center), someone has stacked six one-inch-thick pine boards on top of each other. Each end of the pile rests on two cement blocks that suspend the center of the boards about twelve inches off the floor.

For several moments he glares at the inanimate boards as if attempting to stare down a dangerous opponent intent on his harm. Suddenly, he draws several deep, quick, rhythmic breaths and lunges toward the stack. His arm is raised in the air as though it were a chopping ax, and he lets forth with a piercing yell *(kiyai)*. Almost simultaneously, faster than the eye can follow, his hand strikes the center of the stacked boards with one violent thrust.

Crack! Six one-inch pine boards splinter and fall to the floor, victim to the force of nothing more substantive than human flesh.

An audible sigh of relief is heard from those watching. Some nod in approval while others shake their heads in disbelief. Few, if any, realize that what they have just seen is an ancient spiritual discipline designed to harmonize the body with the energy forces of the universe in order to achieve religious enlightenment.

Pumping Iron with Paranormal Help

Tales abound (some spurious, some true), relating the paranormal feats of adept senseis. Such claims are astounding. Bullets can be caught between one's teeth. Punches can be pulled (i.e., stopped short of striking the body) and yet their effects can still be felt. Psychokinetic phenomena (the movement of material objects by immaterial "mental" power) may be displayed.

These accomplishments have a name: *noi cun*. The source of power for such feats is said to be *ki* (sometimes written as *ch'i*). Ki is widely known in the occult arts as the "life-energy-creative force of the universe."

Advanced practitioners of the martial arts credit ki with enabling them to knock a man down by barely touching him or by merely pointing a finger at him. Some have cultivated ki to such an extent that they can floor a man by their breath or a look from their eyes.

One martial arts practitioner I interviewed said his sensei could place his knuckles on a man's chest and send a burning electric shock through his body, driving him up against a wall.

Most people are interested in the martial arts for less exotic reasons. Concerned with warding off muggers or attaining physical prowess, they spend evenings at a store-front dojo learning kicks and punches. They are more concerned with downing an opponent than with attaining spiritual insight.

Some may be seeking an effective means of self-protection that will enhance a macho image to friends and lovers. But the inherent principles of paganism underlying the martial arts promise the novice he may get more than he bargained for.

Background and Philosophy

Interestingly enough, the centuries-old practices of martial arts are relatively new to the Western world. The boom started when returning World War II servicemen brought back such arts from the Pacific. Later the movie industry churned out films such as *Five Fingers of Death* and *Duel of the Iron Fists*. But it took American actor David Carradine to popularize the arts for the masses. In the 1970s his successful TV series *Kung Fu* helped spin off magazines and T-shirts with an appeal far beyond board breaking.

Martial arts film star Bruce Lee, to whom kung fu was more than a physical practice, explored its spiritual depths until he met an untimely, mysterious death. Carradine told his fans, "When Bruce Lee died, his spirit went into me. I'm possessed."

There are many conflicting historical theories regarding the origin of martial arts. The account stated here is a widely accepted survey that traces the general history of the martial arts and goes back to the dawn of civilization in India.

Three millennia ago in China the arts were developed even more extensively. By the establishment of the Feudal States in 770 B.C., kung fu was widely practiced. Only during the Boxer Rebellion of 1900 were the martial arts partially eliminated from the mainland. In 1928 they were renamed war arts and were accorded national recognition.

Over the centuries various aspects of the arts were modified and eventually evolved into more or less violent types. Northern and southern schools and hard and soft forms also developed. Kung fu was the original all-inclusive term describing the martial arts.

Later specific names were applied to its variations: karate, tai chi, judo, jujitsu, and aikido. In Korea the arts were known as Tae Kwon Do, and they were honed into their highest forms of proficiency in Okinawa. Though one often thinks of the arts as "made in Japan," they have many roots and cultural variations.

Myriad Methods

The original religious philosophy of kung fu dates back as far as 2696 B.C., where it was rooted in the occult forms of divination known as the I-Ching and the "Book of Changes." Lao-Tse, the Chinese sage born in 604 B.C., added further embellishments. His teachings were set forth in a 5,280-word manuscript called *Tao Te Ching*, often called simply "the tao," or "the way" (see entry on Taoism). He taught that salvation could not be found in prayer but rather by the observance of nature, the natural way. As the trees bend with the wind and the rivers follow the path of least resistance, so must man adapt to the rhythm of coexistence with evil and wrong.

The next development in the history of kung fu took place when a monk named Bodhidharma brought Buddhism to China in the sixth century A.D. When he discovered the monks sleeping during his lectures, he introduced exercises to assist them in meditation. Known as *I-chin Sutura*, his system combined kung fu with the philosophical principles of Zen to develop a highly sophisticated form of weaponless fighting. The monks at his Shaolin Temple became famous for their savage abilities of defense, which they employed whenever they were attacked in the course of pilgrimages.

Eventually two schools of martial arts evolved: *Ch'uan Fe* (kung fu) based on the hard (external) school of Buddhism, and other arts founded on the soft (internal) school of Taoism. As martial arts spread beyond the monastery to the fields of war, some of the religious flavor was lost. But the essential belief system behind these disciplines has never been completely abandoned, even today.

After centuries of countless adaptations, the martial arts have evolved into six basic forms by which they are known in the Western world. Other variations exist, but for the sake of brevity, categorizing these six headings will be sufficient.

Kung Fu

Originally used as a colloquialism referring to any martial art, kung fu is considered to be the mother of all such physical disciplines. The alchemists who developed it were said to be literally "possessed" with kung fu. In *The History and Philosophy of Kung Fu*, Earl C. Mederiros states, "Kung fu represents the development of man as a complete person. It combines the theological with the philosophical and blends these with the physical, thus evolving those attitudes that are in keeping with the natural laws . . . a perfect harmony of the physical and metaphysical."

Kung fu is known best for its "hard" school, which emphasizes kicking, striking, and punching with strength and speed. The power is said to be derived from ki and may also be directed toward improvement of one's health as well as for self-defense. But its appeal to many people lies more in its offensive character, which emphasizes force to break force. It also may include the striking of vital points, delayed action "death touches," and the use of psychic powers.

Tai Chi Ch'uan

There is some historical evidence that this martial art, which is increasingly popular with Western women, evolved from the "soft" school of kung fu. There is a separate entry on Tai Chi later in this book, but the following brief summary will help us understand its relationship to the other martial arts.

It was founded by Chang San-feng who meditated on the occult I-Ching while watching a snake and crane fight. Like Lao-Tse, he was interested in the balanced interplay of opposites known as yin and yang. In Tai Chi Ch'uan, these negative (*yin*) and positive (*yang*) principles are supposed to reach a harmonious duality when mind, breath, and sexual energy come together. In this state ki will produce quietness and cure impotency and depression.

All this is achieved by practicing "shadow-boxing" while concentrating on the body's psychic center located below the navel. Participants often arise early to practice the fluid, rhythmic motions of Tai Chi. Some claim it produces natural health (a famous participant was said to have lived for 250 years).

One of the West's foremost Tai Chi teachers, T. T. Liang, states, "The ultimate goal of learning and practicing Tai Chi is to become an immortal." This is accomplished by placing the body in harmony with the laws of nature. Some proponents claim supernatural strength and warn of its devastating power as a combative form.

Karate

For Western men, this is the best known and the most practiced of all the martial arts. Today it is used basically as a form of self-defense and sport fighting, using bare hands, arms, and wrists. American occupation forces brought karate back from Japan where it had been imported from Okinawa and China. It developed in these countries because the Japanese rulers had forbidden their people the use of weapons.

Gichin Funakoshi, who developed it as Shotokan Ryu, emphasized that the student must empty his mind of wickedness in order to react cognitively, and from this philosophy we get the term *karate,* meaning "empty hand." In Okinawa, karate became imbedded with Zen philosophy.

The undercurrent of Buddhism found in some martial arts is illustrated by the emphasis on bowing, breathing exercises, seated meditation, intense concentration, and heightened awareness. Reflective thinking is discouraged—another influence of Buddhism. Since karate is a practice of the spirit, its stated purpose is to unite mind, body, and spirit to achieve the unity envisioned by Zen.

The most distinctive practice in karate is called kata, a choreographed combination of kicks, punches, and breathing techniques. It is like a graceful, yet powerful dance performed alone because the blows are deadly enough to kill. Fortunately, sport karate does not cultivate the intent of taking another life or painfully disabling an opponent. And most instructors do not pursue the spiritual purpose of cultivating ki to achieve union with an internalized god. But it is questionable whether any devotee taught by a traditional sensei may be totally free of the distinctly pagan frame of reference associated with karate.

Aikido

This martial art is the most overtly religious. Literally, *aikido* means "the road to a union with the universal spirit." It was founded by Morihei Uyeshiba, who became concerned that he couldn't control his strength without controlling his mind.

Ultimately, after entering many temples, he arrived at "enlightenment" and viewed himself, in the Buddhist theological concept, as "at one with the universe." At that moment, he declared, "The fundamental principle of the martial arts is God's love and universal love. The true martial arts," he said, "regulate the *ki* of the universe."

All of the body movements of aikido are said to agree with the universal laws of nature and bring to the follower the power of ki, which is inhaled into the lower abdomen and exhaled through the hands. When the innate psychic powers of all men are united with the spirit and body, aikidoists predict the world will be composed of one family.

A tenth-degree black belt aikido instructor from Japan states of his art, "We create a universal harmony that ties together all of the worlds, the phenomenal world we see around us, the world of the kind of spirits we cannot see, and the pure world of energy. This building of harmony and harmonizing the universe with ourselves so we may become one is the essence and ultimate purpose of aikido."

Morihei Uyeshiba (O'senei as he is known by devotees) once described a strange psychic/occult visionary experience of seeing rays come down from the sky. "I felt my body growing larger and filling the entire cosmos. While I was exalted by this vision, I acknowledged suddenly I should not want to win: a martial art should be a form of life."

Judo and Jujitsu

Jujitsu is a blending of kung fu and Japanese martial arts. By the twentieth century it was the Japanese national sport. A basic factor is knowing the vulnerable portions of an antagonist's anatomy and how to attack those areas.

Judo is basically jujitsu minus the killing aspects. It was founded in 1882 by Jogoro Kano, a student of jujitsu. Unlike karate, which may be compared with boxing, the gentler art of judo is similar to wrestling. It employs the use of balance and leverage to throw an enemy. Devotees are warned in some judo manuals that the art should not be learned without the inclusion of meditation exercises. Its founder agrees, calling it a "method of arriving at self-realization."

While it may be true that the various disciplines of martial arts have different forms, they all have similar religious backgrounds and goals. Because of their roots in Taoism and Buddhism, they view the entire universe as an interplay of harmonizing opposites, the yin and yang. These principles are expressed by the relaxed state of movements.

"The way" of Tao is accomplished by yielding and never resisting, and by responding sympathetically to each action of one's opponent. As illustrated in kung fu, each movement is uninterrupted and flowing. The end of one action is the beginning of the next, thus balancing the yin and yang. When the Zen goal of stilled senses is also achieved, this balanced harmony is supposed to help one merge with the Universal Consciousness.

Additional practices include:

- Tae Kwon Do, a sport-oriented form of the martial arts practiced by many Christians
- Muay Thai Kickboxing, a fast-growing competitive sport which originated in Thailand some 3,500 years ago
- Ninjitsu, which is associated with the Eastern pantheism of the Ninja warriors

Assessing the Impact

To Christians, salvation comes by the finished work of the cross, where Christ was sacrificed for our sin. And it is by his resurrection that we have hope of eternal life. Salvation in Zen is achieved by comprehending the divine essence of man, who is a manifestation of the Universal Soul.

Followers of Zen believe that such enlightenment may be shared by sending forth ki to illuminate the spiritual darkness of the world. Whether the form of martial arts one practices is based on the doctrine of naturalism found in Taoism or the doctrine of illusion found in Buddhism, the philosophical basis of both explicitly deny the blood atonement of Christ.

The Christian practitioner of the martial arts must ask himself whether or not any involvement in such physical disciplines implies an inherent approval of the religious principles behind them. He should also take care to be certain his instructor adequately divorces the mystical aspects of the martial arts from their strictly physical components.

In recent years, two Christian groups have emerged which try to help believers sort through some of these issues: The Gospel Martial Arts Union (www.gmaru.org) and Christian Martial Arts (www.christianmartialarts.org).

The Christian Martial Arts group, based in Coral Springs, Florida, has created the following mission statement: "Our prayer is that through this Association, your school will have the freedom to train without compromising your Christian beliefs. You will be able to glorify God with the gifts you've been given just as the Champions for Christ (CMAA/HQ demonstration evangelism team) has been able to do over the last ten years." The group also holds an annual Black Belt Seminar for all black belt students affiliated with CMAA.

Groups like these can help Christians be wise about their involvement in the martial arts.

CHRISTIAN CRITIQUE: The martial arts vary widely, and the instruction students receive depends on the form of discipline studied and the instructor.

Traditional Eastern senseis will possibly present the arts as a religion with meditation techniques and idolatrous trappings. Western instructors will more likely emphasize the initial sport stages and appeal to a more casual fascination with the arts as a fad.

The religious and philosophical roots of most martial arts forms presuppose a pantheistic perception of the cosmos. Even the cautious student runs the risk of being conditioned by the techniques that pursue a goal of impersonal oneness with the universe. The Taoistic and Buddhist overtones represent more than a historical root. These principles are an integral part of fulfilling the ultimate spiritual aims of most art forms.

SOURCES: Erwin de Castro, B. J. Cropeza, and Ron Rhodes, "Enter the Dragon," *Christian Research Journal* (fall 1993): 24–34 and (winter 1994): 24–34; *East-West Journal* (November 1978): 72; William Logan and Herman Petras, *Handbook of the Martial Arts and Self Defense* (New York: Funk and Wagnalls, 1975); Earl Mederiros, *The History and Philosophy of Kung Fu* (Rutland, Vt.: Charles E. Tuttle, 1974); *Newsweek*, 2 January 1978, 40; *Sports Illustrated*, 18 August 1975; Koichi Tohei, *Aikido in Daily Life* (Tokyo: Rikugei, 1966); "Women Liberating Themselves with Karate," *East-West Journal*, September 1976, 14–16.

ACCESS: Martial arts training centers *(dojos)* in most major cities

MEDITATION

This practice, which is found in Judaism, Christianity, and many Eastern faiths
is increasingly popular in our noisy, frenzied world.

True contemplation is not a psychological trick but a theological grace.
CATHOLIC MONK THOMAS MERTON

OVERVIEW: Meditation is one of the most misunderstood words in the vocabulary of contemporary religion. To some people the word evokes images of Christians immersed in prayer to their God. To others it means shaven heads, secret ceremonies, and mind control. For many, meditation seems safe and harmless. After all, the Bible encourages meditation. Other practices of cults and Eastern religions may raise eyebrows, but meditation is seen as possibly beneficial and certainly not dangerous.

Such a conclusion is potentially erroneous. In fact, of all the techniques facilitating the goals of cult philosophy, meditation is probably the one practice that is the most spiritually devastating. Meditation isn't a neutral indulgence. Its benefits or damage depend on why and how one meditates.

The West Embraces an Eastern Practice

According to a *Time* magazine cover story, 10 million Americans meditate regularly. Though the Western world has rediscovered the phenomenon of a contemplative life, meditation is as old as the Hindu Vedic scriptures and the book of Joshua. "This book of the law shall not depart out of thy mouth; but thou shalt meditate therein day and night," the Word of God declares (Joshua 1:8).

Since the words *meditate* or *meditation* appear twenty times in the Old and New Testaments, it is unquestionable that the lost art of biblical meditation is strongly endorsed in Scripture. What then makes it different from the procedures recommended by Transcendental Meditation and other Eastern cults?

The "how" of mystical meditation involves a process of shutting down the mind. While the Bible emphasizes the importance of knowledge as a key to communion with God, the mystic wishes to pacify the will and ego until they no longer function actively. Christianity teaches that the channel of the mind represents one avenue by which God reveals his laws and love. The Creator has gifted man with the capacity of reason, which plays an important role in discerning the will and ways of the Lord. Eastern mysticism considers the mind to be an enemy of the spirit. Therefore, it must be set aside by techniques that cause it to cease functioning.

This assault on the mind may involve a physical or verbal means of stilling its processes. Fasting, posturing positions, long periods of silence, and repetitive mantras are just a few of the techniques employed. The mantra is the most popular and frequently used method. By repeatedly chanting a word or syllable over and over, the neurosensory faculties of the body become fatigued and shut down.

This psychophysiological phenomenon can be illustrated by noticing, when entering a room with a foul odor, that the smell gradually becomes indistinguishable. In a similar manner, repeating a word over and over causes the meditator to lose touch with the objective meaning of the word.

For example, saying the word "chair" in a repetitious fashion for fifteen minutes may actually render the mind incapable of consciously comprehending the relationship between what becomes a nonsensical sound and a material object on which one sits, a *chair*. If the mantra is based on the name of a pagan deity or spiritual principle, an even more powerful and dangerous effect takes place that may actually induce a tranced-out state of altered consciousness.

The "why" of Eastern forms of mystical meditation is predicated on the goal of god-realization and the merging of one's consciousness with the Universal Mind. Once the mind has been emptied of any awareness regarding the objective, external world, the meditator becomes conscious of what appears to be a unifying oneness of reality.

In such a condition, mystical meditators often report a state of joy, peace, and indescribable bliss. If the meditator has previously been coached in a system of religious philosophy by which he can interpret the experience, he readily identifies it as achieving union with Ultimate Reality.

Dangers of Meditation

What really happens when people meditate in ways prescribed by Eastern religions or New Age groups?

The intensity of the experience may trigger biological responses similar to the effect drugs have when creating illusory experiences. It might be that demonic beings seize upon the opportunity of an emptied, unguarded, and defenseless mind to create spiritistic hallucinations. On the other hand, the dormant powers of the human spirit may suddenly be unleashed.

Whatever triggers the reaction, this much is certain. The mystical meditator should not be deceived into thinking that he has communed with the Lord. At best, he has only come face-to-face with his own heart, which the Bible declares to be "desperately wicked" (Jeremiah 17:9-10). At worst, he could have left his mind and body open to an evil invasion by spirit beings associated with the particular discipline employed.

Meditation and the Christian

Is there any place for meditation in the life of a Christian? Yes, if the hows and whys conform to biblical standards.

In fact, meditation is an ancient Christian discipline that has received re-newed attention thanks to the work of Christian thinkers like Richard Foster and Dallas Willard.

These authors have been criticized by Christians who don't look carefully at what they are saying. As Foster repeatedly emphasizes, he is not advocating a mind-emptying, nonrational mystical experience. Rather, he describes a biblical approach to meditation that helps believers deepen their relationship with the living God.

"Christian meditation leads us to the inner wholeness necessary to give ourselves to God freely, and to the spiritual perception necessary to attack social evils," writes Foster in *Celebration of Discipline*, his phenomenally popular 1978 book.

Among the Christian saints from earlier centuries that Foster quotes is Albert the Great, who said, "The contemplation of the saints is fired by the love of the one contemplated: that is, God."

The child of God has no need to twist his limbs or to sit in any particular position in order to properly meditate. The Christian meditator is not trying to empty his mind. Instead, he seeks to fill it with the knowledge of God. Psalm 119 speaks of meditation "all the day" with "understanding" (vv. 97-99). There is no suggestion here of any rigidly ascetic discipline, but rather a natural flow of constant concentration on the things of the Lord throughout the waking hours—working, walking, driving, eating, and talking.

Christians approach meditation differently from Eastern mystics because they believe that the intellect was ordained of God to be a recipient of his truth. God, who is infinite and beyond our complete understanding, has graciously condescended to express himself through the human communicative skill of language.

The living Word became the written Word that we might comprehend enough of the Father's ways to appropriate salvation through his Son. Our relationship to God is based on the experience of his presence and the understanding of his Word by which we properly evaluate the subjective dimensions of conversion.

The root word of *meditation* implies a ruminating process of slowly digesting God's truths. It involves concentrated, directive thought that ponders the laws, works, precepts, word, and person of God. "Meditate on him" is the message of Scripture.

The meditation of man's soul is to be "acceptable in the sight of the Lord," not predicated on some glassy-eyed encounter with an overactive ego. In short, meditation is prayer and communication with the Lord of the universe, not the worked-up state of hyperventilation found in some cults.

Biblical meditation is not formless and aimless. It is the natural process of being constantly absorbed by God's life and love. And it means setting aside the mundane things of this world to concentrate on the kingdom of God. Mystical meditation worships the self as a divine inner manifestation of God. Biblical meditation reaches outward to a transcendent God who lifts us above our sinful inner nature to fellowship with him through the blood of his Son. The Christian who meditates according to the scriptural pattern finds his mind renewed (Romans 12:2). Unlike the mystic whose deepest thoughts lead to darkness, the believer who actively thinks upon those things that are "of good report" (Philippians 4:8) finds comfort and direction for the activities of life.

SOURCES: Richard Foster, *Celebration of Discipline* (San Francisco: Harper & Row, Publishers, 1978); "The Science of Meditation," *Time*, 4 August 2003; Dallas Willard, *The Divine Conspiracy* (San Francisco: Harper & Row, Publishers, 1998).

METROPOLITAN COMMUNITY CHURCH

Excluded from many major denominations, gays and lesbians have started their own church based on an interpretation of Scripture that condones homosexual conduct.

FOUNDER: Troy Perry

OVERVIEW: The Sunday morning service was similar to those held in thousands of churches throughout America every weekend. It included prayers, a Bible reading, a sermon, an offering, and the singing of hymns, including "What a Friend We Have in Jesus."

But the service also featured one activity most churchgoers don't see on Sundays. Following an announcement from the congregation's lesbian pastor, a procession of homosexual couples went forward to the altar to receive communion and a pastoral blessing.

Other church rituals include a holy-union ceremony for gay couples that is similar to the heterosexual marriage ceremonies performed in other churches. (The ceremony has no legal recognition in the United States.)

Welcome to the Metropolitan Community Church, which was founded in

Los Angeles in 1968 and now has more than thirty-five thousand members in more than three hundred congregations in nearly twenty countries.

Finding Fellowship

Troy Perry began preaching at age thirteen, was ordained by a Southern Baptist church by the time he was fifteen, and by eighteen he received an additional ordination from the Pentecostal Church of God of Prophecy denomination.

Even though he suspected he was really gay, he married a woman and had two children. "The church taught that if you married a good woman that would take care of those problems," he said.

It didn't work. After years of trying to separate his homosexuality from his faith, Perry tried to combine them. In the process he lost his family, his ordinations, and nearly his life. After a suicide attempt was unsuccessful, he prayed to God and gradually changed his mind about God and gays: "It was then I knew I could be a Christian and a homosexual."

Perry created a church in his own image. Surprisingly, MCC doctrine is very close to evangelical theology in nearly all respects except for its views on sexuality.

Craig Blomberg, a professor of New Testament at Denver Seminary, gave this intriguing assessment of the MCC: "The Bible calls homosexuality sin, but heterosexual sin is sin, too, and one isn't put up as worse than the other. The MCC is mistaken when it argues that the Bible condones homosexuality. At the same time, MCC is a very conservative group theologically—except for what they say on the homosexual issue. If someone hears the gospel as MCC presents it in their literature, and they trust Jesus for the forgiveness of their sins, then I would say they are saved."

Battling over the Bible

Blomberg isn't the only Christian thinker to acknowledge that MCC theology is largely evangelical except for its views on sex. Where the problem comes in is in the way MCC dismisses biblical teaching found in at least two significant passages:

- Leviticus 18:22 and 20:13. These passages say men who lie with men should be put to death, but MCC says this applies only to Jewish priests.
- 1 Corinthians 6:9. Here Paul says homosexual offenders and other sinners will not inherit the kingdom of God. MCC teaches that the passage condemns only homosexual prostitution and pederasty (sexual relations between men and boys), not loving and responsible homosexual relationships.

To research the MCC, I have attended their services and observed first-hand the eclectic mixture of spirituality and carnality. Though some congregations appear at first glance to be indistinguishable from either liturgical or charismatic worship meetings, the open sensuality seen among the members belies their claim to be no different from other religious groups. Transvestites, transgendered persons, drag queens and others with assorted sexual preferences are all welcomed uncritically amidst a display of open eroticism. Jesus taught in Matthew 7:18 that a good tree bears good fruit and a bad tree bears bad fruit. The warning to false religious teachers in Christ's time seems appropriate for the MCC: "Not everyone who says to Me, 'Lord, Lord,' shall enter the kingdom of heaven; but he who does the will of My Father in heaven" (Matthew 7:21).

SOURCES: John Dart, "Church for Gays Alters Mainline Religions' Views," *Los Angeles Times*, 7 June 1991; Steve Rabey, "A Gay Sanctuary," *Colorado Springs Gazette*, 1 August 1992, E1-3.

ACCESS: Universal Fellowship of Metropolitan Community Churches, 8704 Santa Monica Blvd., Second floor, Los Angeles, CA 90060.

MIND SCIENCES

Sin and physical illness are illusory mental states, according to this movement that has influenced other groups as diverse as *A Course in Miracles* and Unity.

OVERVIEW: "If by Christian you mean that we are saved by the blood of Christ on the Cross, then we're not." That explicit admission by a Church of Religious Science minister points out the essential distinction between the mind science cults and historic Christianity.

Mind science organizations include some better-known groups discussed elsewhere (Christian Science and Unity School of Christianity), as well as other entities that more specifically base their teachings on the ruminations of Ernest Holmes. They go by such names as Religious Science, Divine Science, and Science of Mind.

Drawing upon the metaphysical heritage of Charles and Myrtle Fillmore, Warren Felt Evans, Mary Baker Eddy, and Phineas Parkhurst Quimby, Holmes founded the Institute of Religious Science in 1927. *Science of Mind*, published by Holmes in 1938, is the textbook of mind science teachings, emphasizing that the law and love of God (the "Thing-in-Itself") are perfect.

Applying this theory to living is a nonsupernatural process of "science." Realizing one's inherent self-worth as emanating from a divine spark is the thrust of Holmes's emphasis. "When an individual recognizes his true union with the Infinite, he automatically becomes Christ," he wrote. By using the definitive article *the* when referring to Christ, mind sciences distinguish between Jesus the man and the divine idea of Christ-realization attainable by all men.

Christ's incarnation and divinity are not the only orthodox doctrines denied by mind science cults. In the process of spiritualizing all biblical truth, they also relegate heaven and hell to mental states and suggest that the Resurrection did not produce a bodily risen Lord.

While ignoring scriptural doctrine, mind scientists willingly accept a variety of non-Christian philosophies and sacred books, amalgamating these diverse viewpoints into a syncretistic whole.

In spite of their special emphasis on the contemporary interest in healing and positive thinking, the basic presuppositions of Mind and Religious Science groups differ little from the Gnostic heretics that the apostle Paul confronted nearly two thousand years ago.

SOURCES: Todd Ehrenborg, *Mind Sciences: Christian Science, Religious Science, Unity School of Christianity* (Grand Rapids, Mich.: Zondervan, 1995); Ibid., *Religion, Science or Science of the Mind* (San Juan Capistrano, Calif.: Christian Research Institute, 1979); J. Gordon Melton, *The Encyclopedia of American Religions*, vol. 2 (Wilmington, N.C.: McGrath, 1978).

ACCESS: United Church of Religious Science in Los Angeles and Religious Science International in Spokane, Wash., are both affiliated with the work of Ernest S. Holmes.

See also Christian Science, Unity School of Christianity

REV. SUN MYUNG MOON

See Unification Church.

MORMONISM

Church of Jesus Christ of Latter-day Saints

With a massive PR campaign during the 2002 Winter Olympics and a retitling of *The Book of Mormon,* the Latter-day Saints are on track to portray themselves as mainstream Christians.

FOUNDER: Joseph Smith, born in Sharon, Vermont, December 23, 1805; killed June 27, 1844, Carthage, Illinois. *The Book of Mormon* was published in 1830 and the Church of Jesus Christ of Latter-day Saints was founded April 6, 1830. It was originally named the Church of Jesus Christ. The current official name was adopted in 1837.

TEXT: John 10:16, "Other sheep I have, which are not of this fold," supposedly refers to a Middle Eastern civilization, the Nephites, that migrated to the Americas. Christ preached to them after his resurrection. The Bible is the Word of God only "as far as it has been translated correctly." A Mormon article of faith states that "we also believe the *Book of Mormon* to be the Word of God."

SYMBOL: The angel Moroni, usually perched atop temple spires, with trumpet in hand

APPEAL: Outside observers who do not scrutinize Mormon doctrine may be attracted by their avoidance of unclean physical habits and the seriousness with which members take their faith. They believe in the continuing function of divine revelation that gives a vitality and authority to their faith.

When confronted with the numerous historical and factual inconsistencies of their faith, most Mormons resort to the "burning in the bosom" argument, claiming that their subjective experience lends credence to their claims about their faith and its founder.

OVERVIEW: A year before the 2002 Olympics began, Mormon officials considered spending millions on TV advertising during the games but decided such an effort would look too "corporate."

Instead, the publicity-conscious group decided to keep a low profile, believing that merely appearing normal would be more successful than being too ostentatious.

Mormons found other ways to exploit the Olympics, using the glare of the international media spotlight to continue hammering home the mistaken notion that they are just another mainstream Christian group.

But Mormons can't have it both ways. How can they claim to be a part of a group of mainstream churches that founder Joseph Smith long ago declared to be an "abomination" to God?

Conflicting Images

Newfangled images of Mormons as warm and welcoming are at odds with nearly two centuries of history that show the group to be one of the most exclusivistic and unusual pseudo-Christian religions around.

More traditional images show Mormon missionaries, who almost always come in twos, sport closely cropped hair, and are dressed in near-identical dark suits, white shirts, subdued ties, polished shoes, and plastic name cards with the impressive title "Elder."

Their sincerity is beyond question. And they represent the most basic of human values—patriotism, sobriety, familial responsibilities, and hard work.

While they spend two years of their lives propagating the gospel of Mormonism, these young missionaries are subsidized by their parents, friends, and relatives. Each of them must file a weekly report accounting for every hour of the day.

Their task isn't easy. Only nine of every thousand doors they knock on are opened to them. But it's worth it. In one and a half centuries, the Church of Jesus Christ of Latter-day Saints has grown from six adherents to nearly 11 million members worldwide. In 2000, U.S. News & World Report declared Mormonism the fastest growing faith group in American history.

Why such zeal? Founder Joseph Smith declared that he had a vision of God the Father and Jesus Christ. They revealed to him that all churches and creeds were an "abomination" unto the Lord. He, Smith, was to be a prophet proclaiming a "restored" message of the true gospel.

Today, 60,000 Mormon missionaries garner more than 300,000 converts each year, while the church collects an estimated $4.3 billion annually in donations along with another $400 million from its various corporate enterprises. The wealth of the Mormon empire is conservatively estimated at $8 billion.

Mormon-owned Brigham Young University is the largest private university in the United States, and the Mormons are the largest religious media operator in the world. The twenty-eight-story headquarters in Salt Lake City, Utah, might well bear the inscription *success* emblazoned from its top.

Mention Moonies or Hare Krishna to the average person and he'll respond with disdain. But the word Mormon generally evokes an immediate nod of approval.

The morally austere image is no sham. Mormons are known to eschew tobacco, cigarettes, caffeine, and premarital sex, while revering family life and free enterprise. They have a low cancer rate and score higher than the general populace when it comes to physical fitness.

Who wouldn't admire a religious group that promotes the Boy Scouts and receives "fast offerings" to care for widows as well as the poor and indigent?

The suspicious history and strange beliefs of Mormonism are often overlooked on the assumption that sound morals make a good religion. Most people know little of Mormonism's doctrines and beginnings. They may be familiar with Mormon politicians like Utah Senator Orin Hatch, or perhaps they have heard performances by the internationally recognized Mormon Tabernacle Choir.

Only a few have heard about the odd practices of proxy baptisms and celestial marriages. To truly understand Mormonism, one must sift through all the arcane doctrines and public relations ploys of Latter-day Saints and go back to the small town of Palmyra, New York, in the year 1820.

Seeking Hidden Treasure

Joseph Smith Jr. is revered by millions of Mormons as a seer and prophet. The contemporaries who knew him and his parents were less gracious. Neighbors viewed the Smith family as "illiterate, whiskey-drinking, shiftless, and irreligious."

Joe (as he was known) was said to be indolent, with a penchant for exaggeration and untruthfulness. His mother, Lucy Mack, practiced magic and had visions. His father, Joe Sr., was known as a persistent treasure seeker, always trying to dig up the fabled booty of Captain Kidd. The founder of Mormonism often accompanied his father on these expeditions and was himself fond of the occult, especially divining and fortune-telling by "peep stones."

According to *The Pearl of Great Price*, his official autobiography, Joe was confused and agitated by the profusion of Christian sects who held differing interpretations of the Bible: "I reflected on it again and again, knowing that if any person needed wisdom from God, I did; for how to act I did not know, and unless I could get more wisdom than I then had, I would never know; for the teachers of religion of the different sects understood the same passage of scripture so differently as to destroy all confidence in settling the question by an appeal to the Bible."

Then one day in 1820, while praying in the woods, Joseph Smith received his fabled vision of God and Jesus. In 1823 another personage, an angel named Moroni, appeared at his bedside. The visitor claimed to be the son of Mormon, the departed leader of an American race known as Nephites. Moroni told him about a book of golden plates that contained "the fullness of the everlasting gospel."

Four years later in the hill named Cumorah near Palmyra, New York, Smith unearthed the plates. Buried with them was a pair of large, supernatural spectacles known as the "Urim and Thummim." They were to be used in translating the hieroglyphics on the plates, a language called "reformed Egyptian." (Archaeologists and Egyptologists deny there is any historical evidence to validate the existence of such a form of communication.)

Joseph immediately began his work of translating the plates. He claimed that later during this time John the Baptist (sent by Peter, James, and John) appeared to him and administered a divine ordination. When the translation work was completed (with the help of Oliver Cowdery, an itinerant school-teacher, and Emma Hale, his first and only legal wife) he returned the plates to Moroni. *The Book of Mormon* was published in 1830.

A subtitle, "Another Testament of Jesus Christ," was recently added to make *The Book of Mormon* appear to be more closely linked with orthodox Christianity. On April 6, 1830, Cowdery, Smith, and his brothers, Hyrum and Samuel, officially formed the Church of Jesus Christ, now known as the Church of Jesus Christ of Latter-day Saints.

A Novel Revelation

The Book of Mormon is the cornerstone of Mormon faith. Along with the other Smith volumes, *Doctrines and Covenants* and *The Pearl of Great Price*, it is con-sidered to be a divine revelation superior to the Bible. In actual practice, whenever *The Book of Mormon* contradicts the Bible, the former is considered to be the final authority. What exactly does *The Book of Mormon* contain?

It purports to tell the story of two Middle Eastern peoples who migrated to the Americas. The tale unwinds in a series of books written between 600 B.C. and A.D. 400. An ancient civilization called Jaredites came from the Tower of Babel to Central America.

A wicked group, the Jaredites perished as a result of their own immorality. (I have visited a number of ancient Mayan ruins in Central America where Mormon archaeologists have been engaged in the futile search for evidence to verify Mormonism's outlandish historical claims. At Tikal in Guatemala and Copan in Honduras I have viewed carvings resembling a Star of David, which Mormons say prove their assertions.)

A later group of Jews led by a righteous man named Nephi fled Jerusalem to avoid the Babylonian captivity and ended up in South America. They di-vided into warring factions, the Nephites and Lamanites. The latter annihi-lated the Nephites in a fierce struggle near Palmyra, New York, in A.D. 428. The victory earned them a curse—dark skins.

They continued populating the continent and became the American In-dian race. Before his demise, Mormon, the Nephite leader, compiled a record of his civilization and of the appearance Christ is supposed to have made to them after his resurrection. He described how the Lord met them in South America and commissioned them to institute the ordinances of communion, baptism, and the priesthood. The entire account was recorded on the golden plates that Mormon buried and were found by Joseph Smith fourteen hundred years later.

Reading between the Lines

Before continuing with the historical saga of Smith and his successor, Brigham Young (according to the Utah branch), *The Book of Mormon* deserves some scrutiny, for it claims equality with the Bible. It purports to be the sealed book mentioned in Isaiah 29 and a record of the "other sheep" Jesus spoke of in John 10:16. But its proofs are questionable and its inconsistencies glaring.

While it aspires to be an additional revelation to the Bible, it contains verbatim passages in King James English, though it was supposedly written many centuries before the 1611 Authorized Version. These analogous passages even include some seventeenth-century translators' errors, a strange coincidence for a book supposedly predating the KJV scholars' efforts.

In addition, *The Book of Mormon* credits these New World immigrants with metal-producing capabilities, a claim not confirmed by archaeological research. Mormon even described elephants roaming the Western hemisphere, though no skeletons have ever been found.

The Smithsonian Institution flatly denies any correlation between American archeological discoveries and the information contained in *The Book of Mormon*. A Mormon publication, "Joseph Smith's Testimony," concludes its glowing appraisal of *The Book of Mormon* by citing a total of eleven witnesses. What the pamphlet's author failed to note is that three of them, Oliver Cowdery, David Whitmer, and Martin Harris, were later denounced by Smith. The other eight include five who were related to David Whitmer. Of the final three witnesses, one was Smith's father and the other two his brothers, hardly an objective company of jurists.

Who wrote *The Book of Mormon?* God, Satan, Smith, or another mortal are the only possible sources. Some who doubt its divine inspiration suggest that Smith may have been a fanciful thinker who borrowed King James English and nineteenth-century historical speculation to produce a fictitious novel.

Others contend that one of his converts, Sidney Rigdon, stole a manuscript entitled *Manuscript Story* by Solomon Spaulding, a minister-writer who died in 1816. A few insist Smith's writings bear strong similarity to those of the Rev. Ethan Smith, who authored *View of the Hebrews*. Most evangelical critics espouse the Spalding-plagiarism explanation, noting that Smith always dictated his writing from behind a curtain.

Courting Controversy

No matter who really wrote the book, its revelations and its followers caused quite a stir wherever they went. Mormons were a combative lot, challenging all other sects, and flaunting their polygamous ways. (Smith, it was said, had twenty-seven wives, though one authority estimates Smith may have had sixty or more.)

Persecution drove them from New York to Ohio and then Missouri, where the governor asked them to leave. Smith's clan ended up in Nauvoo, Illinois, where with hard work and dedication, they built the largest city in the state.

He told his followers that Nauvoo meant "beautiful plantation" in Hebrew, and obtained a charter that made it a city-state with its own military.

But Joseph and his brother Hyman ran afoul of the law and ended up in jail in 1844. An outraged mob beset their Carthage, Illinois, cell and murdered both. This tragic, lawless act of intolerance insured instant martyrdom for Smith.

A split immediately followed the shooting. One group, led by his widow, felt that the mantle of leadership should fall on Joseph's sons. They left for Independence, Missouri, to settle on the site where the prophet had declared Christ would return. That group, now known as the Reorganized Church of Jesus Christ of Latter-day Saints, parted ways with some major Mormon doctrines.

Though they claim a common origin and reverence for *The Book of Mormon,* the Reorganized Church repudiates several vital beliefs of the Utah group—i.e., secret rites, a plurality of gods, and sealed marriages. Above all, they claim to be the only legitimate Latter-day Saints body, saying that Joseph Smith appointed his son to succeed in the church presidency. A recently discovered document in Smith's handwriting, dated January 17, 1844, seems to confirm their contention. (See the entry on the Reorganized Church.)

After Smith's assassination, Brigham Young persuaded a majority to follow him on the arduous trek to Utah. In July 1847 Young and his band looked on the Salt Lake Valley and declared, "This is the place." Brigham Young encouraged polygamy, took twenty-five wives, and by the time of his death in 1877 had collected 140,000 followers.

He strongly adhered to the little-talked-about Mormon doctrine of blood atonement. Christ's blood, he believed, could not atone for certain sins. Such deeds required a man's own blood. Another could kill him as a righteous act he described as, "loving our neighbor as ourselves . . . if he wants salvation and it is necessary to spill his blood . . . spill it."

Modern Mormons have suppressed (but not officially repudiated) the doctrine. But they still have stinging memories of the day their second "prophet" ordered his fellow Mormons to attack and slaughter 120 men, women, and children of the Fancher party, who crossed Mormon land on their way to California.

Brigham Young also espoused two other doctrines that Mormons would like to forget. He taught that Adam was actually God who took on a body and came to Eden (in Missouri) with one of his heavenly wives, Eve. This Adam-God (the archangel Michael) begat Jesus by sexually cohabiting with the Virgin Mary in a physical, flesh relationship. "He [Christ] was not begotten by the Holy Ghost," Brigham declared emphatically.

But it was Young's espousal of polygamy that gained Mormons the most bad publicity. He instructed his followers, "The only men who become gods are those who enter into polygamy."

Even today Utah is pocketed with an estimated thirty to fifty thousand fundamentalist Mormons who engage in plural marriages. They are devout in their belief that they will be barred from heaven unless they follow the covenant of polygamy set forth by Joseph Smith in 1843.

In the late 1800s the U.S. Congress became so concerned with the conduct of Mormons that it passed the Edmunds-Tucker Act, threatening to confiscate Mormon property and jail its leaders. The church officially recanted in 1890, and ironically, today most mainline Mormons maintain a pro-family-values image of monogamous bliss.

Key Concepts

Further study of Mormon doctrines reveals plenty of reasons why it would be a big mistake to grant the group its claim of belonging to mainstream Christianity.

Mormons subscribe to the idea of an anthropomorphic God with physical, material dimensions. He is a procreating father (all humans were preexistent spirits he begat) with a divine mother-wife. It is this conviction that undergirds the Mormon emphasis on marriage and parenthood in this life and the next.

Some Mormons believe that Jesus was married to both Mary and Martha and that he bore children on earth. Good Mormons enter their secret temples and don white garments to indulge in esoteric, Masonic-like rituals that seal their marriages for eternity.

The most famous of all Mormon aphorisms declares, "As man now is, God once was; as God now is, man may become." God himself was once procreated in another world, and now humans may aspire to the status of procreator that he has obtained. Adam did right by eating of the forbidden fruit because it made him capable of fathering the human race. In other words, "Adam fell that men might be." The right to godhead is not earned by the grace of Jesus but by being a good Mormon. Followers of Joseph Smith prove their faithfulness by being baptized and married in the temple, being a member of the priesthood, and tracing genealogies. As potential father and mother gods, Mormons will ultimately have their own planets to populate.

All those born prior to Mormonism's founding in 1830 cannot enter the celestial state without a little help from present-day adherents. The church has blasted a tunnel out of Utah granite (capable of withstanding a nuclear explosion) to house the ancestral records of devout Mormons.

Once departed kin have been identified, posthumous proxy baptisms are performed. Mormons spend $10 million a year to maintain the facilities, but for them it is well worth it. Some go through the three-hour ceremony on behalf of a non-relative they have never known. Mormons are universalists and believe that everyone will eventually have immortality, with only baptized

Mormons attaining godhead. (Article of Faith Number Three states, "We believe that through the atonement of Christ all mankind may be saved.")

The priesthood concept, a belief in a restored priesthood of Aaron and Melchizedek, represents one of Mormonism's most distinctive departures from Christian tradition. All Mormon males over fourteen years of age are eligible for the Aaronic priesthood. At twenty years of age they may enter the higher office of Melchizedek and be designated an elder. Until 1978 those with black skins were forbidden this stature. Mormonism's temples (there are now more than one hundred around the world) were off-limits to blacks because Joseph Smith taught that they were the descendants of Cain and therefore cursed. Like its views on polygamy, Mormon views on race were also overturned when church leaders determined the time was right.

The church rejects the doctrine of original sin and believes that sinners are punished on earth for failure in their past spirit lives. Blacks were thus guilty of the preexistent sin of rebelling with Lucifer and barred from the priesthood until Mormonism's leader, First President Spencer Kimball (who died in 1985, succeeded by Ezra Taft Benson), received a "revelation" abrogating this injunction.

Secret Rituals

Most aspects of church structure are seldom known to outsiders. The first president is considered to be a prophetic successor to Smith and thus is a prophet and revelator who speaks in God's name. From there authority descends in a nondemocratic fashion to the president's advisors (two other high priests), the twelve apostles, the presiding quorum of seventy, and the presiding bishopric. Individual members are organized into *wards* of five hundred to one thousand. Wards are consolidated into *stakes*.

Space does not permit a detailed discussion of all Mormon practices. Some of them are as follows: de-emphasis of Easter and the Cross; speaking in tongues and spiritual healing; the ability of individuals to receive private revelations from God; emphasis on Monday as family night; storing of food supplies for times of famine; insistence that the U.S. Constitution is divinely inspired; believing that the state of women is inferior to that of men; opposition to the use of birth control; opposition to interracial marriages; binding temple oaths (breaking them can jeopardize one's hope of eternal life); and belief in the brotherhood of Jesus and Lucifer. Mormons also believe in a three-tiered heaven with separate sections for heathen, non-Mormon Christians, and those with sealed marriages whose earthly matrimonial unions will endure forever.

Some may wonder how such exotic ideas could be compatible with the seeming love and care exhibited by most Mormons. The evangelical Christian questions how such unorthodox theology could produce such pleasant people who knock on doors and warmly present their case. This irony is not so hard to understand when one comprehends why an individual may have joined the Mormon Church.

For one thing, the new Mormon finds an instant social community of God-conscious values. The positive emphasis on Christian virtues and the intense involvement on a layman's level cause most new members to simply overlook the blemished history of the LDS's origins.

Once in the Mormon fold, family pressures often prevent many disillusioned Mormons from forsaking the church, particularly if they are second- or third-generation adherents.

Many people today have a pragmatic approach to religion that tends to see theology as a cumbersome commodity. They want something that *works*, something that will bring them emotional security and shared goals. Mormonism delivers, and for millions that is good enough. While their unorthodoxy—and their success—may alarm us, they should also inspire us to equal or excel them in showing love and concern to searching people.

CHRISTIAN CRITIQUE: Mormonism's main logical fallacy can be found in its contradictory claims that it is the only restored, true church and it is also a mainstream Christian group. But that's hardly the end of Mormonism's problems.

The Mormon church teaches that its concept of salvation must be strictly followed. The highest heaven is open only to faithful Mormons, who will become gods and join in procreative partnership with God who was once as humans are now.

Life on earth is a discipline where one develops one's potential to rule a celestial kingdom with a spouse and children. Marriage and large families on earth are encouraged as part of this evolving process toward equality with Christ, who is the Mormon "elder brother." After death, Mormons in the heavenly realms seek to convert non-Mormons who dwell in the lower realm, so these "gentiles" can also accept the revelations of Joseph Smith.

However, Mormons find themselves in the conundrum of having to modify or deny some of their more embarrassing past doctrines (e.g., blood atonement, the Adam-God concept, polygamy, anti-Negroid beliefs) while according prophetic status to the men who taught such beliefs (i.e., Joseph Smith, Brigham Young, et al.). The priesthood concept is repudiated by Hebrews 7 and 1 Peter 2:9-10. The Aaronic and Melchizedek orders were consummated in Christ, and now all believers are part of a "royal priesthood." The Mormon Jesus is not eternal God-Jehovah (Elohim), able to "save them to the uttermost" (Hebrews 7:25). He is therefore "another Jesus," and Moroni is the false angel of the "accursed" gospel of which Paul speaks in Galatians 1:8-9.

SOURCES: *Christianity Today*, 5 September 1986, 29; *Denver Post*, 1 October 1976, 4BB; Ibid., 1 July 1977, 4BB; Michael Janofsky and Laurie Goodstein,

"In Olympic Glare, a Quieter Mormon Mission," *New York Times*, 20 January 2002, 1, 21; "Joseph Smith's Testimony," Desert News Press, LDS publication; *Journal of Discourses* (Salt Lake City: Bookcraft); Walter Martin, *The Kingdom of the Cults* (Minneapolis: Bethany Fellowship, 1977); *Moody Monthly*, June 1980, 32; *Newsweek*, 21 November 1971, 113–119; Ibid., 1 March 1976, 71; Ibid., 1 September 1980, 68–71; Ibid., 27 April 1981, 87–88; Ibid., 25 November 1985, 87; Richard N. Ostling and Joan K. Ostling, *Mormon America: The Power and the Promise* (San Francisco: HarperSanFrancisco, 1999); Latayne C. Scott, "Mormonism and the Question of Truth," *Christian Research Journal* (summer 1992): 24; Joseph Smith, *Book of Mormon*; Ibid., *Doctrine and Covenants*; Ibid., *The Pearl of Great Price*; *Time*, 11 July 1977, 69; Ibid., 21 October 1977, 38–39; Ibid., 19 June 1978, 55; Ibid., 7 August 1978, 54–55; Ibid., 4 December 1978, 30; Ibid., 23 May 1980, 42–43; Ibid., 24 April 1981, 42; Kurt Van Gorden, *Mormonism* (Grand Rapids, Mich.: Zondervan, 1995); *Vancouver Sun*, 19 April 1980, 5B; Luke P. Wilson, "The Mormon Doctrine of Salvation for the Dead," *Christian Research Journal* (November-December 1997): 22.

ACCESS: The Church of Jesus Christ of Latter-Day Saints, 50 East North Temple Street, Salt Lake City, UT 84150; www.lds.about.com

See also Reorganized Church of Jesus Christ of Latter-Day Saints.

SWAMI MUKTANANDA PARAMAHANSA

SYDA Foundation

When this Indian holy man visited America, he received celebrity endorsements and promoted instant enlightenment to a Hollywood crowd seeking a spiritual fast track.

FOUNDER: Swami Muktananda Paramahansa, born 1908, Mangalore, India; died 1982

TEXT: Hindu scriptures

APPEAL: Muktananda was less secretive and not as ostentatious as most Eastern gurus. This made him appear to be more credible. Followers testified to spontaneous, emotionally and physically charged experiences resulting from his initiation ceremonies. They felt this encounter gave meaning to their lives without having to believe or renounce any religious dogmas.

OVERVIEW: TV star Phylicia Rashad of *Cosby* fame says she "went to the Swami in search of perfection as an actress. What he showed me was not what I had to get, but what I already have. I am just myself, and who I am is a lot."

Est founder Werner Erhard sponsored one of his American tours.

And even John Denver sang the swami's praises. Denver once sang of being "Rocky Mountain High," a possible reference to the drug-induced altitude in his own life. Later he sang about the transcendental bliss he experienced after Swami Muktananda Paramahansa placed his fingers on Denver's closed eyelids.

Baba (father) Muktananda, once surrounded by twenty-five hundred blissed-out showbiz folk who came to do him honor, certainly came a long way from his home in Mangalore, India.

At age fifteen he left his parents to spend more than twenty years seeking spiritual truth. In 1947 he met Guru Bhagwan Sri Nityananda. Nityananda claimed to be a *siddha yogi,* a person whom Hindus believe is a Perfect Master capable of awakening the latent spiritual power of *Shakti.* (Shakti is the Hindu Supreme Mother goddess lying at the base of the spine.) He told Muktananda that man has forgotten his divine nature and that awakening Shakti brings forth God-realization.

Unlike most gurus, who may take years to arouse a student's Shakti power, Nityananda transmitted the experience to Muktananda immediately. He was instantly overwhelmed by rays of light and a hot, burning fever.

This system of enlightenment known as *shaktipat* was passed on to Muktananda. When Nityananda died in 1961, the Shree Gurudev Siddha Yoga Ashram was founded.

Muktananda came to America during his 1970 world tour and was accompanied by Baba Ram Dass (see separate entry). Just before his death in 1982 Muktananda was estimated to have over 300,000 Western followers who experienced shaktipat at his hands.

More than five hundred meditation centers throughout the world carry on the work, including many in the United States. Followers say they have seen visions, heard ethereal sounds, and even, among women, undergone orgasms. (A later controversy that erupted after the swami's death said some of his female followers experienced orgasms by having sexual relations with the holy man.)

"God is within you," Muktananda declared. "Honor and worship your inner being." For Westerners who heard such words in the 1970s, the Swami's version of God-realization was particularly appealing.

CHRISTIAN CRITIQUE: With a brush of his peacock feather fan or the thrust of his fingers into a disciple's eyes (an old Hindu ploy of creating neurological pressure on the retina), Muktananda claimed to awaken the elemental energy force of Shakti.

Followers were admonished to direct their devotion and meditation toward Muktananda with unconditional zeal. In exchange, they received God-realization.

However, the entire system of Siddha Yoga is based on the false premise that a human being can be a channel to God-realization. First Timothy 2:5 states, "There is one God, and one mediator between God and men, . . . Christ Jesus."

The so-called awakening of the *Kundalini* power of Shakti may be the result of an anticipatory psychological response. This experience may also be induced by demon activity.

SOURCES: *People,* 24 May 1976, 83; Ibid., 3 December 1979; Ibid., 9 March 1981, 89; *Time,* 26 July 1976, 78–79; "Update," *SCP Newsletter,* October 1982, 6.

ACCESS: SYDA Foundation, 371 Brickman Road, South Fallsburg, NY 12779. Residential centers are located in the United States, England, Australia, and Mexico. More than five hundred Siddha Yoga centers are located throughout the world. Additional facilities are located in India.

NATION OF ISLAM

Black Muslims

This separatist and sometimes anti-Semitic organization combines
Islamic principles with racial exclusivism.

FOUNDER: Timothy Drew, born in 1886 in North Carolina; successors and leaders of offshoot groups include Wallace Fard, Elijah Muhammad, Wallace Muhammad, Malcolm X, and Louis Farrakhan

TEXT: The Koran. The Bible is also considered a source of truth so long as it is reinterpreted without the "white man's lies."

SYMBOLS: Crescent and star of Islam

APPEAL: Blacks incensed by racism in American culture and Christian churches are vulnerable to the movement's appeal. Youth who feel exploited by a predominantly white society are promised the vision of a black-ruled nation. The call to nationalistic supremacy promotes self-respect based on a strict moral code that produces individual prosperity.

OVERVIEW: In October 1995, hundreds of thousands of African-American men went to Washington, D.C., to attended the Million Man March, an event organized by Louis Farrakhan. Since 1977, Farrakhan has been the leader of the Nation of Islam. Over the past quarter century, he has done more than any other man to change people's perception of the term *Black Muslims*, which once conjured up images of incendiary hate rhetoric directed toward the "blue-eyed devil" white man.

Sports figures like Cassius Clay (who changed his name to Muhammad Ali) and basketball great Lew Alcindor (who changed his name to Kareem Abdul-Jabbar) helped improve the movement's image among edgy whites.

An Early Beginning

In 1913 a North Carolina black man named Timothy Drew arrived in Newark, New Jersey, under the name Noble Drew Ali. He founded the Moorish-American Science Temples on the doctrine that Negroes were of Moroccan (Moorish) origin and that Jesus was a black man killed by white Romans. Many of his teachings were taken from *The Aquarian Gospel of Jesus the Christ,* an occult book written by Levi Dowling.

When Ali died, Wallace Fard, a door-to-door salesman from Detroit, suddenly appeared on the scene, claiming to be Ali's reincarnation. He asserted that he was born in Mecca and had been sent to America to redeem the black man from the "Caucasian devil." One of Fard's spokesmen, Elijah Muhammad (formerly Robert Poole), helped him to found the Nation of Islam. Muhammad insisted that Fard was an incarnation of Allah. By the time Fard mysteriously disappeared from sight in 1935, Muhammad had assumed leadership of the organization.

While incarcerated as a conscientious objector during World War II, Elijah Muhammad, the messenger of Allah, effectively recruited black prisoners for his cause. His message to them was simple: Wallace Fard was God, the Messiah predicted by Christians and the *mahdi* proclaimed by Muslims; the white "beast" (created by a mad black scientist) was allowed to reign for six thousand years, and that period ended in 1914; the time was ripe for the Nation of Islam and the divine, black god-men guided by Allah to arise and claim control over the world.

A New Era

Malcolm X was the mouthpiece of Elijah Muhammad and was an eloquent evangelist until he was murdered by one of Muhammad's rivals on February 21, 1965.

Membership blossomed in the turbulent, racially tense sixties. Dozens of temples were opened in ghetto neighborhoods, usually by acquiring the abandoned churches of white congregations who had fled to the suburbs. *Muhammad Speaks* (later called *Bilalian News*), a newspaper circulated to a half million people, was hawked by well-dressed, militantly organized youth.

Black Muslims bought thousands of acres of farmland to promote self-help enterprises. They opened businesses and projected an image of discipline, cleanliness, and morality.

Though their racial intolerance separated them from the world community of Islam, they did practice some Muslim precepts. Eating pork, gambling, smoking, and drinking liquor were forbidden. Members prayed five times a day facing Mecca.

Women were admonished to respect their husbands and were required to have their heads covered. The Koran was deemed to be the holy scripture of God's prophet, although they also entertained fanciful speculation about the black man having originated on the moon 65 trillion years ago.

Though most critics labeled their theology as "racial hatred," Black Muslims preferred to call their views "social separation." They wanted no part of integration.

Why should they? The white man's day of destruction was coming, and blacks should avoid sharing in his judgment. Heaven and hell were considered irrelevant concepts because the black man in America had already gone through the hell of slavery.

Upon the death of Elijah Muhammad in 1965, his son Wallace took over the movement. His initial lackluster leadership left some followers doubting whether he could adequately fill his father's shoes. His most important accomplishment has been to drop the strident racial invectives that had aroused the fear and dread of whites.

This new image enabled the Black Muslims to gain official recognition as an orthodox Islamic body under the name Community of Islam in the West. Followers are now referred to as Bilalians (Bilal was supposedly the first black convert of the prophet Muhammad). Estimated numbers of adherents in the community now range from 50,000 to 150,000.

Discord and Division

Continuing discord among African-American Muslims resulted in the formation of a new group that uses one of its previous names: The Nation of Islam. This group is headed by Abdul Haleem Farrakhan, who was born Louis Eugene Wolcott. Farrakhan was a nightclub entertainer when he entered Elijah Muhammad's Nation of Islam. He rose rapidly within the organization, but when Muhammad died in 1975 and his son Wallace was appointed the new leader, Farrakhan departed from the group.

While Muhammad's group adopted more moderate positions, Farrakhan kept stoking the flames of racism. This is a prominent feature of his Nation of Islam organization, which has a strict dress code and close-knit security detail. Today Farrakhan's views are regularly featured in radio and TV shows. His Nation of Islam has an estimated membership of 10,000.

CHRISTIAN CRITIQUE: Black Muslims believe that God is black and the black man is a god, and recognizing these "facts" will help blacks to shed the "white man's religion." Black Muslims promote a self-sufficient black economy and demand to have seven or eight states ceded to them in order to establish a black nation. Their stern rules and moral conduct aid them in the rehabilitation of society rejects.

The Black Muslim god is Wallace Fard, believed to be Allah incarnate, the savior of mankind. This is, of course, incompatible with the unique claim to divinity established by Jesus Christ (John 14:6-7; see also Acts 4:12). Peter's vision in Acts 10 leaves no room for any practice of racial superiority. The Bible teaches that all men are sinners and in need of God's saving grace (Romans 3:23; 6:23), no matter what the color of one's skin.

SOURCES: John Bacon, "Muslims Hope Events Lead to Unity," USA Today, 25 February 2000, 3A; "Black Muslims and the Baptist Witness" (Atlanta, Ga.: Home Mission Board, SBC); Christianity Today, 12 May 1980, 29; "Louis Farrakhan and the Nation of Islam," Cornerstone, vol. 26 no. 111, no. 112; Walter Martin, The Kingdom of the Cults (Minneapolis: Bethany Fellowship, 1977); J. Gordon Melton, The Encyclopedia of American Religions (Wilmington, N.C.: McGrath, 1978); Eric Pement, "Louis Farrakhan and the Nation of Islam: Striking a Responsive Chord in the Black Community," Christian Research

Journal (spring 1996): 6–7, 44; William J. Petersen, *Those Curious New Cults* (New Canaan, Conn.: Keats Publishing, 1975); Diego Ribadneira, "American Blacks Rapidly Embracing Islam's Message," *Denver Post*, 2 November 1996, 21A; *Time*, 10 March 1975, 83.

ACCESS: Nation of Islam (Louis Farrakhan), 4855 S. Woodlawn Ave., Chicago, IL 60615; Nation of Islam (John Muhammad), 14880 Wyoming, Detroit, MI 48238

See also Islam, Sufism.

NATIVE AMERICAN SPIRITUALITY

Long suppressed or outlawed, Native American practices are experiencing a resurgence, from sweat lodge ceremonies to mind-altering hallucinogens.

FOUNDER: Most Native American religions have traditional, indigenous origins. The Native American Church for Christian Indians, which uses sacramental peyote in worship ceremonies, was founded in 1918 by tribal peyotists at the suggestion of James Mooney.

TEXT: Religions of the indigenous American people have an oral tradition of original myths and folklore tales about cultural heroes and trickster animals. Some of these have been translated and written down by anthropologists, but many remain unknown to outsiders.

SYMBOLS: Cultural symbols vary from tribe to tribe. Examples are animals, birds, plants, natural phenomena, supernatural beings, cultural heroes and heroines, masks, totems, ceremonial costumes, sand paintings, kachinas, songs, and dances.

APPEAL: People today may sense a primitive wisdom in the religion of Native Americans and may be attracted to the concept of harmony between humans and nature.

OVERVIEW: For centuries, America's first people lived traditional tribal lives that were shaped by ancient religious traditions passed down from generation to generation. These traditions changed after Native Americans encountered white people. At first the two groups lived independently of one another, but in time whites gained control of the continent, oppressing Native American people and outlawing many of their spiritual practices.

In recent years there has been a renewal of interest in the old ways among both Native Americans and spiritual seekers of other races who want to recover ancient practices.

Varied Traditions

Native American spirituality is diverse and varied. Its practitioners ascribe to a variety of beliefs and perform an assortment of rituals.

The shaman—or medicine man—was respected by nearly all Native American groups. The primary religious figure of most tribes, the shaman fulfilled the function of priest, soothsayer, and doctor. Shamans were generally male, though some Great Basin tribes allowed women to hold the office. Eskimo shamans were said to cure sickness by undertaking out-of-body journeys in search of a patient's missing soul, which was then restored to the ailing body.

Shamanistic ability was sought in dreams or visions, usually through totem animals or "power beings," who taught the seeker how to use the magic healing and knowledge bestowed upon him. Shamans sometimes used their powers for less honorable reasons and consequently were feared. In some regions witchcraft and magic were commonplace, as were sorcerers who supposedly could change themselves into animals or birds.

Among some southeastern tribes, elaborate funerary practices supported a belief in ghosts and an afterlife. Each tribe had its own view of the universe, but most believed in a bewildering variety of spirits. Each plant and animal had a guardian spirit that looked after its kind, and many tribes observed strict hunting and fishing rituals to avoid offending the deer or salmon.

Some tribes believe in a single creator, the Great Spirit. Others revere pantheons of minor deities and legendary trickster figures. The Hopi believe in a cyclical series of creations and worlds, while other tribes refute a creation altogether, declaring that the world has always existed.

Vision quests—solitary journeys into the wilderness to encounter spirit guides—were a popular form of maturity rite among many tribes, most notably the Plains Indians. They did not always require the use of drugs. Sometimes a vision was induced by fasting and forced sleeplessness in a secluded spot.

Rituals of endurance in the name of religion were common among many tribes. The Plains Indians still perform the sacred Sun Dance, in which men dance four days without food, water, or sleep. Among the Sioux and some other groups, self-torture was practiced during the Sun Dance. Dancers strained to pull themselves free from ropes tied to wooden skewers piercing their chests and backs.

347

Such old rituals are being practiced with renewed fervor by young adherents of Native American religions in an attempt to recapture the shamanistic mysteries of ancient tribal ceremonies.

Peyote Grows More Popular

Another practice receiving renewed attention is the use of psychedelic drugs. The young, mostly white members of the Peyote Way Church of God worship by trekking into the desert, chewing peyote buttons, and waiting for visions. Peyote is a hallucinogenic cactus used for religious purposes by some Native American people. It is widely used as a sacrament in the Native American Church.

The Peyote Way Church of God was founded by Immanuel Trujillo, who was half Apache and once objected, ironically, to the use of peyote by whites. Claims by his group and the Native American Church that peyote is a part of legitimate religious practices have played an important role in recent legal decisions concerning Native Americans.

Freedom of religion has been slow in coming for Native American people. In a 1983 landmark legal decision, the Forest Service was prevented from building a road along the Siskiyou Mountains. This area had been used for centuries by the Karok, Tolowa, and Yurok tribes for religious purposes. Federal trial and appellate courts determined that Native American use of the wilderness for religious purposes warranted protection under the First Amendment.

A variety of court cases have attempted to deal with the sacramental use of peyote and other psychedelic substances by Native American worshipers. At present, some groups have been granted limited exemptions from U.S. drug laws that would otherwise outlaw these substances

Peyote, similar to LSD and mescaline in both chemistry and effects, originally was little known outside its natural growing range in northeastern Mexico and the Rio Grande valley.

Sixteenth-century Spanish explorers noted the use of the drug among the Aztecs. One commented that "those who eat of it see visions either frightful or laughable. . . . [It] gives them courage to fight and not feel fear nor hunger nor thirst; and they say it protects them from danger."

After the decline of the Aztec civilization, peyote use continued among the Mexican desert tribes, notably the Huichol and Yaqui. It was carried north after the Civil War by Comanche and Kiowa raiding parties and eventually spread to more than fifty tribes.

Peyote use was mixed with Christian concepts that the tribes learned from Catholic and Protestant missionaries. John Wilson, the Caddo-Delaware Indian who founded the Ghost Dance movement in the late nineteenth century, told of his peyote-inspired vision: he said he saw the road "which Christ had taken in his ascent [leading] from Christ's grave to the Moon in the Sky" and was told to walk in this path for the rest of his life.

In 1918 Indian peyote users claiming to be Christians formed the Native American Church at the suggestion of white anthropologist James Mooney. In 1960 an Arizona judge ruled that peyote use by Indians was sacramental. In 1968 the Federal Drug Act limited use of mescaline and peyote to persons at least one-quarter Indian. Legal battles continued throughout the twentieth century.

Peyotism and Indian philosophy were popularized in the 1960s and 1970s by Carlos Castaneda's *The Teachings of Don Juan*. More recently, Lynn Andrews's books and lectures sparked a resurgent interest in Native American religion, this time with a New Age flavor. Though her approach is feminist and does not advocate the use of drugs to obtain self-knowledge, she shares with Castaneda an emphasis on totem spirits and shamanism.

Contemporary Convergence

In these complex technological times, the simpler faiths and lifestyles of the Native American peoples are attractive to disenchanted spiritual seekers.

Movies like Kevin Costner's *Dances with Wolves* have led many Americans to have greater sympathy for the much-abused Native American peoples than for their own government or the white missionaries who tried to convert them to Christianity.

In addition, the growing interest in alternative and holistic medicine has led many to revisit Native American traditions. In 1993 the National Institutes of Health (NIH) established the Office of Alternative Medicine and appointed Dr. Joe Jacobs as its director. Jacobs is a Native American of Mohawk and Cherokee descent.

But such nostalgia about primitive lifestyles is misdirected. The truth is, most modern-day Americans have little interest in the real lives of Native American people, who spent their days concerned with the harsh basics of survival. They fed themselves through hunting, gathering, or crop growing and had to deal with vagaries of natural phenomena that often interfered with a successful hunt or a good harvest. Their religions reflected these realities, and their varied and elaborate rituals were designed to propitiate spirits who might be benevolent one moment and cruel the next.

In contrast, the Bible teaches that true salvation comes from God, not through peyote-inspired visions or spirits in animal forms. God does not expect people to suffer to prove their worthiness.

CHRISTIAN CRITIQUE: Traditional Native American religions served primarily to interpret life, making little distinction between secular and religious aspects of day-to-day living.

Few of these religions acknowledge the Christian doctrines of sin and redemption; rather, man is seen as a part of the whole of nature and not in need of being redeemed by a messiah or savior.

Emphasis is placed on spiritism and pantheism. Spiritual visions are deliberately induced by ingesting peyote and other drugs. A belief in totem animals may lead to occult experiences with demons. Shamanism includes magic and witchcraft-like practices.

SOURCES: *Anchorage Times,* 29 January 1978, B4; *Christianity Today,* 26 June 1981, 37; *Dallas Times Herald,* 14 December 80, 6–14, 31; *Denver Post,* 2 August 1974, 3HH; *East-West Journal,* May 1977, 55; Ibid., June 1984, 30, 36; *Encyclopedia Britannica,* 15th ed., vols. 13 and 26; *Liberty,* May-June 1986, 6; "Medicine Man," 12 April 1993, *People,* 95–96; *New Age Journal* (June 1984): 46; *Rocky Mountain News,* 4 April 1986, 45; George Snyder, "A Native American Renaissance," *San Francisco Chronicle,* 8 September 1992, 1, 10.

ACCESS: www.nativeamericanchurch.com

See also Carlos Castaneda.

NEO-GNOSTICISM

The claims that Jesus Christ gave his followers esoteric, magical teachings
were labeled heresy centuries ago, but such ideas are popular again
with various New Age sects.

FOUNDERS: First-century heretics or earlier mystical religions

TEXTS: Nag Hammadi Codices; miscellaneous Gnostic manuscripts; modern books with conjectures based on ancient texts; the Bible

APPEAL: The main lure of Neo-Gnosticism is secret knowledge not available to the uninitiated.

OVERVIEW: As the infant church sought to formalize its beliefs into a doctrinal structure, the heresy of Gnosticism prompted Paul to write an epistle to the Colossians. Taking their name from the Greek word for knowledge (*gnosis*), the Gnostics taught that Jesus was either a magician, an ascetic, or a sexual deviate who initiated his followers by means of secret ceremonies.

The apostle found it necessary to defend the uniqueness of the person and redemptive work of Christ in the face of suggestions that Jesus was only one of many angelic intermediaries between God and man. He also emphasized that salvation was completed in Christ, countering the legalistic asceticism of Gnosticism (Colossians 2:20-23).

A Different Christ

A major conflict erupted between the orthodoxy of codified beliefs as expressed in the Bible and mystical philosophical concepts held by those who claimed they were the true followers of Christ's esoteric teaching. Orthodoxy eventually triumphed.

Today, however, this early-church heresy is alive and well and debated in prestigious seminaries. Neo-Gnosticism forms the theological foundation for many modern cults and has even formalized a belief structure of its own. Though it has no official organizational apparatus, the tenets of Neo-Gnosticism are held by an increasing number of the educated elite.

Gnostic belief, as expressed in the fourth-century Nag Hammadi Codices and more recent volumes such as *The Secret Gospel, The Gospel of Thomas*, and *The Forbidden Gospel* may be summarized as follows:

- God is actually an abstract figure in an invisible realm.
- The Judeo-Christian Creator is replaced by another deity named Yaldabaoth.
- The serpent in Eden heroically revealed to Adam and Eve secret knowledge that Yaldabaoth had hidden from them.
- The Gnostics guarded this knowledge carefully throughout history; the Flood and the destruction of Sodom and Gomorrah were Yaldabaoth's way of getting revenge upon the Gnostics.
- However, that divine light of gnosis has continued in some enlightened souls even to our present age.

Jesus, according to Gnostic belief, was one of those who possessed a higher consciousness. How he attained this knowledge and what he did with it is a point of conjecture among current Gnostics. Some believe he clandestinely traveled to India to learn the way of the Buddha and the wisdom of the Brahmans.

Others suggest that Christ was actually raised by the hermetic Essenes, who schooled him in mysterious rituals. All Gnostics agree that Christ did not die for man's sin, even suggesting that the Savior tricked Simon of Cyrene into enduring the fate intended for him.

A Dual Appeal

Gnosticism finds fertile ground in two camps. The atheist and agnostic find comfort in believing that Christ was a mere man whose charisma was due to hypnotic techniques or sexual baptismal ceremonies.

The mystically inclined student of Eastern philosophy discovers a presumed harmony between the Gnostic Jesus and the avataristic concept of spiritual leadership as expressed in Hindu texts.

Though Neo-Gnosticism expounds theories too abstract to interest the average person, it does appeal to those whose education has placed them in the upper socioeconomic strata.

As an elitist sect, Neo-Gnosticism is a serious intellectual challenge to Christianity. Those interested in its teachings will acquire an elaborate rationale for rejecting the deity and sacrificial atonement of Christ.

CHRISTIAN CRITIQUE: Orthodox Christian doctrine is refuted and replaced with an alternate explanation for Creation, the Fall, and redemption.

The inspired Scriptures are denied in favor of the "true" teachings of Christ. These esoteric doctrines are available to the adepts of Neo-Gnosticism, who achieve the same level of consciousness as Jesus.

SOURCES: *Denver Post*, 2 December 1977, 6BB; *East-West Journal*, January 1978, 76–87; Michiko Kakutani, "Of Gnosticism and the Spark Within," *New York Times*, 27 September 1996, B8; *Newsweek*, 3 March 1975, 65; *Time*, 4 June 1973, 73; Ibid., 9 June 1975, 46–47.

NEW AGE MOVEMENT

Diverse, eclectic, and adaptable, this movement has profoundly influenced modern thought about politics and spirituality.

FOUNDERS: The New Age movement is rooted in many sources, some ancient, some modern. Marilyn Ferguson, David Spangler, Michael Harner, Jean Houston, Robert Muller, Shirley MacLaine, and others are major theoreticians.

TEXTS: Marilyn Ferguson's *The Aquarian Conspiracy*, Fritjof Capra's *The Tao of Physics*, Shirley MacLaine's *Out on a Limb*, *Dancing in the Light*, and *Going Within*, as well as the writings of Jose Arguelles, Ram Dass, Barbara Marx Hubbard, and many others.

SYMBOLS: Rainbow, globe, lotus flower, mandala, dove

OVERVIEW: The name *New Age* has been around for decades. But what is it, and who started it? Such questions are difficult to answer about a movement that started in small, underground groups but now represents one of the most popular approaches to spirituality.

Equally difficult to pin down is precisely what's new about the current New Age movement. After all, most of the concepts and practices promoted today have enchanted mystics for centuries.

Some of the movement's movers and shakers even suggest that the term *New Age* may be outmoded. *New Age Journal*, a publication that has explored the movement for decades, changed its name to *Body & Soul Magazine* with its March/April 2002 issue. Many book publishers have grown disenchanted with the term, preferring that stores stock their spirituality titles under the "mind-body-spirit" umbrella.

A recent study said the best way to describe the mix of ideas that link together people previously called "New Agers" would be "Lifestyles of Health and Sustainability."

Regardless of what terms one uses, it's clear that *Time* magazine was right years ago when it declared, "A strange mix of spirituality and superstition is sweeping the country."

Another publication entitled *Choices and Connections* declared, "Many of us are still asking what the New Age is. First and foremost, it appears to be an explosion of human curiosity and creativity. It is a time when individuals are passionately seeking to unlock their undiscovered potentials. And while some of this may represent dreams of grandeur, for many it seems to spring from a deep desire to realize the innate goodness that lies within each person."

Cult researcher Ron Rhodes identified the following ten characteristics of the movement in his booklet titled *New Age Movement:*

1. Eclecticism: "New Agers draw from various sources of 'truth.'"
2. Religious syncretism: New Agers blend many religious, philosophical, and mystical views, even if they are contradictory.
3. Monism: "Monism is a theory that sees all reality as a unified whole."
4. Pantheism: The belief that everything that exists is a part of the divine nature.
5. Deification of humanity: Humans, too, are divine beings.
6. Personal and planetary transformation: Personal transformation involves personal awareness of oneness with God, humanity, and the universe.
7. Networking: Connecting with other people, cultures and ideas.
8. Ecological orientation: A commitment to caring for the earth.
9. Belief in a coming utopia: Belief that people and the world we live in are improving.
10. Non-conspiracy: The New Age movement is not a unified, organized

group, but rather a loose affiliation of people who share overlapping values and ideals.

Clearly, contemporary spirituality has undergone a transition that some have called a "paradigm shift in evolutionary consciousness." Successful businessmen consult astrological charts. Yuppie investment bankers talk about past lives. Ethical stock purchasers question a company's worthiness on the basis of its societal contributions. And Republican grandmothers practice martial arts and salve their illnesses with alternative therapies.

Combining New and Old

The New Age is an old adage. Like medieval metaphysicians and ancient Eastern mystics, the New Age movement hails man and his paramount powers as the center of the spiritual universe.

For centuries, people have endeavored to deify themselves and evoke the mysteries of spirituality. The oracles of Greece, the Vedas of the Hindus, and the mysteries of the pharaohs supposed that a secret of existence lay beneath reality. In secluded woods, musty caverns, and passageways of pyramids, these cryptic truths were sought through ritual and ceremony. Today, New Age cults pursue these mysteries of religion in more diverse and ingenious ways.

Implicit in this quest is the assumption that beyond observable reality there is an even more real, hidden universe where unmanifested order is unified into a whole. New Agers believe a "Copernican threshold" must be crossed to uncover the mystery of mankind's relationship to universal spiritual truth. Then the present confrontational system of differing faiths will be replaced with a worldwide oneness of soul and spirit.

Discovering this spiritual symbiosis is the globalistic goal of all New Age religious pilgrimages. Whereas past religions looked outward to the sun, moon, stars, and cosmic forces, those of the New Age who aspire to know hidden truths journey inward to find collective connection with the One Cause. The term *New Age* represents this consciousness, as well as the astrological prediction of the end-of-the-century arrival of an era called the Aquarian Age.

New Age seekers look for a divine being within themselves and strive to be an integral, conscious element of the universe. God becomes the self, and the self becomes God. Marilyn Ferguson, who sums up her support of the New Age movement in *The Aquarian Conspiracy*, describes the New Age as a time for people to unleash the deity within. Ferguson encourages New Agers to "go to the depths of the soul . . . for all that God can do is focused there."

New Age advocates insist that ultimate reality can only be experienced when the mind is stilled of daily distractions. Through New Age practices such as mystical meditation, proponents alter mental states and enter into a collective cosmic consciousness.

In the process, most New Agers adopt the philosophy of relativism, the idea that the meaning of the moment, not predetermined rules, governs behavior. Reality is individualized, created minute by minute. By practicing this theory, New Agers believe they can access enlightening energies and implicit powers to become cocreators with the Divine.

A Growing Presence

New Age beliefs saturate every aspect of American society, from business to sports, education to government. Meditative techniques, such as self-hypnosis, guided imagery, yoga, and centering, are used as part of stress management work strategies. The Human Potential Movement rakes in billions of dollars annually from American companies that urge or require employees to enroll in motivational training seminars.

Beyond the public arena, New Age ideology influences family households with its philosophies of how to achieve self-realization. Housewives hail holistic healing as a new way to tend suffering children. Copulating couples praise pyramid power as a way to channel energy and improve orgasms. Parents and children alike consult astrological charts to foretell their futures.

New Age mind control techniques are employed everywhere. At work and at home, people attempt to achieve self-actualization and manage their lives through visualization. Neurolinguistic trainers observe body language and help clients overcome learning disabilities and insecurities. Creative visualists, frequently found in school systems, use imagery to unleash inner creativity. Teachers encourage ingenuity by asking children to visualize themselves as animals or objects. One teacher instructed students to imagine tiny vultures living inside them, which would grow when the child was bad or diminish when the child was good.

The New Age philosophy that consciousness can be used to influence the body is apparent in the holistic health movement. Some practitioners recommend Rolfing to eliminate ailments by using hands and elbows on connective tissues to achieve bodily "synchronicity."

Still others favor reflexology, viewing the sole of the foot as a microcosm of the body and manipulating key energy points to treat ailments. Polarity therapists teach that sickness results from energy blockages that can be relieved by maneuvering energies around the body.

Most New Age disciples adopt the doctrine that they can cure themselves through positive perception. Some venerate visualization to destroy disease through inner power. Holistic healers advocate therapeutic touching to restore bodily balance and heal the sick. More than fifty nursing schools nationwide teach the therapeutic touch technique. Homeopathy proponents use a theory of like-cures-like and treat the patient with the same substance that sickened him.

Not all of these healing techniques are totally dangerous to one's spiritual health, but problems remain for New Agers who use consciousness to influence the body. The body may also control the mind to the detriment of the entire person. Dr. Carl Raschke, professor of religious studies at the University of Denver, describes the dangers of the Human Potential Movement on a medical and spiritual level. Raschke refers to New Age activity as "the spiritual version of AIDS" because "it destroys the ability of people to cope and function."

A Spiritual Cornucopia

The New Age encompasses many distinct spiritual trends, including psychic phenomena (see separate entry on psychics).

One survey by the University of Chicago revealed that 67 percent of the public claims to have psychic experiences. Psychics seek inner enlightenment through extrasensory perception and psychokinesis, the exertion of energy on an object, event, or situation. Parapsychologists research mental and physical effects of extrasensory occurrences. Clairvoyants receive information from an object or event. Telepathists transfer thoughts into the mental states of others. Rebirthers relive the first moment of their birth and release the trauma to experience a higher self.

Steven Rogat, who teaches New Age psychic seminars, claims intuitive counseling promotes spiritual and physical fitness. Rogat counsels clients on karmic relationships and predicts their futures through dream therapy, numerological consultations, and tarot card readings. A licensed massage technician, Rogat also says magnetic therapy provides relief from menstrual cramps and other bodily discomfort. He routinely rids clients of what he calls "dis-ease" with New Age techniques.

New Age advocates also employ occult divinatory devices to achieve mortal omnipotence. Many consult the Chinese I Ching before making crucial career or personal decisions or commission tasseographers to read tea leaves and calculate kismets. Still others reach for runes to provide answers to dilemmas. People undergoing dream therapy are told they must acknowledge their dreams and commit to realizing them. New Age devotees celebrate auras, supposed fields of multihued colors surrounding one's body as an emanation of one's higher self. Aura advocates have ambiances analyzed to detect health, emotions, and confidence levels.

Pop Culture Phenomenon

Through mass marketing of books, music, and periodicals, New Age philosophies and practices taint every intersection of society. Advocates of New Age consciousness meditate to the sound of New Age music in order to elevate inner excellence.

The public is familiar with the works of Shirley MacLaine, New Age cosmic superstar. Books like Out on a Limb, Dancing in the Light, and Going Within tell the story of her transformation from an agnostic to a believer in the spirit realm, her use of crystals and Hindu mantra chanting for spiritual power, her fascination with yoga and aligning seven spinning wheels of consciousness, called *chakras*, and her reliance on a spirit guide who revealed the law that "everyone is God—everyone." An Academy Award-winning actress, MacLaine released her meditation videotape called *Shirley MacLaine's Inner Workout*. She maintains that exercising the seven batteries of energy permits people to reach ultimate levels of relaxation and higher consciousness.

Oprah Winfrey has been a more important instrument of this movement in recent years, using her popular TV show to introduce many New Age figures to American viewers.

Techniques and Therapies

Some New Agers insist they have encountered their higher selves through a rebirth of their sense of the sacred in near-death experiences.

According to a recent Gallup Poll, 8 to 9 million Americans have reported mystical encounters while temporarily "dead" or on the verge of death. Dr. Raymond A. Moody, a Georgia psychiatrist, says near-death encounters are evidence of life after life. Moody maintains, "Near-death experiences totally transform those who experience them and demonstrate their reality and power."

The cult of the New Age also advocates past-lives therapy to uncover the mystery of previous incarnations. New Agers exercise the strategy to solve current fears and phobias stemming from events in past lives. Dr. Ronald Wong Jue, president of the Association for Transpersonal Psychology, places patients under hypnosis to evaluate past-life memories and dreams. The licensed clinical psychologist believes the material world and the consciousness are interconnected.

Dr. Jue teaches that the past, present, and future can be retrieved by examining linear and mythic time zones of patients. For example, he postulates that someone with a vanity problem may have led a previous Cleopatra-type life. Among Jue's theories is the notion that victims of violent crimes were exploiters in past lives. He attempts to get the client to recognize problems on a mythic level to effect a therapeutic cure.

Still other New Age proponents like the Findhorn Foundation and the Perelandra community communicate with plants, believing them to be inhabited by elemental spirits called *devas*. Plant communicators seek wisdom and guidance from the spirits, whom they believe possess feelings and intelligence.

Other New Agers advocate astral projection to reach spiritual purity. They claim the soul, when propelled into the astral realm, is a temporary manifestation of a higher, eternal spirit that identifies with Christ.

New Age theoreticians are forcing a revolution in the relationship between humans and their macrocosm, with effects as significant as the way Copernicus and Einstein altered their worlds. Understandings of the relationship between body, mind, and spirit will never be the same. Positive visualization, therapeutic healing, guided meditation, and creative imagery all evoke a single, transcendent, unifying force. Instead of Gandhis, Jungs, and Christs to guide the way, there are millions of alternate thinkers, each seeking separation from the past while favoring new explanations of reality. Researcher Carl Raschke said it well. He claims the New Age movement is "essentially the marketing end of the political packaging of occultism . . . a breeding ground for a new American form of fascism."

Assessing the Movement

Critics say this New Age search is really a very old examination of occultism's principles and practices. Reincarnation, astral travel, shamanism, astrology, goddess worship, visualization, and affirmations of inner deity aren't new modes of spirituality. They are ancient ways of claiming to reveal the link between man and God.

In fact, antagonists of the movement say that New Age discoveries aren't really mysteries at all. They are only examples of pagan spiritism rediscovered by those with little sense of religious history and no healthy fear of the unknown.

Simply said, New Age truth is not ultimate but evolving. In fact, any kind of moral absolutism is seen as a dogmatic form of spiritual stagnation. As New Age thinker and writer Marilyn Ferguson puts it, the transformative methods of New Age philosophy "lead to the realization . . . there will be no ultimate answers."

If truth is a constantly changing reality perceived momentarily, then rightness and wrongness are up for grabs as each instance presents itself. Consequently, androgyny (sexual ambiguity) is a preferred state, and homosexuals may be the most enlightened among us.

Some utopians even believe that the New Age rage will evolve into a new world order in which all becomes one. Theology, philosophy, economics, and sociology will unite as common sciences to obliterate all national boundaries. A central authority could then achieve a consolidated consensus concerning all issues of importance to government and religion.

If that sounds a little demagogic, with the potential for Big Brother abuse, never mind. Remember, all is one, one is God, you are one, and you are . . . that's right, God. And since the God in you makes all the decisions, then whatever you decide is right. And if someone disagrees? There's the rub.

The Christian worldview is quite different. God's "shalt nots" are not an oblivious avoidance of each circumstance's merit, but rather a divine perspective that knows the source of ultimate good. Disobedience to God always brings heartache and dysfunction, not because God has arbitrarily ruled it so, but because his character is the stabilizing force of the universe.

Thus, divine law is an extension of divine character. The Ten Commandments weren't meant to be the Ten Suggestions. They represent truth that is fundamental to the perpetuity of human good, just as the laws of thermodynamics are crucial to the continuance of the material universe.

One must wonder what's next on the New Age agenda. When they have exorcised all moral law from society's cognizance, will they next deny gravity its binding role in the universe?

CHRISTIAN CRITIQUE: The New Age promises to unleash people's inner gods and help them attain mortal omnipotence. Advocates attain self-realization by tapping into their subconscious through New Age techniques. They believe the subconscious will conquer all foes and resist all negativism. They restructure perceptions of the world, leading them to a state of personal happiness and power.

Most New Agers conclude God erred by forbidding man to eat of Eden's tree, which they say has the puissance to unleash man's dormant powers. Thus, they blaspheme God's wisdom. Man's problem is not blindness to his innate goodness and potential for divine conduct, but his incapacity for humility in the face of God's omnipotence. Christians believe humanity needs a mass transformation of its value systems and methods of achieving global harmony.

But the transmutability of social institutions and the recasting of human conduct can only occur as individuals are converted by God's grace. Any solution to the human condition that ignores the heart's depravity and God's transcendent wisdom will not usher in a New Age. It can only perpetrate an old lie.

Esoteric half-truths do not lead to God. They are manifestations of the "mystery of iniquity" spoken of in 2 Thessalonians 2:7. The marvelous insights and fascinating knowledge New Agers acquire are the "signs and lying wonders" of Satan and his Antichrist.

SOURCES: Associated Press, "Magic in the Curriculum?" *Colorado Springs Gazette*, 28 February 1999, A14; Craig Branch, "Public Education or Pagan Indoctrination," *Christian Research Journal* (fall 1995): 33–40; *Christianity Today*, 16 May 1986, 17–18; Francis X. Clines, "Mrs. Clinton Calls Sessions Intellectual, Not Spiritual," *New York Times*, 25 June, 1996, A8; *Denver Post*, 23 September 1988, 1F; Marilyn Ferguson, *The Aquarian Conspiracy* (Los Angeles: J. P. Tarcher, 1980); Douglas Groothuis, *Revealing the New Age Jesus* (Downers Grove, Ill.: InterVarsity, 1990); International Transpersonal Conference 1988, notes; Bob Larson, *Straight Answers on the New Age* (Nashville: Thomas Nelson, 1989), 18, 20, 123; "Minding the Store: Influences of the New Age in Business," *SCP Journal* 9, no. 1 (1989); *New Age Journal* (May-June 1988): 67; Ron Rhodes, *New Age Movement* (Grand Rapids, Mich.: Zondervan, 1995); Judith Rosen, "Crossing the Boundaries," *Publishers Weekly*, 27 May, 2002, 25–29.

See also Holism and Alternative Medicine; Human Potential Movement; I AM Institute of Applied Metaphysics; Spiritualism; Trance Channeling.

NICHIREN SHOSHU

Soka Gakkai

These Buddhist reform movements have spread throughout the East and West, attracting the attention of pop stars and the Hollywood elite.

FOUNDERS: Nichiren Daishonen (1222–1282); modern founder, Tsunesaburo Makiguchi (1930–). The cult's main growth occurred under the leadership of Daisaka Ikeda, who was ousted in 1979 due to charges of sexual misconduct and misappropriation of funds.

TEXTS: The *Lotus Sutra* (writings erroneously attributed to Buddha) and *Gosho* (collected volumes of Nichiren Daishonen)

SYMBOLS: Prayer beads, *gongyo* (a booklet with the words of the *Lotus Sutra*), and *butsodon* (black box containing the sacred scroll *Gohonzon*)

APPEAL: Some members are attracted by the admirable goals of world peace, nuclear disarmament, and the abolition of war. Others join in the pursuit of personal desires without moral regard for Christian beliefs or the wishes of others.

OVERVIEW: Western nations are criticized for the hedonistic lifestyles they embrace. How then does one explain the growing popularity of Eastern traditions featuring authoritarian father figures and ascetic rules?

Specifically, how could hundreds of thousands of Americans be attracted by chanting strange syllables while kneeling before a black-lacquered box containing a small, sacred scroll?

But they have been attracted, along with millions of worldwide devotees of the Nichiren Shoshu organization. (Numbers dropped off for a period after a scandal involving charges of misappropriation of funds and sexual misconduct against the group's leader.)

Overall, there may be as many as 30 to 50 million members of the various groups affiliated with these Buddhist reform movements that originated in the thirteenth century.

The Search for a "True Buddhism"

In his search to discover the essence of diverse Buddhist teachings, a thirteenth-century Japanese monk named Nichiren Daishonen claimed to have found the "true Buddhism." It was embodied, he said, in the *Lotus Sutra*, a writing attributed to Buddha but actually written much later.

Nichiren wrote scores of books, but the real growth of his teachings awaited the formation of the *Soka Gakkai* (Value Creation Society) in 1930.

Soka Gakkai is the politically active, evangelistic branch of the organization. It operates a 4.5-million-circulation daily newspaper and has a huge temple near Mount Fuji.

After World War II, the movement grew rapidly under the leadership of Daisaku Ikeda. He made Soka Gakkai a significant force in Japanese politics by establishing its own political party under the name *Komei* (Clean Government) party.

In contrast to Christ's teaching that the chief should be servant of all (Matthew 20:27), Ikeda declared, "You have to have power to do anything at all meaningful."

Powerful Techniques

This power originates in a series of pagan rituals and beliefs. Members are acquired by a conversion technique known as *Shakubuka* (brow-beating), a controversial kind of forced persuasion that borders on brain-washing. A Nichiren Shoshu of America (NSA) document calls it "a merciful method of introducing True Buddhism to nonbelievers."

Once they join, many believers become convinced that NSA holds the keys to world unity and peace. Such laudable goals are to be obtained by chanting *nam-myoho-renge-kyo* (glory to the lotus sutra of the mystical law) before an altar upon which sits the *butsodon* (a black box) containing the *Gohonzon* (sacred scroll). All the while, the devotee fingers the 108 beads of a rosary.

The goal of such devotion is to merge one's self with the essence of Buddha. But curiously, the Nichiren Shoshu group differs from other Buddhist sects in that it elevates Nichiren to a rank higher than the Buddha.

Repeated chanting of the *Diamoku* (worship formula) is said to put one in tune with the rhythm of the universe. As a substitute for psychotherapy, chanting *nam-myoho-renge-kyo* is much easier and cheaper. Perhaps more important, its spiritual goals of working out one's karma take second place to the more immediate purpose of satisfying selfish desires.

"Happy individuals can build a happy world" is NSA's creed, a hedonistic motto that is well received in affluent, Western cultures. If he were alive, Buddha, who taught principles of denial and withdrawal from material pursuits, might look askance on such egocentric goals.

While most of NSA's emphasis is on acquiring wealth, power, and personal happiness, the pagan religious overtones cannot be overlooked by evangelical Christians.

Chanting to the Gohonzon constitutes an idolatrous act, and the belief in its supernatural properties could be a dangerous opening for demonic subjection. The Gohonzon takes the place of God, while implying at the same time a pantheistic version of deity. NSA's espousal of karmic philosophy and reincarnation place it yet another step away from biblical Christianity.

361

The Buddhist goal of fusing one's nature with the universe negates any individual accountability for sin or salvation. While certain material benefits may be incurred by NSA's chanting, forgiveness of sins and conformity with God's moral laws are something that meaningless repetition can never achieve.

CHRISTIAN CRITIQUE: Nichiren Shoshu promotes a Buddhist view of reality while denying Buddha's basic teachings. Salvation is gained through enlightenment and the attainment of Buddhahood. Occult and spiritistic practices of idol worship, shrines, talismans, false scriptures, and repetitious chants are included.

SOURCES: *Christianity Today*, 23 January 1981, 57; *Encyclopedia Britannica*, 15th, vol. 8, 681; Walter Martin, *The New Cults* (Santa Ana, Calif.: Vision House, 1980), 321–350; Pat Means, *The Mystical Maze* (San Bernardino, Calif.: Campus Crusade, 1976), 169–180; *Newsweek*, 5 June 1973, 68; Ibid., 27 August 1973, 60; *Time*, 13 January 1975, 12; Ibid., 1 August 1983, 60.

ACCESS: Two principle groups are Nichiren Shoshu of America, 1401 N. Crescent heights Blvd., West Hollywood, CA 90046, and Soka Gakkai International USA, 4603 Eastern Ave., Mt. Ranier, MD 20712.

NOSTRADAMUS

An insightful prophet to some and a con man to others, this sixteenth-century mystic still fascinates millions who make contemporary applications from his obtuse revelations.

FOUNDER: Michel de Nostredame, called Nostradamus

TEXT: *True Centuries*

APPEAL: Many forms of divination are popular today, and ancient occult wisdom is particularly revered. The idea of forecasting the future holds fascination in an uncertain age. The Third Reich's use of Nostradamus drew the interest of many who had forgotten this "prophet" and his obscure quatrains.

OVERVIEW: After the September 11, 2001, terrorist attacks on America, more people went to church, at least for the next few weeks. This period of uncertainty also spurred more interest in a mysterious sixteenth century man who was said to have predicted the attacks.

A prophecy attributed to Nostradamus and circulated on the Internet proved to be a fake. But that didn't stop a Nostradamus Web site from being the most popular site on search engines like Yahoo and Google, and it didn't stop people from buying tons of books and videos about the celebrated mystic.

A psychiatrist explained the phenomenon to the newspaper USA Today: "People are looking for an explanation," he said.

According to his legion of supporters, Nostradamus supposedly predicted the coming of two antichrists, who materialized as Napoleon and Hitler. Many believe the sixteenth-century physician and mystic made those predictions four hundred years ago and that his prophecy of a third antichrist will also be fulfilled.

Believers in Nostradamus also claim he predicted air travel, air warfare, the space race, electricity, submarines, and even a future bombing of New York City. His book of prophecies, True Centuries, remains popular today. The word century in the book refers to its hundred quatrains, which were written in convoluted language to obscure meaning, since Nostradamus feared prosecution as a magician.

Healer or Master of Hype?

Born in 1503 of Jewish heritage, Nostradamus was influenced by the Catholic Church. Although he attained a doctor's degree and was known as the "healer of the afflicted ones," he studied the occult, alchemy, and magic. He also taught astrology.

Nostradamus predicted the end of the world would occur in 8797. For those worried about nuclear war, he wrote: "In the year 1999 and 7 months, there will come from heaven the great king of terror, to raise again the great king of the Mongols, before and after Mars shall reign at will."

Other physicians of his time deemed him unorthodox for using home remedies. One of the plagues that marked the era killed his wife and children, instigating many years of travel. Nostradamus finally settled in Salon, France, and published his first almanac, which contained prophecies for the pending year. The almanac was so successful that he continued to publish a new one each year thereafter.

Nostradamus's fame as a prophet fired up much controversy. Followers visited him from all parts of France. Catherine de Medici summoned him to the royal court to plot horoscopes for the king and his children, while detractors claimed he represented the devil.

Hitler became fascinated with Nostradamus after Frau Goebbels, wife of the Nazi propaganda minister, introduced him to the Centuries in 1939. During World War II, pamphlets based on a forged Nostradamus prophecy that Germany would win the war were dropped from Nazi aircraft.

Nostradamus said all his visions came from God even though he admitted that the Bible condemned his methods, which included employing the occult.

True Centuries may have been written through necromancy, tarot cards, witchcraft, or psychic inspiration. The Bible clearly reveals that such foretelling is forbidden and that Christ did not make specialized prophecies about future Nazi political regimes.

But you don't have to be a Christian to wonder about Nostradamus. James Randi, a secular skeptic and noted debunker, wrote a 1990 book on the subject called *The Mask of Nostradamus: A Biography of the World's Most Famous Prophet*. His conclusion? More of the same old "classical psychic claptrap"!

CHRISTIAN CRITIQUE: *True Centuries* supports belief in the supernatural and argues that man can look into the future and arrange the present to his advantage.

But Nostradamus's prophecies were likely construed through occult methods; therefore, they may be the work of Satan. Only God knows the future (Ecclesiastes 8:7; see also Revelation 1:8). It cannot be divined by man. The Bible forbids forecasting the future through divination of any kind (Deuteronomy 18:10-12, 14).

SOURCES: Margaret Carlin, "Nostradamus Items Sell Fast," *USA Today*, 18 September 2001, 3D; Erika Cheetham, ed., *The Prophecies of Nostradamus* (New York: Berkley Books, 1973); *The Plain Truth*, April 1983, 33–34; James Randi, *An Encyclopedia of Claims, Frauds, and Hoaxes of the Occult and Supernatural* (New York: St. Martin's Press, 1995); Henry C. Roberts, ed., *The Complete Prophecies of Nostradamus* (New York: Crown, 1982).

ACCESS: The Nostradamus Society of America was formed in 1997 and is "dedicated to the memory of Nostradamus; physician, astrologer, prophet, and humanitarian." www.nostradamususa.com

ODINISM

Norse Neo-Paganism; Asatru Free Assembly; Asatru Folk Assembly

---

In Western Europe and America, Thor and other gods of Norse mythology are a source of inspiration for satanists, racists, and others who embrace these gods' supremacist overtones. In the homelands of such gods, traditionally Christian countries like Denmark now legally sanction marriages in the name of Odin.

FOUNDER: Steven McNallen, a former Catholic, established Asatru Free Assembly in 1971 in Breckenridge, Texas.

TEXT: Norse myths teaching that man can learn wisdom and qualities of strength, courage, honor, joy, and freedom from ancient Norse gods, who share equal status with humans.

A posting on the *Runestone* Web site explains that the Norse groups don't follow any scripture: "There are two real sources of holy truth, and neither expresses itself to us in words. One is the universe around us, which is a manifestation of the underlying divine essence. The other is the universe inside us, passed down from our ancestors as instinct, emotion, innate predispositions, and perhaps even racial memory."

SYMBOLS: Ancient Norse amulets and objects of war, including swastikas, runes, helmets, swords, animal horns, red wooden shields, Viking axes, wooden sculptures of gods and goddesses

APPEAL: Asatru is an individualistic religion based on the arbitrary choice of lenient gods who are like friends one honors and respects. Norse gods make no objectified moral demands of followers; instead, they promise self-indulgent rewards through a loosely structured belief system.

OVERVIEW: Former Roman Catholic Steve McNallen traded Christianity for a form of paganism known as Odinism or Norse Neo-Paganism.

McNallen's search for a different faith started when he was a senior at Midwestern University in Wichita Falls, Texas. McNallen spent ten years researching Norse religions and compiling a collection of pagan prayers before establishing a group called the Asatru Free Assembly (AFA) in Breckenridge, Texas, in 1971.

At its height, the group claimed it had one thousand followers in the United States. The AFA folded in the late 1980s, but then McNallen resurrected it in a slightly different form in 1994, calling it the Asatru Folk Assembly.

Resembling Thor, the macho deity he adulates, the red-bearded McNallen claims to gain strength and wisdom through examples of ancient Norse gods and goddesses and believes man harmonizes more closely with nature by observing changes in the moon and stars.

McNallen and his wife, Madeline Hutter, also a former Catholic, set up an office in their home to publish *The Runestone*, an on-line newsletter that serves as a virtual gathering place for like-minded believers.

Though small, the AFA is just the tip of a Norse neo-pagan iceberg that represents perhaps thousands of people who believe ancient Scandinavian mythology and are affiliated with groups like the Odinist Fellowship, the Odinist Committee in England, or the Asatrufolks in Iceland, all of which were originally created within months of each other and without knowledge of each other's existence.

From Myth to Ritual

Practices vary from group to group, but McNallen and Hutter worship such Norse gods and goddesses as Thor, Odin, Frigga (wife of the one-eyed Odin) and Freya (foremost goddess-representative of the Vanir, a race of fertility gods).

Odin ranks highest among the gods, but mighty Thor is more popular. Thor is Odin's son and god of the sky, thunder, and fertility. He also is responsible for law and order in Midgard, the World of Men.

"Everybody knows Thor," says McNallen who combines seriousness with a sense of humor. "He's the good ol' boy among gods . . . (and) would be the patron god of Texas."

McNallen and Hutter were remarried at a ritualistic festival called an *Althing*, where after a celebratory feast, a huge hammer was burned as an offering to Thor. Visitors came from several states to participate in Viking games, to hear lectures, and to attend *blots* (pronounced "bloats"), ceremonies to worship the gods. To that end, they poured wine upon the ground, chanting, "Hail to you, Freya! Smile on us!"

Wearing long red tunics and silver replicas of Thor's hammer around their necks, McNallen and Hutter honor gods and goddesses by chanting in Old Norse with closed eyes and drinking wine from an animal horn as part of their religious celebration. Traditionally, the honey wine called mead is drunk at such ceremonies, but other drinks are acceptable.

Gods from the North

Vikings once ruled northern Europe all the way to the Mediterranean. They worshiped the Aesir, a pantheon of twelve gods, who ruled the heavens and earth under Odin, variously called the Terrible One, Father of Battle, and the All-Father.

Odin supposedly rides an eight-legged horse and shares his rule with a plethora of other gods and goddesses, a pre-Christian polytheistic belief. In about A.D. 1000 Norse mythology succumbed when Scandinavia fell to Roman religious rule.

In Old Norse, *Asatru* means "belief in the gods." Also known as Odinism, Asatru makes little distinction between Norse deities and mortal man. Followers believe their gods live close to earth and indulge in the experiences of everyday life, like glorified human beings. Asatru stresses that its deities are personifications of the forces of nature. Thor, Odin, and others are friends, never masters. Followers assume positions of equality with their gods, who are revered for qualities of defiance and willpower.

Each Norse deity is responsible for different aspects of the universe. Odin is respected for wisdom, poetry, and magic. Thor, also called Thunder God and the Charioteer, is the farmer's friend, a warrior and toiler. Balder epitomizes courage and goodness.

The Asatru Folk Assembly states, "A religion without a goddess is halfway to atheism." Therefore, Frigga is respected as mother of the gods, and Nerthus is worshiped as Mother Earth, whose wounds man is obligated to heal. Frigga is accorded special honor as the mother of gods. Freya, the "eternal feminine," is respected as the creator of life. For the courageous follower, direct contact with the gods and goddesses is promised, while the less brave can expect less potent contact.

Followers of Asatru believe man is master of his own soul—man, not Jesus Christ, is his own salvation. After death the worthy go to the realm of the gods, called Asgard, while sinners are relegated to eternal gloom, cold, and fog.

The Asatru Folk Assembly also advocates reincarnation, and faithful followers deplore the conversion of Germanic peoples to Christianity. Forces of nature—the moon, solstices, cycles of the year—are celebrated. Displays of courage, speaking out against bureaucracy, hospitality to guests, and preserving the environment are considered religious acts. Loyalty and brotherhood are supreme virtues.

Followers believe they control their destinies by heroic action and that mankind's fate can be molded by taking risks, defending one's rights, and by not compromising one's beliefs. Their code of conduct stresses courage as a primary virtue and advocates the necessity of honoring their ancestors' religion—ancient Norse gods and goddesses, who control all facets of human existence.

Sex is viewed as a vital part of nature to be enjoyed without guilt. In stark contrast to the tenets of Christianity, Neo-pagans feel society is best served when each individual develops his full potential by creating a satisfying sex life. Pagans view sex as a clean, wholesome activity that needn't include matrimony.

Asatru followers accept various forms of worship, avoiding hierarchically determined structures. Members are free to worship whatever god they wish in whatever manner. They believe the only proper expression of self is to experience what they call the rhythm of nature. They do not bow to their gods and goddesses, stressing that equal spiritual footing be shared by the deity and worshiping mortal. Societal skills and human characteristics are revered, rather than Christ's sacrifice on the cross.

Some Asatru Folk Assembly adherents worship daily, using various symbols—cakes, spears, swords, and horns. Steve McNallen says, "I realized . . . we could choose what deities to follow." He also claims the Asatru Folk Assembly performs no animal sacrifices. But in Iceland, where paganism is resurgent, such sacrifices can be approved by the health department and conducted at authorized slaughterhouses.

Small but Influential

Asatru is more widespread than its small membership indicates. While public pagan worship was outlawed in Iceland nine hundred years ago, Nordic paganism was officially recognized in 1972 as a legal religion. People in Iceland recently demanded that plans for a new road be altered to avoid crossing a hill frequented by fairies. Their appeal was honored, the road's course shifted.

Odinists have been accused of being neo-Nazis, though publicly they lament that Nazi Germany used old Norse symbols during its infamous regime. The swastika, principal emblem of Nazism, originally represented both Thor's hammer and the wheel of the sun. Such negative connotations attached to Asatru are aggravated by heavy emphasis on genetic superiority in Odinist literature. Several articles in *The Runestone* observed that "[Psychologist Carl] Jung's original idea was that . . . archetypes were not culturally transmitted but inherited genetically." A member of the Asatru Free Assembly was quoted as saying, "We are not racists, but we are racially aware."

In addition, British writer J. R. R. Tolkien was a big fan of Norse mythology. Many readers see Norse themes in Tolkien's Lord of the Rings novels and the movies based on the books. So even though groups like the Asatru Folk Assembly may seem small, their beliefs are embraced by others around the world.

A recent article in *The New York Times* entitled "Nordic Culture Thrives as Young Seek Out Roots" described an aspect of this culture's renewed popularity: "Now Nordic-language classes are packed, and universities and some high schools are teaching Scandinavian folklore and passing on nautical skills that date from the Vikings. . . . The resurgence is generated by third- and fourth-generation Scandinavian-Americans who are embracing a culture that their grandparents may have tried to play down in an effort to fit into this country. The interest is propelled in some measure by a paradox; merciless parodying in Garrison Keillor's Lake Wobegon chronicles and in the movie 'Fargo' has only fueled interest in their ancestry."

CHRISTIAN CRITIQUE: A section on the *Runestone* Web site spells out this movement's differences from orthodox Christianity:

We are polytheistic. That is, we believe in a number of deities, including Goddesses as well as Gods.

We do not accept the idea of "original sin," the notion that we are tainted from birth and intrinsically bad, as does Christianity. Thus, we do not need "saving."

We do not claim to be a universal religion, a faith for all of humankind. In fact, we don't think such a thing is possible or desirable. The different branches of humanity have different ways of looking at the world, each of which is valid for them. It is only right that they have different religions.

Odinist groups celebrate the forces of nature with feasts. Gods and goddesses of Norse mythology are invited to intervene in life, providing wisdom, strength, courage, and energy.

The Odinist religious system is constructed upon mythology rather than historical fact or biblical truth. It supports reincarnation and proposes that man is master of his soul.

Witches and druids are accepted as legitimate representatives of Asatru, and many gods are esteemed as models to be imitated. Racist overtones refute Christ's promise that all those who believe in him will earn eternal salvation.

Occult overtones introduce the idea of a hidden, divine energy beyond human understanding, an essence that is interdependent with man.

SOURCES: Margot Adler, *Drawing Down the Moon*, rev. ed. (Boston: Beacon Press, 1986); Kevin Crossley, *The Norse Myths* (Holland, N. Y.: Pantheon, 1980); *Denver Post*, 23 May 1975, 3BB; Timothy Egan, "Nordic Culture Thrives as Young Seek Out Roots," *New York Times*, 12 May 2002, 12; *Fort Worth Star Telegram*, 16 December 1985, 13A, 18A; *Oregon Journal*, 22 February 1979, 4.

ACCESS: Asatru Folk Assembly's on-line newsletter, *The Runestone*, can be found at www.runestone.org. Another group, the Asatru Alliance, is located in Payton, Arizona.

ORDER OF THE SOLAR TEMPLE

From the mountains of France to the hamlets of Quebec, the religiously motivated suicides of this little-known group shocked secularized Francophile societies.

FOUNDERS: Luc Jouret and Joseph Di Mambro

TEXT: Jouret's books and taped lectures, including one titled "Fundamental Time of Life: Death"

APPEAL: The world is growing worse, but members of the cult can escape impending doom through death, which leads to a new reincarnation and a better life.

OVERVIEW: Two days before Christmas in 1995, sixteen members of the Order of the Solar Temple died in their compound in the French Alps. Initial reports said the sixteen had committed suicide, but a French investigation found that at least four of the dead cultists, including three young children ages two, four, and six, did not go to their deaths willingly.

In 1997 five more members of the group died in a mysterious blaze outside a village southwest of Quebec City, Canada.

Combined with other deaths and suicides attributed to the group in Europe, the Canadian deaths brought the total number of fatalities to seventy-four.

The deaths happened in a variety of ways: suffocation, sleeping pills, gunfire, and flames. But there was one fact that united them all: the members of this small group believed that conditions in the world were growing worse and that suicide would instantly transport them to a much better place—a new life on a planet called Sirius.

At the time of the Quebec deaths, reports said the group, which once had as many as five hundred members, remained strong and would regroup. But little has been heard of them since 1997. Still, a brief review of the group's history is helpful in understanding the role of deadly cults.

A Complex Lineage

Jo Di Mambro was interested in all manner of esoteric spirituality and was involved with the Rosicrucian Order (see separate entry) for many years. Arrested for swindling, Di Mambro moved to an area near the French-Swiss border and founded the Center for Preparing the New Age in 1973. A small community grew there.

He later shared leadership of the group with Luc Jouret, a charismatic man. Together, the two founded the Order of the Solar Temple, an International

Chivalric Organization of the Solar Tradition, in 1984, and Jouret recruited members from his lectures and radio talks. By the early nineties some members of the group were questioning its beliefs and practices. Di Mambro and Jouret began devising plans for a "transit" to another world and preaching a more apocalyptic message.

The group's rituals included a confession of sins, guided meditation intended to purify members, various prayers, and readings from mystical passages of the Gospel of John. Members came to believe that they were "noble travelers" on this planet who had been reincarnated here to perform a specific mission. This mission involved spreading their message and then reincarnating once again.

This next reincarnation required death. Many members weren't willing to take such a step, but some were. The following is one man's testimony, recorded shortly before he took his own life: "I, a Lightbearer since the most remote times, the time which was given to me on Planet Earth is completed, and I go back freely and willingly to the place from which I came at the beginning of the times! Happiness fills me, because I know that I have fulfilled my duty, and that I can bring back in Peace and Happiness my capitalized energy enriched through the experience which I have lived on this Earth."

It is believed that growing internal dissension and increased criticism from anticult groups led seventy-four devoted members of the group to take their own lives in the nineties. Though some drew comparisons to the mass killings in Jonestown (see separate entry), the Solar Temple deaths were their own unique tragedy.

As French scholar Jean-Francois Mayer put it, "The Solar Temple was engulfed in illusion and its pride led only to nothingness: believing that they would become gods, the blind disciples followed the flute player in a dance of death and hurtled towards their end."

CHRISTIAN CRITIQUE: Only Christ's death is truly redemptive. We cannot improve our lot in the next life by ending our life here. Like the Heaven's Gate, the lies of the Solar Temple were based on the assumptions that earthly life is transitory and illusory and that death is an entry point to a higher spiritual state. Groups like these divorce their followers from any objective view of life and death so that neither state has meaning in literal truth. Thus the passageway to the next incarnation—suicide—holds no moral consequences and has no reprehension because life and death are one. Setting aside such obtuse philosophical reasoning, the truth is that the deaths of sixteen people were the result of the personal megalomania of Di Mambro and Jouret. These men were incapable of managing their own internal demons and unfortunately, convinced others to follow their lead into oblivion rather than face life's vagaries with purpose and hope. These "travelers" were less than noble, and no further states of consciousness in other incarnated forms awaited them—only final judgment before a God who does not view lightly such disregard for the sacredness of life.

SOURCES: John Hall and Phillip Schuyler, "The Mystical Apocalypse of the Solar Temple," *Millennium, Messiahs, and Mayhem*, ed. Thomas Robbins and Susan J. Palmer (New York: Routledge, 1997); Jean-Francois Mayer, "Our Terrestrial Journey Is Coming to an End: The Last Voyage of the Solar Temple," *Nova Religio*, April 1999; www.religiousmovements.lib.virginia.edu/solartem.html.

OSHO

Bhagwan Shree Rajneesh

Neither scandals nor their leader's death have dimmed the devotion of those who still follow this controversial guru.

Never Born, Never Died, Only Visited This Planet
A PLAQUE AT THE SITE IN PUNE, INDIA, WHERE OSHO'S ASHES ARE ENSHRINED

FOUNDER: Shree Rajneesh; born in 1931 as Mohan Chandra Rajneesh; also known as Acharya Rajneesh, Bhagwan Shree Rajneesh, Gautama Buddha, Zorba the Buddha; died in 1990

TEXTS: Hindu scriptures and Rajneesh's books, including *Beyond and Beyond, Above All, Don't Wobble*, and *Meditation: The Art of Ecstasy*

APPEAL: Graduates of consciousness-raising sects in the Human Potential Movement are often looking for a new discipline or experience beyond what they have already encountered. Rajneesh gave them a spiritual rationale for uninhibited self-gratification, especially of the sexual variety. To one unfamiliar with biblical guidelines regarding meditation and self-expression, his therapeutic approach of negating all hang-ups sounds like good advice.

OVERVIEW: In the wake of the September 11, 2001, terrorist attacks on America, experts began debating whether enemies could launch a biological attack on the United States.

But people who had followed the bizarre career of Osho already knew that he had orchestrated the first such biological attack in U.S. history. It was in 1984, and members of his Rajneeshpuram community, who were locked in a bitter battle with their Oregon neighbors, contaminated drinking glasses and a salad bar in a nearby town, causing illness among 751 innocent people.

How could a religious group do something so mean-spirited and potentially deadly? The answers can be found not in the literature of Christian anticult groups but in the pages of *New Age Journal*, which did a blistering exposé of the group in 1992.

In an article entitled "Dance into Darkness," writer Linda Ilene Solomon said, "It was a community built on a guru's promise of love and liberation. But in the end, Rajneeshpuram became a place of guns and paranoia."

Professing Nothing, Doing Anything

To most mystical gurus, sex, drugs, and hedonism are impediments on the path to enlightenment. Not to Bhagwan Shree Rajneesh. "I don't profess anything," he declared, and his disciples acted accordingly. For students of Eastern religions who considered asceticism too confining, this was the way to go.

At first, all one had to do was grab the next plane to Pune, India (a route taken by notables such as Diana Ross, Ruth Carter Stapleton, and fifty thousand others). Once there, all clothes were shed for orange robes. Candidates for Rajneesh's brand of spirituality prostrated themselves the moment Rajneesh entered the room. The seekers then received a new Hindi name and a beaded necklace with Rajneesh's face in a locket.

One important warning: devotees had to wash thoroughly—especially their hair. Guards stood ready to sniff the hair of each entrant, whose every lock had to be clean and free from oil before being allowed into his divine presence. Though he claimed to be a "living God beyond time in a state of continuous bliss," Rajneesh had diabetes and a horrible case of asthma.

Bhagwan's teachings abound in eighty books and more than five hundred tapes. The message is simple: Anything goes. He preaches indiscriminate premarital sex, open marriages, and the abolition of the family, which he says is "the biggest threat to human progress." In his perception of religion, Christianity is a "cult," and even the pope and Mother Teresa receive his castigation. Traditional *sanyasis* (holy men who meditate and renounce the world) may pursue the path to God for years. The Pune guru offers the state of *sanyas*, with all of its bliss, immediately; *neosanyas* he calls it. "Westerners want things quickly, so we give it to them right away." He promises nothing less than "freedom from everything!"

For years the bald and bearded Rajneesh was referred to as India's sex guru. At his resort in Rajasthan State he dispensed *tantric* (sexual) yoga and meditation. Western pilgrims at his Pune *ashram* received more of the same. Adhering to his admonition that "the path to desirelessness is through desire," they would smoke pot, disrobe, dance, jump up and down, and pursue sex however and with whomever they wished.

The sterilization of female members avoided having to cope with one possible consequence of such libertine ways. Such antics attracted followers in five hundred centers worldwide (one hundred of them in the United States).

At one point Rajneesh claimed to have half a million followers, although at most he had about forty thousand devoted *sannyasins*. The estimated income totaled between $5 million and $7 million a year, with Rajneesh being chauffeured about in a Rolls-Royce Silver Shadow.

From Obscurity to Celebrity

Born in 1931 as Mohan Chandra Rajneesh, he was raised as a Jain in a small village in Madhya Pradesh province. (Jainism is an Indian religion emphasizing extreme asceticism.) After receiving a master's degree in philosophy, he served for a while as a professor. In 1966 he left the teaching profession to fulfill what he saw as God's plan for his life—spiritually transforming humanity. In 1971 he took the title Bhagwan Shree Rajneesh, meaning, "The Blessed One Who Has Recognized Himself as God." He established his first *ashram* at Pune, India, in 1974.

The Pune *ashram* usually had approximately five to seven thousand devotees in residence at any given time. As Rajneesh attempted to create a communal theocratic state, area citizens were offended by the way his followers displayed uninhibited sexual affections in public.

Circulated stories about erotic licentiousness and physical violence inside the *ashram* walls eventually provoked harassment from the townspeople. To escape the criticism (and avoid a crackdown from Indian tax officials), Rajneesh packed up his collector's 150,000-volume library and, claiming medical problems, entered the United States—along with twelve tons of luggage.

For years Rajneesh had been seeking "a new site, isolated from the outside world." As the dismantling of the Pune *ashram* was taking place, word surfaced that officials of the Chidvilas Rajneesh Meditation Center had already purchased (with $1.5 million in cash) more than 100 square miles of ranch land near Antelope, Oregon (120 miles southeast of Portland).

Disciples attending his meditation sessions would observe the sex guru sitting motionless for long periods of time as he entered a self-proclaimed period of "speaking through silence." It is now apparent that Rajneesh was formulating plans to establish the world's largest spiritual community on these shores— much to the chagrin of many solid Oregonians!

In August 1981 Rajneesh moved his sect to Rajneeshpuram, a commune built for his followers at a cost of $35 to $40 million. At its peak, the 74,000-

acre commune was home to around four thousand people and included a productive truck and dairy farm. Rajneesh owned ninety-three Rolls-Royces.

Weekly ads in *Time* magazine proclaimed messages such as, "*Repression should not be a word in the vocabulary of a sannyasin* [seeker]." A majority of Rajneesh's followers at this point were well-educated—64 percent had bachelor's degrees and 36 percent had advanced degrees; 22 percent were professionals in psychiatry or psychology.

The guru's teachings were an amalgam of Western psychotherapeutic techniques and Eastern religion. His devotees attended group therapy and practiced meditation. Courses offered at the Rajneesh International University in Rajneeshpuram included "Breath Energy Ecstasy" and "Rajneeshercize."

Meditation at Rajneesh's *ashram* went through five stages, from hyperventilative breathing to Sufi dancing. Participants were often required to wear blindfolds, and many discarded their clothing. Since Rajneesh saw the logical mind as a barrier to spiritual progress, it was stilled by such exercises as staring at his picture without blinking for an hour.

Even his endless list of irrelevant rules was designed to rid one's thinking of the questioning process. He also encouraged "rebirthing," a state of returning mentally and emotionally to the mother's womb before the trauma of birth. Ultimate illumination came when Rajneesh pressed his thumb into the center of the initiate's forehead to awaken the mystical third eye.

A Fractured Kingdom

Rajneesh's kingdom began to fall apart in the early 1980s. Enraged citizens in nearby Antelope were doing all they could to get rid of the cult, which had gained control of the city council and renamed the town *Rajneeshpuram* in 1983.

In November that year the State of Oregon sued, claiming the city of Rajneeshpuram was a theocracy and violated the U.S. Constitution. Although one court ruled the city's incorporation legal in July 1985, a host of other problems overcame the organization. The Indian government still sought $3 million in back taxes from Rajneesh's residence in Pune.

Closer to home, suits and countersuits filed by Oregon and even former followers resulted in increasingly negative publicity. In September 1984 Rajneesh's followers rounded up about two thousand homeless people in major cities across the United States and shipped them to the commune.

Local citizens accused them of attempting to take over the county under the guise of humanitarianism. The final blow fell when Rajneesh himself, arrested as a fugitive in North Carolina, pleaded guilty to illegal immigration charges in 1985 and was ordered out of the United States.

The movement collapsed amid rumors of wiretapping, arson, poisoning, assault, and shady fortunes in Swiss bank accounts. In September 1985 the guru announced his religion was dead, going so far as to claim that "Rajneeshism" had been created by his top aides, who had also tried to poison him. The people of Antelope got their town back, and Rajneesh's thousands of followers scattered, only a few staying at what remained of the nearby commune.

After leaving the United States, Rajneesh was turned away from several other countries. In November 1985 he returned to his original *ashram* in Pune, India, although his current personal secretary said that his followers would try to overturn the court ruling that ordered him to leave the United States. A decade later, his top aides were convicted of conspiring to murder government officials investigating the group's crimes.

In the wake of AIDS, even before he left the United States, Rajneesh's message shifted from advocating free sex to discouraging such behavior, providing condoms and rubber gloves to those followers "who cannot or will not abstain from sex." An article in *The Rajneesh Times*, the movement's newspaper, even discouraged kissing.

Addicted to the pleasures of wealth and adulation, Rajneesh was heard to admit his relief at not having to pretend he was enlightened anymore.

In December 1988 he told ten thousand followers in India that his body had become host to the soul of the ascetic Gautama Buddha, which name he preferred over "Bhagwan." Several days later Rajneesh exorcised himself of that spirit when Gautama disapproved of his use of a Jacuzzi. His new name, he said, was "Zorba the Buddha."

In January 1989 he announced that he had changed his mind about being Buddha and preferred to be called simply "Shree Rajneesh." Later that same year he again changed his name, this time to "Osho." He died of heart failure in January 1990.

A Happy Ending

Things didn't turn out well for Osho or the many people who had followed him, but there was a surprising turn of events for the site of Rajneeshpuram. In 1997 the property was donated to Young Life, the international Christian youth organization, which transformed the former commune into a camp for teens.

After cleansing the property with prayer, Young Life personnel remained concerned about the structure that had served as Osho's residence. To the group's relief, a fire destroyed the structure.

Today, a site that once housed a destructive hedonistic cult is being used for God's glory to teach young people about the Christian life.

Meanwhile, devoted followers in India have kept Osho's flame burning by studying his books and tapes. But recent arguments have divided Osho's disciples. Moderates who want to update Osho's movement have changed the name of their Pune, India, center from Osho Commune International to Osho Meditation Resort and are targeting wealthier visitors. They have also taken down many of the photos of Osho that formerly decorated every available wall. Meanwhile, purists opposed to the changes have set up a rival organization in Delhi called Osho World.

CHRISTIAN CRITIQUE: Osho claimed the goal of God-realization was accomplished when thinking and knowledge had been circumvented. One can live in a constant meditative state, an existence of innate responses to Osho's programmed precepts. Each sannyasin is encouraged to live a sexually vigorous life with spiritual sanction.

But Osho departed from traditional Hindu morality as well as biblical standards of sexuality. In Hinduism God is the universal consciousness, not a person. Human beings are not at the center of determining what conduct is permissible.

Christianity enhances self-identity in contrast to Osho's attempt to destroy one's emotionally protective barriers of self-worth. Meditation should be a concentrative act of the will, not a chaotic, mindless, druglike state of emptying out the consciousness.

SOURCES: Paul Barrett, "Leader," *Gallery*, 21; Howard G. Chua-Eoan, "People: Butt Out, Buddha!" *Time*, 16 January 1989, 78; Satya Bharti Franklin, *The Promise of Paradise: A Woman's Intimate Story of the Perils of Life with Rajneesh* (Barrytown, N.Y.: Station Hill Press, 1992); Roberta Green, "The Rolls Royce of False Prophets," *Eternity*, December 1985, 10; "Guru Wants a Return," *Rocky Mountain News*, 9 February 1988, 110; "A Journey Towards Faith," *Radix*; Neal Karlen, "The Homeless and the Guru," *Newsweek*, 24 September 1984, 35; George Lurie, "Antelope, Ore., Makes a Return," *USA Today*, 30 January 1986, 3A; Art Moore, "From Cult Site to Teen Camp," *Christianity Today*, 15 November 1999, 22–23; *People*, 16 February 1981, 36–38; Ibid., 23 March 1981, 78; "Rajneeshee Leader's Spirit Fiery," *Rocky Mountain News*, 7 September 1987, 166; Linda Ilene Solomon, "Dance into Darkness," *New Age Journal* (November-December 1992): 81–84, 125–129; *Time*, 16 January 1978, 59; Amy Waldman, "Old Rajneesh Commune Lightens Up in Afterlife," *New York Times*, 10 December 2002, A4; "What's in a Few Name Changes?" *Denver Post*, 16 January 1989, 10; Frank Zoretich, "Oregon County Fears," *USA Today*, 18 September 1984.

ACCESS: Osho Commune International, Box 352, Mill Valley, CA 94942

PAGANISM AND NEO-PAGANISM

Today's pagans are reviving ancient practices and recruiting spiritual seekers by the thousands, and they are doing it on the streets, in colleges, and even at military bases.

OVERVIEW: When a group of forty military personnel claiming to be pagans held a public ritual on the country's largest military installation, eyebrows were raised, but no attempts were made to stop the ceremony. One congressman observed, "It is difficult to make the case that encouraging the practice of bizarre rituals makes a positive contribution to combat readiness. What's next? Will armored divisions be forced to travel with sacrificial animals for rituals?"

For many, the word *pagan* conjures up images of primitive people who huddled around huge campfires, perhaps sacrificing animals or children to Satan. Others, such as the congressman quoted above, see paganism as "bizarre."

But to members of the growing worldwide neo-pagan community, their faith is all about finding God—or the Goddess, or many gods—in nature or in themselves. Their rituals, which are allegedly based on centuries-old traditions, are designed to honor the cycles of nature and inspire people to live creatively and harmoniously with those cycles. Such seemingly benign explanations for ancient occultism have boosted the public-relations image of pagans and place them on a legal par with Christians, Jews, and Muslims. The army has even appointed chaplains to oversee pagan ceremonies on at least five bases. In one case a Christian chaplain was forced to take responsibility for overseeing a coven, a job that did not please him.

And many pagans argue that they don't even believe in Satan. That doesn't mean the devil doesn't exist, but people who assume pagans worship the devil are misinformed. This group makes it plain in all their public statements that they worship nature and nature's gods, not the father of evil.

While that may be factually correct, to Christians that assertion is hardly theologically accurate. Whatever claims pagans make to the contrary, their devotion to primordial entities such as Freya and the horned god place them clearly in the category of witchcraft, a practice demanding the death penalty in ancient, theocractic Israel (Exodus 22:18).

A Loose Network

Selena Fox is the founder of Circle Sanctuary, a Wisconsin-based network of contemporary pagans. Fox says there are 250,000 bona fide pagans in the United States but says the movement's influence extends beyond that.

"If we broadened the definition to include those people who consider themselves followers of all forms of Earth-centered or nature-centered spirituality, there would probably be close to a million," she says.

One of the leading pagan figures is Margot Adler, who was raised a "Jewish Marxist atheist" but experienced a conversion to paganism during her youth. During the early 1970s she became a Wiccan priestess (see separate entry on Wicca and witchcraft).

Adler is the author of a book that details the neo-pagan movement. The book is entitled *Drawing Down the Moon: Witches, Druids, Goddess-Worshippers and Other pagans in America Today.*

In that book Adler summarizes the theology of neo-paganism as follows: "The world is holy. Nature is holy. The body is holy. Sexuality is holy. The imagination is holy. You are holy."

CHRISTIAN CRITIQUE: In ancient pre-Christian times, Europe and England were populated with hunting cultures that revered fertility and the power of elemental spirits. The term *pagan* comes from the Latin *pagani*, meaning "those who dwell in the countryside." The original use of the term was not pejorative but descriptive. With the predominance of Christianity after A.D. 1000, the term *pagan* was broadly applied to those associated with non-Christian beliefs, especially witchcraft.

Etymology may have some significance, but theology has eternal significance. Whatever they may be called and however they describe their gods and goddesses, pagans are guilty of violating the first commandment (Exodus 20:3). It is disingenuous to argue that pagans don't worship the devil. That may be true by technical definition, but pagan beliefs in reincarnation, the conjuring of entities, worship of the earth (creation), polytheism, and the lack of moral absolutes places pagans far from the accepted worship of God presented in Scripture. In fact, such practices and beliefs are exactly what the Bible defines as the lies of Lucifer.

PATRIOT MOVEMENT

Combining religiosity and a deep distrust of the government, patriot groups
seek to remake America in their own paranoid image.

*What is it going to take to open up the eyes of our elected officials? AMERICA
IS IN SERIOUS DECLINE. We have no proverbial tea to dump; should we
instead sink a ship full of Japanese imports? Is a civil war imminent? Do we
have to shed blood to reform the current system? I hope it doesn't come to that!
But it might.*

TIMOTHY MCVEIGH, QUOTED IN RICHARD ABANES, *AMERICAN MILITIAS*

*Go up and look legislators in the face, because some day you may have
to blow it off.*

SAMUEL SHERWOOD, UNITED STATES MILITIA ASSOCIATION, QUOTED IN RICHARD ABANES,
AMERICAN MILITIAS

OVERVIEW: After Timothy McVeigh's 1995 bombing of a federal building
in Oklahoma City—an event that up until 2001 was the most destructive act of
terrorism on U.S. soil—people became concerned about the patriot movement.

But unlike many of the groups profiled in this book, the patriot movement
is hard to define. It is made up of numerous groups of individuals who share
common beliefs that center on a deep mistrust of the government.

Among patriot groups are the following: the Militia of Montana, whose
leader John Trochman has links to the racist Aryan Nations Church; Police
Against the New World Order, founded by former Phoenix cop Jack McLamb;
the North American Freedom Council in Booneville, Indiana; the Idaho Sovereignty Association, based in Boise; the Michigan Militia, one of the largest
patriot groups, which claims to have ten thousand members (though most experts think this figure is grossly inflated.)

A guess at the numbers ranges from ten thousand to forty thousand members with organizations in forty states and plans for organizations in all fifty
states, according to *Militia Nation* authors Chip Berlet and Matthew Lyons.

Christian thinker Richard Abanes has written extensively about the
group. In his book *American Militias* (InterVarsity, 1996), he summarized some
of the group's key characteristics:

> Interestingly, patriots have no single leader. The glue binding them
> together is a noxious compound of four ingredients:
> 1) an obsessive suspicion of the government;
> 2) belief in anti-government conspiracy theories;

3) a deep-seated hatred of government officials; and

4) a feeling that the United States Constitution, for all intents and purposes, has been discarded by Washington bureaucrats.

Historic Roots

Suspicion of the government has been a theme in American history since the time of the early colonialists, many of whom came to the New World to escape the power of European monarchs and state-supported religious institutions.

But as American life has grown more complicated and the government has grown more massive and bureaucratic, a growing resentment has emerged among people who feel that they have been left behind, as have some of the nation's founding principles of individual freedom and independence.

In the twentieth century, roots of the later patriot movement could be seen in an earlier, racially based Christian Identity Movement (CIM). As Abanes wrote, "Long before today's militia's, these white supremacists/CIM followers were calling themselves 'patriots.' The goal of white supremacists is to topple the U.S. government so an Aryan nation can be established."

What worries Abanes and others is the use of Christian motifs by groups that have little resemblance to orthodox Christianity: "The beginnings of the patriot/militia movement are inseparably interwoven with the violent Christian Identity Movement (CIM). This network of churches and independent leaders began forming in the 1940s as racists defected from mainstream Christian denominations to organize their own churches. Although they retained a few Christian doctrines, especially those concerning the end times, they adopted additional beliefs built around prejudice and hate."

Both the Christian Identity Movement of the midtwentieth century and the patriot movement of the later decades of the century exploited people's distrust of or anger at the government for their own particular purposes of increasing their membership numbers and cultural clout.

In the 1990s white supremacists became aware of growing numbers of people dissatisfied with the U.S. government. While many of these dissatisfied Americans were not racists, they were considered fair game to be recruited into militias designed to feed antigovernment sentiment. The movement spread and began to include people dissatisfied with the government over issues like abortion and gun control.

Incidents like the August 1992 Ruby Ridge shootings involving white supremacist Randy Weaver and the ill-fated 1993 raid on the Branch Davidian compound in Waco, Texas, were used to justify militias becoming armed groups

A Dangerous Doctrine

Patriot values are disbursed with inflammatory, antigovernment rhetoric that encourages the formation of independent, armed groups of individuals who do not submit themselves to the U.S. government and who see themselves as the only true defenders of the Constitution.

As Abanes suggests, many of these people are driven by religious beliefs. Some are conservative, Bible-believing Christians who have united with racists around the common belief that the end of time as we know it is fast approaching and the triumph of good will be the result.

Conspiracy theories (see separate entry) abound, as Abanes says:

> Many Christian patriots believe the end is near and view Washington politicians as evil conspirators laying the foundation for the soon-to-be-revealed Antichrist, whose reign of terror will end only when Jesus Christ returns to earth in glory. . . .
>
> Since the early 1990s, the national media has devoted countless stories to the increase of antigovernment militias throughout America. Many onlookers wholeheartedly endorse these paramilitary units as constitutionally protected expressions of freedom. Others see them as illegally formed private armies. In reality, the militias are far more complex. They represent the militant arm of the patriot movement, a diverse coalition of persons whose ideology is marked by three elements: rebellion, racism, and religion. The time has come for all Americans to critically examine this movement.

CHRISTIAN CRITIQUE: The blending of Christian doctrine with a doctrine of prejudice and violence is the most obvious difference between the Christian faith and the hatemongering of patriot groups.

There is nothing patriotic or honorable about scapegoating any group of people and singling them out for persecution. Perhaps the worst characteristic of groups that do this is the misuse of religion to justify their unresolved inner rage. There can be no biblical approval for supremacist Aryanism and no glory for those who deem themselves better than others, in the name of God. The Lord's covenant with Noah (Genesis 9:1-17), which established human government, is ratified in the New Testament with the clear command: "Obey the government, for God is the one who has put it there. There is no government anywhere that God has not placed in power. So those who refuse to obey the laws of the land are refusing to obey God, and punishment will follow" (Romans 13:1-2, TLB).

SOURCES: Richard Abanes, *American Militias* (Downers Grove, Ill.: InterVarsity, 1996); Ibid., "America's Patriot Movement: Infiltrating the Church with a Gospel of Hate," *Christian Research Journal* (winter 1997): 15; Michael D. Lemonick, "Montana Family Values," *Time*, 17 June 1996, 32; Mark Potok, "Militant Militia Fringe Is Setting Off Alarms," *USA Today*, 17 April 1996, 4A.

PENITENTES

---

*Self-imposed suffering is the unique characteristic of this group,
which takes identification with the crucifixion of Christ
to the drastic extreme of self-mutilation.*

FOUNDERS: Spanish Catholic immigrants, circa 1700

TEXT: The Bible; folklore

SYMBOLS: Revered religious statues and icons

APPEAL: Adherents share companionship with Christ by reenacting his passion.

OVERVIEW: High in the remote mountain areas of southern Colorado and northern New Mexico live a people caught in a time warp, playing out centuries-old rituals of penance.

Each year at Easter, members of the Brothers of Our Father Jesus—the Penitentes, as they are commonly known—reenact Christ's crucifixion. Their devotion includes painful self-flagellation and stark suffering.

According to some witnesses, actual crucifixions take place every year during Holy Week. Spokesmen for the Brothers deny this claim, but several outsiders who have observed the ritual insist that the ceremony concludes with a man being raised on a cross. There are also tales of literal nails being used and of the participants actually dying, though such versions of this religious drama are hard to verify.

From the Old World to the New

The history of Penitentes can be traced to a fifth-century movement within the Roman Catholic church. Spanish followers of the discipline emigrated to the New World and subsequently retreated to the rugged mountain regions of the Southwest where they were cut off from civilization. Two centuries later, public knowledge of their activities began to emerge. Though the Catholic Church officially denounced their gory activities, the bizarre and clandestine nature of their devotion continued to attract followers.

Unlike their bloodier, better-known counterparts in Brazil and the Philippines, the American Penitentes rigorously guard their secrecy. Eye-witness accounts of present-day cross-bearing, self-whipping, and other torturous acts of penance are hard to verify. Some who claim contact with this strange sect believe that it is currently experiencing a resurgence of interest from those wishing to join its ranks. It has even been suggested that chapters exist in some urban centers of the West. Whether the present fascination with the darker side of occult practices has contributed to such a revival of these ancient masochistic techniques is open to question.

In an age of apathy and contentment, it is not surprising that the sufferings of Jesus would incite fascination in the human spirit. To those who fail to see these agonies as the finished work of atonement, there may still lie the haunting appeal of personally reliving such pain to seek favor with God.

Known Penitentes in America are confined to the active involvement of several thousand Hispanics. But the ritual has an uncanny attraction for new, curious members who seek to share the Lord's passion.

They remind us that the church may have lost a valuable incentive for spiritual fervor by emphasizing the glory of Christ and forgetting that "learned he obedience by the things which he suffered" (Hebrews 5:8).

CHRISTIAN CRITIQUE: Members try to obtain favor with God by self-inflicted penance, but Penitentes believe atonement comes by personal bloodshed rather than Christ's death and suffering.

SOURCES: *Dallas Times Herald,* 12 April 1981, 20–27; "Guarded Secrets of the Penitentes," *Denver Monthly,* May 1980, 24–33; *National Courier,* 16 April 1976, 5.

ACCESS: Ceremonies are practiced in the Philippines, Brazil, and the southwestern United States.

PSYCHICS

They appear on TV and operate profitable telephone lines, but their predictions are usually due to good guessing and a knack for tricking people into volunteering personal information.

OVERVIEW: It's not often that government regulators worry about telephone psychics, but in the case of Miss Cleo, things got so bad they had to act. In 2002 nine states and the Federal Trade Commission sued the phone psychic, who advertised her services on TV and in magazines.

"Miss Cleo (is an) exuberant soothsayer with the Jamaican accent whose television appearances, mostly in late-night commercials, have made her an extrasensory sensation," said an Associated Press report entitled, "Complaints Put Miss Cleo on Hold."

One woman who worked for Miss Cleo's Access Resource Services in Fort Lauderdale, Florida, said her most important job was not to divine the future but to keep callers on the line for twenty minutes. If she didn't, she wouldn't get paid as much as other operators who did.

Investigators also said Miss Cleo had falsified her birth information and was not the "Jamaican shaman" she claimed she was.

Representatives of Access Resource Services said they would cease using Miss Cleo as their spokesperson but would not unplug the profitable phone psychic business.

The Associated Press reported, "Despite recent allegations of deceptive practices against the company fronted by TV pitch-woman and self-proclaimed 'shaman' Miss Cleo, [the company] has seen no drop in business."

Meanwhile, Miss Cleo launched her own psychic dating Web site. "Hello babies!" she said. "After receiving thousands of calls related to love and relationships, it has become apparent to me that people need to take control of their love lives to meet that special someone. As I always say, babies, . . . 'Take back your power!'"

Some trend watchers say the growing popularity of the psychic lines is a sign that a new age of human spiritual development is dawning. Others say the lines are a cruel scam. But most agree the lines' success is due to the deep human desire to reach out and touch somebody.

Psychics are said to have the ability to access information not available to the five senses. Specializing in occult or "hidden" knowledge, psychics are best known for their individual "readings."

Fans of psychic lines say they are doing much good, but critics say they are problem-ridden. One of the dangers cited is the cost of the calls. Ads say people can try the services for free, but some charge up to four or five dollars per minute, a price that can cost regular users hundreds or thousands of dollars a week.

Who Are the Psychics?

Another problem, critics say, is that it is difficult for most callers to assess the reliability and expertise of phone psychics. In fact, most of the people who answer the calls aren't psychics at all, but merely warm bodies who would rather do psychic calls than do telemarketing for magazine subscriptions or vacuum cleaners.

Frederick Woodruff once worked for a psychic phone line and later wrote a tell-all book about the industry. Here's part of what he wrote: "For the last hour I have been inundated with the voices of America's dashed hopes, dilapidated dreams, debilitated romances, and derailed schemes. . . . After a friend explained that he was working for a psychic network out of Florida I decided a job like that would be freaky and fun and convenient, and that I too could make money working out of my apartment as an electronic soothsayer. Forget prayer, mantras, and meditation. People are too busy. Psychics fill a spiritual vacancy that might be left blank if not for the electronic oracles' key-pad accessibility."

An article in *Harper's Magazine* said psychic phone lines grew after regulatory changes transformed the television industry in the 1980s: "The industry took off in 1984 when the Federal Communications Commission deregulated the amount of time broadcast stations could dedicate to advertisements. What seemed at the time to be a minor rule change launched the infomercial industry and its subset: the psychic hot lines."

Celebrities and Pets

When scientists or scholars analyze the specific predictions psychics make, they find that most of the predictions are so general ("There will be a tall stranger in your life," etc.) that it is impossible to verify whether or not they are accurate.

But accuracy isn't the main reason people keep returning to psychics. The thing people are looking for isn't truth but comfort. They want to know that everything will be all right. They want to know that in a world that can be confusing and disappointing, there are good things in their future.

Some of the biggest supporters of psychics are Hollywood celebrities, whose careers are regularly subjected to roller-coaster ups and downs.

Bill Burns is one of the best-known psychics to the stars, according to the magazine *Entertainment Weekly:* "His name is Bill Burns, and Hollywood stars and execs swear by his powers of prediction. Here's a peek behind the curtain: For an hour-long session, costing $275, the barrel-chested 61-year-old Boston native gives insiders a sixth sense about the biz. . . . Working from the name or photograph of a person a client wants 'profiled,' Burns enters a trancelike state. 'I get an instant knowing about who they are in relationship to the question I'm being asked,' he says. 'I can immediately and intuitively visualize the person's motivations, hot buttons, reliability, and integrity.'"

Even more bizarre is a cable television show called *The Pet Psychic,* which airs on the Animal Planet network. Host Sonya Fitzpatrick claims to communicate with animals so she can tell their owners what the pets are thinking.

"If I was an old fake, dear, they wouldn't be spending all this money doing my TV show," says Fitzpatrick.

But when there's money to be made giving people the comfort they desperately want, who says a little fakery won't go a long way?

SOURCES: The Associated Press, "Complaints Put Miss Cleo on Hold," *The Gazette,* 7 April 2002, A16; Gary Cohen, "Psychic Friend," *Entertainment Weekly,* 19 April 2002, 21; Stephen Glass, "Prophets and Losses," *Harper's Magazine,* February 1998, 69–70; Frederick Woodruff, "Call Me Anytime: Revelations of a Telephone Psychic," *Seattle Weekly,* 26 March 1998, 19.

THE RAELIANS

Stories about UFOs and cloning humans are more than science fiction
for this unusual group claiming descent from extraterrestrials.

It is our choice to use our genes the way we want.
RAELIAN DR. BRIGITTE BOISSELIER

FOUNDER: Claude Vorilhon; later took the name Rael

TEXT: Rael's book is entitled *The Book Which Tells the Truth: The Message Given to Me by Extra-Terrestrials.*

SYMBOL: A stylized swastika inside of a Star of David, which Raelians claim is a symbol of infinity

OVERVIEW: In 1973 Frenchman Claude Vorilhon claimed to have been visited by an extraterrestrial being. Adopting the new name Rael, Vorilhon started a movement and wrote a book with the unusual title *The Book Which Tells the Truth: The Message Given to Me by Extra-Terrestrials.*

Many people claim they have been visited by aliens, so Rael's claims didn't cause much of a stir. What did generate worldwide controversy was Rael's belief that the aliens had told him to clone human beings and his determination to use the best science available to do just that.

These ambitions brought the fifty-four-year-old Rael before a Congressional subcommittee investigating the topic of human cloning. Rael reported that his company, CLONAID, was working on human cloning and hoped to soon clone a deceased baby. When the announcement of their supposed success was finally made December 27, 2002, a flurry of media coverage ensued, giving Rael more publicity than he ever dreamed of. But after the press made repeated demands to meet the cloned baby and such requests were stonewalled, interest in CLONAID faded. Today Rael still maintains that one or more cloned babies are alive and well, but their whereabouts remain undisclosed. The opinion of most geneticists is that Rael perpetrated a massive hoax.

Rael's Gospel

Rael's first encounter with an extraterrestrial and his appearance at the hearing on cloning are related events linked by the message of the extraterrestrial.

According to Rael, he was told that the words in the Old Testament book of Genesis, "In the beginning God created," should really be translated as follows: "In the beginning Elohim created and that Elohim means those who came from the sky."

Rael believes that life on earth came into existence when people from another planet created life by scientifically using DNA.

In addition, all the great prophets, including Jesus, were messengers of Elohim (plural, meaning "people from the sky") and their job was to tell the world of the biblical Genesis in preparation for the present age, the Age of Apocalypse.

Apocalypse, meaning "revelation," came to Rael when it did because mankind was finally ready to understand its origins. Mankind is now to build an embassy for the visitation from the Elohim.

Human cloning comes into the picture as part of Rael's interpretation of what this version of Genesis means. This is explained in the first of two divine aims of Raelians. As Susan Palmer writes, "The Raelians have two divinely appointed aims: first, to 'spread the message' (the glad tidings that humanity was created from the DNA of superior extraterrestrial alien scientists, or 'Elohim'); and second, to 'build the Embassy' (welcome Our Creators to earth in around 2035)."

Manipulating the Media

From the beginning, Rael has proven unusually adept at manipulating the media and using it to proclaim his message.

In the seventies the French media covered a lecture Rael gave in Paris which drew a thousand people. He soon became a popular guest on Paris talk shows. His fame spread to the United States in the following years as he was a guest on *Geraldo* in 1991. Geraldo's derisive manner didn't seem to bother Rael at all.

His reputation in France suffered a blow when his Sensual Meditation Camp was reported to be "an unbridled sex orgy where brainwashing was perpetrated and perversions were encouraged." Rael adopted tactics similar to those of Scientologists by suing media individuals and outlets.

In 1992 Rael moved away from much of the controversy and joined his followers in Quebec. Part of his method for attracting followers was to stage controversial events that would attract more media attention.

As Palmer reports, "The first successful action was Operation Condom in 1992, a protest against the Quebec Catholic School Commission's decision to veto condom machines in their high schools. The 'condommobile'—a pink van decorated with flying saucers and condoms—drove up to every Catholic high school in Quebec. The Guides, dressed in white padded suits with swastika medallions, would jump out and distribute ten thousand condoms to bemused teens on recess, who proceeded to return to their classes wearing large pink buttons that read 'Qui aux Condoms a l'Ecole' ('Yes to condoms in school')."

In March of 1997 Rael announced that he had formed a company that would clone children. In September of 2000 he presented women as "cloning mothers." Now his antics were receiving regular coverage in *The New York Times* and other mainstream media.

The announcement was well timed. About the same time, scientists announced the unprecedented cloning of a sheep named Dolly. Now cloning was scientific fact, not science fiction. And the Raelians seemed poised to take cloning to its next step.

After the September 11, 2001, attacks on America, the Raelians again exploited the media by making a well-timed announcement, reported in *The Rocky Mountain News*:

> Two days after the attack, the Raelians issued a news release to say that cloning is a way "to make terrorist attacks inefficient."
>
> That's because whenever a future tragedy occurs, cloning will bring back to life all the victims "as adults, and their personality will be downloaded into their brain."
>
> Genetic banks around the world would contain the genetic code of each individual from their birth—"what primitive people used to call the soul," the Raelians explain. This so-called personality backup would then be downloaded from a PC and into a new clone.
>
> "The person who would benefit from this technology would only, after a tragedy, have the last day missing from their memory," the Raelians say. "This technology would also allow the cloning of terrorists, thus allowing us to try them for their crimes."

As Susan Palmer writes, "All in all, the Raelians' militant demands for respect seem to have paid off. Journalists have become more cautious, and by moving from the dubious twilight of marginal religions into the hot spotlight of avant garde science, the Raelians find their voice is taken more seriously."

SOURCES: Susan J. Palmer, "The Rael Deal," *Religion in the News*, summer 2001, 19; Sheryl Gay Stolberg, "Three Scientists Vow to Clone Humans; Experts at National Symposium Warn Experiments Will Cause Death, Deformity," *Denver Post*, 8 August 2001, 1A; Jean Torkelson, *Rocky Mountain News*, 29 September 2001.

ACCESS: United States Raelian Movement, Box 611793, North Miami, FL 33261

RAINBOW FAMILY OF
LIVING LIGHT

Their summer "tribal gatherings" are a throwback to the hippie
heyday of the 1960s.

OVERVIEW: Every July for the past three decades, thousands of long-haired, tie-dyed members of the Woodstock Nation gather from across the country at a predetermined location for a celebration that is described as "a Gathering of the Tribes."

The gathering is sponsored by a group known as the Rainbow Family of Living Light, but unlike other groups, this one has no headquarters, office, legal representative, mailing address, phone number, or fax machine. Instead, the Rainbow Family is a loose-knit coalition of aging hippies for whom the Age of Aquarius is continuing to dawn.

Many Rainbowers are alumni of the hippie movement. Some have never shorn their long locks or taken other steps necessary to join mainstream society. Rather, they maintain a near-utopian belief that their values of love and freedom, complete with generous amounts of drugs and sex, are the harbinger of a new age of social harmony and cosmic peace.

If this sounds overly optimistic, so be it.

The group began in 1969 after American Garrick Beck visited the deserts of Morocco, where he had a spiritual transformation: "I had a vision of greenery, beautiful water, people dancing and working together," he said. "I saw that what was needed was a living example of people in harmony with each other and with the earth."

When he got back to his home in Oregon, Beck sponsored the first free rock festival near Portland that attracted fifty thousand people. The first Rainbow gathering occurred in 1972, and the event has happened every July since. The events are held in a different location each year. After a site is selected, word is spread person-to-person or, increasingly, over the Internet. One year, confusion resulted in separate gatherings in Alabama and Kentucky.

The gatherings are week-long celebrations of community featuring communal kitchens, child care, areas for artists and homosexuals, and a pervasive feeling of comradeship. There are also communal rituals, including circles featuring prayers to Mother Earth.

However, government officials aren't so enthusiastic about the annual Rainbow events, in part because of forest damage and trash left in each event's wake.

The government has tried to get the Rainbows to seek a legal permit to use the nation's forests, but the group claims such procedures would limit their civic and spiritual freedoms. The group claims it doesn't even have a leader who could formally request a permit.

In 1992 nearly twenty-five thousand people converged at the gathering near Paonia, Colorado. Two people died at that year's event. The 1994 gathering was held in Wyoming. And in 1998 the twenty-seventh annual gathering drew fourteen thousand people to an area near Teagar, Arizona.

"Coming here is like medicine for my spirit," said one attendee. "This is like my family reunion."

SOURCES: Lewis MacAdams, "A Gathering of the Tribes," *Rolling Stone*, 7 December 1993/6 January 1994, 120; Don Terry, "Rainbow Family Takes Colorful Reunion to Arizona," *Denver Post*, 5 July 1998, 8A.

ACCESS: Information about the Rainbow Family's annual gatherings can be found at the unofficial Web site, www.welcomehome.org/rainbow.html.

RAM DASS

Baba Ram Dass; Richard Alpert

One of the enduring spiritual pilgrims of the sixties' spiritual revolution, he is still reinventing himself today.

FOUNDER: Dr. Richard Alpert developed a following in the early seventies with the publication of his book *Be Here Now*.

TEXT: Hindu scriptures

APPEAL: Those who look to drugs as a means of transcending reality see Ram Dass as a psychedelic pioneer who has "been there" and knows what he is talking about. His views on religion, even though they are warmed-over *Raja Yoga* beliefs, are perceived as authoritative because of Dass's past.

OVERVIEW: What Harvard student in the sixties would have suspected that his bespectacled psychiatry professor, Dr. Richard Alpert, would someday become a Hindu guru?

The year was 1961 and a fellow professor named Timothy Leary had started dropping LSD. Alpert literally joined the trip. After six years of getting high, only to come back down to the same problems, Alpert decided to visit India.

There he met a twenty-three-year-old man named Bhagwan Dass. Alpert was so profoundly impressed with Dass that he took up fasting, yoga, and meditation. Eventually, Alpert was taken to Dass's guru, Maharaji, who lived in the foothills of the Himalayas. Dr. Alpert changed his name to Ram Dass, returned to America, and wrote a book entitled *Be Here Now*. It emphasized his philosophy of "living each moment meaningfully."

Ram Dass believes that everyone is on the same spiritual journey to recognize the oneness of all religions and the "truth" that God's spirit resides in each person. A guru is needed to reveal this "truth." A spiritual teacher will suggest the seeker's most expedient way to experience being "here now."

Some might be recommended to indulge in yoga or sex while others are encouraged to meditate or chant mantras. Certain disciples are even given the same psychedelic drugs that failed to satisfy Alpert. Ram doesn't exactly eschew drugs. He credits their role in his own spiritual enlightenment by providing hallucinogenic experiences that paralleled spiritistic descriptions in *The Tibetan Book of the Dead*.

As Ram Dass, Richard Alpert forsook his Jewish upbringing in Boston. (This estranged him from his family, although he tried to change this; in fact, when his father became terminally ill with cancer, Ram Dass served as his caretaker.) Ram Dass left Dr. Alpert far behind, as if his former vocation took place in another incarnation.

He returns to India every other year for a spiritual recharging, and often travels the lecture circuit exuding an apparent happiness he never had during his Mercedes-Benz/private airplane/materialistic days at Harvard. He has even become an activist for the Seva Foundation, a charitable organization he helped found.

In 2002 a new documentary about Ram Dass's life premiered in New York. A *New York Times* writer said *Ram Dass: Fierce Grace* chronicled "his evolution from expelled Harvard professor to giddy LSD proselytizer to best-selling hippie guru to his current conspicuous identity, the survivor of a near-fatal stroke, presenting himself to the camera with his equanimity challenged but intact."

As a father figure from the turbulent days of flower power, Ram Dass brings a message that meshes well into the Eastern/mystical mainstream of contemporary thought.

CHRISTIAN CRITIQUE: Ram Dass has taught that fulfillment comes from avoiding introspection about the past and future. Instead, his disciples are encouraged to acknowledge their inner divinity and oneness with the universal deity. He claims the result is a nonhedonistic compulsion to explore momentary satisfaction.

The Hindu roots of his teachings are incompatible with a Christian worldview. Moral restrictions are ignored in favor of a pleasure principle, which assumes that reveling in "now" is a desirable way to work out one's karma.

The biblical concept of future accountability for sin is replaced by the assumption that inner peace today is more important than preparing for judgment tomorrow.

SOURCES: Michael Almereyda, "A Sober Documentary about an Intoxicating Life," *New York Times*, 24 February 2002, Arts and Leisure, 25, 38; *Circus*, July 1971, 40; Ram Dass, *Be Here Now* (San Cristobal, N.M.: Lama Foundation, 1971); *Denver Post*, 15 May 1981, 35; Jane Sugden, "Ram Dass, Veteran Guru," *People*, 28 September 1987, 79.

ACCESS: The Lama Foundation is a small community that published *Be Here Now* and still maintains some connections with Baba Ram Dass; Box 44, San Cristobal, NM 87564.

RASTAFARIANISM

Combining a reverence for Africa, the ritual use of marijuana,
and a fondness for reggae music, this movement is recognizable thanks
to the "dreadlocks" worn by its adherents.

FOUNDER: Marcus Garvey, a black movement leader in the early 1900s, who stressed black pride, unity, and independence. Garvey urged blacks to accept Ethiopia as their promised land and to recognize their identity with the wandering tribes of Israel.

TEXTS: Rastafarians draw ideology from Marcus Garvey's back-to-Africa admonishments during the 1920s and 1930s, as well as from the Coptic and King James Bibles.

SYMBOLS: Rastas wear dreadlocks, symbolizing the lamb's wool of their god, Haile Selassie. Dreadlocks are also worn to instill fear in white men. Rastafarians and reggae fans often wear red, green, and gold—the colors of the Ethiopian flag, which Bob Marley used as a stage prop in his concerts. Many Rastas are strict vegetarians. Seeing themselves as Jews, they frequently wear yellow Stars of David or lion heads (for the Lions of Judah). Haile Selassie's portrait often adorns the backdrop at reggae concerts.

APPEAL: Rastas believe the Rastafarian ideals of peace, love, and brotherhood will improve Jamaica. Bob Marley once said, "Conditions [in Jamaica] will only improve when the Rastas have the government there." The religion appeals to blacks frustrated with white civilization. Rastafarianism also provides religious justification for smoking pot. Reggae music is passive, vaguely spiritual, and frequently laments injustice and oppression.

OVERVIEW: He popularized sacramental pot smoking and a king/god named Ras Tafari. He used reggae music, also known as "Jah Music," "Roots Music," and "Zion Rock," to introduce his Rastafarian religion to the masses. His stage performances would often find him and his band engulfed in a swirl of smoke from Jamaican *ganja* (pot).

Bob Marley died at the age of thirty-six in 1981 after becoming a figure *Entertainment Weekly* called "the first superstar of reggae." But Marley, whose flag is now carried by his musical son Ziggy, was much more than a musician. He was an ambassador for an entire way of life.

He would display a portrait of the late Ethiopian emperor, Ras Tafari (Haile Selassie). While fans cheered, the black musician would shout a dedication to his god.

Together with his group, the Wailers, Robert Nesta Marley introduced roots-rock-reggae to delighted global audiences in the early 1970s. The word *reggae* is Latin for "to the King." Interwoven in Marley's music are strong Rastafarian messages that encourage the worship of Haile Selassie, smoking of holy herbs, and wearing one's hair in unwashed corkscrew curls called dreadlocks.

Marley believed himself a spiritual leader, chosen to share Rastafarianism with the world. He sang, "Some are leaves, some are branches, I and I [Ras Tafari] are the roots."

Roots of the Faith

The founder of Rastafarianism was Jamaican-born Marcus Garvey, a well-known black leader in the early 1900s. Garvey supported separation of the black and white races. He taught blacks that Ethiopia was their promised land and urged them to identify with the wandering tribes of Israel. His teachings quickly became popular in Jamaica and later in America.

Garvey also prophesied that an African king would be crowned the black messiah-redeemer. In 1930, Prime Regent Ras Tafari announced his lineage to King Solomon and the Queen of Sheba. He was crowned King of Ethiopia and took the name Haile Selassie, which means "Power of the Holy Trinity." Marcus Garvey and his followers hailed him as the long-awaited messiah. Worshiping Ras Tafari, they called themselves Rastafarians or Rastamen.

Rastafarianism is a religious blend of Ethiopian Christianity, Old Testament Judaism, African animism, and spiritualism. The religion has no consistent dogma, nor does it have any official spokesperson who is half as well known as some of the most famous reggae musicians.

To smoke marijuana is considered a biblical mandate and a way of reaching God. Rastas take this idea from 2 Samuel 22:9, which says, "There went up a smoke out of his nostrils, and fire out of his mouth devoured: coals were kindled by it." For the Rastas, marijuana yields spiritual inspiration and a "reasoning of minds" between those who smoke it.

Rastas believe Haile Selassie is the lamb or sacred god of black people. Their dreadlocks are the "lamb's wool" or spiritual symbol of devotion to their creator, Jah. Rastas wear dirty, tattered clothing and live in commune-like dwellings. They practice polygamy and often steal because they don't work. They've been known to attack police officers, refusing to accept them as authority figures.

According to Rastafarian interpretation of the Scriptures, the Western world will be destroyed in the near future. Their god, Haile Selassie, whom they refer to as "Jah," the "King of Kings," and the "Lord of Lords," is the returned messiah. Though Selassie has been dead for more than a decade, Rastas believe he will rise from the dead.

Rastafarians believe they are reincarnated Hebrews, sons and daughters of Jah, and descendants of the biblical Israelites. They feel they are exiled Ethiopians who must struggle to free themselves from the West's capitalistic grasp.

The Few and the Many

According to experts, there are relatively few devoted Rastafarians in the United States today, perhaps as few as three to five thousand. Rastafarians came to the United States in large numbers as part of the general migration of Jamaicans in the 1960s and 1970s.

However, reggae music, Jamaican dreadlocks, and pot smoking have been embraced by many more people who have no significant interest in Jamaican religion. This has led to confusion about the size of the Rastafarian movement in America as well as public image issues about dreadlocked criminals.

True Rastafarians preach a message of peace, love, and brotherhood. But reggae songs like "I Shot the Sheriff" and movies like *The Harder They Come*, starring Rastamen Jimmy Cliff and Carl Bradshaw, contain an undercurrent of violence.

Because of drug usage and the black liberation political messages conveyed in some reggae music, aspects of Jamaican and Rastafarian culture have been involved in crime.

Murders have been committed by ganja-greedy thieves in homes where Haile Selassie is worshiped. Large quantities of "herb" are usually stashed in Rasta homes for the religious ritual of smoking "the wisdom weed," tempting Rasta gunmen and "wolves in sheepskin," non-Rastafarian men who wear dreadlocks, to steal and assault for the valued drug.

Most Rastafarians disavow such violence and try to live decent lives.

Marley's Legacy

Few faiths have been popularized by one person as much as Rastafarianism has been by Bob Marley. The musician was an outspoken advocate of the Jamaica-based political religious cult. As a result, in 1976 an attempt was made on his life by political opponents. The gunmen failed to kill Marley, who died of brain cancer fifteen years later.

But Marley is a curious religious figure. The adulterous musician fathered eleven children by seven different women. He's still considered a prophet and is worshiped by many Rastas, some of whom believe Bob Marley's spirit inhabits other reggae singers or that his son Ziggy, by wife Rita Marley, is his reincarnation.

Born in a poor part of Jamaica, Marley gained worldwide recognition and wealth for his reggae music, whose rhythmic roots originated in Africa. Marley was introduced to Kingston record producers by Jimmy Cliff in 1962.

A year later he formed the group Bob Marley and the Wailers with Peter Tosh and Bunny Wailer. The group embraced Rastafarianism as their religion after Marley claimed Haile Selassie appeared to him in a vision. He then adopted Rastafarian beliefs and used his reggae music as a vehicle for spiritual, cultural, and political expression. Bob Marley and the Wailers merged reggae and Rasta in the minds of modern listeners.

Since Marley's death, the Jamaican reggae world has awaited a new musical messiah to provide hope in a poverty-ridden, restless world. Reggae artists such as Toots and the Maytals, Jimmy Cliff, Sly and Robbie, Black Uhuru, Steel Pulse, Burning Spear, Bad Brains, Ziggy Marley and the Melody Makers, Bunny Wailer, the late Peter Tosh, and of course, Bob Marley, continue to influence reggae fans with Rastafarian messages. Musicians like Sly Dunbar, Robbie Shakespeare, Judy Mowatt, and Yellowman have inspired cult followings since Bob Marley's death.

Many contend that Ziggy Marley will be the next musical messiah. "His spirit is here on earth," says Ziggy of his father. "I feel it around me every day." Three other Marley children—Sharon, Cedella, and Stephen—have also recorded albums of their own.

Peter Tosh, a musician with Bob Marley and the Wailers, did not escape his murderers. Shot to death in September 1986, his murder appeared to be committed by robbers. But it is much more likely his death was related to the drug trafficking he helped generate. Tosh's female bookkeeper and lover had her own theory, claiming Satan killed Tosh because they planned to conceive a baby who would be "a powerful boy with the Star of David on his forehead."

CHRISTIAN CRITIQUE: Rastafarians believe their new Messiah will help overturn capitalist privileges. Said Marley, "Until the philosophy wherein one race is superior and one inferior is permanently abandoned and discredited, there is war."

Jamaicans are serious about their music and message. Reggae lyrics are sung to address political tensions and social grievances. Reggae music is filled with distorted biblical references to extend the Rasta message of black revolution.

Rastafarians revere Haile Selassie as Christ and claim Selassie lives and rules, since no trace of his body, grave, or ashes has ever been found. Bob Marley once expressed disgust over materialism and possessions. Said Marley, "God created the earth for us, but people wonder 'who owns the tree, who owns the ladder, who owns the ganja pipe?'" Yet, when asked about his silver BMW, he replied, "BMW? That stands for Bob Marley and the Wailers. It seemed like the car we were supposed to have."

Those who saw Bob Marley as the Rastafarian prophet now believe his son Ziggy is his incarnation. Says Ziggy, "My father was like the Old Testament. I'm the New Testament." Reggae music conveys messages about a false god, black revolution, and the legalization of marijuana.

SOURCES: Leonard E. Barrett Sr., "The Rastafarians," *Philadelphia Inquirer,* 27 September 1981, 1A–24A; *Billboard,* 1 August 1987, R6, R32–R33; Bob Cannon, "A Reggae Legend for All Countries," *Entertainment Weekly,* 10 May 1991, 80; *Media Update,* 8 July 1988, 12–13; *Rolling Stone,* 25 June 1981, 26–27; Ibid., 24 March 1988, 92; *To the Point,* 21 July 1978, 22–23.

ACCESS: Rastafarians are headquartered on Marcus Garvey Drive in Kingston, Jamaica.

REBIRTHING

This controversial technique to overcome emotional abnormalities has turned
a psychological assumption into a deadly therapy.

OVERVIEW: One can understand the mother's concerns. Jeane Newmaker of Durham, North Carolina, had adopted a young girl named Candace. But the girl was reportedly diagnosed with an attachment disorder that caused her to act out in violent behavior towards her adopted mother.

On April 18, 1999, Jeane took Candace to the home of therapist Connell Watkins so the girl could be subjected to a controversial but increasingly popular process called rebirthing therapy.

Candace was wrapped in a sheet and placed under several large pillows—a situation designed to simulate her mother's womb—so Candace could be "reborn" to her adoptive mother. In addition, Watkins and three other adults pushed against the child to simulate birth contractions.

But buried inside the sheet and pillows, Candace wasn't being reborn; she was slowly suffocating. She screamed and begged for air, yelling that she would die. But the therapists thought the child was merely resisting the healing effects of the therapy. "Go ahead and die," they decreed.

Candace did die that day, but she's not the first to be killed by this strange and unusual technique. Sadly, she probably won't be the last.

Conflicting Claims

Advocates of rebirthing make extravagant claims about the benefits of this therapy. One Web site was extremely enthusiastic about a whole series of unproven claims:

> The rebirthee focuses on maintaining a connection between inhale and exhale, breathing as fully as possible for an hour or more. Your body gets filled with energy and is nourished as it receives more oxygen than it is accustomed to. Toxins are released from the muscles and cells, and exhaled. As the body and cells are cleansed and energized they also release emotional and mental "toxins" that are the result of emotions and traumas that have been suppressed and held in the body.
>
> The rebirthee becomes more aware of thoughts, behaviors, and emotional patterns that are holding them back from living their lives the way they want. Many times just breathing through and releasing the suppressed energy is enough to create a profound psychological/emotional shift for the participant.

The technique is a form of "body work," an increasingly popular form of therapy linking spirituality and physical exercises. Rebirthing gets its name from the assumption that many of people's present-day problems are caused by "birth trauma."

Some advocates add Eastern religious connotations to the procedure. Russell J. Miesemer's Web article, "What Is Rebirthing?" says, "Rebirthing is an American form of prana yoga that is closest to Kriya Yoga. It may be called scientific breathing rhythm or spiritual breathing. Simply described, it is a relaxed, intuitive, connected breathing rhythm, in which the inhale is connected to the exhale, and the inner breath is merged with the outer breath. This merging of pure life energy with air sends vibrations through the nervous system and circulatory system cleaning the body, the human aura, and nourishes and balances the human mind and body."

Others say the technique is closer to Maha Yoga. But regardless of these disagreements, just about all therapy advocates claim it can bring about a spiritual cleansing that is parallel to the Christian concept of spiritual regeneration and being born again.

Many different groups include rebirthing in their arsenal of spiritual techniques. For some, the concept is related to reincarnation and the trauma the soul experiences during its transition to a new body. The occultic principles of *A Course in Miracles* also include recommendations of rebirthing. It is also embraced by members of the Human Potential Movement and followers of disgraced Indian holy man Osho. (See separate entries on all these topics.)

CHRISTIAN CRITIQUE: Psychologists, massage therapists, New Age gurus, and an assortment of self-styled body-work practitioners are among those advocating a return to womblike emotional states as a way to shed a variety of emotional blockages. There is some truth in their theory. Inner-healing advocates like me have seen incalculable value in having certain individuals return to psychological states approximating the earliest and deepest trauma experienced. Bringing Christ into the context of such repressed memories may be an effective remediation for fears and phobias, if pursued as a work of the Holy Spirit's grace.

Rebirthing, on the other hand, is usually enveloped in occult terminology and expectations. Consequently, those who undergo the process may undergo out-of-body experiences, states of at-oneness with the universe, and visionary encounters with spirit guides. Whereas Christian healing gently prods the emotions to evoke long-denied states of psychological wounding, rebirthing forcefully invokes terrorized states without any accompanying spiritual comfort. Secular rebirthing is often a manipulative counterfeit for the changes brought about by the new birth in Christ experienced by those who trust in

God's Word. It is a demonic substitute for the true rehabilitation of internalized hurts through prayer and the guided process of inner healing.

SOURCES: Peggy Lowe, "Therapists Get 16 years: Women Plan to Appeal Convictions in Death of 10-Year-Old Candace in Rebirthing Therapy," *Rocky Mountain News*; www.gospelcom.net/apologeticsindex.

REIKI

The human body is not matter but energy, according to this ancient healing technique that makes phenomenal claims for the alleviation of sickness and suffering.

Five principles for Reiki practitioners:

Just for today I will give thanks for my many blessings;
Just for today I will not worry;
Just for today I will not be angry;
Just for today I will do my work honestly;
And just for today I will be kind to my neighbor and every living thing.
MIKAO USUI

OVERVIEW: The room is decorated with pastel colors and illumined by the soft glow of scented candles. In the background soothing New Age music is playing. Nearby, a small water fountain bubbles and gurgles.

The patient enters and lies down on the cushioned table. For the next hour, a process involving touch, prayer, and spiritual healing will supposedly heal the physical and emotional pains that have troubled this middle-aged woman for years.

Welcome to the brave new world of Reiki, an ancient therapy that has been dusted off and spruced up for a new generation of hurting and spiritually hungry seekers.

According to the *New Age Almanac*, "Reiki, also known as the Usui Shiko Ryoho System of Healing, is described as the art of applying, through a precise technique, the universal life energy (ki) to promote healing and wholeness. Using what is conceived to be the self's natural healing energy through a technique of the systematic laying of hands, reiki attempts to apply natural vital energy in a systematic treatment."

Author Elizabeth Severino says *Reiki* is a Japanese word meaning "vital life force energy directed by universal spiritual guidance—the energy of living."

Ancient and New

Advocates say Reiki is an ancient Eastern system of healing, but the techniques used today have little resemblance to any historic practices researchers have been able to uncover.

Rather, Reiki's history goes back to the nineteenth century, when a mysterious man named Mikao Usui began promoting its principles. Usui said he was a Christian teacher (other sources call him a teacher or a monk), but his ideas about spiritual energy owe more to Eastern sources, especially the Buddhism he studied, than they do to the Bible.

After attending college in America, Usui returned to his native Japan to study the Chinese and Sanskrit languages, thus enabling him to study traditional Buddhist documents. After a celebrated, twenty-one-day fast, he emerged with the principles and practices that define Reiki today.

According to the *New Age Almanac*, Reiki healers are taught three levels of knowledge:

> In the first-degree program the student is taught the history of reiki and the basic format of reiki laying-on-of-hands treatment for both oneself and others.
>
> The second-degree, a program for graduates of the first degree only, includes further energy activations and the teaching of special techniques for use with deep-seated emotional and mental conditions.
>
> The third-degree program, taught by the grand master(s), is for the person who wants to become a Reiki master/teacher. It includes all of the advanced techniques, with special emphasis on the new master's personal growth and enlightenment.

Although many people find temporary relief from their pain by using Reiki techniques, they should be cautious about Reiki's anti-Christian roots.

CHRISTIAN CRITIQUE: I have debated several Reiki practitioners, and each of them claimed some supernatural source for their cures. Indeed, those who are best at Reiki don't need to actually touch the client, they only pass their hands over the body to redistribute the energies. When doing so, they often enter into light or deep trance states and become spirit mediums. Though some give testimonies of miraculous cures from Reiki, the occult source of this practice and the metaphysical approach of those who use it make it more likely that a demonic relief of symptoms took place rather than a true healing.

SOURCES: J. Gordon Melton, Jerome Clark, and Aidan A. Kelly, *New Age Almanac* (Detroit, Mich.: Visible Ink Press, 1991).

REINCARNATION

This teaching, found in many non-Western faiths, says souls return to earth for repeated lives until enough good works are accumulated to circumvent the endless cycles of transmigration.

OVERVIEW: An article published in *People* magazine in 2000 discussed the latest spiritual memoir from Shirley MacLaine, who has openly talked about her belief in reincarnation for many years:

Her latest book, *The Camino*, reveals that during a spiritual trek in Spain, she learned that in a former life she and the Holy Roman Emperor Charlemagne had been lovers. She describes the King of the Franks, who died in 814, as a "lusty" man who "loved to swim."

As luck would have it, she says she met up with him again in this lifetime, reincarnated as the late Swedish Prime Minister Olaf Palme.

She reports the two had an affair and though they "fit in every way," he was concerned about how the press would perceive their union. If journalists had known it was a relationship that had withstood 1,200 or so years, surely they would have been understanding.

Years ago MacLaine was seen as an oddball, a voice crying in the wilderness about reincarnation. Today the actress doesn't feel so alone. Many people in the West now ascribe to the belief that souls inhabit many bodies over the course of the centuries.

Exploring Past Lives

"Say a prayer to your higher self and Almighty God. Your mental body will leave your physical body and come back down in this life having the answers to the questions you have posed."

This monologue was delivered by a psychiatrist who practices "past-life therapy." His patient wanted to know why she was blind in one eye.

Under a hypnotic state, she supposedly regressed in time and saw herself in New York. Her mental journey had taken her back to 1943 when she found herself in the body of another person hurling a bottle at her lover's face.

As the psychiatrist moved her forward in time, she once again saw her boyfriend, this time with a patch over his eye. Now she was ready to return to her body. The answer was plain. She had committed a sin of violence in her last reincarnation, and in this life she had to be punished in order to work out her karma.

What lesson had she learned? "My higher self says I must learn to control myself in this life," she replied to the psychiatrist.

This story is true. Whether the facts are accurate is open to question. The only certainty is that practitioners of past-life therapy have their calendars full of appointments. It seems in our age of stress and tension, there are those who eschew any thought of assuming personal responsibility for the consequences of their conduct. It's much easier to blame everything on a former existence.

John Ankerberg and John Weldon discussed past-life therapy (PLT) in their 1996 book, *Encyclopedia of New Age Beliefs*:

> Past-life therapy (PLT), or so-called "reincarnation" therapy is more widely practiced than most people might think. . . . Hundreds—possibly several thousand—therapists use this method. The field has professional societies and journals, such as the Association for Past-Life Research and Therapy, and the *Journal of Regression Therapy*.
>
> "Past-life" therapy employs hypnosis to place the individual into a trance state for a specific purpose. That purpose is to send the individual "back" into his supposed former lives in order to resolve hidden emotional or spiritual conflicts that are allegedly affecting his physical, emotional, or spiritual health today. . . .
>
> The basic conclusion of our own research into reincarnation is that its experiences and phenomena result from several factors:
> 1) suggestions of the therapist;
> 2) inventions or delusions of the patient;
> 3) spiritistic manipulation of the mind.

But PLT is only one example of the West's growing interest in reincarnation. The belief that a therapist can help one explore one's previous lives shows that many Westerners have abandoned Christian understandings of life and death. This paradigm shift is one that has been a long time coming.

Hindus have believed in reincarnation for centuries. Now many Westerners are following the same karmic path of fatalism. Belief in reincarnation is on the rise, and the classic inquiry, "Who am I?" has been replaced by the puzzling question, "Who was I?"

With the shift away from ecclesiastical directives and moral absolutism, our society has a desperate need to explain the nature of its existence. Historically, the deterioration from faith to hedonism has not always resulted in atheism. Man generally seeks something that will satisfy the spiritual vacuum left by the denial of God as a guiding force in his life. The growth of interest in occult phenomena illustrates that Western man has traded in his unbelief for a new system of order and meaning.

Astrology, psychic predictions, and parapsychological investigations are pillars of this new "religious" system, with reincarnation as a major part of its foundation.

Found in Many Faiths

A variety of faith groups and cults consider reincarnation to be an essential aspect of their teachings. Scientology proposes to remove the traumas of past lives by the use of a device called an E-meter (see separate entry on Scientology). Almost all of the important Eastern religions base their quest for higher consciousness on the premise of reincarnation. Other groups espousing this belief include Rosicrucianism, Unity School of Christianity, Hare Krishna, Theosophy, and Urantia.

But belief in reincarnation itself is not confined to exotic cults. Nearly three quarters of Americans consider this concept—human events experienced in the past being passed on to future lives—to be a reasonable probability.

The word *reincarnation* takes its root from the word *incarnation*, or *in carnis* in Latin, which means "in the flesh." Reincarnation refers to the cyclical evolution of each man's soul as it passes into another body after death. The process continues until the soul has reached a state of perfection and merges back with its source.

In the theory of reincarnation, the soul can only inhabit another human body. Transmigration, the Hindu doctrine from which reincarnation originated, teaches that each successive cycle may result in the soul's incorporating itself into organic or inorganic life, meaning anything from a monkey to a rock. Where the soul ends up next depends upon the karma it accumulated in its previous incarnations.

Western advocates of rebirthing (see separate entry) have generally emphasized reincarnation rather than transmigration because they know that the principles of the latter might be rejected by the more educated adherent. The average American would not necessarily be offended by the possibility of reincarnating as a respectable human being, but the thought of coming back as a pig or a bug is hardly enticing.

The doctrine of karma has found surprisingly easy acceptance among Westerners. (See the entry on Hinduism for a more extensive analysis of this concept.) In the earliest Hindu texts karma connoted an act of ritual significance. In later writings it was modified to illustrate how events in this life affect the quality of life in the next incarnation.

Eventually, karma came to represent the immutable law of sowing and reaping, with pronounced punishment in future lives as a purification from evil in this life or in past lives. It was hoped that this refining process would permit the soul to be worthy of reabsorption into the Universal Soul from which it came. In India the teaching of karma justified the prejudices of the developing social strata, resulting in the infamous caste system.

The Untouchable had no hope of bettering his lot. His miserable destiny had been predetermined by a former existence. Likewise, the priestly Brahmin class saw no need to extend acts of kindness to the less fortunate. To do so would interfere with the karma of those beneath the Brahmins and bring disrespect upon the privileges of their class, a status that they deserved because of their conduct in previous incarnations.

A Recurring Concept

The Indian subcontinent is not entirely responsible for promoting the theory of reincarnation. Gnostic cults of the first century and early challengers of the new Christian faith also flirted with the idea. They took their cue from the philosophy of Plato, who put forward the concept of dualism, which had also been discussed by earlier Greek philosophers. Plato viewed the spirit as a positive entity encased in the evil "prison house" of the body. Therefore, man's spirit longs to be free from its captor and to return to its Source, fading into the nebulous consciousness of the Universal Soul.

Spiritualism's resurgence in the 1800s formally introduced reincarnation to Westerners. The foremost twentieth-century advocate was Edgar Cayce (see separate entry). Cayce, who had a church-oriented background, was at first hesitant to adopt the belief. However, his spiritual teacher, Arthur Lammers, convinced Cayce that reincarnation was an evolutionary process by which one could attain the perfection of Christ.

Lammers insisted that Jesus taught reincarnation to his disciples, but the belief had been deliberately omitted as Bible translations passed from one language to another. Eventually Cayce came to believe that biblical phrases refuting reincarnation, such as "resurrection of the dead" and "last judgment day" were "meant to be understood symbolically rather than literally." In the end, Edgar Cayce ridiculed the idea that Christ was "offering a hit-or-miss, one-chance-only hope of survival."

One of today's foremost secular "experts" on reincarnation is Dr. Ian Stevenson. A Montreal-born psychiatrist, Stevenson became interested in reincarnation while serving as chairman of the department of psychiatry at the University of Virginia School of Medicine.

Stevenson has carefully documented approximately two thousand reported cases of reincarnation, each of which he has attempted to account for with logical explanations. While most of these stories have been fraudulent or have resulted from parapsychological phenomenon, Stevenson remains intrigued by those examples that appear to be legitimate.

Stevenson theorizes that mental stress in this life could be alleviated if the traumas of previous existences could be identified—a view that is echoed by Scientologists. He even goes so far as to suggest that parents who believe in reincarnation have a head start on child-rearing. If the parents accept the fact that the baby had a history before conception, they will give the child greater respect as an individual, and that, says Stevenson, "could greatly reduce parental guilt."

Not everyone accepts Stevenson's ideas, but many do. For example, the Children's Past Lives Web site (www.childpastlives.org) features this endorsement from Dr. Harold Lief, as cited in the *Journal of Nervous and Mental Disease:* "Either Dr. Stevenson is making a colossal mistake, or he will be known as the Galileo of the 20th century."

An Enduring Appeal

Why have teachings about reincarnation been received so readily? On the surface, some of its claims do sound reasonable to those not grounded in biblical theology. First of all, since every man senses his own sinfulness outside of Christ, he must have a way to cope with the burden of unrighteousness.

Reincarnation promises an eventual freedom from the confines of moral guilt. It also provides a future opportunity to finish every worthy goal in this life that remains uncompleted at death. The talented achiever may be convinced that any application of his skills will come to fruition in the next life, if not this one.

Above all, reincarnation seeks to provide the ultimate answer for understanding suffering and injustice. As Robert Morey points out in his book *Reincarnation and Christianity,* "The ancient philosophers used the theory of karmic reincarnation to explain away such things as birth defects, physical handicaps, low IQs, retardation, personality traits, etc., because they had no knowledge of genetics or the DNA code. They assumed that all babies should normally be born in perfect health and that all birth defects had a mystical or religious explanation, thus giving a mystical quality to an obviously genetic problem."

Morey goes on to point out that since the "mentally and physically handicapped are receiving the karma they deserve, they have been left to suffer."

What Morey so clearly illustrates is that the explanation of reincarnation only perpetuates the problem. Is it any wonder that health care and social services are seldom seen in the East, except where Christian missionaries have brought a healing hand? To be a Good Samaritan, according to reincarnation, would only interfere with the divine order of karmic punishment.

Assessing Reincarnation's Claims

Apart from any appraisal of reincarnation in the light of scriptural scrutiny, mere logic dismisses most of its claims. If successive lives are designed to bring about moral refinement, then what good does it do to be punished for something you can't remember having done?

If a finite number of souls is assumed to exist as an extension of the Universal Soul, with some of them being purified and reabsorbed, then why is the world population increasing? The global birth rate obviously exceeds the death rate, so where do all those newly reincarnated souls come from? (Some reincarnationists tenuously argue that this discrepancy is made up by the addition of souls from other planets.)

If the essence of karma is to rid humanity of its selfish desires, then shouldn't there be a noticeable improvement in human nature after all the millennia of reincarnations? If people such as the Marquis de Sade and Attila the Hun were on an evolutionary moral ascent, then why did we still have Hitler and Charles Manson?

For some people, reincarnation seems to remove any incentive to excel morally, since there will always be a second chance. One needs only to look at the lands where karmic philosophy and theories of transmigration have held sway for centuries to see the subhuman view of life fostered by these teachings.

If other people's suffering is the result of sin in their lives, then what recompense is there for the pain endured by malformed children whose broken limbs were deliberately twisted to make them more useful to professional begging syndicates? Why lift a man from the gutter to clean his sores and feed his belly if some impersonal, unforgiving law of retribution is perpetuating his hunger? What eventual economic and social price will the West pay someday when it reaps the whirlwind of its fascination with the essence of karmic thought in reincarnation? Will we too create a generation callously indifferent to human misery because all concepts of ultimate accountability have been swept from our culture and replaced by the philosophy "I'll do better the next time around"?

Unexplainable cases of cognition and other phenomena that seem to support reincarnation continue to baffle those who seek scientific validity of claims regarding past lives. In the strictest sense, there is no objective way to verify or deny such occurrences.

But some tales of former existences are obviously fraudulent. People with low self-esteem have been known to invent marvelous stories in which they were persons of power, beauty, and nobility in another age. But what about those cases where an individual recounts in precise detail a number of verified facts concerning another place or time about which he presumably knew nothing?

Intuitive recall (*déjà vu*, as it commonly known) is the experience of having done something or having been somewhere before. Could this explain the phenomenon of reincarnation? It should be noted that the human subconscious mind contains an incalculable record of sights and sounds, most of which have long since been forgotten.

Movies, TV programs, photographs, songs, and literature may provide bits and pieces from which the mind composes the image of a person or place, creating the feeling that it all happened in precisely the same way at some other time in the past.

Even though the person or place may not be consciously recalled, the mind may have been imprinted with the memory of an instance with striking similarity. Some psychologists have also speculated that cases of déjà vu result when the experiential memory functions of the brain go slightly out of phase. In this case, one really has been there before—a split second earlier.

Spontaneous recall, the memory a child may have concerning a previous life, is often intriguing but seldom verifiable. Most cases reported by researchers such as Dr. Stevenson involved children raised in cultures with a predisposition towards belief in reincarnation. Considering the vivid imagination of most youngsters, it would take little parental encouragement to spin a tale of fascinating proportions. The resulting doting attention would enable even a child's mind to construct a very believable scenario.

What about the case of the PLT client we discussed earlier? Did hypnotism actually help her regress to a previous life in New York circa 1943? Hypnosis is an unreliable technique to judge qualitatively. Deeply imbedded memories may surface, which may seem to validate reincarnation. A good novel or an impressive film, long since forgotten, may set the stage for a compelling story the hypnotist accepts as a first-person account. Under hypnosis, the subject has a tendency to be suggestively guided by the hypnotist, who may bring forth information that he in part has unwittingly planted. In summary, hypnosis is hardly a reliable investigative tool to probe the proofs of reincarnation.

The greatest danger in using hypnosis to verify reincarnation is the subject's spiritually vulnerable condition, in which the trance state could be manipulated by demonic forces. The information about another life being impressed upon the mind may come from an alien spiritual source. Since evil spirits have existed far back beyond the span of recorded history, they could easily construct a verifiable time, person, and place, because they were there! Such an explanation would indeed seem legitimate, since a demon could supernaturally provide any data necessary to apparently confirm a previous existence. And the person who experienced the recall could honestly claim to have had no means of secretly or unwittingly obtaining such information.

People may be led to assume that if the facts are correct, the phenomenon of spontaneous recall verifies reincarnation. But confirming a particular circumstance does not automatically verify that it actually took place. If the source of the information is evil and if the application of it is unbiblical, nothing is proven except that Satan is supernaturally able to manipulate one's consciousness. The spiritual source of reincarnation episodes needs to be tested (1 John 4:1), and the accuracy of the facts in question must be verified.

CHRISTIAN CRITIQUE: In spite of these problems, advocates of reincarnation in the West still proclaim its virtues. Often they delude Christians by buttressing their claims with seemingly supportive quotes from Scripture. While acknowledging that the Bible does not explicitly teach reincarnation, they do cite a few verses that appear to support their theories. These references are listed here, along with the orthodox Christian perspective on each passage.

1. "This is John the Baptist; he is risen from the dead; and therefore mighty works do shew forth themselves in him" (Matthew 14:2). Although some have suggested that Jesus was a reincarnation of John the Baptist, the Bible doesn't endorse their claim. Even by the tenets of reincarnation, such a proposition would not have been possible, because Jesus was a grown adult when John was beheaded.

2. "Jesus said unto them, Verily, verily, I say unto you, Before Abraham was, I am" (John 8:58). If Jesus had actually suggested he was a reincarnation of Abraham, the Jews would have dismissed him as a lunatic. Instead, they tried to kill Christ because they knew that his claim to be the "I Am" before Abraham was an assertion of his eternally existent deity.

3. "For this [Melchizedek], king of Salem, priest of the most high God, who met Abraham returning from the slaughter of the kings, and blessed him; To whom also Abraham gave a tenth part of all; first being by interpretation King of righteousness, and after that also King of Salem, which is, King of peace; Without father, without mother, without descent, having neither beginning of days, nor end of life; but made like unto the Son of God; abideth a priest continually" (Hebrews 7:1-3). Melchizedek is merely presented as a type of Christ, whose priesthood is a point of comparison with that of Jesus. Even if one accepts Melchizedek as theophany (an Old Testament appearance of Christ), which I do not, such a conclusion would still not endorse a belief in reincarnation.

4. "If ye will receive it, this is [Elijah], which was for to come" (Matthew 11:14). To say that John the Baptist was a reincarnation of Elijah is to ignore his own answer to those who raised this possibility. "I am not," he emphatically declared (John 1:21). Luke plainly records that John came in the "spirit and power" of Elijah's style of ministry (see Luke 1:17).

5. "There was a man of the Pharisees, named Nicodemus, a ruler of the

Jews: The same came to Jesus by night, and said unto him, Rabbi, we know that thou art a teacher come from God: for no man can do these miracles that thou doest, except God be with him. Jesus answered and said unto him, Verily, verily, I say unto thee, Except a man be born again, he cannot see the kingdom of God. Nicodemus saith unto him, How can a man be born when he is old? can he enter the second time into his mother's womb, and be born? Jesus answered, Verily, verily, I say unto thee, Except a man be born of water and of the Spirit, he cannot enter into the kingdom of God. That which is born of the flesh is flesh; and that which is born of the Spirit is spirit. Marvel not that I said unto thee, Ye must be born again. The wind bloweth where it listeth, and thou hearest the sound thereof, but canst not tell whence it cometh, and whither it goeth: so is every one that is born of the Spirit" (John 3:1-8). Jesus clearly indicates in this passage that he is speaking of a spiritual, not a natural birth. The emphasis is upon God's requirement for entrance into his kingdom, not a succession of cyclic rebirths on a journey to nirvana.

In contrast to the attempt made by reincarnationists to justify their beliefs by quoting certain Scriptures, the Bible is filled with proof texts that deal a fatal blow to any hopes of an evolving soul. Here are some passages that may be cited to refute reincarnation:

1. "For me to live is Christ, and to die is gain" (Philippians 1:21). The "gain" through death that the apostle Paul speaks of expresses his longing to be *immediately* with Christ.

2. "We are confident, I say, and willing rather to be absent from the body, and to be present with the Lord" (2 Corinthians 5:8). To leave this body is to be instantly in the presence of Jesus, not floating around the realms of the spirit world, waiting in line for another body to inhabit.

3. "But [Stephen], being full of the Holy Ghost, looked up stedfastly into heaven, and saw the glory of God, and Jesus standing on the right hand of God, And said, Behold, I see the heavens opened, and the Son of man standing on the right hand of God. . . . And they stoned Stephen, calling upon God, and saying, Lord Jesus, receive my spirit" (Acts 7:55-56, 59). Before he was stoned, Stephen beheld Christ awaiting him in glory. And at the moment of his death, Jesus received Stephen's spirit—he did not have to perfect his karma through any further lives.

4. "Jesus said unto him, Verily I say unto thee, To day shalt thou be with me in paradise" (Luke 23:43). The thief on the cross received the promise of paradise that very day; he didn't get a lecture on how he'd be punished in the next life for the sins that lead to his crucifixion.

5. "Because he hath appointed a day, in the which he will judge the world in righteousness" (Acts 17:31). How could the certainty of God's judgment be specified for an appointed day if varying numbers of reincarnations would be necessary for each person before all mankind could be perfected?

6. "Then shall the dust return to earth as it was: and the spirit shall return unto God who gave it" (Ecclesiastes 12:7). Solomon in his wisdom declared that the destination of man's spirit is not another body but an appearance before God to be judged.

7. "But we know that, when he shall appear, we shall be like him; for we shall see him as he is" (1 John 3:2). The expectation of every Christian is to be like Christ at the resurrection, not to acquire multiple identities through a series of reincarnations.

8. "To him that overcometh will I grant to sit with me in my throne" (Revelation 3:21). The redeemed of Christ look forward to being joined with Christ at death, reigning with him, instead of being indistinguishable, absorbed into an impersonal essence.

9. "As Jesus passed by, he saw a man which was blind from his birth. And his disciples asked him, saying, Master, who did sin, this man, or his parents, that he was born blind? Jesus answered, Neither hath this man sinned, nor his parents: but that the works of God should be made manifest in him" (John 9:1-3). When the disciples echoed a popular notion similar to the principles of karma, Jesus succinctly stated that the man's blindness since birth was in no way associated with either his moral conduct or that of his parents.

Matters of Life and Death

These Scriptures indicate that reincarnation and the teachings of the Bible are mutually exclusive. No false claim of countless opportunities of reformation can stand alongside the finished work of Christ's redemption. The sacrifice of Christ on the cross and the shedding of his blood cannot be compatible with a system of belief that denies his atonement.

The law of karma inhibits any freedom of the will to determine a life of obedience to God's plan. It is a selfish concept that sees no merit in sacrifice for the welfare of others; only despair and resignation—not hope—are its result. Reincarnation offers no loving God, no forgiving grace, and it robs the Almighty of his attribute of mercy.

The apostle Paul told Timothy to avoid any false doctrine (see 1 Timothy 1:3-4). Reincarnation surely qualifies in this regard, for it seeks to replace the hope of the Christian faith—the Resurrection. Paul's great treatise on the Resurrection, found in 1 Corinthians 15, states without compromise, "If Christ be not raised, your faith is in vain" (v. 17).

It is no wonder that a fatalistic gloom permeates any religious system that upholds reincarnation. As Paul put it, "If in this life only we have hope in Christ, we are of all men most miserable" (1 Corinthians 15:19). It is the promise of eternal life with Jesus immediately beyond the grave that brings worth and meaning to serving Christ in this life.

Daniel foreshadowed the hope of Christ's victory over death by reminding the reader that either everlasting shame or everlasting life await all who die (see Daniel 12:2). Jesus affirmed the same alternatives in John 3:36 and offered the proof of his own body to substantiate his promise. He invited Thomas to place a hand in his side (see John 20:27) and challenged his disciples to touch him, to feel his flesh and bones (see Luke 24:39).

Such infallible proofs were witnessed by hundreds of his followers over a period of forty days, removing any doubts that he had conquered man's last enemy—death. Instead of directing his followers to prepare for successive reincarnations, Jesus instructed them to prepare for the day when they too would be raised from the dead to be with him forever (see 1 Thessalonians 4:17)!

REORGANIZED CHURCH OF JESUS CHRIST OF LATTER DAY SAINTS

Once a doctrinally unorthodox offshoot of the larger Mormon church, the RLDS has moved closer to mainstream Christianity in recent years.

FOUNDER: Joseph Smith III in 1860; based upon the church founded by his father, Joseph Smith Jr., in 1830

TEXTS: The Bible, *The Book of Mormon*, *The Doctrine and Covenants*

SYMBOL: A stylized oval globe, the center circle depicting the Christ child standing between a reclining lion and a small lamb, with the caption "Peace"

APPEAL: Saints members believe in the importance of their work and the uniqueness of their history and calling. Their emphasis on human-oriented service and their hopeful vision of the future, as expressed in the Zion ideal for a future utopia, is attractive.

OVERVIEW: In 1985 Emily Fern "Bunny" Spillman, a 73-year-old grand-mother from Denver, Colorado, was among the first group of women to be or-dained as elders by the Reorganized Church of Latter Day Saints, also called the Saints Church or the RLDS. Spillman and her companions are empowered to preach, administer sacraments, and counsel fellow members, activities pre-viously reserved for male elders.

The RLDS decision to break with tradition came after the church's presi-dent, Wallace B. Smith, presented a written revelation to delegates at a con-ference in Independence, Missouri. Accepting the document as the mind and will of God, the delegates voted to accept women into the priesthood. (Some observers have cynically suggested the real reason behind Smith's revelation is that the headship of the RLDS has always been hereditary, and the current prophet-president has no sons, only daughters.)

Still, Spillman's ordination accentuates the doctrinal differences between the RLDS and the better-known Church of Jesus Christ of Latter-day Saints—also called the Mormons—which still bars women from ordination. (See sepa-rate entry on the Mormons.) This and other differences have increased in re-cent years.

Mormon Roots

Wallace B. Smith traces his ancestry to Joseph Smith Jr., founder of both the RLDS and Mormon churches. The textual basis of both faiths is the work known as *The Book of Mormon*, which Joseph Smith Jr. claimed to have trans-lated from golden plates given to him by the angel Moroni.

Several years earlier as a teenager, Joseph Smith had seen a vision during which Jesus Christ told him all churches were an abomination and that Smith should join none of them. Smith was directed to wait until God chose to use him to "restore the fullness of the everlasting Gospel of Christ again to the earth."

Joseph Smith may have seemed an unlikely prophet for the latter days, and his *Book of Mormon* may be nothing more than a preposterous compilation of fiction and plagiarized Bible quotes. But today, Smith and his book are revered by the Mormons and the RLDS as foundations of their respective faiths.

The history of the two churches diverged during the early nineteenth cen-tury when a schism occurred within the Latter-day Saints over such doctrines as plural marriage for Mormon men, baptism of the dead, and the plurality of gods. In 1844 after Joseph Smith and his brother Hyrum were killed by a mob while in jail in Carthage, Illinois, the Latter-day Saints divided into factions.

About ten thousand members followed Brigham Young westward, eventu-ally settling in Salt Lake City, Utah. But the majority of the Saints scattered, waiting until Smith's young son, Joseph III, could fulfill the prophecy that named him to succeed his father.

In 1860 Joseph Smith III assumed leadership of the Latter Day Saints at age 27. The church added the word *Reorganized* to its name, further distinguishing it from the sect that had traveled to Utah. According to an RLDS pamphlet, the church set about "regathering its scattered members, without 'adding to' or 'taking from'" any of the original tenets established by the church when it was organized in 1830 in Fayette, New York.

Today the Reorganized Church of Jesus Christ of Latter Day Saints has a nationwide membership of nearly 250,000 and is established in many foreign countries. Church headquarters are located in Independence, Missouri.

A Different Path

The RLDS proclaims itself the true Latter Day Saints church, rejecting as heresy many of the more flamboyant tenets of Mormonism.

Members of the RLDS profess doctrines that sound more like mainstream Christianity. In fact, in recent years the group has grown increasingly orthodox in its theology and practices.

The RLDS affirms "a belief in God and more particularly in Jesus Christ, the Son who came to earth for the purpose of redeeming humankind." The Holy Spirit is described as "the living power and presence of God, which has been experienced in the lives of persons and of the church down through the ages."

God is seen as personal, "the creator and sustainer of the universe," who nevertheless takes time to intervene in history and to reveal himself to his followers. The Saints member reasons that, while he cannot fully comprehend God, "the fact that God has been experienced in various ways is evidence of God's desire to be known." Ways in which God has revealed himself include "miracles," as well as spiritual experiences of individuals and groups.

Written records of spiritual experiences of the RLDS president-prophets become part of *The Doctrine and Covenants*. This text dates back to 1828 and is a compilation of documents that the church accepts as inspired statements representing "the mind and will of God" and as a standard of church laws and practice.

Each new president-prophet is obligated to write down what he considers to be God's will for the church. After various RLDS councils and quorums have read these documents, a vote is taken, and approved sections are added to *The Doctrine and Covenants*.

The Bible, *The Book of Mormon*, and *The Doctrine and Covenants* are the three standard books on which the church is founded. All are considered inspired scriptures. But since God's process of self-revelation continues even today, man's discernment of the scriptures is never quite complete or final.

The RLDS emphasizes its two priesthoods. The Aaronic priesthood is concerned with temporal activities, such as those attended by priests, deacons, and teachers. The more exalted Melchizedek priesthood consists of the elders and the high priests. Examples of its duties are ministering to others, preaching, teaching, administering church laws, and directing church affairs. Members may be called to serve in either priesthood by "church officials responding to the spirit of inspiration and discernment."

Sacraments among the Latter Day Saints consist of the blessing of infants; baptism, for children aged eight; confirmation, by the laying on of hands; the Lord's Supper or Communion service; marriage; administration or anointing of the sick; ordination to the priesthood; and patriarchal blessing, given privately by the laying on of hands.

The RLDS church believes it is destined to do God's work among his people. Part of this conception is expressed by the ideal of Zion. According to the Saints, their church "is called to gather the covenant people into signal communities where they live out the will of God in the total life of society."

The Saints recognize the potential partnership between the church and government agencies, community organizations, and businesses. They work with these groups in cooperative ventures to improve the quality of life.

Signs of Growth

The Reorganized Church of Jesus Christ of Latter Day Saints may be a much more palatable faith than its larger sister church headquartered in Utah. Many of Mormonism's best qualities are present with few of the fanciful rites.

According to *Christianity Today*, which published an article entitled "In Search of Respectability" about the evolution of a number of heretical groups, the RLDS has been "one of the most striking examples of doctrinal transition in recent years."

The group does not claim to be the only true church, but rather says it is one church among many. In addition, it has downplayed distinctive Mormon doctrines like salvation by works and proxy baptism.

The RLDS is still based upon Joseph Smith and *The Book of Mormon* and still relies upon divine revelations bestowed upon leaders for its direction and growth. But there are signs that at least some members of the RLDS are no longer equating these strange revelations with God's holy Word.

"Where the church as a whole is headed is difficult to determine at this point," said *Christianity Today*, "but president Wallace B. Smith . . . has come a long way since the days of his great-grandfather, Joseph Smith, Jr."

CHRISTIAN CRITIQUE: The six objectives for the RLDS, adopted in 1966 and restated in 1973, refer to the interpretation of the "Zionic concept" in world terms. Other concerns included evangelism, emphasis on the value of individuals, and the growth of world understanding.

The RLDS reveres Joseph Smith Jr. and his direct descendants as their prophet-presidents. The church accepts the scriptural validity of *The Book of Mormon* and *The Doctrine and Covenants* and denies biblical inerrancy, saying it has lost certain passages through human editing. The incarnation of Jesus is minimized because the Saints see man as an eternal and preexistent being.

RLDS has established an unbiblical priesthood that claims access to divine mysteries. Salvation is based on good works. Spiritual experiences and divine revelations are ways to know the Word of God, leaving open the possibility of evolving spiritual truth.

SOURCES: *An Introduction to the Reorganized Church of Jesus Christ of Latter-Day Saints* (Independence, Mo.: Herald Publishing); *Rocky Mountain News*, 18 November 1985; Ruth A. Tucker, "In Search of Respectability," *Christianity Today*, 5 February 1990, 16–17; *Who Are the Saints?* (Independence, Mo.: Herald Publishing).

ACCESS: The Auditorium, Box 1059, Independence, MO 64501.

See also Mormonism.

ROSICRUCIANISM
AMORC

Claiming to possess secret knowledge, this group promises to help people use cosmic forces to master life.

FOUNDER: According to the movement's tradition, Christian Rosenkreuz (1374–1484). AMORC claims that its origins are found in ancient Egyptian "mystery schools." Modern American Rosicrucianism was founded in 1915 by Dr. H. Spencer Lewis.

TEXT: Various geometric and hieroglyphic symbols, along with the hidden, esoteric knowledge of the Kher-Hebs, who are said to be the Masters of ancient Egyptian mystery schools

SYMBOLS: Foremost among their symbols is the "Rosy Cross" (a Christian cross with a rose in the center). Rosicrucians claim that Christians chose the cross as an "arbitrary symbol." To the AMORC, the cross represents "the body of man," with the rose symbolizing "man's soul unfolding and evolving."

APPEAL: Extensive use of advertising entices the prospective member to "develop your psychic power of attraction." Ads proclaim that great thinkers like Isaac Newton, Francis Bacon, and René Descartes were Rosicrucians and suggest "they were inspired and moved by the teachings and knowledge of Rosicrucianism."

OVERVIEW: Have you ever wanted to "connect yourself to the universe"? According to a promotional brochure published by the Rosicrucians, you can do just that:

> You can harness virtually unlimited powers of insight, creativity, and spirituality. You can attract people and events into your life, speed your body's natural healing processes, create harmony around you, and much more. These powers are universal. All you have to do is learn how to draw upon the higher knowledge already within you.
>
> Using time-honored techniques that allow you to gradually develop your inner abilities, the Rosicrucian Order has created a successful system of personal, home-based study that will help you discover your inner wisdom and strengths while enhancing your physical, mental, and spiritual well-being.
>
> The Rosicrucian Order is a world-wide educational and philosophical organization. It is not a religion, and does not require a specific code of belief or conduct.

How does this spiritual correspondence course work, and where does its inspiration come from? Answers to such questions aren't easy to come by.

A Sect of Secrets

Who they are, where they come from, and what they really believe are matters of controversy surrounding most secret organizations. With Rosicrucians, these uncertainties are amplified by the volumes of undocumented literature they distribute.

They insist that their belief is not a religion, not an occult organization, has no relationship with Freemasonry, and has nothing to do with spiritism.

Though there is ample evidence to refute these assertions, Rosicrucians still claim they are nothing more than a "fraternal order" with the intent of awakening "the dormant, latent facilities of the individual whereby he may utilize to a better advantage his natural talents and lead a happier and more useful life."

This statement of purpose seems laudable, but it obscures the somewhat tainted history and esoteric practices that dominate Rosicrucian beliefs. If we define religion as "a system of faith and worship," then Rosicrucianism surely qualifies.

Those who begin a study of its teachings soon discover that self-advancement is no mere psychological goal. It is dependent upon a complex system of doctrines, rituals, and ceremonies laced with Judaic and Christian concepts, based on pagan mythology and occult practices.

Through the Ages

In the seventeenth century, a work entitled *Fama Fraternitatis* appeared in Germany. The book described the religious discoveries of Christian Rosenkreuz, who claimed to have traveled to Egypt and uncovered the mystery of the "rose cross." Though historical dates for his existence are available (1378–1484), Rosicrucians claim that the name Christian Rosenkreuz was symbolic, enabling them to assert a much earlier origin for their order.

Wherever their prior historical roots may lie, Rosicrucian societies flourished in seventeenth- and eighteenth-century Europe. Some evidence indicates they exchanged ideas with Freemasonry. Current-day Rosicrucians deny this philosophical cross-pollination. Freemasonry does include a Rose Croix degree, and there appears to be a historical link between these two closed societies.

Rosicrucians claim that their order first came to the United States in 1694 under the leadership of Grand Master Kelpius, who was connected with a European lodge.

After a time of flourishing activity (Benjamin Franklin and Thomas Jefferson are said to have been Rosicrucians), the order went into a self-proclaimed period of "outer silence" lasting 108 years. Secret work continued, but overt knowledge of the organization awaited a twentieth-century resurrection. In 1909 order literature states that Dr. H. Spencer Lewis met with officials of the French Rosicrucian Order.

Dr. Lewis was initiated and returned to spark a revival of the order in America. His efforts continued until his "transition" (the Rosicrucian term for death) in 1939 when his son, Ralph, took over.

What Rosicrucian literature fails to mention is Lewis's contact with the occult group Ordo Templi Orientis (OTO) and the infamous British spiritualist Aleister Crowley. (Crowley was a homosexual, a murderer, and a practitioner of black magic. He sought to violate every moral law possible and actually renamed himself "Beast 666.")

Lewis founded the Ancient and Mystical Order of Rosae Crucis (AMORC) in 1915. Apparently he was not at all embarrassed to receive the endorsement of the OTO, in spite of its unsavory practices. Religious researcher J. Gordon Melton claims that various emblems of the AMORC, including the Rose Cross symbol, were actually borrowed from Crowley's periodicals. Such information makes even more suspect AMORC's statement that it does not endorse any occult or superstitious beliefs.

Several other Rosicrucian orders exist, including the Rosicrucian Fellowship, founded by Max Heindel, and the Societas Rosicruciana, an American variant, which requires its members to be Masons. Since AMORC is the largest and most visible representative order, this discussion will be limited to it.

To validate its authenticity (and perhaps to obscure its recent checkered history), AMORC insists its roots extend back to ancient Egypt. In 1500 B.C. Pharaoh Thutmose III is said to have established certain "mystery schools" of the Great White Lodge. His successor, Amenhotep IV, is claimed to be the "most enlightened man of his time" and the object of much AMORC reverence.

No substantial evidence exists to connect these ancient rituals with a continuing observance leading to modern Rosicrucian practices. AMORC justifies this link by declaring that during certain periods of inactive cycles of "outer silence," Rosicrucian ceremonies and rituals were kept alive by secret practices. Therefore, with or without historical evidence, one cannot test the belief system. Its validity is asserted regardless of reason or proof.

Myth, Legend, and Pseudoscience

Modern AMORC beliefs are a mixture of Egyptian religious tenets, paranormal and psychic interests, and pseudoscientific pursuits based on alchemy. Members attempt soul travel, development of inner "intuition," and healing, and they also conduct chemical experiments.

The absorbing nature of this approach permits Rosicrucians to encompass almost every form of mystical-transcendent experience, from water witching to mind control

Training for members takes place primarily by correspondence through a series of mail-order *Mandamus*, which are secret, sealed instructions. Neophytes are warned never to reveal the content of such literature nor to explain to outsiders their clandestine ceremonies. "Simply tell them you study one night a week," new members are instructed. "Always emphasize that AMORC is *not* a religion."

The facts indicate otherwise. Members are encouraged to construct what is essentially an altar (they call it a *telesterion*) in their homes. Emblems may include incense, an ankh, candles, and idols of Egyptian deities and rulers. A document entitled "Confession to Maat" may be hung on the wall (*Maat* is supposed to be Egyptian for *truth*). The affirmation begins, "Homage to thee, Great God, thou Master of all Truth, I am pure." Neophytes are told they are petitioning the "forty-two principal gods . . . expressions of the principal god, the Sun-God, AMEN-RA."

Each lesson gradually introduces more AMORC theology. Since the neophyte affirms he is pure, there is no need for sins to be forgiven. Only "psychological obstacles" are acknowledged, and these are "confessed" to oneself. Prayers are made to "the God of your heart." The penalty for bad *karma* one has accumulated can be expiated by the law of *AMRA*. (A check donated to AMORCA is suggested.) God is defined as the "Supreme Intelligence," a form of "pure energy," "The First Cause of All." This Brahmanistic-type deity is totally impersonal and is also said to be a "number endowed with motion."

The Bible takes a special drubbing from AMORC. Genesis is dismissed as "a beautiful poem." The New Testament is said to be devoid of the most important, private teachings of Jesus. Several books are recommended in the stead of Holy Scripture, such as *The Secret Doctrines of Jesus, The Book of Jasher,* and other volumes supporting reincarnation.

Bible beliefs are replaced with a concoction of teachings about the lost continent of Atlantis and a race of Negroes called Lemurans. Jesus is said to be the highest initiate of the Sun Period, and the Holy Spirit is the foremost initiate of the Moon Period.

Though AMORC officially denigrates spiritism, the sealed instructions encourage members to contact departed spirit masters. These are called "psychic contacts with soul personalities" who are now part of "the Universal Soul." These "personalities" are said to be in need of an "identity" to find expression; therefore, the neophyte becomes that "physical medium." Christian theology would view this phenomenon as an example of demonic control when the "personality" (evil spirit) enters (possesses) the "physical medium" (body) of the unsuspecting initiate.

In this perspective it is perhaps appropriate that AMORC denies that its "Rosy Cross" represents the Christian crucifix, since the cross of Christ symbolizes the defeat of Satan's kingdom.

CHRISTIAN CRITIQUE: This group's aim is to help people achieve "an understanding of natural, cosmic laws as the only means of mastership of life."

The esoteric ceremonies of Rosicrucianism lead its followers into ancient Egyptian secret rites that may result in demonic phenomena, including possession and spirit conjuration. Initiation rituals are verbally affirmed with the words, "So mote it be," a standard oral oath of witchcraft cults.

SOURCES: AMORC, "History of the AMORC," "Master of Life," "Who and What Are the Rosicrucians?" "Rosicrucian Initiation—Neophyte Guide," "Recognition," miscellaneous literature; Ibid., *Master Monograph, The Celestial Sanctum,* and *Rosicrucian Digest* (March 1975), various publications; Walter Martin, *The Kingdom of the Cults* (Minneapolis: Bethany Fellowship, 1977); J. Gordon Melton, *The Encyclopedia of American Religions* (Wilmington, N.C.: McGrath, 1978), 177–184.

ACCESS: The Rosicrucian Order, 1342 Naglee Avenue, San Jose, CA 95191

SATANISM

Once a dark and secretive practice, satanism is both open and evangelistic in its campaign to attract those who want to codify their anger toward God into a belief system embracing all human vice.

OVERVIEW: The ceremonial chamber is set up like an elaborate stage for a dramatic play. Lighting is dark and dismal with only a few candles piercing the gloom. Symbols of Satan decorate the room.

A priest and selected helpers are the main characters, and the play's participants are the onlookers. They are often attired in dark, hooded robes. Success hinges upon the strength of the participants' beliefs and magical abilities.

During the ensuing ritual, the priest and onlookers will recite blasphemies. Other rituals also incorporate pornography and sexuality, and some feature a naked woman lying on an altar.

This description might sound like the opening pages of a mystery novel or the setup for a teen slasher movie. But it's not. It comes from the pages of a how-to guide for satanists entitled *The Satanic Ritual*. The book, written by Anton LaVey and published in 1972, is a companion book to LaVey's *The Satanic Bible*, which has helped popularize satanism in the United States.

The terms *satanic* and *demonic* are tossed around with regrettable casualness these days. Some people use these terms to describe anything they think differs from true Christian teaching.

But we need to remember that popular movements like paganism and Wicca (witchcraft) are not ostensibly satanic. It is true that Satan may delude the people in these groups as well as followers of other false religions. But these groups don't even acknowledge the existence of Satan, let alone worship him.

Hard-core satanists, on the other hand, believe in the devil with all their hearts and worship him with all the devotion that Christians show for God.

Unfortunately, I have known many young people who became satanists after dabbling in occult-themed pop music, role-playing games, and even rebellion against their parents.

In dealing with the phenomenon of contemporary satanism, we need to realize that Satan is alive and well, and he is doing everything he can to lure people to his side. On the other hand, God is still more powerful than Satan, and he can help rescue people who have fallen into the devil's clutches.

A Fallen Angel

One of the key Bible passages about Satan, or Lucifer, is found in the prophecy of Isaiah 14:12-15 (NIV):

How you have fallen from heaven,
O morning star, son of the dawn!
You have been cast down to the earth,
you who once laid low the nations!
You said in your heart,
"I will ascend to heaven;
I will raise my throne
above the stars of God;
I will sit enthroned on the mount of assembly,
on the utmost heights of the sacred mountain.
I will ascend above the tops of the clouds;
I will make myself like the Most High."
But you are brought down to the grave,
to the depths of the pit.

This passage illustrates a central point about Satan and satanism. Lucifer's rebellion against God began with his desire to "ascend to heaven" and rise above God. Today many satanists desire the same thing. They want to transcend their narrow, broken existence and exult in spiritual power.

Then as now, God harshly judges those who rebel against his will and seek to outsmart him. There have always been those who sought to serve Satan. Centuries ago, the town of Salem, Massachusetts, was thrown into a frenzy when many who lived there were charged with demonic influences and witchcraft—accusations that many scholars say appear to have been exaggerated.

Recent centuries have seen a revival in satanism that continues to exert a powerful influence today. In late nineteenth-century France a renewal of interest in satanism accompanied a generalized cultural decadence that followed years of revolution against the power of Christian churches and traditional customs. And in early twentieth-century England a mysterious magician named Aleister Crowley called himself "The Great Beast 666" and flouted conventional morality (see separate entry on Crowley).

In America a renewed interest in satanism emerged from the post-World War II era and the turbulent decade of the 1960s counterculture. During this period, rock bands like the Rolling Stones sang songs about Satan, new groups like the Church of Satan were founded in San Francisco, and figures like mass murderer Charles Manson claimed to be following the dictates of the devil.

LaVey's Legacy

One of the key figures in America's satanic revival was Anton LaVey (1930–1997), a former animal trainer and carnival employee who authored *The Satanic Bible,* founded the Church of Satan, and is generally regarded as the father of contemporary "populist" satanism in America.

LaVey originally gained a reputation as an expert in hypnotism and mentalism. But on April 30, 1966, the occult holiday of Walpurgisnacht (the witches' sabbath announcing the transition from winter to spring), LaVey shaved his head and announced the formation of the Magic Circle, a secret ritualistic group from which he eventually organized the Church of Satan.

LaVey, with his shaven head and mesmerizing looks, was a master of media manipulation. He talked to the media about worshiping with a nude woman on the altar in his black house in San Francisco. He also let it be known that actress Jayne Mansfield had been associated with his church. He even had a small acting role as the devil in the phenomenally popular movie *Rosemary's Baby*.

Behind all the showmanship, LaVey was serious about satanism. He taught that Satan was an archetypal image of humanity's baser instincts, a dark image invented by the church to scare people into conversion. Whatever his actual beliefs about the existence of Satan, he milked the metaphor of Lucifer effectively.

LaVey died in 1997, and Blanche Barton succeeded him as the church's administrative head. The group refuses to release membership statistics, but the Church of Satan is not a numerically significant movement in the United States today.

However, the worship of the devil as a malevolent being is real, and I am personally aware of many cases where youthful dabblers have wound up getting more involved with the prince of darkness than they ever intended.

The Youth Connection

Some of the best-documented instances of modern satanism involve teenage dabblers in the satanic arts. Youthful dabblers are invariably white, middle class, and acting out of some form of rebellion against their parents.

I wrote about this phenomenon in my book *Satanism: The Seduction of America's Youth*. In that book I discussed some telltale signs of involvement in satanism among youth:

- An unhealthy preoccupation with fantasy role-playing games like Dungeons and Dragons (D&D)
- An interest in Ouija boards and other occult games
- A preoccupation with psychic phenomena like telepathy, astral projection, Tarot cards, I Ching, and parapsychology
- An addiction to horror movies that have main characters who kill and maim
- An obsession with heavy-metal music, particularly bands like Marilyn Manson, Slayer, Venom, King Diamond, and other groups that evoke satanic symbolism
- An affinity for satanic paraphernalia, including posters of black-metal bands, skulls, knives, chalices, black candles, and robes

- An inclination to write poems or letters about satanism or to sketch designs of upside-down crosses, pentagrams, the number 666, names of the devil, or skulls and other symbols of death
- An attraction to satanic literature and such books as *The Satanic Bible*, the *Necronomicon*, the writings of Aleister Crowley, or keeping a private journal such as a *book of shadows* (a self-designed secret chronicle of satanic activities and ideas)
- An involvement with friends who dress in black, greet each other with the satanic salute (index and pinkie finger extended, with palm facing inward), speak and write backwards, or organize secret meetings

Parents are right to be concerned about their children's possible involvement in satanism, but they don't need to become irrational or repressive.

Beware of the temptation to search a child's room or screen his mail, which would breach his trust in you. Don't suddenly demand that every offensive poster come off his wall and every distasteful record album go into the garbage. Precipitous action will instill further anger and rebellion.

Instead, be alert for additional clues of satanic involvement. Ask prudent questions of your child's peers, teachers, and acquaintances. Above all, don't assume satanism can't intrude upon your family.

Satanism and Self-Indulgence

As with Satan's original rebellion against God, many who turn to the devil today do so because they believe they can have their needs met more easily than they could any other way, including through Christianity.

In many cases there is a connection between satanism and drug abuse. For many participants in satanic ceremonies the lure of drugs is an enticement attracting them to satanism. Once involved in the cult, the use of drugs, along with hypnotic suggestion, becomes a form of brainwashing. Satanic cult leaders know that even though their philosophy is based on moral anarchy, they must maintain cohesiveness with their followers. Drugs render the devil's devotees addictively dependent and less likely to abandon their allegiance to Satan.

My own research library contains news media and other reports about scores of documented cases of killings involving devil worship, including many cases that have gone to court and involved lurid testimonies of bizarre rituals requiring human sacrifice.

In the long run, the lure of satanism is selfishness, as one can see in the following nine "Satanic Statements" from LaVey's *Satanic Bible*:

1. Satan represents indulgence, instead of abstinence.
2. Satan represents vital existence, instead of spiritual pipe dreams.
3. Satan represents undefiled wisdom, instead of hypocritical self-deceit.
4. Satan represents kindness to those who deserve it, instead of love wasted on ingrates.

5. Satan represents vengeance, instead of turning the other cheek.
6. Satan represents responsibility to the responsible, instead of concern for psychic vampires.
7. Satan represents man as just another animal, sometimes better, more often worse than those that walk on all fours, who, because of his "divine spiritual and intellectual development," has become the most vicious animal of all.
8. Satan represents all of the so-called sins, as they all lead to physical, mental, or emotional gratification.
9. Satan has been the best friend the church has ever had, as he has kept it in business all these years.

To adequately understand satanism, one needs to distinguish between its variants, all very different in how they approach the nature and source of evil. There are essentially five categories:

1. Classic satanism—They worship the devil as a literal being and believe that Lucifer is indeed Lord, and his throne was usurped by Christ. As Luciferians, they are devoted to returning the Dark Lord to his rightful place as ruler of the universe.
2. Self-styled satanism—Mostly rebellious youth who are looking for an excuse for moral revolt. They piece together various sources of the dark arts, from black magic to witchcraft, and develop their own system of appeasing Satan. Many borrow their ideas from *The Satanic Bible* and *The Necronomicon*.
3. Church of Satan—Disciples of Anton Lavey vehemently deny the existence of a literal devil and instead say that Satan is an archetype representing the basest instincts of human nature. They choose carnal indulgence as the way to liberation.
4. Clandestine satanism—These shadowy devotees operate underground in secret groups and are responsible for some unsolved crimes of child abduction and murder. They are criminal by nature and engage in ritual abuse to control and program their victims
5. Ritual satanism—Drawn by the psychodrama of ceremonies, these followers of the dark side regularly engage in debaucheries as a form of empowerment and sexual gratification. They are careful to avoid detection for engaging in illegal activities such as ritual animal sacrifices.

ACCESS: Church of Satan, Box 210666, San Francisco, CA 94121

SATHYA SAI BABA

To thousands of followers, this Indian teacher is a god and a miracle worker with the power to create matter out of nothing.

FOUNDER: Sathya Sai Baba, born in 1926 as Satyanarayana Raju Pratsanti Nilayam in India

TEXT: Hindu scriptures

APPEAL: Unlike most Indian gurus who claim to have achieved God-realization, Sai Baba produces apparent miracles as a proof of his atavistic claims. His powers are seemingly greater than those of other *siddhis*, and he performs his feats more frequently. Those who do not believe in the devil or are unaware of the extent to which his powers may be manifested will be impressed by Sai Baba. They must decide if the source of his phenomena is satanic, psychic, divine, or mere trickery.

OVERVIEW: In 1995 Alice Ross, a Canadian pastor in a Religious Science church, traveled to Puttaparti, India. When she came back to the United States, she couldn't contain her excitement about Sathya Sai Baba, a famed holy man who seemed to be able to perform miracles.

"He does miracles way beyond anything Jesus has done," she told a newspaper reporter. "What Baba did was reconfirm my faith and belief that there is a loving presence and an infinite intelligence working toward our common good."

But researcher Dale Beyerstein, who has written a book about the so-called holy man, wasn't so sure. "I think he's pretty scary," said Beyerstein. "A couple of years ago, six of his former followers were killed in his bedchamber."

Such divergent opinions are common when it comes to Sathya Sai Baba, who continues to spread his fame through supposedly supernatural acts. But are these divine miracles or showbiz magic?

We've all seen the magician who gestures with his hands and out pops a bird. But he generally has on a coat, and you wonder just what he had up his sleeve. What would you think of a man wearing no sleeves who waves his hand and produces a U.S. gold coin minted in the year of your birth?

That feat, which took place in India, is just one officially recorded "miracle" of Sathya Sai Baba, perhaps the most unusual guru of this century. Since his own sympathetic biographers provide the major source of information regarding Sai Baba, much of this chapter is based on their account. Consequently, what is known about his background is undocumented, leaving some of his claims open to the possibility they are based more on legend than fact.

A Punjabi Prophet?

The forerunner of Sathya Sai Baba, Sai Baba of Shirdi, was born in the mid-1880s in Hyderabad State, India. Before his death in 1918 he had convinced area devotees and skeptics alike that he was an incarnation of God, an *avatar*.

Legends declare that he cured leprosy, cast out spirits, appeared in animal as well as human forms, and was especially fond of holy ash, which he produced out of thin air by a gesture of his hand. The ash, called *udhi,* was used for curing ailments and miraculous purposes. When he died, mourners wondered whose body would be the recipient of his next incarnation. Though countless Indian gurus lay claim to the office of avatar, Hindu theology clearly states that only one incarnation of God may exist at one time.

Entering on the stage of potential avatars, Sathya Sai Baba was born in 1926 in Prasanti Nilayam, India. Even before his birth as Satyanarayana Raju (his given name), strange things happened in his home. Musical instruments would twang unaided in the night, and unseen hands would pound rhythms on a *maddala* (drum).

On a certain occasion after his birth, he was laid on top of some bedclothes on the floor. His parents noticed movement in the cloth and looked to see a cobra entwined about the baby's body. Incredibly, no harm came to the child. (Later, devotees took this to mean that his incarnation also included the role of Sheshiara, Lord of Serpents.)

As a youngster, Satyanarayana would produce candy and fruit for his friends—out of an empty bag. When asked how these and other paranormal feats were performed, he explained that an invisible helper named Grama Sakti obeyed his will to give him whatever he wanted. At age 13 he suffered a scorpion bite (though no one could find the culprit) and lapsed into a coma.

Shortly after he came out of the coma, he exhibited different personalities, and various voices spoke from his body. Some of these entities quoted lengthy portions of Hindu scriptures that the boy had never learned. His parents consulted a witch doctor, who failed in an attempt to exorcise any evil spirits from the lad. Two months and fifteen days after the scorpion bite, he suddenly started producing objects out of the air with a mere flick of his hands. "I am Sai Baba," he declared. No one knew who he was talking about.

Eventually, people in the village of Prasanti Nilayam learned of Sai Baba of Shirdi and became convinced that Satyanarayana Ruja was an incarnation of the late Hindu saint. From then on, Satyanarayana became known as Sathya Sai Baba. (*Sa* means "divine," *ai* means "mother," and *Baba* means "father"—"the Divine Mother/Father.")

Tales of Miracles Spread

Tales of Sai Baba's miracles began to abound. To convince men of his reincarnation as Sai Baba of Shirdi, he related conversations that were known only to the departed guru's disciples. He also supernaturally produced articles of devotion that had been placed at the shrine of the Shirdi tomb many miles away.

Whether or not any or all of the supposed miracles attributed to Sai Baba are true is open to question. Such claims either represent exaggerated legends or phenomenal psychic feats. Consider these examples of Sai Baba's powers:

- Flower petals thrown on the floor fall in the pattern of his name.
- Pendants, chains, rings, necklaces, and photographs can be plucked from the air by his bare hands and are then dispensed as gifts to devotees.
- Disciples name a fruit, and it instantly appears on a tree.
- Food supplies are multiplied.
- A blinding ray of light streams from his forehead.
- Cancer is cured.
- *Devas* (Hindu for "angels") hand him a carved glass bowl that materializes out of nothing.
- Idol statuettes suddenly appear.
- Psychic surgery is performed.
- Rocks turn into candy.
- A flower bud is transformed into a diamond.
- Demons are driven out.
- And a man is raised from the dead in a fashion that bears striking similarity to Christ's miracle in Luke 8:40-56.

Sai Baba's favorite "miracle" is to produce sacred ash from his waving hand. The ash (*vibhuti*, he calls it) is said to represent the regenerative aspect of the Hindu god Shiva. When given to devotees, the ash becomes a curative powder for all sorts of ailments. At Shiva's annual festival, Baba always performs two miracles. One is the creation of a mound of ash from a small urn. The other miracle that Baba performs at Shiva's festival is more repulsive to the Western mind. Hindus sometimes worship Shiva in the form of a *lingam*. Though intellectual Hindus have elaborate explanations about the philosophy of lingams, these objects are actually fertility symbols. The most common form is that of an elongated oval, the shape of a phallus.

During the annual Shiva observance, Sai Baba may speak for an hour or more, then he writhes and twists in apparent pain. His temperature rises to 104 degrees. Suddenly he ejects an object from his mouth—a five-by-three-inch solid lingam. He has been known to spit out as many as nine lingams on one occasion.

What is the purpose of such paranormal phenomena? A chronicler of Sai Baba's life put it this way: "The miracles of Christ must be taken on faith; those of Sai Baba you can see for yourself." In other words, Sai Baba's miracles are the pudding-proof of the "truths" he teaches. As one writer explained, "[Baba's miracles] build our faith . . . toward the production of a divine edition of ourselves."

A Hindu Huckster?

Sai Baba's theology is classical Hinduism. Each person is essentially *atma* (soul/ spirit), an entity that is formless. It is manifested in five sheaths (spiritual essences). Each atma is divine but has forgotten its god-nature.

"Man is not born in sin," Baba declares. Eternal bliss is only possible by conquering earthly desires to reveal the spark of divinity. "If you realize the atma-principle, you become God himself," according to Baba.

There are three ways to attain this: *karma* (action), *jnana* (knowledge), and *bhakti* (devotion to a guru). The latter is Sai Baba's preference. In his perception, the *Sadguru* (God-realized guru) *is* God to the disciple. Only by putting himself completely in the hands of Baba may the devotee be guided to the knowledge of God-love. But who guides the hands of Sai Baba?

As Sai Baba stands before his disciples, red silk robe flowing and Afro crinkled like a circular mop, he evokes tears and sighs of awe.

The contrast between Jesus and Sai Baba is apparent. Though the latter lays claim to being Christ, the avatar for our age, the proofs of divinity offered by each are distinctly dichotomous. Sai Baba's feats may not need an element of faith. But a man who claims to be God and then regurgitates replicas of sex organs brings into question the motive of his miracles. Charlatan or psychic, Sai Baba will need more than holy ash to cure what ails him.

CHRISTIAN CRITIQUE: Baba's miracles are intended to validate his claims of divinity and cause devotees to submit to his wishes and teachings. By thus concentrating on their guru (Baba), who is the form of God, disciples are said to become more placid and realize their own oneness with the Supreme.

Baba teaches that scriptures are partially effective spiritual guidebooks, but devotion to the *Sadguru* is the easiest and quickest way to the knowledge of God.

Sai Baba's miracles, though impressive, are limited in scope and degree. When confronted with this inconsistency of his presumed omnipotent nature, he argues that man has accumulated too much karmic sin to heal all those who seek relief.

When Christ's resurrection and power over death is brought up in regard to Baba's own eventual demise, Baba insists he has conquered death too. By this he means that he has the power to choose his time and manner of death as well as his next incarnation. The fallacy of this rationale is self-evident.

SOURCES: Robert Eckhart, "Pastor and Skeptic Debate Authenticity of Sai Baba," *Paradise Post* (British Columbia), 6 July 1996; H. Murphett, *Sai Baba, Man of Miracles* (York Beach, Me.: Weisser, 1977); Sai Baba Center and Book Store, "Who Is Sai Baba?" "Sathya Sai Baba Speaks," miscellaneous materials; Arnold Schulman, *Baba* (New York: Pocket Books, 1975).

ACCESS: S.A.I. Foundation, 14849 Lull St., Van Nuys, CA 91405; *Sathya Sai Newsletter*, 1800 E. Garvey Ave., West Covina, CA 91791; in India, Prasanti Nilayam (Home of the Supreme), Anantapur District, Andhra Pradesh; Brindavan, Kadugodi, Near Whitefield, Bangalore, Karnataka State

SCIENTOLOGY

Is Scientology scientific? religious? Critics say it's a high-pressure business making millions from devoted, dependent followers.

In all the broad Universe there's no other hope for Man than ourselves.
L. RON HUBBARD, FROM HIS JOURNAL, 1967

Scientology's may be the most debilitating set of rituals of any cult in America.
RESEARCHERS FLO CONWAY AND JIM SIEGELMAN

FOUNDER: L. Ron Hubbard (1911–1986) founded Scientology, created all its major teachings, and closely controlled the organization until his death. Hubbard was a recluse during his final years, possibly trying to avoid testifying in numerous lawsuits against the group.

TEXT: Hubbard wrote *Dianetics: The Modern Science of Mental Health*, as well as numerous other Scientology books and science-fiction novels. Before he died in 1986, he delivered more than three thousand taped lectures, so it will be many years before we see the end of new Hubbard books. Scientology says Hubbard gave the world more than 40 million written and spoken words.

SYMBOL: Scientology uses a modified Christian cross that has eight branches instead of four, symbolizing the group's "eight dynamics" (self, group, survival, etc.). Another major symbol is "the bridge." The organization teaches that by taking its many courses, individuals may cross the bridge that separates their current limited life from a life of limitless possibilities.

OVERVIEW: Many people know little more about Scientology than this: big-name entertainers like John Travolta and Tom Cruise have worked overtime to portray the group in a favorable light.

The first contact many have with Scientology comes when they are offered a "free personality analysis" at one of the group's offices in cities around the world.

Who would suspect that the questions on the personality test are part of a Church of Scientology recruiting program? And why be skeptical of "an applied religious philosophy" that offers "a clear, bright insight to help you blaze toward your mind's full potential"? After all, Dianetics (meaning "through the soul") promises to reveal "the single source of all man's insanities, psychosomatic illnesses, and neuroses."

Painting a Positive Picture

Through its celebrity supporters and its aggressive advertising campaigns, Scientology portrays itself as the perfect blend of science and religion.

Whatever it is, it isn't cheap. An hour of Scientology counseling can cost hundreds of dollars. Some former members say they were required to spend more than $250,000 on a never-ending series of classes and counseling sessions.

In 1991 Time magazine published a cover story on the group. "Scientology: The Cult of Greed," shouted the cover headline. Inside, investigative reporter Richard Behar called the organization "a depraved yet thriving enterprise" and showed "how the growing Dianetics empire squeezes millions from believers worldwide." As Behar wrote, "The Church of Scientology . . . portrays itself as a religion. In reality, the church is a hugely profitable global racket that survives by intimidating members and critics in a Mafia-like manner."

Until his death in 1986, reclusive founder L. Ron Hubbard oversaw all Scientology activities with guru-like control from an offshore fleet of ships.

A Sci-Fi Faith?

Before Hubbard founded Scientology he was a struggling science fiction writer. People who knew him in the 1950s claim they once heard him say that if a person really wanted to make money, he would start a religion.

In 1950 he published *Dianetics: The Modern Science of Mental Health*. It was an instant success. The book was Hubbard's psychotherapeutic alternative to the techniques of modern mainstream psychiatry. But when the medical community responded with alarm, Hubbard transformed his theories into a religion, with *Dianetics* as the "scripture" of his new movement.

The Church of Scientology was founded in Washington, D.C., in 1955. Hubbard sought tax-exempt status and freedom from governmental interference for his organization. Scientology was eventually granted tax-exempt status in the United States, but it is still denied such benefits in Germany and other European countries. Its recognition as a church saves the organization millions of dollars in taxes.

In his 1952 book entitled *Scientology: A History of Man* Hubbard even adapted the words of Jesus as found in Matthew 11:5 to describe his new teaching: "This is useful knowledge. With it the blind again see, the lame walk, the ill recover, the insane become sane and the sane become saner. By its use the thousand abilities Man has sought to recover become his once more."

Since then, Scientology has blossomed. The organization claims millions of members in dozens of countries (though some defectors say that current membership may be less than 700,000).

The church reports that more than 16 million copies of *Dianetics* have been sold. Hubbard's reputation as an explorer, science fiction writer, and parabotanist (he was one of the first to expound the idea of communicating with plants) enlarged to make him the worldwide spokesman for this fast-growing cult.

Still, some of Scientology's teachings sound like the far-fetched story lines from one of Hubbard's many sci-fi novels. In 1985 one of the many lawsuits brought against the organization by former members resulted in the release of secret Scientology teachings to the general public.

Unlike many Christian groups who try to give away Bibles, Scientology closely guards its scriptures. One of the group's many lawyers referred to the group's teachings and techniques as "trade secrets."

Here's how an Associated Press story summarized the group's ideas:

> Seventy-five million years ago, Earth was called Teegeeach and was among 90 planets ruled by Xemu, who spread his evil by thermonuclear bombs. . . .
>
> Xemu, attempting to solve overpopulation problems, destroyed selected inhabitants of the planets and implanted the seeds of aberrant behavior in their spirits to affect future generations of mankind. . . .
>
> Beings from the planets were taken to at least 10 volcanoes on Earth where H-bombs far more powerful than any in existence today were detonated, destroying the beings but freeing their spirits, called thetans. . . .
>
> The thetans were trapped in a compound of frozen alcohols and, during a 36-day period, Xemu "implanted" in them the seeds of aberrant behavior for generations to come.

Devoted Scientologists pay tens of thousands of dollars to study such material, which is part of the group's upper-level training called OT III.

Making People Clear

It's difficult to understand Hubbard's teaching without a crash course in Scientology nomenclature. The church published a dictionary with seven thousand definitions for the use of over three thousand Dianetic words.

Hubbard taught that mankind is descended from a race of uncreated, omnipotent gods called thetans, who gave up their powers to enter the Material-Energy-Space-Time (MEST) world of Earth. Gradually, they devolved by reincarnation to become humans who could not remember their deified state. Scientologists are encouraged to awaken their dormant thetan potential by removing all mental blocks called engrams, which are best described as emotional hang-ups, comparable to repressed memories stored in the subconscious.

Engrams are said to be traumatic experiences from past lives. The "analytical mind" reasons, but the "reactive mind" simply records engrams, which impede spiritual progress. Dianetics teaches the techniques for removing (clearing) all engrams. One of Scientology's goals is to "clear the planet," and the group looks at all non-Scientologists as "preclear" (PC).

The technique Scientologists use to discover and clear engrams is called auditing. This process uses a galvanometer called an E-Meter, which costs hundreds of dollars. The device measures the resistance to electric current by recording galvanic skin responses. As with a polygraph (lie detector), the instructor (auditor) asks a series of questions while the student holds the two "tin cans" of the E-Meter in his hands. Scientologists insist the auditing procedure is like a church confessional.

By removing engrams and becoming clear, Scientologists can realize their true personhood, achieving total power and control over all aspects of life.

While *Today's Health* contends that Scientology attracts the "weak, confused, lonely, and emotionally ill," there are others who genuinely look to Dianetics for altruistic reasons. Scientologists have tried to keep a clean image, publicly eschewing drugs, adultery, and premarital sex. Members are usually well-scrubbed, respectable, middle-class types. The Church of Scientology does not have regular church services and does not believe in prayer or many of the practices people expect from a church. Church ministers wear the conventional black clerical with white collar and even sport crosses, though they point out it isn't representative of Christ's crucifix. Scientologists talk at length about their antidrug-abuse program, called Narcanon, and their efforts with prisoners and the mentally retarded.

A Fighting Faith

When their teachings and tactics are questioned, Scientologists are not prone to turn the other cheek.

In the 1950s Hubbard declared war on the psychiatric establishment, which ridiculed his ideas. Today Scientologists still organize protests against psychiatric drugs.

During the 1970s Scientology battled the U.S. government, which had long denied the organization the tax exemptions routinely granted to religious groups.

Scientologists went so far as to infiltrate and install wiretaps in the offices of a number of federal agencies, including the IRS, a perennial church foe.

Scientology leaders even devised an elaborate plot to take over parts of the federal government.

The plot came to light after eleven church members, including Hubbard's third wife, Mary Sue, were convicted of stealing government documents and attempting to cover up their activities. Mary Sue Hubbard was sentenced in federal court to four years in prison for her role in a conspiracy to plant church spies in government agencies, steal government documents, and bug at least one government meeting.

L. Ron Hubbard turned his back on his wife, declaring that she was part of a "rogue" operation that was not acting on the organization's behalf. But no amount of denials can conceal the fact that Scientology is unusually ruthless in its attacks on perceived enemies. Over the years, Scientology lawyers have gone after ex-members, journalists, and so-called "cult-watching" groups.

In the 1990s Scientology set its sights on a Chicago group called the Cult Awareness Network (CAN), which had referred to Scientology as a cult. Lawyers affiliated with Scientology helped bring a successful lawsuit against CAN, which was saddled with a judgment of $1.1 million and was forced to declare bankruptcy. Ultimately, a Scientology supporter bought CAN's name and resources. After that, people who called CAN for information on Scientology never heard it called a cult again.

L. Ron Hubbard died January 24, 1986, at age seventy-four. He had spent the last two years of his life on a remote and meticulously manicured 160-acre ranch in California. Heber C. Jentzsch assumed leadership of the movement.

One of Hubbard's survivors was his eldest son, Ronald E. DeWolf, who changed his last name to remove any associations with his father. Even before Hubbard's death, DeWolf referred to him as "one of the biggest con men of this century," a black-magic practitioner who concocted his theories while under the influence of drugs. DeWolf, now a Christian, also says his father had many mistresses and was plagued by venereal disease.

Lights! Camera! Scientology!

In 1973 Scientology founder L. Ron Hubbard said celebrities could help "forward the expansion and popularization of Scientology." By 1998 *The New York Times* was writing about how successful the organization was. In an article entitled "Scientology's Star Roster Enhances Image," reporter Douglas Frantz wrote, "More than any church that has begun on the religious fringe, the Church of Scientology has cultivated a potent roster of celebrity members . . . in its struggle to win acceptance as a mainstream religion and spread its message at home and abroad."

One of the biggest Scientology celebrities is actor John Travolta, who made a movie out of Hubbard's one-thousand-plus-page 1982 novel, *Battlefield Earth: A Saga of the Year 3000*. The reviews were mixed.

"A Planetary Disaster," read the headline in *Time* magazine, where critic Richard Schickel called the film "the worst movie in living memory."

Another critic called the film "a gritty, ugly, obnoxiously loud, unimaginative crap-heap of a film piled high with implausibilities and shoddy production values."

The film swept the 2001 Razzie Awards, the satirical bad-movie honors which are presented annually by the Golden Raspberry Foundation. *Battlefield Earth* won Razzies for worst picture, worst director, worst actor, worst supporting actor, worst supporting actress (Travolta's Scientologist wife, Kelly Preston), and worst screen couple (a unique award given to "John Travolta and anyone sharing the screen with him in *Battlefield Earth*.")

"It was actually a cake walk for jurors," said Golden Raspberry Foundation spokesman John Wilson. "*Battlefield* was truly wretched."

Ministering to Scientologists

Scientology claims to be a church which respects all religions. It also claims to be compatible with Christianity and uses a modified Christian cross as one of its symbols. Try asking members if they ever go to a Scientology church service and what happens there. See if their experience in the group matches what the Bible says about the Christian life.

Scientology promises that it will help its followers experience freedom, but ironically, many of these people become increasingly dependent and indebted to the church. Talk to members about what true freedom is, and ask them if that's what they're experiencing.

Scientology has one of the most elaborate systems of terms and technology of any modern cult. Don't get bogged down in all the confusing nomenclature. Instead, continually ask members what they mean when they use obscure terms. By doing so you might be helping them see beyond Hubbard's sci-fi fantasy world and regain contact with the real world outside the Church of Scientology.

CHRISTIAN CRITIQUE: The Bible teaches that humanity is sinful, but Scientology teaches that we are sinless and good. This tenet is consistent with the Dianetic belief that man is descended from the gods and may someday evolve to reclaim his thetan potential. Still, Scientology teaches that people aren't quite good enough; rather, they need the church's training to achieve real freedom.

Scientology also claims to support religious freedom, but such freedom often applies only to its members. Ex-Scientologist Jon Atack is one of the most insightful critics of the group. In his book, *A Piece of Blue Sky*, he discussed its animosity for Christianity:

> Despite its claims to be nondenominational, and to welcome members of all religions, Scientology is essentially anti-Christian. In confidential

materials Hubbard attacked Christianity as an "implant," and said that Christ was a fiction. He railed against "priests." . . . . Certain basic Christian values are despised by the Scientologist, who considers them misconceived. Humility is supplanted by self-pride. Searching self-criticism is considered dangerous. . . . Material wealth is a virtue. Charity creates dependence. In Scientology, there is no concept of God, nor of grace. The Scientologist is in every respect a self-made Thetan.

Hubbard claimed that his teachings were compatible with Christianity, but he also declared Dianetics to be "the spiritual heir of Buddhism in the Western world." The regal, thirty-room mansion and fifty-seven-acre estate the church occupies in England symbolize Scientology's success on earth. But Christians who are preparing for life after death feel a sense of compassionate concern for those who fruitlessly search for meaning in nonexistent past lives.

Other questionable doctrines and practices include astral travel, regression to past lives, and the "urge toward existence as spirits."

ACCESS: Scientology's world headquarters and its Celebrity Centre are in Los Angeles. The group also has a major presence in Clearwater, Florida, where many of its highest-level courses are offered. There are offices in many cities, where free personality tests are offered as a way of introducing people to the group.

SOURCES: Richard Behar, "Scientology: The Cult of Greed," *Time*, 6 May 1991; Ronald DeWolf, *Madman or Messiah?* (Secaucus, N.J.: Lyle Stuart Inc., 1987); Jody Veekner with Steve Rabey, "Building Scientopolis: How Scientology Remade Clearwater, Florida—and What Local Christians Learned in the Process," *Christianity Today*, 4 September 2000.

SELF-REALIZATION FELLOWSHIP

Paramahansa Yogananda

Though he died half a century ago, this Indian guru was a pioneer in the movement to meld Eastern philosopy and Western society.

"Aims and Ideals of Self-Realization Fellowship"

To disseminate among the nations a knowledge of definite scientific techniques for attaining direct personal experience of God.

To teach that the purpose of life is the evolution, through self-effort, of man's limited moral consciousness into God Consciousness; and to this end to establish Self-Realization Fellowship temples for God-communion throughout the world, and to encourage the establishment of individual temples of God in the homes and in the hearts of men.

To reveal the complete harmony and basic oneness of original Christianity as taught by Jesus Christ and original Yoga as taught by Bhagavan Krishna; and to show that these principles of truth are the common scientific foundation of all true religions.

To point out the divine highway to which all paths of true religious beliefs eventually lead: the highway of daily, scientific, devotional meditation on God.

To liberate man from his threefold suffering: physical disease, mental inharmonies, and spiritual ignorance.

To encourage "plain living and high thinking"; and to spread a spirit of brotherhood among all peoples by teaching the eternal basis of their unity: kinship with God.

To demonstrate the superiority of mind over body, of soul over mind.

To overcome evil by good, sorrow by joy, cruelty by kindness, ignorance by wisdom.

To unite science and religion through realization of the unity of their underlying principles.

To advocate cultural and spiritual understanding between East and West, and the exchange of their finest distinctive features.

To serve mankind as one's larger Self.

PARAMAHANSA YOGANANDA

OVERVIEW: If Paramahansa Yogananda (whose names mean "highest swan" and "bliss through divine union") were alive today with access to the media, he would be one of the most popular Eastern gurus.

Had he not died in 1952 after founding the Self-Realization Fellowship (SRF), the thousands of worldwide adherents of the SRF might be part of a much larger company of devotees.

Yogananda came to the United States in 1920 to address the International Congress of Religious Liberals. His subsequent lectures across America attracted a wide following out of which he formed the SRF in 1935. The appeal of SRF teaching is essentially Hindu, with the "realization" of God coming when one achieves "cosmic consciousness." To arrive at this state, one must pursue yogic disciplines, including exercises, daily meditation, and abstinence from meat and alcohol.

The foremost practice facilitating transcendence beyond the illusory material world is *Kriya Yoga,* described as a "highly scientific technique for the control of subtle life currents."

As a Hindu Yogananda taught that "cosmic consciousness" could ordinarily be attained only after a million years of reincarnations. With Kriya Yoga, the same results can be obtained in only three years with "intelligent self-effort." As a benefit the SRF devotee "is gradually freed from *karma* or the lawful chain of cause-effects equilibriums."

Yogananda boasted that thirty seconds of Kriya Yoga "equals one year of natural spiritual unfoldment." In addition, this esoteric mastery of breath control promises "continuous oxygenation of the blood . . . enabling the heart to become quiet."

SRF also teaches that it presents a truer message of Christianity than is found in churches. Christians need to be concerned about such claims, since SRF teaches a Westernized version of Hinduism that has little compatibility with orthodox Christianity.

Still, it is clear that the group's token appreciation of Christianity has added to its appeal in the West. As Yogananda once said, "Change yourself and you have done your part in changing the world. Every individual must change his own life if he wants to live in a peaceful world. The world cannot become peaceful unless and until you yourself begin to work toward peace. It is only by removing hate from our hearts that we can live a Christlike life."

In addition, SRF received valuable endorsements from former Beatle George Harrison, who was a life-long supporter of the group. After Harrison's death in 2002, the estate of the guitarist and so-called "spiritual Beatle" donated the proceeds from a reissued version of the song "My Sweet Lord" to SRF.

As a testimony to the Yogananda's application of Kriya Yoga, SRF officials report that "even 20 days after death, Paramahansa Yogananda's body was apparently devoid of impurities." Whatever the state of his corpse, his teaching did not alter the finality of death.

SOURCES: "Harrison Still Giving to Charity," *Rolling Stone*, 14 February 2002, 24; Paramanhansa Yogananda, *Autobiography of a Yogi* (Los Angeles: Self-Realization Fellowship, 1972); *People*, 6 October 1975; *Undreamed-of Possibilities* (Los Angeles: Self-Realization Fellowship, 1971).

ACCESS: Self-Realization Fellowship, 3880 San Rafael Ave., Los Angeles, CA 90065. Other groups started by SRF disciples include the Self Realization Church of Absolute Monism, the Temple of Kriya Yoga, and the International Church of Ageless Wisdom.

SETH

See Trance Channeling.

SHINTO

Closely linked to its native Japan, this ancient faith is shrouded in legend and secrecy while exerting powerful influence on the political life of a modern, technocratic society.

Let us be grateful for Kami's grace and ancestors' benevolence, and with bright and sincere heart, perform religious services.
THE GENERAL PRINCIPLES OF SHINTO LIFE, 1956

OVERVIEW: When Japan's emperor Hirohito died in the late 1980s, the world was able to see portions of a secretive ritual that had not been performed in more than half a century.

After the emperor's death, his son, Crown Prince Akihito, was expected to observe a year-long period of mourning. Then, according to an article in *Time* magazine, ancient Shinto ceremonies were performed: "Wearing white silks and a plumed headdress, Akihito will dish out food for his numerous 'guests'—Japan's 8 million kami, or gods. Then he will retreat behind a screen, where the spirit of the sun goddess will invite him to enter her womb. When he emerges, according to Shinto belief, he will no longer be an ordinary human. He will be the living embodiment of Ninigi-no-mi-koto, the god of the ripened rice plant—and the newly deified emperor of Japan."

For many Westerners, such rituals seemed like a strange way to do both religion and politics. But for the Japanese, who have observed Shinto rituals for centuries, the ceremonies surrounding the transition of power made perfect sense.

Gods and Shrines

Shinto comes from the Chinese word *Shen-tao,* which means "the way of the gods." People who practice Shinto believe the rituals they follow connect them with the gods that have inhabited Japan's islands since the dawn of time.

Unlike Buddhism, Islam, or Christianity, which each had founders who articulated their faith's key teachings, Shinto arose gradually over a series of centuries as ancient mythical traditions were finally codified in the eighteenth century.

Prior to this, people engaged in a variety of localized religious rituals. Shinto brought some order and uniformity to this diversity. And while there are no revealed scriptures, two books are considered sacred: *Ko-ji-ki,* the "records of ancient matters," and *Nihongi,* the "chronicles of Japan."

A major focus of Shinto rituals is the worship of *kami,* a term which refers to things believed to be sacred and pure, including local gods and forces of creation, local natural features such as sacred mountains and rivers, and Japan's emperors.

In the nineteenth century, the Japanese emperor was restored and Shinto became a state religion. But after the Japanese defeat in World War II, Western powers demanded that the emperor renounce any claim to divinity and that Japan cease to support Shinto as a state religion. While this led to a diminishing of observance of Shinto, the faith still remains strong in Japan.

Since it lost its status as a state religion, Shinto has been just one of many spiritual options available to the Japanese people. Today, the practice of ancient Shinto rituals happens mainly at local shrines, often in conjunction with the observation of seasonal holidays associated with agriculture (such as spring planting, fall harvesting, etc.). These connections to the natural world are a fundamental aspect of Shintoism, which teaches that Japan's islands were the first part of the world to be created.

There is a grand imperial shrine located at Ise, which is two hundred miles southwest of Tokyo. But even though this is the most sacred spot in all of Japan, there is little emphasis on people making pilgrimages there.

With 30 million adherents and more than a dozen sects, this three-thousand-year-old religion still holds fearful power over many in Asia. Known as "the way of the spirits," state Shinto still wields control in governmental matters and the daily life of millions in Japan. Devotion to the Kami may be hard for Westerners to understand, but to the faithful, these forces must be constantly appeased with food, water, and incense on a daily basis.

Shintoism not only errs in its embrace of potentially demonic forces in the name of the Kami, but as a religious system it differs from Christianity in its view of humanity's condition. We are not, in Shintoism, the result of a divine creation by a God who exists and whose Son came here in the form of a human to reconcile us. We are, instead, an extension of and part of nature, just as the sun, moon, wind, trees, and mountains. Indeed, Shinto holds sacred those things in which there is no animation.

CHRISTIAN CRITIQUE: Since Shinto literally means "the way of the gods (Kami)," the Christian critic understandably wants to know what gods are worshiped. There are many gods in Shintoism, but supreme is the Sun-God, the Anaterasu-omi Kami. He is one of three in a divine triad, quite obviously a perversion of the Christian Holy Trinity. Like in the Judeo-Christian tradition, there are ten commandments, or precepts, guiding the daily lives of those who follow the Shinto way. But unlike the ardent moral quantification of Mosaic law, Shinto's demands are more akin to moral suggestions than divine revelation. What is clearly missing when compared with biblical faith are specific prohibitions of sexual, social, and religious conduct. "Do not forget that the world is one great family" is the closest that Shintoism comes to a Christian ethic.

Most telling of Shinto's unorthodoxy is a proverbial Shinto saying: "The first and surest means to enter into communion with the Divine is sincerity. If you pray to a deity with sincerity, you will surely feel the divine presence." The Bible, by contrast, warns that "Satan himself is transformed into an angel of light" (2 Corinthians 11:14).

Perhaps even more serious evidence against the group is Shinto's unsavory past, which includes affiliation with sorcery, divination, ritualism, and magic. Even though Shinto has no congregational worship or coherent theology, these occult aspects are enough of a warning to avoid its lure.

SOURCES: Harry Anderson with Bradley Martin and Rich Thomas, "Japan's Sacred Rice God: An Ancient Ritual and a Modern Trade Dispute," *Newsweek*, 17 October 1988, 48.

ACCESS: International Shinto Foundation, New York Center, 777 United Nations Plaza, Suite WCRP-9A, New York, NY 10017; Tenrikyo Mission Headquarters in America, 2727 E. First Street, Los Angeles, CA 90033

SIKH DHARMA

3HO Foundation; Yogi Bhajan

This offshoot group of the Sikh faith has spread around the world and generated considerable criticism for alleged sexual indiscretions.

FOUNDER: Yogi Bhajan

OVERVIEW: His full name is Siri Singh Sahib Bhai Sahib Harbhajan Singh Khalsa Yogiji, which he understandably shortened to Yogi Bhajan. As one of the popularizers of this offshoot of the Sikh faith, he came to America in 1969, where he has encountered both praise and problems.

He has been accused of being a womanizer, demanding group massages from female attendants with whom he takes turns sleeping. The charges stem in part from his mystical view of sex, which he teaches in the *tantric* tradition.

In fact, Yogi Bhajan claims to be the "only living master of *tantrism*." More than five thousand followers (he claims 250,000) have joined his nearly 140 Sikh Dharma U.S. *ashrams*. Bhajan's disciples arise at 3:30 A.M. for a day of meditation and to practice *Kundalini Yoga*. This system of yoga is supposed to be a simplified way of attaining spiritual enlightenment by releasing energy that travels up the spine.

Another title claimed by Yogi Bhajan is Supreme Religious and Administrative Authority of the Sikh Religion in the Western Hemisphere. Sikhism (see separate entry) is a monotheistic faith combining elements of Hinduism and Islam and seeking God-realization through meditation.

Indian Sikh officials aren't so certain that Yogi Bhajan, a once obscure Delhi airport customs officer, deserves to be the leader of Western Sikhism, "the holiest man of this era." They view with suspicion his luxurious ways (e.g., the over $100,000 a year he spends in lecture fees).

The manner in which the democratic principles of Sikhism are merged with the autocratic, sexually explicit style of Bhajan's 3HO (Healthy, Happy, Holy) Foundation is looked upon with equal skepticism.

In addition to indulging in nude massages and rapid breathing techniques, couples are instructed to stare into each other's eyes (or at a picture of Bhajan) while chanting *Ek Ong Kar Sat Nam Siri Wha Guru*, the repetition of God's name in a "sacred" language.

Though yoga has never been an essential practice of Sikhism, Bhajan insists that for his disciples to experience the "infinity of God," they must position their arms and fingers in precisely patterned angles.

"The man who ties a turban on his head must live up to the purity of the whiteness and radiance of his soul," Bhajan proclaims from his forty-acre ranch near Espanola, New Mexico.

The traditional Sikh symbols are uncut hair, symbolic daggers, combs, bracelets, and special chastity underwear (these are the "five Ks" discussed in greater detail under "Hinduism"). Critics wonder if Bhajan may have eliminated this special garment, which ensures moral purity, in his zealous pursuit of tantrism.

SOURCES: *Columbus (Ohio) Dispatch,* 12 December 1978; Mary Frei, "Former Sikhs Tell Why They Left New Mexico Religious Commune," *Journal North (Albuquerque),* 9 February 1984; J. Gordon Melton, *The Encyclopedia of American Religions,* vol. 2 (Wilmington, N.C.: McGrath, 1978); *Newsweek,* 21 April 1975; *Time,* 5 September 1977, 34–35.

ACCESS: Sikh Dharma, Box 35330, Los Angeles, CA 90035

SIKHISM

Founded five hundred years ago in India, the Sikh faith
has many disciples in the West.

OVERVIEW: You can understand the elementary school teacher's concern. During a basketball game on a playground in Livingston, California, a fifth grader jumped up to shoot a basket. There was nothing unusual about that. What surprised the teacher was that under his shirt the boy was wearing a small dagger in a sheath.

After being sent to the principal's office, the student explained. The dagger is a sacred symbol to the Sikh religion—much like a cross is to Christians. It cannot be removed, even while bathing. It symbolizes the Sikh faith's teaching that people must defend the weak and the oppressed.

"It's not a weapon," said the student's mother. "It's a sacred symbol."

When this event caught national attention in 1994, few Americans had ever heard of the Sikh religion. But now, with more than 250,000 Sikhs in the United States, more people are hearing about this exotic faith every day. Pop star Shania Twain makes no secret of her devotion to Sant Mat, a strain of

Sikh mysticism that advocates hours of daily meditation and lengthy journal keeping as the path to self-realization.

And thanks to U.S. laws and court decisions, many Sikh students are now permitted to wear their sacred daggers when they attend school—in spite of post-Columbine fears about student violence.

A Historic Indian Faith

Sikhism originated five centuries ago in the Punjab region of northern India. The Indian city Amritsar is still the sacred headquarters of the faith, which claims nearly 20 million adherents in India.

The Sikh tradition began with a teacher named Guru Nanak (1469–1539), a saint and poet who preached about the need for loving devotion to God at a time when growing numbers of Muslims were present in a traditionally Hindu area. He taught about a God who was formless and nonanthropomorphic. Technically, Sikhism is monotheistic, but its ideas about God differ significantly from Christian teaching.

Guru Nanak recruited a small group of disciples who studied his teaching and meditated on the divine name (Punjabi Nam). Anyone who did this was called a *sikh*.

After Guru Nanak's death the movement split, but in the eighteenth and nineteenth centuries the faith was helped by a series of Sikh princes and military commanders who made Sikhism an unofficial state religion. This secular support ended with the British victory in the first Anglo-Sikh war, which gave the British control of the Punjab region.

Now the Sikh faith had to find other ways to grow, which it did through a series of reform movements. The most influential of these movements was the Singh Sabha, which developed an effective response to Christian missionaries who were stepping up their work in the Punjab.

The Singh Sabha transformed a formerly informal faith into a well-organized and theologically defined movement that helped Sikhism spread in the twentieth century. But the process hasn't always been peaceful. After Sikhs were denied the opportunity to create an independent Sikh homeland in Khalistan, a militant movement within the faith was attacked by the Indian army. The militants responded by assassinating Indian prime minister Indira Gandhi in 1984.

Through such acts, Sikhs have attempted to show that they are distinct from India's predominant Hindu faith. But in fact, Sikh teaching resembles Hinduism in many ways.

Sikh Teaching

Like many Hindus and Buddhists, Sikhs believe in the concept of karma and the idea of reincarnation. Through many successive incarnations, a soul can achieve spiritual merit and escape the veil of *maya*, or "illusion," which keeps so many people shrouded in spiritual darkness.

God is one (not many, as in Hinduism) and is the creator of the cosmos. But this God cannot be perceived in human or any other form. Instead, God is understood as supreme guru, and only God's name *(Nam)* can be understood by those who would seek to worship.

In order to escape the destructive effects of maya, Sikhs practice meditation, communal worship and concentration on the divine name to achieve more spiritual states of consciousness.

A group of strict Sikhs known as Khalsa saints devoutly follow a code of behavior known as "the Five Ks," which are:
1. *kesa* (or uncut hair coiled underneath a turban)
2. *kangha* (a ceremonial comb for the hair)
3. *kacha* (specialized short pants)
4. *kachu* (a unique metal bracelet)
5. *kirpan* (a sacred sword)

As with Hinduism, Sikhism is a religion that denies the inherent sinfulness of humanity. God is within each person—"deep within the self," as Guru Amar Das has said. But Sikhism is more codified than Hinduism. According to the Sikh Code of Conduct, a true follower is "any human being who faithfully believes in: (i) One Immortal Being, (ii) Ten Gurus, from Guru Nanak Dev to Guru Gobind Singh, (iii) The Guru Granth Sahib, (iv) The utterances and teachings of the ten Gurus and, (v) the baptism bequeathed by the tenth Guru, and who does not owe allegiance to any other religion." It also departs from Hinduism and Islam by declaring that rituals, pilgrimages, and idols are forbidden.

CHRISTIAN CRITIQUE: The most critical belief of Sikhism contradicts Christianity by adopting a universalistic belief that God is the same God for all religions and that cycles of births and deaths are necessary to merge with the godhead. Sikhism can have no accommodation with Christianity, which teaches an incarnated Savior. Sikhs are adamant that "God cannot take human form. He neither has father, nor mother, nor sons nor brothers." Sikhism is also a religion of works, not grace: "The five cardinal vices are: Kam (lust), Krodh (anger), Lobh (greed), Moh (worldly attachment) and Ahankar (pride). If one can overcome these, they will achieve salvation."

SOURCES: Carol J. Castaneda, "Sacred Blade at Heart of School Dispute," *USA Today*, 11 August 1994, 2A; Jonathan Z. Smith, ed., *The HarperCollins Dictionary of Religion* (San Francisco: HarperSanFrancisco, 1995); *Time*, 9 December 2002.

ACCESS: Sikh Council of North America, 95-30 118th St., Richmond Hill, NY 11419

SILVA INTERNATIONAL

Silva Methods; Silva Mind Control

Change your life in forty-eight hours? That's the unsupported promise this group makes for the power of mind over matter that it offers.

FOUNDER: Jose Silva

OVERVIEW: The introductory lectures certainly seem harmless enough. And the come-on is directly to the point: "In 48 hours you can learn to use your mind to do *anything* you wish."

That "anything" presumably includes waking up without clocks, increasing powers of memory, improving creativity, solving problems, and developing ESP.

The Silva Basic Lecture Series, offered by Texas-based Silva International (formerly Silva Mind Control) is the brainchild of Jose Silva, a Laredo, Texas, hypnotist who began mental experiments in 1944.

His investigations were based on the assumption that the mind can generate more energy and function more effectively at a lower, "subjective" state of brain wave frequency. Silva proposes to teach the student how to maintain alert consciousness while deriving the supposed benefits of deeper states of consciousness.

Alphagenics, the science of investigating and measuring brain waves, has classified four levels of consciousness: *beta,* the waking state of conscious actions; *alpha,* the state of relaxation and meditation; and *delta* and *theta,* subtler levels of the mind that Silva Mind Control purports to unlock.

Proponents of Silva methods contend that at the delta level one has the capacity to achieve "cosmic awareness, enlightenment . . . Christ awareness." Such religious overtones are just part of the occultic, mystical nature of Jose Silva's techniques.

In recent years much attention has been given to the differences between the left and right sides of the brain. Silva, like other New Age cultists, claims that the right brain—the intuitive, "spiritual," feeling side—is too often neglected as we favor the left side, which is more rational and logical.

According to Silva, Jesus came to free us from our left-brain fixation and teach us the value of our God-given, right-brain abilities. Silva sees himself as one of the fortunate "10 percenters," the 10 percent of the population who can effectively use both brain hemispheres. This is an interesting example of combining recent scientific findings—although the left-brain/right-brain dichotomy is still questioned by many scientists—with religious teaching to give Silva International the feel of being hip and relevant.

Most people who are attracted by Silva's glowing prospects see no harm in quietly listening to a prerecorded cassette that features a soothing voice giving instructions on how to relax. I have had the opportunity to attend public presentations promoting Silva's methods. These sessions make no attempt to obscure the close association that "psychorientology" has with practices such as hypnosis, yoga, TM, biofeedback, and various paranormal phenomena. At one such meeting I watched a promotional film that likened Silva's techniques to the powers exercised by spiritualistic mediums. Most people are apparently more fascinated than frightened by such associations.

Millions of people in more than one hundred countries have plunked down hundreds of dollars each to embark on the forty-eight-hour-long course. (Advanced courses offer intense involvement in occult practices.) These people have responded to the Silva Method appeal, which promised to teach them how to stop smoking, sleep without medication, awake without alarm clocks, relax, relieve nervousness, improve memory and creativity, use dreams to detect information to solve problems, and develop true ESP.

Silva lectures openly court the development of extrasensory and clairvoyant powers. Students are also taught that dilemmas in life can be solved by mentally visualizing a "laboratory." Once this fantasized room has been "furnished," the subject is told to mentally solicit "laboratory technicians" (counselors). Sometimes Silva parlance refers to these assistants as "spirit guides" or "guardian angels." Christians can hardly feel comfortable with the close parallel such "counselors" have to the spiritistic phenomenon of demonic manifestations.

Silva lectures also take over where positive thinker Norman Vincent Peale leaves off, adding a dash of Christian Science as the clincher. Negative thoughts are forbidden in favor of positive perceptions, which, according to Silva, actually have the power to alter reality.

But these "positive beneficial phrases" may become a system of salvation by works, since the illusion of evil need only be negated by merely pronouncing it out of existence. Thus, the methodology of the Silva lectures becomes a mental exercise more suited for manipulation by visualized "counselors" than by a suffering Savior.

SOURCES: Walter Martin, *The New Cults* (Santa Ana, Calif.: Vision House, 1980); Javier Rodriguez, "Wired for Success," *Denver Post*, 20 August 1989; Jose Silva and Philip Miele, *The Silva Mind Control Method* (New York: Simon and Schuster, 1977); Silva International, various publications and promotional literature.

ACCESS: Silva International, Inc., P.O. Box 2249, 1407 Calle del Norte, Laredo, Texas 78044-2249

See also New Age Movement, est, and The Forum.

SNAKE HANDLERS

They risk their lives in the name of Jesus, but does Christ really require his followers to perform deadly deeds as a proof of faith, or are such foolhardy actions the work of the devil?

FOUNDER: George Hensley, Holiness circuit preacher who in 1909 started snake handling in Tennessee and died of a snakebite in 1955

TEXT: Snake handlers' faith is based on Mark 16:17-18 of the King James Version of the Bible, which reads, "These signs shall follow them that believe; In my name shall they cast out devils. . . . They shall take up serpents; and if they drink any deadly thing, it shall not hurt them."

SYMBOLS: The snakes symbolize danger, which, when conquered, earns approval from God. Strychnine symbolizes the harmful drink spoken of in Scripture. If a person drinks it successfully, the favor of God is bestowed on him.

APPEAL: The snake-handling churches appeal to people living in austere rural areas, people who are forbidden popular entertainment or glamour. Those attracted to snake handling are the devout who feel the need to publicly demonstrate their faith by participating in a dangerous ceremony.

OVERVIEW: Bearing a deadly diamondback rattlesnake on his shoulders, a man known as Prince performs a religious dance in Jesus' name at the Holiness Church of God. He steps on a second dangerous snake with his bare right foot. With his other foot, he rakes the squirming ends of the snake as the clatter of the creature ensues. Oblivious to the bleeding wound on his hand, Prince steadily chants, "Praise the Lord" with mounting fervor.

Prince then returns the snakes to their boxes and walks behind the church's pulpit. He lifts a jar of liquid he claims is laced with strychnine to his lips and takes a gulp. Next he picks up a soft drink bottle filled with flammable liquid. The wick is lit, and Prince deliberately holds its fiery flames under his chin. Like other snake handlers, Prince believes dancing with snakes, drinking poisonous substances, and exposing his flesh to fire will provide eternal life.

But Prince found an early death instead of everlasting life. He was arrested for violating a North Carolina law against handling snakes. He defied authorities and continued to conduct religious services with the slithering serpents. Bitten on the thumb by a rattlesnake in Tennessee, Prince refused medical attention and died two days later. Other snake handlers have died as a result of their dangerous practices.

The Reverend Liston Pack witnessed two deaths in his church. Pack and his fellow Holiness Church of God members meet each week to pray, handle snakes, and drink strychnine. Known as the "Snake Man" in eastern Tennessee, Pack claims his faith in his religion was shaken only once. That was in 1973 when he watched his brother, Buford Pack, and the church's founder, Jimmy Williams, die writhing in pain after drinking strychnine. The incident only temporarily shook his faith, and he continued to handle snakes and drink strychnine.

Snake handling is practiced primarily in rural areas from Georgia to Ohio among congregations of independent, fundamentalist churches that often adhere to "Jesus only" doctrines. The practice is prevalent in the Appalachian hills of West Virginia, and it started in 1909 when George Hensley, a Holiness circuit preacher, began the practice of snake handling in Tennessee. Hensley died in 1955 of snakebite, but the ritual of snake handling lives on.

The Jesus Church at Micco, West Virginia, is a center for snake handling, strychnine-drinking worshipers, who take their biblical support from Mark 16:17-18 of the King James Version of the Bible. Their faith is based on a stone-cold reading of the words, "If they drink any deadly thing, it shall not hurt them," which is why the group drinks strychnine. They also interpret the words "They shall take up serpents" to mean they must handle poisonous snakes.

Snake handlers sing a song called "I Know the Bible's Right, Somebody's Wrong" as live rattlesnakes clatter in their clutches. These mountain people engage in ceremonies that last for hours and intensify in volume and emotion. The music and rhythmic clapping of hundreds of hands creates a religious fervor of enormous magnitude. The people jerk involuntarily, as if possessed.

Snake handlers raise their arms high and cry out Jesus' name as serpents glide everywhere. Then they pick up Eastern diamondbacks and timber rattlers and copperheads and dance with them. The idea behind the practice is that true faith in God protects believers from harm.

A middle-aged man with neatly combed hair holding two thick rattlesnakes in his hand explained, "The Lord told us what we could do, and that's exactly what we're doing." He and others believe snakes won't bite them and that successfully handling the venomous reptiles yields religious power and the approval of God. After the ceremony, the congregation gathers around a table spread with food.

Beyond handling serpents and fire and drinking harmful substances, snake handlers believe in casting out devils, speaking in tongues, and laying hands on the sick. An anointing or blessing ceremony is performed during religious services to protect the snake handlers from being bitten.

Says one handler of the blessing, "When I get anointed, I get numb all over." When members feel the anointing start to break, they put the snakes down.

One snake handler, Dewey Chafin, has been bitten ninety-one times.

Most other snake handlers have been bitten several times. Those who are bitten refuse medical treatment, believing the matter is in God's hands. They maintain that God has more power to heal than doctors. Sometimes they triumph over the poison. Other times they die.

A snakebite is not viewed as a sign of sin or punishment. According to one advocate, "That's just the way God wants it. This is a suffering life, and you have to suffer if you want to reign with him."

This philosophy conflicts with the Christian belief that God can work through people in the medical profession. Self-inflicted suffering is not commanded by God, as snake handlers believe. Snake handlers presumably play a game that leads many to disillusionment and death.

Some snake handlers may turn to their church's strange worship to offset their austere lives in a region that was economically devastated by the coal industry's demise. Their church provides the guidelines and structure by which they live their legalistic and rigid lives. The church strictly forbids seeing movies, smoking and chewing tobacco, women wearing makeup, and men growing beards or long hair. The monotony of their lives can be broken by flirting with death under the guise of religion. Handling poisonous snakes permits them to release energy and feel alive.

Snake handlers claim they don't worship serpents. Yet the poisonous snakes are treated with the utmost reverence and respect, housed in the homes of church members and well fed. The snakes are carefully returned to their natural habitats in the fall. Explains Bishop Kelly Williams of the Micco Jesus Church, "Snakes, too, have the right to live. God gave it to them."

The pastor of a Tennessee snake-handling church also denies reverence for the reptiles. He speaks of God's role in the practice. Says the reverend, "I never test my faith. I am as afraid as you are of snakes, but perfect love casts out fear, and when you overcome fear you can pick up the serpent."

His philosophy strays from Christian theology because God does not ask anyone to jeopardize life in order to obtain God's love. Dancing with poisonous snakes and drinking strychnine is no way to worship God. It's radical cult behavior that can result in a death that parallels suicide.

Some snake handlers allow their young children to handle snakes too, which could end in fatality. In such cases, the snake handlers would be committing murder. Junior Church, a snake handler, permits his children to handle snakes. He asserts, "I'd rather lose a child now and have it go to heaven than keep it 100 years and have it go to hell."

CHRISTIAN CRITIQUE: The practice of this religion involves struggling rural people manipulating deadly serpents because of what they falsely believe to be a biblical mandate. If they can handle the snakes, they've overcome the weakness of fear and find favor in God's eyes.

But God doesn't ask us to put ourselves in danger or endure self-inflicted suffering to win his approval. Snake handlers misinterpret the Bible to create danger and excitement in their lives. Jesus told the Devil, "Thou shalt not tempt the Lord thy God" (Matthew 4:7), a prohibition against Christians taking part in such life-threatening activities.

SOURCES: Associated Press, "Deadly Snakes Slither Their Way into Fundamentalist Ritual," *The Tampa Tribune-Times*, 6 December 1998, 19; *Charisma*, October 1985, 102; *Christianity Today*, 12 July 1985, 56; Dennis Covington, *Salvation on Sand Mountain: Snake Handling and Redemption in Southern Appalachia* (Reading, Mass.: Addison-Wesley, 1995); *Denver Post*, 15 July 1977, 8BB; *Phoenix Gazette*, 29 December 1984, D3; *Rocky Mountain News*, 27 October 1982, 50; *US*, 18 July 1983, 35.

SPIRITUALISM AND SPIRITISM

Communing with the dead, which is prohibited in the Bible, is a pop-culture craze today, with assorted psychics claiming the ability to transmit information from "the other side."

FOUNDER: Spiritualism is the outgrowth of Spiritism, a universal pagan practice outside the Judeo-Christian tradition. The National Spiritualistic Association of Churches, the oldest and largest of Spiritualistic bodies, was formed in 1893. Also prominent among the nearly twenty Spiritualist denominations are the International General Assembly of Spiritualists and the National Spiritual Alliance of the U.S.A. Hard-core membership of Spiritualist churches probably numbers less than ten thousand, though church officials estimate there are more than a half million adherents.

TEXTS: Books by Andrew Jackson Davis, as well as *Oahspe* by John Newbrough and the *Aquarian Gospel of Jesus the Christ* by Levi Dowling. Shirley MacLaine's many best-sellers, including *Dancing in the Light*, *It's All in the Playing*, and *Going Within* are popular examples of how Spiritualism finds expression in the New Age movement.

SYMBOLS: The Spiritualist creed, affirming "the belief in personal survival of death, which can be demonstrated by mediumship."

451

APPEAL: Spiritualism capitalizes on the distraught emotions of those who have suffered the loss of loved ones and desire to communicate with them after death. The spirits that are contacted may offer to reveal the past, prophesy the future, and divulge spiritual "truths." The bereaved, the curious, and those fascinated by the paranormal may be enticed to experience the apparent proof of an afterlife.

OVERVIEW: The daily, half-hour TV show is a cross between *Oprah* and backroom palm reading. It's called *Crossing Over with John Edward,* and it is seen by millions of viewers all over the country. *The New York Times* calls the program "a new genre of television: the psychic talk show."

During the show, host John Edward is both tough and tender as he calls out to members of his studio audience, presumably with messages from their dead loved ones.

"Does 'Dr. Zhivago' have any meaning to you?" he asks audience members.

"Somebody in your family is a very heavy smoker," he says to another.

When audience members respond to such clues, he sits down next to them and begins giving further clues from "the other side." Many of Edward's comments miss their target, but occasionally he says something that brings audience members to tears.

One time he asked an audience member if their departed loved one ever told a joke about celery. No, but there was an onion joke once, and that was close enough for Edward, who will spend fifteen minutes on a single person if he is making a connection and the encounter is providing good entertainment for the home viewing audience.

Welcome to the new world of spiritualism—when TV talk-show hosts claim to commune with the dead while the cameras roll.

Seeking Solace

The methods may be novel, but there's nothing new about spiritualism, an ancient practice that is condemned in the Bible. I once visited with a woman who claimed to be an evangelical Christian and also claimed she had communed with the spirit of Elvis. When I expressed doubt about this, she responded with absolute certainty: "But it is Elvis! I was his fan for years. I know his voice and mannerisms. I'm telling you, it is Elvis Presley who comes to see me at night."

Before Elvis Presley's death in 1977, this woman had idolized him. When he died, it was as though a loved one had passed away. Now, she felt comforted thinking that his spirit was reappearing to console her in her grief.

"I don't believe it's a masquerading demon," she insisted. "Elvis always tells me to worship God. He just talks to me, touches me, and assures me that he's gone to be with Jesus." It was no small task to convince her that whatever was appearing to her had nothing to do with the person or spirit of Elvis Presley.

Though her situation was unique, I have counseled scores of individuals who feel they are communicating with the actual presence of a departed friend or relative. In a time of sorrow and confusion, they are tempted to look past death's veil for some seemingly objective "proof" that those for whom they grieve continue their existence in another realm. Occurrences of communicating with the dead seem to "confirm" for those left behind that they will eventually be reunited with their loved ones. These occurrences also supposedly provide information about life beyond the grave.

A Recurring Fascination

After a period of decline due to the onslaught of scientific rationalism, Spiritualism is once again on the rise. Our post-Christian age has produced a biblically illiterate populace unaware of Scripture's stern denunciations of attempting to seek knowledge or comfort by contacting the spirit world.

Such conduct in Old Testament times was punishable by exile or death (see Leviticus 20:6, 27). Today these laws are seen only as the unenlightened injunctions of a theocratic state. In the 1970s the late Arthur Ford, a Disciples of Christ minister, served as a medium to perform seances on live television. Episcopal bishop James A. Pike endorsed Ford's blasphemy by seeking to contact his son, who had committed suicide while on LSD. Pike wrote a best-selling book, *The Other Side,* which explored his burgeoning fascination with paranormal realities. Pike's ecclesiastical superiors neither censored nor defrocked the bishop for daring to attempt what cost King Saul his kingdom and his life (see 1 Chronicles 10:13)!

The Oldest Religion?

Spiritualism and Spiritism may be humankind's oldest religions. From the shamans of primitive cultures and the seers of ancient paganism to the psychics who frequent today's TV talk shows, these religions have a history in almost every culture.

In the strictest sense of the term, *Spiritism* is the overt worship of spirit beings, exemplified by voodoo practitioners in Haiti, macumba devotees in Brazil, and black-magic advocates in Africa. *Spiritualism,* on the other hand, generally refers to activities designed to contact the dead and is consistent with the practice of necromancy.

However, since any form of contact with spirit beings results in a deeply felt sense of devotion, obeisance, and honor for these entities, there is little real difference between Spiritism and Spiritualism. So for practical purposes, any technical semantic distinctions will be ignored in this entry. The term *Spiritualism* will be understood to also encompass the activities of most Spiritists, with the focus on organized Spiritualism as it exists in Western culture.

Psychic activity in the eighteenth century centered on the life and work of

Emanuel Swedenborg (see separate entry on Swedenborgianism), as well as the experiments of Franz Anton Mesmer. Mesmer's investigations into hypnotism and magnetic healing sparked the interest of a shoemaker named Andrew Jackson Davis.

In 1843 Davis was hypnotized, and while in a trance he displayed clairvoyant abilities and experienced visions. He philosophized about a system containing six spheres of existence in the afterlife, through which humans progress upward. Davis's theories were explained in *Principles of Nature: A Divine Revelation* and *The Voice of Mankind*, books still revered by Spiritualists.

A more precise birthday of modern Spiritualism is March 31, 1848. The site was the residence of John Fox in Hydesville, New York, near Rochester. Mrs. Fox became aware of some strange rapping sounds emanating from upstairs and from the cellar. Mrs. Fox's two daughters, fifteen-year-old Margaretta and twelve-year-old Kate, claimed they were communicating with a disincarnate entity they called Mr. Splitfoot. Splitfoot informed them he was actually Charles B. Roena, a peddler who had been murdered in the house some years earlier. The sisters worked out a code (one tap meant no and three taps meant yes) with Splitfoot. Newspaperman Horace Greeley endorsed the "Rochester rappings," as they were called, and hundreds of curiosity-seekers descended on the Fox home.

All across the country and the world, other mediums began making similar claims, and Spiritualism entered its golden age. Advocates included such renowned figures as James Fenimore Cooper, Sir Arthur Conan Doyle, Elizabeth Barrett Browning, Daniel Webster, and William Cullen Bryant. It was even rumored that Abraham Lincoln's wife was holding seances in the White House.

In 1888 the Fox sisters confessed that the rappings were accomplished by a method of cracking their toes. (Margaretta, who had become an alcoholic and a convert to Roman Catholicism, later retracted her confession and was readmitted into Spiritualism's good graces.) Despite this damaging admission, the Fox home in modern Lilydale, New York, is still considered a mecca of Spiritualism and bears a shrine marker declaring, "There is no death."

Spiritualism was introduced to England and Germany in the 1850s; in the United States mediums flourished during the years 1880–1920. Today, according to the National Spiritualistic Association, there are nearly 150 churches in its membership in America.

Communicating with the Other Side

The essence of Spiritualism is talking with or receiving information from beings who have departed this life. Communication beyond the grave takes place at a seance. Interested parties gather in a darkened setting, since the entities are said to be less likely to appear if there is too much light or too many people.

They are even less likely to appear if some nonbelievers are present at the seance.

Ectoplasm, the foul-smelling, milky-white substance that exudes as an "umbilical cord" from the medium's mouth, is said to be an energy form that will not function properly without darkness. Since ectoplasm may be the essence out of which the *apparition* and/or *voice trumpet* (the video and audio of the spirit world) emanate, seances are always held in dimly lit surroundings.

What goes on at a seance is unpredictable, though certain occurrences are standard fare. As the participants sit quietly in a circle, lights may appear, ghosts may materialize, a trumpet may convey the message of disembodied speech, objects may levitate, and the medium may be taken over by a spirit *control* who answers the inquiries of those who have gathered.

The spirit guide, who generally is already known (*familiar*) to the medium, may control his subject's mind or subject the medium to a trance state. The voice and personality of the medium then change as the spirit imposes his will and character upon his vehicle of communication.

Mediums usually specialize in a particular type of spiritistic phenomenon. While a trance state is the type most commonly effected, others may use automatic handwriting, table tipping, or actual materializations. In the latter case, either facial or full bodily dimensions appear, and the spirit is often recognizable to someone at the seance.

This presumed visitation by a loved one seems incontrovertible proof of life after death, especially if the spirit relates information known only to the grieving participant.

Testing the Claims

What is the source of such eerie events? Some are unquestionably fraudulent. The contrived activities of magicians and hucksters have long been the nemesis of "respectable" Spiritualists. Swindlers have often preyed upon those who are bereaved and have staged seances for handsome fees. Henry Sedgwick, founder of the Psychical Research Society, which investigates the claims of supernaturalism, remained a skeptic until his death.

However, the history of Spiritualism presents too many bona fide claims to dismiss such evidence outright. Only the non-Biblicist who ignores the sorcery of Pharaoh's magicians (Exodus 7:11, 22) and the signs and wonders of the Antichrist (Revelation 13) would conclude that the feats described by the Spiritualists are beyond the realm of possibility.

Some researchers and certain Christian writers feel that some paranormal happenings at seances may be attributed to the extraordinary psychic abilities of the medium. It has been speculated that a universal subconscious mind exists and that certain highly skilled experts can plug into the information it contains, much like getting information out of a computer. Such ESP and telepathy may enable some mediums to draw knowledge out of the seeker's subconscious.

However, certain documented cases of seances exist where the information exchanged was beyond the realm of any conscious or unconscious ideation of those present. While it may be arguable that the spirit of man possesses latent, untapped powers, two things seem certain: First, God never condones or promotes the exploration of these powers, especially when telepathic phenomena violate the moral sovereignty of another person's mind. Second, most phenomena of Spiritualism seem to exist in a realm that defies naturalistic explanation and confounds the investigations made by scientists and parapsychologists. Most evangelical observers would acknowledge that some Spiritualists genuinely communicate with spirit beings. The serious student of the Bible believes such entities are fallen angels, the demonic emissaries of Satan's kingdom of darkness.

It should be noted that some Spiritualists claim there are biblical pretexts for their activities. The Transfiguration in Matthew 17 is viewed as an example of spirit materialization. Pentecost is said to have been "the greatest seance in history."

In fact, Spiritualists believe that Jesus was the master medium of all time. They hold that the stone was levitated from his tomb and that his own disincarnate entity materialized before the gaze of the disciples. One Spiritualistic writer suggests that "by a slight change of name, 'medium' for 'prophet,' 'clairvoyant' for 'discernment of spirits,' 'psychic phenomena' for 'miracles,' 'spirit lights' for 'tongues of fire,' the close affinity of the two systems [Spiritualism and biblical Christianity] becomes apparent to all sincere investigators and students."

Gordon Lewis, Christian apologist and cult expert, has observed that this word game "makes the Bible endorse what its writers emphatically opposed! The prophets received their messages, not from the spirits of the dead, but from God. Spirits were discerned (1 Corinthians 12:10), not by clairvoyant apprehension, but by their teaching of Jesus Christ (1 John 4:1-3). Biblical miracles, unlike Spiritualistic phenomena, took place in nature and in broad daylight. They served not to entertain nor comfort individuals, but to establish God's redemptive program."

Having discarded objective biblical truth on the basis of subjective, speculative spirit communication, Spiritualism has developed its own belief structure.

Though many Spiritualists prefer to consider themselves Christians, the National Spiritualistic Association of Churches officially decrees that Spiritualists are not Christians. (They also disavow any endorsement of belief in reincarnation.) That is to be expected since one of their spokesmen has declared, "Advanced spirits do not teach the atonement of Christ."

Seeking to mimic Christian forms of worship, Spiritualistic churches conduct services that resemble the church gatherings of most denominations. There are, however, some significant differences. Though furnishings may include a pulpit, pews, crucifix, and organ to accompany singing, members receive "spirit greetings" in place of the pastoral blessing. The presiding minister's sermon may be delivered while in a trance. Psychic readings replace prayer, and familiar hymns such as "Just As I Am" and "Holy, Holy, Holy" have subtle lyric changes to avoid affirming Christian doctrine.

Spiritualism is a system of theories based on whatever information has been supplied by spirit beings who range from the profane and blasphemous to the refined and intellectual. Over the years, organized Spiritualistic churches have codified their beliefs into "Seven Principles" and "Nine Articles." These doctrines are listed below, allowing Spiritualists to speak for themselves as to their view of God and spiritual realities:

Seven Principles
1. The Fatherhood of God;
2. The Brotherhood of Man;
3. Continuous Existence;
4. Communion of Spirits and Ministry of Angels;
5. Personal Responsibility;
6. Compensation and Retribution Hereafter for Good or Evil Done on Earth; and
7. A Path of Endless Progression.

Nine Articles
1. We believe in Infinite Intelligence.
2. We believe that the phenomena of Nature, both physical and spiritual, are the expression of Infinite Intelligence.
3. We affirm that a correct understanding of such expression and living in accordance therewith constitute true religion.
4. We affirm that the existence and personal identity of the individual continues after the change called death.
5. We affirm that communication with the so-called dead is a fact scientifically proven by the phenomena of Spiritualism.
6. We believe that the highest morality is contained in the Golden Rule: "Whatever ye would that others should do unto you, do ye unto them."
7. We affirm the moral responsibility of the individual and that he makes his own happiness or unhappiness as he obeys or disobeys Nature's physical and spiritual laws.
8. We affirm that the doorway to reformation is never closed against any human soul here or hereafter.

9. We affirm that the precept of Prophecy contained in the Bible is a divine attribute proven through Mediumship.

What the articles and principles do not tell about Spiritualist beliefs may be summarized in the following statements: Every human is a divine child of God, no less a part of the Infinite Intelligence than was Christ. There is no actual hell, no ultimate judgment of a human's life. The crucifixion of Jesus was no more than "an illustration of the martyr spirit." Original sin, miracles, and the Virgin Birth have no place in Spiritualism.

New Forms of an Old Technique

In recent years the older forms of Spiritualism—such as seances—have declined in favor of the newer and more entertaining forms. Author and medium James Van Praagh, whose book *Talking to Heaven* was a national best-seller, lectures huge crowds. Beginning with open-ended statements like "Someone here has lost a son," Van Praagh peppers his audiences with questions. He says he receives assistance from four spirit guides, but he's wrong as often as he's right. His devoted fans are very forgiving, but ABC's *20/20* was more critical. *Skeptic Magazine* has also criticized Van Praagh's methods, saying he has merely updated old vaudeville tricks.

Another popular form of Spiritualism is trance channeling (see separate entry), which has been advocated by such notables as Oscar-winning actress Shirley MacLaine, who has repeatedly talked about the role of spirit guides in her life. Usually these are said to be departed human beings who speak through channelers, who are like human telephones connecting the living to the spirit world. MacLaine's favorite channeler, Kevin Ryerson, is a prominent figure in her many best-selling books. (Note that the old word *medium* is abandoned in favor of the more contemporary, scientific-sounding *channeler*.) According to MacLaine, her spirit guides communicate to her using the electromagnetic frequencies of Ryerson's body.

MacLaine's spirit guides have also spoken to her without using a channeler. On one occasion they—at her request—took possession of her so she could give an electrifying stage performance. MacLaine also claims that her guides have validated their authenticity by revealing intimate details about her life, details no living being could know.

As with the New Age movement in general, MacLaine's belief system is a hodgepodge of various cult and occult practices. While she claims that some spirit guides are departed human beings, she says that other entities have never been incarnated. (The older forms of Spiritualism usually had no interest in spirits that had not at one time been human beings.) MacLaine also rather unorthodoxly combines her Spiritualism with her now-famous belief in reincarnation. (Some of her guides are, she says, people she has known in her past lives.)

Classic Spiritualism, practiced by fairly conventional people who seek to contact the spirit of a departed loved one, may be waning, but the New Age movement with its "any belief may be valid" attitude encourages a new form of Spiritualism, a form that focuses on obtaining power. MacLaine's account of her mesmerizing stage performance, in which her guides "permeated" her legs and arms during her dance numbers, encourages many people to seek out these benevolent guides and the power they can provide. While the Elvis devotee described earlier may have merely wanted assurance that the much-loved Elvis was indeed still alive in some way, most New Age–influenced people are seeking power, not comfort.

Delving into Secret Things

What can we conclude about channelers and mediums, whose receptivity to vibrations from the spirit world welcomes poltergeists (ghosts), apports (movements of objects by psychokinetic means), and clairvoyant powers to see beyond the five senses?

Their search for secret knowledge violates God's prohibitions on such behavior: "The secret things belong unto the Lord" (Deuteronomy 29:29). Luke 16:19-31 clearly illustrates that an unbridgeable gulf separates the dead from the living. There is no comfort the "initiates of a higher order" have to offer that has not already been offered by the Holy Spirit, the Comforter. The capricious messages of ghostly apparitions at mysterious seances can never promise more than the One who conquered the grave and who assures every Christian of the certainty of life after death.

Spiritualists are generally not devious individuals, though many are enticed into the darker realms of black magic. They are often kindly people who make warm friends and vow to promote morality for the common good. But their good intentions cannot remove the sting of death. Death is the result of sin, and only by facing that fact squarely through repentance can the resurrection promise of Christ offer hope.

CHRISTIAN CRITIQUE: Spiritualism is defined by the National Spiritualistic Association of Churches as "the Science, Philosophy, and Religion of a continuous life, based upon the demonstrable fact of communication by means of a mediumship, with those who live in the Spirit World."

Contact with the dead is presumed to bring consolation to the living. The information obtained from departed spirits is said to produce spiritual growth and moral advancement. In this way sin and wrong conduct will be overcome by personal effort.

The key test of any spirit's validity has nothing to do with the accurateness of its information but rather its views regarding Jesus Christ. Prayer is the only "spirit world contact" sanctioned by God, and the Holy Spirit is to be the only guiding source of spiritual information.

Scripture abounds with prohibitions regarding the practices of Spiritualism (Leviticus 19:31; Deuteronomy 18:10-11; 1 Chronicles 10:13; 2 Chronicles 33:6; Isaiah 8:19; Galatians 5:19-21; 1 Timothy 4:1). The Bible warns of lying spirits, and the Spiritualist has no gauge to objectively determine the credibility of his sources, since the biblical standards for discerning spirits have been discarded. The hope of reformation in the hereafter removes the urgency of correct moral choice in this life. Messages from subjectively identified spirits takes precedence over the revelation of Christ's gospel.

Spiritualism's main tenet is but the paraphrase of Eden's serpent, whom Christ identified as a liar and a murderer (John 8:44): "Ye shall not surely die" (Genesis 3:4). The apostle Paul clearly condemned the mediumship of Barjesus (Acts 13), declaring that one who participates in such sorceries is a "child of the devil."

SOURCES: Chris Ballard, "Oprah of the Other Side," *New York Times Magazine*, 29 July 2001; Edmund Gruss, *Cults and the Occult* (Grand Rapids, Mich.: Baker, 1980); Gordon Lewis, *Confronting the Cults* (Nutley, N.J.: Presbyterian and Reformed, 1966); Walter Martin, *Kingdom of the Cults* (Minneapolis: Bethany Fellowship, 1977); J. Gordon Melton, *The Encyclopedia of American Religions*, vol. 2 (Wilmington, N.C.: McGrath, 1978); Bob Morris, "Looking for Solace in a Spirit World," *New York Times*, 16 December 2001; William Petersen, *Those Curious New Cults* (New Canaan, Ct.: Keats, 1977); Josh Wolk, "Tomb Reader," *Entertainment Weekly*, 14 September 2001, 57–59.

ACCESS: The National Spiritualistic Association offices are in Washington, D.C. Those training for ordination as a Spiritualist minister attend the Morris Pratt Spiritualist Institute in Whitewater, Wisconsin. Spiritualism is more prevalent in Europe than in the United States, especially in France and the United Kingdom. It also has a stronghold in South America, particularly in Brazil, which may have more practitioners of Spiritualism than any nation in the world.

See also Ascended Masters; New Age Movement; Trance Channeling; Voodoo, Santeria, and Yoruba.

SRI CHINMOY

This Indian guru has mixed piety and publicity in an effort to gain attention for his teachings.

FOUNDER: Sri Chinmoy; born 1931, West Bengal, India; came to the United States in 1964

TEXT: Hindu scriptures and Chinmoy's own books

APPEAL: Despite his campaign to get publicity for himself, Chinmoy's personal lifestyle is less extravagant than that of most imported gurus. His following (though small) is more fervent. The laid-back image gives him the appearance of being more genuine.

OVERVIEW: Born Chinmoy Kumar Ghose in 1931 in Chittagong, India, Chinmoy later added the honorific title *Sri* to his name. He came to America in 1964 at a time when many American young people were looking East for wisdom and inspiration.

Chinmoy had the advantage of being endorsed by influential musicians like Carlos Santana and John McLaughlin. At one point, Santana, who was the lead guitarist and guiding force of the rock group that bore his name, even adopted the name *Devadip*, a Hindu word meaning "the lamp of the light of the Supreme." This name was given to him by his guru, Sri Chinmoy.

Santana was not the only musician to devote himself to Chinmoy's teaching. McLaughlin called Sri Chinmoy "Perfection . . . a Divine Being." McLaughlin began his concerts with meditation and sang metaphysical lyrics that sometimes praised Chinmoy with unabashed devotion.

Though Chinmoy's actual following never grew much larger than a thousand fully committed disciples, such high-profile endorsements helped him stand out from the crowd and contributed to his far-ranging influence. He talked with the pope and lectured at Yale. He made friends with former Russian leader Mikhail Gorbachev. And in a stroke of "enlightened" genius, Chinmoy even established a headquarters at the United Nations, where he supervised the bimonthly U.N. meditation program.

Hyping Hinduism

The Hindu doctrine of yoga is at the heart of Chinmoy's system of salvation. Students go through a process that may include hatha yoga, vegetarianism, and meditation. Chinmoy's way to God is through devotion and surrender to one's guru. Though such a mentor may not be absolutely essential, Chinmoy told followers that having a private tutor is certainly the quickest way to achieve the enlightenment he himself had known since age twelve.

Chinmoy advocated that a guru take a disciple through *siksha*, the yielding of one's life to this teacher. Chinmoy's ritual of siksha began with a trance state during which the disciple's eyes rolled back into their sockets, leaving only the whites visible. This state of meditative bliss (known in Hinduism as *samadhi*) had a powerful effect on disciples who knelt before Chinmoy.

Finally, the devotee received a portion of Chinmoy's soul in exchange for unswerving service from that day forth. Those who have undergone siksha claim the experience is so overwhelming they never again doubt Chinmoy's authenticity as a spiritual leader.

A Renaissance Guru

Chinmoy claims to have prolific creative talents. He claims to have completed over sixteen thousand paintings in a single day, though such a pace would mean an incredible two paintings per second! (Altogether, Sri Chinmoy has exhibited more than 130,000 paintings and drawings around the world.) Another phenomenal output is his record of 843 poems during one twenty-four-hour period. He has published seven hundred books and pamphlets, as well as two periodicals, *Chinmoy Family* and *Aum*.

His athletic accomplishments have also been phenomenal. Trying to show people how to push themselves to the limit, he has participated in triathlons, marathons, and the very strenuous ultramarathons. Many of his followers are long-distance runners. More circus-like in nature are his amazing feats of weight lifting, including lifting an elephant—not bad for a man who is only five-foot-seven. In 1988 the fifty-seven-year-old guru staged an event at a California shopping center where he lifted two members of the San Francisco 49ers football team.

But some of these events backfired, bringing Chinmoy jeers instead of praise. A profile of the guru published in the *Wall Street Journal* said, "He craves publicity. The Sri Chinmoy Center has a staff of publicists responsible for alerting the media when the guru is going to stage a stunt. They are dogged in their efforts to gain recognition for their leader, whom they describe as 'Atlas holding up the world.'"

Chinmoy's mission to America is a deliberate blending of the East and West. "There are two aspects of God," he declares. "One is realization and the other is manifestation." To him, Eastern disciples bring the realization of God, while the Supreme's manifestation is seen in Western approaches to spirituality.

Perhaps part of the reason he never achieved a fraction of the following generated by fellow Hindu Deepak Chopra is because he doesn't promise instantaneous enlightenment. Potential followers are warned that they may spend a dozen or more years before they experience their oneness with the Supreme (Chinmoy's designation of God).

CHRISTIAN CRITIQUE: The guru-student relationship is central to Chinmoy's teachings. Total submission to one's guru facilitates the process of God-realization. His spiritual path is more in line with traditional Hinduism than some other yoga masters, lending emphasis to his selective approach of quality over quantity of disciples.

Jesus plainly stated that he was the only way to God (John 14:6), and this access is through his redemptive death. Chinmoy seeks to replace the mediatory status of Christ by putting a human channel (himself) between God and man. Chinmoy's doctrine of submission to a guru is the same lie of self-deification the serpent expounded in Eden.

SOURCES: James T. Areddy, "Sri Chinmoy Seeks to Claim a Title: Stunt Man Supreme," *Wall Street Journal*, 13 January 1989, 1; "Celebrities Uplifted by Inner Strength," *Toronto Glove and Mail*, 28 October 1988, A18; *Denver Post*, 6 May 1977, 3BB; *People*, 2 December 1976, 50.

ACCESS: Centers in the United States, Canada, Europe, and Australia.

See also Yoga and Frederick Lenz.

SUFISM

The most exotic variant of Islam proposes to reach God
not through the Five Pillars of the mainstream faith but by entering
trance states induced by dancing.

FOUNDER: Melvana Celaleddin Rumi, who established the tradition in Konya, Turkey, in 1273; Pir Vilavat Inavat Khan is the current director and president of the Sufi Order.

TEXT: Islamic scriptures, Gnostic texts, and many recent books on Rumi

SYMBOL: The *samazen* (pupil) posing with the circular skirt preparing for circumambulations (walking meditation)

APPEAL: Sufism is a way to ecstatically experience oneness with God, if one assumes that the mystical trance state achieved by dervishes is a form of communion with God. The counterculture fascination with consciousness-expanding modes of religion provides a fertile environment of curiosity among the young, which has led some to experiment with Sufism.

OVERVIEW: The Sufis, whose name comes from the wool, or *suf*, of their undergarments, are a mystical Islamic branch rooted in the ascetic pietism of Muhammad's followers. Al-Hasan of Basra (643–728) was an early advocate of Sufism, as was Melvana Celaleddin Rumi, a Turkish mystic who lived in the thirteenth century.

Sufism's emphasis is on union with God through meditation and ritual rather than koranic obedience. Combining Islamic doctrines with Christian and Gnostic beliefs, they have developed a pantheistic theology with a spiritual hierarchy of *awliya* (saints). Chief of these is Qutb, the Pole of the World. Sufi leaders known as sheikhs are held to be saints, and many of them practice celibacy, though it is not a requirement of their office.

While the average Muslim is content in submitting to the will of Allah, the Sufi wants an immediate, ecstatic experience of oneness with God. The means to accomplish this is a once-secret rite of twirling dance maneuvers.

It was Rumi who adapted Asian shamanistic practices and formed a ritualistic approach to Islam. Rumi watched a goldsmith one day and as a result was brought into a state of whirling ecstasy. He developed a special dance routine requiring a twirling motion. To master this choreographed movement 1,001 hours of training are required. His disciples have become known as "whirling dervishes" (*dervish* means "beggar" in Turkish). Until recently, dervishes were illegal in their native Turkey, a ban imposed by Kemal Ataturk, who considered their beliefs an impediment to his modernization schemes.

Dervishes turn for an hour or more at a time without any sign of fatigue, repeating the name of Allah in prayer to the accompaniment of a musical beat. Eventually they enter an unconscious trance state and fall on the floor, an act that is supposed to represent an "awakening from indifference."

This esoteric "metaphysics of ecstasy" was formerly a path available only to initiates. Now Sufis are performing in public, and their beliefs and practices are being openly explained. The dervish ritual is presented as a way for the teacher to expel from the pupil "gross energy," which would otherwise hinder his spiritual progress. The costume worn is a white skirt that represents a shroud and a high felt hat that symbolizes a tombstone.

Among the eight Sufi precepts are a concentrated breathing technique, returning to God from the material world, and being aware of the divine presence. "When you turn," says a foremost Sufi devotee, "you do not turn for yourself but for God . . . so the light of God may descend upon the earth."

In America, Sufism has attracted thousands of adherents. The Sufi goal of higher consciousness through chants and meditative dancing blends well into the mystical landscape of contemporary religious cults.

CHRISTIAN CRITIQUE: Sufi literature declares, "The greatest principle of Sufism is *Isha Allah Ma'bud Allah*, God is love, lover, and beloved." Harmony with all the world's religions and peoples is said to be accomplished by each individual contemplating the immanence of God.

However, Sufism virtually ignores the question of sin and redemption. Its lack of fixed doctrinal structure means that belief resides in a subjective, mystical interpretation of truth. The awliya could be classified as familiar spirits (demons), and Qutd, a personification of Lucifer. Dervish trance states exhibit the characteristics of biblically defined demonic possession.

SOURCES: *Denver Post*, 29 August 1975, 3BB; Ibid., 14 May 1976, B-9; Ibid., 14 January 1977, 5BB; Ibid., 25 February 1977, 5BB; J. Gordon Melton, *The Encyclopedia of American Religions* (Wilmington, N.C.: McGrath, 1978); Sufi advertisements in occult journals; *Time*, 16 April 1979, 52; J. Isamu Yamamoto, "Expanding Sufi Horizons," 1983, Spiritual Counterfeits Project pamphlet.

ACCESS: Sufi Order, Box 574, Lebanon Springs, NY 12114; International Association of Sufism, 25 Mitchell Blvd., Suite 2, San Rafael, CA 94903

See also Islam; Nation of Islam.

SWEDENBORGIANISM

This fascinating man said the Bible needed to be reinterpreted,
and he used occultic means to do so.

OVERVIEW: His body had been laid to rest for more than two hundred years in Sweden's Uppsala Cathedral, but only recently did his skull join the rest of his bones. The Swedish Royal Academy of Science paid three thousand dollars at a Sotheby's London auction to purchase the head of Emanuel Swedenborg, an eighteenth-century mystic, scientist, and religious philosopher. Swedenborg's remains were considered so valuable that an official diplomatic pouch was dispatched to return the skull to Swedenborg's homeland.

Emanuel Swedenborg (1688–1772) was born the son of a pious Lutheran minister. He grew up to be a dynamic intellectual who circulated in the highest echelons of government and academia. His expertise in the field of geology earned him an appointment as a college professor and a membership in the Swedish Diet. Swedenborg traveled widely and gained a reputation as an expert in the field of metallurgy and crystallography.

At the age of fifty-two his life changed abruptly when he answered what he felt was a divine calling to become a revelator of the symbolic meanings in Scripture.

Swedenborg developed mediumistic abilities (automatic handwriting and clairaudience—hearing something not actually audible to others) and practiced astral travel—journeying to the spirit world to communicate with good and evil angels (deceased humans). The messages from these beings convinced him that the Bible needed special interpretation.

This led him to write a commentary on the Bible as well as several lengthy treatises, including *Arcana Coelestia: The Earths in the Universe*. His visions included conversations with persons whom he identified as Luther, Calvin, St. Augustine, and the apostle Paul. (The latter would not have taken kindly to him, because Swedenborg's theology proposed eliminating the Pauline Epistles from the Bible, along with much of the Old Testament.)

Today, Swedenborgian ministers, who represent one of the three main branches of the Church of the New Jerusalem, generally consider Swedenborg's writings to be "divinely inspired." The "truth" he brought is said to represent "the second coming of Christ."

In Swedenborg's theological system, those who die enter an intermediate state where they prepare for heaven or hell. In hell, one becomes an evil spirit, but in heaven an angelic status awaits. Either existence is a spiritual state since there is no bodily resurrection. In this life after death, each soul retains the physical appearance of early adulthood as it was lived on earth.

The historic Christian concept of the Trinity is discarded, along with the Vicarious Atonement—an "abomination" and "mere human invention," according to Swedenborg. Christ's death on the Cross is described as "a climax of a life of service," not "a debt of blood." The person of the Holy Spirit is specifically denied, and Jesus Christ is God alone, an "indivisible . . . Divine Essence" manifested as three principles.

This unique form of Spiritualism is practiced by approximately twenty thousand Americans and at least a hundred thousand others worldwide, with the largest concentrations in England.

SOURCES: *Denver Post*, 16 January 1976, 3BB; *Eternity*, May 1981, 44–45; Walter Martin, *The Kingdom of the Cults* (Minneapolis: Bethany Fellowship, 1977); J. Gordon Melton, *The Encyclopedia of American Religions*, vol. 2 (Wilmington, N.C.: McGrath, 1978).

ACCESS: Swedenborg Foundation, 320 N. Church St., West Chester, PA 19380, www.swedenborg.com; General Convention of the New Jerusalem in the U.S.A., 48 Sargent St., Newton, MA 02158; General Church of the New Jerusalem, Bryn Athyn, PA 19009

TAI CHI AND QIGONG

These exercises from the East promise health and spirituality;
but while they seek to free the body, they may enslave the soul.

It's a perfect therapy for the diseases of modern civilization.
KENNETH COHEN, AUTHOR OF *THE WAY OF QIGONG*

OVERVIEW: Tai Chi (pronounced tie-CHEE, and sometimes spelled Tai Ji) is an ancient form of Chinese boxing. Qigong (chee-GONG) is a form of dance from the same country. Together, these two forms of spiritual exercise have taken parts of the West by storm. Like Kung Fu, both have been altered by ambitious promoters who market them to spiritually hungry and trend-conscious Americans. But both still retain elements of the spiritual heritage that gave birth to them.

Meditative Maneuvers

According to legend, seven centuries ago, a Taoist monk named Chang San-feng was inspired by watching a snake and crane fight each other. Chang was particularly impressed by the creative ways the snake avoided the crane by twisting and turning his lengthy body.

Chang incorporated the snake's moves into a new regimen he devised called Tai Chi. But at this point, the legends diverge. Was Tai Chi originally intended as a method of combat, or was it designed to be a discipline like meditation, said to promote both physical and spiritual health?

One thing is certain. The technique is catching on in America, according to an article in *USA Today:* "The ancient Chinese discipline is moving out of martial arts studios and into gyms, health spas and even workplaces across the country. And at the New York Health and Racquet Club in Manhattan, spokeswoman Jennifer Stein also reports a growing audience for tai chi. 'We get a lot of stressed out business people,' Stein says. 'They say that after tai chi classes they leave the gym feeling relaxed and great.'"

Regardless of its mixed history, today Tai Chi is popular as a form of exercise, a natural stress reducer, and a spiritual discipline. People who use it only to stretch their muscles may not realize that the discipline involves a tradition of spiritual and philosophical assumptions, but many devoted disciples are attuned to these underlying themes.

Tai Chi is a form of moving meditation that is steeped in Taoist spiritual philosophy and characterized by slow, dancelike body movements that are pleasing to the eye and calming to the mind. As with many Eastern belief systems, Tai Chi emphasizes harmony with nature and promises to create positive by-products in body, mind, and spirit.

Those who are most devoted to Tai Chi say it promotes physical health, longevity, and even immortality. One Web site is even more specific in its claims: "Tai Chi might well be considered the world's oldest stress reduction program. For the most part stress is understood to be a mental/emotional situation expressed through the physical body. Anxiety, worry, fear, and a host of related negative mental states can and do cause serious physical symptoms including increased blood pressure, impaired organ function, and accumulated tension in the muscles and joints which can lead to arthritis and other joint afflictions."

The Web site also explains how bodily movements are used to achieve nonphysical results: "Tai Chi, like contemporary Western psychiatry, understands that it is very difficult to directly influence the mental/emotional state. So what has developed over the centuries is a very simple yet highly sophisticated method of influencing mental/emotional changes through body experiences."

One of the signs of Tai Chi's acceptance in the West is how it has been employed in a multimillion dollar advertising campaign for the pain-relief drug Celebrex. Apparently the drug maker feels the image of ordinary-looking Americans doing Tai Chi in a park portrays the image of health and happiness it is looking for.

The Key to Qi

While TV commercials promote Tai Chi, Qigong is promoted by TV stars like Regis Philbin, well-known athletes, and other Western celebrities who find its combination of dance and meditation to be relaxing and reinvigorating.

An article in *Newsweek* magazine described a typical group of practitioners: "At the instructor's gentle urging, the students raise their hands above their heads, pause and then push them down past their stomachs while breathing deeply and rhythmically. They repeat the move for 15 minutes, then sit down to meditate for 10 more. . . . And because it's less strenuous and methodical than yoga or Qigong's martial-arts cousin, tai chi, it's more accessible to the sick and the elderly. While improving posture and circulation, Qigong can also lower blood pressure and tone the immune system by countering the effects of stress."

There has been a flood of books, magazine articles, instructional videos and other products based on Qigong, and teachers have offered seemingly innumerable variations of the relatively simple ancient practice. But the one spiritual assumption that provides the foundation for all the varied approaches is this: the body is composed of invisible channels called meridians, and these meridians can be used to *gong* (develop) the body's *qi* (inherent vital energy).

Many experts have found that the practice of Qigong does induce something that has been called the "relaxation response." But perhaps part of this response is based on the belief that the practice works.

The real question is whether similar benefits could be derived by an equal amount of time devoted to stretching, swimming, cycling, walking, or other nonaggressive exercises that aid the joints and tone muscles. If so, is the philosophical overlay of Tai Chi and Qigong necessary for success? Probably not, which raises the question, Can the occult teachings regarding spirituality be divorced from the musculoskelatal benefits? They can, but if they are not, the Christian must ask if it's wise to subject one's self to such occult indoctrination to achieve physical betterment.

CHRISTIAN CRITIQUE: Like practicing yoga, submitting to a discipline with embedded unbiblical teachings for the sake of some goal apart from the belief system is an unacceptable spiritual risk. There can be no compromise with a worldview rooted in ideas that oppose God's Word. In fact, many Tai Chi and Qigong instructors incorporate Buddhist indoctrination, Taoistic principles, and divinatory practices such as I-Ching. In addition, both disciplines are based on the belief in *Jing* (the essence of life), *Qi* (energy), and *Shen* (spiritual force). This alignment with Eastern metaphysics cannot be compatible with the Christian who desires "to keep himself unspotted from the world" (James 1:27).

SOURCES: Cathy Hainer, "A Widening Appreciation for Benefits of Tai Chi," *USA Today*, 15 May 1997, 10D; Brad Stone, "Cultivating Qi: More and More Westerners Are Discovering Qigong, an Ancient Amalgam of Dance and Meditation with a Range of Physical Benefits," *Newsweek*, 28 July 1997, 71.

TAOISM

Equal parts philosophy and religion, this Chinese faith claims
to help followers find "the Way."

FOUNDER: Lao Tzu, a hermit-philosopher who was a contemporary of
Confucius

TEXT: *Tao-Te-Ching*, the classic text of Taoism, is readily available today.

OVERVIEW: Lao Tzu lived at the same time as Confucius in the fifth and
sixth centuries before Christ. Other than that, not much is known about this
man, except that he wrote an influential book called *Tao Te Ching*, which provided the intellectual framework for a philosophy known as Taoism.

Lao Tzu was a government scribe who quit his job and retired from the
world into a comfortable seclusion. He spent the remaining years of his life as a
hermit in a mountainside hut, where he could reflect on the nature of the
world and his thoughts about life.

He also wrote down many aphorisms concerning how rulers should regulate the lives of their people. The following brief passage serves as a sample:

> Not to honor men of worth will keep the people from contention; not to
> value goods which are hard to come by will keep them from theft; not to
> display what is desirable will keep them from being unsettled of mind.
>
> Therefore in governing the people, the sage empties their minds but
> fills their bellies, weakens their wills but strengthens their bones. He
> always keeps them innocent of knowledge and free from desire, and
> ensures that the clever never dare to act.
>
> Do that which consists in taking no action, and order will prevail.

For centuries Lao Tzu was viewed primarily as a philosopher, political
thinker, or great teacher. He probably would have been surprised to realize that
centuries after his death, his simple philosophy was christened as a religion and
adopted as the official state religion by fifth century Chinese rulers.

As a result of this decision, Taoism is now regarded, along with Buddhism
and Confucianism, as one of the three great religions of China. Still, there are
times where Taoism seems more like a philosophy than a faith, and certainly
many students who read the *Tao Te Ching* did not become devoted Taoists.

Promoting Social Tranquillity
In the entry on Tai Chi and Qigong, we saw that these ancient Chinese practices are promoted as keys to calm and relaxation. In a sense, Taoism can be

seen as a philosophy for social and community life that promotes calm throughout the culture.

The rulers of China's Han dynasty certainly felt Taoism could help them achieve the utopian "Grand Tranquillity" they believed they were called to provide their people.

Over the centuries, Taoism developed from a book of ideas into a well-organized social movement that provided a host of specific steps for realizing social calm. This phase of Taoism continued from the fifth to the thirteenth century, when China was overrun by Mongol invaders. During the following centuries, calm was at a premium, and Taoism became a more individualized and ritualized form of faith and worship.

Things got even worse for Taoists in the twentieth century, when the faith was outlawed by the new Communist rulers. But government suppression couldn't stop this popular movement, and today Taoism survives as a branch of philosophy, a form of religious liturgy, and a school of Eastern mystical thought. It's impact on Chinese traditions and institutions is inestimable.

Which Way Is the Right Way?

When Jesus came to earth, he proclaimed that he himself was "the way, the truth and the life." Lao Tzu had made similar claims for his philosophy of life five centuries earlier.

According to Lao Tzu, he was merely pointing the way to the Tao, which he described as the way, the truth, or the path. According to Lao Tzu, the Tao embodies ultimate reality, and people must orient their lives around its principles if they are to achieve personal peace and social harmony.

Like Jesus, Lao Tzu also employed images from the natural world to make his case. He used the water flowing in rivers or the blood flowing in people's veins to illustrate the power of the Tao flowing through all areas of life.

He even worked out a detailed cosmology in which parts of the world were said to correspond to various facets of human life. In time, some of these ideas would be formalized in the concepts of yin and yang, which are seen as the complementary light and dark sides of reality.

In many ways, the forces of the Tao would work their will no matter what humans did. The main thing for people to do was to orient their lives around the Tao in accordance with the "Three Jewels" of compassion, moderation, and humility.

But there were disputes about how this should be done. Some critics have charged that Taoism is a faith of passivity and apathy. Such criticisms cite comments of Lao Tzu like this one: "The man of superior virtue never acts, and yet there is nothing he leaves undone." The Chinese government has continued to oppose Taoism because of fears that it promotes laziness and lack of appropriate involvement in social life.

There are also clear cases of conflict between Taoist teaching and Christian belief. Taoism describes divinity as an impersonal and uninvolved force, but Christianity teaches that God is personal and deeply involved in the world, from the first moments of creation to the present day. And of course, Jesus is the ultimate sign of the personality of God and his intervention in human affairs.

In addition, Christianity emphasizes activity, and Jesus himself commissioned his followers to go into the world and spread his message. Taoists, in contrast, often honor inactivity, and they seldom promote evangelism on behalf of their beliefs.

The most severe contradiction between Christianity and Taoism is the belief that the Tao is the First-Cause of the universe and the force that flows through all life. This is blatantly opposed to the Bible, which declares that Christ is above all, the head of every principality and power, the one by and for whom all things were created (Colossians 1:16-18).

CHRISTIAN CRITIQUE: To the Taoist, prayer is pointless for there is no God to hear or to act upon such petitions. All life's answers are to be found through inward meditation and outward observation. This directly opposes the biblical admonition of Proverbs 3:5 that it is better not to lean on one's own understanding, but to acknowledge God in all things. The ubiquitous Yin Yang symbol of Taoism has invaded our culture with its message of harmonizing opposites—the light Yang (male, energetic, aggressive, hard) and the dark Yin (feminine, supple, calm, cool). These two opposing forces in nature are said to best reside in balance, as the symbol indicates. To the Taoist, light and dark, good and evil reside in equilibrium. But the Christian is commanded to overcome evil with good (Romans 12:21).

ACCESS: Healing Tao Centers claim forty thousand members worldwide. For information write Taoist Esoteric Yoga Center & Foundation, P.O. Box 1194, Huntington, NY 11743; for additional information about Taoism contact Living Tao Foundation, P.O. Box 846, Urbana, IL 61801.

TEMPLE OF SET

Founded in 1975, this congregation is an offshoot
of Anton LaVey's Church of Satan.

OVERVIEW: The biblical principle "pride goes before a fall" apparently applies not only to Bible-quoting televangelists but also to leaders of satanic churches. That, at least, is the conclusion of Michael Aquino, a former leader in the Church of Satan, a congregation founded by magician and media darling Anton LaVey (see separate entry).

LaVey founded the Church of Satan in San Francisco in 1966. According to Aquino, as the congregation grew from a local phenomenon and LaVey became a national celebrity, LaVey apparently lost his head.

Aquino's decision to develop his own sect of satanism was described in the Temple of Set's "General Information and Admissions Policies" (updated February 17, 2002):

> It . . . proved to be a misfortune of modern Satanism that, en route to divinity, the psyche is prone to superficial egotism. The Church suffered periodically from petty crises and scandals. . . . In 1975 [LaVey] made a decision to redesign it as a non-functional vehicle for his personal expression and financial income. This decision was emphatically rejected by the majority of the Priesthood, who immediately resigned from the Church in protest and denied its legitimacy as the true Church of Satan henceforth. The senior Initiate, Michael A. Aquino, invoked the Prince of Darkness in quest of a new Mandate to preserve and enhance the more noble concepts which the Church of Satan had conceived and outlined. That Mandate was given in the form of *The Book of Coming Forth by Night*—a statement by that entity, in his most ancient semblance as Set, ordaining the Temple of Set to succeed the Church.

Though the Temple was founded in 1975, Aquino claims it has prehistoric roots that go back to the times of predynastic Egypt: "Images of Set have been dated to [around] 3200 BCE, with astronomically-based estimates of inscriptions dating to [around] 5000 BCE."

While it's difficult to build an entire spiritual philosophy around a couple of supposed ancient archeological finds, that's what Aquino has done. He claims the Temple's beliefs originated "in mankind's first apprehension that there is 'something different' about the human race—a sense of self-consciousness that places humanity above all other known forms of life."

474

Among Aquino's ambitious claims are the following statement: "The Temple of Set is an institution unlike any you have previously encountered. The Temple is designed as a tool for personal empowerment and self cultivation. To decide whether such a tool is a valuable one for you, you should consider the philosophy of the Temple, the concept of Set, the obligations and responsibilities which a Setian assumes, and what the Temple looks for in a candidate."

Setian Philosophy

Although Aquino claims to be a mouthpiece for an ancient philosophy, he occasionally revises that statement of philosophy. One recent revision of the statement sought to make the group more socially acceptable. Earlier versions had stated clearly that the Temple of Set considers itself part of other "movements dedicated to the Prince of Darkness," "occultism," and "Black Magic." The group's latest statement of beliefs, however, aims for a more mainstream appeal:

Temple of Set seeks above all to honor and enshrine consciousness. We wish to apprehend what makes us each individually unique and use this gift to make ourselves stronger in all facets of our being. To do this we preserve and improve the tradition of spiritual distinction from the natural universe, which in the Judeo/Christian West has been called Satanism, but which is more generally known as the Left-Hand Path.

The Left-Hand Path is a process for creating an individual, powerful essence that exists above and beyond animal life. It is thus the true vehicle for personal immortality.

The components of this path include antinomianism (the "denial and rejection of the herd-mentality"); individuality; control ("the ability to recognize, start, and complete great quests distinguishes the Initiate from the 'occultnik' who seeks to parody greatness by mindlessly muttering a few incoherent 'spells'"); black magic (the "formula is 'my will be done', as opposed to the White Magic of the Right-Hand Path, whose formula is 'thy will be done'"); and a belief in Set.

Aquino also tries to distance his group from images of satanism found in contemporary popular culture: "Regretfully there still exist some individuals whose idea of 'Satanism' is largely a simple-minded synthesis of Christian propaganda and Hollywood horror movies. The Temple of Set enjoys the colorful legacy of the Black Arts, and we use many forms of historical Satanic imagery for our artistic stimulation and pleasure. But we have not found that any interest or activity which an enlightened, mature intellect would regard as undignified, sadistic, criminal, or depraved is desirable, much less essential to our work."

One of the few acknowledgments made by the group that it is playing with fire is the following brief warning: "The Black Arts are dangerous in the same way that working with volatile chemicals is dangerous. This is most emphatically not a field for unstable, immature, or otherwise emotionally or intellectually weak-minded people."

An Individualistic "Congregation"

Even though one might think that the Temple of Set's main purpose is to host regular gatherings, that is not the case. "The deliberately individualistic atmosphere of the Temple of Set is not easily conducive to group activities on a routine or programmed basis," says the group's statement. "There are no congregations of docile 'followers'—only cooperative philosophers and magicians."

Though regularly scheduled events are not publicized, the Temple does host some events in San Francisco. Those Setian groups that do meet are sometimes referred to as "Pylons" (supposedly named after the gates of ancient Egyptian temples). In addition to national meetings, there are local gatherings and communication between the various Aquino groups.

The annual membership fee for the Temple of Set is $70, and members are assured that their affiliation with the group will be kept confidential: "Your admission is known only to the Priesthood," says the group's statement.

The Temple says it is looking for initiates who possess the following characteristics:

- a realization that the world isn't fair or loving
- a sense of wonder at one's own being
- a willingness to learn, to go to school
- a desire to make yourself into something better
- intellectual ability as well as access to scholarly data you are capable of handling
- magical ability
- a sense of humor
- an ability to privately acknowledge your fears, prejudices, and problems, as well as to forgive your honest mistakes
- a willingness to share with others what you have found, in the right place and time—and to be silent when it is not the right place and time

Many of these ideals (except for the one about magic) are embraced by mainstream groups like the Boy Scouts. But the Temple of Set is no typical organization.

CHRISTIAN CRITIQUE: On several occasions I have debated publicly with leaders in the Temple of Set, including Zena Lavey, Anton Lavey's daughter who forsook her father before his death and adopted the teachings of his rival, Aquino. The contrast between Church of Satan philosophy (i.e., that Satan does not literally exist) and Setian doctrine was distinct in all these dialogues. The Temple of Set truly believes in the personality of Satan (Set) and that a personal relationship with this dark force can be sought. Setians speak in hushed tones of feeling the presence and power of Set in the same way Christians speak of Christ's nearness. While satanists of the LaVey variety may sometimes be seen as misfits seeking attention by embracing evil, Setians are a serious threat to the church because they actively pursue the invocation of Satan's company to direct their lives in every way.

ACCESS: P.O. Box 470307, San Francisco, CA 94147; www.xeper.org

THEOSOPHY

Blending occultism, Eastern theology, and showbiz savvy, movement
founder Madame Blavatsky paved the way for other gurus
to preach transcendentalism in the West.

FOUNDER: Madame Helena Petrovna Blavatsky, born in Russia in 1831, daughter of Peter Hahn, descendant of German nobles; she died in 1891 while living in exile in Germany. Blavatsky founded the Theosophical Society in New York in 1875 with Henry Olcott, aided by William Quan Judge.

TEXTS: Writings of Madame Blavatsky, including *The Secret Doctrine, Isis Unveiled, Cosmogenesis,* and *Anthropogenesis.* Though Blavatsky's books are considered divinely inspired, other books and authors are also revered: *Ancient Wisdom* by Annie Besant; *Ocean of Theosophy* by William Judge; *At the Feet of the Master* by C.W. Leadbeater; and *Elementary Theosophy* by L.W. Rogers. The religious philosophy of Theosophy is rooted in Hindu texts (Vedas, Upanishads, Bhagavad Gita) and other occult sources.

SYMBOL: A combination of religious designations, including the ankh (an Egyptian fertility symbol), a backward swastika (which portrays energy), the Sanskrit word *om* (meaning "oneness"), and the Jewish Star of David.

APPEAL: Its lack of official public dogma makes Theosophy attractive to religionists who take a universalistic view. Many people find its inclusion of mystical elements (such as vegetarianism, yoga, and mahatmas) a way to incorporate Eastern ideas into a Western tradition without turning to a more extreme cult such as Hare Krishna. Those enamored by psychic phenomena may be intrigued by stories regarding the supposed occult powers possessed by Blavatsky.

OVERVIEW: Theosophy has never been a large and popular movement. During its heyday in the late 1800s and early 1900s, it had no more than a hundred thousand followers, who varied widely in their commitment to the group.

In 1995 the Theosophical Society reported to have 30,000 members worldwide, including 4,300 members and 140 centers in the United States, and approximately 400 members and 18 centers in Canada.

Part of the society's problem of small numbers had to do with Helena Petrovna Blavatsky, the group's controversial founder. Although she briefly attracted the interest of celebrities like inventor Thomas Edison and poet W. B. Yeats, she offended many others. Another problem was the group's shaky historical grounding. Blavatsky claimed to be receiving messages from the Great White Brotherhood, but researchers found that many of her ideas came from the fantasy novels of Edward Bulwer Lytton.

But the importance of this group was never based on the size of its membership. Rather, as a *Time* magazine writer said, the group's main contribution was how it prepared America for an influx of esoteric and Eastern non-Christian faiths: "Theosophy . . . helped soften up the American mind for the revelations of more bizarre and sinister charismatic teachers."

A Unique History

Helena Petrovna Blavatsky was born in 1831 of an aristocratic Russian family. She exhibited psychic tendencies at an early age, a portent of things to come. Her marriage at age seventeen to a much older czarist general lasted only three months. Her perfidious marriage vows were symptomatic of her basic lack of moral character.

After her divorce from the elderly Mr. Blavatsky, Helena Petrovna proceeded to travel widely. While visiting the United States, she became intensely involved in Spiritualism. She also claimed that during her journeys to Tibet she had made contact with disembodied higher spiritual beings whom she called *mahatmas*. Blavatsky told how these masters of the spirit world had guided her entire life through letters and messages. Her home even contained an altar to the mahatmas.

In New York Helena Petrovna met Colonel Henry Steel Olcott, who shared her occult interests. Along with another of her admirers, William Quan Judge, the three formed the Theosophical Society in 1875. Blavatsky's first book, *Isis Unveiled*, became the society's central document, and a year later *The Secret Doctrine* was added to the Theosophical "canon."

Blavatsky traveled to India in 1879 and declared that the Theosophists' headquarters would be in Adyar, a suburb of Madras. It was there that the vocal and written communications she received from the mahatmas became more frequent.

However, during a visit to England in 1884, Blavatsky's Spiritualistic messages came under closer scrutiny. She was accused of being a magician, a hypnotist, and a charlatan. The prestigious Society of Psychical Research investigated her claims and found them to be considerably lacking in credibility. This blow to Blavatsky's veracity nearly destroyed Theosophy.

But one major accomplishment of her stay in London was meeting Annie Besant, a radical activist. Besant joined the society, and her oratorical skills brought about a resurgence in Theosophy's growth. She eventually became head of the society after Blavatsky's death in 1891.

Biographers report that Mrs. Blavatsky swore fluently in several languages, went through two marriages and many lovers, and gave birth to an illegitimate child. She exhibited a violent temper and was addicted to hashish. Of her ability to sway masses to accept her teachings, she once declared that people "in every part of the world have turned into asses at my whistle and have obediently wagged their long ears as I piped the tune."

Blavatsky's corrupt character hardly qualified her to inaugurate a global religious movement with the motto "There is no religion higher than truth." Yet the Theosophical Society owes its conception to her guiding hand. Through the years, her mix of Hinduism and Spiritualism attracted the likes of George Bernard Shaw, Thomas Edison, William Butler Yeats, and Jawaharial Nehru. Such access to influential people gave Theosophists power beyond their numbers. But the organization eventually dwindled in size, partly due to strife from internal dissension.

A Plethora of Gods

Though Blavatsky owed a debt of gratitude to Spiritualism for sparking her early endeavors, she eventually became an ardent foe of it. According to her, Spiritualists were erroneously engaged in contacting the lower levels of psychic entities. Helena Petrovna was more concerned with directives from the ruling masters of the spirit world.

Foremost among these deities is a being known as the Lord of the World. Under his authority are a trinity of Buddhas and a variety of "rays" and emanating spirits, including Master Morya and Master Koot Hoomi. Master Jesus is considered to be a reincarnation of Lord Krishna, the Hindu deity. The cosmological status now held by Christ had once been filled by the Greek god Apollonius. The desired destination of man's soul is *devachan*, which means "heaven" to Theosophists. Hell is known as *kamaloka*, a purgatory type of existence where souls await another chance in a new reincarnation. Even the most evil offender need not fear a permanent, final, divine judgment. "Man is a god in the making," wrote one leading Theosophist.

To outsiders, Theosophy presents a benign image of religious liberals intent only on fulfilling three major tenets: (1) forming a universal brotherhood of humankind; (2) investigating the unexplained laws of nature and the latent powers of humans; and (3) encouraging a comparative study of religion, science, and philosophy. A closer look at Theosophical thought reveals a complicated system of cosmological theories based on Hindu doctrine. Blavatsky's universe contains a pantheistic plethora of gods, lesser deities, and *devas* (which are "angels" in Hinduism), arranged in a hierarchical pattern based on numerological symmetry.

Both humans and earth are destined to evolve through seven stages. Earth is in its fourth cycle and humans are in their fifth root race, from which point they will evolve upward spiritually. The human body is composed of seven qualities: divine, monadic, spiritual, intuitional, mental, astral, and physical. To evolve spiritually, humans must raise their consciousness beyond earth's material plane with the aid of occult phenomena and the mahatmas.

A Struggle for Leadership

Though Helena Petrovna had once been toasted as a "world traveler, multilinguist, psychic, knowledgeable occultist, and altruist," she died as a lonely, obese, and miserably sick woman who was considered a fake and was deserted by most of her followers.

With Blavatsky gone, Henry Olcott and William Quan Judge struggled for control of the society. They eventually split into two factions. Olcott, who was more interested in Eastern occultism, ended up directing the European branch of the society. Before his death in 1907, Olcott claimed to receive messages from the mahatmas indicating Besant was next in line to lead the flock.

In the United States, Judge tried to synthesize Western philosophy with occult theories. He split with the Olcott/Besant division of the society in 1895. Shortly after Judge died in 1896, Katherine August Westcott Tingley (bearing three names from three marriages), a Spiritualist with amazing occult powers, took over the American branch of Theosophy.

Most of today's Theosophists belong to the Olcott/Besant wing, though a smaller group faithful to the Judge/Tingley branch continues, with headquarters in Altadena, California. The Theosophical Society of America, with headquarters in Wheaton, Illinois, keeps close ties with the British Theosophical Society and encourages modern Theosophists to dabble in contemporary occult phenomena, such as Kirlian photography, and paranormal practices, like psychokinesis.

Dismissing Christianity

Though Theosophy seeks to encompass all religions, the Christian message understandably receives considerable drubbing. Theosophists have no need for the Cross because karma and reincarnation guide their search for redemption. The atonement of Christ is dismissed as a "pernicious doctrine" perpetuating the deplorable idea that "wrong-doing by one can be set right by the sacrifice of another." After all, the incarnation of Christ had no unique significance since, according to Theosophy, "christs and saviors of the age have been appearing at propitious times since humanity began existence."

Theosophy's foremost leaders have led undistinguished lives, it has historically been rocked by scandal and internal dissent, and its teachings have been tinged by the dark, spiritistic arts. Yet Theosophy survives, indeed thrives, in the fertile soil of today's disenchantment with materialism.

A leading Theosophist once declared, "Theosophy evokes a philosophy so profound and recondite, trying to explain it to someone is impossible. It takes years—lifetimes." And, I might add, it also takes rose-colored glasses to overlook the foibles and fables of its founders.

CHRISTIAN CRITIQUE: "We are seekers of truth," a former leader of the society declared, but what brand of "truth" does this group promote?

Though the esoteric teachings of Theosophy constitute a complex system of doctrines based on Hinduism and various mystery cults, members insist their society represents a philosophy and not a religion. Theosophy espouses goals of world peace, brotherhood without distinction of sex or creed, and investigation of occult and paranormal phenomena that presumes to reveal unexplained laws of the universe.

Though Blavatsky officially denigrated Spiritualism in her later years, the realm of psychic powers is of special interest to Theosophists. Theosophy comes from the Greek *theosophia*, meaning "divine wisdom." In reality, theosophical thought is merely a modernized version of the pantheistic Gnostic teaching so sternly condemned by the apostle Paul in his letter to the Colossians. The supremacy of Christ as extolled in Colossians 2:10 ("the head of all principality and power") is reduced in Theosophy to a "Christ principle" apart from Jesus. This cosmic Christ-consciousness is claimed to be attainable by all men, since in Besant's words, "all men become Christs."

By asserting that humanity is but "a spark of the divine fire," Theosophy deifies the created and denigrates the Creator. Instead of walking "in the light" and knowing that "the blood of Jesus Christ his Son cleanseth us from all sin" (1 John 1:7), Theosophists flounder in the darkness of reincarnation beliefs, which they call "the religion of self-respect."

SOURCES: David Gates, "A Bunch of Balmy Swamis," *Time*, 20 February 1995, 66; *Herald Weekend Magazine*, 7 December 1980, 16–20; Walter Martin, *The Kingdom of the Cults* (Minneapolis: Bethany Fellowship, 1977); Marian Meade, *Madame Blavatsky: The Woman Behind the Myth* (New York: Putnam, 1980); J. Gordon Melton, *Encyclopedia of American Religions*, vol. 2 (Wilmington, N.C.: McGrath, 1978); *Newsweek*, 24 November 1975, 10; Peter Washington, *Madame Blavatsky's Baboon* (New York: Schocken, 1995).

ACCESS: International Headquarters are in Adyar (Madras), India. U.S. headquarters: The Theosophical Society in America, P.O. Box 270, Wheaton, IL 60189.

See also Anthroposophical Society.

TRANCE CHANNELING

The ancient practice of necromancy has been retitled trance channeling, but it still has the same purpose of reaching out to touch the dead via a human medium.

FOUNDERS: Various channelers who claimed to communicate with entities in the spirit world.

TEXT: Traditions of witchcraft, pagan oracles, and modern Spiritualism all mingle. Shirley MacLaine's many books are among the most popular and influential works that focus on channeling.

APPEAL: An estimated 23 percent of Americans believe in reincarnation, according to a *USA Today* poll, and 14 percent believe in mediums. Receiving advice from spiritual mentors, who claim to have intellectual superiority and advanced knowledge, provides comfort for the confused and distressed.

OVERVIEW: Why am I here? What is my purpose in life? To answer such questions, scores of Americans are resorting to *trance channeling*—communication with spirit entities through human contacts.

Some seek material gain. Others want advice about marital situations, career changes, and spiritual growth. Still others, disillusioned with organized religion and seeking to fill a spiritual void, stretch imagination and credibility, trying to contact beings from other planes of existence.

One thing that's clear is that channeling has continued to grow in popularity as the authority of Christianity had waned for many Americans.

Linking Living and Dead

Channelers have assumed a mythical quality because they receive communication from other planes of existence. Channeling has been part of human culture for as long as history has been recorded. The enigmatic theory that the dead can communicate with the living across dimensions unknown to humans has persisted in all cultures. At various times and in different places, channelers have been known by other names: priests, gurus, prophets, saints, and holy ones.

The bodies of channelers supposedly are commandeered by entities from the spirit world. The channeler often enters an altered conscious or unconscious state, which allows the transformation of the personality into a spirit guide. Channelers claim such guides have a hot line to universal truth. Mediums usually predict the future, while channelers concentrate on the present.

Referred to as "pioneers of the psyche," trance channelers envision a world brimming with healthy, happy, enlightened people who have found the answer to an ancient dilemma—how to live peaceably together.

Carl Raschke, professor of religious studies at the University of Denver, says of trance channeling, "It's a form of mass hypnosis that is leading to mass acceptance of the irrational." Marcello Truzzi, head of Eastern Michigan University's Center for Scientific Anomalies Research, says, "It's a democratization of the supernatural. Everyone is their own priest . . . their own god."

Multiple Channels

Just as TV has evolved from three major networks to cable with dozens of offerings, so trance channeling has begun to offer seekers a variety of options in recent decades.

Actress-author Shirley MacLaine is undoubtedly one of the most popular and influential fans of channeling. MacLaine (see more about her in the entry for the New Age Movement) served as a forerunner of an army of popular mediums, who became channelers to entities from the spirit world.

In her book *Dancing in the Light*, MacLaine focused national attention on J. Z. Knight, a successful Washington State channeler who serves Ramtha, a thirty-five-thousand-year-old male spirit. Knight goes into a deep, cataleptic trance, claiming to leave her body so the powerful spirit can enter. Ramtha calls himself "the Enlightened One" and says he once conquered Atlantis as a warrior. Claiming to hail from the lost continent of Lumeria, Ramtha talks for hours and marches around grandly when summoned by Knight.

J. Z. Knight admits to earning millions of dollars through Ramtha. During her heyday she employed a staff of fourteen to organize seminars and to publish tapes and brochures. Thousands of people have paid up to $1,700 each to hear Ramtha preach New Age self-reliance mingled with Eastern mysticism. Ramtha claims there is no right or wrong, just individual reality. He says, "The kingdom of God is within us all. Everyone has the power to master his destiny and achieve his desires through positive thinking."

Another well-publicized channeled entity called Seth was said to speak through Jane Roberts, who began receiving messages from Seth in 1963. According to Roberts, Seth described himself as "an energy personality essence no longer focused in physical reality."

Seth's primary message through Roberts over a twenty-year affiliation was that each of us creates our own reality by our beliefs and desires. He commanded supplicants, "Enjoy yourself! Listen to your own inner wisdom." Seth proclaimed that reality is self-created through beliefs; thus, changing one's belief alters reality. Each of us supposedly has counterparts, entities who once lived and others who live now, all of whom become facets of the personality and form a "greater self."

A group called Seth Network International (SNI) sought to connect those who believed in Roberts's readings. From 1992 to 1999, SNI's president was Lynda Dahl. She stepped down following the death of her partner, leaving the group in some disarray and declaring its programs "inactive." Remaining members of SNI created a Web site, www.sethnet.org.

A lesser known channeler was the Reverend Laura Cameron-Fraser, an Episcopal priest in Seattle who was forced from her church for believing a spirit named Jonah spoke through her. She found it illogical that God stopped talking to human beings and said, "I have reason to believe that Jesus Christ's voice is being heard today through channeling." Cameron-Fraser also claims the Bible was written by trance channelers and that Old Testament prophets were channelers.

Elsewhere, a trance channeler known only as Susie communicated with a spirit called Enoch, who believed that retarded children are reincarnated souls in a state of bliss who "choose to come and see the world through these blissful eyes. . . . It is their choice." Susie, a recovered alcoholic and cocaine addict who shunned publicity, would enter an altered, unconscious state and then permit her personality to dissolve into one of seven "guides." She charged forty-five dollars for a private session and conducted free public seminars.

Barbara Rollinson-Huss of Broomfield, Colorado, wanted to build a research center for spiritual training on forty-four acres in Colorado Springs. Even though the acreage was near the NORAD missile site, Rollinson-Huss was unconcerned. Her spirit guide told her that NORAD wouldn't be there much longer. Rollinson-Huss charged eighty-five dollars per session and claimed to channel information from dolphins. During one channeling session, Rollinson-Huss claimed that she channeled an Oriental spirit who spoke with a Chinese-American accent. Then the spirit of Jesus, followed by Buddha, allegedly came upon her. And last I checked, NORAD was still firmly in place.

Some critics think channeling results from self-hypnosis, which involves relaxation, concentration, turning inward, and focusing upon certain words, sounds, or images. The goal is to change one's state of consciousness. New Age advocates of channeling support the philosophy that each of us is part of a Universal Mind, and that makes possible talking with departed spirits about mundane human matters.

No significant scientific understanding of channeling has verified its claims to transcend time and space. Still, Wall Street investors have consulted channelers for stock market guidance, and even the United States Army has reportedly investigated the military implications of extrasensory perception (ESP). Communicating with spirits is lucrative. At one time Shirley MacLaine was charging people three hundred dollars each to attend her seminars called "Connecting with the Higher Self."

CHRISTIAN CRITIQUE: Practitioners of trance channeling claim it breaches the spiritual chasm between life on earth and life after death, providing spiritual, moral, and financial help from allegedly advanced entities.

Channelers adhere to the New Age idea that Jesus Christ was not divine, only one of many prophets who came to earth to educate mankind. God is within each person, who directs and controls his own destiny. Human channels can intervene in the spirit world and summon spirit entities to communicate with the living for mundane purposes.

It was for such activities that God required the life of King Saul (1 Chronicles 10:13). Known as necromancy in Scripture, trance channeling was considered an abomination by God (Deuteronomy 18:11).

SOURCES: *Denver Post*, 23 June 1985; *New Age Journal* (November-December 1987); *New Realities*, March-April, 1988; *Time*, 15 December 1986; *USA Today*, 28 January 1987.

See also New Age Movement; Spiritualism and Spiritism.

TRANSCENDENTAL MEDITATION (TM)

One of the more popular Eastern religious practices of the 1960s, TM has extended its mystical reach into education, business, and politics.

FOUNDER: Maharishi Mahesh Yogi, born in 1911 as Mahesh Brasad Warma in Jabalpur, Madhya Pradesh, India

TEXT: Hindu scriptures, including the Bhagavad Gita, which the Maharishi views as an "indispensable" religious document

SYMBOLS: The letters TM and images of the Maharishi

APPEAL: Most seekers do not turn to TM because they are searching for religious truth. Instead, they are looking for a means of attaining inner peace and cessation of stress with the minimum commitment of time and discipline. TM claims to have phenomenal psychophysiological benefits and offers release from feelings of guilt.

OVERVIEW: Many people in the West didn't know much about Eastern religions until the 1960s, when four long-haired men known collectively as the Beatles traveled to India to study with a holy man named Maharishi Mahesh Yogi. That wouldn't be the last time the Maharishi (devout disciples insist "the" must be dropped) revealed his intuitive grasp of publicity and marketing.

Even though the words *transcendental* and *meditation* are deeply connected to a host of Eastern religious traditions and practices, the Maharishi spent a good part of the 1970s claiming these words had nothing to do with religion. The claims were all part of a campaign to have TM used in public schools, prisons, and other facilities where religious indoctrination was prohibited.

But on October 9, 1977, the pretense that TM "isn't a religion" ceased to be defensible. On that day U.S. District Judge H. Curtis Meanor issued an extensive eighty-two-page opinion upholding a plaintiff's claim regarding the religious nature of transcendental meditation. In Judge Meanor's words, "No inference was possible except that the teachings of SCI (Science of Creative Intelligence) and TM and the *puja* are religious in nature. No other inference is permissible or reasonable, especially because the court is dealing with the meaning of the constitutional term and not with a factual dispute." Seventeen months later the United States Court of Appeals for the Third Circuit, sitting in Philadelphia, affirmed this ruling.

The legal opinion regarding TM was valuable to Christians who were concerned about its incursions into various government-funded institutions. TM's seventeen government grants were halted, including a grant for $21,540 from the Department of Health, Education and Welfare to train 150 high school faculty members in teaching TM.

Even though the movement suffered a string of setbacks like this one, TM hasn't faded away. Instead, it remains popular in many quarters and has extended its influence in the worlds of business and politics. And of course, it has continued to court celebrities, who help give it legitimacy. U.S. senators, sports idols, movie stars, businessmen, and even doctors continue to tout TM's benefits.

To a generation raised on commercials for quick-relief products, expediency is all important. Thus, when an M.D. advises, "no technique of meditation is as effective as TM in producing deep rest and consequent psychophysiological integration," who really cares about the intrinsic pagan nature of such a practice? After all, the highly publicized benefits of TM allegedly include relief from insomnia, normalization of weight, beneficial effects on asthma, faster reaction time, broader comprehension, the curbing of alcohol and drug abuse, criminal rehabilitation, improved athletic performance, increased intelligence quotients, and improved ability to focus attention.

From Anonymity to Fame

Maharishi Mahesh Yogi was born Mahesh Brasad Warma in 1911 in Jabalpur, Madhya Pradesh, India. At thirty-one years of age he graduated from Allahabad University with a degree in physics. He worked for a while in a factory until crossing paths with Swami Brahamananda Saraswati, Jagadguru, Bhagwan Shankaracharya of Jyotir Math (commonly known as Guru Dev, meaning "Divine Teacher"). In 1956 he adopted the name Maharishi, which means "Great Sage."

Guru Dev had left his home at age nine to seek enlightenment. Under the teachings of Swami Krishanand Saraswati he achieved his God-realization and became known as an *avatar*, a manifestation of the divine. Guru Dev had revived a technique of meditation that originated from the Hindu monastic tradition of Shankara, a philosopher who established the practice in the ninth century A.D. For twelve years, Maharishi was the favorite student of Guru Dev.

When his spiritual mentor died in 1953, Maharishi retreated to a Himalayan cave for two years. In 1958 he ended up in Madras, where during a lecture he spontaneously announced a plan to spread TM all over the world. He formed the International Meditation Society and headed for the West. In Los Angeles in 1959, he chartered the Spiritual Regeneration movement. He finally settled in a London apartment, where nothing much happened until 1967.

Flower power was in bloom, but the sex- and drug-crazed ways of the

Beatles had brought the Fab Four disillusionment and frustration. George Harrison met the Maharishi and persuaded John, Paul, and Ringo to join him on a pilgrimage to India. There the Beatles, with Mia Farrow in tow, sat at the Maharishi's feet to be schooled in the ancient Vedic practice of Transcendental Meditation. The Rolling Stones and the Beach Boys joined the bandwagon. Of the latter group, Mike Love and Al Jardine became TM teachers. Brian Wilson augmented the faith of his comrades by lyrically declaring, "Transcendental Meditation, it works real good / More, much more than I thought it would." With such celebrity endorsements, the Maharishi confidently boasted, "I shall bring fulfillment to the hippie movement."

The Maharishi pocketed a week's pay from his followers (a substantial sum for a Beatle!) and blitzed the United States with a lecture tour. The disarming smile of this giggly guru dominated magazine covers and TV talk shows. With flowers in hand he repeated the basic theme that the mind has a natural tendency to seek happiness.

But peace and serenity are only possible if one passes beyond the normally experienced states of consciousness: sleep, dreaming, and wakefulness. Man must learn to "meditate" so he can "transcend" to the fourth state of "bliss consciousness," a condition of "pure awareness" where one is tuned in to "creative intelligence."

The promises were euphoric. Maharishi confidently predicted that just one percent of the population practicing TM in any locality would reduce crime and empty hospitals. Many victims of stress and hypertension gave glowing testimonials. Some argued that such relief was merely due to an anticipatory attitude aided by the forty minutes of restful posture that TM required each day. But supporters seemed to far outnumber detractors until the bubble of optimism burst.

Troubles for a Guru

"We were wrong," the Beatles concluded, with John accusing the Maharishi of being a "lecherous womanizer." The Maharishi's following was nearly defunct, and crowds no longer seemed charmed by his Hindu platitudes. Though he had once hobnobbed with celebrity luminaries, the Maharishi headed home with the pronouncement, "I know that I have failed. My mission is over."

His stay in his Rishikesh, India, ashram was cut short by a government-launched financial inquiry, so he set up shop in Fiuggi Fonte, an Italian resort community. There he decided to revamp his entire approach and vocabulary. His resplendent beard and hypnotically dark eyes disappeared from American TV screens. But not for long.

The Maharishi began to change his tactics. Religious terminology was dropped in favor of psychological and scientific language. The Spiritual Regeneration movement became the Science of Creative Intelligence (SCI), and the Maharishi presented an image of a friendly psychotherapist rather than a Hindu monk. His inner circle may have heard him call the Bhagavad Gita "an anchor for the ship of life sailing on the turbulent waves of time." But outsiders only heard the oft-repeated litany, "It's not a religion."

The ruse worked. By the mid-1970s, more than a million Americans had tried TM. Seven thousand teachers were propagating the Maharishi's gospel in more than one hundred U.S. centers. The group's income jumped to over $20 million a year as thirty to forty thousand followers a month joined the movement to meditation.

For an introductory fee that at the time ran from $55 for college students to $125 for adults (now increased), everyone was guaranteed inner peace. Best of all, there was no renunciation of materialism or desire, as in the Buddhist tradition, and no repentance of sin or reformation of character, as in the Christian tradition. All around the world, in prison cells and military barracks, TMers gathered twice a day to chant their mantras. The Maharishi was virtually deified as a yogi who had achieved "a perpetual fourth state of consciousness" with an "awesome" clarity of mind.

Though TM has popularized the terms *meditation* and *mantra*, most people are still a little vague about their precise definitions. To understand their usage in TM, it is necessary to decipher the religious framework of the Maharishi's entire system.

Assessing TM's Religious Roots

The religious philosophy of the Maharishi is rooted in Vedic Hinduism. God is a pantheistic, pervasive "Absolute Being" (*Brahman*). Even a person's inner self is part of this divine being. In Christianity, a person's dilemma is separation by sin from a transcendent deity. The Maharishi sees a person's foremost problem as alienation from his "True Being." Salvation is derived by contacting this inner state of pure consciousness. Meditation is the key to transcending (going beyond) the three levels of normal consciousness (discussed earlier) to the fourth state, where one is cognizant of his soul's true nature.

Three additional levels exist: cosmic consciousness, complete God consciousness, and Unity consciousness. Beginners in TM hear only about the first two, but the Maharishi's ultimate goal is to lead all humanity to Unity consciousness. At that point, the "mediator" (one who practices TM) is liberated from the karmic cycles of reincarnation by achieving sinlessness.

For the present, the Maharishi is content with introducing adherents to the fourth level of consciousness. But what the mediator may not realize is that the interpretation of the process is based on assumptions that represent a systematic approach to Hindu theology. At the heart of this hypothesis is the mantra. Representatives of the Maharishi insist it is only a vibratory sound with "no denotative meaning." On the contrary, Hindu tradition says that such words or syllables have supernatural powers, often invoking a deity who is believed to embody the sound.

TM as prescribed by the Maharishi requires the mediator to sit with eyes closed in a quiet, relaxed position, twenty minutes in the morning and again in the evening. All the while his mind repeats the Sanskrit word deemed to be his personal mantra. This mantra is the means of diving to the depths of the mind's ocean, delving into ever subtler recesses of thought. No mental discipline is necessary. The mantra does it all. Just let the mind go out of gear and coast to its desired destiny of fulfillment.

In the process, one's deepest thoughts emerge and dissipate like tiny champagne bubbles. As the incantation progresses, the mediator is supposed to be relieving tension and disposing of stress. When the source of all thought is reached, the chanter has available "a reservoir of energy, intelligence, and happiness." Only 73,500 minutes of meditation later, the faithful have hope of absolute union with the Being, provided they never meditate before bed or after a meal.

Mantras aren't easy to acquire. The introductory fee is a mandatory requirement. Every mediator must also undergo an initiation ceremony that is distinctly idolatrous in nature. The mediator, with fruit, flowers, and a white handkerchief in hand, takes off his shoes and enters a candlelit room. Then the instructor directs the mediator to lay these items on a flower-banked altar that features a color portrait of Guru Dev. Incense pervades the atmosphere. Finally, the teacher kneels before the altar and begins to sing in Sanskrit. The mediator may stand or kneel as he listens to this ten-minute recitation.

When TM first became popular, most people didn't question this part of the ceremony. They were told it was "not a religious observance" but merely an opportunity for the teacher to "express his gratitude to the tradition from which TM comes." Apprehensive students were said to be "witnessing" the ritual, "not participating." Christian researchers weren't placated by this innocuous tale and persisted in their attempts to uncover the truth about the proceedings. What they discovered came as no shock.

The TM initiation song is actually a devotional Hindu hymn called a *puja* (which means "worship"). Guru Dev's picture represents a *muri*, the literal embodiment of God in corporeal form. While singing the puja, the instructor first invokes the favor and presence of the Hindu gods. Then he presents seventeen offerings to Guru Dev before finally praising him (personified in his picture idol) as an incarnation of deity. Among the lines recited are: "To lotus-born Brahma the Creator, to Shakti, . . . I bow down. At whose door the whole galaxy of gods pray . . . Guru, I bow down . . . the teacher of the truth of the Absolute, the Shri Guru Dev, I bow down."

After this incantation the teacher leans toward the mediator and whispers a mantra in his ear. The secret word is supposed to be his own specialized mantra, chosen for him by a Maharishi-trained instructor. The mantra must never be divulged to an outsider, even a spouse, or it will lose its magical powers. The mediator's own particular temperament, personality, and profession have presumably been analyzed to determine the mantra that will produce the appropriate psychic vibrations. In fact, investigation has shown that only sixteen TM mantras actually exist, and these are dispensed according to age.

Does the mantra really work? Though the Maharishi's organizations publish volumes of information about research studies, most non-TM scientists are skeptical. No findings exist that have been subject to the proper objective controls that could substantiate the claims of TM. The American Association for the Advancement of Science evaluated TM's stress-reducing capabilities. Tests concluded that the Maharishi's meditation techniques "produced no measurable change whatever in the body's basic metabolism, and further, TM did not induce a unique state of consciousness."

New Ventures

Always seeking new opportunities for income and the promotion of their beliefs, followers of the Maharishi spent the late 1980s supporting a major promotional program for Ayurvedic medicine. Kicked off at the Maharishi Center for Ayur-Veda in Fairfield, Iowa, which is adjacent to Maharishi International University, the effort appealed to people interested in holistic health by selling a wide range of products. Sales were handled by Maharishi Ayurvedic Products International, which had offices in Colorado Springs.

In the 1990s TM disciples turned increasing attention to politics, establishing the Natural Law Party. The party's candidate in the 1996 U.S. presidential election was John Hagelin, but he spent much of his time on the campaign trail dealing with controversies concerning his religious views. He only received a miniscule portion of the popular vote.

In 2002 residents of Vedic City, Iowa (the name now given to the large constellation of educational and business ventures based near Fairfield), even issued their own money, called Raam Mudra. Designed primarily as a publicity event to promote Vedic City's plans to build a TM theme park, the stunt only further divided devotees from local residents.

Beneficial or Troubling?

Evangelical critics charge that even if positive effects could be proven, there are dangerous spiritual consequences. To begin with, TM conditions the mediator's view of reality and religion, predisposing him toward an Eastern concept of humans and God. The guilt of sin can be neutralized by inducing a false sense of serenity, replacing the stress caused by conviction.

Demonic phenomena may result because spiritual defense mechanisms become ineffective when the mind enters a state of passivity. Some mediators report a "blackout phenomenon," waking up hours after starting to chant, unable to remember what has happened. In addition, some advanced mediators exhibit neuroses and psychoses resulting from the practice of "unstressing," the procedure of shedding karma from one's present and past lives through prolonged meditation.

To counter such criticisms, Maharishi has tried to further refurbish his image. God-name mantras have been dropped, and the organization of the group has been subdivided. The TM empire now includes: World Plan Executive Council, Student International Meditation Society, American Foundation for Creative Intelligence, American Meditation Society, Maharishi International University, Maharishi European Research University, Institute for Fitness and Athletic Excellence, Affiliated Organizational Conglomerate, and other related ventures. The Maharishi directs the activities of all these organs from his international headquarters in the Swiss village of Seelisberg.

As the number of new converts plunged to an estimated low of four thousand per month in the late seventies, TM launched its most controversial aspect—the Sidhi program. (*Sidhi* is a Sanskrit term denoting supernatural, occultic powers. The Maharishi has adopted this variant spelling for trademark purposes.) A *Sidha* (one who has completed Sidhi training) spends from three to five thousand dollars to reach an enlightened state of infinite compassion. He is also supposed to have the ability to walk through walls, become invisible, and levitate.

Advanced mediators claim to have mastered dematerialization and flying, "just like Peter Pan." In mattress-filled rooms ("landings are unusually bumpy"), the Maharishi's most ardent followers say they begin by hopping, then floating, in preparation for flight. Leaders claim that thousands have mastered the art, but they have repeatedly turned down offers of up to ten thousand dollars from members of the press to witness a mediator in flight. The validity of the Sidhi program is undercut by the Maharishi's preferred forms of transportation—his two Rolls-Royces and a private helicopter that await outside his residence.

By promoting such bizarre phenomena as flying, the Maharishi may have lost his hold on mainstream America. But he seems oblivious to any indication that his welcome has been outworn. From his head office in the "International Capital of the Age of Enlightenment," a decree went forth: "Society will soon be characterized by harmony and happiness. Through the Science of Creative Intelligence, education will be ideal, producing fully developed citizens. Through the Transcendental Meditation programme, health will be perfect. There will be peace in the family of nations."

In 1984 a three-week "Taste of Utopia" conference gathered Maharishi disciples from thirty countries to infuse a troubled world with a force they called "positivity." The conference, held in TM's university in Fairfield, Iowa, gathered seven thousand mediators (seven thousand is approximately the square root of one percent of the world's population, supposedly a number of some significance). Devotees claimed that "positivity" was really effective during that period, since the U.S. stock market rose, three nations showed a decrease in traffic fatalities, and there were fewer war deaths. (One wonders if the word *coincidence* ever occurred to the mediators.)

Whether TM's vaunted relief from tension will enhance the world's moral virtue, as claimed by this pronouncement, is yet to be proven. The mantras may give mediators an improved sense of well-being. But it remains to be seen whether such positive feelings will also produce individuals who act in accordance with sound ethics.

TM's ethics have been seriously questioned in the past. In 1987 a U.S. district court found two TM organizations guilty of fraud and negligence and ordered them to pay damages to Robert Kropinsky, who said TM had not made good on the promises that chanting would reduce stress, improve his memory and health, and enable him to levitate and otherwise manipulate the laws of nature.

CHRISTIAN CRITIQUE: The public posture of TM insists that the Maharishi's mantras open the mind to a state of "bliss consciousness" that unleashes creative impulses and reduces stress. In the place of suffering and salvation, TM promotes health and happiness. Supposedly, when there is one TM teacher for every one thousand citizens on earth, social ills and conflicts will cease.

The esoteric aims of TM are to introduce the meditator to the underlying Hindu theological precepts (i.e., "all is one" and humans are gods). As for those who do not practice TM, the Maharishi says, "There will not be a place for the unfit . . . in the Age of Enlightenment."

TM practitioners who go on to advanced stages will ultimately experience a merged unity with pure Being and may possibly become unwitting mediums for evil spirits. (Though the Maharishi acknowledges the existence of demons, he cautions against any contact with them.)

In addition, the TM initiation ceremony violates the first commandment. Matthew 6:7 denounces the chanting of mantras. Maharishi Mahesh Yogi's monist view of the universe is not compatible with the scriptural presentation of a personal God, who as Creator is distinct from his creation.

Christian meditation is an outward concentration on the Word and ways of God, whereas TM is a passive, selfish, inward withdrawal from reality. The repetitive sensory stimulation dulls the conscious mind and makes it vulnerable to evil invasion. Christ's blood atonement is rejected in the Maharishi's statement, "[TM] is the only way to salvation and success in life: there is no other way."

SOURCES: *Christianity Today,* 9 April 1976, 17; *Junior Statesman* (Indian youth magazine published in Calcutta), 20 January 1968; *Liberty,* May-June 1979, 14–15; Maharishi Mahesh Yogi, *Science of Being and Art of Living* (Bergenfield, N.J.: New American Library, 1963); Ibid., *On the Bhagavad-Gita: A New Translation and Commentary* (Baltimore: Penguin, 1976); Ibid., *Meditations of Maharishi Mahesh Yogi* (New York: Bantam, 1968); Ibid., *Transcendental Meditations* (New York: Delacorte, 1975); "Manipulative Metaphysics," *Christianity Today,* 20 February 1987, 54; Pat Means, *The Mystical Maze* (San Bernardino, Calif.: Campus Crusade for Christ, 1976); *Newsweek,* 7 January 1974, 73–35; Ibid., 13 June 1977, 98–100; David Pitt, "Meditators Money Fails at Transcendence," *Denver Post,* 30 April 2002, 5A; *Province* (Vancouver, B.C.), 28 October 1978, 21; Steve Rabey, "Maharishi, Inc.," *Christian Research Journal* (winter 1997): 48; *Right On,* November 1975, 8–14; *Rolling Stone,* 3 June 1976, 10; *SCP Newsletter,* November 1977; Jack Sparks, *The Mind Benders* (Nashville: Thomas Nelson, 1977); *Time,* 23 October 1972, 102–105; Ibid., 13 October 1975, 71–74; Ibid., 8 August 1977, 75; *TM Newsletter,* July-August, 1976; TM, miscellaneous promotional literature; *USA Today,* 4 March 1985, 11A; "Utopian Thinking in Iowa," *Newsweek,* 2 January 1984, 31.

ACCESS: TM Centers are in more than one hundred countries and hundreds of U.S. cities. World Plan Executive Council, P.O. Box 370, Lake Shandelee Rd., Livingston Manor, NY 12758; world headquarters, Maharishi International Capital of the Age of Enlightenment, Acrogyadham, Maharishi Nagar, Ghaziabad, U.P. 201304, India.

UFOS

Starry-eyed devotees say earth is being visited by aliens from other planets who have superior intelligence and will save humanity from an apocalypse.

TEXT: Various occult and pagan writings are cited as metaphoric references to UFOs. Some claim that Ezekiel 1 is a biblical account of UFOs.

APPEAL: It is becoming increasingly obvious that mankind's dilemmas need an external solution. Those who refuse to seek a transcendent God may assume that extraterrestrials of a higher technological and spiritual state may be able to save humanity. Curiosity about the unknown creates a mystical fascination with UFOs.

OVERVIEW: Ken Arnold could hardly believe his eyes. There, just outside the window of the small aircraft he was piloting, were nine metallic discs floating in the air. They darted about with incredible speed and maneuverability.

When Arnold landed, he immediately reported the incident. "What did they look like?" he was asked. More than half a century later his answer is still the descriptive preference of those who have had similar experiences—flying saucers.

The staple of science fiction literature for years, UFOs, or unidentified flying objects, have experienced a resurgence in popularity. TV shows like *The X-Files* and movies like *Close Encounters of the Third Kind, E.T., Contact,* and *Independence Day* helped this resurgence, as did the popularity of a place called Roswell.

Roswell is a New Mexico city, the site where an alien space ship allegedly landed in 1947. Journalist Julia Duin reports: "Although all military records pertaining to the so-called 'Roswell Incident' have been 'lost,' there's a mood in our culture to believe Roswell is Ground Zero in the search for extraterrestrial life. . . . The issue goes beyond science or astronomy. Dig deep into any study of alien appearances and a spiritual dimension appears."

Some are even hoping to move questions of whether alien life exists from science fiction to science. A 1999 decision by the National Aeronautics and Space Administration provides government funding for alien investigations. As *The New York Times* reported, "NASA gave new prominence today to its search for extraterrestrial life by appointing a Nobel laureate to head its recently formed Astrobiology Institute, dedicated to studying the origin, distribution and destiny of life in the universe."

Strange Encounters

Alleged sightings of UFOs have occurred at random times and locations throughout the world, but the phenomena do bear similarities. The craft are usually described as being circular, cylindrical, or spherical in shape, with flashing lights and luminous brilliance. They change color and shape, appear and disappear, and seemingly defy the laws of physics. In just a few seconds they can accelerate from a resting position to speeds clocked at several thousand miles per hour and then make a ninety-degree turn in midair. In their wake, they leave vile odors, mutilated animals, radiation burns, charred landing spots, and various kinds of electrical interference.

Dr. J. Allen Hynek has long been considered one of the world's ranking experts on UFOs. He has classified these appearances according to the following categories of "close encounters":

1. observation of a UFO within five hundred feet
2. physical traces left behind
3. actual contact with the occupants
4. abduction or examination by these beings

Hynek says the evidence concerning all four kinds of encounters is overwhelming, and in some cases irrefutable. Actual contact with the occupants of a UFO is the "close encounter" referred to in the film titled *Close Encounters of the Third Kind*. This was just one of many immensely popular movies focusing on extraterrestrial beings.

Investigating Truth Claims

With all the talk these days about UFOs and the widely circulated stories of people who claim to have communicated with the occupants of such aircraft, people are being forced to take these strange events seriously.

UFO tales must either be explained or explained away. If they are not real phenomena, then they should be dismissed without further consideration. If such occurrences are legitimate, then the nature and origin of UFOs need to be determined. Christians have an additional concern as to how these appearances may affect the spiritual future of mankind.

Are UFOs real? Most alleged sightings are not real and are easily dismissed as mistakenly identified planets, rocket launchings, weather balloons, and atmospheric phenomena. The Air Force Project Blue Book was able to provide a rational explanation for all but 700 of 12,600 cases of sightings between 1947 and 1969.

Other reports are not as easy to dismiss. What of the cases where UFOs have torn off treetops, ricocheted bullets, and razed thousands of acres of forest in the Soviet Union? What about the hundreds of reports from responsible citizens claiming to have seen and heard unexplainable objects zooming across the sky? Why do these flying machines often hover near power lines, bodies of water, and military installations? Can such a diversity of situations with striking similarities all be dismissed as hallucinatory speculations or imaginations run wild?

If UFOs are from some unknown human source, who is responsible for them? Only the industrialized nations could possibly have access to the kind of antigravitational technology necessary for such phenomena. If any advanced nation does have knowledge of such secrets, how has such information been so well hidden for so long? Supposing that such expertise does exist, only satanic influence would lead men to wreak such havoc and terror on their own unsuspecting countrymen.

The most commonly accepted theory regarding the origin of UFOs is that of ETIs (extraterrestrial intelligences). Unofficially, the U.S. government presumes that such aircraft must come from other planets. When the *Voyager* spacecraft rose beyond earth's gravity, it carried on board a twelve-inch copper LP title, "Sounds of Earth." The record's ninety minutes of playing time included numerically coded explanations of our geology, chemistry, and mathematics.

Psychologist Leo Sprinkle of the University of Wyoming division of counseling and testing, who is also a consultant for the Aerial Phenomena Research Organization, claims that he has hypnotized over fifty people who say they have been aboard UFOs. Professor Sprinkle reports that these subjects are able to recall their stellar voyages in minute detail.

The accounts of ETI contacts seem to fit a pattern. A person is usually engaged in some ordinary activity when suddenly a UFO is sighted and they investigate out of curiosity. As the humanoid occupant of the UFO approaches them, the person is usually frightened at first. Then the creature gives reassuring gestures to calm the earthling and proceeds to give him a physical examination by passing a probe over his body. Some victims tell of sexual encounters with their captors. They usually report that communication with the ETI takes place nonverbally by telepathy. They say that the aliens insist they are benevolent agents sent to help humankind and assist us in understanding the deeper nature of spiritual truth. The alien conveys a brief summary of something approximating occult philosophy and then hypnotizes or places the person in a trance to wipe the abduction experience from their memory.

God and UFOs

Accepting the existence of extraterrestrial beings necessitates subscribing to one of two explanations for their origin: the evolutionary hypothesis or a belief in other God-created stellar civilizations. The option of nontheistic evolution is not available to the Christian. The simplest, single-cell organism known to exist is still far too complex to have spontaneously evolved by chance somewhere in the universe. The Bible teaches that God alone is the Creator of life, and the feasibility of conscious beings springing forth from nonorganic life is not scripturally supportable.

On the other hand, since there is no specific Bible verse prohibiting the possibility of extraterrestrial life, some argue that this omission leaves open the option that God may have created beings on other planets. Proponents of this theory insist that in the vastness of space there must surely be other races of creatures to whom God has given life. "We're so small and insignificant compared to the infinite realm of the universe," the argument goes, "how dare we be so egotistical as to assume we are alone?"

In his book *The High Frontier: Human Colonies in Space*, Princeton physicist Gerald K. O'Neill put it this way: "The idea that we as intelligent life are unique is of course absurd. The more we learn about the origins of life, the more we realize that the conditions under which life first began on earth must have been duplicated many times over in other parts of the galaxy."

If God did choose to create intelligent beings on other planets, they too would be tainted by Adam's sin, which affected the entire cosmos. They would be fallen creatures like human beings and thus possibly have the same technological limitations that we do. If sin's retrogressive impact on man's advancement has prevented us from going to visit them, how could they possibly come to us? If for some reason sin has not invaded their race, would God permit such an unfallen civilization to contact us and thus be contaminated by our sin? The answer to both of these questions is decidedly negative. If extraterrestrial beings do exist, surely the Lord would have told us without equivocation. It seems that such a crucial matter would be discussed somewhere in the Word of God.

Since it appears likely that neither human agencies nor extraterrestrial creatures are the source of UFOs, we are left to consider whether they are of supernatural origin. Author, lecturer, and UFO expert Robert Achzenner has put it this way: "I have come to these conclusions. The unknown objects and their manifestations are real; they are intelligently controlled; and no government authority or scientific agency knows what they are, where they are from, or why they are here."

One thing appears certain: We are not alone in the cosmos. Something or someone is out there. Professor Leo Sprinkle expressed his view of the situation like this: "My guess is that they're more than just a physical phenomenon, that they're a psychic or spiritual phenomenon too." J. Allen Hynek said these aliens may come from a "parallel reality." He concluded, "I suspect that a very advanced civilization might know something about the connections between mind and matter that we don't."

Is it possible that this "parallel reality" is angelic in origin? Such a presumption cannot be excluded, since the Bible does warn us that in the end times "great signs shall there be from heaven" (Luke 21:11). Likewise, the prophet Joel declared that God would "shew wonders in the heavens" (2:30). There are some committed believers who suggest that a percentage of UFOs are "chariots" of the Lord's "hosts." Others wonder if perhaps the Rapture of the saints will take place when living Christians board flying saucers and are whisked away to be with the Lord. Another possibility often stated is that

UFOs are evidences of God's angelic army, amassing for the war in heaven that has been prophesied for the last days.

Analyzing the Encounters

To discuss whether or not UFOs are of godly origin, we need to divide the phenomena into two categories: encounters of the first kind (sightings), and encounters of the third kind (contact).

Third-kind encounters do not appear to be angelic. The conduct of UFO occupants (for example, sexual assaults and induced trance states) and the metaphysical message they bring is contrary to the activity that would be expected of unfallen angels. Whenever they appear in Scripture, angels of the Lord always carry out specific, divine missions. Their purpose is to convey a glorious revelation of God's plan (for example, the announcement of Christ's birth to the shepherds in Luke 2:9-14) or to execute the Lord's wrath and judgment (the destruction of Sodom and Gomorrah in Genesis 19:12-17). Above all, as evidenced by Revelation 22:8-9, they never draw attention to themselves. True angels of the Lord speak only when divinely commissioned to do so, with the intent of directing man's attention to God.

Having ruled out the probability of angelic encounters of the third kind, what may be said of UFO encounters of the first kind (sightings)? Obviously, if no direct, personal contact is made with the occupants of such craft, no objectively conclusive statements can be made. But inferences can be drawn from the nature of such visitations.

The occurrences of poltergeist phenomena and feelings of terror experienced by observers suggest demonic rather than angelic visitation. When God intervenes supernaturally, it is to bring comfort and peace, unless there is a clear reason for his wrath to be exhibited. What can be said of blips disappearing from radar screens and flashing oval objects floating through distant skies? While neither God nor Satan can be positively identified as the source, the latter seems a far more likely culprit.

The descriptions given of UFO occupants usually include grotesque features and oddly shaped bodies. They may have enlarged heads, slits for eyes, ethereal forms, and antennae sticking out of their skulls. Most accounts describe beings that bear a distinct resemblance to the "familiar spirits" described in classical Spiritualism.

When UFO visitors speak, their message brings neither solace nor information in conformity with God's Word. They talk of cosmic awareness and transcendence to higher spiritual planes. Their discourses never glorify Christ as God and Creator. Instead, the humans they contact are told to prepare for an age of peace that will be ushered in by these unidentified aliens.

UFO occupants also encourage participation in a variety of psychic practices: astral projection, psychokinesis, automatic handwriting, clairvoyance, and levitation. Sin, judgment, and the redemptive work of Christ are never mentioned. Their words, their actions, and their appearances betray the concealed satanic origin of these beings.

If it can be concluded that the majority of UFOs are of demonic origin, then what is their ultimate purpose? Couldn't the devil just as easily accomplish his ends by another means, or do UFOs serve a unique roll in the master plan of Satan to deceive mankind?

An interesting insight was provided by Jacques Vallee, a Frenchman who served as a consultant to the film *Close Encounters of the Third Kind* and who has a master's degree in astrophysics and a doctorate in computer science. As an exponent of UFO investigations, he concluded that such phenomena are creating "a willingness to believe in extraterrestrial life." He goes on to point out that "attitudes on the subject among scientists, the media, and the public have totally changed in twenty years. We can rationalize this change or we can recognize it for what it is—the result of a shifting of our mythological structure."

It may be that UFOs are reeducating mankind to accept a casual familiarity with paranormal activity. This conditioning process will be completed under the reign of the Antichrist. During that time fire will fall from heaven, a fatal wound will be healed, and an inanimate image will live and speak (Revelation 13:13-15). The apostle John explains that such miracles will be used to deceive humanity into following the Antichrist (Revelation 13:14).

Many people would like to think that human beings today are more advanced than the primitive pagans of antiquity. But is the mythology of gods, goddesses, and superbeings really any different from the fascination with contacting humanoids from distant planets? The Greeks built their altar to the unknown god, while we erect giant dish antennae to probe the heavens in search of some distant trace of extraterrestrial life, seemingly indicated by a pulsing radio wave. Perhaps the persistent Old Testament warnings against any communication with "familiar spirits" applies to modern interest in UFOs as well.

CHRISTIAN CRITIQUE: People are curious about UFOs; they want to understand them and find out if their supposed occupants are of a higher state of evolution. If so, some people think, communications with them may reap certain scientific benefits.

But those with a secular interest in UFOs fail to consider the possibility that such phenomena may be supernatural and demonic in nature. From that standpoint, Satan may be using UFOs to prepare the modern world to accept a casual familiarity with supernatural phenomena. This would facilitate the Antichrist's reign, and until then, create a milieu in which evil spirits may operate more freely.

The Bible does not give the slightest hint that extraterrestrials exist. Scripture indicates that God created only two kinds of beings—angels and humans.

In addition, Romans 8:19-23 indicates that the Fall in Eden had cosmological effects. The death of Christ at Calvary was distinctively for the descendants of Adam; how many other times would he have needed to give his life to redeem other civilizations?

SOURCES: *Anchorage Times,* 1 January 1978, B5; *Denver Post,* February 1978, 34, 38–39; J. Allen Hynek, *The UFO Experience* (New York: Ballantine, 1972); Warren Leary, "Search for Life beyond Earth Gets a Leader," *New York Times,* 19 May 1999, A16; *Newsweek,* 21 November 1977; *SCP Journal* 1, no. 2 (August 1977); *To the Point (South Africa),* 15 September 1978.

ACCESS: Many groups are interested in UFOs. One of the most popular today is the International UFO Museum and Research Center, 114 N. Main Street, Roswell, NM 88202, (505) 625-9495, www.iufomrc.com. Others include Association of Sananda and Sanat Kumara, Box 35, Mount Shasta, CA 96067; and Cosmic Circle of Fellowship, 4857 N. Melvina Ave., Chicago, IL 60630.

See also the Aetherius Society.

UNIFICATION CHURCH

Rev. Sun Myung Moon

This group claims that Jesus failed in his redemptive mission on earth—
and now it will finish that work.

FOUNDER: Sun Myung Moon, born January 6, 1920, in Kwangju Sangsa Ru, Korea, which is now controlled by Communist North Korea

TEXT: *Divine Principle,* by the Reverend Moon. Moon's revelations are said to be the "things to come" referred to in John 16:13.

SYMBOL: A square surrounded by a circle. Four spokes radiate from the outer circle to the center where they meet a smaller darkened sphere inside the square. This inner circle radiates spokes to the edge of the square.

APPEAL: Many Moonies are former evangelicals or frequent churchgoers. Their frustrations with hypocrisy and lack of dynamic leadership led them to

Moon. In the Unification Church they discover authority, a nonjudgmental, accepting kind of love, and a vision for world unity and peace.

OVERVIEW: "The cross is the symbol of the defeat of Christianity." I was stunned at that statement and wondered if the speaker really meant what he said. The Reverend Sun Myung Moon had harangued the audience through his Korean interpreter for over two hours. His message was filled with many theological absurdities, but this last statement topped them all. "The cross is the symbol of the defeat of Christianity," he repeated.

Full-page newspaper ads had stirred my curiosity. "Christianity in Crisis— New Hope for America," the headlines declared. The year was 1973, and few people had yet heard of this militant messiah. The word *Moonie* had not yet entered the average person's vocabulary. Today, the Reverend Moon, "Lord of the Second Advent" to his disciples, stirs international controversy.

Did Moon actually intend to ridicule the cross of Christ as representing the hallmark of Christianity's failures? Yes. And perhaps even more surprising, Moon has cultivated relationships with evangelical Christians in his never-ending bid for mainstream acceptance.

A Modern Messiah?

Moon went on to explain the theology that hatched this conclusion. Before Adam had a conjugal relationship with Eve, she was sexually seduced by the serpent, none other than the archangel Lucifer. The evil offspring of this union (Cain) became the seed from which Communism sprang. Abel, Adam's child, started the lineage resulting in the spiritual democracies of South Korea and the United States.

With the bloodline of humanity tainted by Eve's sexual sin, God's original purpose in creating Adam and Eve was thwarted. He had wanted them to procreate children for the perfect human family; therefore, Christ came to earth as a man to correct Adam's failures.

Moon says that Jesus of Nazareth was the bastard offspring of Zechariah and Mary. "Jesus is not God himself," he states. Since God intended for Christ to redeem mankind spiritually and physically, he needed to marry, father children, and begin rearing the perfect family. But before he could find the "Eve" he searched for, the Jews killed him. As a result, his death on the cross fulfilled only half of God's plan, the spiritual redemption of man.

Since then, God has searched for two thousand years to find someone who would redeem the human race by becoming the True Parent—the Third Adam, who must have a sinless life and be completely dedicated to God's will. If he qualifies, he will succeed where the First Adam (in Eden) and the Second Adam (Christ) failed.

Such theological assertions are only a small part of the highly unorthodox worldview held by Rev. Moon. He could easily be ignored as another Oriental fanatic, were it not for the fact that over 3 million people worldwide, including an estimated fifty thousand in the United States, make his doctrinal fantasies their supreme spiritual authority.

As a result, this millionaire industrialist from South Korea has enslaved the minds of thousands of young people, stripped them of their personal belongings, and pressed them into virtual servitude. In doing so, he has amassed a fortune for himself and his church.

Moon's bold denouncement of Christ's crucifixion is only one of his many notable and outlandish statements. He has also been quoted as follows:

"I will conquer and subjugate the world. I am your brain."

"He [God] is living in me. I am the incarnation of himself."

"I want to have members under me who are willing to obey me even though they may have to disobey their own parents."

"In restoring a man from evil sovereignty, we must cheat."

"Master [Moon] here is more than any of those people [saints and prophets] and greater than Jesus himself."

To Save the World

How did Rev. Moon develop the egomania that led to such pretensions of self-deification? He was born in 1920 as Yong Myung Moon and was reared in a Presbyterian family. His clairvoyant inclinations in childhood climaxed at the age of sixteen when Moon claims he had a vision of Jesus. He claimed that Christ commissioned him to fulfill his interrupted task of physically saving humanity. Moon married his first wife in 1944 and began gathering a following. After meeting Park Moon Kim, a self-proclaimed messiah, Moon changed his name from Yong Myung Moon (Dragon Shining Moon) to Sun Myung Moon (Sun Shining Moon).

Moon spent the next few years in prison. He says he was persecuted for opposing Communism, though his contemporary critics claimed that accusations of ritual sex practices were the real reason behind his incarceration. In 1954 his wife divorced him. Shortly after that, he officially organized the Unification Church in Korea. Three years later he published his spiritual manifesto, *Divine Principle*. Meanwhile, he searched for the perfect woman. His marriage to a fourth wife, Hak Ja Han (some say he never divorced number two before going on to number three), was proclaimed as the "marriage of the Lamb" prophesied in Revelation 19. Such eccentricities brought charges of moral improprieties and excommunication from the Presbyterian Church.

This rebuke certainly didn't affect Moon's business success. His Korean conglomerates of munitions, tea, and titanium accumulated an estimated worth of $20 million. His next target for money and Moonies was the United States, where he headed in the early 1970s.

Pursuing the American Dream

The stage had already been set for Moon in 1959 when Young Oon Kim, an associate, brought Moon's message to America via an English translation of *Divine Principle*. Spiritualistic medium Arthur Ford extolled Moon as the New Age voice of religious thought.

Once he arrived in America, Moon wasted no time in getting on with his job in high style. He purchased a million-dollar headquarters complex and a posh residence in upstate New York. Moon added the New Yorker Hotel and Tiffany Building to his real estate portfolio, and there were rumors of overtures to buy the Empire State Building. A large-circulation newspaper called *News World* was launched, and nationwide tours heralded Moon's message.

Moon also started a newspaper in the nation's capital called *The Washington Times*. It is read by some conservative Christians who prefer it to the perceived liberal bias of *The Washington Post*, but the *Times* has been a money pit for Moon. In a 1982 speech celebrating the paper's tenth anniversary, Moon said, "I have invested close to $1 billion in this newspaper during the past ten years." Interestingly, *The Washington Times* covered Moon's speech but omitted this intriguing statement!

Moon also sought mainstream acceptance by hobnobbing with political leaders. He defended the beleaguered Richard Nixon and was photographed with Hubert Humphrey and Ted Kennedy. His political aspirations were as exaggerated as his spiritual goals. He wanted nothing less than to organize a religious party and institute a worldwide, theocratic rule.

Provoking Strong Reactions

As Moon and his followers gained the attention of a skeptical press, a national controversy erupted. Parents charged him with brainwashing and hired deprogrammers to rescue their children from his clutches. Questions were raised regarding the legality of immigrant status for his Korean followers. Moonies swarmed Capitol Hill to cajole members of Congress. Meanwhile, other followers invaded shopping centers and airports, hawking flowers and candles to the tune of millions of dollars every year. Not so long ago, all this would have seemed like the plot line from a novel. In this case, fact is indeed stranger than fiction, providing an interesting commentary on the religious climate of America.

It can't be denied that Moon's teachings strike a responsive chord with many. Young people disillusioned with the institutional church and yearning for security within an authoritarian structure have provided much of the fuel for his spiritual wildfire. Invited to a weekend retreat of flattery, smiles, and "love bombing," potential Moonies hear nothing of Moon or his claims. It is later that the cult tactics of sensory deprivation, physical exhaustion, and intense indoctrination are used to introduce neophytes to their "true Father and Mother"—Mr. and Mrs. Moon.

Moon has also sought support from evangelicals by portraying himself as a paragon of family virtues. In 1997 Moon took out full-page ads in major newspapers to promote "Blessing '97," an event dedicated to "family values." "You may think of me as a man surrounded by controversy," he said in the ads. "We are not trying to promote me as an individual or expand the Unification Church as an institution. Our goal is to bring together all peoples and all religions in an effort to strengthen families."

But Moon has more than enough family problems of his own. According to an explosive 1998 article in *People* magazine, "Divorce, drugs, jail, a nasty custody battle—family woes lay bare the dark side of the Rev. Sun Myung Moon." According to the article, Moon's oldest son and the church's heir apparent, Hyo Jin, has been arrested for drunk driving, has been divorced, and has been charged with spouse abuse. Most of Moon's eleven other surviving children also lead troubled lives.

A Convoluted Theology

Moon's theological scheme is based on a scope of history divided into an Old Testament Age, a New Testament Age, and the present Completed Testament Age. The latter requires a new revelation of truth to supplant the Bible, and Moon's 536-page *Divine Principle* fills the bill. It was dictated to him by God, he explains, through the process of automatic handwriting. Its "truths" were compiled only after Moon had conferred in the spirit world with Buddha, Jesus, and other notable religious figures. All of them bowed in acquiescence to Moon, imploring him to bring humanity the unuttered revelations supposedly mentioned by Jesus in John 16:13. Moon also reserves the option of continuing to add supernatural revelation or adjusting his "divine principle" at a future date.

Central to Moon's belief system is the concept of a Third Adam, the messiah and lord of the Second Advent. Moon declares that this world savior will "appear in the East," that he will unify all religions, and that his birth date (determined by numerological calculation) was sometime about 1920. More specifically, this messiah must come from an Oriental land populated by Christians. He will be persecuted by the masses who reject him. Like John the Baptist, who came as Elijah, this "lord" will appear in a physical body.

Though Unification Church leaders are careful to avoid publicly naming Moon as this messiah, the deductive conclusions are inescapable. The suffering, torture, and bloodshed he claims to have endured in Communist prisons are supposed to be further proof of his redemptive mission.

Moon neither confirms nor denies that he is the Promised One but does purport to have personally conquered Satan. The present battle line between good and evil, God and the devil, is the thirty-eighth parallel between North and South Korea. Since the Almighty has chosen the United States as the bulwark against satanic Communism, it is Moon's duty to reverse America's moral and spiritual decline.

Moon promises more than a message. It is his duty to take up where Christ left off. The union with his present wife is presumed to result in a new humanity, unpolluted by Lucifer's bloodline. Do Moon's failed marriages disqualify him to be the messiah? "No!" Moonies respond emphatically. Moon's mission to save humanity is so crucial that more than one perfect woman could have been the "True Mother." God prepared three "Eves," and they all failed. Hak Ja Han is *the* Mother of humankind, the final chosen of God.

Sin, in Moon's estimation, results from corrupted physical genes, not a corrupted spiritual heritage and corrupt moral choices. Salvation results from being born of his perfect physical genes or entering a marital union chosen and blessed by him. Knowledgeable critics describe a doctrine called "blood cleansing"—removing Lucifer's genetic interference—which, when the cult was small, was accomplished by having female members engage in sexual intercourse with Rev. Moon. The dramatic growth of the cult necessitated that this premise be expanded to include purification for any male who has had relations with a woman "cleansed" by Moon. Now, those who totally submit to his authority may consider their devotion to be a spiritual kind of purification not requiring sexual activity.

The absolution Moon offers may require members to turn over all their financial assets to the Unification Church. Any child may be removed from personal parental guidance and placed under the church's corporate care. Prior marriages have to be ended and resolemnized by Moon. Those who are single must wait until they have completed seven years of service to Moon before he chooses a mate for them. Some do not meet their future marriage partner until the day of the wedding and are not allowed to consummate the union until forty days thereafter. To conserve Moon's time and energy, mass wedding ceremonies are held, where hundreds or even thousands of men and women are joined in matrimony at one time.

There are many other strange beliefs held by Moon. In some cases, members are encouraged to isolate themselves from all contact with parents and past associates. Mother and Father Moon are the True Parents (the term "heavenly Father" is reserved for God) and the only ones worthy of devotion. In exchange for this submission, all the necessities of life are provided. Food, clothing, and accommodations—everything from toothpaste to trousers—are served up commune-style for those members who forsake everything and pound the streets selling wares to augment church income. A minimum quota is suggested (such as $100 or more per day), though some ex-members claim to have brought in as much as $1,600 in one outing. Estimated totals indicate this approach brings in about $1 million every five days. Deliberate misrepresentation ("heavenly deceit") is used when a customer inquires regarding the destination of the proceeds. People are far more inclined to give to a "drug rehabilitation program" or to "feed starving children" than to fill the coffers of a self-anointed messiah. Members have also been known to solicit from wheel-chairs in order to enhance the sympathetic motives of potential contributors.

Problematic Practices

Moon's theology is a mixture of Christian concepts and Spiritualistic practices. He teaches that heaven is a realm of the spirit world. Hell is inconsequential, because it will "pass away as heaven expands." A person's destination after death depends on his spirit's "quality of life on earth; by the degree of goodness we build into them through our actions." Unlike the Christian promise of immortal perfection, Moon insists that in the afterlife his followers will experience the same "desires, dislikes, and aspirations as before death."

Any spot sprinkled with soil from Korea is considered to be holy ground. Evil spirits may be expelled by a sprinkling of "holy salt"; an application may be surreptitiously applied from behind whenever someone who is considered evil enters a Unification Church center.

Sunday mornings are set aside to pay homage to the True Parents. Rising at 5:00 A.M., the Church Family bows three times before a picture of the Reverend and Mrs. Moon. A pledge follows, in which members vow to do whatever is necessary to bring about Moon's will on earth. At times, prayer sessions (with petitions directed to Moon himself) become loud, frenzied affairs. Observers report seeing some devotees sob and wail, pounding their fists on the floor in explosive outpourings of grief and exclamations of victory. Moonies were described by one reporter as jerking spasmodically "in spiritual transport, like participants in a voodoo ceremony."

Such dramatic experiences are better than receiving a humiliating tirade from Moon. To those who fail his goals, the True Father is merciless. He scathingly attacks slothful members, accusing them of not helping to build the kingdom of heaven on earth.

From the beginning, occult practices have overshadowed Moon's approach. He admits to communicating with familiar spirits by means of seances. Though the Christian ordinances of baptism and communion are avoided, the Unification Church accepts clairvoyance, automatic handwriting, and mediumistic trances. Moon confidently predicts, "As history approaches its end point, more and more people will have spiritual and psychic experiences."

He promises followers that those who are completely surrendered to his precepts will witness spirit materialization of their Father (Moon). Certain members claim to have observed this phenomenon while others credit Moon with the ability to read their minds. Some initiates have been lured by dreams in which Moon and his wife have appeared to call them to service in the church. Ironically, those who consider forsaking Moon's teachings are warned that such actions may result in satanic possession.

Public Image

For a time Moon fell out of grace with Seoul's new governmental leaders, and favorable mention of him in the press was barred in his homeland. Many Koreans seemed genuinely embarrassed by Moon's image.

In the United States, public consciousness of his unsavory tactics is better known than the tactics of most cults. This has created a plethora of problems. Some of his church-owned buildings in New York have been declared taxable. The U.S. Immigration and Naturalization Service has recommended that Moon be deported, based on the falsified credentials of his wife's application for permanent resident alien status. A federal grand jury in New York handed down a twelve-point indictment charging Moon and an aide with tax evasion. In 1982 a court found him guilty of conspiracy to avoid taxes on $162,000 in personal income.

In 1984 Moon was sent to the Federal Correctional Institution in Danbury, Connecticut, for eleven months. (The Danbury facility has a reputation as a "country club" prison, more like a college dorm than a typical prison.) After his release he was to serve for seven months at Brooklyn's Oxford Project Halfway House, but during this period he was allowed to conduct his church business. While Moon's detractors were and are many, it became clear with his short (and relatively painless) imprisonment that his political and financial clout had made him, at least to some degree, above the law.

A curious sidelight on the case: Many organizations—including the National Association of Evangelicals, the National Council of Churches, and the American Civil Liberties Union—filed amicus briefs with the court, voicing their sympathy with Moon. Jerry Falwell was one of many religious leaders who claimed that Moon's prosecution was an assault on religious freedom.

Moon's aide, Mose Durst, claimed that all this publicity did not hurt the Unification Church. Rather, he says, membership jumped from 5 to 6 percent nationwide. This is essential for the church, since it must somehow make up for the estimated 50 percent attrition rate of disillusioned followers. So long as America remains a society of rootless youth, Moon's vision of hope for the future will continue to attract a sizable following. In fact, Moon's disciples are so confident of the days ahead that Mose Durst now openly declares Moon to be the "second Messiah," succeeding Jesus.

A Global Empire

The Moon empire is more widespread than most people know. The Unification Church invested at least $70 million in Uruguay and has therefore gained considerable control in that country. Because of Moon's anti-Communist stance, the church made powerful friends. The church purchased Banco de Credito, the third largest bank in Uruguay, plus the country's largest luxury hotel in Montevideo. Added to this impressive list of holdings, the Moonies also own three printing presses in Uruguay, a newspaper, and huge amounts of farmland.

Elsewhere in South America, Moonies had less success. Brazilian riots ousted them from that country, and the church gained little power or influence in Bolivia, Chile, and Paraguay.

Closer to home for Moon, the church operates two hotels in Communist North Korea, and in 2002, a Moon-funded auto plant opened near the coastal city of Nampo.

In the United States, the group operates numerous fishing businesses in Virginia and Massachusetts and has enormous real estate holdings throughout the country. The fishing businesses were controversial for a time, because as "church boats" they were tax-exempt, even though they were clearly commercial in nature. Paragon House, a book publishing firm in New York, was begun in 1984, with prominent scholars on its editorial board. A number of front organizations help to channel church money toward various anti-Communist movements.

CHRISTIAN CRITIQUE: Moon's literature states, "In the work of restoration [humankind's salvation], God worked to find one individual who could overcome his evil nature, and on the foundation of that person's faith to find a family around him, a society, a nation, and finally to restore the whole world."

Christianity apparently holds no hope since God has discarded it as a corrupt and outdated religion. God is pictured as a sad creature, surrounded by evil and estranged from his creation. Moon is the man who will cheer God's heart by accomplishing what Christ failed to do: redeem man physically from the curse of the serpent's sexual seduction of Eve.

The God depicted in *Divine Principle* is neither omnipotent nor sovereign in earth's affairs. It assigns a female nature to the Holy Spirit and ridicules Christ's resurrection—blasphemies of the highest order. Moon's doctrine of sinless perfection by "indemnity" (forgiveness of sin by works on Moon's behalf), which can apply even to deceased ancestors, is a denial of the salvation by grace offered through Christ (Galatians 1; Ephesians 2:8-9). The warning in Matthew 24 regarding false prophets is clearly fulfilled in Moon's doctrines and claims to spiritual authority.

SOURCES: *Circus,* 13 April 1976, 50–53; *Denver Post,* 1 February 1974, 6FF; Ibid., 5 December 1975, 5BB; Ibid., 18 February 1977, 8BB; Ibid., 3 March 1978, 4, 5BB; Ibid., 8 May 1981, 5BB; Chris Elkins, *Heavenly Deception* (Wheaton, Ill.: Tyndale, 1980); Ronald Enroth, *The Law of Cults* (Chappaqua, N.Y.: Christian Herald Books, 1979); Laurie Goodstein, "35,000 Couples Are Invited to a Blessing by Rev. Moon," *New York Times,* 28 November 1997,

A11; Don Lattin, "Moon Proclaims Himself New Messiah," *San Francisco Chronicle*, August 1990; *Media Spotlight*, January-March 1986, 1; *Newsweek*, 26 march 1975, 63; Ibid., 14 June 1976, 60–66; Ibid., 19 May 1980, 27; *People*, 20 October 1975, 7–9; *Psychology Today* 2, no. 8 (August 1976): 16–21; Edward Schumacher, *New York Times* News Service, "Rev. Moon's Uruguay Ties," *Dallas Morning News*, 26 February 1984; Sun Myung Moon, *Divine Principle* (New York: Unification Church, 1973); Ibid., *New Hope* (New York: Unification Church, 1973); *Time*, 10 November 1975, 44; Ibid., 14 June 1976, 45; Ibid., 28 February 1975, 42; Ibid., 19 December 1975, 13–16; Ibid., 12 March 1976, 45; Ibid., 8 October 1976, 59–62; Ibid., 20 July 1979, 38–40; Alex Tresniowski, "Moonstruck," *People*, 21 September 1998, 89–92; "The Unification Church—Who We Are," introductory pamphlet; J. Isamu Yamamoto, *Unification Church* (Grand Rapids, Mich.: Zondervan, 1995).

ACCESS: Holy Spirit Association for the Unification of World Christianity (The Unification Church), 4 W. 43rd. St., New York, NY 10036

UNITARIAN UNIVERSALIST ASSOCIATION

In an age when consumers are king, this association offers members a spiritual smorgasboard from which they can choose their own beliefs.

OVERVIEW: Most churches have an official doctrinal statement, but not this one. Instead, this church promotes principles that affirm the inherent worth and dignity of every person, the wisdom of the world's religions, and the importance of rationality and "the responsible search for truth and meaning."

As an outgrowth of the eighteenth-century Enlightenment movement, which included beliefs like rationalism and antisupernaturalism, Unitarian thought has historically attracted leading intellectuals, such as poet-essayist Ralph Waldo Emerson.

In 1959 the Unitarian Church merged with the Universalist Church, and today the combined group claims slightly fewer than two hundred thousand members in nearly one thousand churches.

Some might see the behavior of Unitarians as schizophrenic. On one hand, members laud the selfless sacrifice of Christ's crucifixion and often quote Scripture. On the other hand, they repudiate the Virgin Birth, the Atonement, and the Nicene, Chalcedonian, and Apostles' Creeds. They reject the Trinity affirmed in those creeds in favor of a unitary God. There are no sacraments observed by the members, who hold Jesus to be no more than a great prophet. And they subscribe to the doctrine that all souls will ultimately be saved. Their aim, according to the charter of the Universalist Church, is to "promote harmony among adherents of all religious faiths, whether Christian or otherwise."

Such inclusiveness has prevented the association from being accorded official recognition by national Christian bodies (for example, the National Council of Churches), though some Unitarians do belong to local ministerial groups.

Since the truth of God is said to be revealed in the sacred writings of all great religions, the philosophy of Unitarians is reduced to little more than an ethical system of morality. Heaven and hell are anathema to Unitarians, and the doctrine of the Atonement is said to be "offensive" and "unbiblical."

Present-day members differ as to whether they should classify themselves as Christian. Their adherence to universal truth as declared in the teachings of all prophets of all ages renders the terms *Christian* and *Unitarian* to be mutually exclusive.

More recently, president William Sinkford actually touched off a furor by suggesting that the association might consider reinserting the word "God" to accommodate what he called a "vocabulary of reverence." He argued that his denomination contained no "hint of the holy" and no way to discuss "human agency in theological terms." His statements caused concern among atheists and humanists who had found comfort in Unitarian circles. (Only 3 percent of Unitarian congregations call themselves "Christian.") What such ideas will do to a sect which currently blends elements of Buddhism, world religions, and scientific rationalism is yet to be seen.

SOURCES: *Christianity Today*, 2 August 1972; Walter Martin, *The Kingdom of the Cults* (Minneapolis: Bethany Fellowship, 1977); J. Gordon Melton, *The Encyclopedia of American Religions*, vol. 2 (Wilmington, N.C.: McGrath, 1978); Unitarian Universalist Association documents.

ACCESS: Unitarian Universalist Association, 25 Beacon Street, Boston, MA 02108

UNITY SCHOOL OF CHRISTIANITY

*Its language may sound Christian, but this group's message
is metaphysical and syncretistic.*

FOUNDERS: Founded in 1889 by Charles and Myrtle Fillmore of Kansas City, Missouri. Myrtle died in 1931, Charles in 1948. Their son Lowell served as the leader of Unity for many years. Current president J. Thomas Zender is the first CEO in Unity's history who never had a relationship with the Fillmores.

TEXT: The Bible, though passages are spiritualized and allegorized to fit Unity teachings. Sacred writings of all world religions are accepted. Charles Fillmore wrote: "Unity believes there is good in every religion on earth and that we should keep our minds open."

SYMBOLS: A circle with wings on both sides and the word *Unity* across the front; the several-storied tower that rises above the Unity Village complex; a light shining at night from a lone window, symbolizing "The Light that Shines for You," a reference to Silent Unity's constant prayer vigil.

APPEAL: Christian terminology is used to promote syncretistic, metaphysical beliefs. Some with a poor mental perspective on life may be uplifted by Unity's emphasis on love and positive emotions. Their restoration to psychological health would undoubtedly accrue certain physical benefits. In addition, Unity's optimistic attitude toward material prosperity may have compelled some toward greater financial gain.

OVERVIEW: "This has been a message from Unity," the announcer intones. It certainly sounds good. Who wouldn't want such a pleasant approach to life? Just think of it. No more guilt, disease, or financial worries. Every problem solved. Why not send a letter to the Missouri address and find out what it's all about?

This is the way many people every year fall prey to the pseudo-Christianity of Unity, a small but influential group based at Unity Village in Lee's Summit near Kansas City, Missouri.

The group promotes its message through radio and TV promotions and a slick, well-financed printing operation. Print projects include periodicals like *Wee Wisdom* (discontinued in the early nineties), which applies to Sunday school children, and Ernest Wilson's book *Have We Lived Before?*, which hones in on adults ripe for reincarnation teachings. Such media exposure has paid off. Unity's mail-order approach has reached an estimated 6 million "readers and followers" worldwide, with approximately one thousand centers in several countries.

To the casual observer, Unity's beliefs may seem like nothing more than "power of positive thinking" homilies. But those acquainted with the fertile ground of late nineteenth-century pantheistic philosophy will readily see Unity's similarity to Christian Science and New Thought. That is to be expected. A Belfast, Maine, clock maker, Phineas Parkhurst Quimby, fathered all three religions. His theories of animal magnetism and mental healing were plagiarized by Mary Baker Eddy (Christian Science founder) as well as Julius and Annetta Dresser and Warren Felt Evans (New Thought creators).

Charles and Myrtle Fillmore adopted their brand of Quimby's teachings to launch Unity in 1889. (The actual name *Unity* was designated in 1895.) Myrtle claimed she was tubercular until she learned, "I am a child of God; therefore I do not inherit sickness." Charles, a cripple with tuberculosis of the hip, had explored Spiritualism and Hinduism. Both later testified that living by Christian Science and New Thought principles cured their ills.

Eventually, the Fillmores split with the other two groups on minor points of theology. The Fillmores dropped the Christian Science belief that matter is not real. They added a reverence for Jesus and the doctrine of reincarnation to New Thought philosophy. In fact, Charles Fillmore believed he was a reincarnation of the apostle Paul.

Reincarnation is one of Unity's least publicized but most distinctive doctrines. Charles and Myrtle borrowed heavily from the Hindu teachings of Swami Vivekananda from India. But sensing that the idea of soul transmigration back to an animal form might not set well with Westerners, they insisted that reincarnation could only occur in human bodies. Several Bible references are used to justify this teaching, such as the instances where Christ is called the Son of David. To Unity, this is an indication that Jesus had been previously incarnated in King David.

Confronting such scriptural perversion with proper biblical exegesis would be pointless. Charles Fillmore declared that the Bible is only one of many sacred books to be revered. He went so far as to suggest that the Word of God is an inferior form of revelation for those "who are not themselves in direct communication with God."

An Unorthodox "Christianity"

It should, therefore, come as no surprise that the belief system of Unity severely departs from orthodox Christian doctrine. As in Christian Science, God is said to be a principle of love, and his Son is only an example of how we too can come to our own Christ-consciousness. Since, according to Fillmore, there are other "spiritually illuminated persons" who can "help one get started on the right path for finding God," Christ does not have an indispensable role in Unity's perception of salvation.

Unity believes that "atonement means reconciliation between God and man through Christ." Such an evangelical-sounding statement is clarified by the qualification that "reconciliation means a reuniting of our consciousness with the God-consciousness." The traditional Christian position is that reconciliation should be based on forgiveness of sin and removing the barrier of rebellion between man and God. In Unity, redemption isn't necessary because evil and sin do not exist. Since God is in everything, including plants and inanimate objects, this premise of pantheism does away with both the devil and man's fallen unregenerate nature.

The average person who explores Unity probably never delves that deeply into its theology. Many participants experience the benefits of its principles without necessarily adhering to its more refined doctrines. Initiates are discouraged from leaving their own churches, though they later encounter pressure to more closely align themselves with Unity Centers (some of which are called churches). Most inquirers are attracted by the core of Unity, which is called Silent Unity. This group handles prayer requests and apparently expresses genuine concern for people who bring their problems to them. Each year Silent Unity receives an estimated 2.5 million requests for help. Letters from Silent Unity recommend "affirmation" or "mediations" to get inquirers' thinking back into the right mode to solve their problems. By thus adjusting their mind to the "divine mind," physical ills and difficulties will vanish.

But will they? For some, the answer is decidedly yes. Those with physiological or emotional symptoms resulting from mental stress are bound to experience some relief by adopting a positive outlook on life. Even organic disorders may have the healing process accelerated by the right frame of mind.

But such a commonly accepted fact of medical science is a long way from Fillmore's belief that "thoughts of disease will produce microbes of destruction." Still, there is no doubt that many are impressed with the religious warmth by which Unity's emotional guidance is dispensed.

Psychological aid is a worthy merit, but it should never take the place of adherence to spiritual truth rooted in objective revelation. The question is not whether Unity works but how it works without having any biblical basis for its benefits.

CHRISTIAN CRITIQUE: Charles Fillmore viewed physical ills and failure as an outgrowth of mental disequilibrium. He said one must overcome this by affirming that God is the source of all desirable values and that God and man are inseparable. The divine mind of God is said to be present in all men, and perfection (as attained by Jesus) is possible by acknowledging this inner divinity and removing the illusion of sin.

But Unity's goal of harmony with the mind of God ignores the scriptural truth that union with God requires a penalty for sin and the shedding of blood.

In the words of Charles Fillmore, "The number and seriousness of our past mistakes do not matter to God. He holds no grudges and has no account book."

A mere affirmation denying the existence of evil does not eradicate its effect on the soul. Fallen humanity bears guilt for transgression, and good thoughts and beneficent feelings will not suffice to remove the consequences of divine judgment.

SOURCES: Kenneth Boa, *Cults, World Religions and You* (Wheaton, Ill.: Victor, 1977); *Daily Word*, Unity devotional publication, various issues; *Denver Post*, 29 November 1975, 5BB; Charles Fillmore, "The Adventure Called Unity," "Talks on Truth," "Jesus Christ Heals," "Prosperity," miscellaneous writings; Walter Martin, *The Kingdom of the Cults* (Minneapolis: Bethany, 1965); *Unity—A Way of Life*, Unity periodical, various issues.

ACCESS: Unity School of Christianity, 1901 NW Blue Parkway, Unity Village, MO 64065; www.unityworldhq.org

See also New Age Movement.

URANTIA

This new revelation wants to supplant orthodox Christianity with the perspective of extraterrestrial beings.

FOUNDER: Dr. Bill Sadler, to whom *The Urantia Book* was delivered by seven spirit beings in 1934. A group of thirty-seven people, called the Forum, studied the original manuscripts before incorporating the Urantia Foundation in 1950. John Hales is the current president.

TEXT: *The Urantia Book*, a 2,097-page volume said to be written by celestial beings and communicated by automatic handwriting (an occult practice). It was first published in Chicago in 1958.

SYMBOLS: Three concentric circles

APPEAL: For those who do not accept biblical infallibility, *The Urantia Book* provides a fascinating disclosure of esoteric and cosmological information. The curious or speculative mind not rooted in Christian doctrine can easily be drawn into it.

OVERVIEW: Disciples of *The Urantia Book* describe it as "the finest worldview of religion available to contemporary man." And they claim their book was personally delivered by superhuman, extraterrestrial beings. Its 2,097 pages are said to be the "finest major divine revelation since the coming of Christ to our planet."

Is it any wonder Urantia followers devoutly believe they are "custodians of the greatest message ever given to man"? Urantia teaches that all previous religious concepts are outdated for our age. (In contradiction, their promotional literature insists that membership in other churches or religious organizations is compatible with membership in Urantia.)

Urantia proposes to augment established religious precepts with a new understanding of man's evolutionary ascent. To accomplish this end, the organization is structured around societies (ten or more dedicated followers who study *The Urantia Book*) chartered by the Urantia Brotherhood. The Brotherhood is described as "a voluntary and fraternal association of believers in the teachings of *The Urantia Book*."

The Urantia Foundation is the nonprofit, tax-exempt entity that is custodian of *The Urantia Book*. Since the book was first published in 1955, more than 100,000 copies have been sold.

A five-member board of trustees who are appointed to life terms manages the foundation. Thirty-six members of the general council govern the affairs of the brotherhood. The societies claim a domestic and foreign active membership of about one thousand. Members I have met have been well-educated individuals of the upper socioeconomic strata. Since the brotherhood admittedly seeks quality rather than quantity, it may be assumed that Urantia's scope of influence exceeds its actual numbers.

The Urantia Book expounds a strange psychic revelation based on the cosmological view of our universe as seen from the perspective of beings from another world. The foreparts of the book include an analysis of our earth (Urantia, as it is known by these extraterrestrials) and its super-universe, *Havona*. In addition to descriptions of spirit entities, names of celestial designations are given, which describe places such as Salvington, Nebadon, and the Isle of Paradise. There are actually three Trinities—the *Paradise Trinity*, the *Ultimate Trinity*, and the *Absolute Trinity*. The Paradise Trinity is supreme, consisting of the Universal Father, the Eternal Son, and the Infinite Spirit.

Most importantly, the book includes a discussion of what it calls the hidden years of Christ, from age twelve to his public ministry. It purports to show the "religion of Jesus," not the "religion about Jesus."

A Complex Cosmos

The *Urantia Concordex,* a companion of the *Urantia Book,* claims that the planet Urantia (Earth) is part of a local universe of 10 million habitable worlds, known as Nebadon. Erect bipeds of neighboring planets refer to Urantia as the "World of the Cross," a disturbed, disorderly planet elevated by a great ruler, whom Earth inhabitants call Jesus Christ.

The *Concordex* claims Jesus of Nazareth was actually the mortal incarnation of Michael of Nebadon, who sacrificed himself to elevate Urantia to a place of honor and interest, and will one day reclaim leadership of the cosmos of Nebadon. The *Urantia Concordex* also claims that an eight-foot-tall Adam was, like Jesus, sent to Urantia to uplift the human race thirty-eight thousand years ago.

The *Concordex* also contends that the Christian church is "in the larval stage of the thwarted kingdom." The only hope for Earth inhabitants is to tune into an energy source called the Thought Adjuster, a fragment of God sent to inhabit the souls of Urantia mortals. Upon death, one's Thought Adjuster and soul rejoin to ascend into eternity.

According to Urantia, Jesus is *a* son of God who perfected his divinity by seven incarnations among various creatures of the universe. His seventh incarnation on Urantia as Joshua ben Joseph was intended to teach us that we, too, are sons of God. Before that, Jesus was known as Michael of Nebadon. He is not to be equated with *the* Eternal Son of the Paradise Trinity. Jesus is merely number 611,121 in the evolving scheme of Creator Sons who form and rule local universes. His three years of ministry ended in his crucifixion, but according to Urantia, the cross was unnecessary since "the Father in Paradise did not decree, demand, or require the death of his Son. All of this was man's doing, not God's."

Dismissing Christ and Christians

Urantia may claim to welcome Christians into its membership, but *The Urantia Book* denies most cardinal doctrines of Christianity. In *The Urantia Book* all major world religions are said to have monotheistic compatibility. The fall of man is dismissed as a "distorted story," since Adam and Even actually "carried on in the Garden for one hundred and seventeen years." The bodily resurrection of Christ is refuted: "His material or physical body was not part of the resurrected personality. . . . The body of flesh in which he lived . . . was still lying there in the sepulcher." Above all, the New Testament concepts of blood atonement and redemption from original sin are dismissed as the expression of a "primordial ghost fear." In the place of these essential Christian beliefs, Urantia proposes a system of soul transmigration, with humans gradually ascending from animal to human to God.

The Urantia Book is so expansive that an exhaustive analysis is impossible. Listed below are a few more areas where *Urantia* departs from Christian belief:

1. Prayer is not to be attempted until one has "exhausted the human capacity for human adjustment." In addition, "words are irrelevant to prayer."
2. The biblical doctrine of atonement (Hebrews 9:22) "unnecessarily encumbered Christianity with teachings about blood and sacrifice."
3. The home is seen as a "sociologic institution," and the belief that marriage is a sacred state is called "unfortunate." "Deity is not a conjoining party" in marriages that dissolve.
4. Mankind's parents were named Andon and Fonta, who procreated Sontad.
5. Adam, Solomon, and David were not in the direct line of ancestry of Joseph, the father of Jesus.
6. Jesus adopted the term "Son of Man" at age fifteen after reading a passage in the so-called Book of Enoch.
7. During his twenty-eighth and twenty-ninth years on earth, Jesus toured the Roman world, accompanied by the natives from India.
8. The indwelling Christ is not essential to salvation, since "Jesus does not require his disciples to believe in him but rather to believe with him."

In addition to these problems, impersonal as well as personal concepts of a deity are expounded without any acknowledgment of inconsistency. In some instances, both Unitarian and Trinitarian views seem to be considered acceptable.

The only ultimate guide to faith is reliance on the indwelling Thought Adjuster instead of consulting objective revelation. Thought Adjusters are said to be "undiluted . . . parts of Deity" who guide humans on the path of spiritual progress through countless lifetimes on other planets, "universe upon universe until [humans] actually attain the divine presence of [their] Paradise Father."

Christians faced with such a philosophical outlook may find it difficult to present the unique claims of Christ, since the Urantia member's inclusive view will seem to accept any doctrinal viewpoint. But a careful study will clearly illustrate that *The Urantia Book* contains contradictory, extrabiblical information opposing the most crucial of Christian precepts.

CHRISTIAN CRITIQUE: Urantia literature says the foundation aims to improve "comprehension of Cosmology and the realization of the planet on which we live to the universe of the genesis and destiny of man and his relation to God, and of the true teachings of Jesus Christ."

Urantia revelation is held to be superior to Scripture. Humans are not a unique creation by God but an evolving being, ascended from the animal kingdom, destined to become an angelic spirit being and eventually a god. Humans only need to acknowledge that a portion of God's Spirit (the Thought Adjuster) dwells within them. Moral accountability is replaced with the Hindu idea of merging with God by soul Transmigration. Paul's Epistle to the Colossians responds succinctly to such Gnostic-originated concepts that suggest Jesus is only one among many spirit beings who serve as intermediaries between God and humans.

SOURCES: Clyde Bedell, *Concordex of the Urantia Book* (Santa Barbara, Calif.: Clyde Bedell Estates, 1986); Karl Cates, "Jose D. Cepeda," *The Iskander*, 11 May 1986; Martin Gardner, *Urantia: The Great Cult Mystery* (Amherst, N.Y.: Prometheus, 1995); J. Gordon Melton, *The Encyclopedia of American Religions*, vol. 2 (Wilmington, N.C.: McGrath, 1978), 119; Elliot Miller, "The Urantia Book," Christian Research Institute, 1979; *SCP Newsletter* 7, no. 3 (August 1981); Urantia Foundation, "Leavening Our Religious Heritage," "Our Task," "The Urantia Book," "Basic Concepts of the Urantia Book."

ACCESS: The Urantia Foundation, 533 Diversey Parkway, Chicago, IL 60614; Fifth Epochal Fellowship, 529 Wrightwood Ave., Chicago, IL 60614

VAMPIRISM

For those attracted to the darker side of occultism, vampires are a contemporary, blood-hungry reality, not the sharp-fanged misanthropes seen in the movies.

OVERVIEW: For decades Hollywood has been fascinated with vampire lore. In 1931 Hungarian actor Bela Lugosi set the standard for the definitive Dracula with his memorable line, "Good eve-en-ing . . . "

Lugosi's character was based on literature's most famous vampire—Count Dracula in Bram Stroker's 1897 novel, *Dracula*. And it's from Lugosi's original *Dracula* film that many people got their first image of vampires as creatures of the night that stay alive after death by ingesting the blood of the living. Among the fictional misconceptions conveyed by these movies are ideas such as these:

- Vampires must continue to drink blood or they die.
- A vampire's power lasts only from sunset to sunrise.
- During daylight hours the body must rest in the earth where it was buried.

The most misleading fallacy is the fabled method of vanquishing a vampire. Lugosi's classic *Dracula* film taught that garlic and wolfsbane (a plant that grows in central Europe) would help, but only a stake through the heart as the vampire slept in his coffin would really do the job.

More recently, modern literature and movies have romanticized the image of the debonair bloodsucker who sweeps women off their feet and ravishes them. The novels of Anne Rice have transformed the legends of the original Dracula into an image of eroticism and sensuality. Rice's popularization of sexy blood lust reached a peak when her 1976 novel *Interview with the Vampire* hit the big screen, featuring Hollywood hunks Brad Pitt and Tom Cruise as the leading vampires. For all its decadence and perverse sexuality, *Interview with the Vampire* conveyed an enticing creepiness.

Demonic behavior glamorized in such a way comes across as all too alluring to youth looking for another cheap thrill. As I sat in the darkened theater watching *Interview with the Vampire*, I wondered how many young people would become vulnerable to demon possession or would pursue meddling with demons because of this movie.

The History of Vampirism

The real Dracula, Vlad Dracula, was a fifteenth-century Romanian monarch, a hero to his country. Dracula's father got his title from membership in the crusading Order of the Dragon. He really did live in a Transylvanian castle from which he taxed local merchants.

His reign of savagery against the invading Ottoman Turks led to his assuming the name of Vlad Tepes, or Vlad the Impaler. He was said to have impaled military challengers on upright wooden stakes, creating what was called the "forest of the impaled." This barbarianism was done to intimidate his foes, and it worked. When the Turks marched into Dracula's province of Wallachian in the summer of 1462, they were horrified to see twenty thousand of their fellow soldiers rotting on stakes, forming a two-mile-long wall of corpses. They immediately retreated.

In addition to intimidating his opponents, Vlad used his butchery to support his own brand of family values. Promiscuous women were skinned alive. Hats were nailed to the heads of visiting dignitaries who had failed to show respect by taking off their hats.

It's hard to see how a historical figure like Vlad Dracula morphed into the figure portrayed in literature and film, but this mythical character has a powerful allure for many spiritually confused young people.

What makes vampirism particularly dangerous is its mystical attachment to the supernatural. Teenagers often feel powerless during their betwixt and between years. Vampirism offers access to a spiritual force beyond human attainment. This allure is often coupled with video and role-playing vampire games which can be an ongoing part of their lives.

Understanding the contemporary interest in vampires may be no more mysterious than the obvious supernatural character of vampires. Because of their defiance of death and religious dogma, vampires are a way of grasping at the unknown.

In addition, vampires aren't bound by time and space limitations. They appear and disappear at will, emerging from the mist to provoke our deepest fears and suspicions. Vampires, if understood in this way, are indeed the most mysterious of all the aliens among us.

Vampire Cults

The recent surge of interest in the macabre has led to the mainstreaming of the idea of vampires. Not only do Anne Rice and Stephen King have books that have topped the best-seller charts, fashion has taken on the vampire look. Some nightclubs even have vampire nights.

On a more troublesome level, some bizarre cults have sprung up around the vampire theme. Such groups tend to attract kids who are marginal in their social skills and lack the structure of a healthy family and church life.

Members of contemporary vampire cults believe that drinking blood will give them longevity, vitality, and even supernatural powers. After some involvement in the cult they may graduate to a belief that drinking blood is essential to sustaining life. This horrid belief might not be of much interest to most people were it not for the fact that some vampire cult members are putting their beliefs into action. As a result, innocent people have been murdered in what law enforcement officials have described as vampire-related cult crimes.

One of the most famous cases happened in 1996 when teenage vampire killers murdered Richard and Ruth Wendorf in Eustis, Florida, a town located about thirty miles northwest of Orlando. Police arrested five teens. One of them was the slain couple's fifteen-year-old daughter.

Reality or Fantasy?

What's the truth surrounding the vampire myth? Unfortunately, it seems to be a matter of fantasy becoming reality only in the minds and lives of vampire cult members. I've talked with scores of youth who claimed to be vampires. In truth, the majority of those were emotionally disturbed individuals whose Dracula fantasies enabled them to escape their dysfunctional personal lives.

Others who claim to be vampires are actually satanic blood-drinking cultists. They consume blood to ceremonially enforce their beliefs and show off their Luciferian bravado. One young man I talked to was named Antonio. As a teenager he had been a member of a satanic vampire cult. His involvement began with the drinking of animal blood. "The blood was usually collected in a chalice and passed around to be shared in rituals mocking Christian communion," he told me. At first, the blood rituals made him nauseous. But as he told me, "After doing it several times the repulsiveness wore off. I began looking forward to the bloodiest part of each new ceremony."

Some vampire cultists are sadomasochists, who have twisted the pain/pleasure responses in their brains. But a select few of these "creatures of the night" are in constant pursuit of the emotional and spiritual reinforcement of blood drinking.

One alarming spiritual reason to be concerned about the rise of vampirism among the young is the passing on of diseases, such as AIDS. More importantly, because Scripture prohibits such acts (Genesis 9:4), participation opens a dark door to the world of evil spirits. The spiritual transmission of demons can occur when blood is ritually shared. An unsuspecting youth who experiments with such activity out of curiosity may get more than he bargained for.

VEDANTA SOCIETY

Swami Vivekananda

This influential and pioneering Hindu missionary group introduced many in the West to beliefs from the East.

OVERVIEW: The increasing influence of mystical thought on Western religious values owes a debt of gratitude to the first Hindu guru to be widely accepted as a legitimate spokesman for the East—Swami Vivekananda (1863–1902).

In 1893 he addressed the Parliament of Religions in Chicago and took the conference by storm. His subsequent national exposure via lecture tours led to his founding of the Vedanta Society in 1894, which was the first official Hindu organization to be established in the Untied States. The proliferation of many current Eastern-based religious groups is the fruition of this landmark event.

Named Narendranath Datta at the time of his birth, he later assumed the *swami* name of Vivekananda ("Bliss of Discrimination" between the real and the illusory) and became a devoted disciple of the Bengali holy man Sri Ramakrishna, who served as a priest in Calcutta's Kali Temple. Ramakrishna often experienced *samadhi* (the bliss of altered trance consciousness) and concluded that all gods and religions were but multiple manifestations of the one Absolute. He then pursued the path of *Vedanta* (the goal of knowledge based on the *Vedas*, the sacred Hindu scriptures) and developed an intellectual approach to Hinduism based in part on charitable works of mercy. Vivekananda viewed Ramakrishna as an *avatar* worthy of the kind of devotion shown Christ by his apostles. Upon the holy man's death, Vivekananda founded the Ramakrishna Mission in Calcutta.

Through the Vedanta Society, Vivekananda was able to favorably influence many prominent figures, including authors Aldous Huxley and Gertrude Stein. While insisting on the primacy of Hinduism, Vivekananda told them, "We accept all religions as true." Those who view Vivekananda's influence on Western religious thought in favorable terms might do well to visit personally both the Kali Temple and the Ramakrishna Mission in Calcutta. Kali, the blackened goddess of death, stands draped in a necklace of human skulls and holds a bloody severed head in one hand. These ghoulish remains are all that is left of the lovers she seduced and beheaded. Near the entrance of the Kali Temple I witnessed bloody goat sacrifices before a phallic *lingam* (genital replica).

Not far away at the Ramakrishna Mission Temple, I watched poor peasants bow before an idol, offering the deity the little money they had. The idol's favor meant more to them than obtaining food to sustain the lives of their children.

Transporting a cleaned-up version of this pagan spiritual heritage to the West was the Vedanta Society's ultimate goal, and most religious experts now acknowledge that it opened up the door to the West's ideological move toward the East.

But such idolatrous practices as those described above cannot be obscured by intellectual discourse regarding the "existence of the One Cause" or "merging the self with Reality."

SOURCES: J. Gordon Melton, *The Encyclopedia of American Religions*, vol. 2 (Wilmington, N.C.: McGrath, 1978); *SCP Newsletter* 5, no. 3 (April-May 1979).

ACCESS: 5423 S. Hyde Park Blvd., Chicago, IL 60615.

VOODOO, SANTERIA, AND YORUBA

Originating in Africa and traveling to the Caribbean, these tribal traditions blend witchcraft, Christianity, and folk superstitions into a spiritually deadly concoction.

FOUNDERS: African slaves who imported occult tribal beliefs to the Caribbean.

TEXT: Oral traditions only.

SYMBOLS: Fetishes, icons, voodoo dolls. Other symbols protect the wearer against poisoning, death hexes, evil spirits, sickness, injury, and accidents.

APPEAL: The statement is often made that voodoo helps Haitians face the crushing poverty in their country. While such religious eccentricities may attract illiterate masses in the Caribbean, the appeal in the United States is much different. Voodoo and Santeria lure a dark part of the human psyche that covertly craves uninhibited behavior and revenge.

OVERVIEW: Haitians call it voodoo. Cubans and other Latinos refer to it as Santeria. Brazilians christen it Macumba. Trinidadians call it Shango. Others call it Yoruba.

Regardless of the name, all of these practices are derivatives of tribal African religious practices that have become increasingly popular in the United States. They are sources of worry for some who say they are responsible for increasing violence, murder, and spiritual enslavement wherever they are practiced.

Voodoo in Fantasy and Fact

The dangerous cult of voodoo has been glorified by such movies as *The Serpent and the Rainbow* and *Angel Heart*, but this tradition is more than merely fictional.

Voodoo has become increasingly popular in this country. Some cities have pharmacies where customers can purchase snakeskin, dried bird claws, bones, roots, incense, statues, candles, and other paraphernalia to use in voodoo spells and potions. People use the crude drugs and voodoo magic to ward off evil spirits, gain control over other people, win lawsuits, and advance in the business world.

Surprisingly, voodoo thrives in many parts of America. A colony in South Carolina called the Oyotunji African Yoruba Village boasts of its return to old African ways and the practice of witchcraft. Village founder Walter Eugene King (also known as King Oba) discovered voodoo during a 1954 visit to Haiti.

Known to anthropologists as *vodoun*, voodoo is a system focusing on a distant god known as the Grand Master, who manifests himself through various rituals. He has a pantheon of spirits, such as benevolent ones invoked by *rada* rites and harsher spirits invoked by bloody *petro* rites. The harsh spirits supposedly are crude and malicious when possessing someone.

Voodoo has played a powerful role in Haitian politics. The notorious slave revolt of 1791 began one August evening at a voodoo ceremony. Participants pledged allegiance to Satan if their nation would be freed from the French. Nearly two centuries later, voodoo was a major factor in the rise and fall of the Haitian Duvalier dynasty. At first voodoo frightened and intimidated the people into submission, then it enraged them into violence and destruction.

"Papa Doc" Duvalier ruled Haiti for fourteen years, dying in 1971. He used voodoo to instill fear in the Haitians and to strengthen his power. When he became president in 1957, many peasants believe he was the incarnation of the voodoo god Baron Samedi, the spirit of death and one of the malevolent spirits of the voodoo pantheon.

Duvalier often dressed in black suits and donned voodoo trappings to encourage that belief. Duvalier also named his security force *Tontons Macoutes* after the legendary Haitian bogeyman who snatched naughty children. To impress his followers with his voodoo power, he changed the Haitian flag to red and black, the colors of voodoo secret ceremonies. During his reign, Duvalier's minions murdered thousands of Haitians. He claimed to sleep in a tomb once a year to commune with spirits.

Jean-Claude Duvalier inherited his father's dictatorship in 1971 and continued the vicious, despotic voodoo regime of demonism. As Jean-Claude

"Baby Doc" Duvalier's dynasty disintegrated, he summoned, in vain, voodoo priests to help him control the unrest. He finally fled Haiti in 1986. Now that Baby Doc is gone, the new rulers have changed the black and red flag to red and blue.

A 1996 article in Christianity Today says voodoo remains a powerful force in Haiti: "Haitian Protestants and Roman Catholics may not agree on much theologically, but they both admit that the religion of Voodoo (or Vodou) and its practices still have a profound influence on Haitian society. . . . Although Haiti is about 97 percent Christian, Voodoo has a centuries-old grip on the country's populace."

From Haiti to America

Recent years have seen a growing number of Voodoo practitioners in the United States.

Walter Serge King was a wiry voodoo visionary who lived in New York. The son of a follower of Marcus Garvey (an early 1900s black-movement leader who taught blacks that Ethiopia was their promised land), King yearned to rediscover his cultural roots, so he became an African dancer in a traveling troupe. He studied ballet, wandered through black Africa, and roamed Haiti.

Upon returning to New York, King became a well-known figure in black nationalist groups. When most black leaders were advocating political power, King pushed for a broader cultural nationalism, but he knew he couldn't unite a deeply religious group of blacks without a powerful catalyst. He decided voodoo was that spiritual catalyst. King was initiated into a voodoo cult in Cuba in 1959, after which he returned to New York City. He then opened the first temple devoted to pure African voodoo and acted as "Chief Bab" (short for *babalawo*, or priest).

While voodoo is popular in Mississippi and Louisiana, Santeria flourishes in Florida. Practicing voodoo is particularly popular in New Orleans and is growing in America among refugees. Another center that reaches out to Americans who may have little background in the subject is the Voodoo Spiritual Temple, located in the French Quarter in New Orleans. Known for its openness to people who are not of African or Caribbean lineage, the temple has introduced many residents and guests in Louisiana to the mysteries of voodoo.

Santeria's Controversial Sacrifices

When police investigated the 1986 mutilation and murder of a baby in Connecticut, they soon discovered links to the centuries-old Santeria religion. Surrounding the baby were pennies, fruit, and other trinkets, indicating involvement of the Caribbean religious cult.

Santeria is especially popular in Dade County, Florida, where a third-grade student skipped school to become a Santeria priestess. The girl's initiation rites took three to four weeks, according to religious experts, and she was legitimately excused from school. The Cuban form of voodoo traces its roots to Africa, calls for the sacrifice of animals to saints, and uses chanting and bathing in its initiation rites.

Santeria's ways are secretive, the size of its membership unknown. Devotees argue that they've been victimized by unequal law enforcement and religious persecution. Some feel they've been painted as bloodthirsty pagans. Says Gene Bailly, a Santerian priest, "Santeria has a bad name. People think it's witchcraft, think it's Satanism. It's misinformation." He calls Santeria a deep, ancient religion. The Santeria cult originated among black slaves the Spanish brought to Cuba. Forced to embrace Catholicism, the slaves held on to their religious roots by transferring the characteristics of their own gods to Christian saints.

In Miami, religious stores in Cuban neighborhoods sell candles, Roman Catholic icons, and live animals for sacrificial rites. Law enforcement officials say animal sacrifice rituals in the Miami area are so common the river's cleanup boat picks up an average of one hundred carcasses a week. *Santeros,* or priests, slaughter animals as an offering of blood to appease their gods. In exchange, they hope to be blessed with good fortune. Explains one Santeria advocate, "The saints have to be fed, and blood sacrifice is one of the ways you feed them." Palo Mayombe, a black magic offshoot of Santeria, is more malevolent, often using human skulls obtained by grave robbing.

Like Santeria, Yoruba also practices animal sacrifice. Additional Yoruba rituals include ecstatic dancing, ancestor worship, and the use of varied offerings in order to appease the gods.

Appeasing the Gods

While differences exist between voodoo and Santeria, the two cults have several gods and rituals in common. Each sect also believes that all events in this world are shaped by divine forces outside of it.

A major voodoo philosophy is, "Take care of the gods and they will take care of you." For example, during the year that they wear nothing but white garments as a form of purification, Santeria initiates learn their religion's secret ceremonies, study the Yoruba language so they can address their gods in the god's own tongue, and learn the favorite foods and drinks of their gods.

Ogun, the god of iron and war, supposedly likes roosters and male goats for dinner, and his favorite drink is rum. Erzlie, the voodoo god of life, craves desserts, especially decorated cakes and crème de menthe. Damballah desires champagne, whereas other voodoo gods settle for Coca-Cola.

I have personally witnessed voodoo worshipers become possessed by a spirit that has entered their bodies, after which they usually shriek or howl. Some violently shake or writhe, as if experiencing an epileptic fit. Sometimes the possessed person passes out and falls to the ground. While in the trance, some worshipers walk over broken glass or burning coals. Others place their hands in burning oil or alcohol. Voodoo advocates vow that if worshipers show no bodily harm after such ordeals, it proves that the spirits have entered their bodies.

Voodoo may be partially accountable for the AIDS outbreak in Haiti. Because voodoo priests use cadaver components in various potions and powders and because human blood is used in sacrificial worship, some AIDS experts believe the disease has been spread by contact with these contaminated remains. It seems to be the reason why AIDS is so common in Haiti but not on other Caribbean islands.

Voodoo is an occult religion rooted in satanism. To tempt spirit possession is also to tempt serious spiritual risk. The Bible teaches us to drive spirits out, not ask them in. God calls us to offer our bodies as holy, living sacrifices, not to appease spirits by making gifts of dead animals. An attempt to consort with spirits brought about King Saul's end; perhaps the same judgment befell the Duvaliers in Haiti.

CHRISTIAN CRITIQUE: People practice voodoo to appease their gods and bring good fortune on themselves. Some practice voodoo to instill serious negative psychological effects on others.

The Bible teaches us to tread on demons, not invoke them (Luke 10:19). In occult voodoo practices, possession is invited. Voodoo offers blood sacrifices to appease spirits, but the Lord doesn't require us to kill for him. Also, using voodoo malevolently to further one's social or professional position is evil and selfish behavior.

While many who practice voodoo also practice Christianity, voodoo's distant "Grand Master" deity and its pantheon of spirits conflict with the biblical teachings.

SOURCES: *Dallas Life Magazine*, 15 July 1984, 29; *Drug Topics*, 3 May 1982, 56; *National Observer*, 20 November 1975, 20; *Newsweek*, 22 June 1981, 44; Ibid., 17 February 1986, 46; *OMNI*, December 1987, 132–133; *Press (Atlantic City, New Jersey)*, 21 March 1986, 6; *Rocky Mountain News*, 8 December 1984; Ibid. 23 March 1986, 30; *Seattle Times/Seattle Post-Intelligence*, 25 November 1984, B14; *Stuart (Florida) News*, 8 February 1981, A5; *USA Today*, 1 June 1987, 2A; *Vancouver Sun*, 1 February 1980, 7L; "Voodoo's Hold Seems Unshakeable," *Christianity Today*, 17 June 1996, 56.

ACCESS: Voodoo Spiritual Temple, 828 N. Rampart Street, New Orleans, LA 70116.

See also Black Magic; Macumba, Umbanda, and Condomble; Wicca and Witchcraft.

THE WAY INTERNATIONAL

Combining non-Trinitarian theology and Pentecostal practices,
this once-growing group has suffered significant losses.

OVERVIEW: Ordained as a Protestant minister, Victor Paul Wierwille (1916–1985) began developing his own theological ideas in the 1940s after a period of intense Bible study. Among his controversial conclusions were his views that Jesus Christ was not God and the Holy Spirit was an impersonal force.

In 1951 Wierwille says he spoke in tongues, a practice he said was proof of the presence of the Holy Spirit. Two years later, he began presenting his Power of Abundant Living Class, and in 1955 he founded The Way, Inc., renamed The Way International in 1975. Wierwille informed his followers: "God told me he would teach me the Word as it has not been known since the first century, if I would teach it to others." He would later say, "About 85 percent of what is believed as being Christian is not Christian if the Bible is right."

Housed at the Wierwille family's farm near the tiny town of New Knoxville, Ohio, The Way grew rapidly during the 1970s as young people interested in both the charismatic movement and the Jesus movement flocked to the farm to study the Bible and speak in tongues. The group was best known for its summer Rock of Ages festivals, which incorporated expository preaching and rock music. Some of the festivals were attended by more than ten thousand people. Rock bands like Takit and the Take a Stand Caravan presented music and drama.

Apart from these annual gatherings, The Way spread its message through a network of small local fellowships that met in members' homes and were overseen by a small but efficient network of regional leaders. Members (known as Wayers) read books by Wierwille, such as *Jesus Christ Is Not God* and *Receiving the Holy Spirit Today*. They also studied the founder's teaching by watching a series of films based on his Power of Abundant Living Class. Wayers revered Wierwille as their "Father in the Word" and believed that no one had taught the Bible with such truth and power since the birth of the New Testament church.

After completing their studies, the most dedicated Wayers became ambassadors in the Word over the World (WOW) missionary outreach. Through their efforts, The Way gained as many as thirty-five thousand members by the 1980s. Then a number of crises challenged the group.

Crises and Confusion

Wierwille died of cancer in 1985, the same year the Internal Revenue Service revoked the group's tax-exempt status. New president L. Craig Martindale took over leadership of the group and replaced Wierwille's classes with his own "The Way of Abundance and Power" classes.

Many members thought Martindale's changes had gone too far, and some members left to form their own rival groups based on Wierwille's original teaching. These groups include John Lynn's Christian Educational Services and Chris Geer's The Way of Great Britain.

Over the years, The Way endured criticism that its theology was heretical, that its control over members' lives was too authoritarian, that its leaders had engaged in widespread and inappropriate sexual activity with members, and that the group's reliance on heavily armed security guards was a sign of growing rancor and paranoia within the group.

In 1994 an even more bizarre crisis confronted the group. Martindale said no Word over the World ambassadors would be commissioned that year because the WOW's ranks harbored many homosexuals. Martindale condemned homosexuality, calling it "devil-spirit possession," but interestingly, The Way had also worked to develop a biblical rationale for adultery. According to the Christian Research Journal, "Their arguments included: women who traveled with Jesus and Paul supplied them with sex because it satisfied their legitimate needs; men have needs for sex with a variety of women and God provides for this; all things are lawful when done in faith (Rom. 14:21-23); stringent laws are done away with when one is born again (Col. 2:20-21); God punished David for killing Uriah, not for having sex with Bathsheba; and the Bible's word for 'adultery' has a spiritual, not a physical meaning."

Such arguments may persuade hard-core Wayers who long ago submitted their critical thinking faculties to the group's leaders. But for others who question not only its teaching on sex but its more basic errors on the nature of Jesus and the Holy Spirit, The Way is seen as a path to error, not biblical truth.

CHRISTIAN CRITIQUE: Wierwille claimed that "Jesus Christ is not God but the Son of God. . . . If Jesus Christ is God, we have not been redeemed. . . . Jesus Christ was not literally with God in the beginning; neither does he have all the assets of God." Among other unbiblical teachings, Wierwille claimed the following: four criminals (not two) were crucified next to Jesus; only believers after Pentecost will be saved, and they must remain dead until the final resurrection; water baptism is discouraged in favor of the holy spirit (he lowercases the h and the s); baptism with accompanying speaking in tongues is encouraged and, unlike its spontaneous charismatic counterpart, taught. (Members were initially encouraged to cultivate this glossolalia for thirty minutes every morning as an indispensable part of salvation.) Christians who counter The Way must be wary of their inclusive use of evangelical terminology (e.g., "born again," "Jesus Christ our Savior") and insist on clear biblical definitions of any theological matters discussed. Though many of The

Way's followers are sincere, their belligerence may stem from a disillusioned background in orthodox but sterile churches. The best approach for evangelism is not strident counterattacks but a compassionate example of Christian faith that will cause Wierwille's disciples to question if The Way really *is* the Way of John 14:6.

SOURCES: John P. Juedes, "A Special Report: Sweeping Changes in The Way International," *Christian Research Journal* (summer 1996): 6–7, 44.

ACCESS: The Way International, P.O. Box 328, New Knoxville, OH 45871

WHITE SUPREMACY

See Ku Klux Klan.

WICCA AND WITCHCRAFT

Persecuted for centuries, witches now enjoy growing mainstream acceptance and governmental approval, from the military to the IRS.

SYMBOLS: Pentagram, pentacle (five-pointed star), the ankh

APPEAL: Serious students of witchcraft are often people who feel humanity is out of control, unaligned with the cycles of nature. They turn to witchcraft for healing and to become one with their environment. They believe knowledge is power through which they can control their lives, destinies, and the world.

OVERVIEW: The gathering was small—about twenty people—and the rituals were far from novel, as a *Time* magazine writer reported: "The high priestess lifts her arms to the crescent moon, her bright silver pentagrams shimmering in the light of a burning cauldron. About her stand hooded figures, some with long forked staffs bearing stag horns and hawk feathers, animal skins and other talismans."

What made this gathering unique was the people who attended it: army colonels, sergeants, captains, and privates stationed at Fort Hood in Killeen, Texas, the nation's largest military base.

"What's next?" asked a Republican congressman. "Will armored divisions be forced to travel with sacrificial animals for satanic rituals?"

Fort Hood's wiccan rituals provoked controversy, but they also demonstrated an important point. After centuries of persecution and death, witches have now gone mainstream.

From Hatred to Acceptance

An estimated 9 million women and girls met death by fire between the years of 1300 and 1700 for practicing witchcraft. In the eighteenth century, nineteen suspected witches were killed in Salem, Massachusetts.

But despite such extreme countermeasures, the occult rituals of witchcraft are widely practiced today around the world. No longer threatened with death, witches enjoy a degree of respectability in America's spiritually lenient society.

Because some witches are reluctant to announce their pagan affiliations, it's difficult to get precise figures of how many are involved in organized witchcraft in the United States today. Estimates range from 250,000 to a million or more. Witchcraft is officially recognized as a religion by the IRS, which has granted tax exemption to groups such as the Church and School of Wicca ("seekers of wisdom"). At one Midwestern university, five hundred students enrolled in a course in witchcraft.

According to *New York Times* writer Gus Niebuhr, "Encouraged by Federal court rulings recognizing witchcraft as a legal religion, an increasing number of books related to the subject and the continuing cultural concern for the environment, Wicca—as contemporary witchcraft is often called—has been growing in the United States and abroad. It is a major element in an expanding 'neo-pagan' movement whose members regard nature itself as charged with divinity."

Present-day popularity has also been aided by positive pop culture portrayals of witches, as *Entertainment Weekly* pointed out in 1998: "In its opening weekend, *Practical Magic*, starring Nicole Kidman and Sandra Bullock as her enchanted but lovelorn sister, earned $13 million and the No. 1 spot at the box office. The WB debuted *Charmed*, about a tart triumvirate of sorceresses (Shannon Doherty, Alyssa Milano, and Holly Marie Combs), and it topped overhyped *Felicity* as the network's highest-rated series premiere. Meanwhile, on *Buffy the Vampire Slayer*, Willow (Alyson Hannigan) has gotten downright witchy, casting spells and restoring lost souls."

Ancient Roots

The history of witchcraft is sketchy because ceremonies and beliefs are orally communicated. Witchcraft rituals have been traced to worship of the Greek goddess Artemis, the Roman goddess Diana, the Egyptian moon goddess, and the fertility goddess of the Canaanites. Many modern witches believe in two primary deities: Hecate, the Greek goddess of ghosts, and Pan, the god of the woods and shepherds. Witches insist that their Pan, even though horned and cloven-hoofed, is not the same as the Lucifer condemned in Scripture.

Some cartoon images of witches are based on fact. In previous centuries, old women living on edges of villages were responsible for healing, midwifery, and counseling people. They kept cats to control mice-ridden medieval cottages and used broomsticks as weapons while gathering herbs in the forest. Dark cloaks were common dress. Toads provided a glandular secretion that was used as an anesthetic. Ancient recipes for "flying ointment" included belladonna and aconite, powerful hallucinogens.

No longer resembling the stereotypical hags in Shakespeare's *Macbeth*, today's witches are physicians, police officers, secretaries, merchants, mechanics—even ministers. Their credo is, "If it harms none, do as you will." Witches claim they don't practice evil magic, since they believe anything sent out will return threefold. They also adhere to the tenets of reincarnation and karma.

Witches identify themselves as pagans, druids, and wiccans. Such terminology as earth or nature religion, positive magick, the craft, the craft of the wise, wisecraft, goddess worship, wimmin religion, and shamanism is also associated with witchcraft groups. Resurgence of neopagan witchcraft is partially traceable to the 1960s feminist movement and the environmental protection movements. Margot Adler, author of *Drawing Down the Moon*, an exhaustive study on witches and druids in America, says, "Neopaganism is partly a response to a planet in crisis. People today are looking for a religion that ties in with the natural world."

Individuals and Groups

Many wiccans practice their faith as individuals with no connection to a larger group. For those who do worship together, many groups follow these typical practices.

Meetings attended by thirteen members (a *coven*) are held weekly at a *covenstead*, generally a leader's home. Larger meetings, called *esbats*, occur on special days of celebration (*sabats*, a term first used in 1662). Each coven is usually autonomous, except for those groups that owe their initiation to another witch's assembly. Membership is by invitation, and progress occurs in degrees.

Some ceremonies begin with members shedding their clothing to become *skyclad*, believed to permit easier release of the body's energy. An imaginary circle is drawn around the coven with a ritualistic dagger called an *athame*.

Candles are lit and incense is burned on an altar. A priest or priestess moves to each point of the compass to summon the four guardians, symbolic of the elements of earth, air, fire, and water. Such rituals come from the *Black Book* or *Book of Shadows*. Witches might intone:

> *Queen of heaven, Queen of hell,*
> *Horned Hunter of the night.*
> *Lend your power unto the spell,*
> *Work my will by magic rite.*

Ceremonial activities include hexes and healing by the laying on of hands. "Love spells" can be cast upon reluctant suitors. Spirits are called upon to answer questions and speak through mediums. Animal sacrifices may end the ceremonies, though most mainstream "respectable" witches deny such activity.

A Modern Revival

Gerald Gardner, who was born in England in 1884 and died in 1964, did more than any other modern individual to revive witchcraft. Gardner was an occultist, an initiate of the secretive Ordo Templi Orientis, and a friend of British satanist Aleister Crowley, from whom he borrowed certain practices. Though poorly educated, Gardner pursued anthropology on his own and studied occultism with the daughter of Theosophist Annie Besant. Publication of his book *Witchcraft Today* led to a revival of interest in the cult in England.

Witchcraft in America was revived by Dr. Raymond Buckland, an anthropologist, and his wife, Rosemary, who studied under Gerald Gardner and brought his brand of Wicca to America in the 1960s. Witch Sybil Leek, who started with Gardnerian rituals, also came to America in the 1960s and established several covens. The Religious Order of Witchcraft was incorporated in 1972 in New Orleans, Louisiana, by Mary Oneida Toups, its high priestess.

In the early 1970s Gavin and Yvonne Frost of New Bern, North Carolina, opened the Church and School of Wicca, one of the most visible and active witchcraft movements. Gavin and Yvonne pay less attention to traditional witchcraft deities, promoting instead the development of psychic powers. Their basic message is that any suppression of the body's desires is unnatural and unwise. The Frosts also promote the Gardnerian concept of astral sex with spirit partners (*incubus* or *succubus*).

Several other witchcraft groups have gone public. The Church of the Eternal Source centers on ancient Egyptian culture and occultism. Members have been attracted by the archeological significance of Egypt, leading them to spiritual encounters with Egyptian deities. The Church of All Worlds is nature-oriented and promotes a symbiotic relationship between humans and earth through a form of pantheism. The Radical Faerie Movement consists of gays and lesbians, who connect their sexual choices with aged pagan nature religions.

Most participants of the occult don't get involved with high-profile witchcraft. Instead, they read the books and study the ceremonies of organized witchcraft, then invent their own brand of the craft. Usually they combine elements of witchcraft with black magic and self-styled satanism. The resulting mixture is dangerously combustible.

CHRISTIAN CRITIQUE: Witches claim they seek to understand the connection between man and his environment, but they do so without any reference to God or his revealed truth. One witch has explained the craft as follows: "To obtain knowledge. To have the power and use it to achieve balance. To discover truths . . . possibly unleash the gods and goddesses within us all."

Reincarnation is crucial to the witchcraft idea that good and evil are returned through karma. The elemental forces conjured are demons, and the horned deity revered is the devil.

Witchcraft denies biblical doctrines of heaven and hell, original sin, and the denunciation of demons. Scripture repeatedly denounces witchcraft (Leviticus 19:26; Deuteronomy 18:10-11; Galatians 5:20).

Though white witches claim to be benevolent, all such association with the spirit world is forbidden by the Bible.

SOURCES: *Calgary Herald*, 22 October 1983; Suna Chang, "Rhymes with Rich . . . from *Practical Magic* to *Charmed*, the Witch Is Back All over Hollywood," *Entertainment Weekly*, 30 October 1998, 12; S. C. Gwynne, "I Saluted a Witch: An Army Base in Texas Becomes the Hotbed for Earth-Goddess Worshippers Called Wiccans," *Time*, 5 July 1999, 59; *Insight Northwest*, October-November 1984; *Moody Monthly*, January 1983; Gustav Niebuhr, "Witches Cast as the Neo-Pagans Next Door," *New York Times*, 31 October 1999, 1, 28; *US*, 23 June 1981; *U.S. News and World Report*, 7 November 1983.

ACCESS: Church and School of Wicca, P.O. Box 297, Hinton, WV 25951-0297; Artemisian Order c/o Oriethyia, P.O. Box 7184, Capital Station, Albany, NY 12224; additional groups and covens are located worldwide.

See also Paganism; Black Magic; Macumba, Umbanda, and Condomble; and Voodoo, Santeria, and Yoruba.

WORLDWIDE CHURCH OF GOD

*In a stunning turnaround, this formerly heretical group
has embraced biblical Christianity.*

FOUNDER: Herbert W. Armstrong, born in 1892 in Des Moines, Iowa; founded religion in Eugene, Oregon, in 1934; died in January 1986.

TEXT: Emphasis on Old Testament Scriptures regarding feasts and dietary laws

SYMBOLS: "The World Tomorrow," the theme of media broadcasts.

APPEAL: Conservatively inclined people concerned about moral decay were attracted by Armstrong's denunciation of social evils and calls for biblical allegiance. WCG broadcasts and publications contained a measure of truth that drew disaffected members of traditional churches. The absence of overt fund solicitation and the sobering style of their news commentaries gave a respectability that concealed the true nature of church activities and doctrines.

OVERVIEW: A book like this can be discouraging to anyone concerned about the significant growth of aberrant religious groups. There are so many ways for cults to depart from the path of truth, and once they have done so, their errors multiply. That's why it is so refreshing to observe the positive changes in the Worldwide Church of God, an organization that has long been a cause for alarm.

But don't take my word for it. Read the opening paragraphs from a May 1997 press release issued by the National Association of Evangelicals and entitled "NAE Accepts Worldwide Church of God: Transformed Church Finds Acceptance and Fellowship in Evangelical Community." The release begins as follows:

> The Board of Directors of the National Association of Evangelicals (NAE) has voted overwhelmingly to accept the Worldwide Church of God (WCG), headquartered in Pasadena, CA, into membership. The application process included examination of doctrinal changes which have taken place in the once-controversial denomination.
>
> "NAE is founded on the premise that the Bible is the inspired, the only infallible, authoritative Word of God. I respect Joseph Tkach and the leadership of the Worldwide Church of God who did not rest in the refuge of their historically held doctrines, but sought the Truth through careful study of the scriptures—even at significant cost to the denomination," said NAE President Don Argue. "And we thank God for his faith-

fulness to them. We appreciate the gracious and open manner in which this church's leaders answered questions about the struggles that led them to a biblically-based theology."

WCG members once followed the teachings of church founder, Herbert W. Armstrong, who rejected the Trinity as a pagan doctrine, while also insisting that tithing and observance of the Old Testament Sabbath were necessary for salvation, among numerous other old covenant practices. After Armstrong's death in 1986, denominational leaders began to study and reflect on the validity of the church's teachings. In light of the Word of God in the Bible, they could not find support for many of the denomination's most controversial doctrines.

Transformations like this have been disappointingly rare during my decades of covering cults and new religious movements. In order to understand what an about-face this is, we need to review the group's history.

Marketing a Message

The orchestra swells, the music crescendos, and a deep-throated voice intones, "The World Tomorrow, with Garner Ted Armstrong." Or at least that's what used to be said before Garner Ted's philandering with money and women (a reported two hundred) resulted in a four-month exile from the group in 1972 and final expulsion in 1978. Octogenarian Herbert W. Armstrong went back on the tube himself and reclaimed total autocratic control over the then sixty-eight thousand members of the Worldwide Church of God (WCG), an organization whose interests included Ambassador College campuses in Pasadena, California; Big Sandy, Texas; and St. Albans, England.

Herbert W. Armstrong was known for his frequent association with distinguished officials and world governmental leaders. He traveled aboard a private jet, a symbol of the opulent lifestyle for which he had been criticized. Armstrong fancied himself an international statesman and had gained access to prominent international leaders (like Egypt's Sadat, Israel's Begin, and India's Gandhi) by bestowing philanthropic gifts. Critics charged him with having thirty thousand dollars worth of carpet in his office and lavishing five hundred thousand dollars on the Vienna Symphony, which performed at the opening of his extravagant, $11 million Ambassador Auditorium.

Armstrong, self-styled prophet of the "one true church," started out as an advertising salesman in Des Moines, Iowa. After being influenced by the teachings of an Adventist offshoot, his wife convinced him that salvation was only possible by keeping all of God's commandments.

These injunctions were later to become an integral part of WCG doctrine: Sabbath keeping, following Old Testament kosher laws, and observing Jewish feasts. Other precepts adopted by Armstrong were rejection of the Trinity, noninvolvement in governmental affairs, denial of hell as a place of eternal torment for humans, annihilation of the wicked, and Anglo-Israelism, a belief that caused him to split with the Church of God (Seventh Day).

His background in promotion alerted him to the possibilities of media exposure. From an initial broadcast on a 100-watt station in 1934, the Armstrong empire grew to include scores of radio and TV outlets (five hundred in Garner Ted's heyday). In addition, *The Plain Truth*, a slick, four-color monthly magazine (which once had a circulation of 2 million in five different languages), enticed future church recruits. Its patriotic, morally concerned editorial slant catered to middle Americans. And *Quest* magazine, an expensive, glossy, bimonthly public relations vehicle dedicated to "the pursuit of excellence," was published by Ambassador International Cultural Foundation, a WCG front organization.

To people frustrated with crime, pornography, and political uncertainty, WCG promised a brighter "world tomorrow," which would not be achieved until the day of Christ's return.

Enigmatic Teachings

WCG downplayed the beliefs that made this homegrown sect an enigma. Some of these strange doctrines were modified earlier during the group's campaign for mainstream acceptance. Others remained intact until the group's more recent transformation.

These teachings included: a form of triple-tithing to underwrite the church, church festivals, and special funds; hesitation to seek physicians and surgery; implicit requirements that members dissolve post-divorce marriages, a dictum repealed in 1976; and condemnation of recognizing birthdays as well as Easter and Christmas. Since the group held to a view of progressive theology, claiming "no final understanding of the Word of God" and asserting a "willingness to incorporate new understanding," other doctrines were introduced.

It was Armstrong's belief in Anglo-Israelism that drew the most theological attention. Though Herbert denied it, his doctrine closely resembled the theory expounded by Canadian Richard Brothers, a psychic visionary who lived in London in the eighteenth century. (His ideas were later popularized in 1840 by Scotsman John Wilson.)

Ignoring sound rules of linguistics and hermeneutics, the theory suggests that England (Ephraim) and the United States (Manasseh) are what is left of the so-called Ten Lost Tribes of Israel. Ancient Judah and Israel are believed to be two separate entities; the former are Jews as they are known today. After the Assyrian captivity, Israel migrated northward to eventually become the Anglo-Saxons of British heritage.

Armstrong taught that the promises of God to his chosen people had been transferred to America and the United Kingdom. He also declared that Queen

Elizabeth sits on the throne to which Christ will return. Although sound Bible scholarship questions whether or not Israel and Judah should be separated and debunks the idea that any tribes were ever lost, the WCG maintained that the British Coronation Stone of Scone was actually brought to the Emerald Isle by the prophet Jeremiah. Armstrong believed the war of Armageddon was near and that Germany (modern Assyria) would lead a ten-nation confederation into this battle.

Worldwide Church of God members had no fear of the coming conflagration. God's "true church" (i.e., WCG) was to be raptured, perhaps from Petra (the ancient rock city south of the Dead Sea in Jordan). When would all of this take place? Armstrong variously set the dates for 1936, 1943, 1972, and 1975, though the WCG today officially refutes such date setting. When the 1975 date passed without prophetic fulfillment, Armstrong imposed a permanent silence on the issue. He had already erred in 1965 by declaring that Jerusalem would remain in Gentile hands until the return of Christ. The Six Day War in 1967 changed all that.

Increasing Scrutiny

If a predisposed view of Jewish history and a predilection for expensive tastes had been his only shortcomings, Herbert W. Armstrong might have been dismissed as easily as any other religious zealot. However, because his ubiquitous broadcasts and publications reached an estimated 150 million people weekly, he brought closer scrutiny.

When speaking of his "conversion," the elder Armstrong declared, "God called me . . . for the most important commission in 1900 years." That message, as he explained, teaches the born-again experience is a process, not an instantly imputed act. "We are not yet born of God—only heirs—only begotten," he emphasized.

Armstrong insisted one cannot be truly "saved" in this life, since redemption will not be completed until the resurrection. According to him, "salvation cannot be opened to humanity until Jesus unseats Satan and restores the government of God to this planet." In the meantime, some WCG followers lived in fear of offending God and losing their salvation, careful not to miss a church feast or fall short of their financial obligations to the WCG.

Perhaps the most dangerous of Armstrong's doctrines was the contention that deity is an attainable goal for humans. One WCG publication insisted, "We are to be changed from physical to spiritual [a denial of the bodily resurrection] . . . into the spirit of God. We must be God. Blasphemy? No. Believe it or not, you are a potential omnipotent power. You were born to become God!"

Note that the writer doesn't say *a god*. He says *God*. This view, of course, robs Christ of his unique position as eternal God. Humans, who were created by Christ, are thus elevated from their finite position to a status equal with infinite God. Armstrong also believed that man would someday join God in recreating the entire universe.

Garner Ted's sexual misconduct drove away many members, who left to form splinter groups. The younger Armstrong said his father had rebuffed several attempts at reconciliation. Garner Ted left WCG to lead the Church of God International, based in Tyler, Texas. This group had as many as five thousand members and annual revenues of $2 million.

After Garner Ted's departure from the WCG, top church leaders resigned, and for a time the government placed Herbert's purse strings in receivership, an action the California courts later ruled was "ill-conceived litigation." In addition, his closest associate and heir apparent, Stanley Rader, left his position as treasurer and board member. (In 1980, Rader reportedly drew a salary of $350,000 to serve as the church's executive manager.)

Other scandals caused additional problems. At age ninety-two, Herbert W. Armstrong was divorced after a seven-year marriage to his wife Ramona, aged forty-five. The litigation reportedly cost the church more than $5 million in legal fees. Transcripts of court proceedings reportedly indicated that Armstrong's sexual misconduct extended even to incest. It was also revealed that Ramona and Herbert had had a sexual relationship for three years prior to their marriage.

A New Chapter

Herbert W. Armstrong died in 1986 at the age of ninety-three. Just before he died he published his last book, *Mystery of the Ages,* which he claimed contained seven mysteries revealed to him by God.

Armstrong's designated successor was Joseph Tkach, who oversaw a then ninety-two-thousand-member organization. Four spokesmen replaced Armstrong on "The World Tomorrow" telecast. And for a time, membership and income continued to grow.

Though the church prospered after Armstrong's death—membership grew by seven thousand, and annual income grew from $140 million in 1985 to $163 million in 1988—Armstrong's legacy of misguided teaching continued to mislead the undiscerning.

Then in 1995 Tkach died and was replaced by his son, Joseph Tkach Jr. Both the Tkaches set the WCG on an ambitious course that would bring it into line with orthodox Christian doctrine. But this transformation came with a huge cost. Membership declined, many ministers departed, and splinter groups broke off in order to continue their commitment to Armstrong's unorthodox doctrines.

The story of the Worldwide Church of God is still being written today. But the group's recent history is an example of the power of God to bring wayward groups to the truth.

CHRISTIAN CRITIQUE: Herbert W. Armstrong believed that the true church and its pure message had been underground for 1,900 years. Then, just prior to the return of Christ, he had been called of God to bring a message that would dispel the confusion of all other false denominations who consider themselves Christians.

Armstrong claimed the Worldwide Church of God was the only legitimate representative of the gospel of Christ. But instead, the church followed a mix of unorthodox teachings.

But right before Joseph Tkach Jr. became the leader of the WCG in 1995, the church had begun a process of study and reflection, which continued under his leadership. The result of the process was an admission that the church practiced unorthodox views. This led to an aggressive and successful effort to stamp out heresy and embrace the truth.

SOURCES: *Christianity Today,* 17 December 1971, 6–9; Ibid., 1 April 1977, 20–24; Ibid., 20 February 1981, 41; Ibid., 15 January 1988; *Eternity,* May 1981, 15; J. Michael Feazell, *The Liberation of the Worldwide Church of God* (Grand Rapids, Mich.: Zondervan, 2001); *The Good News,* July 1976, 28; Roy Knuteson, "The Final Testimony of Herbert W. Armstrong," *The Discerner,* April-June 1986, 9; Doug LeBlanc, "The Worldwide Church of God: Resurrected into Orthodoxy," *Christian Research Journal* (winter 1996): 7; *The Plain Truth,* April 1977, 3; Ibid., May 1977, 39; *Time,* 15 May 1972, 87; Ibid., 4 March 1974, 50; Ibid., 15 June 1978, 54; Ibid., 23 February 1981, 54; Ibid., 27 January 1986, 78.

ACCESS: Worldwide Church of God, 300 W. Green St., Pasadena, CA 91129; and additional foreign offices; www.wcg.org

YOGA

Barely known in the West a few decades ago, yoga has become the spiritual discipline of choice for those seeking a physically conditioned outer life and a more reflective inner life.

FOUNDER: The principles and practices of yoga developed as ascetic and physical means to achieve the spiritual purposes of Hinduism.

TEXT: The Hindu Vedic scriptures provide the theological and philosophical basis for yoga's presuppositions.

APPEAL: Humans have become the victims of their modern diets. Obesity and a sedentary lifestyle have become an increasing focus of concern for those who value their health and physical appearance. Yoga seems like an exotic and less strenuous way of restoring youthful vigor.

OVERVIEW: Her face is fresh and her body is incredibly slim. She looks like the model for a health food ad. The calisthenics she has just led you through are guaranteed to knock off the pounds overnight. For an exercise instructor, she certainly lives what she preaches. But how does she stay in such good shape?

Almost anticipating that question, she informs her students, "Now I want to show you how to *keep* those muscles toned and make sure the fat *stays* off. Sit on the floor and cross your legs. Now, put your shoulders back. Close your eyes. Take a deep breath, and as you let it out say, '*Om.*' Let the *m* string out . . . like humming. This will help you to relax. Then we'll try some other yoga positions."

When I first began researching this subject decades ago, people were surprised to encounter yoga in their exercise classes. Today there are no such surprises, as millions have embraced this ancient form of exercise. In an age of stress and busyness, yoga is being practiced in YWCAs and YMCAs, public schools, health spas, and churches.

Most people have a naïve openness to Eastern religions and have assumed yoga to be nothing more than an exotic way to achieve a beautiful body. But yoga is much more than a series of muscular maneuvers designed to relieve tension. It is a practice based on mystical doctrines that emerged from Hindu tradition as much as five thousand years ago. Yoga, taken from the Sanskrit word *yuj*, meaning "to join," literally means "union with God." Which God?

A 2001 cover story in *Time* magazine tried to explain why yoga seems to work so well for so many people. The explanation included both scientific and spiritual elements:

The Scientific: Breathing exercises have been shown to decrease blood pressure and lower levels of stress hormones. Stretching the body through various poses promotes better drainage of the lymphatic vessels, the body's waste-removal system. Holding postures may build muscle tone, which enhances physical well-being and protects delicate joints against injury.

The Mystical: Enlightenment and good health require the free flow of the life force (prana) and the proper balance between the seven major energy hubs (chakras). (An eighth chakra, or aura, surrounds the body and encompasses the other seven.) The three lower chakras serve the body's physical needs, while the five upper chakras are associated with the spiritual realm.

Firmer Muscles and God-Realization

A major text on yoga states, "The aim of all yoga is realization of the Absolute Brahman." This Eastern concept of God is difficult for many Westerners to understand. The Bible presents a personal, anthropomorphic God to whom we are personally, morally responsible. The God of yoga is an impersonal deity who pervades the universe as an energy force. Hindu belief teaches that God (*Brahman*) is unknowable, inexplicable, and at the same time present in all living things.

Sometimes Brahman is referred to as the Universal Being, the Supreme Absolute, or Pure Consciousness. Whatever the name, his manifestation to men is known through the Hindu god *Shiva*. And it is Shiva, the Hindu divinity who is the manifestation of destruction, who plays an integral part in the practice of yoga.

One of the basic beliefs of yoga is the dichotomous view of a material (physical) body and a so-called subtle (spiritual) body. The Bible does teach that the flesh and the spirit are enemies (Romans 7:18-19; Galatians 5:13-16). But Scripture does not say that the physical body is inherently evil. It only states that the flesh is more easily tempted to sin. Yoga, on the other hand, teaches that the spiritual body is held in bondage by the physical body. Consequently, the positions are intended to manipulate the skeletal and muscular structure in such a way as to release the spiritual body for its goal of *yoga*, or union, with God.

The primary concern of yoga is to heighten God-consciousness by elevating the awareness of the spiritual body. At no time does it seek to convert the human spirit, assuming that it is intrinsically good. Christ promises to regenerate our spirits (John 3:1-7) and give us the Holy Spirit, that we might have power and victory over flesh. This promise is fulfilled by placing our trust in Jesus, not by contorting our limbs.

Swami Vishnudevananda, a foremost exponent of yoga and author of *The Complete Illustrated Book of Yoga*, succinctly explains the purpose of yoga: "It is the duty of each developed man to train his body to the highest degree of perfection so that it may be used to pursue the spiritual purposes. The expression of the spirit increases in proportion to the development of the body and mind in which it is encased. The aim of all yoga practice is to achieve truth wherein the individual soul identifies itself with the supreme soul of God."

How is this accomplished? Swami Vishnudevananda declares, "The supreme power of nature" is a coiled serpent lying at the base of the spine. She is the goddess Shakti, whom Hindus believe is "the giver of immortality and eternal happiness." But Shakti can only fulfill her promise by achieving union with Shiva, her consort. (Shiva is one member of the Hindu Trinitarian godhead including Brahma, Vishnu, and Shiva.) Shiva is said to reside at the center of the forehead between the eyebrows.

The purpose of yoga is to arouse the serpent powers of Shakti (sometimes called *kundalini*) so that she rises through the *sushumma*, a hollow canal said to be running through the spinal cord. On the ascension, Shakti passes through six *chakras*, or spiritual energy centers. The seventh chakra, her destination, is Shiva. Once Shakti merges with Shiva, union, or yoga, is achieved. The next goal is permanent union to become a liberated soul and be unlimited by time and space—at one with God. The person who accomplishes this goal then possesses all powers, psychic abilities, and sinless perfection.

Different Approaches

How does all this affect the average soccer mom or harried business executive who seeks to use yoga to reduce stress and increase health?

There are four forms of yoga: *Karma Yoga* (spiritual union through right conduct); *Bhakti Yoga* (union with the Absolute by devotion to a guru); *Juana (Gyana) Yoga* (access to God through knowledge); and *Raja Yoga* (God-realization through mental control). Raja Yoga has three subdivisions, one of which is *Hatha Yoga*, the practice most familiar to the general public. Hatha Yoga is in turn divided into eight stages:

1. body purification
2. postures
3. *mudras* (postures that produce psychic energy)
4. breath control
5. stilling the mind
6. concentration
7. meditation
8. union with God (Shiva)

Body purification, for example, can involve belching air, vomiting water, swallowing a fifteen-foot long cloth, or running a string up the nose, through the nasal cavity, and out the mouth. These procedures are known as *kriyas*. The meditative aspects of yoga are designed to still the senses by gazing at an object without blinking (referred to as *tratak*). Some yoga meditations involve the recitation of a *mantra* (the resident name of a Hindu deity) and Hindu prayers.

Most people who begin yoga assume that the positions are mere techniques to calm the body and improve physical fitness. But yoga has distinctly religious purposes involved in every aspect of it. The postures (*asanas*) are sometimes designed with a devotional intent, such as the *soorya namaskar*, or sun exercises. They are to be practiced by facing the rising sun and repeating the twelve names of the Lord Sun. Other positions are named after gods (like the Baby Krishna and Lord Nataraja poses) and animals (lion, scorpion, cobra, etc.). Western yoga instructors often de-emphasize these religious overtones, but such departure cannot lessen the ultimate result.

Swami Vishnudevananda states, "Hatha Yoga prescribes physical methods to begin with so that the student can manipulate the mind more easily as he advances, attaining communication with one's higher self." Some might argue that although Raja Yoga (the distinctly religious discipline of which Hatha Yoga is a part) has a spiritual intent, Hatha Yoga may be practiced free of these consequences. Again the Swami warns, "Many people think Hatha Yoga is merely physical exercise. But in reality there is no difference between Hatha Yoga and Raja Yoga."

The postures of Hatha Yoga are designed to condition the mind to experience an altered state of consciousness. Each pose is presumed to be tuning the body, glands, and psychic nervous system to a level of spiritual susceptibility and altered awareness. Hindu yoga teachers have long defined this discipline as religious both in goal and practice. Can it then be casually disassociated from its pagan origins simply because a Western teacher redefines its intent?

Once the yoga novice has learned a few basic postures, she is quickly introduced to the breathing exercises (*pranayamas*). She may be told that these are for relaxation or clearing of the lungs. However, this aspect of yoga is actually designed for the purposes of controlling what is called *prana*. This so-called "vital breath" is said to be a form of soul energy that originates with the Universal Life Force (God, Brahman) and permeates all living matter.

Prana, sometimes called *ki*, is supposed to be the source of psychic energy and the fount of all extrasensory phenomena experienced in advanced states of yoga. Prana is localized in the chakras, the spiritual energy centers through which Shakti rises on the way to her psychosexual union with Shiva. The chakras regulate prana and thereby manipulate one's willpower and all bodily functions. Yoga's breathing exercises control prana, a practice claimed to be beneficial in ridding the body of diseases. Prana may also be transmitted as a spiritualistic healing force by the laying on of hands and connecting one's mind with "the cosmic power of god."

Claims and Concerns

It should be obvious that Hatha Yoga promises more than supple limbs and relief from tension. Yoga's ultimate purpose is union with Brahman and acquiring the resultant peace and harmony which Hindus believe comes from such God-realization. The supposed consequence of this achievement is the complete cessation of sickness, evil, stress, and domination of the spirit by the body. In this state, perfect souls may then unite immortally with God.

Such goals are certainly admirable. But are they attainable? The answer is no when they are compared to a Bible-based view of God, man, and the concept of union with God. Scripture teaches that a chasm of sin separates us from our Creator. This gulf can only be spanned by an act of reconciliation to God through believing in the death of his Son. Any attempt to merge or unite one's consciousness with an "Ultimate Reality" would encounter the sin barrier and thus be thwarted.

It is not the human merit of ascetic disciplines that brings harmony with God. It is by the blood of Christ that the separation brought about by Adam's disobedience is eradicated. Faith in the saving power of that blood can bring true union with God and his will.

Yoga advocates are certainly to be admired for their devotion to healthy bodies. Many who strenuously oppose the religious overtones of yoga are themselves gluttonous specimens of the junk-food syndrome. Many people consume inordinate amounts of coffee, sweets, and soft drinks, and they certainly may find some immediate physical benefits of yoga. Even unprecedented numbers young people are having difficulty with obesity and stress. As a result increasing numbers of school teachers are having their students perform yoga.

Care for one's physique is important, but not at the risk of aligning oneself with pagan principles. The popularity of yoga presents a formidable challenge to Christians who ought to make their bodies a welcoming place for the Holy Spirit to reside (1 Corinthians 3:16-17; 6:19-20).

CHRISTIAN CRITIQUE: The original intent of yoga, a variant of Hinduism, was to achieve spiritual union with the impersonal Supreme Absolute deity. It may be argued that most Westerners derive physical benefits from it without entanglement in such theological premises. However, there is always the possibility that one may be drawn to experiment with the deeper stages, which are distinctly religious in nature.

The book *Yoga, Youth and Reincarnation* states, "Yoga is accomplished when the individual spirit merges with the Universal Spirit [God] in a spirit of oneness." It is poor logic to assume that commitment to a religious system of false gods may be excused by divorcing part of the system from its ultimate aim (i.e., doing yoga exercises for physical reasons independent of their intended integration into a methodology of spiritual merit by "works").

The Christian's concept of peace with God is based on reconciliation to the Lord, not union with a Brahmanistic pantheon. Spiritual favor and righteousness come from what Christ has done for us (Ephesians 2:8-9), not the positions we do for him. Yoga ultimately strives for the deification of man and his spiritual enlightenment. It also promises release from the endless cycles of reincarnation, an unbiblical teaching.

SOURCES: Patricia Leigh Brown, "Latest Way to Cut Grade School Stress: Yoga," *New York Times*, 24 March 2002; "The Science of Yoga," *Time*, 23 April 2001, 56–57; Jess Stearn, *Yoga, Youth and Reincarnation* (New York: Bantam, 1963); Swami Vishnudevananda, *The Complete Illustrated Book of Yoga* (East Brunswick, N.J.: Bell, 1960).

ACCESS: Yoga centers and teachers are located in most major cities.

See also Meditation, Sri Chinmoy.

YORUBA

See Voodoo, Santeria, and Yoruba.

ZEN BUDDHISM

See Buddhism.

RECOMMENDED READING

The books listed here represent sources of information about world religions, alternative spirituality, and cults for the reader who wishes to investigate more thoroughly a particular group or teaching.* Not all of these resources are written from an evangelical perspective.

Abanes, Richard. *Cults, New Religious Movements and Your Family: A Guide to Ten Non-Christian Groups Out to Convert Your Loved Ones.* Wheaton, Ill.: Crossway, 1998. The author presents a comprehensive analysis of the ten most threatening cults to family members. The primary purpose is to shine the light of biblical truth on each group and expose the dangers to those who are searching.

Abdul-Haqq, Abdiyah Akbar. *Sharing Your Faith with a Muslim.* Minneapolis: Bethany, 1980. This book is for anyone who is serious about sharing the truth of the gospel to Muslims. It is written by a Christian whose father was a convert from Islam.

Adair, James R., and Ted Miller, eds. *We Found Our Way Out.* Grand Rapids: Baker, 1964. A Christian book containing testimonies of people who have come out of religious groups such as Mormonism, Jehovah's Witnesses, Christian Science, Rosicrucianism, Humanism, Theosophy, and Agnosticism.

Agency for Cultural Affairs. *Japanese Religions: A Survey.* Tokyo: Kodansha International, 1972, 1981. A non-Christian book distributed by the Agency for Cultural Affairs in Japan discussing all of the major religions popular in Japan today. Included are the different sects of Buddhism, Hinduism, and Shintoism, as well as Christian groups that have followings in Japan. An excellent secular resource.

Amano, J. Yutaka, and Norman L. Geisler. *The Infiltration of the New Age.* Wheaton, Ill.: Tyndale, 1989. An insightful look at New Age thought and how it has permeated our society.

Anderson, Einar. *The Inside Story of Mormonism.* Grand Rapids: Kregel, 1973. A Christian approach to Mormonism. The author shares his own testimony of how he left the Mormon Church and became a Christian. Mormon history and Mormon doctrine are discussed from a Christian perspective with biblical answers.

*Portions of the above list were provided by: Religions Analysis Service Inc., 5693 Geneva Ave. N., Oakdale, MN 55128; 1-800-562-9128. Its catalog of books and tracts exposing cults and unscriptural teachings in the light of God's Word is itself an excellent resource for further reading.

Anderson, J. N. D. *The World's Religions.* Grand Rapids: Eerdmans, 1976. This is the fourth edition of a book that has been a reliable study guide for more than twenty-five years. Its aim is to summarize the origin and teaching of seven main non-Christian religions. Each chapter is written by a different author.

————. *Christianity and Comparative Religions.* Downers Grove, Ill.: Intervarsity, 1970. A Christian book discussing comparative religions and Christianity. It does not deal with specific religions.

————. *Christianity and World Religions.* The author answers some difficult questions relating to the uniqueness of the Christian revelation. This is a complete revision and expansion of his *Christianity and Comparative Religion.*

Ankerberg, John, and John Weldon. *Encyclopedia of Cults and New Religions.* Eugene, Oreg.: Harvest House, 1999. This exhaustive volume provides in-depth treatment of more than fifty aberrant groups. The doctrinal appendix is especially helpful.

————. *Encyclopedia of New Age Beliefs.* Eugene, Oreg.: Harvest House, 1996. This major work is designed to help you understand the broad spectrum of New Age beliefs in comparison with traditional Biblical beliefs and practices. A valuable reference book.

————. *The Secret Teachings of the Masonic Lodge.* Chicago: Moody, 1990. An eye-opening, carefully researched book looking at the beliefs, rituals, and teachings of the Masons. Things you need to know from the Christian perspective.

Beaver, R. Pierce, et al., eds. *Eerdman's Handbook to the World's Religions.* Grand Rapids: Eerdmans, 1982. A new revised edition by a number of consulting editors. An excellent introduction to religions of the world. Beautifully illustrated with over two hundred color photos, maps, charts, and a forty-six-page glossary.

Beckwith, Francis. *Baha'i.* Minneapolis: Bethany, 1985. A Christian response to Baha'ism, the religion which aims toward one world government and one common faith. A remarkably incisive work; brief yet thorough.

Beckwith, Francis J., et al. *The Counterfeit Gospel of Mormonism.* Eugene, Oreg.: Harvest House, 1998. This book was written in response to the position that there isn't much difference between Mormonism and Christianity. The book covers in detail the radically opposing doctrines and practices of the two, with a presentation of the gospel to Mormons.

Benware, Paul N. *Ambassadors of Armstrongism.* Nutley, N.J.: Presbyterian and Reformed, 1977. A Christian approach to Armstrongism, including a brief history of the Worldwide church of God and a summary of the teachings of the Worldwide Church of God on Scripture, God, the Holy Spirit, Christ, angels, humans, sin, salvation, the church, and eschatology.

Berry, Gerald L. *Religions of the World.* New York: Barnes and Noble, 1956.

Berry, Harold J. *Unity School of Christianity: What They Believe*. Berry has done objective research into the background and present-day beliefs of Unity.

Bjornstad, James. *Counterfeits at Your Door*. Ventura, Calif.: Gospel Light, 1979. From a Christian perspective, cult expert Jim Bjornstad examines the teachings and proselytizing efforts of the Jehovah's Witnesses and the Mormons.

———. *The Moon Is Not the Sun*. Minneapolis: Bethany, 1976. A Christian treatment of the Unification Church of Sun Myung Moon. It contains good documentation on the major teachings of the Unification church and some advice on how to witness to a Moonie.

———. *Sun Myung Moon and the Unification Church*. A reasoned biblical look at the Moonies and their teachings. A helpful, informative, readable little book.

Boa, Kenneth. *Cults, World Religions, and the Occult*. Wheaton, Ill.: Victor, 1990. This is a revised and expanded version of *Cults, World Religions, and You*. An easy-to-understand guide to major religions and cults and the occult as well as other new cults. Includes the history of each, their teachings, and how to respond to them.

———. *Cults, World Religions, and You*. Wheaton, Ill.: Scripture Press, 1977. A short introduction to all the major religions and cults from a Christian perspective. Discusses non-Christian religions of the East, pseudo-Christian religions of the West, occult religious systems, and new religions and cults. A brief but adequate introduction to cults and religions.

Bowman, Robert M. Jr. *Understanding Jehovah's Witnesses: Why They Read the Bible the Way They Do*. Grand Rapids: Baker, 1991. The focus of this book is on understanding Jehovah's Witnesses, not attacking them. Bowman points out the truth in love.

Breese, David. *Know the Mark of the Cults*. Wheaton, Ill.: Victor, 1980.

Brooke, Tal. *One World*. End Run Publishing, 2000. This book is described as a "special millennial edition" of *When the World Will Be As One*, with 40 percent new material and over 190 graphics, pictures, and photos. Further, "this new updated edition reveals the deep forces behind the present worldwide transformation and how it could affect life as we know it."

Bubeck, Mark I. *Overcoming the Adversary*. Chicago: Moody, 1984. A practical handbook that shows how to be strong in the Lord, how to appropriate the power of the Holy Spirit, and how to put on the whole armor of God. Good reading to be applied and triumph to be claimed.

———. *The Satanic Revival*. San Bernadino, Calif: Here's Life, 1991. A resurgence of devil worship has exploded across the United States. This book reveals what is happening and provides practical tools to use against this plague.

Burks, Thompson. *Religions of the World.* Cincinnati: Standard, 1972. This book is good to use in an adult education or Sunday school class. It is divided into thirteen chapters which can be combined for a ten-week session of lessons. Includes good study outlines, and discusses Judaism, Islam, Hinduism, Buddhism, and primitive religions.

Chafer, Lewis Sperry. *Satan: His Motives and Methods.* Grand Rapids: Kregel, 1991. This classic study has again been made available at a time when satanism is on the rise and the occult is capturing headlines. This study exposes the Great Deceiver under the searchlight of the Scriptures.

Chandler, Russell. *Understanding the New Age.* Grand Rapids: Zondervan, 1993. A revised, updated, revealing analysis of the New Age by a former religion writer for the *Los Angeles Times.* Includes helpful index and discussion guide.

Chang, Lit-sen. *Zen-Existentialism: The Spiritual Decline of the West; A Positive Answer to the Hippies.* Nutley, N.J.: Presbyterian and Reformed, 1969. An extensive, in-depth treatment of Zen Buddhism and Christianity from a biblical perspective.

Conway, Flo, and Jim Siegelman. *Snapping.* Philadelphia: J. B. Lippincott, 1978.

Cowan, Marvin W. *Mormon Claims Answered.* Salt Lake City: Published by the author, 1975. A good technical treatment of the origin and history of Mormonism, its doctrines concerning God and the Bible, and a very careful study of the *Book of Mormon.* It also has an extensive section on salvation from an orthodox Christian point of view.

Decker, Ed. *Decker's Complete Handbook on Mormonism.* Eugene, Oreg.: Harvest House, 1995. This is a relatively new book, an all-in-one-volume specifically created for those who want a clear, concise overview of Mormonism. A landmark reference guide.

————. *The Question of Freemasonry.* Lafayette, La.: Huntington, 1992. This booklet is part of the Huntington House Salt Series and provides a brief but well researched critique of Freemasonry. Decker shows why no Christian should want to be a Mason.

————. *What You Need to Know about . . . Masons.* Eugene, Oreg.: Harvest House, 1992. A provocative book which takes a behind-the-scenes look at Masonic beliefs and rituals. It isn't just another fraternal organization but a separate religion.

Decker, Ed, and Dave Hunt. *The God Makers.* Eugene, Oreg.: Harvest House, 1994. A shocking expose of what the Mormon Church really believes. Gives an account of the theology, goals, and secrets of Mormonism and is written in readable style. Good for both pastors and laity.

Dencher, Ted. *Why I Left Jehovah's Witnesses.* Fort Washington, Penn.: Christian Literature Crusade, 1966. An excellent book on the doctrines of Jehovah's Witnesses and the internal workings of the organization, including the testimony of Dencher, who used to be a Jehovah's Witness. This is a good book for a Christian to study, but since its tone is somewhat sarcastic, it would not be wise to share it with a Jehovah's Witness.

Dickason, C. Fred. *Angels: Elect and Evil.* Chicago, Moody, 1995. A clearly outlined discussion of the angels of God, fallen angels, demons, and the chief fallen angel, Satan. A rewarding doctrinal study.

Drummond, Richard H. *Guatama the Buddha: An Essay in Religious Understanding.* Grand Rapids: Eerdmans, 1974. A lengthy treatment of the life and teachings of Buddha from a Christian perspective. It also deals with the general concepts of Eastern thought.

Edwards, Christopher. *Crazy for God: The Nightmare of Cult Life.* Englewood Cliffs, N.J.: Prentice-Hall, 1979. The testimony and life history of a young man who joined the Unification Church. He explores the time he spent as a Moonie, the deprogramming he went through, and his final release from the cult. Not necessarily from a Christian point of view.

Eidsmoe, John. *Basic Principles of New Age Thought.* Green Forest, Ark.: New Leaf Press, 1991. As a university law professor, Eidsmoe teaches the reader how to counter the New Age threat to civilization itself. He shows how a false gospel is being woven into the fabric of modern society.

Elkins, Chris. *Heavenly Deception.* Wheaton, Ill.: Tyndale House, 1980. The testimony of a man who was raised a Christian but joined the Unification Church. After being a Moonie for some time, he was freed from the bondage he had experienced in this cult.

Enroth, Ronald. *The Lure of the Cults.* Chappaqua, N.Y.: Christian Herald Books, 1979. Instead of dealing systematically with individual cults, Enroth explores the sociological and psychological characteristics of cults and explains how to help someone who is in a cult.

———. *Youth, Brainwashing, and the Extremist Cults.* Grand Rapids: Zondervan, 1977. An introduction to a sociologist's view of the cults. Case histories are presented along with a discussion of characteristics of cultic activity from a Christian perspective.

Enroth, Ronald, et al. *A Guide to Cults and New Religions.* Downers Grove, Ill.: InterVarsity, 1983. Covers some of the lesser known cults, as well as some better known cults.

Evans, Christopher. *Cults of Unreason.* New York: Dell, 1973. A non-Christian book which deals with some of the more mystical and pseudo-scientific cults. Most of the book is devoted to a study of Scientology and is considered to be the best current treatment of this cult from a non-Christian perspective.

Franz, Raymond. *Crisis of Conscience.* Atlanta: Commentary Press, 1983. Written by a former member of the governing body of Jehovah's Witnesses, this book offers a penetrating view of that group's supreme council. This is an excellent book with a personal side that reveals the conflict that goes on when someone changes allegiance.

————. *In Search of Christian Freedom.* Atlanta: Commentary Press, 1991. This book is a sequel to Franz's *Crisis of Conscience* and provides an even more comprehensive view of the Jehovah's Witnesses by a man who is the nephew of a former president of the group. A very thorough examination with unparalleled sources of information. A challenge to Christian freedom.

Fraser, Gordon H. *Is Mormonism Christian?* Chicago: Moody, 1977. An old book that has been consistently updated since its first printing. It treats all the major doctrines of Mormonism from a Christian point of view, including the restoration of the church, the Mormon genealogy, God, Jesus Christ, the Holy Spirit, the doctrine of man, the priesthood, baptism, baptism for the dead, salvation, the lost tribes of Israel, and the sects of Mormonism.

————. *The Sects of the Latter-day Saints.* Eugene, Ore.: Industrial Litho, 1978. From a Christian perspective, this book deals with the major sects of the Latter-day Saints, especially the Reorganized Church of Jesus Christ of Latter Day Saints. It also analyzes the different polygamous sects of Mormonism.

Fry, George, James Kin, Eugene Sanger, and Herbert Wolf. *Great Asian Religions.* These four coauthors, who have lived and labored in Asia, introduce the country's seven great religions and approach them from three different disciplines: theology, history, and literature.

Garabedian, John H., and Orde Coombs. *Eastern Religions in the Electric Age.* New York: Grosset and Dunlap, Workman, 1969.

Geer, Thelma "Granny". *Mormonism, Mama, and Me.* This is a unique approach to Mormonism, written by one who had been raised in the "real" Mormonism. "Granny's" personal style makes every chapter a pleasure to read.

Geisler, Norman. *False Gods of Our Time.* Eugene, Ore.: Harvest House, 1985. Excellent analysis of atheism, pantheism, polytheism, and other anti-Christian philosophies that provide the theological background for most cults.

Gomes, Alan W. *Unitarian Universalism.* Grand Rapids: Zondervan, 1998. This book is in the Zondervan Guide series. Although the Unitarian Universalist

Association (UUA) is not a large or well known religious group in America, it is important because it is a "politically correct" movement which is prevalent in politics and on college campuses. It is known for its tolerance of "alternative life styles" and beliefs, including homosexuality, radical feminism, and abortion on demand. To this group, the Bible is a myth and Jesus Christ is one of many inspirational, but fallible teachers. A well researched study.

Great Religions of the World. Washington: National Geographic Society, 1971.

Groothuis, Douglas. *Confronting the New Age: How to Resist a Growing Religious Movement.* Downers Grove, Ill.: InterVarsity, 1988. Teaches Christians how to: witness to New Age adherents; identify New Age influences in business seminars; expose New Age curriculum in public schools; discern New Age influences in many areas; and how to confront the New Age.

————. *Revealing the New Age Jesus: Challenges to Orthodox Views of Christ.* Downers Grove, Ill.: InterVarsity, 1990. The New Age movement spreads more and more confusing ideas about the identity of Jesus Christ. Groothuis examines the claims made by New Age thinkers and demonstrates how the Bible gives the true picture of Jesus Christ.

————. *Unmasking the New Age.* Downers Grove, Ill.: InterVarsity, 1986. In the last ten years the New Age has shifted out of the counterculture into the mainstream of society. This book helps Christians become more alert and discerning about how to respond to this aggressive movement.

Gruss, Edmond C. *Apostles of Denial: An Examination and Exposé of the History, Doctrines, and Claims of the Jehovah's Witnesses.* Grand Rapids: Baker, 1978. The best documented treatment of the Jehovah's Witnesses from a Christian point of view. Gruss, who was a Jehovah's Witness himself, includes his own testimony at the end of the book.

————. *Cults and the Occult.* Phillipsburg, N.J.: Presbyterian and Reformed, 1980. A brief study meant to be used in an adult education or Bible class situation. It deals with Jehovah's Witnesses, Mormons, Christian Scientists, Unity, Armstrongism, Spiritualism, astrology, Baha'ism, Rosicrucianism, Ouija boards, Edgar Cayce, the Unification Church, and concludes with a Christian perspective on cults and the occult.

————. *The Jehovah's Witnesses and Prophetic Speculation.* Nutley, N.J.: Presbyterian and Reformed, 1972. This thoroughly documented book deals specifically with the Jehovah's Witnesses' propagation of false prophecies regarding the end of the world.

————. *We Left Jehovah's Witnesses: Personal Testimonies.* Phillipsburg, N.J.: Presbyterian and Reformed, 1992. Testimonies of converted Jehovah's Witnesses. Much of the material is documented, and pages from the Watchtower Society publications have been reproduced.

Hansen, Carol. *Reorganized Latter Day Saint Church: Is It Christian?* Refiner's Fire Ministries, 2000. This book is a revised and expanded version of Hansen's original book. It contains a wealth of information on the RLDS Church including its real history, cultic teachings and practices, as well as personal testimonials from former members.

Hefley, James C. *The Youth-Nappers.* Wheaton, Ill.: Scripture Press, 1977. A brief Christian review of some new cults such as Unification Church, Hare Krishna, Divine Light Mission, Transcendental Meditation, Children of God, and others.

Hesselgrave, David J., ed. *Dynamic Religious Movements.* Grand Rapids: Baker, 1978. An excellent Christian book discussing cultic religions in other countries, including Africa, Europe, the Far East, the Mideast, North America, South America, and Southeast Asia.

Hexham, Irving, and Karla Poewe. *Understanding Cults and New Religions.* Grand Rapids: Eerdmans, 1986. The authors argue that new religions are in fact neither very new nor very religious. They outline key features of Eastern and Western religions that are evident in new religions—a fresh approach to the study of cults.

Heydt, Henry J. *A Comparison of World Religions.* Fort Washington, Penn.: Christian Literature Crusade, 1967. A historical survey dealing with Judaism, Christianity, Hinduism, Zoroastrianism, Shintoism, Taoism, Jainism, Buddhism, Confucianism, Islam, and Sikhism. Chapter three gives a topical comparison of all these groups, and chapter four shows the distinctive superiority of Christianity.

Hoekema, Anthony A. *Christian Science.* Grand Rapids: Eerdmans, 1974. Taken from *The Four Major Cults* and extensively updated.

————. *The Four Major Cults.* Grand Rapids: Eerdmans, 1963. A classic work on the major cults such as Jehovah's Witnesses, Mormonism, and Christian Science.

————. *Jehovah's Witnesses.* Grand Rapids: Eerdmans, 1974. Taken from *The Four Major Cults* and extensively updated.

————. *Mormonism.* Grand Rapids: Eerdmans, 1974. Taken from *The Four Major Cults* and extensively updated.

Hopkins, Joseph. *The Armstrong Empire.* Grand Rapids: Eerdmans, 1974. A Christian perspective on Herbert W. Armstrong and the Worldwide Church of God. It deals extensively with the background of Armstrong and the church and includes a brief survey of WCG doctrines.

Hunt, Dave. *The Cult Explosion.* Eugene, Oreg.: Harvest House, 1980. A thoroughly scriptural, psychological, and sociological perspective on the rise of the cults. Some of the topics covered are: altered states of consciousness, the ultimate lie, beyond morality, authoritarianism and responsibility, spirit communication, and the battle for the mind. This book does not deal with cults individually or in a systematic way.

―――. *Occult Invasion.* Eugene, Oreg.: Harvest House, 1998. This book gives you the skills you need to recognize the subtle incursions of the occult and provide tools you can use to halt its destructive advance. Very comprehensive.

Kemperman, Steve. *Lord of the Second Advent: A Rare Look inside the Terrifying World of the Moonies.* Ventura, Calif.: Regal, 1981. An excellent testimony of a young man who joined the Moonies. He describes his experiences of being deprogrammed twice and how he finally came to be released from the cult.

Koch, Kurt. *Between Christ and Satan.* Grand Rapids: Kregel, 1971. This work is a classic on demonic activity in the world today. It discusses fortune telling, magic, spiritism, healing miracles, and occult literature. The analysis is based on 193 case studies in light of the Word of God.

―――. *Christian Counseling and Occultism: The Counselling of the Psychically Disturbed and Those Oppressed through Involvement in Occultism. A Practical, Theological and Systematic Investigation in the Light of Present Day Psychological and Medical Knowledge.* The author of this book has written a number of books on demonology, Satan, and occultism. This is an in-depth work and is well documented. A part of his ministry included dealing with those suffering from demon affliction and the occult.

―――. *Demonology, Past and Present.* Grand Rapids: Kregel, 1973. An invaluable help to Christians and to pastors who are confronted with the problems of those who have experimented with any kind of occult practices.

―――. *The Devil's Alphabet.* Grand Rapids: Kregel, 1971. The author's years of ministry and study on demonic and occultic activity qualify him to discuss forty-seven forms of occultism. He also covers the freedom available in Christ and gives New Testament teaching on deliverance and victory.

―――. *Occult ABC.* Translated by Michael Freeman. Literature Mission Aglasterhausen, 1980. Distributed by Grand Rapids International Publications. Brings the reader to an awareness of occult movements and Satan's devices. It deals with abuses, ideologies, parapsychology, rock music, and other practices.

―――. *Occult Bondage and Deliverance: Advice for Counseling the Sick, the Troubled, and the Occultly Oppressed.* Grand Rapids: Kregel, 1971. This book sounds a clear warning against dabbling in various phases of the occult. A valuable feature includes a definition of terms in the occult world.

Larson, Bob. *Larson's Book of Spiritual Warfare*. Nashville: Nelson, 1999. This encyclopedic reference answers questions about demons, the devil, deliverance, angels and the supernatural. A comprehensive approach to satanism, occultism, and exorcism.

————. *Straight Answers on the New Age*. Nashville: Nelson, 1989. A definitive reference on the New Age movement. This is a comprehensive volume written by one of the foremost experts on the New Age. It answers commonly asked questions and includes a glossary of terms and an exhaustive index.

Lewis, Gordon R. *Confronting the Cults*. Grand Rapids: Baker, 1966. A standard reference work on the major cults, including Jehovah's Witnesses, Mormonism, Christian Science, Unity, and Spiritualism. From a Christian perspective, Lewis provides theological answers to cultic claims. For the Christian layperson confronted by members of cults. Questions and teaching hints at the end of each chapter makes this a tool for group discussions.

————. *What Everyone Should Know about Transcendental Meditation*. Ventura, Calif.: Regal Books, 1975. A brief treatment of Transcendental Meditation from a Christian perspective.

Lincoln, C. Eric. *The Black Muslims in America*. Grand Rapids: Eerdmans, 1993. In the wake of recent events relating to Black Muslims, this timely update (third edition) provides fascinating reading and challenge to keep abreast of this group that is still in the process of developing.

Lindsey, Hal. *Satan Is Alive and Well on Planet Earth*. Grand Rapids: Zondervan, 1972. This well-known book exposes the dangers in playing with forces from the "other side."

Lutzer, Erwin W., and John F. DeVries. *Satan's "Evangelistic" Strategy for This New Age*. Wheaton, Ill.: Victor, 1989. Satan is enlisting people to stand with him in his final assault on God. His recruitment tool is the New Age movement. This book presents a Christian defense against "four spiritual flaws."

MacGregor, Lorri. *What You Need to Know about Jehovah's Witnesses*. Eugene, Oreg.: Harvest House, 1992. An effective teaching tool about the contradictory beliefs of Jehovah's Witnesses in light of Scripture.

Magnani, Duane. *The Watchtower Files: Dialogue with a Jehovah's Witness*. Minneapolis: Bethany, 1985. Documentation from over 150 Watchtower publications. One of the most thoroughly researched studies on the history and the doctrines of this group.

Maharaj, Rabindranath R., and Dave Hunt. *The Death of a Guru*. Philadelphia: A. J. Holman, 1977. This book is the poignant autobiography of Rabi R. Maharaj, who was a Hindu from a long line of Brahmin priests and gurus. He describes his life as a Hindu and his struggle to choose between Hinduism and Christ.

Mangalwadi, Vishal. *The World of Gurus.* Chicago: Cornerstone, 1992. Guruism has been a powerful religious movement worldwide since the early 1960s. This is an in-depth look at the historical background and philosophical aspirations of guruism.

Marsh, C. R. *Share Your Faith with a Muslim.* Chicago: Moody, 1975. A perspective on Islam giving its history, doctrines, and explaining how to share Christ with a Muslim.

Martin, Walter. *Jehovah of the Watchtower.* Minneapolis: Bethany, 1982. A re-release of Martin's classic on the Jehovah's Witnesses, originally published by Moody. Martin deals with the history and doctrines of Jehovah's Witnesses and provides biblical responses to each of the group's major doctrines.

———. *The Kingdom of the Cults.* Minneapolis: Bethany, 1975. This is the classic Christian volume on the major traditional cults. A 1982 edition is completely updated with current documentation.

———. *The Maze of Mormonism.* Santa Ana, Calif.: Vision, 1978. An expansive revision of Martin's 1962 classic by the same title is perhaps the best Christian treatment of the major teachings of Mormonism.

———. *The New Cults.* Santa Ana, Calif.: Vision, 1980. An excellent treatment of some newer cults. The history of each cult and its leader is discussed along with each individual belief in the areas of God, Jesus Christ, humans, salvation, and Scripture. Cults covered include: the Way International, Hinduism, est, the Children of God, the Ascended Masters, Silva Mind Control, Church of the Living Word, and Foundation of Human Understanding.

———. *The Rise of the Cults.* Santa Ana, Calif.: Vision, 1980. A revision and update of the 1955 classic. Condensed from *The Kingdom of the Cults.*

———, ed. *Walter Martin's Cults Reference Bible.* Santa Ana, Calif.: Vision House, 1981. A unique volume explaining the texts of the Old and New Testaments (King James Version), used by the major cults in support of their own teachings. Martin gives the cultic misinterpretation and the biblical Christian response to each passage. Also included are essays on all of the major cults, charts comparing the teachings of the major cults, a dictionary of terms used by the cults, a brief essay on interpreting the Bible, and biblical helps for those witnessing to members of the cults.

Mather, George A., and Larry A. Nichols. *Dictionary of Cults, Sects, Religions and the Occult.* Grand Rapids: Zondervan, 1993. This is a significant reference book which includes not only well known groups (i.e., Jehovah's Witnesses, Mormons,

Islam, etc) but other groups not as well known but those which are increasingly more visible and invasive. It gives the beliefs and practices of the various cults and religions, their history, and many illustrations and charts, as well as a bibliography, for each of the groups and movements. A good resource to refer to when information is sought about the many groups on the scene today.

McDowell, Josh, and Don Stewart. *Handbook of Today's Religions.* Nashville: Nelson, 1983. This book is a reference work written for all concerned Christians who desire a discerning, broad-based knowledge of the major cults and belief systems that oppose Bible-based Christianity.

McElveen, Floyd C. *The Mormon Illusion.* Ventura, Calif.: Regal, 1977. A traditional Christian treatment of Mormonism, discussing Mormon history, sacred scriptures, and major doctrines.

McKenney, Tom C. *Please Tell Me . . . Questions People Ask about Freemasonry— and the Answers.* "In his latest book, McKenney has compiled the questions most often asked by the public concerning the cult-like nature and anti-Christian activities of the Masonic movements."

Means, Pat. *The Mystical Maze.* San Bernardino, Calif.: Campus Crusade for Christ, 1976.

Melton, J. Gordon. *The Encyclopedia of American Religions.* 2 vols. Wilmington, N.C.: McGrath, 1978.

Miller, Calvin. *Transcendental Hesitation.* Grand Rapids: Zondervan, 1977. An in-depth treatment of Transcendental Meditation, with discussion of Eastern mysticism compared to a biblical worldview.

Miller, Elliot. *Crash Course on the New Age Movement.* Grand Rapids: Baker, 1989. Penetrates New Age vocabulary, discusses crystals, channeling, claims of the New Age movement and New Age science. Examines *The Aquarian Conspiracy*, looks at holism versus reductionism, and provides Christian answers.

Miller, William McElwee. *The Bahai Faith: Its History and Teaching.* South Pasadena, Calif.: William Carey Library, 1974. The best book on the Baha'i faith in the English language from a Christian perspective.

————. *Ten Muslims Meet Christ.* Grand Rapids: Eerdmans, 1969. Testimonies of Muslims who have accepted Christ, and a description of the persecution they have suffered in their native Muslim lands.

Milmine, George E. *The Life of Mary Baker G. Eddy and the History of Christian Science.* Grand Rapids: Baker, 1937. A classic biography of Mary Baker Eddy, explaining how she developed her cult by taking the teachings of Christian Science from previous writers and thinkers.

Montgomery, John Warwick, ed. *Demon possession: A Medical, Historical, Anthropological, and Theological Symposium: Papers Presented at the University of Notre Dame, January 8–11, 1975, under the Auspices of the Christian Medical Society.* Minneapolis: Bethany, 1976. Montgomery is a Christian lawyer and writer. This is a well written book in eight sections, each one a paper presented at the University of Notre Dame, from a medical historical, anthropological, and theological perspective on the subject of demon possession.

———. *Principalities and Powers: The World of the Occult.* Minneapolis: Bethany, 1975. A fascinating look at the paranormal, the supernatural, and the hidden things. A thoroughly dependable look at the "unnatural" occurrences that have captivated the minds of millions of Americans.

Morey, Robert. *How to Answer a Jehovah's Witness.* This book stresses taking the offensive in confronting the door-to-door "salesperson" of the Jehovah's Witnesses. It is an effective handbook.

———. *The Islamic Invasion: Confronting the World's Fastest Growing Religion.* Eugene, Oreg.: Harvest House, 1992. One of Christianity's clearest communicators on Muslim beliefs, Morey gives the insight one needs to understand Islam and the challenge it poses today.

———. *Reincarnation and Christianity.* Minneapolis: Bethany, 1980. An excellent treatment of reincarnation with biblical answers. Written for Morey's doctrinal treatise, it displays good scholarship and documentation.

Needleman, Jacob. *The New Religion.* New York: E. P. Dutton, 1970. A non-Christian review of the main teachings of major religions as well as some of the newer cults. The section on Zen Buddhism is particularly good.

Neill, Stephen. *Christian Faith and Other Faiths.* Downers Grove, Ill.: InterVarsity, 1984. The author offers an analysis of all the great religions, as well as Christianity. This book will provoke discussion and challenge the reader.

Palmer, Bernard. *Understanding the Islamic Explosion.* Beaverlodge, Alberta: Horizon House, 1980. A Christian perspective on Islam, the problems in the Middle East (e.g., the oil embargo), and how they relate to the Christian.

Penton, M. James. *Apocalypse Delayed: The Story of Jehovah's Witnesses.* Toronto: University of Toronto Press, 1997. As a longtime member of the group, now expelled, James Penton offers a comprehensive overview of the Jehovah's Witnesses in three different contexts: historical, doctrinal, and sociological. A valuable book.

Petersen, William J. *Those Curious New Cults.* New Canaan, Conn.: Keats, 1975. An evangelical treatment of some major new cults, as well as Spiritualism, witchcraft, Satanism, and astrology. A brief section on Scientology is included.

Rawlings, Maurice S. *Life Wish (Reincarnation: Reality or Hoax?).* Nashville: Nelson, 1981. A Christian perspective on the major teachings of reincarnation contrasted with biblical truth.

Reed, David A., ed. *Index of Watch Tower Errors, 1879–1989.* Grand Rapids: Baker, 1990. This book is an essential tool in dealing with the beliefs and practices of the Jehovah's Witnesses. The teachings are chronological, and a second index organizes by subjects.

Reisser, Paul C., Teri K. Reisser, and John Weldon. *New Age Medicine.* Downers Grove, Ill.: InterVarsity, 1987. Originally published as *The Holistic Healer.* A Christian perspective on New Age medicine: holistic health, reflexology, acupuncture, and popular theories in New Age medicine. A checklist of what to watch for in a neighborhood healer.

Richardson, Don. *Eternity in Their Hearts.* Ventura, Calif.: Regal, 1981. A good perspective on the biblical view of the origin of religions, including folk religions from preliterate societies.

Ridenour, Fritz. *So What's the Difference?* Ventura, Calif.: Regal, 1979. A brief introduction to some of the major religions and cults, including Buddhism, Mormonism, Unitarianism, Roman Catholicism, Christian Science, Protestantism, Jehovah's Witnesses, Islam, Hinduism, and Judaism. This book is especially compiled to work well for adult education.

Rhodes, Ron. *Counterfeit Christ of the New Age Movement.* The question, "Who do people say the Son of Man is?" is what has separated cults and the occult from authentic Christianity. Now we are faced with the New Age "Cosmic Christ." The author warns Christians to react thoughtfully, with their minds prepared by God's Word, to all ideas that do not confess Christ as the only Lord.

———. *The Culting of America.* Eugene, Oreg.: Harvest House, 1994. A cult researcher and author of a number of books, Ron Rhodes takes a look at why cults have been so successful at spreading darkness across our land, through Hollywood connections, public school influence, powerful dominance in American business, health, and much more.

———. *Reasoning from the Scriptures with the Jehovah's Witnesses.* Eugene, Oreg.: Harvest House, 1993. The author shows Christians how to turn the tables on the Jehovah's Witnesses who spread their errors. An excellent, hands-on reference guide with Scripture comparisons, tactics, and arguments.

Rhodes, Ron, and Marian Bodine. *Reasoning from the Scriptures with the Mormons.* Eugene, Oreg.: Harvest House, 1995. These cult experts help you understand the main points of Mormonism and equip you to ask strategic questions that challenge the Mormons.

Rosten, Leo, ed. *Religions in America.* New York: Simon and Schuster, 1963. A standard non-Christian review of the major cults and religions in the United States. However, since the articles were contributed by each group, religion, or cult concerned, the teachings represented are not necessarily objective.

Rudin, James, and Marcia Rudin. *Prison or Paradise?* Philadelphia: Fortress, 1980.

Saal, William J. *Reaching Muslims for Christ.* Chicago: Moody, 1991. Whether you are a novice in Muslim outreach or already involved at a higher level, you will find this field-tested counsel to be both fascinating and helpful.

Samples, Kenneth, Erwin de Castro, Richard Abanes, and Robert Lyle. *Prophets of the Apocalypse: David Koresh and Other American Messiahs.* Grand Rapids: Baker, 1994. Former members of the staff of the Christian Research Institute and the *Christian Research Journal*, these authors look at various groups and leaders and tell why they are dangerous. Its main emphasis is on the Branch Davidians. It is a relevant book for today.

Schnoebelen, William. *Masonry: Beyond the Light.* Chino, Calif.: Chick Publications, 1991. Get the facts from someone who learned that utter darkness lies behind the light of Masonry. The author studied hard to achieve the thirty-second degree of Masonry but discovered more ungodliness the higher he climbed.

Scott, Latayne C. *The Mormon Mirage: A Former Mormon Tells Why She Left the Church.* Grand Rapids: Zondervan, 1979. The author does a good job of approaching Mormonism from a Mormon's point of view. Much of what Mormons believe today differs from the historical documents.

Shah, Douglas. *The Mediators.* Plainfield, N.J.: Logos, 1975. A popular Christian treatment of Transcendental Meditation, mysticism, Zen, yoga, and other Eastern movements and religions.

Shorrosh, Anis A. *Islam Revealed: A Christian Arab's View of Islam.* Nashville: Nelson, 1988. This book is the result of the author's study and research he conducted for two debates with one of the foremost Islamic spokesmen in the world.

Sire, James W. *Scripture Twisting: Twenty Ways the Cults Misread the Bible.* Downers Grove, Ill.: InterVarsity, 1980. This book by a popular author lists twenty ways the cults misread the Bible. The author deals with misquotations as well as misinterpretations.

Smith, F. LaGard. *Crystal Lies: Choices in the New Age.* Ann Arbor, Mich.: Vine, 1989. This book is a detailed look at what the New Age promises and what it really delivers. It will assist Christians as they confront the "spiritual supermarket" of ideas and practices represented by the New Age movement.

————. *Out On a Broken Limb*. Eugene, Oreg.: Harvest House, 1986. A response to Shirley MacLaine about the meaning of life and the afterlife. Smith uses his background in law to examine the case against the philosophies and trendy Westernized versions of Eastern mysticism presented in Shirley MacLaine's book.

Smith, Houston. *The Religions of Man*. New York: Harper and Row, 1958. A classic, brief treatment of the major world religions from a non-Christian point of view.

Sparks, Jack. *The Mind Benders*. Nashville: Nelson, 1979. A church historian's point of view of the Unification Church, the Way, Children of God, Transcendental Meditation, Divine Light Mission, Hare Krishna, and the Peoples Temple. Sparks is a conservative evangelical Christian who uses the writings of the early church and the creeds of the church councils (along with the Old and New Testaments) to refute the major teachings of these cults.

Spencer, James R. *Beyond Mormonism: An Elder's Story*. Grand Rapids: Chosen, 1984. Spencer is a former Mormon and a respected elder, yet he was troubled by many questions. This is a compelling account of leaving Mormonism and the struggles involved.

Spittler, Russell P. *Cults and Isms*. Grand Rapids: Baker, 1962. An old but still useful book on some of the major cults, including Mormonism, Spiritualism, Christian Science, Jehovah's Witnesses, Unity, Theosophy, Baha'ism, Zen Buddhism, Anglo-Israelism, astrology, Father Divine, Rosicrucianism, Swedenborgianism, modernism, humanism, Unitarianism, Universalism, liberalism, and neo-orthodoxy.

Stoner, Carroll, and Jo Anne Parke. *All God's Children*. Radnor, Penn.: Chilton, 1977. Written by two journalists, this book is a non-Christian observation of people involved in some of the new cults. It explains the teachings of new cults and why they may be dangerous for young people.

Storms, E. M. *Should a Christian Be a Mason?* Fletcher, N.C.: New Puritan Library, 1980. This book, in its fourteenth printing, has been used to lead many out of Masonry. The subject is set forth in a clear and thought-provoking manner.

Strohmer, Charles. *What Your Horoscope Doesn't Tell You*. Wheaton, Ill.: Tyndale, 1988. A biblical response to the confused world of astrology.

Sumrall, Lester. *Where Was God When Pagan Religions Began?* Nashville: Nelson, 1980. A discussion of the biblical texts related to the rise of world religions, with biblical responses to the major tenets of these faiths.

Tanenbaum, Marc H., Marvin R. Wilson, and A. James Rudin., eds. *Evangelicals and Jews in Conversation on Scripture, Theology, and History*. Grand Rapids: Baker, 1978. An objective portrayal of the differences between Judaism and Christianity, especially between modern Judaism and evangelical Christianity. This is a very good resource book, using the format of a conversational interchange.

Tucker, Ruth A. *Another Gospel.* Grand Rapids: Zondervan, 1989. An evangelical perspective on fifteen of the largest and most dangerous cults, plus twenty-one smaller but equally critical cults.

Watson, William. *A Concise Dictionary of Cults and Religions.* Chicago: Moody, 1991. This is an excellent resource containing information on literally hundreds of cults, movements, and religions. There are three sections: dictionary, bibliography, and ministries.

Weldon, John. *The Transcendental Explosion.* Irvine, Calif.: Harvest House, 1976. An excellent, in-depth research treatment on the history and teachings of Transcendental Meditation.

Weldon, John, and Clifford Wilson. *Occult Shock and Psychic Forces.* San Diego: Master Books, 1980.

White, Mel. *Deceived.* Old Tappan, N.J.: Revell, 1979. A Christian analysis of the People's Temple in Guyana, explaining how such a tragedy could happen and how to watch out for other groups that may be similar.

Whitehead, John W. *The Stealing of America.* Westchester, Ill.: Crossway, 1983. Are we in danger of losing many hard-won freedoms? Whitehead, president of the Rutherford Institute and a lawyer, thinks so. The Rutherford Institute participates in free speech and free exercise issues.

Williams, J. L. *Victor Paul Wierwille and The Way International.* Chicago: Moody, 1979. The best single-volume treatment of the history and teachings of the Way International, with a biblical response.

Yamamoto, J Isamu. *Buddhism, Taoism and Other Far Eastern Religions.* Grand Rapids: Zondervan, 1998. This book in the Zondervan Guide series concentrates on the Far Eastern religions and their mystical beliefs, including Nirvana and annihilation.

———. *Hinduism, TM, and Hare Krishna.* Grand Rapids: Zondervan, 1998. This particular book in the Zondervan Guide series starts with the root religion of Hinduism. TM, a Hindu-based movement, became popular in the sixties as a way of therapy and psychological well-being, after it was endorsed by the Beatles and the Beach Boys. Another Americanized form of Hinduism is Hare Krishna. It is important to know about these Eastern religions and their impact on North America.

———. *The Puppet Master: An Inquiry into Sun Myung Moon and the Unification Church.* Downers Grove, Ill.: InterVarsity, 1977. An appraisal of the teachings of the Unification Church with a biblical response. Yamamoto especially emphasizes a sociological perspective.

INDEX

ABOUT THE AUTHOR

Bob Larson is the world's foremost expert on cults, the occult, and alternative spirituality. He has lectured in more than eighty countries and has appeared on TV shows such as *The Oprah Winfrey Show*, *Larry King Live*, *The O'Reilly Factor*, and *Politically Incorrect*. Several television networks have produced documentaries about his work, including MSNBC, The Learning Channel (TLC), The Discovery Channel, A&E, and the British Broadcasting Corporation (BBC). He has been featured in major national newspapers such as the *Los Angeles Times*, *The New York Times*, and *The Washington Post*.

Bob has written thirty books—both fiction and nonfiction—translated into more than a dozen languages. He has written extensively about alternative spirituality and the occult, including *Satanism: The Seduction of America's Youth*; *Extreme Evil: Kids Killing Kids*; *Straight Answers on the New Age*; *In the Name of Satan*; *UFOs and the Alien Agenda*; and *Larson's Book of Spiritual Warfare*.

Bob recently completed his twentieth year of hosting a live, call-in radio show, *TALK-BACK with Bob Larson*, which was broadcast across the United States and Canada. He hosts a weekly television series, *Bob Larson Presents: Spiritual Freedom*, a program aired worldwide on hundreds of stations and the Internet.

Drawing on his more than twenty years of experience investigating supernatural phenomena, Bob presents Spiritual Freedom conferences to educate people about the influences of evil. He has also established and trained Do What Jesus Did (DWJD) Spiritual Freedom teams in more than one hundred cities worldwide to heal victims of abuse and spiritual bondage; he teaches Take Your Life Back seminars to address issues of personal growth for those in the business community; and he offers personal coaching for spiritual discovery and development. In addition, Bob is the founder of the Spiritual Freedom Church, an affiliation of congregations around the world dedicated to the mission of Luke 4:18: to preach the gospel, heal the brokenhearted, and set the captives free!

For more information, contact:
Bob Larson
P.O. Box 36A
Denver, Colorado 80236
(303) 980-1511
www.boblarson.org